Research Anthology on Combating Denial-of-Service Attacks

Information Resources Management Association
USA

Published in the United States of America by
IGI Global
Information Science Reference (an imprint of IGI Global)
701 E. Chocolate Avenue
Hershey PA, USA 17033
Tel: 717-533-8845
Fax: 717-533-8661
E-mail: cust@igi-global.com
Web site: http://www.igi-global.com

Library of Congress Cataloging-in-Publication Data

Names: Information Resources Management Association, editor.
Title: Research anthology on combating denial-of-service attacks /
  Information Resources Management Association, Editor.
Description: Hershey, PA : Information Science Reference, an imprint of IGI
  Global, [2020] | Includes bibliographical references and index. |
  Summary: "This book examines the latest research on the development of
  intrusion detection systems and best practices for preventing and
  combating cyber-attacks intended to disrupt business and user
  experience"-- Provided by publisher.
Identifiers: LCCN 2020004123 (print) | LCCN 2020004124 (ebook) | ISBN
  9781799853480 (hardcover) | ISBN 9781799853497 (ebook)
Subjects: LCSH: Denial of service attacks. | Computer networks--Security
  measures.
Classification: LCC TK5105.59 .D46 2020 (print) | LCC TK5105.59 (ebook) |
  DDC 005.8/7--dc23
LC record available at https://lccn.loc.gov/2020004123
LC ebook record available at https://lccn.loc.gov/2020004124

British Cataloguing in Publication Data
A Cataloguing in Publication record for this book is available from the British Library.

The views expressed in this book are those of the authors, but not necessarily of the publisher.

For electronic access to this publication, please contact: eresources@igi-global.com.

List of Contributors

Table of Contents

Section 2
Detection and Prevention: Intrusion Detection Systems and General Strategies

Section 3
Detection and Prevention: Internet of Things and Smart Devices

Preface

As more and more businesses, organizations, governments, and schools become reliant on technology and online services to engage customers, store data, and more, it is increasingly imperative that measures are constantly being taken to protect against the vulnerabilities that these services render. Denial-of-Service Attacks (DoS attacks) and Distributed Denial-of-Service Attacks (DDoS attacks) have become significant concerns recently. Used to flood a targeted host or network with traffic until the target can no longer respond or crashes, these attacks cost organizations worldwide time and money as they scramble to block the attack and make their services accessible once again. For certain businesses, this can cause lost revenue as frustrated customers, unable to access products, take their business elsewhere. For other organizations, including banks, these attacks mean costly disruptions and hamper the usability and easy access to information that society has become accustomed to. Further revealing the severity of these attacks is the fact that they can often be used to mask and deflect attention away from a secondary, potentially even more harmful, attack, such as stealing personal data.

The *Research Anthology on Combating Denial-of-Service* seeks to address these issues by offering the latest methods, techniques, and strategies for the detection, mitigation, and prevention of DoS and DDoS attacks. Compiled into a one-volume reference work, the book collects a selection of reprinted IGI Global book chapters and journal articles that have been handpicked by the editor and editorial team of this research anthology in order to present in-depth coverage of the use of botnets in attacks, the general strategies and newest technologies being used in their prevention, and the detection and mitigation of these attacks within certain vulnerable systems, including but not limited to the internet of things, vehicular ad-hoc networks, and smart grids. While covering techniques that include machine learning, blockchain technology, defense mechanisms, and intrusion detection systems, the extensive research contained within this book empowers security and data professionals, academicians, researchers, and students with both broad and detailed perspectives on cutting-edge developments.

The *Research Anthology on Combating Denial-of-Service Attacks* is organized into five sections that provide comprehensive coverage of important topics. The sections are:

1. Botnets;
2. Detection and Prevention: Intrusion Detection Systems and General Strategies;
3. Detection and Prevention: Internet of Things and Smart Devices;
4. Detection and Prevention: Social Media and the Cloud; and
5. Detection and Prevention: Smart Grid, Vehicular Ad-Hoc Networks, and Wireless Sensor Networks.

The following paragraphs provide a summary of what to expect from this invaluable reference tool.

Section 1, "Botnets," starts this comprehensive reference source by investigating botnets and their use in conducting Denial-of-Service Attacks. Detection and mitigation technologies such as machine learning techniques are also highlighted in addition to botnet impacts on e-commerce and the Internet of Things particularly analyzed. Opening this section is the chapter "Inevitable Battle Against Botnets," by Prof. Ibrahim Firat from the University of Reading, UK. This chapter aims to review working principles of botnets and botnet detection mechanisms in order to increase general knowledge about botnets. The following chapter, "Denial-of-Service and Botnet Analysis, Detection, and Mitigation," authored by Prof. Sobana Sikkanan from the Adithya Institute of Technology, India and Prof. Kasthuri M. from the PSNA College of Engineering and Technology, India, provides a systematic analysis of the causes of DoS attacks, including motivations and history, analysis of different attacks, detection and protection techniques, various mitigation techniques, and the limitations and challenges of DoS research areas. The next chapter, titled "Denial-of-Service (DoS) Attack and Botnet: Network Analysis, Research Tactics, and Mitigation," written by Prof. Kavita Sharma from the National Institute of Technology Kurukshetra, India and Profs. Arushi Arora and Sumit Kumar Yadav of Indira Gandhi Delhi Technical University for Women, India, describes how the consequence and hazards showcased by Denial of Service attacks have resulted in the surge of research studies, commercial software and innovative cogitations. Another chapter within this section, "Detection of Botnet Based Attacks on Network: Using Machine Learning Techniques," authored by Prof. Prachi from the The NorthCap University, India, proposes a new model to detect botnet behavior on the basis of traffic analysis and machine learning techniques. In the following chapter, "Detecting DDoS Attacks on Multiple Network Hosts: Advanced Pattern Detection Method for the Identification of Intelligent Botnet Attacks," by Prof. Reda Alhajj from the University of Calgary, Canada & Global University, Lebanon; Prof. Konstantinos F. Xylogiannopoulos from the University of Calgary, Canada; and Prof. Panagiotis Karampelas from the Hellenic Air Force Academy, Greece, an advanced pattern detection method is presented that is able to collect and classify in real time all the incoming traffic and detect a developing slow and low DDoS attack by monitoring the traffic in all the hosts of the network. Another chapter in this section, "Botnet Threats to E-Commerce Web Applications and Their Detection," by Profs. Rizwan Ur Rahman and Deepak Singh Tomar from the Maulana Azad National Institute of Technology, India, scrutinizes to what degree botnets can cause a threat to e-commerce security. One of the concluding chapters, "Botnet and Internet of Things (IoTs): A Definition, Taxonomy, Challenges, and Future Directions," authored by Profs. Rosni Abdullah and Kamal Alieyan from the Universiti Sains Malaysia, Malaysia; Prof. Ammar Almomani of Al-Balqa Applied University, Jordan; Prof. Badr Almutairi from the Majmaah University, Saudi Arabia; and Prof. Mohammad Alauthman of Zarqa University, Jordan, discusses IoT, botnet in IoT, and various botnet detection techniques available in IoT. In the final chapter of this section, "Successful Computer Forensics Analysis on the Cyber Attack Botnet," by Prof. Chellappan C. from the GKM College of Engineering and Technology, India; Prof. Kavisankar Leelasankar of Hindustan Institute of Technology and Science, India; and Prof. Sivasankar P. from the National Institute of Technical Teachers Training and Research, India, an analysis to find the real mastermind to protect the innocent compromised system and to protect the victim system/organization affected by the botnet cyberattack is undertaken.

Section 2, "Detection and Prevention: Intrusion Detection Systems and General Strategies," provides the latest research for combating DoS and DDoS attacks through the use of Intrusion Detection Systems, as well as by utilizing the newest methods, techniques, and technologies for stopping general attacks. The first chapter in this section is "Visualization Technique for Intrusion Detection," by Profs. Mohamed Cheikh, Salima Hacini, and Zizette Boufaida from the Constantine 2 University, Algeria. In this chapter, a new technique for detecting DoS attacks is proposed; it detects DOS attacks using a set of classifiers and visualizes them in real time. The next chapter, "Association Rule-Mining-Based Intrusion Detection System With Entropy-Based Feature Selection: Intrusion Detection System," authored by Prof. Devaraju Sellappan of Sri Krishna Arts and Science College, India and Prof. Ramakrishnan Srinivasan from the Dr. Mahalingam College of Engineering and Technology, India, demonstrates an association rule-mining algorithm for detecting various network intrusions. In the following chapter, "Security Integration in DDoS Attack Mitigation Using Access Control Lists," by Prof. Kavita Sharma from the National Institute of Technology Kurukshetra, India and Profs. Sumit Kumar Yadav and Arushi Arora of Indira Gandhi Delhi Technical University for Women, India, the authors propose a DDoS mitigation system through access list-based configurations, which are deployed at the ISP (Internet Service Provider's) edge routers to prohibit DDoS attacks over ISPs' networks traffic. Another chapter in this section, "A Survey on Denial of Service Attacks and Preclusions," written by Profs. Nagesh K., Sumathy R., Devakumar P., and Sathiyamurthy K. from Pondicherry Engineering College, India, proposes various types of attacks and solutions associated with each layer of OSI model. The next chapter, "DDoS Attacks and Defense Mechanisms Using Machine Learning Techniques for SDN," by Profs. Mayank Dave, Rochak Swami, and Virender Ranga from the National Institute of Technology, Kurukshetra, India, illustrates how DDoS attacks affect the whole working of SDN. The objective of this chapter is also to provide a better understanding of DDoS attacks and how machine learning approaches may be used for detecting DDoS attacks. In one of the closing chapters of this section, "Global Naming and Storage System Using Blockchain," authored by Profs. Chanti S., Taushif Anwar, Chithralekha T., and V. Uma of Pondicherry University, India, an overview of blockchain technology is provided and a brief introduction to blockchain-based naming and storage systems is given in order to handle the challenges of DoS/DDoS attacks. A concluding chapter, "Performance Evaluation of Web Server's Request Queue against AL-DDoS Attacks in NS-2," authored by Profs. Manish Kumar and Abhinav Bhandari from Punjabi University, India, presents various simulation scenarios for comparison and estabilshes that queue scheduling policy can be a significant role player in tolerating the AL-DDoS attacks. The final chapter of this section, "Evaluation of the Attack Effect Based on Improved Grey Clustering Model," by Profs. Chen Yue, Lu Tianliang, Cai Manchun, and Li Jingying from the People's Public Security University of China, China, presents a model that could evaluate the effect of the denial-of-service attack precisely. It is also shown that the model is viable to evaluate the attack effect.

Section 3, "Detection and Prevention: Internet of Things and Smart Devices," examines the threat of DoS and DDoS attacks on the Internet of Things, as well as methods to protect and secure the Internet of Things, as well as smart devices such as smartphones. Opening this section is the chapter, "Security in IoT Devices," by Profs. N. Jeyanthi, Shreyansh Banthia, and Akhil Sharma of VIT University, India. This chapter provides a general survey of the prevailing attack types along with analysis of the underlying structures that make these attacks possible, which would help researchers in understanding the DDoS problem better. A following chapter, "Cyber-Physical System and Internet of Things Security: An Overview," authored by Profs. Christian Steger and Thomas Ulz from Graz University of Technology, Austria and Ms. Sarah Haas from the Infineon Austria AG, Austria, intends to give an overview of current research regarding the security of data in industrial CPS and the Internet of Things. In the next chapter, "Advanced Network Data Analytics for Large-Scale DDoS Attack Detection," by Prof. Konstantinos F. Xylogiannopoulos from the University of Calgary, Canada; Prof. Panagiotis Karampelas from the Hellenic Air Force Academy, Greece; and Prof. Reda Alhajj from the University of Calgary, Canada, a novel method is introduced, which is based on a data mining technique that can analyze incoming IP traffic details and early warn the network administrator about a potentially developing DDoS attack. In a concluding chapter of this section titled "Malware Threat in Internet of Things and Its Mitigation Analysis," by Prof. Brij Gupta from the National Institute of Technology, Kurukshetra, India and Prof. Shingo Yamaguchi from Yamaguchi University, Japan, malware's threat in the internet of things (IoT) is introduced and then the mitigation methods against the threat are analyzed. In another closing chapter, "Zero-Crossing Analysis of Lévy Walks and a DDoS Dataset for Real-Time Feature Extraction: Composite and Applied Signal Analysis for Strengthening the Internet-of-Things Against DDoS Attacks," written by Prof. Witold Kinsner from the University of Manitoba, Canada & Telecommunications Research Laboratories (TRLabs), Canada and Prof. Jesus David Terrazas Gonzalez from the University of Manitoba, Canada, a comparison between the probability similarities of a Distributed Denial-of-Service (DDoS) dataset and Lévy walks is presented. In the final chapter of this section, "Taxonomy of Distributed Denial of Service (DDoS) Attacks and Defense Mechanisms in Present Era of Smartphone Devices," by Profs. Kavita Sharma and B. B. Gupta from the National Institute of Technology, Kurukshetra, India, an explanation on DDoS attacks and the nature of these attacks against Smartphones and Wi-Fi Technology is provided and a taxonomy of various defense mechanisms is presented.

Section 4, "Detection and Prevention: Social Media and the Cloud," focuses on securing social media and the cloud against DoS and DDoS attacks and presents models and frameworks for their detection and mitigation. Opening this section is the chapter titled "The Improved LSTM and CNN Models for DDoS Attacks Prediction in Social Media," by Profs. Rasim M. Alguliyev, Ramiz M. Aliguliyev, and Fargana J. Abdullayeva from Azerbaijan National Academy of Sciences, Azerbaijan, which presents classifiers based on Convolutional Neural Network (CNN) and Long Short-Term Memory (LSTM) to address this problem domain, and to predict the occurrence probability of the DDoS events the next day, the negative and positive sentiments in social networking texts are used. To verify the efficacy of the proposed method an experiment is conducted on Twitter data. The next chapter, "The HTTP Flooding Attack Detection to Secure and Safeguard Online Applications in the Cloud," authored by Profs. Dhanapal A. and Nithyanandam P. of VIT University, Chennai, India, offers a solution for detecting a HTTP flooding attack in the cloud by using the novel TriZonal Linear Prediction (TLP) model. The solution is implemented using OpenStack and the FIFA Worldcup '98 data set for experimentation. The next chapter, "DOS Attacks on Cloud Platform: Their Solutions and Implications," by Prof. Rohit Kumar from Chandigarh University, India, presents DOS threats and methods to mitigate them in varied dimensions. The following chapter, "Denial of Service (DoS) Attacks Over Cloud Environment: A Literature Survey," authored by Profs. Thangavel M., Sindhuja R., and Nithya S. from Thiagarajar College of Engineering, India, discusses DOS attack in the cloud and its types, what tools are used to perform DOS attack and how they are detected and prevented. Finally it deals with the measures to protect the cloud services from DOS attack and also penetration testing for DOS attack. In a concluding chapter, "Distributed Denial of Service Attacks and Defense in Cloud Computing," authored by Profs. Gopal Singh Kushwah and Virender Ranga of the National Institute of Technology Kurukshetra, India, a classification of various types of DDoS attacks is presented, and techniques for defending these attacks in cloud computing are discussed. Moreover, a conceptual model based on extreme learning machine has been proposed to defend these attacks. In the final chapter of this section, "Comparing Single Tier and Three Tier Infrastructure Designs against DDoS Attacks," by Prof. Akashdeep Bhardwaj from the University of Petroleum and Energy Studies, India and Prof. Sam Goundar of CENTRUM, Graduate Business School, Lima, Peru, the resilience to withstand against DDoS attacks is measured for real user monitoring parameters, compared for the two infrastructure designs and the data is validated using T-Test.

Section 5, "Detection and Prevention: Smart Grid, Vehicular Ad-Hoc Networks, and Wireless Sensor Networks," concludes this book by offering strategies for detecting and preventing DoS and DDoS attacks in smart grids, vehicular ad-hoc networks (VANET) and wireless sensor networks (WSN). In the first chapter in this section, "Denial of Service Attack on Protocols for Smart Grid Communications," authored by Prof. Swapnoneel Roy from the University of North Florida, USA, a denial of service (DoS) attack known as the clogging attack has been performed on three different modern protocols for smart grid (SG) communications. Solutions to protect these protocols against this attack are then illustrated along with identifying the causes behind the occurrence of this vulnerability in SG communication protocols in general. In the next chapter, "Security for AMI Application," written by Prof. Jun-Ho Huh of Catholic University of Pusan, South Korea, security tests have been tested under the smart grid environment and several DDoS (distributed denial of service) attack scenarios were developed for experiments. In the following chapter, "IP-CHOCK Reference Detection and Prevention of Denial of Service (DoS) Attacks in Vehicular Ad-Hoc Network: Detection and Prevention of Denial of Service (DoS) Attacks in Vehicular Ad-Hoc Network," by Prof. Karan Verma from the Central University of Rajasthan, India, an efficient detection method is proposed to detect UDP flooding attacks, called Bloom-filter-based IP-CHOCK (BFICK). A prevention method using IP-CHOCK is also proposed to prevent DoS, called reference broadcast synchronization (RBS). Another chapter titled "A Detailed Study on Security Concerns of VANET and Cognitive Radio VANETs," authored by Profs. M. Manikandakumar, Sri Subarnaa D. K., and Monica Grace R. from the Thiagarajar College of Engineering, India, classifies the securities and their prevention mechanisms in overcoming these security issues in VANET and Cognitive Radio VANET perspectives. A concluding chapter, "Design and Development of Secured Framework for Efficient Routing in Vehicular Ad-Hoc Network," by Prof. Mamata Rath from Birla Global University, India; Prof. Bibudhendu Pati from Rama Devi Women's University, India; and Prof. Binod Kumar Pattanayak from Siksha 'O' Anusandhan (Deemed to be) University, India, presents a Secured and Safety Protocol for VANET (STVAN), as an intelligent ad-hoc on demand distance vector (AODV)-based routing mechanism that prevents the DoS and improves the quality of service for secured communications in a VANET. The final chapter, "UWDBCSN Analysis During Node Replication Attack in WSN," by Profs. Harpreet Kaur and Sharad Saxena from Thapar University, India, considers the security of sensor nodes which are harmful to different types of mischievous attacks like denial of service attack and describes how to deal with these types of attacks.

Although the primary organization of the contents in this work is based on its five sections, offering a progression of coverage of the important concepts, methodologies, technologies, applications, social issues, and emerging trends, the reader can also identify specific contents by utilizing the extensive indexing system listed at the end. As a comprehensive collection of research on the latest findings related to tools, technologies, and methods that can be utilized to block DoS and DDoS attacks, the *Research Anthology on Combating Denial-of-Service Attacks* provides researchers, cybersecurity professionals, security analysts, IT specialists, academicians, students, and all audiences with a complete understanding of the development of models and frameworks that offer solutions for the prevention of these attacks. Given the vast number of issues concerning DoS and DDoS attacks and their social and economic impacts in countries around the world, this extensive book addresses the demand for a resource that encompasses the most pertinent research in technologies being employed to globally bolster the detection and mitigation of these specialized attacks.

Section 1
Botnets

Chapter 1
Inevitable Battle Against Botnets

Ibrahim Firat
University of Reading, UK

ABSTRACT

It is undeniable that technology is developing and growing at an unstoppable pace. Technology has become a part of people's daily lives. It has been used for many purposes but mainly to make human life easier. In addition to being useful, these advancements in technology have some bad consequences. A new malware called botnet has recently emerged. It is considered to be one of the most important and dangerous cyber security problems as it is not well understood and evolves quickly. Communication of bots between each other and their botmaster results in the formation of botnet; this is also known as a zombie army. As botnets become popular among cybercriminals, more studies have been done in botnet detection area. Researchers have developed new detection mechanisms in order to understand and tackle this growing botnet issue. This chapter aims to review working principles of botnets and botnet detection mechanisms in order to increase general knowledge about botnets.

INTRODUCTION

When it comes to talk about cyber security and its possible consequences, botnet is one of the most common word that pops in people's mind who are specialised in cybersecurity. Botnets can be considered as network of bots as they consist of more than one bot working together. Botnets use command and control (C&C) communication channels to talk with the cybercriminal who controls them. During this communication process, bots receive commands from the cybercriminal and then report back to that cybercriminal. This is one of the most distinctive characteristics of botnets which separates them from other malwares. Botnets have different architectures and cybercriminals choose any of these architectures depending on their purposes. Cybercriminals have a range of different options ranging from client-server model to peer-to-peer networks (Botnet, 2018). In general, botmasters try to collect more devices as possible to increase the strength of botnet. Through infection process, botmasters add new devices to their army. Botmasters infect new devices by using viruses, worms, trojan horses and many other malicious techniques. Once a device gets infected by any of the mentioned malicious technique, it

DOI: 10.4018/978-1-7998-5348-0.ch001

becomes a part of the botnet and can be labelled as a bot. Bots can be any device as long as cybercriminals can infect them such as computers and smartphones. On the other hand, it is well known that botnet detection is an on-going problem. It is very challenging to detect botnets as they use small amounts of computing power and they can update their behaviours. They can be very dangerous as they are capable of carrying out distributed denial-of-service (DDoS) attacks, stealing sensitive data and performing a number of different malicious behaviours. They can cause a range of different and serious problems if they are not successfully detected and neutralized. To be more precise, leakage of sensitive data can lead to conflicts at different levels. If cybercriminals leak government secrets, this can cause a crisis at a national level. On the other hand, DDoS attacks can make important online services unavailable. For example, if cybercriminals decide to perform DDoS attacks on online banking system, this can lead to money transaction problems, money fraud and even more serious financial issues. These are only some of the few problems that botnets can cause. Therefore, it is important to detect and understand botnets. This chapter aims to increase the knowledge about botnets by giving information about different types of botnets with their uses and formation. Also, it aims to explain botnet's working principles, architecture, life-cycle, possible threats, infection and detection processes.

BACKGROUND

Many researches have been done in the areas of botnets and botnet detection in order to strengthen the domain knowledge about botnets and protect innocent users from possible attacks of botnets. Cooke et al. published a paper in order to draw attention to the current botnet problem and determine the origins and structure of bots and as well as botnets. The authors stated that, monitoring IRC communication or other command and control activity was not sufficient enough to detect botnets effectively. The authors concluded the paper by describing a system which was able to detect botnets with advanced command and control mechanisms by using secondary detection data from more than one sources (Cooke, Jahanian & McPherson, 2005). In 2014, Sebastián García presented three new botnet detection methods in his PHD thesis. These detection methods were SimDetect, BClus and CCDetector. SimDetect method focused on finding structural similarities, BClus focused on clustering network traffic based on connection patterns and CCDetector focused on training a Markov Chain to detect similar traffic in unknown networks. Also, he presented a new model for botnet behaviour analysis in the given network (Garcia, 2014). On the other hand, Muthumanickam K. et al. proposed a decentralized three phased botnet detection model for the detection of P2P based botnets. The first phase was the identification of P2P node, second phase was about collecting suspicious P2P nodes together and the final phase was the detection of botnets (Muthumanickam, Ilavarasan & Dwivedi, 2014). This is followed by a study in which the authors compared the outputs of three popular botnet detection methods by executing them over a range of different datasets (Garcia, Grill, Stiborek, Zunino, 2014). In another study, the authors proposed a new technique to detect botnet activity with the help of machine learning. The authors detected botnet activity based on traffic behavior analysis by identifying network traffic behavior. Also, the authors worked on the feasibility of locating botnet activity without having access to a complete network flow by identifying behavior based on time intervals (Zhao, Traore, Sayed, Lu, Saad, Ghorbani & Garant, 2013). In another paper, the authors presented an event-driven log analysis software that helped researchers to detect botnet activities and identify if an end-user's machine has become part of the botnet (Ersson & Moradian 2013). In another study, the researchers presented a method which used artificial fish swarm algorithm and a support vector machine together. The presented method was used to classify important features which determined the patterns of botnets (Lin, Chen & Hung, 2014). On the other hand, for the early detection of botnets, the authors presented a new method for recreating botnet's port scanning patterns with the help of simple text classifier which illustrates these patterns like a matrix. Then, these patterns were used to train a hidden Markov model for early detection of botnets (Kim, Lee, Kang, Jeong & In, 2012). In another study, the authors proposed large scale and wide area botnet detection system which made use of a range of different techniques to eliminate the challenges imposed by the use of NetFlow data (Bilge, Balzarotti, Robertson, Kirda & Kruegel, 2012). In a recently published paper, the authors made a study about DDoS attacks which were launched by botnets. The authors stated that the geospatial distribution of attacking sources follows a similar pattern which enables prediction of future attacks. Also, the authors mentioned about an attacking trend where different botnets execute DDoS attacks on the same victim (Wang, Chang, Chen & Mohaisen, 2018). In a different research, the authors used machine learning algorithm to determine connections which belong to a botnet. In order to maximise detection rate of botnets, the authors found feature set according to the connections of botnets at their C&C (Alejandre, Cortés, & Anaya, 2017). On the other hand, a researcher invented a new national cyber-firewall called "Seddulbahir" against 21 different cyber-attacks (Sari, 2019). The researcher used artificial neural network radial basis function to set rules which can be used in the detection processes of these possible attacks (Sari, 2019). Lastly, the same author proposed a different study about the importance of context-aware intelligent systems of Fog Computing on analysing IoT data. The author stated that use of Fog Computing to analyse IoT data can help cybersecurity professionals to detect, mitigate and prevent possible attacks earlier (Sari, 2018).

BOTNET DEFINITION

A botnet is a collection of bots which usually communicate with a bot controller and other bots continuously. This is also known as a zombie army (Cooke, Jahanian & McPherson, 2005). The bot controller is also referred as botmaster. Botnets can be considered as networks of devices which are under control of malware (bot) code (Gu, Perdisci, Zhang & Lee, 2008). Generally, the term botnet itself means network of infected end hosts (bots) which are in control of botmaster (Rajab, Zarfoss, Monrose & Terzis, 2006). Usually, bots are not physically possessed by a botmaster and can be placed in several locations around the world. Botnets are capable of carrying out different types of malicious activity. In some cases, these activities can be very dangerous. They aim a range of different profiles changing from individual users to businesses. Therefore, they are considered to be one of the most serious cyber security problems.

BOTNET TYPES

Recently, the numbers of botnets have risen sharply, and new types of botnets have emerged. Botnets can be classified as IRC-Based, HTTP-based and Peer to Peer (P2P) botnets depending on Command and Control (C&C) architecture or communication protocol used.

Peer to Peer (P2P) Botnets

Peer to Peer (P2P) botnets have emerged recently as attackers noticed the weak points of using traditional centralised botnets (Wang, Aslam & Zou, 2010). P2P botnets make use of decentralized C&C structure. Mostly, usage of centralised servers resulted in a single point of failure for the network which makes it even easier to take down servers (Wang, Aslam & Zou, 2010). In P2P botnets, bots can act as C&C servers and as well as clients (Vormayr, Zseby, Fabini, 2017). Every bot is connected to each other, and the botmaster can only control the whole botnet when there is a flow of commands between connected bots. So, there is a potential for every bot to become a potential C&C server (Vormayr, Zseby, Fabini, 2017). Moreover, the communication between botnet elements would not be disrupted regardless of losing members of botnet (Wang, Aslam & Zou, 2010). Also, it is harder to detect, shutdown or monitor P2P botnets compared to other kinds of botnets. Another definition of P2P botnets was done by G. Gu, et al. (Gu, Perdisci, Zhang & Lee, 2008). The authors mentioned about commands which were transferred through push/pull mechanism. The bots use this mechanism to receive command files which were generated by botmaster. P2P bots stay in touch with adjacent bots to get commands and send "Keep Alive" messages to other members of the botnet in the network. Trojan.Peacomm botnet and Stormnet are examples of Peer to Peer botnets (Wang, Aslam & Zou, 2010).

The first known P2P botnet was Storm Worm and it appeared in 2007 (Van Ruitenbeek & Sanders, 2008). Attacks of this botnet mostly rely on social engineering techniques and it uses infected email attachments to trick users on opening them (Van Ruitenbeek & Sanders, 2008). These attachments contain Trojan horses which infect user's computers. After infecting the computers of users, the trojan horses try to establish a communication with others in the Storm Worm botnet and download the full payload (Van Ruitenbeek & Sanders, 2008). At the end, infected computers become a part of the botnet and start to receive commands and execute them consecutively.

IRC-Based Botnets

IRC protocol allows different kinds of communications such as point to point or point to multi-point to take place (Rajab, Zarfoss, Monrose & Terzis, 2006). The flexibility of this protocol and the presence of open-source implementations allow third parties to modify it for different uses. This is the reason why botmasters prefer IRC protocol as a botnet control mechanism (Rajab, Zarfoss, Monrose & Terzis, 2006). Internet Relay Chat (IRC) is a text-based messaging protocol between people who are connected with the internet (Liu, Xiao, Ghaboosi, Deng & Zhang, 2009). IRC servers are interconnected and transfer messages between each other. They are designed to set a communication between hundreds of clients by using more than one server (Liu, Xiao, Ghaboosi, Deng & Zhang, 2009). Multiple IRC (mIRC) is a situation of transferring communications between clients and a server to ones who established communication with the channel (Liu, Xiao, Ghaboosi, Deng & Zhang, 2009). IRC bots are capable of managing access lists, moving files, sharing clients and more (Liu, Xiao, Ghaboosi, Deng & Zhang, 2009).

HTTP-Based Botnets

Network-level signatures are easier to set up as existing network monitoring infrastructures can be used. These days, malwares use network connections to carry out their malicious activities such as getting malware updates or spamming. According to the findings, approximately 75% of malware samples produce HTTP traffic (Perdisci, Lee & Feamster, 2010). HTTP (hyper-text transfer protocol) botnets make use of HTTP protocol and do not pursue connection with a Command and Control (C&C) server (Lee, Jeong, Park, Kim & Noh, 2008). BlackEnergy is an example of HTTP-based botnets and mainly used for DDoS attacks. This botnet provides an easy control of web-based bots which are capable of carrying out different attacks (Lee, Jeong, Park, Kim & Noh, 2008).

ORIGINAL USE OF BOTNETS

Bots (IRC Bots) were originally used in Internet relay Chat (IRC) channel management (Oikarinen & Reed, 1993). Back in time, when Internet was a new piece of technology, Internet Relay Chat was used to communicate with new people all over the world. A typical Internet Relay Chat network allows users to communicate with each other and consists of different numbers of servers which are located at different geographical locations (Canavan, 2005). In 1993, a legitimate IRC bot known as Eggdrop was written by Robey Pointer to monitor a single channel (Canavan, 2005). It was written in C and used in execution of TCL scripts which were added by users to improve the functionality (Canavan, 2005). Eggdrop was considered as a non-malicious bot. It was used to coordinate legally transferred files, imposing channel admin commands and playing games (Grizzard, Sharma, Nunnery, Kang & Dagon, 2007). Also, early IRC bots were used to keep servers up and running by preventing them from shutting down due to inactivity in the servers. An expansion in the numbers of servers resulted in a term known as netsplit (Canavan, 2005). The term "Netsplit" is disconnection of a node from its previous connection. When the IRC Channel Operator loses its connection, another channel member was assigned as Channel Operator (Canavan, 2005). Some people took advantage of this and carried out attacks to cause netsplits in order to obtain Channel Operator status and use it for malicious purposes (Canavan, 2005). Those people modified server attack scripts to carry out malicious attacks on both individual users and other devices. These attacks include Denial of Service attacks (DDoS) and even more (Canavan, 2005).

HOW BOTNETS INFECT OTHER DEVICES?

Botnets are considered to be one of the most important threats to the internet community. They are capable of carrying out different types of attacks which are all very dangerous. Usually bots infect other vulnerable hosts by using exploitation tools in order to expand both their network and capabilities. Bots infect other vulnerable systems by taking advantage of software vulnerabilities, trojan insertion, use of different kinds of viruses and worms and use of social engineering skills to download malicious bot code (Feily, Shahrestani, & Ramadass, 2009). Also, recent studies showed that new bots have several exploit vectors to make exploitation process better and more efficient (Rajab, Zarfoss, Monrose & Terzis, 2006). In another research, the authors stated that the process of transferring malicious software to the victim's computers has changed a lot (Bailey, Cooke, Jahanian, Xu & Karir, 2009). These days, attackers prefer multiple automated propagation vectors instead of single propagation vector as single propagation vectors may need a manual installation (Bailey, Cooke, Jahanian, Xu & Karir, 2009). In addition, the authors mentioned about a movement away from using random scanning to robust "hitlists" such as list of hosts and email lists (Bailey, Cooke, Jahanian, Xu & Karir, 2009). Also, instead of looking for vulnerable services, attackers started to look at vulnerable applications and vulnerable users (Bailey,

Cooke, Jahanian, Xu & Karir, 2009). In another study, the authors mentioned about attackers who made use of P2P networks to infect new computers as there was no centralised server which made exchange of malicious content easier (Wang, Aslam & Zou, 2010). Recently, the number of P2P malwares which have been used in this infection process has increased significantly (Wang, Aslam & Zou, 2010). These P2P malwares include active and passive P2P worms. Active P2P worms try to infect other computers in the network while passive worms stay in local file sharing directory and spread between other computers. After this infection process, the botnet is ready to be controlled by a botmaster as they are able to communicate through P2P protocol.

FORMATION OF BOTNETS

To explain this process in a simpler manner, the formation of botnets can be investigated in two phases. The first one is collection of bots. So, this phase involves infecting or tricking users. This can be achieved with the help of viruses, worms or other kinds of malwares. Increasing the number of infected devices will increase the capabilities of the botnet. The second phase is more about actions which are needed to be taken in order to form the botnet.

A botnet named *FrankenB.* can be used as an example to develop a better understanding on formation of botnets. In the formation process of *FrankenB.* botnet, a single web-based C&C server with an encryption is preferred. In order to build *FranklinB.* botnet, following steps are followed (Cho, 2003):

- A domain is taken and required environment is established.
- The host is connected to ADSL link with a static IP address.
- A web site which will act as front face to hide the C&C of the botnet is built on that host. The web site contains MySQL database and a directory found at the roof of the web server. There are two main files in this directory. One of them is the main script which bots connect to communicate with C&C and get further commands and the second one is another script which is used by botmaster to command *FrankenB.*
- Bots join to the C&C server with HTTP and send data inside a POST. Usually, HTML method is the most used one to submit data which is needed to be processed by a web server. Posts usually preferred when a user completes a form and submits it. Also, use of HTTP communication mechanism between bots and C&C makes the detection process even more difficult.
- As simple web site traffic is unencrypted the communication within botnet is visible. However, encryption can be used to overcome this problem. *FrankenB.* makes use of SSL certificate to protect transferred data.
- After that, bots find their C&C and they start to give reports and receive commands. It is important to make sure that this is done securely. This can be done by using encrypted POST. Also, the bots learn to build a trust to the SSL certificate of the C&C server.
- For security reasons it is important to make sure that only *FrankenB.* bots can communicate with the botnet. To address this issue, a simple authentication with a secret password can be used.
- After all of these steps, the botnet is ready for use. It can be used for many purposes such as email spamming.

LIFE CYCLE OF BOTNETS

Although there are many different types of botnets, it is possible to investigate their life-cycle in five main phases. The following paragraphs will examine these phases and their explanations (Feily, Shahrestani, & Ramadass, 2009):

1. Initial Infection
2. Secondary Injection
3. Connection
4. Malicious Command and Control
5. Update and Maintenance

Figure 1. Life cycle of botnets

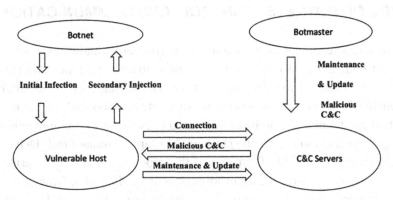

During the first phase, attackers try to find vulnerable points of machines and exploit them. This infection process can be achieved by using different types of malwares or exploitation techniques. In the second phase, infected hosts invoke a script which is also known as shell-code. With the help of FTP, HTTP or P2P, the shell code gets the bot binary from a predetermined location. Once the bot binary downloads itself on the infected machine, the computer starts to execute malicious code. This is followed by the connection phase. In this phase, command and control (C&C) channels are set up. This connects the infected computer which is also referred as zombie to the C&C server. As soon as C&C channels are set up successfully, the infected computers become part of the botnet. The malicious command and control phase is about botmaster commanding the botnet remotely. In this phase, infected computers receive commands from the botmaster and execute them. The last phase is about updating and maintaining the bots. It is important to keep botnets updated as the botmaster may be willing to add new functionality or new attacking techniques to overcome new detection mechanisms.

In another study, instead of five phases, the researchers examined the life-cycle of botnets under three phases (Hachem, Mustapha, Granadillo & Debar, 2011). These phases are (Hachem, Mustapha, Granadillo & Debar, 2011):

- Spreading and Injection: In this phase, the authors mentioned about the ability of botnets to spread, infect and inject themselves into new systems. They also mentioned about the how botnets spread between machines. Mostly, attackers make use of social engineering techniques and malicious email distribution to spread botnets between machines. According to the reports, there was an increase in spam and malware in 2010 on social networks compared to previous years. In addition, use of other botnets, software vulnerabilities and instant messaging which includes a computer worm that spreads by messaging are other ways of infecting and spreading between machines.
- Command and Control: The authors mentioned about the necessity of C&C for communication between botnet and botmaster. Also, the authors stated different models, and topologies for implementing C&C channel.
- Botnet Applications: This phase in about legitimate and illegitimate actions of botnets. The illegitimate actions include DDoS attack (Distributed Denial of Service), spamming and espionage.

ARCHITECTURE OF BOTNETS, CONTROL, AND COMMUNICATION

Botnets have certain characteristics which separates them from other malwares. One of these characteristics is the usage of Command and Control (C&C) channels to set a communication within botnet. This gives an opportunity to botmaster to take control of the botnet. Botnets have internal communication protocols which enable them to establish communication between bots and the botmaster. Simply, IRC (Internet Relay Chat) communication protocol, is created to establish a communication between clients and server by using communication channels (Hachem, Mustapha, Granadillo & Debar, 2011). It creates a connection for clients and agents. The flexibility of this protocol made itself a perfect choice for third parties as it can be customised for different purposes (Hachem, Mustapha, Granadillo & Debar, 2011). HTTP (Hypertext Transfer Protocol) communication protocol works on the basis of request-respond ideology. The bots create queries for the HTTP server and botmaster talks to them by giving commands (Hachem, Mustapha, Granadillo & Debar, 2011). Also, some of the botnets use P2P communication protocols. The idea is to create nodes which act both as client and server.

Moreover, the mentioned Command and Control channels can be updated and controlled for different purposes (Feily, Shahrestani, & Ramadass, 2009). Botmasters make use of a range of different Control and Command topologies and communication methods to overcome defence mechanisms and any legal shutdowns. These topologies have their own advantages and disadvantages. The following paragraphs will examine some of the communication topologies that botnets use.

Centralised Topology

Botnets which make use of centralised topology has a central point which transfers messages between clients. Usually, botmaster assigns a host to be the central point of all botnets (Hachem, Mustapha, Granadillo & Debar, 2011). This host can be either an infected machine or a legitimate public service provider (Hachem, Mustapha, Granadillo & Debar, 2011). As an advantage of using centralised topology, there is less delay in time taken to transfer messages between clients as messages only need to pass from a few hops (Bailey, Cooke, Jahanian, Xu & Karir, 2009). This is very useful topology to implement, as it is very easy to use and gives opportunity of customisation for different needs. However, centralised topologies come with some disadvantages. Firstly, centralised systems are easy to detect as most of the clients are connected to the same central point and secondly, discovery of this central point will result in detection of whole system (Bailey, Cooke, Jahanian, Xu & Karir, 2009).

Peer to Peer (P2P) Topology

P2P botnet communication has many advantages compared to other communication topologies. Firstly, it is hard to damage communication in P2P communication systems (Bailey, Cooke, Jahanian, Xu & Karir, 2009). Therefore, compromise of a single bot does not put whole botnet into a damage. Also, compared with other topologies, P2P topology is harder to get detected by detection mechanisms (Hachem, Mustapha, Granadillo & Debar, 2011). But, construction of P2P systems is complex and not easy. So, it may be time consuming to build it up and there may be some delays in message delivery (Bailey, Cooke, Jahanian, Xu & Karir, 2009).

Unstructured Topology

Unstructured botnet communication can take P2P communication concept and modify it in an extreme way that only a single bot is only aware of one other bot (Bailey, Cooke, Jahanian, Xu & Karir, 2009). In order to send a message, Internet is randomly scanned, and the message is passed along when another bot is detected (Bailey, Cooke, Jahanian, Xu & Karir, 2009). This communication type is very simple to design and loss of one bot would not damage the whole botnet (Bailey, Cooke, Jahanian, Xu & Karir, 2009). However, time taken to deliver a message would be very long and there is no guarantee of delivery of the message (Bailey, Cooke, Jahanian, Xu & Karir, 2009).

Star C&C Topology

Formation of centralised C&C topology has led to formation of star C&C topology and can be considered as an extension of centralised topology. The star topology makes use of a single centralised C&C resource to establish a communication with all bot agents and each bot receives commands from the central C&C point (Kavitha & Rani, 2015). Star topology will allow a direct communication between the C&C and the bot which results in a fast transfer of instructions (Ollmann, 2009). However, if the central C&C is damaged in some way, this will damage the whole botnet (Ollmann, 2009).

Multi-Server C&C Topology

Multi-Server C&C topology is considered as a logical extension of the star C&C topology. Multi-server C&C topology uses several servers to command bot agents (Kavitha & Rani, 2015). Using multiple servers for communication resulted in no single point of failure which is an advantage as a failure in one of the C&C servers would not prevent botmaster from controlling the whole botnet (Ollmann, 2009). Also, spreading servers wisely among different geographical regions will increase the speed of communication between botnet elements (Ollmann, 2009). However, building up multiple C&C servers is not easy and requires extra work.

Hierarchical C&C Topology

Hierarchical topology includes dynamics of principles used in compromise and subsequent propagation of bot agents themselves (Kavitha & Rani, 2015). In hierarchical C&C topology, some bots act as proxy servers for C&C servers (Hachem, Mustapha, Granadillo & Debar, 2011). One of the advantages of using this topology is that bots do not know the location of the whole botnet which makes evaluation of actual size of the botnet even harder (Ollmann, 2009). However, as commands pass from multiple communication branches, it becomes harder for botmaster to control the botnet simultaneously and this increases time latency issues (Ollmann, 2009).

Random C&C Topology

Random topology has no centralised C&C infrastructure and makes use of bot agents to transfer commands (Kavitha & Rani, 2015). Also, having no centralised C&C infrastructure makes it resistant against shutdowns. However, it is very easy to enumerate other members of the botnet by screening a single host (Ollmann, 2009).

POSSIBLE THREATS

These days, botnets are considered to be one of the most serious cyber security problems as they are capable of doing many illegal activities. These illegal activities can aim different profiles ranging from individual users to companies and even governments. Therefore, botnets have become favourite toy of hackers and other cybercriminals. Mostly, botnets are used for DDoS attacks (Distributed Denial of Service), password cracking, click fraud and email spamming, etc. According to the recent studies, DDoS attacks have started to become one of the leading disturbances of the global internet (Ioannidis & Bellovin, 2002). In a typical DDoS attack, a single system is flooded by massive amounts of traffic/request which are generated from different sources. This makes it even harder to stop incoming attacks. The aim is to overload the system and make it unavailable to its users. DDoS attacks include many compromised systems targeting a single system and usually these systems are infected by using Trojan horses or other malwares. In another research, the authors stated that botnets are the reason for approximately 70% to 90% of world's spam (Liu, Xiao, Ghaboosi, Deng & Zhang, 2009). Simply, a spam can be defined as a form of message which is sent to users who did not specifically asked for it. Usually, bots open the SOCKS v4/v5 proxy on infected hosts to be able to send spams (Liu, Xiao, Ghaboosi, Deng & Zhang, 2009). Botnets can also leak sensitive data from the infected machines as they are able to retrieve sensitive information in addition to normal traffic (Liu, Xiao, Ghaboosi, Deng & Zhang, 2009). So, user's passwords, usernames and other sensitive information are in danger. Not only that, botnets can also be used for keylogging. This is a process where bots record keystrokes and report them to their botmaster. According to the researches, botnets have started to develop more complex manner of finding and leaking important financial data (Pappas, 2008). This can result in loss of huge amounts of financial savings. Recently, botnets have started to play a role in identity theft with a process known as Phishing mail. These mails contain legitimate URLs which ask users to enter their personal information. Moreover, botnets can also be used for click-fraud. For example, they can be used to increase click through rate (CTR) artificially as they can be commanded to click on specific hyperlinks continuously. In some serious cases, these illegal activities of botnets may lead to government conflicts, shutdown of companies and other serious events. Furthermore, cybercriminals can use botnets to take control of some the most important public sectors and this can have very bad consequences. For example, taking control of health sector can affect hospitals and as a result, sick people who stay in these hospitals as cybercriminals are able to alter patient records and even affect machines which are used to treat sick people. On the other hand, performing an attack on education sector can have impact on students and as well as on the income of governments. Some governments mostly relay on tax generated from education sector as a source of income. If cybercriminals manage to perform attacks on the education sector of governments, this can discourage students from studying in these countries and therefore decrease the amount of income of these governments generated from education sector. For the companies, cybercriminals can use botnets to perform attacks and obtain confidential information which can be sold to other companies by these cybercriminals. To sum up, botnets are very dangerous. Cybercriminals can use them according to their needs. The only limit is their imagination. Therefore, new methods must be invented to detect, mitigate, traceback and neutralise these attacks before they start.

DETECTION OF BOTNETS

As botnets have become a huge problem in cyber security world, experts have started to invent new detection mechanisms to detect botnets before they launch a new attack and reduce the amount of damage they can give. Until now, many different methods have been proposed and tried. The following paragraphs will examine some of these methods:

Honeypots

Honeypots are recognised by their ability to detect threats, aggregate malwares and observe behaviours of attackers (Liu, Xiao, Ghaboosi, Deng & Zhang, 2009). Honeypots observe behaviours of attackers by letting subnets act as being infected by a Trojan which also allows identification of controlling hosts (Cooke, Jahanian & McPherson, 2005). As there are more honeynet tools on Linux, most of the researches are Linux-based researches (McCarty, 2003). Therefore, the number of tools which support honeypot deployment on Windows is very low which allowed attackers to dismantle the honeypot and take advantage of this (Liu, Xiao, Ghaboosi, Deng & Zhang, 2009). A honeynet consists of more than one honeypot working on a single network and is used to screen large networks. Some researchers conducted a study about producing a reactive firewall to protect compromises of honeypots (McCarty, 2003). The inbound attacks on compromised ports can be prevented as those ports are detected by such a firewall (McCarty, 2003). It is important to block incoming traffic carefully, as attackers download toolkits after an invasion (McCarty, 2003). These toolkits can be used as pioneer pieces of work in further researches. On the other hand, attackers have responded to this honeypot trap situation by finding new ways of avoiding them. They have invented new methods to detect these honeypots. A group of researchers have found a way of detecting honeypots with the help of intelligent probing on public report statistics (Bethencourt, Franklin & Vernon, 2005). In addition to this, another group of researchers have invented another way of detecting honeypots by using independent software and hardware (Zou & Cunningham, 2006). Also, they proposed a way of finding and removing infected honeypots with the help of peer to peer botnets (Zou & Cunningham, 2006).

Signature-Based Detection

Signature-based detection uses passive traffic monitoring to locate botnets. Behaviours and signatures retained from existing botnets are used in botnet detection. Simply, it is about gathering information from the traffic packets and comparing it with patterns found on database collected from existing bots (Liu, Xiao, Ghaboosi, Deng & Zhang, 2009). It can be really simple to compare every byte in the packet, but this comes with some disadvantages. These disadvantages are (Kugisaki, Kasahara, Hori & Sakurai, 2007):

- Detection of unknown botnets would not be possible.
- The database of signatures should be updated regularly which results in increase in management costs and decrease in performance.
- The database of signatures should be pathed with a pace or new bots may launch new attacks before that.

Another example of signature-based detection is Snort, which is an open source intrusion detection system (Snort - Network Intrusion Detection & Prevention System, n.d.). Snort is programmed with a set of behaviours or signatures to log traffic which is assumed to be suspicious (Snort - Network Intrusion Detection & Prevention System, n.d.).

Anomaly-Based Detection

Anomaly-based detection uses network traffic anomalies to locate botnets. These anomalies are high network latency, high volumes of traffic, traffic on unusual ports and any other unusual system behaviour which shows presence of bots (Feily, Shahrestani, & Ramadass, 2009). Unlike signature-based detection mechanisms, anomaly-based detection mechanisms can detect unknown botnets. However, it cannot detect IRC networks which may be a botnet but not active yet as there are no anomalies (Feily, Shahrestani, & Ramadass, 2009). In order to overcome this issue, an algorithm presented by a group of researchers. They used TCP-based anomaly detection with IRC tokenization and IRC message statistics to create a mechanism which can also locate client botnets (Binkley & Singh, 2006). Moreover, another algorithm which uses passive analysis of flow data located in transport layer for detection and characterisation of botnets was proposed by the researchers (Karasaridis, Rexroad & Hoeflin, 2007). On the other hand, Gu et al. presented a BotSniffer which makes use of network-based anomaly detection to determine C&C channels in a local area network (Gu, Zhang & Lee, 2008).

DNS-Based Detection

DNS-based detection is more like anomaly-based detection as same anomaly detection algorithms can be used on DNS traffic (Feily, Shahrestani, & Ramadass, 2009). Bots send DNS queries to be able to access the C&C server where they initiate communication and receive commands. Therefore, it is convenient to detect botnets by doing DNS monitoring on DNS traffic to detect anomalies (Feily, Shahrestani, & Ramadass, 2009). Choi et al. presented a study about anomaly-based detection where they screened group activities in DNS traffic (Choi, Lee, Lee & Kim, 2007). According to their findings, botnet queries can easily be differentiated from legitimate ones (Choi, Lee, Lee & Kim, 2007). The authors distinguished botnet queries from legitimate ones by looking at these features (Choi, Lee, Lee & Kim, 2007):

1.   Only bots send DNS queries to the domain of C&C server.
2.   Bots act and move around together simultaneously. This also includes their DNS queries.
3.   Botnets make use of Dynamic DNS for their C&C servers whereas legitimate hosts do not use them frequently.

The researchers have used these features to propose a new algorithm which determines botnet DNS queries. They also invented an anomaly-based detection mechanism which detected C&C server migration and was more durable compared to other detection methods as it could detect any kind of bot or botnet by checking group activities on DNS traffic (Feily, Shahrestani, & Ramadass, 2009). In addition, it can also detect botnets with encrypted channels as it uses information from IP headers, however this approach requires high processing time (Feily, Shahrestani, & Ramadass, 2009). In 2005, a researcher presented a mechanism which detected domain names with high or temporally concentrated DDNS query rates in order to determine C&C servers of botnets (Dagon, 2005). However, this detection method can be fooled by using faked DNS queries (Feily, Shahrestani, & Ramadass, 2009). Also, in another research, it is proven that this method produces high false positive rate as it misclassifies legitimate domains which use DNS with short time-to-live (TTL) (Villamarín-Salomón, & Brustoloni, 2008).

Mining-Based Detection

Mining-based detection is more about detection of C&C traffic of botnets. As botnets communicate with their botmasters via C&C channels, it would be an intelligent move to detect C&C traffic. However, botnets use normal protocols for C&C communications which do not produce any anomalies such as high volume of traffic or high network latency (Feily, Shahrestani, & Ramadass, 2009). Therefore, it would be difficult to detect C&C traffic of botnets by using anomaly-based detection techniques. Here, mining-based detection comes into play which is a very effective way of detecting C&C traffic of botnets. In 2008, the authors proposed an approach to detect C&C traffic of botnets by using a technique known as multiple log-file mining which is a good example of flow-based botnet traffic detection (Masud, Al-Khateeb, Khan, Thuraisingham & Hamlen, 2008). In order to detect C&C traffic of botnets, the authors introduced multiple log correlation. The researchers correlated two host-based log files temporarily to detect botnet activity in a host machine (Masud, Al-Khateeb, Khan, Thuraisingham & Hamlen, 2008). Then, with the help of data mining techniques, the authors obtained relevant features from these log files and used them in C&C traffic detection of botnets (Masud, Al-Khateeb, Khan, Thuraisingham & Hamlen, 2008). As the mentioned approach does not need access to payload content, it works perfectly in situations where payload is encrypted or not available (Masud, Al-Khateeb, Khan, Thuraisingham & Hamlen, 2008). In another study, the authors proposed a detection mechanism known as Botminer which did not require any prior knowledge and still detect botnets regardless to C&C botnet protocol and structure (Gu, Perdisci, Zhang & Lee, 2008). Botminer groups similar communication and malicious traffic together and carries out cross cluster correlation to detect hosts with similar communication and attacking patterns (Gu, Perdisci, Zhang & Lee, 2008). Also, studies proved that Botminer has low false positive rates and can detect real world botnets such as IRC-based and P2P botnets etc (Gu, Perdisci, Zhang & Lee, 2008).

Detection With Machine Learning and AI

Detection mechanisms which employ machine learning or artificial intelligence aim for identification and classification of network traffic generated by botnets as they communicate with their botmaster and each other. Recently, many studies have been done in this area as capabilities of machine learning and artificial intelligence have realised by the researchers. Zhao et al. proposed a study in the area of botnet detection using machine learning where they analysed traffic behaviour of botnets by classifying network traffic behaviour (Zhao, Traore, Sayed, Luu, Saad, Ghorbani & Garant, 2013). The authors worked on the practicability of detecting botnet activity without seeing the complete network flow by grouping behaviour based on time intervals (Zhao, Traore, Sayed, Luu, Saad, Ghorbani & Garant, 2013). Also, they focused on behavioural analysis of Peer to Peer C&C channels (Zhao, Traore, Sayed, Luu, Saad, Ghorbani & Garant, 2013). As an advantage, the mentioned method can analyse encrypted network communication protocols as traffic analysis methods do not bound up with the payload of packets. On the other hand, Nogueira et al. used Artificial Neural Network to figure out licit and illicit traffic patterns (Nogueira, Salvador & Blessa, 2010). The authors trained multi-layer neural network with TCP connection-based features to detect HTTP-based botnet (Nogueira, Salvador & Blessa, 2010). Also, it is mentioned that the proposed method has low false positive detection rate and high accuracy of detecting HTTP botnets (Nogueira, Salvador & Blessa, 2010). Moreover, Venkatesh et al, proposed a new approach for botnet detection using Multilayer Feed-Forward Neural Network with an adaptive learning rate (Venkatesh & Nadarajan, 2012). The approach was based around extraction of TCP related features as HTTP-based botnets use TCP connections for communication purposes (Venkatesh & Nadarajan, 2012). The authors used bold driver back-propagation algorithm to optimise the learning rate coefficient during weight updating process (Venkatesh & Nadarajan, 2012). Studies have showed that, actively learned neural networks had better identification accuracy with less false positives (Venkatesh & Nadarajan, 2012). In another research, the authors proposed a new detection framework with three detection models where different machine learning classifiers are inspected for each model (Alenazi, Traore, Ganame & Woungang, 2017). The first model analyses applications and removes malicious ones while the second model controls regularity in timing of DNS queries of bots and uses this in the detection of botnets (Alenazi, Traore, Ganame & Woungang, 2017). The last model focuses on the characteristics of DNS domain names and determines algorithmically created domains and fast flux ones which are considered to be footprints of HTTP-based botnets (Alenazi, Traore, Ganame & Woungang, 2017).

CONCLUSION

Nowadays, building or purchasing botnets have become very easy. An individual person who knows how to use a computer and has no prior knowledge about botnets can purchase a botnet from black market with a very low price. Giving such a power to someone without required knowledge may result in a huge disaster. In addition, there publicly available support tools which let criminal people to build their own personal botnets for different purposes. This increases the number of botnets and threats in cyber security world. As botnets become more popular among cyber criminals, the use of botnets has peaked. They have started to build new kinds of botnets to overcome detection mechanisms created by experts. There is an invisible race between hackers and experts. Experts try to beat hackers by generating new ways of detecting and neutralising botnets while hackers try to build newer models of botnets to increase variety. Therefore, it is very important to increase awareness among individual users. Individual users need to know how botnets operate and how to protect themselves from possible threats. This is very important as botnets can target different profiles. They can aim big companies as well as individual users and even governments. The awareness of individual users can be increased with little training sessions. It will be useful to teach users how to protect themselves. Users should know the use of anti-virus software, anti-spyware or firewalls. Otherwise, they may become a part of botnet without them knowing. This will create a big threat against their identity, personal information or even financial data. This book chapter aims to increase knowledge about botnets and make individual users more familiar with the concepts related to botnets.

REFERENCES

Abu Rajab, M., Zarfoss, J., Monrose, F., & Terzis, A. (2006, October). A multifaceted approach to understanding the botnet phenomenon. In *Proceedings of the 6th ACM SIGCOMM conference on Internet measurement* (pp. 41-52). ACM. 10.1145/1177080.1177086

Alejandre, F. V., Cortés, N. C., & Anaya, E. A. (2017, February). Feature selection to detect botnets using machine learning algorithms. In *Electronics, Communications and Computers (CONIELECOMP), 2017 International Conference on* (pp. 1-7). IEEE. 10.1109/CONIELECOMP.2017.7891834

Alenazi, A., Traore, I., Ganame, K., & Woungang, I. (2017, October). Holistic Model for HTTP Botnet Detection Based on DNS Traffic Analysis. In *International Conference on Intelligent, Secure, and Dependable Systems in Distributed and Cloud Environments* (pp. 1-18). Springer. 10.1007/978-3-319-69155-8_1

Bailey, M., Cooke, E., Jahanian, F., Xu, Y., & Karir, M. (2009, March). A survey of botnet technology and defenses. In Conference For Homeland Security, 2009. CATCH'09. Cybersecurity Applications & Technology (pp. 299-304). IEEE doi:10.1109/CATCH.2009.40

Bethencourt, J., Franklin, J., & Vernon, M. K. (2005, August). Mapping Internet Sensors with Probe Response Attacks. In *USENIX Security Symposium* (pp. 193-208). USENIX.

Bilge, L., Balzarotti, D., Robertson, W., Kirda, E., & Kruegel, C. (2012, December). Disclosure: detecting botnet command and control servers through large-scale netflow analysis. In *Proceedings of the 28th Annual Computer Security Applications Conference* (pp. 129-138). ACM. 10.1145/2420950.2420969

Binkley, J. R., & Singh, S. (2006). An Algorithm for Anomaly-based Botnet Detection. *SRUTI, 6,* 7–7.

Botnet. (2018, September 22). Retrieved from https://en.wikipedia.org/wiki/Botnet

Canavan, J. (2005, October). The evolution of malicious IRC bots. In *Virus Bulletin Conference* (pp. 104-114). Academic Press.

Cho, M. (2003). *Mixing Technology and Business: The Roles and Responsibilities of the Chief Information Security Officer.* Retrieved from SANS Institute: SANS Institute: https://www.sans.org/reading-room/whitepapers/assurance/mixing-technology-business-roles-responsibilities-chief-information-security-of-1044

Choi, H., Lee, H., Lee, H., & Kim, H. (2007, October). Botnet detection by monitoring group activities in DNS traffic. In *Computer and Information Technology, 2007. CIT 2007. 7th IEEE International Conference on* (pp. 715-720). IEEE. 10.1109/CIT.2007.90

Cooke, E., Jahanian, F., & McPherson, D. (2005). The Zombie Roundup: Understanding, Detecting, and Disrupting Botnets. *SRUTI, 5,* 6–6.

Dagon, D. (2005, July). Botnet detection and response. In OARC workshop (Vol. 2005). Academic Press.

Ersson, J., & Moradian, E. (2013). Botnet Detection with Event-Driven Analysis. *Procedia Computer Science, 22,* 662–671. doi:10.1016/j.procs.2013.09.147

Feily, M., Shahrestani, A., & Ramadass, S. (2009, June). A survey of botnet and botnet detection. In *Emerging Security Information, Systems and Technologies, 2009. SECURWARE'09. Third International Conference on* (pp. 268-273). IEEE. 10.1109/SECURWARE.2009.48

Garcıa, S. (2014). *Identifying, Modeling and Detecting Botnet Behaviors in the Network* (Unpublished doctoral dissertation). Universidad Nacional del Centro de la Provincia de Buenos Aires.

Garcia, S., Grill, M., Stiborek, J., & Zunino, A. (2014). An empirical comparison of botnet detection methods. *Computers & Security, 45,* 100-123.

Grizzard, J. B., Sharma, V., Nunnery, C., Kang, B. B., & Dagon, D. (2007). Peer-to-Peer Botnets: Overview and Case Study. *HotBots, 7,* 1–1.

Gu, G., Perdisci, R., Zhang, J., & Lee, W. (2008). *Botminer: Clustering analysis of network traffic for protocol-and structure-independent botnet detection.* Academic Press.

Gu, G., Zhang, J., & Lee, W. (2008). *BotSniffer: Detecting botnet command and control channels in network traffic.* Academic Press.

Hachem, N., Mustapha, Y. B., Granadillo, G. G., & Debar, H. (2011, May). Botnets: lifecycle and taxonomy. In *Network and Information Systems Security (SAR-SSI), 2011 Conference on* (pp. 1-8). IEEE. 10.1109/SAR-SSI.2011.5931395

Ioannidis, J., & Bellovin, S. M. (2002, February). Implementing Pushback: Router-Based Defense Against DDoS Attacks. In NDSS (Vol. 2). Academic Press.

Karasaridis, A., Rexroad, B., & Hoeflin, D. A. (2007). Wide-Scale Botnet Detection and Characterization. *HotBots, 7,* 7–7.

Kavitha, D., & Rani, S. K. (2015). Review of Botnet Attacks and its detection Mechanism. *International Journal of Innovative Research in Computer and Communication Engineering, 3,* 2377-2383.

Kim, D. H., Lee, T., Kang, J., Jeong, H., & In, H. P. (2012). Adaptive pattern mining model for early detection of botnet-propagation scale. *Security and Communication Networks, 5*(8), 917–927. doi:10.1002ec.366

Kugisaki, Y., Kasahara, Y., Hori, Y., & Sakurai, K. (2007, October). Bot detection based on traffic analysis. In *Intelligent Pervasive Computing, 2007. IPC. The 2007 International Conference on* (pp. 303-306). IEEE. 10.1109/IPC.2007.91

Lee, J. S., Jeong, H., Park, J. H., Kim, M., & Noh, B. N. (2008, December). The activity analysis of malicious http-based botnets using degree of periodic repeatability. In *Security Technology, 2008. SECTECH'08. International Conference on* (pp. 83-86). IEEE. 10.1109/SecTech.2008.52

Lin, K. C., Chen, S. Y., & Hung, J. C. (2014). Botnet detection using support vector machines with artificial fish swarm algorithm. *Journal of Applied Mathematics*.

Liu, J., Xiao, Y., Ghaboosi, K., Deng, H., & Zhang, J. (2009). Botnet: Classification, attacks, detection, tracing, and preventive measures. *EURASIP Journal on Wireless Communications and Networking, 2009*(1), 692654. doi:10.1155/2009/692654

Masud, M. M., Al-Khateeb, T., Khan, L., Thuraisingham, B., & Hamlen, K. W. (2008, October). Flow-based identification of botnet traffic by mining multiple log files. In *Distributed Framework and Applications, 2008. DFmA 2008. First International Conference on* (pp. 200-206). IEEE. 10.1109/ICDFMA.2008.4784437

McCarty, B. (2003). Botnets: Big and bigger. *IEEE Security and Privacy, 99*(4), 87–90. doi:10.1109/MSECP.2003.1219079

Muthumanickam, K., Ilavarasan, E., & Dwivedi, S. K. (2014). A Dynamic Botnet Detection Model based on Behavior Analysis. *International Journal on Recent Trends in Engineering & Technology, 10*(1), 104.

Nogueira, A., Salvador, P., & Blessa, F. (2010, June). A botnet detection system based on neural networks. In *Digital Telecommunications (ICDT), 2010 Fifth International Conference on* (pp. 57-62). IEEE. 10.1109/ICDT.2010.19

Oikarinen, J., & Reed, D. (1993). *Internet relay chat protocol* (No. RFC 1459).

Ollmann, G. (2009). *Botnet communication topologies*. Academic Press.

Pappas, K. (2008). *Back to basics to fight botnets*. Academic Press.

Perdisci, R., Lee, W., & Feamster, N. (2010, April). *Behavioral Clustering of HTTP-Based Malware and Signature Generation Using Malicious Network Traces* (Vol. 10). NSDI.

Sari, A. (2018). Context-Aware Intelligent Systems for Fog Computing Environments for Cyber-Threat Intelligence. In *Fog Computing* (pp. 205–225). Cham: Springer. doi:10.1007/978-3-319-94890-4_10

Sari, A. (2019). Turkish national cyber-firewall to mitigate countrywide cyber-attacks. *Computers & Electrical Engineering, 73*, 128–144. doi:10.1016/j.compeleceng.2018.11.008

Snort - Network Intrusion Detection & Prevention System. (n.d.). Retrieved from http://www.snort.org/

Van Ruitenbeek, E., & Sanders, W. H. (2008, September). Modeling peer-to-peer botnets. In *Quantitative Evaluation of Systems, 2008. QEST'08. Fifth International Conference on* (pp. 307-316). IEEE. 10.1109/QEST.2008.43

Venkatesh, G. K., & Nadarajan, R. A. (2012, June). HTTP botnet detection using adaptive learning rate multilayer feed-forward neural network. In *IFIP International Workshop on Information Security Theory and Practice* (pp. 38-48). Springer.

Villamarín-Salomón, R., & Brustoloni, J. C. (2008, January). Identifying botnets using anomaly detection techniques applied to DNS traffic. In *Consumer Communications and Networking Conference, 2008. CCNC 2008. 5th IEEE* (pp. 476-481). IEEE. 10.1109/ccnc08.2007.112

Vormayr, G., Zseby, T., & Fabini, J. (2017). Botnet communication patterns. *IEEE Communications Surveys and Tutorials*, *19*(4), 2768–2796. doi:10.1109/COMST.2017.2749442

Wang, A., Chang, W., Chen, S., & Mohaisen, A. (2018). Delving into internet DDoS attacks by botnets: Characterization and analysis. *IEEE/ACM Transactions on Networking*, *26*(6), 2843–2855. doi:10.1109/TNET.2018.2874896

Wang, P., Aslam, B., & Zou, C. C. (2010). Peer-to-peer botnets. In *Handbook of Information and Communication Security* (pp. 335–350). Berlin: Springer. doi:10.1007/978-3-642-04117-4_18

Xie, Y., Yu, F., Achan, K., Panigrahy, R., Hulten, G., & Osipkov, I. (2008). Spamming botnets: Signatures and characteristics. *Computer Communication Review*, *38*(4), 171–182. doi:10.1145/1402946.1402979

Zhao, D., Traore, I., Sayed, B., Lu, W., Saad, S., Ghorbani, A., & Garant, D. (2013). Botnet detection based on traffic behavior analysis and flow intervals. *Computers & Security*, *39*, 2–16. doi:10.1016/j.cose.2013.04.007

Zou, C. C., & Cunningham, R. (2006, June). Honeypot-aware advanced botnet construction and maintenance. In *Null* (pp. 199-208). IEEE. doi:10.1109/DSN.2006.38

ADDITIONAL READING

Al-Hammadi, Y., & Aickelin, U. (2010, January). Behavioural correlation for detecting P2P bots. In *Future Networks, 2010. ICFN'10. Second International Conference on* (pp. 323-327). IEEE. 10.1109/ICFN.2010.72

Chen, C. M., Ou, Y. H., & Tsai, Y. C. (2010, December). Web botnet detection based on flow information. In *Computer Symposium (ICS), 2010 International* (pp. 381-384). IEEE. 10.1109/COMPSYM.2010.5685482

García, S., Zunino, A., & Campo, M. (2012). Botnet behavior detection using network synchronism. In *Privacy, Intrusion Detection and Response: Technologies for Protecting Networks* (pp. 122-144). IGI Global. doi:10.4018/978-1-60960-836-1.ch005

Saad, S., Traore, I., Ghorbani, A., Sayed, B., Zhao, D., Lu, W., . . . Hakimian, P. (2011, July). Detecting P2P botnets through network behavior analysis and machine learning. In *Privacy, Security and Trust (PST), 2011 Ninth Annual International Conference on* (pp. 174-180). IEEE 10.1109/PST.2011.5971980

Strayer, W. T., Walsh, R., Livadas, C., & Lapsley, D. (2006, November). Detecting botnets with tight command and control. In *Local Computer Networks, Proceedings 2006 31st IEEE Conference on* (pp. 195-202). IEEE. 10.1109/LCN.2006.322100

Wang, B., Li, Z., Li, D., Liu, F., & Chen, H. (2010, May). Modeling connections behavior for web-based bots detection. In *e-Business and Information System Security (EBISS), 2010 2nd International Conference on* (pp. 1-4). IEEE. 10.1109/EBISS.2010.5473532

KEY TERMS AND DEFINITIONS

AI: AI stands for artificial intelligence. Artificial intelligence is a form of intelligence which is used by machines to carry out activities associated with humans. Learning new things or adapting to changes in an environment can be example to human associated activities.

Bot: A botnet consists of more than one bot working together in an accordance. If a botnet is considered as an army, then a bot can be considered as a single soldier in that army.

Botmaster: Botmaster is the cyber-criminal/attacker who owns the botnet and responsible for its actions. In other words, botmaster is a person who controls the botnet.

Command and Control (C&C) Server: Command and control (C&C) server is used to set communication with systems which are infected by malwares. C&C servers are controlled by cybercriminals who own those malwares. Botnets make use of these C&C servers, and botmasters use them as communication channels to be able to command their botnets.

Domain Name System (DNS): Domain name system (DNS) translates domain names into IP addresses so browsers can understand and load the required contents.

Honeypot: Honeypots let subnets act as being infected by a Trojan to be able to observe behaviors of attackers. This helps professionals to detect threats and aggregate malwares.

Markov Chain: Markov chain is a sequence of possible events and the probability of each event happening is determined by the state in the previous events.

Peer-to-Peer (P2P) Network: Peer-to-peer (P2P) networks consist of peers that are connected to each other with the internet. Files can be shared between systems and every computer has the probability of becoming a client and a file server.

This research was previously published in Applying Methods of Scientific Inquiry Into Intelligence, Security, and Counterterrorism edited by Arif Sari; pages 111-137, copyright year 2019 by Information Science Reference (an imprint of IGI Global).

Chapter 2
Denial-of-Service and Botnet Analysis, Detection, and Mitigation

Sobana Sikkanan

https://orcid.org/0000-0001-8237-7140
Adithya Institute of Technology, India

Kasthuri M.
PSNA College of Engineering and Technology, India

ABSTRACT

The internet is designed for processing and forwarding of any packet in a best effort manner. The packets carried by the internet may be malicious or not. Most of the time, internet architecture provides an unregulated path to victims. Denial-of-service (DoS) attack is the most common critical threat that causes devastating effects on the internet. The Botnet-based DoS attack aims to exhaust both the target resources and network bandwidth, thereby making the network resources unavailable for its valid users. The resources are utilized by either injecting a computer virus or flooding the network with useless traffic. This chapter provides a systematic analysis of the causes of DoS attacks, including motivations and history, analysis of different attacks, detection and protection techniques, various mitigation techniques, the limitations and challenges of DoS research areas. Finally, this chapter discusses some important research directions which will need more attention in the near future to guarantee the successful defense against DoS attacks.

INTRODUCTION

In the modern era, our daily life depends on Internet applications for all our necessary activities. Some humans are using this internet in a destructive manner and some others use this in a constructive manner. Cloud computing has an impact on the growth of internet word even though the process of designing and computing of a cloud environment is complicated (Kumar, 2018). The complexity of the cloud-computing

DOI: 10.4018/978-1-7998-5348-0.ch002

process leads to insecure digital data processing (Feng, Chen, & Liu, 2010). A collection of hijacked devices connected through the internet represents a Botnet which creates some safety and security issues. Bailey, Cooke, Xu, and Karir (2009) stated that the detection and mitigation of these botnet threads is a complicated process. Botnet cyber-attacks such as Denial-of-Service (DoS) and Distributed Denial-of-Service (DDoS) attacks are introduced to steal a victim's personal information (Aamir & Zaidi, 2013).

Initially, the DoS attacks were introduced against web applications. The first DoS attack was initiated by the hijackers in the late 1990s and it becomes a significant danger to all the web applications (Bencsáth & Vajda, 2004). As said by (Gresty, Shi, & Merabti, 2001), DoS controls the web pages for a predefined amount of time to collect all the personal information and introduces some revenue lost even in the offline condition. In business environments, companies try to knock off their competing companies from the business market with the help of these DoS attacks. Pappalardo (2005) revealed that online extortion via DoS attacks is increasing during the past decades. Attackers controlled the victim's online businesses using DoS attacks and threatened them to give payments for their protection.

In recent network scenarios, most of the companies, organizations, and government sectors are looking forward to transferring all or parts of their information to the cloud (Gonzales D, Kaplan J.M, Saltzman E, Winkelman Z, & D., 2017; Wong, 1998). The introduction of cloud technology allows the organization to transfer a lot of information with the least capital cost. DoS aims to attack widely used public sectors such as Banking services and e-commerce sites. DoS attack introduces some massive security threats to some government organizations such as India in 2012 (Register., 2012), the USA in 2015 (Incapsula., 2015), Brazil in 2016 (Corero., 2016) and Ireland in 2017 (Silicon., 2017). DoS attackers used some malware techniques to hack the details of customers of U.S based banks in 2012 (Networks, 2012). HSBC bank in the U.K was in the hit list of DoS attack during 2016 (Guardian., 2016). E-commerce sectors such as Bitcoin websites were also affected by DoS attacks in 2017 (Coindesk., 2017). Recent years DoS causes a significant impact on social websites like eBay, Amazon, Buy.com, Capital one bank, SunTrust bank, and Microsoft. The above discussions reveal that protecting the network from the DoS attack becomes an important issue (Arunadevi, 2018). The inability of the network security mechanism in detecting the DoS attack indicates the lack of security services in the government structure.

A lot of DoS detection and prevention techniques were introduced in the past decades (Jayanthi, DileepKumar, & Singh, 2016; Sharma & Gupta, 2018; Shrivastava, Sharma, & Rai, 2010). But still, DoS remains a significant challenge to network security systems because of its implementation complexity (Amit & Santhithilagam, 2019). Different types of DoS attacks and the different defense mechanism involved in detection and prevention process leads to the development of a structural approach to the DoS defense mechanisms (Arushi Arora, Sumit Kumar Yadav, & Sharma, 2018; Douligeris & Mitrokotsa, 2004). Linear predictor model (Al-Anzi, Yadav, & Soni, 2014; Gupta et al., 2010),web referrals (Desai, Patel, Somaiya, & Vishwanathan, 2016) and multivariate data analysis to measure the low and high rate DDoS attack (Arushi Arora et al., 2018; Bhushan, Banerjea, & Yadav, 2014; Hoque, 2016) are some of the existing approaches to prevent proposed the DDoS attack. In 2018 Yadav, Sharma, and Arora (2018) proposed a list-based DDoS mitigation system configurations. This mitigation software are developed by the edge router of the Internet Service Provider (ISP) to rule out DDoS attacks into and from the ISPs' networks.

This chapter discusses in detail about the causes of DoS and DDoS, different types of DoS attacks, the motivation of different DoS attacks, available protection, and mitigation techniques and the challenges associated with modern techniques. The chapter also gives some research directions to overcome the DoS and DDoS security attacks. This chapter is organized as a combination of seven subdivisions.

Subdivision 1 presents the introduction about the botnet, DoS and the motivation behind the DoS attack. Subdivision 2 describes the botnet basics, causes, and controlling mechanisms. Subdivision 3 describes in detail about the fundamentals of DoS attack, Phases of DoS, classification of existing DoS attacks and their detection techniques. Different classifications of DoS prevention techniques are presented in subdivision 4. Subdivision 5 provides a clear idea about the mitigating effects of DoS. Subdivision 6 discusses the existing DoS challenges on various systems. Finally, Subdivision 7 gives a summary of this chapter and suggests some ideas for the future design considerations for avoiding DoS.

Motivation Behind DoS

In practice understanding the motivation behind the occurrence of DoS attacks is difficult. Illicit cyber activities are the headlines on daily news in the past three decades and more efforts are taken in preventing and dealing with such attacks. Increase in the number of network users increases the possibility of the occurrence of illegal activities. The attackers in the remote hidden places are trying to control and access the victim systems to perform their attack (Cohen & Felson, 2016). Identifying the attackers and their motivation of attack is a complicated process; hence explanations about why does occur are based on the assumption obtained from existing evidence. A secured organization must be capable of identifying the initiator of the attack and their motivation in order to handle and prevent the DoS attacks. Most of the DoS attacks are initiated by the attackers only for fun or for some specific goals. Some of the common motivations for the DoS attacks are listed out by Bhale (2016).

1. **Financial Motivations**: This is the most prevalent reason behind an organized attack. The attackers implement their financial attacks in three different ways:
    a. **Data Breach**: A data breach is a security attack that accesses the users' information without authorization. Intestinally the motivators' theft the identity proves and financial information's such as bank details or credit card details, personal health information and intellectual property. *The attacker gangs are well organized and circulate the gathered information in a supply chain basis. The dark web act as a market place for hackers to sell the stolen data to those who want to commit fraud activities.* A data breach is a security incident in which information is accessed without authorization. Ponemon Institute carried out a study regarding the data beach and revealed that the average total cost of a company's data breach is about $3.86 million.
    b. **Financial Demands**: Here the main reason for introducing a DoS attack is to gain money. Hackers attack victim's laptops or computers or mobile phones and freeze it. Then they access the details without the victim's permission and disrupt the victim's services and blackmail with financial demands to avoid disruption. Criminals may also reveal the security details of the individuals by sending emails in the name of reputable bankers and advise them to change of bank account login details (Kramer L, 2015). In some scenarios, the attackers try to initiate a DoS attack against some reputed companies or organizations and disturb their websites and make it unsuitable of operation then demand ransom money in order to stop their attack. Some attackers demand ransom money by threatening the company that they are going to initiate an attack against the company's website.
    c. **Anticompetitive Business Practices**: Cyber-attackers introduce a DoS attack to take over the control of a competitor's company websites. Then they disturb the services supported by

the target company and reduce their rate of sales. These types of DoS attacks are most common in online gambling websites. In some situations, the attackers first initiate their attack against the companies' web pages and make them unusable. Then they demand a considerable amount of money in order to stop their attacks. Sometimes the attackers claim some money by threatening them that they are planning to initiate DoS attack against their web pages.

2. **Nonfinancial Motivations:** Other than financial motivations some hackers involve in hactivism or protest for misusing a computer system or network for a politically or socially motivated reasons. The hackers introduce new attacks for some specific purposes such as to demonstrate the techniques or tools developed by them. Sometimes the DoS attack is initiated by the competitors in order to demolish the sales, damage the reputation and customer relationships of the opponent company. In the recent scenario, the government introduces the DoS attack against other governments as a weapon of war.

3. **To make a Political or Social Point:** 'Hacktivists' launching a DoS attack against the companies involving in activities they do not concur with. The time needed for initiating this type of attack is so short so that it is challenging to realize the attacks and stop them. Sometimes because of the hacktivists cyber-attacks, even the political bodies and Government organizations are forced to stop carrying out their normal activities. Beyond this, terrorist also attack their targets with the help of this hacking. Some attackers try to hack the web defacement of unsecured servers. Government websites are commonly attacked by some people, organizations or another government who do not like to support the ideas of this government.

4. **For the Intellectual Challenge:** This type of attack aims to create a wrong impression of an organization. The criticism may be against a political party or a particular person. The motivations behind the attacks are as follows.

    a. **Fights Between Attackers**: Sometimes the attackers who involved in Internet-based malicious activities use a DoS attack against opponent group's infrastructure and operations, and catch their businesses. A user having a small idea about the internet may download and run a program that performs a DoS attack. This helps an average computer user to take over a large company. Some attackers perform DOS attacks on another user's personal network for sacrificing their personal vengeance.

    b. **Self-Induced Attacks:** In some situations, the company or organization employees may introduce some server configuration problems by mistake thereby introduce DoS attacks.

    c. **Without Any Reason:** Sometimes the victims never understand the motivation of the DoS attack introduced in their system.

BOTNET DETECTION AND MITIGATION

Introduction

Understanding the motivation of the botnet security attack, make the readers to gain some insightful knowledge about the business models and know the immediate actions needed against the attack. This section describes the basics of a botnet attack, the motivation behind this attack and how to overcome this attack using some security algorithms (Kreuzer, 2016). Botnets refer to the networks of "bots and the term Bot, is derived from the short form of the word "robot". The Bots refers to a collection of remotely controlled, compromised software robots that run without human involvement. As said by Stevanovic and Pedersen (2015), in nature the Botnets are always under the control of a set of malicious software scripts designed to perform some predefined functions repeatedly to interfere or misuse a wide range of Internet-based services (Alomari et al., 2016; Alomari, Manickam, Gupta, Karuppayah, & Alfaris, 2012). Botnet malware integrates the components of viruses, worms, spyware and other malicious software (Vacca, 2013). The Botnet can be used for launching a variety of cybersecurity attacks such as financially motivated crimes, steal sensitive information of a target, *Denial of Service* (DoS) attacks, sending spam e-mails, and some ID or password theft. In the beginning, the Bots introduced for performing some repetitive operations in order to reduce time consumption. Bots used for legal activities in an automated manner are termed as benevolent Bots, and those used for malicious activities are termed as malicious Bots (Alomari et al., 2012). The essential concepts in the Botnet attack are;

- The bot starts automatically without the user's interaction (Csanádi, 2007).
- Bot perform a task or set of tasks, under the command and control (C&C) of a malicious remote administrator known as Bot master or master host (Schiller & Binkley, 2011).

The botnet introduces a massive security attack on internet applications, so it is necessary to use effective detection techniques. Though various research and commercial efforts are taken by the researches, the botnet attacks still continue to grow in size and complexity (Mahjabin, Xiao, Sun, & Jiang, 2017). In (Fielding, 2007), it is discussed that before five years at least a quarter of the world's computer networks was affected by a botnet attack. But till now there is no well-defined remedy for the botnet attacks against the security of the Internet services (CIOinsight, 2011). The Shadower Foundation (2012) survey approximated that around 6000 C&C servers, with an average of 2200 active C&C servers per day are affected by this attack. In practice, spam e-mails are responsible for the creation of botnets when the users open the link or e-mail; it downloads malicious software that their controls the specified computers and make them act as a botnet client.

Botnet Motivations

At first, the primary motivation of hackers is sharing software and information over other computers using viruses and worms. The growth of the internet allows internet users to begin online shopping and online banking facilities. The attackers exploit these online facilities for their financial gain instead of spending more time to disturb the victim's network services. In practice, the credit/debit card numbers, social security numbers such as Aadhar or PAN, and their online passwords are stolen by the Malware. The botmaster collects the stolen information and utilizes them for initiating their own financial attacks or sell the details to other attackers. Now a day's with spam emails, hardware installation on victim systems are also used for the financial gain (Massi, Panda, Rajappa, Selvaraj, & Revankar, 2010).

The main motivations of botnets are as follows (Bhale, 2016):

- **Identity Theft:** This aims to extract the user's personal data and credentials for getting financial benefits without their knowledge. The personal identity information includes passwords of e-mail accounts, online shopping, net banking, and social networks (Massi et al., 2010).
- **Spam Email:** Using spammer the attacker is able to support mass mailing services thereby reduces the computational complexity and increases the power of botnets.

- **Click Frauds:** The botmaster opens some online clicks on the victim's web page and tempts them to open their advertisement and make them participate in online games or purchases thus again money.
- **Denial of Service attack (DoS):** Botnets here try to control and occupy a considerable amount of victim's bandwidth and effectively utilize them to achieve multiple gigabytes of traffic load so as to initiate an attack against social websites to access political or military contexts.

Origination of Botnet Threat

Over a decade, growth in the number of malware practices are unmeasurable (Bonguet & Bellaiche, 2017). Day by day the complexities of malware software techniques get improved. The number of malware specimens or signatures identified by the anti-malware software providers reveals the growth of the crime. The malware may be either polymorphic or metamorphic. In polymorphic malware is a fixed code sequence is used to modify the malware binary code during transmission but the code remains unchanged. Whereas in metamorphic malware is changed for every transmission process. As explained previously the malware practices are introduced to gain financial benefit using various fraud schemes.

Various terms related to malware practices are mentioned below.

1. Computer Virus

   Computer virus exists in an executable file that combines itself to increase its number and spreads like a flu virus to other systems by copying itself again and again. In practice, using removable devices and network files in the affected host leads to the spreading of computer virus (Hogben, Plohmann, Gerhards-Padilla, & Leder, 2011). In general, a computer virus is a malicious program used to alter the operation of the victim host. It inserts itself to the legitimate code in order to execute itself. It has a capability of corrupting system software data and introduces unexpected effects on the system software.

2. Computer Worm

   A computer worm is capable of spreading itself actively without the use of any removable devices. It automatically searches the network and identifies other vulnerable hosts and infects them. This can be done by exploiting vulnerabilities in the host operating system or in the software's installed in the host. Some worms affect the victim host directly without the use of any predefined destructive schedule. In some places, the worms spread across the communication channels and act as an active carrier. The worms can also indirectly affect the system or network by consuming more power and bandwidth and introduce instability to the victim systems and networks (Hoque, 2016).

3. Trojan Horse

   Here the user is pretended to install or execute the Trojan horse software as legal software for general purposes. Then it implements its own malicious activities (Hogben et al., 2011). Trojan Horse is a vicious code that ruses in the form of a new application. Like computer viruses, Trojan Horse is not capable of spreading itself. By claiming the victim to free the victim's computer viruses, Trojan Horse introduces its own attack. Depending upon the breaching and damaging procedure of Trojan horse, it is classified as Remote Access Trojans, Data Sending Trojans, Destructive Trojans, Proxy Trojans, FTP Trojans, Security software disabler Trojans, and Denial-of Services (DoS) Trojans.

4. Spyware, Keylogger, Sniffer

These types of malware are used to extract secured data from a remote system. These attacks are enabled by weakening the functions of the operating system. Spyware is malicious software designed to extract data from the victim system. Example of such an activity are stealing credit card details, the behavior of users, stealing software serial numbers, etc. A key logger is another type of malware used to capture the official documents. Origination of Sniffer starts from network analysis process; the aim is to listen to traffic in a malicious environment and capture the essential official documents (Hogben et al., 2011).

5. **Rootkit**

A rootkit is a malicious software tool to secure specific malicious process from being detected or disabled by the host. A rootkit is a collection of tools; it is a combination of two words "root" and "kit". Here, the word root indicates an administrative account on Linux or UNIX systems, and it indicates the software used as a tool to implement the attack. Rootkit introduces its attack by enabling administrative access to a computer network. The presence of Rootkit in the victim hosts is for a longer duration, so it is challenging to remove it (Hogben et al., 2011). The rootkit controller can be capable of remotely executing and changing system configurations and file contents.

Botnet Control and Communication Architecture

The server computer which generates the required directives to the victim devices infected with ransomware or rootkits is named as command and control server (C&C server). C&C server is responsible for connecting all the responsible devices for initiating DDoS attacks, stealing and deleting victims' data, earning money through forgeries. Comparing previous decades, today the lifetime of the C&C server is reduced by following some cloud computing and automated domain generation algorithms (DGAs). Hence even the white hat malware feels hard to locate the C&C server location. Figure 1 gives an idea about the general structure of the Botnet. The life cycle of bot includes four different cycles such as creation, infection, rallying, weighting, and execution (Bhale, 2016). Figure 2 depicts the lifecycle of Botnet.

- The master creates or updates Botnet software's in the creation cycle, and it is suitable for remote locations.
- In the infection cycle, the victim's devices are infected by using vulnerable software's, Trojan horse or by sending email attachments. The infected victim is technically named as a zombie.
- In rallying cycle, the zombie device tries to contact C&C server either in point to point or in centralized topology. In point, to point topology, the device identifies the peer machine and joins the victim network. In centralized topology, Internet Relay Chat (IRC) server or HTTP server is responsible for generating the zombie. Bot C&C servers are capable of supporting multiple addresses and also respond immediately to any other bot requests.
- In the waiting cycle, the network will wait until it receives a command from the C&C server. Thus there must be very less traffic between master and bot.
- After receiving a command from the master in the execution cycle, the C&C server sends typical commands such as sending spam, scanning for new victims and flooding Dos attacks.

Figure 1. Botnet architecture

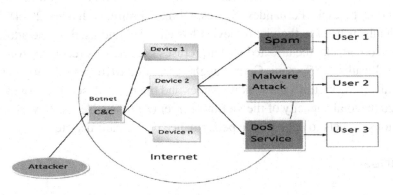

Figure 2. Botnet lifecycle

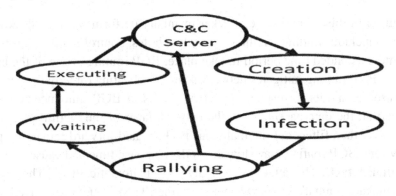

DOS ATTACK DETECTION

Introduction

In a cloud computing scenario, DoS becomes one of the most significant cyber-attack. DoS uses powerful and simple attack mechanisms to introduce a massive amount of threats to current Internet services (Mahjabin et al., 2017). The person who initiates the DoS attack blocks the resources of victim networks thereby disturbs their Internet services either permanently or temporarily. DoS attack is introduced by flooding unnecessary Internet applications to the victim systems; overload them; prevent them from processing their legitimate requests. Flooding of DoS attacks from different attackers at the same time to make them as a more troublesome attack is termed as Distributed Denial of Service (DDoS). The main target of the DoS or DDoS executers is to take over the control of the cloud server and access the web servers such as online bank transactions or credit card transactions from the user's service (Baheti & Gill, 2011). The victim's memory is also accessed by the attackers to threaten the victims by sending blackmails and activism.

DoS attack affects the website of a typical user by merely stopping the display of their personal contents. It affects the business environments by ceasing online systems and makes them stop responding. It also controls the industrial system by retrieving their sensor information(NCSC, 2018). Riquet, Grimaud, and Hauspie (2012) analyzed the presence of DDoS attack in the security software's and concluded

DDoS remains undetected by IDS and Firewall. The DoS or DDoS attacks on networks can be either direct attack or indirect attack (Fernandes, Soares, Gomes, Freire, & Inácio, 2014). In direct attacks, the security mechanisms used in the victim device has encoded and used by the attackers. Whereas in indirect DoS or DDoS attacks the affected system refuses the requests received from other services in the same network. Results of (Somani, Gaur, Sanghi, & Conti, 2016) reveals that with server network DoS attacks also affect the victim's network resources and the network service providers. The main aim of DoS is to utilize the total capacity of the victim's server (Antunes, Neves, & Veríssimo, 2008). Next, DoS inject malicious packets to degrade the performance of the victim system.

Attack Scenarios

The three different phases and their implementation of the DoS attacks can be set in three different scenarios. The scenarios are a manual attack, agent–handler attack and automatic attack.

1. **Manual Attack:** In this scenario, the attacker manually performs all the attacking process. The manual process includes finding out the security loopholes, controlling the victim machines. This takes some more extended time period to take place. BGP routing is one of the best examples of manual attack. BGP routing mitigates network layer DoS beating directly focusing the IP address of the victim server and its corresponding network links. A BGP announcement is sent from the router to divert all the data packets from the network layer of the victim system to the victim's server. The server then filters out the malicious packets, and forward remaining packets towards the victim system. BGP routing may slow down the response time and cause data leakage.
2. **Agent–Handler Attack:** This attack is basically a semiautomatic attack. The supervisor and the agents communicate manually to know about each other. The instruction received from the attacker decides the type of attack, the duration and the victims of the attack. But identifying and employing the supervisor network is an automatic process. The supervisor, machine, and agents either directly or indirectly communicate with them.
    a. In the *direct communication* method, the supervisor's IP address is added to the attack code. The agent thus knows the supervisor's identities for their later communications. The agent knows this IP address with the help of the compromised agent machine. In practice this type of communication is identifiable and it is easy to reveal the DOS attack using the backtracking method.
    b. *Indirect communication* uses internet relay chat (IRC) channels to enable communication between the supervisor and the agents. IRC makes it challenging to reveal the DOS attacks.
3. **Automatic Attack**: In this scenario, all the essential communications such as attack phases and attack requirements are automatic. At any time without any communication, the attacker can attack the victim system without the knowledge of the supervisor and agents. The compromised system has the attack code, which contains all the requirements of the attack and executes it to initiate the attack. The attackers use the existing back-doors to alter the attack code and introduce a new type of attack every time.

Attack Strategies and Mechanisms Involved in Different Attack Phases

A well-planned DoS attack, force the victim systems to shut down or make them run at dangerous conditions. Now a day's medical services, banking services, and air travel services are under the control of the internet for their effective communication. DoS attacks DNS root servers directly and introduce terrible internet attacks. DoS structure is shown in figure 3 consists of three different phases of operation and four different types of components. The components are the attacker, multiple control masters, slaves, agents or zombies, and the victim server.

Figure 3. Structure of DoS attack

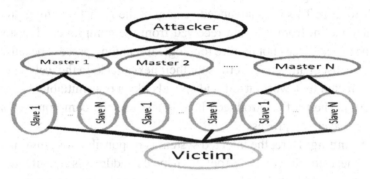

The functions performed in the three phases are as follows,

1. **Phase I**: **Recruiting Attack Armies**: Phase I initiates the botnet self-propagating programs (Sun, Yan, Xiao, & Yang, 2009) is used by the attackers for this purpose. They mainly concentrate on affecting devices having poor security support (Staniford, Paxson, & Weaver, 2002). The techniques used to identify the victim devices are mentioned in research papers(Weaver, 2001).

    Some of the widely used techniques are as follows.

a. **Random Scanning:** In this scanning process, previously affected victim systems randomly choose an IP address and infect that new system. The best example of this method is the well-known worm Code-Red (CRv2) (Moore & Shannon, 2002). In this method, the systems are typically expected to be in different networks, so the data traffic is heavy. There is no synchronization between the systems; this leads to the introduction of more number of duplicate data. The detection possibility of attack increases as the number of infected systems increases.

b. **Hitlist Scanning:** The first process in this technique is to list out the systems that are more vulnerable. It generates a warms and propagate it throughout the list and infect half of the listed systems. The hit list is prepared in several ways; if it is generated by port scans for a longer duration, then it is known as stealthy scanning. In distributed scanning, the already infected systems are used to prepare the Hitlist. Web-crawling and public surveys are the other alternative methods used by the attackers to generate the Hitlist in advance. The increase in the transmission of the Hitlist between hosts increases the detection possibility.

c. **Permutation Scanning:** In this method, the list of victim IP addresses is shared among the network devices with the help of preselected key formed from a 32-bit pseudorandom permutation list. If a device is infected by this permutation scanning, it begins to infect the next system randomly chosen from the list. Self-coordination among the victim systems eliminates the possibility of multiple probing of the same IP address. Frequent monitoring of the new infection decides the stopping point of probing. This leads to a reduction in duplicate infection and an increase in infection rate. Combination of Hit-list scanning and permutation scanning leads to the invention of partitioned permutation scanning. Here, the permutation list is split into two halves whenever the infected system identifies a new target. One half of the list is kept by the infected system and the other half is sent to the newly infected system. If the permutation list of the infected system reduces below a certain level, the scanning method returns back to standard permutation scanning method.

d. **Topological Scanning:** This is an advanced version of the Hitlist scanning process. Here a worm identifies its new victim from the data received from the compromised system. In peer-to-peer based attack, the attacker does not require topological scanning process because the compromised systems itself has a list of attractive victims for their next attack. In the web server–based infection, the infection is created by a worm itself and spreads like a transmittable disease to infect victims (Chen & Ji, 2007). The traffic introduced here is less and the compromised system decides the initiation of a new scanning process.

e. **Local Subnet Scanning:** Here, the infected system is responsible for pointing out the new victim systems in its subnet using the concealed details in local IP addresses and infecting them. In practice, this method is jointly used with the other previously explained scanning processes. Subnet scanning is capable of infecting the systems in the same subnet even though they have firewall protection. In specific the local subnet scanning runs behind a firewall and tries to infect the systems protected by the firewall. The compromised system may initiate its scanning process with local subnet scanning, finds out the vulnerable systems in its network and continue the attacking procedures by switching to any one of the previously explained scanning techniques in order to continue the attack in the offline network.

2. **Phase II: Propagation.** After generating the attacking army, the next step is to propagate the code. This process must have the details about the victim's information, duration and time of the attack. The three different ways of propagation are as follows,

a. **Central Source Propagation:** As shown in Figure 4 (a) the central server is responsible for propagating the attack code to the victims. A considerable amount of traffic generated in the central server makes this an easily discoverable attack. Identifying the central server and remove it from the network may help to stop a DoS attack.

b. **Back-Chaining Propagation:** Here the victim system downloads the attack code directly from the attacker. Figure 4 (b) depicts the method employed by the attacker to establish a connection with the victim network. File Transfer Protocol (FTP) is widely used for the connection establishment (Patrikakis, Masikos, & Zouraraki, 2004).

c. **Autonomous Propagation:** In autonomous propagation, there is no need to initialize the prior connection to the victim system, or no communication is needed with the server system. Whenever the attacker has the attack code, it can be propagated the victim system (Figure 4 (c)). The direct connection for a limited period makes this more challenging to discover the attack.

Figure 4. Mechanisms of Phase II Attack

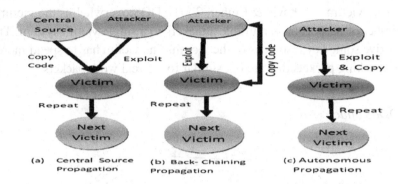

3. **Phase III - Attack:** The attacker controls and instructs the slave devices to initiate and execute their attacks. The initiation and execution of DoS attacks are categorized into several procedures. A spoofed IP address hides the root location of the attackers. This spoofed IP does not allow the victim devices to sort out the malicious software's thus; it is difficult to identify the attacker (Mahjabin et al., 2017). During the DOS attack phase, the network response slowly for opening files, executing files or accessing web contents. Sometimes the occurrence of the attack leads to unavailability of the required web pages.

Classification of DoS attack

The aim of the DoS attack is to utilize the victims' network resources and restrict the intended user's access to their network resources. Figure 5 illustrates the different classification of DoS attacks.

1. Infrastructure Level Attacks
    Bandwidth, computing resources, and routing equipment decide the infrastructure of a Network. In this attack, the victim system receives a number of fake requests and overwhelms the resource capacity. This leads to performance degradation and damages the system. Deka, Bhattacharyya, and Kalita (2017) pointed out some widely used infrastructure level attacks.

Figure 5. Classification of DoS attack

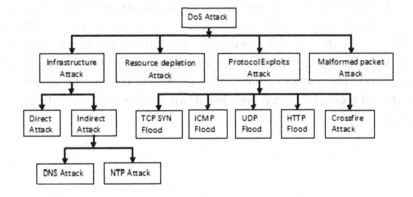

a.   **Direct Attack:** A direct Denial-of-Service attack makes the resources unavailable for the usage of the authorized victim (Mirkovic & Reiher, 2004). DOS overwhelms the victim's resources by sending a number of packets from multiple attackers to a single victim system. These high quantity packets arrive some key resources of the victim. The victim has to spend more time period to handle these attacking packets that are not similar to the real work packets.

Figure 6. Direct DDoS attack

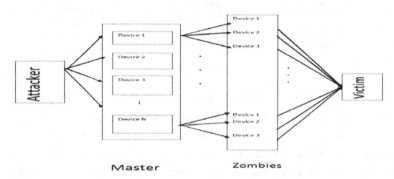

b.   **Indirect Attack**: In this attack, the compromised victim networks are forced to participate in a DoS attack. The target resource is filled with a burst of requests from the attacker to the victim system. The most commonly used reflection mechanisms are discussed below (Deka et al., 2017).

   i.   **DNS Amplification Attack**: The primary motivation of this attack is to utilize the vulnerable aspect of a DNS to strengthen the DoS attack on a larger scale. Here, a number of recursive DNS servers send a number of UDP packets in order to flood a victim network. The rise in data traffic results in the catastrophic effect. Here, the reflected responses from the attacker are used to occupy the bandwidth of the spoofed source IP addresses(Peng, Leckie, & Ramamohanarao, 2007). The effort spent by the attacker is very less in this attack, but it can be capable of introducing a lot of damage because it cannot be easily identified at an initial stage.

   ii.   **NTP (Network Time Protocol) Amplification Attack**: The attack process of NTP amplification attack is the same as that of the DNS amplification attack (Graham-Cumming & John, 2014) with some modifications. A Network Time Protocol is used to synchronize the clocks of the connected machines in between the client and server(Mills, 2016). Initially, the DoS attacker sends MON_GETLIST command to the NTP server. Then the NTP server sends a response to the last 600 queries previously made to the server. Hence the amount of response message is approximately 19 times more than that of the query messages (Graham-Cumming & John, 2014). These amplified messages are then flooded to the victim systems available in the spoofed source IP address and slow down the access between the legitimate users and the server.

Figure 7. Indirect DDoS attack

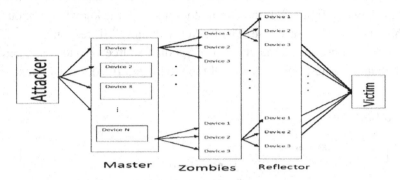

2. Resource Depletion Attacks

The main motive of this attack is to smash all the significant resources (memory, CPU and socket) of the victim system and making them reject legitimate requests from the original server. The amount of resource exhaustion increases as the strength of attack increases. Resource depletion attack may be implemented by utilizing the network, transport, and application layer protocol or by using their malformed packets. Resource depletion based DoS attacks targets three different types of resources such as storage and processing resources, energy resources and bandwidth. By using an efficient congestion based defense method, the victim can prevent these types of attacks.

3. Protocol Exploited Attacks

The weakness of the network layer protocol is identified using some protocol-based attacks. In this type of attack, the resources such as memory and CPU of the victim are exploited by the attacker without their knowledge. The transport layer and network layer protocols such as Transmission Control Protocol (TCP), User Datagram Protocol (UDP) and Internet Control Message Protocol (ICMP) are utilized for this purpose. They have some impact on the Hypertext Transfer Protocol (HTTP) and Session Initiation Protocol (SIP) during the execution of the attack. The different types of protocol exploited attacks are analyzed and compared in (Zargar, Joshi, & Tipper, 2013).

a. **TCP SYN Attack**: In this method, the attacker uses the normal three-way handshaking process for the connection establishment. In three-way handshaking for every TCP connection, there must be a consecutive acknowledgement between the two devices. Until the connection establishment or timeout in identifying the client, the handshake information must be stored in the server. After this attack, the victim server rejects the connection request from a legitimate and valid user. Further, using a 3-way handshaking process the attacker flood up plenty of SYN packets and spoofs of the victim resources. Thereby making the server to deny the establishment of legitimate connections. The attacking process can be done by using compromised networks. Here, the compromised source network performs the successful SYN attack by ignoring the SYN+ACK packets received from the victim (Deka et al., 2017).

b. **UDP Flood Attack:** UDP flood attack has become the most common DoS attack today. The attacker's army floods a massive amount of UDP packets to some random ports on the target networks. First, the target network identifies the type of application of the UDP packet in the particular port. If the port is free, then it initiates the transmission of the ICMP response packet as shown in figure 8. If the victim does not have the knowledge about the application, then the server sends a response. The packet with an ICMP response sent from the attacker and victim occupies all the bandwidth of spoofed source IP address. Thereby the attacker overwhelming the network resources of the victimized IP addresses (Deka et al., 2017).

Figure 8. UDP flood attack

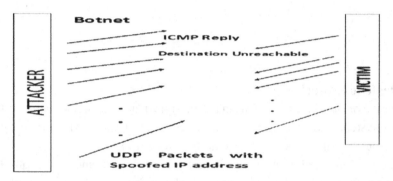

c. **ICMP Flood**: ICMP flood is aping based DoS attack and this attack is also known as the ping flood or a Smurf attack. Here, the attackers' flood a massive number of IP layer protocol ICMP's request packets (ICMP_ECHO_REQUEST) to a server. The ping message packet is used to identify the availability of the remote host. The ICMP packet is normally delivered to the broadcast IP address. All the systems connected to the network will receive this request message and they will reply with ICMP_ECHO_REPLY packet to the spoofed target source address. The attacker uses an intermediate network in order to overwhelm the victim network. The attackers break down the server's TCP/IP stack and force the victim's resource to saturate. The server now rejects and stops responding to the service requests and TCP/IP requests from the genuine users.

d. **Crossfire Attack**: In crossfire attack, a set of spoofed IP addresses and their advertisement areas are identified by the controller of botnet attacker. Then it sends a tremendous amount of request packets to these addresses and occupies their bandwidth (Kang, Lee, & Gligor, 2013). The concentration of these request packets on a carefully chosen network servers flood these packets and disconnect the intended target network server from the Internet. Crossfield attack doesn't receive any messages and it is impossible to differentiate the legitimate packets from the low-intensity request packets. Thus the network and target servers are unable to detect this crossfire attacks.

e. **HTTP Flood Attacks:** This attack aims to capture the resources of web servers by spreading a vast HTTP GETs and POSTs packet. This is the second most commonly occurred flood operation that happens in the application layer (Deka et al., 2017). Overwhelming the victim's resources make the victim server to refuse the request from legitimate servers. To enable this attack, the attacker enables a TCP connection using its botnets' IP address. Resolution in the response attached to the link makes it difficult to detect and mitigate this attack.

4. **Malformed Packet Attacks**

The main aim of this attack is to collapse the functioning of the victim system using duplicate packets. Some of the examples of these attacks are a land attack, IP packet option attack, Ping of death attack and Teardrop attack. The inland attack, the attacker uses the victim's IP address as the IP address of the packet and thus generates an infinite loop. In the packet option filed attack, the value of the optional field of the IP packet is randomized. Thereby increase the time needed by the victim to analyze the received packets and thus overwhelms the victim's resources. Ping of death attack aims to consume the resources by flooding a maximum size packet throughout the network without the help of the botnets. teardrop attack introduces a DoS attack by introducing manipulation errors in the offset value of the fragmentation and reassembly of the data packets. Thus creates invalid data packets and reboot the victim system.

Detection Techniques

Carl, Kesidis, Brooks, and Rai (2006) presented a survey report on DoS detection techniques. The DoS detection techniques are aimed to detect and differentiate legitimate data packets and malicious data packets. Activity profiling, sequential change point detection, and wavelet analysis are the common categories of DoS detection techniques.

1. **Activity Profiling**

In activity profiling, an active profile is generated by examining the network traffic inside the header of the packet. Successive packets having identical header fields represent the network flow. The elapsed time between the successive packets decides the average packet rate. The network activity depends on the ratio between the sum over the average packet rates of all inbound and outbound flows decide the total network activity. The dimensional problem is avoided by using the clustering concept (Carl et al., 2006). Communications Individual flows with similar characteristics can be grouped in a cluster. The activity level is decided by using the summation of constituent flows of the clusters. Increase in activity level indicates the presence of DoS attack and the corresponding attack rate (Alenezi & Reed, 2012).

a. **Traceback Processing**: In traceback processing method a packet having irregular supply is sent over the internet (Krishan Kumar, Sangal, & Bhandari, 2011). Because of the vulnerability of the internet architecture identifying the attacker is very difficult. The various methods involved in this trace backing method are as follows,

i. **IP Traceback Technique:** This is one of the essential processes in protecting against DDoS attacks with the help of IP spoofing. This technique is mainly used to identify the origin of the packets (Krishan Kumar et al., 2011). Normally the DoS attack is initialized by multiple IP sources, so it is complicated to precisely identify the source IP address (Sivabalan & Radcliffe, 2013). The IP traceback technique is basically classified into proactive and is a reactive approach.

ii. **Reactive Approach**- This approach is categorized into IDS and Non-IDS assisted. Host-based IDS and Network-based IDS schemes are the basic types of IDS assisted scheme.

iii. **Proactive Approach**: Here, the attack path is reconstructed by and identified by traceback the packets in the network (Bhale, 2016; Menezes, 2007). The information here is classified into in-band and out-of-band information.

iv. **Packet Marking Technique**: In this method, the attacker misleads the victim to take unprotected path direction using probabilistic packet marking (PPM) and Deterministic packet marking (DPM) (Krishan Kumar et al., 2011) methods.

v. **Probabilistic packet marking (PPM)**: When the packets cross each other the router marks the packets (Law, Lui, & Yau, 2005). Approximately 677 attackers try to misguide the victims using mislead marking information (Krishan Kumar et al., 2011). Then the victim decides the path of the attacking packet. The marking may be either node marking or edge marking. In node marking the victim uses the router IP address, whereas in edge marking the victim uses the edge of the paths to forward attacking packets.

vi. **Deterministic packet marking (DPM)**-In DPM technique, the router assigns a unique id to mark the incoming packets. Compared with PPM method DPM converges quickly, needs less overhead and less complicated computation.

The traceback technique provides minimum scalability and needs high storage cost. The performance of the legacy router is also reduced.

b. **Entropy Variation**: Entropy variation technique dynamically detects and predicts the random features of the network traffic. It describes the spreading characteristics and concentration of traffic. The entropy variation is defined as the random variation in the flow of packets on the router. LAN routers are supervising the network traffic randomly and if the entropy level drops below the predefined threshold, it makes an alarm. The DoS attacks can also be distinguished from the regular traffic by using the information distance. The information distance of the DoS attack flows always less than the given threshold. This confirms the presence of DoS attack and the router discards the packets received from the attackers before they reach the victim systems (Kamboj, Trivedi, Yadav, & Singh, 2017).

c. **Sequential Change-Point Detection Technique**: In this technique using different network parameters such as an address, port, and protocol some filtering is applied to the victim networks (Carl et al., 2006). The filtering parameters are calculated for a particular duration of time.

i. **Intrusion Detection and Prevention System (IDS/IPS)**: This technique uses some application software's to monitor and intimate the doubtful events of the network to the administrator. The different types of IDS/IPS techniques are signature-based detection, anomaly detection, etc.(Yu, Tian, Guo, & Wu, 2014)

ii. **Signature-Based Detection**: In signature Based intrusion detection, a set of rules or signatures are defined to detect the type of the packet. Each user is assigned with an individual signature in order to differentiate it from the spurious users. According to the amount of traffic on the network, the signature is used or not used. If the load is lower than the low load threshold (LLT), then all the traffics are blocked to cross the network. If the load is above the LLT, then the spurious packets are identified by using the signature and delayed. If the traffic load reaches a high-level threshold (HTL), then the doubtful users are not allowed to cross the network (Patcha & Park, 2007).

iii. **Anomaly (or Behavioral) Detection**: An abnormal activity of the network is determined by this anomaly detection technique. Some of the existing anomaly techniques are data mining, statistical modeling and hidden Markov modeling (Pimentel, Clifton, Clifton, &

Tarassenko, 2014). In this technique, the user behaviors are periodically collected as data and some statistical tests are applied to the data to decide whether the data is legitimate or not.

d.   **Wavelet Analysis:** The input signals are processed in the form of spectral components in wavelet analysis. Here the time-varying anomalous signals are separated from the wavelets and by analyzing the spectral energy the anomalies can be determined. Mirkovic and Reiher (Mirkovic & Reiher, 2004) applied this analysis to four different anomaly types: measurement failure, attacks, flash crowds, and network failures.

PREVENTION AGAINST DOS ATTACKS

In modern network applications, DDoS attacks put a massive threat to the victim's resources and the network bandwidths. This section describes some of the available DDoS prevention techniques used to ensure the regular operation of the victim (Mahjabin et al., 2017).

Service Level Agreement (SLA)

In SLA, a legal agreement is established between the server and the client (Kandukuri, Paturi, & Rakshit, 2009) to provide a confident and trusted connectivity. The SLA aims to provide privileged user access; regulatory compliance; data location assurance to store and process data and proper encryption to support data segregation.

Prevention Using Filters

The prevention against DDoS is achieved by introducing various filtering techniques. The filtering techniques mainly applied in the router in order to allow only the legitimate user access across the network. In real time applications, Ingress/egress filtering (Senie & Ferguson, 1998), Route-based packet filtering (Park & Lee, 2001), Hop-count filtering and History-based filtering (Jin, Wang, & Shin, 2003) techniques are used for preventing DoS.

Source Address Validity Enforcement (SAVE) protocol

The server router periodically updates the source information to the destination router using SAVE protocol. Then, all the destination routers update their routing table using the current information and filter out the unwanted users. However, the updating routing table consumes some time period and sometimes it is not possible to filter out all the spoofed IP addresses (Li, Mirkovic, Wang, Reiher, & Zhang, 2002).

Honeypots

Honeypots/honeynets imitate the legitimate victim system and attract the attackers. Thus the attacker misunderstands the honeynet as the legitimate victim. Thus, the original legitimate system remains unaffected. Honeypot extracts the information about the attack activity and software tools used for the attack. Using this information it detects and prevents the DoS attack and its attackers (Krämer et al., 2015).

Load Balancing

Load balancing approach balance the load among different systems thereby avoids the overloading of one user (McMullin, 2016). If the server encounters any DDoS attack, the server reroutes the incoming traffic to another un-attacked server. Thus it ensures flexibility thereby increases maximum uptime and optimal productivity. Load balancing technique needs some extra bandwidth to handle the critical connections. It is also essential to have a sufficient number of duplicated servers and data centres to avoid single point failure.

Prevention based on Awareness

A real-time application such as IoT needs some user awareness regarding the botnet-based DDoS attacks. Since the IoT devices have inadequate security mechanisms, the users must be capable of taking prevention measures by own (Mahjabin et al., 2017). Thus the user ensures its own security against the zombie of the attacking army. Some of the initiatives from the user side are continuously changing the source IP address (Geng & Whinston, 2000), disabling unusual UDP echo services (Herzberg, Bekerman, & Zeifman, 2017), continuous change in the user password (Mahjabin et al., 2017).

DDOS MITIGATION

Mitigating DDoS attacks is a typical problem in our latest network environment. To eliminate a DoS attack basically, four general requirements are needed (Latanicki, Massonet, Naqvi, Rochwerger, & Villari, 2010). The first requirement is to identify the type of attack as early as possible and determine the impact of the attack on the network and its effect. Second, mitigate the DoS effects using suitable techniques. Third, if the technique used in the second step is not efficient to try to migrate safeguard the network server. Fourth, choose a set of rules to effectively allocate the bandwidth to the users in order to safeguard the resources. Some of the widely used mitigation algorithms are discussed below (Bonguet & Bellaiche, 2017).

1. **Push-Back:** Most network congestion occurs due to the presence of malicious attacks. Ioannidis and Bellovin (2002) described the concept of controlling congestion using a push-back mechanism. In this mechanism, the incoming packets are identified by using congestion signature matching process. The rate-limiter receives the packets and decide whether it can forward the packet or discard the packets. Push- Back Daemon receives the dropped packets and update the rate limit and congestion signatures periodically.
2. **Router Throttling:** This technique concentrates on preventing DoS attack in the upstream data transmission. Here, the routers are portioned in order to regulate the packet rate of the server. In (Yau, Lui, Liang, & Yam, 2005) the authors proposed an improved K-level max-min fairness theory to verify whether the controlling mechanism is highly effective in identifying the attacker or not. This method efficiently controls the traffic of the server below its design limit of a DDoS attack. The router throttling model is shown in figure 9.

Figure 9. Router throttling model

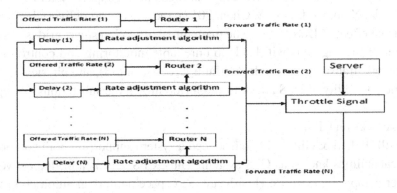

3. **SDN-Based DDoS Defense:** The Software Defined Network (SDN) options such as a global view of the network, centralized control, dynamic updating, and forwarding process, traffic analysis supports the network to detect a protect the DDoS attacks. SDN separates the control and data planes for processing this leads to a new SDN attack activity. Some of the DDoS attacks will affect the SDN itself so preventing the network becomes complex.

4. **Big Data Analytics:** Large enterprises like Google and Facebook have to access more amounts of data from a cloud network. This mitigation technique is the starting point of the development of the concept of Big Data (Lohr, 2012). The required packets from the clouds are collected and analyzed in network servers. Since big data process massive amount of data, it is essential to prevent DoS attack. Govinda and Sathiyamoorthy (Govinda & Sathiyamoorthy, 2014) clustered the traffic into flash traffic, interactive traffic; latency-sensitive traffic, non-real time traffic and unknown traffic. Then these traffics are analyzed using Hadoop and the unknown traffics are separated from the big data traffic. The unknown traffic is considered as the DDoS attack and eliminated using efficient technology.

5. **Statistical Machine Learning.** Here the topmost attacks are identified by using a Support Vector Machine (SVM) technique (Dean & Ghemawat, 2008).This SVM intimates about the DDoS attack to the system administrators and data owners to take necessary actions to prevent DDoS attack. The customers are able to know the attack even if the cloud providers are unwilling to reveal the attack information.

DoS/DDoS Attacks to Other Systems

The previous section discusses the DoS or DDoS attacks on conventional systems. This section focus on DoS or DDoS attacks on some non-traditional systems, for example, smart grids, CPS, smart homes and IoT applications (Mahjabin et al., 2017).

1. DoS/DDoS Attacks on Smart Grids

   Developing a smart infrastructure using the traditional power grid is known as smart grids. The smart grid technique integrates the traditional electric power supply system with Information and Communication Technologies (ICT) (Wang & Lu, 2013). The smart grid has distributed power source and automated maintenance as well as operating ability. This improves the capacity, reliability, efficiency, and quality of the existing traditional power supply system (Arnold et al., 2010). As stated in (Liu, Xiao, Li, Liang, & Chen, 2012), the smart grid delivery becomes damaged by some significant effect of DoS attack. The main threat of DoS in smart grid is introducing a delay in the transfer of message this will leads to unreliable monitoring and controlling of the victim systems. Network, transport, data link (Medium Access Control), and physical layers of the smart grids have the possibility of DoS attack through flooding in the substations (Wang & Lu, 2013).

2. DoS/DDoS Attacks on CPSs
   Baheti and Gill (Baheti & Gill, 2011) introduced a system supporting both computational as well as physical capabilities known as CPS system. Thus, CPS acts as a bridge between the physical and the cyber computing systems. Healthcare, aerospace and urban automobile are some of the critical systems controlled, coordinated and monitored by CPS systems (Rajkumar, Lee, Sha, & Stankovic, 2010). DoS introduce some significant threats against these trusted communications. Thus introducing a robust CPS system against DoS attack is a future research issue.

3. DoS/DDoS Attacks on Smart Homes
   In a recent network scenario, the concept of controlling our home appliances with the help of the internet from remote places becomes popular. Home having devices connected is known as a smart home. Since smart homes depend on internet services even though it provides high security, it can be hacked and affected by malicious DoS attacks. Confidentiality, integrity, authentication, authorization, non-repudiation, and availability are the essential properties of a perfect smart home application (Mantas, Lymberopoulos, & Komninos, 2011).

4. **DoS/DDoS Attacks on IoT Systems**
   As stated by (Heer et al., 2011) Internet of Things (IoT) is a technology that interconnects different network units to perform a task. The entities of the IoTs are called ''highly heterogeneous'' networked entities or the ''technology to provide connectivity to anything'' (Strategy & Unit, 2005). The tremendous growth of the IoT results in good as well as bad effects. The bad effects are due to the unawareness of the network security issues to the manufacturers. Since the IoT devices are used in different essential fields such as rescue service, health care service, between vehicles, it is essential to use an effective authentication method to protect IoT from DoS attacks.

CONCLUSION AND FUTURE SCOPE

Conclusion

In the future, most of the network activities and network resources will definitely utilize the cloud computing process and it increases the need for security. DoS is becoming an advanced method of attacking a network and restrict legitimate users from accessing the resources. So it is essential to develop a solution that must include different defense activities to ensure different DoS attacks. Restriction of DDoS attacks improves the survival of the network under consideration. But it is necessary to totally prevent the occurrence of DoS instead of identifying the occurrence. This chapter discussed the basics of Botnet, DoS, the issues and challenges in handling these attacks, Detecting and Preventing the DoS attack in various environments. This chapter presented a review of the existing DoS detection and prevention approaches developed by several types of research. The importance of DoS mitigation and resource optimization in the government and private network has been highlighted. Even though some enough research has gone into detecting and preventing DoS attacks, it should still be noted that it needs some extra work to identify and overcome different types of DoS attacks. We hope that this chapter will open doors for the development and deployment of new research areas in the DoS attack area.

Future Scope

Still, some new research areas which need improvement are there during the DOS attacks. The following are the new research directions in the field of DoS.

1. **Software Defined Network (SDN) Infrastructure:** The use of SDN will reduce the impacts of attackers. Making the mitigation techniques more effective and using the techniques in a flexible manner is more essential. In the future, it is essential to focus on the detection method to mitigate both spoofed and non-spoofed attacks in an SDN environment.
2. **Defense System**: Effectiveness and efficiency of a DDoS defense system depend on the location and positioning of the system in any network. The network must have a sufficient number of defense points near the source end, victim end or between both the ends. When a DoS attack occurs in a network, the defense system must be capable of handling a vast volume of data traffic, especially in the Internet environment. The researchers need to introduce an adaptive defense system when the attacker is continuously modifying their flooding tools.
3. **Cross-Layer Design DoS Attacks:** Nowadays different DoS detection techniques are used for detecting DoS attack in different layers of Open Systems Interconnection (OSI) layers. Cross-Layer DoS detection technique aims to provide a common DoS detection technique to detect and identify the DoS attackers on any layer of the OSI layers. This mechanism aims to mitigate and minimize the negative impact on the victim network.
4. **Distributed Cooperative Approach**: Performance of a DoS detection system can be improved by introducing a cooperative detection among the target system so as to spread the DoS attack alert information to other devices in the network.
5. **The DDoS Problem on World Wide Web:** Wireless applications such as WSN, WLAN, MANET and multimedia communications on wireless platforms are also affected by DDoS attack like wired networks; such as Session Initiation Protocol (SIP) flood attacks in Voice over IP (VoIP). Therefore, protecting these specific services from a DOS attack will require significant research interest in the future.

REFERENCES

Aamir, M., & Zaidi, M. A. (2013). A survey on DDoS attack and defense strategies: From traditional schemes to current techniques. *Interdisciplinary Information Sciences*, *19*(2), 173–200. doi:10.4036/iis.2013.173

Al-Anzi, F. S., Yadav, S. K., & Soni, J. (2014). Cloud computing: Security model comprising governance, risk management, and compliance. *Proceedings of International Conference on Data Mining and Intelligent Computing (ICDMIC)*. 10.1109/ICDMIC.2014.6954232

Alenezi, M., & Reed, M. J. (2012). Methodologies for detecting DoS/DDoS attacks against network servers. *Proceedings of the Seventh International Conference on Systems and Networks Communications—ICSNC*.

Alomari, E., Manickam, S., Gupta, B., Anbar, M., Saad, R. M., & Alsaleem, S. (2016). *A survey of botnet-based DDoS flooding attacks of application layer: Detection and mitigation approaches. In Handbook of Research on Modern Cryptographic Solutions for Computer and Cyber Security* (pp. 52–79). IGI Global. doi:10.4018/978-1-5225-0105-3.ch003

Alomari, E., Manickam, S., Gupta, B. B., Karuppayah, S., & Alfaris, R. (2012). *Botnet-based distributed denial of service (DDoS) attacks on web servers: classification and art.* arXiv preprint arXiv:1208.0403

Amit, P., & Santhithilagam, P. (2019). DDoS Attacks at the Application Layer: Challenges and Research Perspectives for Safeguarding Web Applications. *IEEE Communications Surveys and Tutorials*, *21*(1), 661–685. doi:10.1109/COMST.2018.2870658

Antunes, J., Neves, N. F., & Veríssimo, P. J. (2008). *Detection and prediction of resource-exhaustion vulnerabilities.* Paper presented at the 19th International Symposium on Software Reliability Engineering. 10.1109/ISSRE.2008.47

Arnold, G. W., Wollman, D. A., FitzPatrick, G. J., Prochaska, D. E., Lee, A., Holmberg, D. G., & Simmon, E. D. (2010). *NIST Framework and Roadmap for Smart Grid Interoperability Standards Release 1.0*. Academic Press.

Arora, Yadav, & Sharma. (2018). Denial-of-Service (DoS) Attack and Botnet: Network Analysis, Research Tactics, and Mitigation. In *Handbook of Research on Network Forensics and Analysis Techniques* (pp. 117-141): IGI Global.

Arunadevi, R. (2018). Experimentation Of Denial Of Service Attack In Wireless Local Area Infrastructure Network Using Loic Tool. *Journal of Engineering Research and Application*, 51-55.

Baheti, R., & Gill, H. (2011). Cyber-physical systems. The Impact of Control Technology, 12, 161-166.

Bailey, M., Cooke, E., Jahanian, F., Xu, Y., & Karir, M. (2009). *A survey of botnet technology and defenses.* Paper presented at the Cybersecurity Applications & Technology Conference for Homeland Security. 10.1109/CATCH.2009.40

Bencsáth, B., & Vajda, I. (2004). *Protection against DDoS attacks based on traffic level measurements.* Paper presented at the International Symposium on Collaborative Technologies and Systems.

Bhale, K. M. (2016). *Botnet Detection Tools and Techniques: A review*. Centre for Cyber Security Institute for Development and Research in Banking Technology.

Bhushan, M., Banerjea, S., & Yadav, S. K. (2014). *Bloom filter based optimization on HBase with Map Reduce*. Paper presented at the International Conference on Data Mining and Intelligent Computing (ICDMIC).

Bonguet, A., & Bellaiche, M. (2017). A Survey of Denial-of-Service and Distributed Denial of Service Attacks and Defenses in Cloud Computing. *Future Internet, 9*(3), 43. doi:10.3390/fi9030043

Carl, G., Kesidis, G., Brooks, R. R., & Rai, S. (2006). Denial-of-service attack-detection techniques. *IEEE Internet Computing, 10*(1), 82–89. doi:10.1109/MIC.2006.5

Chen, Z., & Ji, C. (2007). Optimal worm-scanning method using vulnerable-host distributions. *International Journal of Security and Networks, 2*(1-2), 71–80. doi:10.1504/IJSN.2007.012826

CIOinsight. (2011). *Botnets still a major threat.* Retrieved from http://tinyurl.com/cw5bypo

Cohen, L. E., & Felson, M. (2016). *Social Change and Crime Rate Trends: A Routine Activity Approach. In Classics in Environmental Criminology* (pp. 203–232). CRC Press.

Coindesk. (2017). *Bitcoin Gold Website Down Following DDoS Attack* [Press release]. Author.

Corero. (2016). *DDoS Attacks Plague Olympic & Brazilian Government Websites* [Press release]. Author.

Csanádi, L. C. G. (2007). *Cyber war: Poor man's weapon of mass destruction, and a new whip in the hands of the rich.* Academic Press.

Dean, J., & Ghemawat, S. (2008). MapReduce: Simplified data processing on large clusters. *Communications of the ACM, 51*(1), 107–113.

Deka, R. K., Bhattacharyya, D. K., & Kalita, J. K. (2017). *DDoS Attacks: Tools, Mitigation Approaches, and Probable Impact on Private Cloud Environment.* arXiv preprint arXiv:1710.08628

Desai, M., Patel, S., Somaiya, P., & Vishwanathan, V. (2016). Prevention of Distributed Denial of Service Attack using Web Referrals: A Review. *International Research Journal of Engineering and Technology,* 1994-1996.

Douligeris, C., & Mitrokotsa, A. (2004). DDoS attacks and defense mechanisms: A classification. *Proceedings of the 3rd IEEE International Symposium on Signal Processing and Information Technology.* 10.1109/ISSPIT.2003.1341092

Feng, J., Chen, Y., & Liu, P. (2010). *Bridging the missing link of cloud data storage security in AWS.* Paper presented at the 7th IEEE Consumer Communications and Networking Conference. 10.1109/CCNC.2010.5421770

Fernandes, D. A., Soares, L. F., Gomes, J. V., Freire, M. M., & Inácio, P. R. (2014). Security issues in cloud environments: A survey. *International Journal of Information Security, 13*(2), 113–170. doi:10.100710207-013-0208-7

Fielding, J. (2007). *25% of all computers on botnets.* Retrieved from http://tinyurl.com

Geng, X., & Whinston, A. B. (2000). Defeating distributed denial of service attacks. *IT Professional, 2*(4), 36–42. doi:10.1109/6294.869381

Gonzales, D., Kaplan, J.M., Saltzman, E., Winkelman, Z., & D., W. (2017). Cloud-trust–A security assessment model for infrastructure as a service (IaaS) clouds. *IEEE Transactions on Cloud Computing, 5*(3), 523–536.

Govinda, K., & Sathiyamoorthy, E. (2014). Secure traffic management in cluster environment to handle DDoS attack. *World Applied Sciences Journal, 32*(9), 1828–1834.

Graham-Cumming, J. (2014). *Understanding and mitigating NTP-based DDoS attacks*. Retrieved from http://blog.cloudflare.com/understanding-and-mitigating-ntp-based-ddos-attacks

Gresty, D. W., Shi, Q., & Merabti, M. (2001). *Requirements for a general framework for response to distributed denial-of-service*. Paper presented at the 17th Annual Computer Security Applications Conference. 10.1109/ACSAC.2001.991559

Guardian. (2016). *HSBC Suffers Online Banking Cyber Attack* [Press release]. Author.

Gupta, B. B., Joshi, R. C., Misra, M., Meena, D. L., Shrivastava, G., & Sharma, K. (2010). Detecting a wide range of flooding DDoS attacks using linear prediction model. In *IEEE 2nd International Conference on Information and Multimedia Technology (ICIMT 2010)* (Vol. 2, pp. 535-539). IEEE.

Heer, T., Garcia-Morchon, O., Hummen, R., Keoh, S. L., Kumar, S. S., & Wehrle, K. (2011). Security Challenges in the IP-based Internet of Things. *Wireless Personal Communications, 61*(3), 527–542. doi:10.100711277-011-0385-5

Herzberg, B., Bekerman, D., & Zeifman, I. (2017). *Breaking down Mirai: an IoT DDoS Botnet analysis, 2017*. Academic Press.

Hogben, G., Plohmann, D., Gerhards-Padilla, E., & Leder, F. (2011). *Botnets: Detection, measurement, disinfection, and defense*. European Network and Information Security Agency.

Hoque, N., Bhattacharyya, D. K., & Kalita, J. K. (2016). FFSc: a novel measure for low-rate and high-rate DDoS attack detection using multivariate data analysis. In Security and Communication Networks. Wiley Online Library.

Incapsula. (2015). *Analysis of Vikingdom DDoS Attacks on U.S. Government Sites*. Retrieved from https://www.incapsula.com/blog/vikingdom-ddos-attacks-us-government.html

Ioannidis, J., & Bellovin, S. M. (2002). *Implementing Pushback: Router-Based Defense Against DDoS Attacks*. Paper presented at the NDSS.

Jayanthi, M. K., DileepKumar, G., & Singh, M. (2016). Network Security Attacks and Countermeasures Security and Forensics for 2019. IGI Global

Jin, C., Wang, H., & Shin, K. G. (2003). Hop-count filtering: an effective defense against spoofed DDoS traffic. *Proceedings of the 10th ACM conference on Computer and communications security*. 10.1145/948109.948116

Kamboj, P., Trivedi, M. C., Yadav, V. K., & Singh, V. K. (2017). *Detection techniques of DDoS attacks: A survey*. Paper presented at the International Conference on Electrical, Computer and Electronics (UPCON), 2017 4th IEEE Uttar Pradesh Section 10.1109/UPCON.2017.8251130

Kandukuri, B., Paturi, V., & Rakshit, A. (2009). Cloud Security Issues. *Proceedings of the 2009 IEEE International, Conference on Services Computing*, 517–520.

Kang, M. S., Lee, S. B., & Gligor, V. D. (2013). *The crossfire attack*. Paper presented at the Security and Privacy (SP), 2013 IEEE Symposium on.

Krämer, L., Krupp, J., Makita, D., Nishizoe, T., Koide, T., Yoshioka, K., & Rossow, C. (2015). *Amppot: Monitoring and defending against amplification DDoS attacks*. Paper presented at the International Workshop on Recent Advances in Intrusion Detection. 10.1007/978-3-319-26362-5_28

Kramer, L. K. J., & Makita, D. (2015). AmpPot: monitoring and defending against amplification DDoS attacks. *Proceedings of the international workshop on recent advances in intrusion detection.* 10.1007/978-3-319-26362-5_28

Kreuzer, M. (2016). *Botnets – Structural analysis, functional principle and general overview*. Retrieved from https://blog.mi.hdm-stuttgart.de

Kumar, K., Sangal, A., & Bhandari, A. (2011). *Traceback techniques against DDOS attacks: a comprehensive review*. Paper presented at the 2nd International Conference on Computer and Communication Technology (ICCCT). 10.1109/ICCCT.2011.6075132

Kumar, R. (2018). DOS Attacks on Cloud Platform: Their Solutions and Implications. In Critical Research on Scalability and Security Issues in Virtual Cloud Environments (pp. 167-184). IGI GLobal.

Latanicki, J., Massonet, P., Naqvi, S., Rochwerger, B., & Villari, M. (2010). *Scalable Cloud Defenses for Detection, Analysis, and Mitigation of DDoS Attacks*. Paper presented at the Future Internet Assembly.

Law, T. K., Lui, J. C., & Yau, D. K. (2005). You can run, but you can't hide: An effective statistical methodology to trace back DDoS attackers. *IEEE Transactions on Parallel and Distributed Systems, 16*(9), 799–813. doi:10.1109/TPDS.2005.114

Li, J., Mirkovic, J., Wang, M., Reiher, P., & Zhang, L. (2002). *SAVE Source address validity enforcement protocol*. Paper presented at the INFOCOM 2002. Twenty-First Annual Joint Conference of the IEEE Computer and Communications Societies.

Liu, J., Xiao, Y., Li, S., Liang, W., & Chen, C. P. (2012). Cybersecurity and privacy issues in smart grids. *IEEE Communications Surveys and Tutorials, 14*(4), 981–997. doi:10.1109/SURV.2011.122111.00145

Lohr, S. (2012). The age of big data. *New York Times, 11*(2012).

Mahjabin, T., Xiao, Y., Sun, G., & Jiang, W. (2017). A survey of distributed denial-of-service attack, prevention, and mitigation techniques. *International Journal of Distributed Sensor Networks, 13*(12). doi:10.1177/1550147717741463

Mantas, G., Lymberopoulos, D., & Komninos, N. (2011). *Security in smart home environment Wireless Technologies for Ambient Assisted Living and Healthcare: Systems and Applications*. IGI Global. doi:10.4018/978-1-61520-805-0.ch010

Massi, J., Panda, S., Rajappa, G., Selvaraj, S., & Revankar, S. (2010). *Botnet detection and mitigation. presented on Proceedings of Student-Faculty Research Day, CSIS*. Pace University.

McMullin, M. (2016). *DNS load balancing and DDoS attacks*. Retrieved from https://kemptechnologies.com/blog/load-balancing-and-ddos-attacks/

Menezes, J. P. (2007). *The botnet menace*. Retrieved from https://www.itworldcanada.com/article/the-botnet-menace-and-what-you-can-do-about-it/8454

Mills, D. L. (2016). *Computer network time synchronization: the network time protocol on earth and in space*. CRC Press.

Mirkovic, J., & Reiher, P. (2004). A taxonomy of DDoS attack and DDoS defense mechanisms. *Computer Communication Review*, *34*(2), 39–53. doi:10.1145/997150.997156

Moore, D., & Shannon, C. (2002). Code-Red: a case study on the spread and victims of an Internet worm. *Proceedings of the 2nd ACM SIGCOMM Workshop on Internet measurement*. 10.1145/637201.637244

NCSC. (2018). *National Cyber Security Centre: Understanding denial of service (DoS) attacks*. Retrieved from https://www.ncsc.gov.uk/guidance/

Networks, A. (2012). *Leading U.S. Banks Targeted in DDoS Attacks* [Press release]. Author.

Pappalardo, D., & Messmer, E. (2005). *Extortion via DDoS on the rise*. Network World.

Park, K., & Lee, H. (2001). On the effectiveness of route-based packet filtering for distributed DoS attack prevention in power-law internets. *Computer Communication Review*, *31*(4), 15–26.

Patcha, A., & Park, J.-M. (2007). An overview of anomaly detection techniques: Existing solutions and latest technological trends. *Computer Networks*, *51*(12), 3448–3470. doi:10.1016/j.comnet.2007.02.001

Patrikakis, C., Masikos, M., & Zouraraki, O. (2004). Distributed denial of service attacks. *The Internet Protocol Journal*, *7*(4), 13–35.

Peng, T., Leckie, C., & Ramamohanarao, K. (2007). Survey of network-based defense mechanisms countering the DoS and DDoS problems. *ACM Computing Surveys*, *39*(1), 3, es. doi:10.1145/1216370.1216373

Pimentel, M. A., Clifton, D. A., Clifton, L., & Tarassenko, L. (2014). A review of novelty detection. *Signal Processing*, *99*, 215–249. doi:10.1016/j.sigpro.2013.12.026

Rajkumar, R., Lee, I., Sha, L., & Stankovic, J. (2010). *Cyber-physical systems: the next computing revolution*. Paper presented at the Design Automation Conference (DAC), 2010 47th ACM/IEEE. 10.1145/1837274.1837461

Register. (2012). *Anonymous Turns Its DDoS Cannons on India* [Press release]. Author.

Riquet, D., Grimaud, G., & Hauspie, M. (2012). *Large-scale coordinated attacks: Impact on the cloud security*. Paper presented at the Sixth International Conference on Innovative Mobile and Internet Services in Ubiquitous Computing (IMIS). 10.1109/IMIS.2012.76

Schiller, C., & Binkley, J. R. (2011). *Botnets: The killer web applications*. Elsevier.

Senie, D., & Ferguson, P. (1998). Network ingress filtering: Defeating denial of service attacks which employ IP source address spoofing. *Network*.

Sharma, K., & Gupta, B. B. (2018). *Taxonomy of Distributed Denial of Service DDoS Attacks and Defense Mechanisms in Present Era of Smartphone Devices*. *International Journal of E-Services and Mobile Applications*, 58–74.

Shrivastava, G., Sharma, K., & Rai, S. (2010). The detection & defense of DoS & DDos attack: a technical overview. In *Proceedings of ICC* (pp. 274-282). Academic Press.

Silicon. (2017). *Irish Government Websites Taken Down By DDoS Attacks* [Press release]. Author.

Sivabalan, S., & Radcliffe, P. (2013). *A novel framework to detect and block DDoS attack at the application layer.* Paper presented at the IEEE 2013 Tencon-Spring. 10.1109/TENCONSpring.2013.6584511

Somani, G., Gaur, M. S., Sanghi, D., & Conti, M. (2016). DDoS attacks in cloud computing: Collateral damage to non-targets. *Computer Networks, 109,* 157–171. doi:10.1016/j.comnet.2016.03.022

Staniford, S., Paxson, V., & Weaver, N. (2002). *How to Own the Internet in Your Spare Time.* Paper presented at the USENIX security symposium.

Stevanovic, M., & Pedersen, J. M. (2015). *An analysis of network traffic classification for botnet detection.* Paper presented at the 2015 International Conference on Cyber Situational Awareness, Data Analytics and Assessment (CyberSA). 10.1109/CyberSA.2015.7361120

Strategy, I., & Unit, P. (2005). ITU Internet Reports 2005: The internet of things. Geneva: International Telecommunication Union (ITU).

Sun, B., Yan, G., Xiao, Y., & Yang, T. A. (2009). Self-propagating mal-packets in wireless sensor networks: Dynamics and defense implications. *Ad Hoc Networks, 7*(8), 1489–1500. doi:10.1016/j.adhoc.2009.04.003

The Shadower Foundation. (2012). *The Shadower Foundation.* Retrieved from http://www.shadowserver.org/wiki/

Vacca, J. R. (2013). *Network and system security.* Elsevier.

Wang, W., & Lu, Z. (2013). Cyber security in the smart grid: Survey and challenges. *Computer Networks, 57*(5), 1344–1371. doi:10.1016/j.comnet.2012.12.017

Weaver, N. (2001). *Warhol worms: The potential for very fast internet plagues.* Academic Press.

Wong, Q. (1998). *Salesforce Pushed Silicon Valley Into the Cloud* [Press release]. Author.

Yadav, S. K., Sharma, K., & Arora, A. (2018). Security Integration in DDoS Attack Mitigation Using Access Control Lists. *International Journal of Information System Modeling and Design, 9*(1), 56–76. doi:10.4018/IJISMD.2018010103

Yau, D. K., Lui, J., Liang, F., & Yam, Y. (2005). Defending against distributed denial-of-service attacks with max-min fair server-centric router throttles. *IEEE/ACM Transactions on Networking (TON), 13*(1), 29-42.

Yu, S., Tian, Y., Guo, S., & Wu, D. O. (2014). Can we beat DDoS attacks in clouds? *IEEE Transactions on Parallel and Distributed Systems, 25*(9), 2245–2254. doi:10.1109/TPDS.2013.181

Zargar, S. T., Joshi, J., & Tipper, D. (2013). A survey of defense mechanisms against distributed denial of service (DDoS) flooding attacks. *IEEE Communications Surveys and Tutorials, 15*(4), 2046–2069. doi:10.1109/SURV.2013.031413.00127

KEY TERMS AND DEFINITIONS

Denial of Service: An interruption in an authorized user's access to a computer network, typically one caused with malicious intent.

Botmaster: A person who controls a bot or botnet.

Botnet: A network of private computers infected with malicious software and controlled as a group without the owners' knowledge (e.g., to send spam).

Cross-Layer Design: A protocol design that leverages on the interactions and dependencies between different layers of the networking protocol stacks to achieve better performance. MANET (mobile ad hoc network)—self-configuring and self-maintaining network in which nodes are autonomous and distributed in nature.

Internet of Things (IoT): The internet of things, or IoT, is a system of interrelated computing devices, mechanical and digital machines, objects, animals or people that are provided with unique identifiers (UIDs) and the ability to transfer data over a network without requiring human-to-human or human-to-computer interaction.

Smart Grids: An electricity supply network that uses digital communications technology to detect and react to local changes in usage.

Software-Defined Networking (SDN): The physical separation of the network control plane from the forwarding plane, and where a control plane controls several devices.

This research was previously published in Forensic Investigations and Risk Management in Mobile and Wireless Communications edited by Kavita Sharma, Mitsunori Makino, Gulshan Shrivastava and Basant Agarwal; pages 114-151, copyright year 2020 by Information Science Reference (an imprint of IGI Global).

Chapter 3
Denial–of–Service (DoS) Attack and Botnet:
Network Analysis, Research Tactics, and Mitigation

Arushi Arora
Indira Gandhi Delhi Technical University for Women, India

Sumit Kumar Yadav
Indira Gandhi Delhi Technical University for Women, India

Kavita Sharma
National Institute of Technology Kurukshetra, India

ABSTRACT

This chapter describes how the consequence and hazards showcased by Denial of Service attacks have resulted in the surge of research studies, commercial software and innovative cogitations. Of the DoS attacks, the incursion of its variant DDoS can be quite severe. A botnet, on the other hand, is a group of hijacked devices that are connected by internet. These botnet servers are used to perform DDoS attacks effectively. In this chapter, the authors attempt to provide an insight into DoS attacks and botnets, focusing on their analysis and mitigation. They also propose a defense mechanism to mitigate our system from botnet DDoS attacks. This is achieved by using a through access list based configuration. The artful engineering of malware is a weapon used for online crime and the ideas behind it are profit-motivated. The last section of the chapter provides an understanding of the WannaCry Ransomware Attack which locked computers in more than 150 countries.

DOI: 10.4018/978-1-7998-5348-0.ch003

INTRODUCTION

In recent years, changes in cybercrime techniques have become more pronounced and menacing. One of the evident examples is DDoS (Distributed Denial-of-Service) Attacks, which are now appearing with a new twist, using IoT (Internet of Things) to expand their target area (Bhatt et al., 2017; Yadav et al., 2018). IoT has impacted the digital technology in a way, altering how we think or live (Dey et al., 2017). The technology promises to ease our living by providing convenience and practically improving our communication with our surroundings (Jain & Bhatnagar, 2017; Elhayatmy et al., 2018). The concept of "Anonymity of Internet" is used in the cyber attacks, changing their scale and scope. The Internet is one area where assiduousness is mandatory and security should be a priority. "The Internet is becoming the town square for the global village of tomorrow" was rightly stated by Bill Gates, co-founder of the Microsoft Corporation. The Internet provides us with a huge range of resources and services and has become a platform for numerous commercial activities like online banking, online shopping, publicity, marketing, advertising etc. (Tayal, 2017). The Internet is an open platform when compared to the current circuit-switched networks (ATMs, the analog telephone network, etc.); hence this makes it easier for attackers to enforce a cyber attack on devices connected to the Internet. The reason behind this is that the former is implemented in software using general-purpose computing hardware. Also, standardized and open technologies using servers are reachable through the Internet. Therefore, services like these suffer from internet threats just like HTTP-based services (Mukherjee et al., 2016). This chapter will focus on the Denial-of-Service attacks (Carl et al., 2006) and Botnet analysis (Alejandre et al., 2017), their detection (Park & Lee, 2001) and mitigation (Zhang et al., 2016). It has been appropriately said by Art Wittmann that, "As we've come to realize, the idea that security starts and ends with the purchase of a prepackaged firewall is simply misguided", therefore, in this chapter hybrid mitigation techniques for DoS attacks and botnets are presented (Shrivastava et al., 2010).

Man is a curious being. From the very beginning, communicating and curiosity have encouraged and led to underground research. Over these years, online financial transactions, attackers have shifted their focus from communicating to commercialization and monitory profits. Most computer systems that belong to large organizations contain valuable information about the users or business activities. The attackers are well experienced and know the methods for information retrieval, its location, and extraction for financial gain. Therefore, to protect their resources, organizations are setting up system security, staffing and defensive technologies to protect their information and computer systems (Matallah et al., 2017; Yamin & Sen, 2018). This can reduce the risk of successful attacks but it does not cure the problem completely (Kimbahune et al., 2017). Some attackers, on the other hand, are attracted to individual machines because of lack of security measures taken by the user.

The first section of the chapter explains the DoS attack types; DoS attack techniques along with its symptoms and defense techniques (Desai et al., 2016; Saha et al., 2016). The attacker of a DoS attack prevents the utilization of the resources by the user. In the attack, the bandwidth of the user is reduced and the network is flooded, thereby disrupting a service. Distributed attacks also came into existence soon after Denial of Service attacks. In Distributed attack, separate sites are used for execution to as Distributed Denial-of-Service (DDoS) attacks. The types of DoS attacks that are explained in the chapter are Denial-of-service as a service, Advanced persistent DoS (APDoS) and Distributed DoS (Mirkovic & Reiher, 2004; Feinstein et al., 2003) after which its symptoms are listed. These symptoms comprise of speed issue or slow *network performance,* unreachable websites, drastic number of spam emails or email bomb attack, networking wire issue, connection failure issue and internet access denial for a long period of time. DoS attack techniques including Internet Control Message Protocol (ICMP) flood, attack tools (Kumar et al., 2009) that are Predators Face, Rolling Thunder, *MyDoom, Stacheldraht* and Low Orbit Ion Cannon, Peer-to-peer attacks, application-layer floods (*LAND* attack, *XDoS*), Degradation-of-service attacks (Poturalski et al., 2010), permanent denial-of-service attacks, reflected/spoofed attack, Distributed DoS attack, DDoS extortion, Nuke, Telephony denial-of-service (TDoS), Teardrop attacks, (S)SYN flood, R-U-Dead-Yet? (RUDY), Shrew attack and sophisticated low-bandwidth Distributed Denial-of-Service Attack is explained in detail along with various research work done on these attacks (Long & Thomas, 2001; Gupta et al., 2010)). The defense techniques (Hasbullah & Soomro, 2010) and the solutions proposed on these attacks are then presented. The defense techniques include an amalgam of attack detection, response, and traffic classification. These defense techniques function to block traffic that is identified as illegitimate or illegal and allow traffic that on the other hand is identified as legitimate or illegal (Senie & Ferguson, 1998). Some of the defense techniques that are explained in this chapter are upstream filtering, DDS based defense, blackholing and sinkholing, firewalls, routers, IPS based prevention, switches and application front-end hardware.

The focus of the chapter then shifts to botnets (Cooke et al., 2005). A network of robots can be defined as the botnet. It refers to a number of devices that are connected to the internet and can be used to perform attacks like the DDoS attack, sending of spam and stealing of data. It consists of compromised networks wherein each compromised device is referred to as a "bot." In the second section of this chapter, botnets are explained in detail. Botnets are now rented out as commodities for a number of purposes, by *cybercriminals* (Danchev & Dancho, 2010). These bots over the time have progressed to dodge their detection. Its application and architecture models including peer-to-peer and client-server model are discussed in the chapter (Ullah et al., 2013). In peer-to-peer model, digital signatures might be used by these, for example, a botnet can be controlled by a person who has access to a key of that network (Kang et al., 2009). Newer botnets communicate with a server, which is centralized. In a client-server model, botnets are operated by using Internet Relay Chat (IRC) networks, domains, and websites. Infected clients await incoming commands from the server as they access a predetermined location (Ollmann & Gunter, 2009). The person having the key of the botnet may send commands to the server, which is further forwarded to the clients. The results of the command executed are then sent back to that person called the bot herder. After the architecture, common botnet features of e-mail spam, spyware, Bitcoin Mining, Distributed denial-of-service and click fraud are listed. Botnet detection techniques (Mathews et al., 2016) are discussed along with various researches done on these techniques. The first detection technique that is discussed is the Honeypot-based botnet detection technique that is further divided into low-interaction honeypots and high-interaction honeypots (Provos et al., 2007). The second detection technique that is explained in the chapter is the network-based botnet detection technique wherein different models like BotMiner (Gu et al., 2008), SBotMiner (Yu et al., 2010) and BotSniffer (Gu et al., 2008) are elaborated. The differences in the implementation can sometimes be used to identify the botnets. For example, some botnets use services like DynDns.org, No-IP.com, and Afraid.org that are free Domain Name System (DNS) hosting services which themselves do not host attacks. They point to a *subdomain* towards an Internet Relay Chat server. This server caters to the bots. Rather, they provide the reference points, which can be, removed (Choi et al., 2007). These can incapacitate an entire botnet. Countermeasures like these to curb botnets are discussed along with the exiting software(s) that fulfill this purpose like the Norton AntiBot.

The authors then propose a botnet DDoS mitigation system through access list based configurations. They are designed at the ISP (Internet Service Provider's) edge routers in order to prevent DDoS attacks over ISPs' network traffic. Access Control Lists secure the system by restricting user and device access to a network using packet filtering. The last section of the chapter provides an understanding of the WannaCry Ransomware Attack, which locked the computers in more than 150 countries. In total, the chapter covers the following topics and focuses on:

- **Denial-of-Service Attack:**
  - Types of DoS attacks
  - DoS attack techniques
  - DoS attack symptoms
  - DoS attack defense techniques
- **Botnets:**
  - Botnet architecture
  - Botnet applications
  - Botnet features
  - Botnet detection techniques
  - Countermeasures against botnets
- An approach to secure a network from botnet DDoS attacks using access control lists
- **Case Study:** WannaCry Ransomware Attack

BACKGROUND

In a denial of service attack, the attacker prevents the utilization of resources of an authenticates legal user. In other words, services are disrupted by flooding the network. This also reduces the bandwidth provided to the user. According to 2004 CSI/FBI survey report[1], 17 percent of respondent's detected DoS attacks directed against them, with the respondents indicating that DoS was most common and costly cyber attack on them, even before the theft of proprietary information. These DoS attacks can be classified into two general forms listed below:

- **Crashing Attacks:** Sending the target information leading to a crash.
- **Flooding Attacks:** Flooding the target with traffic, depriving the legitimate users of the services.

Distributed attacks also came into existence soon after Denial of Service attacks. In such attacks, separate sites are used for execution to as Distributed Denial-of-Service (DDoS) attacks. In a distributed denial-of-service (DDoS) attack, which is a cyber attack, a large number of IP addresses that are unique are used. Thousands of IP addresses may be used by the perpetrator. The scale of DDoS has risen tremendously after it was discovered. In 2016, it exceeded a terabit per second. In the past years, the tools, methods, and techniques used for DDoS attacks have improved and have become more sophisticated and effective. This has made difficult to trace and find to the real attackers. The attacking techniques have become so advanced that the present technologies have to surrender to such large-scale attacks. A DoS attack resembles a group of people standing at the entry door or gate to a movie theatre, having valid tickets. The normal service is said to be disrupted when they are not being let in. Usually high-profile web servers of high-profit organizations, multi-nationals, finance companies etc. are targeted by the cybercriminals. Blackmailing and activism in the form of ransom may be done. Incoming traffic is flooded into the system in a distributed denial-of-service (DDoS) attack. Numerous unique IP addresses are used for DDoS attack. This effectively creates problems like:

- Blocking one IP address doesn't curb the attack
- Differentiating or distinguishing between legitimate and illegitimate traffic from user and attacker respectively is very tedious
- Involvement of IP address spoofing which defeats ingress filtering

The number of savages abusing the internet for their mean purposes has increased with the popularity of the internet. Bots are the most common choice to attack networks. In other words, a bot is nothing but a type of malware. A bot is written and programmed in a way to access the Internet and hijack the hosts. Botnets are used as a kick-start for denial of service (DoS) attacks, sending spam and junk mails. It is also used as a platform to host scam pages. Usually, the victim is tricked to install the bot himself. This is generally achieved by taking advantage of software or browser vulnerability. A channel called the command and control channel is then established by the bot with compromised machine. As the name suggests its function is to send commands to the compromised machine thereby taking the full control., This feature of bots separates it from other types of malware. A malicious entity, called the bot-master is used to control all other bot-infected machines. The whole system is referred to a botnet.

There are many traditional means of defense against bots that are available in the market, for example, installation of anti-virus software on the end users' machines. Unfortunately, these methods do not provide enough protection against attacks like DDoS, which is becoming more efficient with its evolution. It is mainly because of the reason that this antivirus software's have been programmed and made based on the already known samples, making the defense difficult. In order to keep up with the fast-rising malware, a large number of defense systems that are host-based have come into play. The behavior of unknown programs is captured by using static or dynamic analysis techniques. However, these systems have a disadvantage of runtime overhead and are problematic in practice. Installation of a platform for analysis is also required by every user. It is desirable to have a network-based detection system for host-based analysis technique, in order to supervise and identify the symptoms of traffic on computers that are bot-infected. The next section gives an insight of the chapter.

INSIGHT OF THE CHAPTER

In this chapter, an overview of DoS attack types is given after which, DoS attack techniques are elaborated in a tabular form by the authors. Its well-known symptoms and defense techniques are then listed. The types of DoS attacks that are explained in the chapter include Denial-of-service as a service, Advanced persistent DoS (APDoS) and Distributed DoS. Some of the DoS attack techniques that are explained in the chapter include Internet Control Message Protocol (ICMP) flood, attack tools that are Predators Face, Rolling Thunder, *MyDoom, Stacheldraht* and Low Orbit Ion Cannon, Peer-to-peer attacks, application-layer floods (LAND attack, *XDoS*), Degradation-of-service attacks, Distributed DoS attack, DDoS extortion, Nuke, Telephony denial-of-service (TDoS), Teardrop attacks, (S)SYN flood, Shrew attack, sophisticated low-bandwidth Distributed Denial-of-Service Attack etc. The defense techniques and the solutions proposed on these attacks that are presented include a composition of attack detection, response, and traffic classification such as upstream filtering, DDS based defense, blackholing and sinkholing, firewalls, routers, IPS based prevention, switches, and application front-end hardware. A detailed explanation of botnets is then presented in the chapter. Its application and architecture models including peer-to-peer and client-server model are discussed. Some of the common botnet features such as e-mail spam, spyware, Bitcoin Mining, Distributed denial-of-service, etc. and its detection techniques like honeypots, BotMiner, etc. are discussed in the section following architecture models. The authors then propose a botnet DDoS mitigation system through access list based configurations. In the section below an analysis on DoS attacks is done.

DENIAL-OF-SERVICE (DOS) ATTACKS

Denial-of-service attacks have used several techniques to crash or hang up machines with large volumes of traffic. The attackers may scan millions of computer devices connected to the internet and search unsecured ports and other loopholes. Daemons on intermediate machines are then installed through batch processes, which then wait for orders from master machine. The section below focuses on types of DoS attacks, their symptoms and defense techniques along with various research works done in the field. The types of DoS attacks are listed below.

Types of Denial-of-Service Attacks

A few prominent examples show the different types of DDoS techniques that hackers use: This section elaborates on the various types of DoS attacks such as DDoS, Advanced persistent DoS (APDos), Denial-of-service as a service, which is as follows:

- **Distributed DoS:** In this cyber attack, more than one unique *IP address,* crossing over a thousand, are used. These multi-person attacks are harder to deflect, due to more number of devices involved. DDoS attacks target the network infrastructure. They fill it with a large volume of traffic. A Trojan usually infects these systems using a Denial of Service (DoS) attack. Figure 1 shows a botnet DDoS attack.
- **Denial-of-Service as a Service:** These are the "booter" or "stresser" services that are now provided by some of the vendors and accept payment over the web. Unauthorized denial-of-service attacks can be performed by these services by allowing technical access of the attacker to the tool without understanding its use. The next section lists the symptoms of DoS attacks identified by US-CERT.
- **Advanced Persistent DoS (APDoS):** These attacks require a specialized monitoring and present an obvious and growing threat involving massive network layer DDoS attacks. Characteristics of APDoS attacks include tactical execution, large computing capacity, advanced reconnaissance and extended period persistence. An APDoSis more likely to be led by exceptionally artful and skilled actors having high-level resources and capacity. APDoS attacks have proved to be a clear threat. They require a lot of monitoring and defensive services. In the section below, the symptoms of DoS attacks have been listed.

Figure 1. Botnet diagram showing DDoS attack

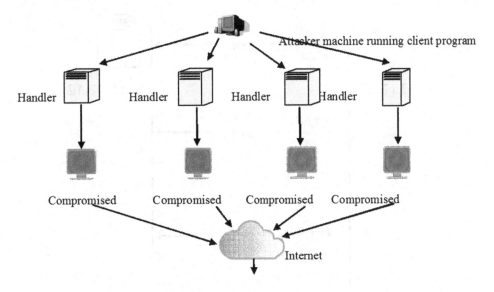

Symptoms of Denial-of-Service Attacks

Symptoms of a denial-of-service attack have been identified by the United States Computer Emergency Readiness Team (US-CERT)[2]. These are as follows:

- Speed Issue or slow *network performance.*
- Website not reachable or reachability issue.
- A drastic number of spam emails or email bomb attack.
- Networking wire issue, connection failure issue.
- Internet access is denied for a long period of time.

In the following section, DoS attack techniques have been elaborated in a tabular form along with their description.

DoS Attack Techniques

A broad spectrum of programs is used to commence DoS-attacks. In this section, various DoS attack techniques are listed in table 1. Figure 2 shows the structure of a land attack (Damon et al., 2012) and Figure 3 shows the architecture of a normal BitTorrent swarm (Hoßfeld et al., 2011).

The section below gives an overview of the techniques providing defense against DoS attacks.

Figure 2. Structure of land attack

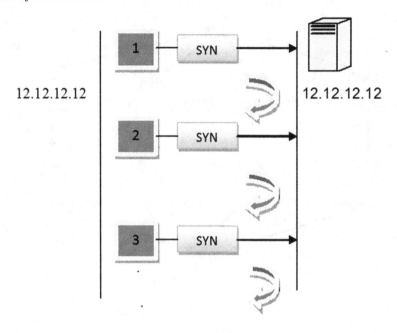

Figure 3. Architecture of a normal BitTorrent swarm

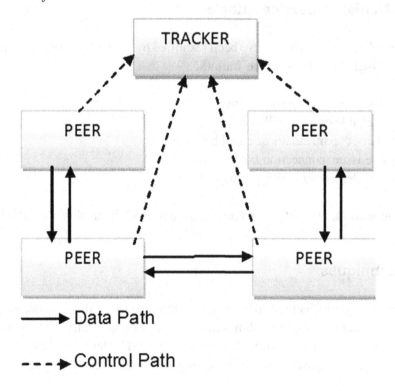

Table 1. DoS attack techniques

DoS ATTACK TECHNIQUES	DESCRIPTION
Attack tools	Government Communications Headquarters has PREDATORS FACE and ROLLING THUNDER tools built for DDoS. In MyDoom[3] the attacks are launched without the system owner knowing it whereas Low Orbit Ion Cannon (LOIC)[4] is used with user's consent. Stacheldraht[5] uses a layered structure. A client program is used by the attacker to connect to handlers.
Application-layer floods	Various exploits affect the memory of the system by eating up all the available memory or taking up all the disk space. Application level attacks focus their attack on one or a few applications, e.g. LAND attack, XDoS, etc. Some examples of application specific targets Web-based email apps, WordPress, Joomla, and forum software. Figure 4 shows the percentage of application layer attacks[6].
Degradation-of-service attacks	These attacks disrupt websites for time and can be more difficult to detect than a regular zombie invasion. It causes more concentrated floods, slowing server response times.
Distributed DoS attack	It is a cyber attack similar to DoS attack using numerous unique IP addresses.
DDoS extortion	A ransom is asked from the user of the attacked system against the warning of carrying out a larger attack or leaking the user information stored on it. The ransom is usually paid in Bitcoin[7].
Internet Control Message Protocol (ICMP) flood	In this type of flooding, a huge amount of IP packets are sent, affecting the bandwidth of the network. The packets never reach the required destination, as the address sending the packets is dummied with that of the victim. The "ping" command from Unix-like hosts is used to flood the network with ping flooding.
Nuke	The computer is slowed down and finally halted by sending invalid ICMP flood packets to the target in this attack via a modified ping utility. This is done by repeatedly sending corrupt data.
Peer-to-peer attacks	In this attack, the attacker plays the role of a "ringmaster". It instructs clients to connect to the website of the victim and disconnect to their peers.
Permanent denial-of-service attacks	It is an attack that damages hardware of a system such as memory crash, ports failure etc.
Reflected/spoofed attack	It requires sending counterfeit requests of a particular type to thousand of systems that will then reply to them.
Telephony denial-of-service (TDoS)	Calls have become inexpensive and automated with the introduction of Voice over IP. Through caller ID, spoofing fake calls can be placed.
Teardrop attacks	This attack can crash various operating systems as it involves sending mangled IP fragments because of which overlapping of packets occurs. The target machine cannot reassemble these packets because of a bug in TCP/IP fragmentation reassembly (Marin & Gerald, 2005).
(S)SYN flood	In this attack, a number of TCP/SYN packets, with counterfeit source address are sent by the host. Therefore, the response to legitimate requests never comes, causing saturation of half-open connections. (Lemon & Jonathan, 2002). The SYN-ACK communication process involves three steps. It is like handshake protocol which involves SYN & ACK message packet sending and receiving.
R-U-Dead-Yet? (RUDY)	The sessions on the web server are denied by making them unavailable to the victim web applications.
Sophisticated low-bandwidth DDoS Attack	This attack aims at a fatal flaw of the target machine by sending complicated requests to the system.
Shrew attack	This attack disrupts TCP connections by using short synchronized bursts of traffic.
UDP Flood	User Datagram Protocol is a networking protocol wherein flooding of packets is done on random ports of the target machine. They then report back with an ICMP packet.
Ping of Death	Ping of death overwrites the IP packet by sending packets larger than the maximum capacity. Large packets are fragmented across multiple IP packets. They are then reassembled and the resulting packet causes servers to reboot or crash.
Slowloris	Slowloris establishes a low bandwidth consuming connection with the target machine and keeps it open for a long time, affecting its web server. This is achieved using partial HTTP requests that are sent to the target machine and remain uncompleted.

Figure 4. Percentage targets of application-layer attacks

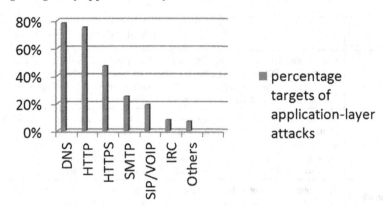

DoS Attack Defense Techniques

The defense techniques include a combination of attack detection (Jin et al., 2004), traffic classification (Douligeris et al., 2004) and response tools. Their purpose is to block traffic that they identify as illegitimate and allow traffic that they identify as legitimate. A list of techniques is given below in Table 2.

The next section gives an overview of botnets.

Table 2. List of DoS attack defense techniques

DEFENSE TECHNIQUES	DESCRIPTION
Application front end hardware	It is used along with routers and switches analyzing data packets as they enter the system. These data packets are then categorized as a priority, regular, or dangerous.
DDS based defense	It can address both protocol and rate-based attacks by blocking a DoS attack with legitimate content but bad intent.
Blackholing and sinkholing	In blackholing routing, traffic to the attacked IP address is forwarded to non-existent server i.e. a 'black hole'. In sinkholing, traffic is forwarded to a valid IP address for the analysis purpose which then rejected the Bad Packets.
Firewalls	They can prove to be very useful in a simple attack as they can cater to a simple rule which denies all incoming traffic from the attacker.
Routers	Routers reduce the effects of flooding and are set manually. They have some rate-limiting and Access Control List capability.
IPS based prevention	Intrusion Prevention System (IPS) works on the principle of content recognition. They find their use if the attacks have footprints associated with them. It cannot block DoS attack which is based on the behavior.
Switches	Most switches support access control list capabilities to detect and reform DoS attacks.
Upstream filtering	Different methods like proxies, digital cross-connects, tunnels etc. separating the unwanted traffic and sending only the 'good' traffic to the server. It uses the concept of "cleaning center" or a "scrubbing center".

BOTNETS

In the section below, botnet application, its architecture, features, detection techniques and ways to mitigate have been mentioned (Liu et al., 2009).

Botnet Application and Architecture

Botnets are now rented out as commodities for a number of purposes, by *cybercriminals*. It consists of compromised networks wherein each compromised device is referred to as a "bot". These bots over the time have progressed to dodge their detection. Figure 5 depicts typical botnet architecture. The two botnet architectures are as follows:

1. Client-Server Model
    Initially, botnets on the internet used this architecture to fulfill their task. Clients that are infected by the attack await incoming commands from the server as they access a location which is already specified. These commands generated by the person operating the botnet called as the bot herder are then further forwarded to the clients. Power engines of the botnets include Internet Relay Chat (IRC) networks, domains, or websites. These commands are then performed by the client the result obtained is reported back to the bot herder.

2. Peer-to-Peer
    Now, the bot herders have started to input traffic and malware on P2P networks as a result of detection of Internet Relay Chat (IRC) botnets. Digital signatures might be used by these bots allowing only a person with access to the key of the botnet network to control the botnet. Newer botnets communicate with a centralized server, where command distribution server and a client who receives commands, both are performed by a P2P bot.

Figure 5. Architecture of a Botnet

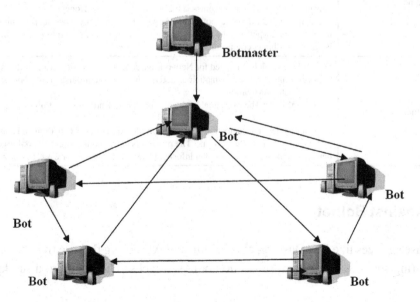

Common Botnet Features

The common botnet features are listed in Table 3.

Botnet detection techniques have been listed in the section below.

Table 3. Common botnet features

COMMON BOTNET FEATURES	DESCRIPTION
Distributed denial-of-service	In order to connect to the network, the victim receives a lot of requests by the bots.
Spyware	Private and confidential information like bank account and credit card numbers is sent to the creator of the Spyware who could further misuse or sell the data.
Bitcoin Mining	This feature generates profits for the operator of the botnet.
E-mail spam	E-mail messages are disguised as messages from people. In reality, they are malicious.
Click fraud	User's computer visits websites without his/her knowing it. Fake web traffic is hence created for monitory benefits and commercial gain.

Botnet Detection Techniques

The common detection techniques for botnet are mentioned in Table 4.

Table 4. Botnet detection and Identification techniques

BOTNET DETECTION TECHNIQUES	DESCRIPTION
Honeypot-based botnet detection	A honeypot is a resource, used to detect and deflect unauthorized use of information system (Weiler, 2002). The two types of honeypots are: • Low-interaction honeypots: They affect only the frequently requested services by attackers. Hosting multiple virtual machines is easy in this case. E.g. Honeyd • High-interaction honeypots: They provide more security by being difficult to detect. A number of honeypots can be used by using virtual machines. Therefore, restoration of honeypots is quick after being compromised.
Network-based Botnet Detection	Some of the models proposed for Network-based Botnet detection are as follows: • BotMiner: To identify malicious activity manner accomplished by a bot, BotMiner performs a cross-cluster correlation. • SBotMiner: The main goal of the approach is to find a group of bots that generate low rate traffic. • BotSniffer: This detection approach can identify both C&C (Command and Control) servers and infected hosts in the network. The process is carried out using network-based anomaly detection and without any known information about signatures or C&C server addresses.

Measures Against Botnet

Some botnets use services like DynDns.org, No-IP.com, and Afraid.org that are free Domain Name System (DNS) hosting services which themselves do not host attacks. They point to a subdomain towards

Figure 6. Distribution of botnet C&C servers in Q4 2016[8]

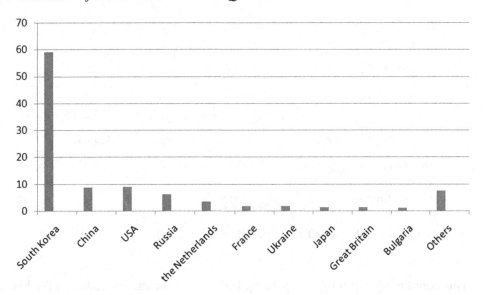

an Internet Relay Chat server. This server caters to the bots. Rather, they provide the reference points, which can be removed. The attacks are not hosted by these free DNS services. Rather, they provide the reference points which can be removed. These can incapacitate an entire botnet. Some botnets inherit the properties of customized versions of famous protocols and hence are based on them. The differences in implementation can be analyzed in order to detect the botnets. Software to counter botnets has now been released by computer and network security companies, e.g. Norton AntiBot. In the next section, solutions and recommendations to botnet DDoS attack have been proposed.

BOTNET DDOS ATTACK: SOLUTIONS AND RECOMMENDATIONS

In the above section, we studied that botnet is a group of hijacked devices that are connected to the internet. Each device injected with malware that is hidden from the owner of the device and is controlled by a remote region. Figure 6 shows the distribution of botnet Command and Control (C&C) servers in quarter 4 of 2016. A botnet DDoS attack may have multiple origins, i.e. it may be controlled by multiple individuals working in a coordinated manner. Many solutions have been proposed to prevent and to defend against botnet DDoS attack. One of the effective solutions proposed was using dynamic reconfiguration in 5G Mobile Networks (Pérez et al., 2017). Solutions in cloud computing environment have also been proposed (Somani et al., 2017; Osanaiye et al., 2016) that presented a conceptual cloud DDoS mitigation framework. Blackholing at ixps was another effective technique proposed (Dietzel et al., 2016).

From various sources, botnets-for-hire are available. Their services are usually auctioned and traded among attackers. Figure 7 shows the distribution of unique DDoS attack targets. We propose a botnet DDoS mitigation system through access list based configurations. They are deployed at the ISP (Internet Service Provider's) edge routers in order to prevent DDoS attacks over ISPs' network traffic. Access Control Lists secure the system by restricting user and device access to a network using packet filtering. The efficiency of the system is strongly dependent on the responsiveness of ISPs in implementing

Figure 7. Distribution of unique DDoS attack targets by country, Q3 2016 vs. Q4 2016[9]

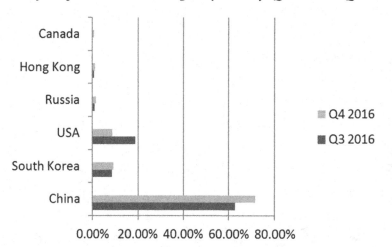

the system. This coordinated effort by participating ISPs filters out attacks, reducing the load on other routers. Most attacks can easily be stopped close to their point of origin, once each ISP has been implemented in the system. The suspicious traffic is first filtered out based on their source IP address. The first technique spawned as much traffic with different spoofed IP addresses as possible and the second technique generated without spoofed IP addresses. After the testing, it was observed that the bulk of malicious DDoS traffic can be effectively filtered out using proper configuration and filtering rules on the routers. Hence, this mechanism efficiently eliminates bogus traffic from their source, ensuring that high priority packets pass through the network and reach the destination and such services are not denied to the clients. Figure 8 classifies the defense mechanisms against network/transport-level DDoS flooding attacks based on their deployment location in a simple network of Autonomous Systems (AS). Figure 9 shows different areas for performing DDoS response and detection.

Setting up the Environment

To test the setup, we were required to generate DDoS traffic ourselves. To generate a lot of traffic to the attacked host, we used two different techniques. We used hping2 as the main tool for generating traffic.

Figure 8. A classification of the defense mechanisms against network/transport-level DDoS flooding attacks based on their deployment location in a simple network of Autonomous Systems (ASs)

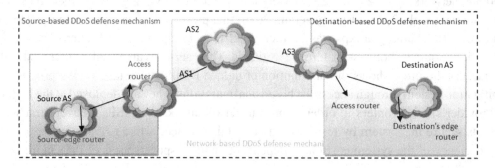

Figure 9. Different areas for performing DDoS response and detection

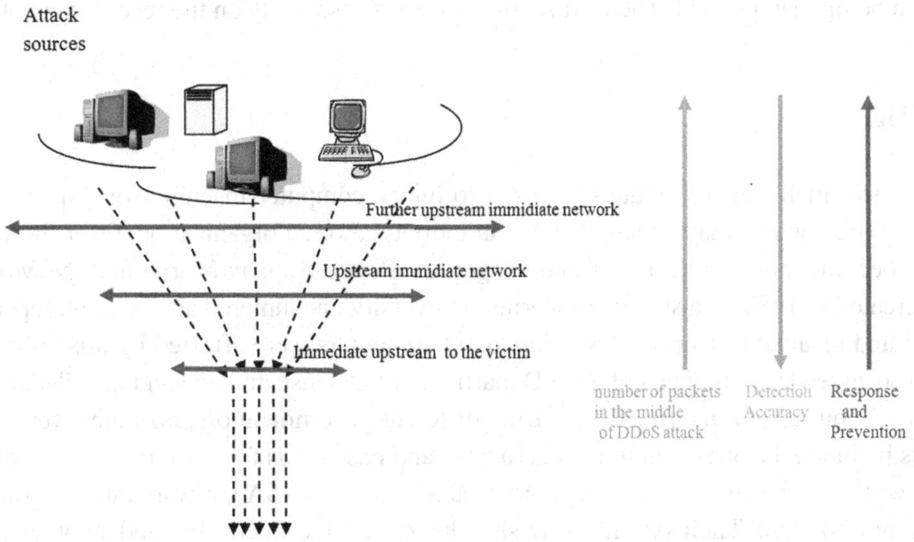

Hping is a TCP/IP packet crafter that is command-line oriented. It can be used for creating IP packets containing UDP, TCP or ICMP payloads. Using the command line, all header fields can be controlled and modified.

Filtering Rules 1

Only traffic with source addresses belonging to the customer network should be accepted by the ISP edge router. Any source address outside of the customer's network is readily a spoofed IP address. This is required to be implemented on the part of the ISP to prevent customers from participating in such malicious activities. Only traffic with source addresses other than the customer network address-block should be accepted by customer network.

Filtering Rules 2

As opposed to the previous filtering where the source address is filtered, the destination address or port is checked and filtered for filtering. Whatever is not included in the permit list will be rejected. Most of the time ICMP echo and echo-reply packets are allowed to pass through the network as it is an important tool for network troubleshooting and for checking connectivity. However, care must be taken when allowing ICMP traffic coming from the external networks. Although it has been a recommended practice to block known malware ports to prevent misuse of the network through such programs and to reduce the chances of individual computers participating in such activities as zombies, this system of ingress-filtering implicitly blocks any traffic targeted at ports not utilized by the publicly accessible server and thus effectively prevents unused ports from being manipulated. Emsisoft, an anti-malware vendor, has a publicly viewable list of such malware ports. It can be seen from the list that even some well-known ports have been exploited and used to run malicious activities. So, by explicitly allowing access only to specific ports where verified services are being provided is the most effective way to prevent networked systems from being manipulated. The next section covers a case study on the recent WannaCry attack.

CASE STUDY

In a cyber attack, malicious techniques are used to hijack computer machines or a network from an autonomous source, which may be handled, by an individual or an organization. Over the years, these attacks have become more sophisticated and dangerous. Robert Tappan Morris and the Morris Worm which was created in 1988 by a student of Cornell University encountered an error and repeatedly replicated itself and resulted in Denial of Service. 6000 computers were affected by this cyber attack. In 1999, a teen accessed the computers of a US Department of Defense division and installed a 'backdoor' on its servers. Thousands of internal emails from different government organizations were intercepted by him. This included the ones containing usernames and passwords for various military computers.

James used this information and was able to steal a piece of NASA software that cost the space exploration agency $41,000. Their systems were shut down for three weeks. In 2000, another 15-year-old boy named Michael Calce caused problems in the cyberspace by unleashing a number of Distributed Denial of Service attack on leading commercial sites like Amazon, Yahoo!, CNN and eBay. The attack resulted in a $1.2 Billion dollar damage bill. In 2009, a security breach was detected in Google's Chinese headquarters. Intellectual property was stolen, and various Google's servers were accessed by the hackers forcing it to shifts its headquarters to Hong Kong.

One of the biggest data breaches occurred on 3rd October 2013, when Adobe claimed that customer credit card records and login data were stolen and the source code of Adobe's software- Photoshop, Adobe Acrobat Reader, and ColdFusion was exposed. The hackers removed information relating to 2.9 million Adobe customers, including customer names, encrypted credit or debit card numbers, expiration dates, and other information relating to customer orders from the systems. The economic impact of cyber attacks is explained in CRS Report for Congress (Cashell et al., 2004). One of the research works done on cyber attacks by Carnegie Mellon Software Engineering Institute explains their tracking and tracing (Lipson & Howard, 2002). Countermeasures and challenges of cyber attacks were also presented in one of the research works (Li et al., 2012). In a brief issue, cyber attacks on US companies in the year 2014 have been mentioned (Walters & Riley, 2014). In this section, a case study of Wannacy Ransomware Attack is presented.

WannaCry Ransomware Attack

On 14 May'17, computers across the world were hit by a cyber attack, which resulted in locking up of the machines. The files and important documents of the users were held for ransom. The cyber attack mainly focused on government organizations, hospitals, health centers, and multinational companies. Ransomware is a type of Malware (harmful software) that hijacks a system. The user cannot access this system unless the ransom is paid. The ransom is usually paid in Bitcoins.

This type of ransomware was called "WannaCry". The attack halted the systems running banks, transportation, and other multinationals. In total, the cyber attack affected 200,000 victims in more than 150 countries. According to the Japan Computer Emergency, Response Team Coordination Center, a nonprofit group, at 600 locations in Japan was affected which in total included 2,000 systems. The attack

Figure 10. Most affected countries of the WannaCry Ransomware

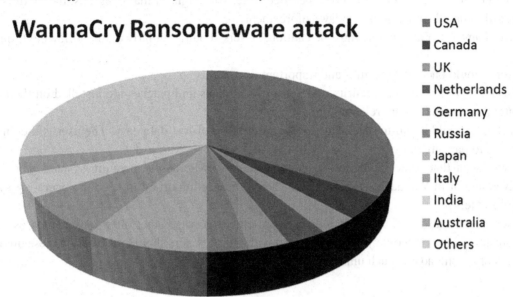

also shut down various social media sites disrupting its access. In addition, many people could not take their online driving tests in some regions as the transportation sites of the police department were also affected. Russia's interior ministry and companies including Spain's Telefonica and FedEx corporation in the US where some of the companies that were hit. Multinationals like Hitachi and Nissan Motor Co were also affected. Chinese media reported 29,372 institutions were infected along with hundreds of thousands of systems. Because schools and universities tend to have old and slow computers with less security and use old versions of operating systems, hence they were the hardest hit. In Indonesia, the locking down of systems affected the hospitals, as the files on the systems could not be accessed. This caused delays. Although, South Korea had a very small amount of cases. Figure 10 shows the percentage of most affected countries.

The idea behind this cyber attack was to trick the user to run a malicious code. In most cases, ransomware affected the systems through the links and attachments that were generally forwarded through e-mail. These e-mails are called phishing e-mails. The malware is hidden in these e-mails in the form of links and attachments. Once this piece of code is run, the malware takes over the system leaving the victim helpless. The important files and documents in the system are then held for ransom. All these files are encrypted by the malware and a message for ransom appears. In order to decrypt these files, the ransom has to be paid. The data may be lost if the ransom is not paid. The key for the encryption is only known to the attacker. People are mining for Bitcoins and various other forms of currency. Cryptocurrency has taken the world by storm. Cryptocurrency in some places has been accepted as a payment for goods and services. Figure 11 shows how do Bitcoins work. When this cyber attack occurs, the malware takes over the computer and the demands of the attacker are mentioned explicitly. Usually, the wallpaper of the affected system is changed. It contains a message specifying the amount to be paid and the method through which it is to be paid in order to recover the files. The attackers mostly demanded between $300 and $500 to remove the malicious ransomware. In addition, the price was doubled if the required amount was not paid within the specified time. Although, in many regions, the victims were discouraged to pay the ransom by the law enforcement.

To avoid any cyber attack, one must be cautious. Users should regularly do the following things:

- Users should back up their files and important documents.
- Users should ensure that security and anti-virus updates and patches are installed on their computer as soon as they are released.
- Backups should be up-to-date. This makes restoration of lost data easy. The user is then not required to pay any ransom.
- It was seen that some loopholes in older versions of Microsoft operating systems were taken advantage of in WannaCry cyber attack. Therefore, it is important to keep the operating system up-to-date.
- Users should also look for malicious or spam email messages that often masquerade as emails from companies or people you often interact with online. Users should not click on these unknown links or download any such unknown files.

Figure 11. Working of Bitcoins

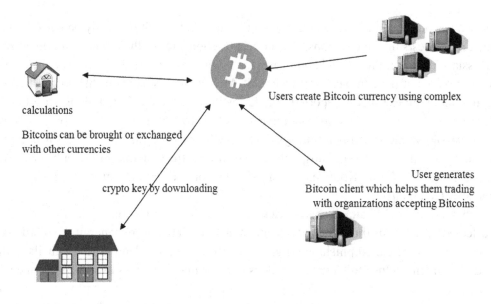

calculations

Bitcoins can be brought or exchanged with other currencies

Users create Bitcoin currency using complex

crypto key by downloading

User generates Bitcoin client which helps them trading with organizations accepting Bitcoins

Business organization accepts payments through Bitcoins and sells to users using unique crypto key

The challenge for hospitals was to keep patient data private, secure access to sensitive areas like operation theatres and ensure smooth operations. Some of the steps taken include:

- **Hiring Experts:** All top private hospitals have cybersecurity experts to secure patient information and private hacking.
- **Dedicated Fund:** Hospitals spend anywhere between Rs20 Lakh and Rs 2 Crore for cybersecurity.

- **Strong Password:** Access to Sensitive areas and equipment is controlled with strong passwords.
- **Regular Monitoring:** In a few cases, third-party agencies specializing in cybersecurity are engaged to periodically monitor safeguards.

The Reserve Bank of India (RBI) asked banks to follow instructions issued by Nation' cybersecurity unit CERT-in to prevent the worm from creeping into their systems. Some ATM is running on old the Microsoft Operating System was shut as a precaution.

FUTURE RESEARCH DIRECTIONS

Although users can take, steps to minimize the threat posed by DDoS attacks there are several reasons for concern about the future. Over the time, hackers will become more tempted and may use new fast-growing technologies to plan an attack and overwhelm victims with traffic. This may also overcome the proposed technique or packet filtering techniques. The key to protecting devices is keeping antivirus signatures up-to-date to prevent any future attacks like WannaCry Ransomware. As a part of our future work, detectors in various sub-networks can be introduced. These detectors communicate amongst themselves and warn other sub-networks if they are under attack. For this, we may use multi-agent system approach which has often been used in artificial intelligence. Another challenge is to develop a hypothesis to trace back the source of the attacks since the attacks follow a common pattern. Also, the performance of the technique proposed in this paper needs to be compared with other techniques that are currently being used in terms of false-alarm possibility and response time.

Another evolution in malware would be brought in IoT in the form of thingbots. Thingbots are a variant of botnets that are made up of contaminated IoT devices. These IoT devices can be controlled and supervised to:

- Theft of important sensitive information
- Launching of the attacks
- Other activities that come under cyber crime

In recent years, such activities of thingbots have been observed possessing a threat to cybersecurity. Therefore, there is an urgent need to address IoT related vulnerabilities, especially:

- IoT security
- Adherence to high standards in IoT devices
- Manufacturer and ISP levels should have best standards practice

A cryptocurrency is a value that can be cryptographically secured, and digitally represented and transmitted via the Internet. It is interoperable i.e. it is convertible and transferable. Interoperability is a more practical and credible outcome that requiring less damage to the incumbent. The future development in cryptocurrency is shown in Table 5.

Table 5. Developments in cryptocurrency

DEVELOPMENT AREA	DESCRIPTION
Online Shopping	Bitcoin wallets are now available in most of the leading online shopping websites. It was observed that 2.3 billion people now shop on Amazon using Bitcoins.
Education	Cryptocurrency transactions will soon be moving beyond the digital boundaries and will be accepted as investment opportunities.
Prioritizing privacy	It is very easy to find the details and spending habits of the sender of Bitcoins participating in a transaction. In the future cryptocurrencies like Monero will gain more popularity because of its privacy settings.
Significant capacity	Researchers are working on new algorithms (Ahuja & Yadav, 2013) (Bhushan, Gupta & Yadav, 2016) (Bhushan & Yadav, 2014) (Kamal 2016) (Tayal 2016) and programs in order to overcome blockchain issues. This will expand the reach of cryptocurrencies beyond its present limitations.

CONCLUSION

Botnet DDoS attack is currently one of the most cardinal threats on the Internet. Moreover, its early detection is also a big challenge. This is mainly because of the characteristics and volume of traffic change at a rattling pace. Therefore, updating the filtering rules and antivirus software is of utmost importance. This chapter mainly included an overview of DoS attacks and botnets. It further improves the measuring and understanding of botnet DDoS attacks and how to deal with them. We also proposed a defending methodology against botnet DDoS attacks. The case study of WannaCry ransomware attack showcases the current situation of malware existing and how much preparation we are for these attacks. In this chapter, the authors did an analysis on DoS attacks like Denial-of-service as a service, advanced persistent DoS (APDoS) and Distributed DoS is done. An overview on DoS attacking methodologies including attack tools, Low Orbit Ion Cannon, application-layer floods (LAND attack, XDoS), Degradation-of-service attacks, Nuke, Distributed DoS attack, Peer-to-peer attacks, DDoS extortion, R-U-Dead-Yet? (RUDY), Shrew attack, Internet Control Message Protocol (ICMP) flood, Telephony denial-of-service (TDoS), Teardrop attacks, (S) SYN flood and so on. The defense techniques and the solutions proposed in these attacks were then presented. Botnet application and architecture models including peer-to-peer and client-server model were successfully discussed in the chapter. Common botnet features of e-mail spam, spyware, Bitcoin mining, distributed denial-of-service and click fraud and botnet detection techniques were listed.

It was also seen that the bulk of malicious DDoS traffic could be effectively filtered out using proper configuration and filtering rules on the routers. This mechanism efficiently eliminates bogus traffic from their source and based on the type of packet and the volume of traffic at that instance, it is either allowed to pass through the network to the targeted host or queued or completely dropped at the destination. This ensures high priority packets to pass through the network and reach the destination and such services are not denied to the clients. From the above, it can be seen that proper filtering of packets at the point of origin can greatly reduce the amount of malicious traffic going through a network. Once such packets are filtered, they do not reach their intended destination. A coordinated effort across all ISPs would reduce such malicious packets and ultimately reduce the load on targeted hosts and the target network. This also prevents the individual internet users from participating in such activities. A case study on WannaCry Ransom Attack was also done.

REFERENCES

Ahuja, Y., & Yadav, S. K. (2013). Statistical Approach to Support Vector Machine. [IJEAT]. *International Journal of Engineering and Advanced Technology*, 2(3), 556–559.

Alejandre, F. V., Cortés, N. C., & Anaya, E. A. (2017, February). Feature selection to detect botnets using machine learning algorithms. In *Proceedings of the International Conference on Electronics, Communications and Computers (CONIELECOMP)*. 10.1109/CONIELECOMP.2017.7891834

Bhatt, C. M., Dey, N., & Ashour, A. (2017). Internet of Things and Big Data Technologies for Next Generation Healthcare (Vol. 23).

Bhushan, M., Gupta, A., & Yadav, S. K. (2016). Big Data Suite for Market Prediction and Reducing Complexity Using Bloom Filter. *The Human Element of Big Data: Issues, Analytics, and Performance*, 281.

Bhushan, M., & Yadav, S. K. (2014). Cost based Model for Big Data Processing with Hadoop Architecture. *Global Journal of Computer Science and Technology*, 14(2-C), 13.

Carl, G., Kesidis, G., Brooks, R. R., & Rai, S. (2006). Denial-of-service attack-detection techniques. *IEEE Internet Computing*, 10(1), 82–89. doi:10.1109/MIC.2006.5

Cashell, B., Jackson, W. D., Jickling, M., & Webel, B. (2004). The economic impact of cyber-attacks. *Congressional Research Service Document,* Retrieved from http://www.au.af.mil/au/awc/awcgate/crs/rl32331.pdf

Choi, H., Lee, H., Lee, H., & Kim, H. (2007, October). Botnet detection by monitoring group activities in DNS traffic. In *Proceedings of the 7th IEEE International Conference on Computer and Information Technology* (pp. 715-720). 10.1109/CIT.2007.90

Cooke, E., Jahanian, F., & McPherson, D. (2005). The Zombie Roundup: Understanding, Detecting, and Disrupting Botnets. *SRUTI*, 5, 6.

Damon, E., Dale, J., Laron, E., Mache, J., Land, N., & Weiss, R. (2012, October). Hands-on denial of service lab exercises using slowloris and rudy. In Proceedings of the 2012 information security curriculum development conference, 21-29. doi:10.1145/2390317.2390321

Danchev, D. (2010). Study finds the average price for renting a botnet. *Zdnet.com*. Retrieved from http://www.zdnet.com/article/study-finds-the-average-price-for-renting-a-botnet/

Desai, M., Patel, S., Somaiya, P., & Vishwanathan, V. (2016). Prevention of Distributed Denial of Service Attack using Web Referrals: A Review. *International Research Journal of Engineering and Technology*, 3(4), 1994–1996.

Dey, N., Ashour, A. S., & Bhatt, C. (2017). Internet of Things Driven Connected Healthcare. In Internet of Things and Big Data Technologies for Next Generation Healthcare (pp. 3-12). doi:10.1007/978-3-319-49736-5_1

Dietzel, C., Feldmann, A., & King, T. (2016, March). Blackholing at ixps: On the effectiveness of ddos mitigation in the wild. In *Proceedings of the International Conference on Passive and Active Network Measurement* (pp. 319-332). 10.1007/978-3-319-30505-9_24

Douligeris, C., & Mitrokotsa, A. (2004). DDoS attacks and defense mechanisms: Classification and state-of-the-art. *Computer Networks, 44*(5), 643–666. doi:10.1016/j.comnet.2003.10.003

Elhayatmy, G., Dey, N., & Ashour, A. S. (2018). Internet of Things Based Wireless Body Area Network in Healthcare. In Internet of Things and Big Data Analytics Toward Next-Generation Intelligence (pp. 3-20). doi:10.1007/978-3-319-60435-0_1

Feinstein, L., Schnackenberg, D., Balupari, R., & Kindred, D. (2003, April). Statistical approaches to DDoS attack detection and response. In DARPA Information Survivability Conference and Exposition (pp. 303-314). doi:10.1109/DISCEX.2003.1194894

Gu, G., Perdisci, R., Zhang, J., & Lee, W. (2008, July). BotMiner: Clustering Analysis of Network Traffic for Protocol-and Structure-Independent Botnet Detection. *USENIX Security Symposium, 5*(2), 139-154.

Gu, G., Zhang, J., & Lee, W. (2008). BotSniffer: Detecting botnet command and control channels in network traffic. In *Proceedings of the Network and Distributed System Security Symposium*, San Diego, CA.

Gupta, B. B., Joshi, R. C., Misra, M., Meena, D. L., Shrivastava, G., & Sharma, K. (2010). Detecting a Wide Range of Flooding DDoS Attacks using Linear Prediction Model. In *Proceedings of the 2nd International Conference on Information and Multimedia Technology (ICIMT 2010)* (Vol. 2, pp. 535-539).

Hasbullah, H., & Soomro, I. A. (2010). Denial of service (DOS) attack and its possible solutions in VANET. *International Journal of Electrical, Computer, Energetic, Electronic and Communication Engineering, 4*(5), 813–817.

Hoßfeld, T., Lehrieder, F., Hock, D., Oechsner, S., Despotovic, Z., Kellerer, W., & Michel, M. (2011). Characterization of BitTorrent swarms and their distribution in the Internet. *Computer Networks, 55*(5), 1197–1215. doi:10.1016/j.comnet.2010.11.011

Jain, A., & Bhatnagar, V. (2017). Concoction of Ambient Intelligence and Big Data for Better Patient Ministration Services. *International Journal of Ambient Computing and Intelligence, 8*(4), 19–30. doi:10.4018/IJACI.2017100102

Jin, S., & Yeung, D. S. (2004, June). A covariance analysis model for DDoS attack detection. In *Proceedings of the IEEE International Conference on Communications* (Vol. 4, pp. 1882-1886).

Kamal, S., Ripon, S. H., Dey, N., Ashour, A. S., & Santhi, V. (2016). A MapReduce approach to diminish imbalance parameters for big deoxyribonucleic acid dataset. *Computer Methods and Programs in Biomedicine, 131*, 191–206. doi:10.1016/j.cmpb.2016.04.005 PMID:27265059

Kang, J., & Zhang, J. Y. (2009, May). Application entropy theory to detect new peer-to-peer botnet with multi-chart CUSUM. In *Proceedings of the Second International Symposium on Electronic Commerce and Security* (Vol. 1, pp. 470-474). 10.1109/ISECS.2009.61

Kimbahune, V. V., Deshpande, A. V., & Mahalle, P. N. (2017). Lightweight Key Management for Adaptive Addressing in Next Generation Internet. *International Journal of Ambient Computing and Intelligence, 8*(1), 50–69. doi:10.4018/IJACI.2017010103

Kumar, R., Arun, P., & Selvakumar, S. (2009, March). Distributed denial-of-service (ddos) threat in collaborative environment-a survey on ddos attack tools and traceback mechanisms. In *Proceedings of the IEEE International Advance Computing Conference* (pp. 1275-1280).

Lemon, J. (2002, February). Resisting SYN Flood DoS Attacks with a SYN Cache. In *BSDCon* (pp. 89-97).

Li, X., Liang, X., Lu, R., Shen, X., Lin, X., & Zhu, H. (2012). Securing smart grid: Cyber attacks, countermeasures, and challenges. *IEEE Communications Magazine, 50*(8), 38–45. doi:10.1109/MCOM.2012.6257525

Lipson, H. F. (2002). Tracking and tracing cyber-attacks: Technical challenges and global policy issues. Retrieved from https://resources.sei.cmu.edu/library/asset-view.cfm?assetid=5831

Liu, H. (2010, October). A new form of DOS attack in a cloud and its avoidance mechanism. In *Proceedings of the 2010 ACM workshop on Cloud computing security workshop* (pp. 65-76). 10.1145/1866835.1866849

Liu, J., Xiao, Y., Ghaboosi, K., Deng, H., & Zhang, J. (2009, December). Botnet: Classification, attacks, detection, tracing, and preventive measures. *EURASIP Journal on Wireless Communications and Networking, 2009*(1), 1184–1187. doi:10.1155/2009/692654

Long, N., & Thomas, R. (2001). Trends in denial of service attack technology. *CERT Coordination Center.* Retrieved from https://resources.sei.cmu.edu/library/asset-view.cfm?assetid=52490

Marin, G. A. (2005). Network security basics. *IEEE Security and Privacy, 3*(6), 68–72. doi:10.1109/MSP.2005.153

Matallah, H., Belalem, G., & Bouamrane, K. (2017). Towards a New Model of Storage and Access to Data in Big Data and Cloud Computing. *International Journal of Ambient Computing and Intelligence, 8*(4), 31–44. doi:10.4018/IJACI.2017100103

Mathews, M. L., Joshi, A., & Finin, T. (2016, February). Detecting botnets using a collaborative situational-aware idps. In *Proceedings of the Second International Conference on Information Systems Security and Privacy* (Vol. 1, pp. 290-298). 10.5220/0005684902900298

Mirkovic, J., & Reiher, P. (2004). A taxonomy of DDoS attack and DDoS defense mechanisms. *Computer Communication Review, 34*(2), 39–53. doi:10.1145/997150.997156

Mukherjee, A., Dey, N., Kausar, N., Ashour, A. S., Taiar, R., & Hassanien, A. E. (2016). A disaster management specific mobility model for flying ad-hoc network. *International Journal of Rough Sets and Data Analysis, 3*(3), 72–103. doi:10.4018/IJRSDA.2016070106

Ollmann, G. (2009). Botnet communication topologies. *Retrieved from* http://www.technicalinfo.net/papers/PDF/WP_Botnet_Communications_Primer_(2009-06-04).pdf

Osanaiye, O., Choo, K. K. R., & Dlodlo, M. (2016). Distributed denial of service (DDoS) resilience in cloud: Review and conceptual cloud DDoS mitigation framework. *Journal of Network and Computer Applications, 67,* 147–165. doi:10.1016/j.jnca.2016.01.001

Park, K., & Lee, H. (2001, August). On the effectiveness of route-based packet filtering for distributed DoS attack prevention in power-law internets. *Computer Communication Review*, *31*(4), 15–26. doi:10.1145/964723.383061

Pérez, M. G., Celdrán, A. H., Ippoliti, F., Giardina, P. G., Bernini, G., Alaez, R. M., ... Carrozzo, G. (2017). Dynamic Reconfiguration in 5G Mobile Networks to Proactively Detect and Mitigate Botnets. *IEEE Internet Computing*, *21*(5), 28–36. doi:10.1109/MIC.2017.3481345

Poturalski, M., Flury, M., Papadimitratos, P., Hubaux, J. P., & Le Boudec, J. Y. (2010, September). The cicada attack: degradation and denial of service in IR ranging. In *Proceedings of the IEEE International Conference on Ultra-Wideband* (Vol. 2). 10.1109/ICUWB.2010.5616900

Provos, N., & Holz, T. (2007). *Virtual honeypots: from botnet tracking to intrusion detection*. Pearson Education database.

Saha, S., Nandi, S., Verma, R., Sengupta, S., Singh, K., Sinha, V., & Das, S. K. (2016). Design of efficient lightweight strategies to combat DoS attack in delay tolerant network routing. *Wireless Networks*.

Senie, D., & Ferguson, P. (1998). Network ingress filtering: Defeating denial of service attacks which employ IP source address spoofing. *Network. Retrieved from* https://buildbot.tools.ietf.org/html/rfc2267

Shrivastava, G., Sharma, K., & Rai, S. (2010, December). The Detection & Defense of DoS & DDoS Attack: A Technical Overview. In *Proceeding of ICC* (Vol. 27, p. 28).

Somani, G., Gaur, M. S., Sanghi, D., Conti, M., & Buyya, R. (2017). Service resizing for quick DDoS mitigation in cloud computing environment. *Annales des Télécommunications*, *72*(5-6), 237–252. doi:10.100712243-016-0552-5

Tayal, D. K., & Yadav, S. K. (2016). Fast retrieval approach of sentimental analysis with implementation of bloom filter on Hadoop. In *Proceedings of the 2016 International Conference on Computational Techniques in Information and Communication Technologies (ICCTICT)* (pp. 14-18). IEEE. 10.1109/ICCTICT.2016.7514544

Tayal, D. K., & Yadav, S. K. (2017). Sentiment analysis on social campaign "Swachh Bharat Abhiyan" using unigram method. *AI & Society*, *32*(4), 633–645. doi:10.100700146-016-0672-5

Ullah, I., Khan, N., & Aboalsamh, H. A. (2013, April). Survey on botnet: Its architecture, detection, prevention and mitigation. In *Proceedings of the 10th IEEE International Conference on Networking, Sensing and Control (ICNSC)* (pp. 660-665). 10.1109/ICNSC.2013.6548817

Walters, R. (2014). Cyber attacks on US companies in 2014. *Heritage Foundation Issue Brief, 4289*.

Weiler, N. (2002). Honeypots for distributed denial-of-service attacks. In *Proceedings of the Eleventh IEEE International Workshops on Enabling Technologies: Infrastructure for Collaborative Enterprises* (pp. 109-114).

Yadav, P., Sharma, S., Tiwari, P., Dey, N., Ashour, A. S., & Nguyen, G. N. (2018). A Modified Hybrid Structure for Next Generation Super High Speed Communication Using TDLTE and Wi-Max. In Internet of Things and Big Data Analytics Toward Next-Generation Intelligence (pp. 525-549). doi:10.1007/978-3-319-60435-0_21

Yamin, M., & Sen, A. A. A. (2018). Improving Privacy and Security of User Data in Location Based Services. *International Journal of Ambient Computing and Intelligence*, 9(1), 19–42. doi:10.4018/ IJACI.2018010102

Yu, F., Xie, Y., & Ke, Q. (2010, February). Sbotminer: large scale search bot detection. In *Proceedings of the third ACM international conference on Web search and data mining* (pp. 421-430). 10.1145/1718487.1718540

Zhang, H., Cheng, P., Shi, L., & Chen, J. (2016). Optimal DoS attack scheduling in wireless networked control system. *IEEE Transactions on Control Systems Technology*, 24(3), 843–852. doi:10.1109/ TCST.2015.2462741

ENDNOTES

[1]   See http://www.crime-research.org/news/11.06.2004/423/

[2]   See https://www.us-cert.gov/ncas/tips/ST04-015

[3]   MyDoom is a type of a computer worm, which affects MS Windows.

[4]   Low Orbit Ion Cannon is a torture testing and DoS attack application developed by Praetox Technologies

[5]   Stacheldraht is a malware acting as a DoS attack agent.

[6]   See http://www.thewhir.com/web-hosting-news/cloud-and-application-layer-increasingly-popular-attack-targets-report

[7]   Bitcoin is a cryptocurrency that is accepted and used globally. The transactions are decentralized.

[8]   See https://securelist.com/ddos-attacks-in-q4-2016/77412/

[9]   See http://www.csoonline.in/analysis/ddos-attacks-q4-2016

This research was previously published in the Handbook of Research on Network Forensics and Analysis Techniques edited by Gulshan Shrivastava, Prabhat Kumar, B. B. Gupta, Suman Bala and Nilanjan Dey; pages 117-141, copyright year 2018 by Information Science Reference (an imprint of IGI Global).

Chapter 4
Detection of Botnet Based Attacks on Network:
Using Machine Learning Techniques

Prachi

The NorthCap University, India

ABSTRACT

This chapter describes how with Botnets becoming more and more the leading cyber threat on the web nowadays, they also serve as the key platform for carrying out large-scale distributed attacks. Although a substantial amount of research in the fields of botnet detection and analysis, bot-masters inculcate new techniques to make them more sophisticated, destructive and hard to detect with the help of code encryption and obfuscation. This chapter proposes a new model to detect botnet behavior on the basis of traffic analysis and machine learning techniques. Traffic analysis behavior does not depend upon payload analysis so the proposed technique is immune to code encryption and other evasion techniques generally used by bot-masters. This chapter analyzes the benchmark datasets as well as real-time generated traffic to determine the feasibility of botnet detection using traffic flow analysis. Experimental results clearly indicate that a proposed model is able to classify the network traffic as a botnet or as normal traffic with a high accuracy and low false-positive rates.

INTRODUCTION

Scalability in computer networks, its architecture and a variety of software applications allows people to carry out their most mundane of tasks to most complex activities from remote locations in time efficient manner with great ease. There is the tremendous change in people's daily lives and business model of organizations across the world. More and more people are getting connected to the Internet in order to complete their daily chores and get benefits of the new business model. Although Internet brings lots of new ways to reach the end users it also brings the risk associated with it. Unfortunately, criminals have gained these revolutionary technological advances to commit offenses against an individual or groups

DOI: 10.4018/978-1-7998-5348-0.ch004

of individuals in order to physically or mentally harasses victim for personal gains using modern tele-communication systems in form of Cyber Crimes (Shrivastava, 2016). Acceleration in growing usage of Internet and technological advances leads to integration of information from multiple sources that reflects scaling of volume and type of information (Matallah et al., 2017). Constant advancement in Next Generation Internet enhances the requirement of secure and efficient communication against the new sort of challenges posed by the emerging applications (Kimbahune et al., 2017). In recent times, botnets are used to launch a number of distributed cyber-attacks such as ransomware, Distributed Denial of Service (DDoS) (Shrivastava et al., 2010), distributed computational tasks, spam emails, etc. The high infection rate, a large number of unlawful activities and strong comebacks make botnets one of the most destructive attacks (Cox, 2013; David, 2012). Destruction impact of the botnet is becoming more and more critical nowadays (Guntuku, 2014).

In general, botnets can be characterized based on the characteristics of Command & Control server that is used for the communication between the bot-master and bot-client. Command & Control server facilitates a bot-master to issue some queries and waits for their responses in a time efficient manner while evading the security measures deployed by the victim to detect a botnet. Although, the different types of command and control are presented in literature two of them are most significant: centralized and distributed. In case of the distributed botnet, individual bots are hard to detect and hence increase the resiliency of botnet. However, both of them have their own benefits and drawbacks. To address their drawbacks, peer-to-peer botnets came into existence. Till date, these are most robust and hard to detect by most of the existing security mechanisms.

Although a significant number of security solutions have been developed in recent past in terms of firewall and cryptographic solutions they have their limitations in terms of security solutions. Defense solutions that identify network intrusions are another way of identifying the recent type of attacks (Shrivastava et al., 2016). The research community is actively working towards detection of botnets and a number of detection techniques have been proposed in the literature. Botnet mitigation techniques can be classified into 2 categories: active botnet detection and passive botnet detection.

Active botnet detection involves all sorts of analysis techniques that inform Command &Control server or bot-master either directly or indirectly about botnet analysis. Although, active botnet detection techniques appear promising they suffer from the drawback of early detection. Once identified, they can easily circumvent any actions taken against the botnets.

During passive analysis of network traffic, the analysis is performed without interrupting the activity of botnet. In such type of scenario, network activities are traced (Shrivastava, 2017). Most common technique in a passive analysis is the inspection of network packets. Parameters of network packets are analyzed against a large database of malicious behavior for identification of botnets. Packet inspection techniques can be easily incorporated into existing Intrusion Detection Systems (IDS). Intrusion Detection System is considered as most effective technology against the network attacks by identifying and analyzing the traffic (Denning, 1987). Most of the Intrusion Detection System designed for botnet detection is rule-based. Performance of such Intrusion Detection System depends on the rule set defined by the experts (Zhang et al., 2005; Roesch, 1999). In this type of Intrusion Detection System, signatures of incoming network traffic are compared against signatures of previously identified botnets. Such detection mechanism may work well for existing botnet but fail against rapidly changing network traffic. Such dependencies make rule-based Intrusion Detection System inefficient, time-consuming and tedious process against botnets.

Behavior or anomaly based Intrusion Detection System (Huang et al., 2016) cannot perform the complete inspection of packets when network flow is high. Techniques such as packet filtering and packet sampling increase the possibility of missing malicious packets. Moreover, behavior-based IDS increase a large number of false alarms.

In order to counter these issues, analysis of flow records can be considered as one useful technique. In case of flow-based analysis, the headers of several packets are aggregated in a flow and then flows are analyzed (Strayer et al., 2008; Zhao et al., 2012). Consequently, flow-based analysis uses only packet headers, behavior-based packet analysis use payload and some of them use a combination of both (Zeidanloo et al., 2010; Wurzinger et al., 2009). To evade behavior-based packet analysis techniques, attackers started employing data encryption techniques on the data embedded in the messages.

Haddadi et al., 2016 used traffic analysis techniques for detection of the botnet. Traffic traces of normal and malicious traffic for evaluation of botnets were generated by setting HyperText Transfer Protocol and Domain Name System communication with publically available domains of authentic web server and botnet Command & Control server. Features were extracted from the packet header and machine learning algorithms (Naïve Bayes and C4.5) were employed for detection of botnets. The proposed approach is able to achieve the Detection rate of 97% and False Positive Rate of 3%.

Authors investigated four different botnet detection systems: packet based detection system, flow-based detection system, BotHunter (The unique network defense solution that quickly isolates the infected machines and helps you to determine who actually owns your system) (Gu et al., 2007) and Snort (IDS) (Roesch, 1999). After analyzing the botnet traffic on CTU-13 (13 botnet datasets) (Gracia et al., 2014), authors concluded that flow based botnet detection system outperformed all other detection systems.

Therefore, this chapter aims to design a detection model that doesn't use payload but only packet headers in order to detect the botnet. Machine learning techniques will be used to automate the process of botnet detection because flexibility and automated learning capability of machine learning algorithms provide them an edge over other mitigation methods.

We will use a flow exported tool to extract the important features from the network traffic. Exporter tools are generally used to aggregate the network packets into flows. Netflow (Cisco IOS Netflow, 2017), is a standard by CISCO for the collection of IP-flow. This chapter uses its open-source version, softflowd (softflowd, 2017) to collect data in form of flows. Later on, machine learning is applied to differentiate botnet and normal traffic.

BACKGROUND

In current times, detection of botnets has been one of the prominent research areas of researchers. Although a number of techniques are present in literature, a majority of them are not able to detect the recent type of botnets. Previously proposed botnet detection methodologies majorly focused on the analysis of payloads for mischievous content. Payload examination approaches consume more data because they require a massive amount of data. Also, bots nowadays use techniques such as data encryption and code obfuscation to hide their malicious content.

A framework is presented in 2007 for detection of botnets, named as BotHunter, based on the Snort to implement a rule-based Intrusion Detection System (Gu et al., 2007). This framework relates bot activities with alarms from the Snort Intrusion Detection System. This framework exploits the concept that bots perform similar sort of actions during their lifecycle, for example, scanning of the host, infection with some sort of virus, download of binary, connection with Command & Control server, etc. BotHunter closely monitors the traffic of a network to identify the different phases of botnet lifecycle. Thereafter, BotHunter performs the analysis of payload on the basis of different rules of the Snort and correlation engine of BotHunter is used to calculate the score. The score determines the amount of probability that network is infected by a bot. BotHunter possesses high accuracy when a bot covers all the phases of its lifecycle. Although such type of system provides quite accurate results they don't scale well with voluminous and varied network traffic. Moreover, it can't cope up with encrypted data as it is based on payload analysis.

A botnet detection system was proposed (Strayer et al., 2008) on the basis of network behavior. Authors particularly focused on Internet Relay Chat-based Command & Control activities by examining different flow characteristics of Internet Relay Chat flows such as packet timing, bandwidth, and burst duration. This approach is divided into four different phases: During the first phase, filtering is applied on the generated traffic to differentiate Internet Relay Chat from normal traffic by eradicating traffic that is possibly normal Internet Relay Chat. Filters are designed by taking into consideration the commands of Internet Relay Chats bots, white and blacklists of Internet domains and some of the network flow characteristics. During the second phase, clustering is applied to filtered flows using machine learning algorithms on the basis of pre-defined network applications clusters. Authors didn't specifically mention which machine learning techniques have been used in this paper during this stage. Thereafter, clustered flows are passed on to correlator stage. During the third stage, clustered flows are again clustered according to similarity among characteristics. Consequently, the topological analysis is applied on the correlated flows in order to identify the common controller. Flows that belong to the common controller are analyzed by a human analyst to evaluate whether they belong to a botnet or not. As preciseness of this approach is dependent on the expertise of a human analyst, this is a noticeable drawback of the proposed approach.

Authors have used classification for filtering the traffic and clustering is used to identify different activities. Authors were successfully able.

BotMiner was developed in 2008 for detection of the botnet on the basis of group behavior analysis of individual bots that belongs to a single botnet (Gu et al., 2008). It analyzes and clusters the similar behavior that is being performed continuously on a group of machines in the network for detection of the botnet. They first applied clustering in order to group the behavior for a similar type of communication and later on applied activity clustering. Network flows of popular safe protocols were filtered from the network traffic to increase the accuracy of detection. Consequently, the second phase of clustering is applied to group flows according to the malicious activities identified by the Snort. After applying both types of clustering, BotMiner associates bots that possess similar behavior and perform malicious activities. During this process, BotMiner was able to detect most of existing popular botnets with a detection rate of 99% and false positive rate of approximately 1%.

BotSniffer was proposed on the concept of network-based anomaly detection when there is no previous knowledge of Command and Control server signatures (Gu et al., 2008). This approach can be used to identify both, the Command & Control server as well as the bots. It worked on the assumption that all the bots that belong to the same botnet depict strong synchronization and spatial as well as the temporal correlation between their response behavior as well as activities. The proposed system captures this strong correlation among activities and responses of several bots that belong to a single botnet and utilized various statistical techniques to identify botnets with a restricted number of false positives and false negatives. Authors have evaluated the proposed approach on a large number of real-world network traces.

A system was proposed for detection of general botnets such as Internet Relay Chat and Peer-to-Peer based botnets (Zeidanloo et al., 2010). This approach focused on the similarity in behavior as well as communication pattern among multiple bots that belongs to a single botnet. Moreover, this work doesn't rely on any previous knowledge about the botnets or their signatures.

Authors used classification and clustering to distinguish between normal and botnet traffic.

In 2012, authors presented a methodology for botnet detection by observing network traffic characteristics (Zeidanloo et al., 2012). This approach works very similar to that of BotMiner. The proposed methodology was divided into 3 different stages: filtering, detection of malicious activity and monitoring of network traffic. These different stages are used to group the different types of bots by their group behavior. Proposed approach segregates the flows in six hours' time period. However, effects of different size of flow intervals were not presented. Therefore, the correctness of this approach is not identified.

All the group behavior-based approaches are not suitable for early detection of botnets because they require botnets to perform malicious activities before their detection. Additionally, group behavior-based approaches assume that multiple machines are infected by botnet on the monitored network. Subsequently, this methodology became infeasible if a single system is affected by the botnet on the monitored network.

An approach that detects botnet on the host end without requiring the group behavior analysis was presented (Giroire et al., 2009). Authors worked upon the assumption that bot needs to frequently communicate with its bot-master to perform its desired function. Frequent communication is required between bot-master and bot-client in form of commands and responses. Therefore, there is a form of regularity in communication among bot and its bot-master that may be spread over a large span of time. This sort of communication can be easily captured by monitoring the incoming and outgoing network traffic to/from mischievous destinations with some sort of regularity in time. In order to distinguish normal destination from the malicious ones, the author designed a white-list of authentic destinations. The persistent feature is used to capture the temporal regularity of visited destinations. Botnet detection is implemented by identifying persistent communication from/to non-white listed source/destinations beyond a certain level of threshold. Performance evaluation of proposed approach on real-world network traffic generated the low number of false positives.

On the basis of correlation among commands and responses of monitored traffic, network nodes of a monitored network are evaluated to determine their relation to botnets (Wurzinger et al., 2009). It finds responses within network traffic and then observes the earlier traffic for recognizing the corresponding commands. On the basis of command and responses patterns, detection models are build to identify similar sort of activity and presence of botnet. However, the models generated in this form are specific to the particular type of botnets. In order to evaluate the performance of proposed methodology, 18 models were automatically generated for the different type of botnets say, Internet Relay Chat (IRC) System, Hyper Text Transfer Protocol (HTTP) and Peer-to-Peer (P2P) and their performance was evaluated on publicly available datasets. Performance results depict low false positive rate during evaluation.

Authors have used packet payload information for detection so such type of systems can easily fail when encryption is employed in botnet traffic.

An anomaly-based system was presented (Arshad et al., 2011) that doesn't require any prior information about signatures of bots, addresses of Command & Control and botnet protocols. In the proposed approach, inherent characteristics of botnets were used. In general, all the bots connect to their bot-master, receive and then execute those commands. It became obvious that all the bots that belong to a single botnet receive same instructions. This results in the similarity between NetFlow characteristics and thereby they perform the same type of attacks. This method clusters bots that possess alike net flows and attacks in various time windows and perform the correlation to identify all the hosts that are infected by a botnet. Authors this paper evaluated proposed method against various normal and malicious network traces available over the Internet.

A system was designed for detection of botnets using flow intervals and traffic behavior analysis (Zhao et al., 2012). Features extracted with the help of packet headers were used with classifiers for detection of botnets. Network flow features along-with Bayesian network and decision trees were used for detection of botnets. Authors focused on Peer 2 Peer (P2P) botnets that utilized Domain Name System (DNS) technique and Hyper Text Transfer Protocol (HTTP). The proposed technique was evaluated on the combination of malicious and normal traffic that is collected from various sources LBNL datasets were used for normal traffic and malicious from traces from Honeynet Project. Evaluation results clearly depict that detection rate is above 60% while the false positive rate is below 5%.

A system for detection of Hyper Text Transfer Protocol (HTTP) based botnets on the basis of traffic flow using multilayer feed-forward neural network was proposed (Kirubavathi & Anitha, 2016). They focused on features such as packet ratio, the initial length of packets for detection of botnets. In general, HTTP based botnets don't maintain a persistent connection with Command &Control server but bots send the periodical request to the Command & Control server in order to download all the instructions given by Command & Control server. Authors extracted Transmission Control Protocol features from packet headers. Different botnets are simulated in a laboratory for performance evaluation of the proposed system.

Some researchers used active DNS probing on a large scale to evaluate the query of DNS characteristics based on the values of DNS cache (Ma et al., 2015). However, this method raises high-security alarms and increases the probability of detection by the attackers.

Studies by various researchers on detection of periodic communication in HTTP and their limitations were reviewed (Eslahi et al., 2015). Authors proposed three measures for determining the different communication patterns on the basis of periodicity. The levels of periodicity were explored in order to characterize the traffic for botnets by matching the likeness among messages. Authors were able to detect communication of Hyper Text Transfer Protocol botnet with 80% accuracy. However, this work suffers from the problem of a large number of false positives. Therefore, it became necessary to combine it with other features for better results.

A number of security threats launched by attackers at the network level (Suriya & Khari, 2012). Author classified the attacks in 2 major categories: active attack and passive attack. Further, authors presented a number of security issues that should be taken into consideration while designing a secure routing protocol for networks (Miglani et al., 2017).

The vulnerable features of mobile ad-hoc network and various security measures such as cryptography, intrusion detection system, secure protocols, etc., are reviewed so that they can be used to secure the network nodes against these vulnerabilities (Saini & Khari, 2011).

The numbers of techniques used by attackers to attack web applications that are running on victim system to retrieve confidential and sensitive details are discussed (Khari & Kumar, 2016). Attackers can exploit the vulnerabilities of web applications via a number of attacking techniques such as SQL Injection, cross-site scripting, etc.

A paper was presented where different types of web applications vulnerabilities are presented (Khari & Sangwan, 2016). Authors also discussed various dynamic and static analysis approaches proposed by researchers to tackle against these types of vulnerabilities. Particularly, authors focused on the research done by researchers on cross-site scripting attack.

A novel user authentication technique is presented in order to prevent unauthorized access to the database during SQL Injection attack (Khari & Kumar, 2016). In case of SQL Injection attack, the attacker exploits the vulnerabilities of web applications to gain access to admin credentials hence control of the entire website. In this paper, authors present a SQL Injection Protector for Authentication where salt and the hash value of username and password are used while authentication in addition to username and password. Since these values are created during the dynamic time so an attacker will not be able to get access to these values.

Various methodologies presented by researchers such as IDS, black hole testing, etc to prevent against SQL Injection attacks were discussed (Khari & Karar, 2013).

It is clear from the above discussion that a number of researchers have presented different botnet detection techniques by a variety of methods. However, most of them were able to detect a specific type of botnet either Internet Relay Chat Based or Hyper Text Transfer Protocol based or Peer-2-Peer-based. In this chapter, the objective of the author is to propose a botnet detection system that can identify all types of botnets with high accuracy and low false positives.

MAIN FOCUS OF THE CHAPTER

This section discusses the advantage of using flow analysis during detection of botnets, generation, and collection of the botnet and normal traffic and different type of machine learning algorithms used for network flow analysis.

Most of earlier presented work focuses on payload analysis that analyzes contents of TCP or UDP protocol based payloads to identify the malicious behavior. This type of analysis offers high accuracy when compared with many other algorithms but also suffers from a number of limitations. Payload-based analysis techniques are resource consuming operations that consume lots of time while performing the analysis. Such techniques fail when the amount of network traffic is quite high. Additionally, new bots started used data encryption, code obfuscation techniques in order to hide the content from the user and hence defeat the purpose of packet inspection techniques. Furthermore, packet inspection techniques also raise the concern regarding violation of privacy.

Flow analysis techniques counter most of the concerns raised by payload inspection techniques. Flow analysis techniques are based on the concept that all bots within a botnet exhibit similar behavior. These techniques use flow generation tools to consolidate data according to the information in packet headers. Network behavior is characterized by a set of features. Therefore, these features can be used to differentiate the normal traffic from the botnet traffic. The flow-based analysis doesn't use payload, so this technique is invulnerable to code encryption and code obfuscation techniques.

Therefore, this chapter explores the possibility of detecting botnets with the help of packet headers. Network traffic is aggregated in form of flows to extract useful features from network traffic. Later on, an effective machine learning model will be designed to detect botnets in real time with high accuracy. Our proposed work is divided into different phases: Dataset collection, Flow extraction, Flow Analysis and Feature extraction

Data Collection

To design a machine learning based botnet detection system, a dataset is required in order to train the models. The dataset should also comprise of real-world network traffic with all the essential features. During analysis, selected models will be evaluated on the ISOT dataset (Saad et al., 2011) from University of Victoria. The ISOT dataset is a collection of various normal and malicious botnet dataset available online on many public sites. To represent the non-malicious data, normal data in ISOT comprises of 2 different datasets i.e. Traffic Lab at Ericsson Research in Hungary and from Lawrence Berkeley National Lab. The malicious dataset actually comprises of 2 different botnets: storm and waledac. In addition to this, the CTU (Gracia et al., 2014) dataset by CTU University is used for botnet traffic dataset. Further, Zeus botnet is used to capture data in real time. Zeus botnet is very popular botnet to steal sensitive details. In addition to above-collected data, Alexa Internet, Inc (Alexa, 2017) is used to gather normal traffic. This site displays 500 benign sites. Softflowd (open source version of NetFlow (a CISCO software)) is also used to capture the traffic in real time. In order to homogenize the network traffic, TCPRelay is used to replay the trace files of these datasets. In the end, the replayed traffic is captured with the help of Wireshark.

Flow Extraction

In order to build the flows out of the captured data, nfcapd and nfdump (NfDump, 2017) are used. Nfdump is an open source and user-friendly flow exporter that can work with a number of NetFlow versions. It can easily export flows out of already captured traffic and real-time traffic captured with the help of softflowd. As input, it can use live network traffic as well as pre-captured data in form of pcap files to extract the important features. By default, nfdump extract 48 features from the flows.

Flow Analysis

In order to classify the flows as botnet or normal, it is important to analyze values of a set of attributes. Functioning of the proposed approach is divided into 2 phases: training and detection phase. Classifiers were trained with the help of malicious and non-malicious attributes values during the training phase for segregation of data in two different classes: normal and malicious. Once the training phase is complete, detection phase starts observing the traffic network and classifies the flows on the basis of the value of different attributes. Whenever attributes show malicious values then flows are flagged as suspicious.

For the analysis purpose, three most prominent machine learning algorithms (Alpaydin, 2004): SVM, Random Tree and REPTree are used to distinguish the botnet and normal traffic accurately:

1. **Support Vector Machine:** In Support Vector Machine, each data instance can be classified according to a hyperplane. The objective of this algorithm is to determine an optimal hyperplane to ensure the biggest minimum distance between training examples.
2. **Random Tree:** This algorithm repeatedly classifies the dataset by randomly selecting a subset of features at each node for constructing the trees. This algorithm creates a number of trees and in the end, each tree makes a vote. This algorithm decreases the risk of over-fitting. It works efficiently even on large datasets and possesses high accuracy even if a large amount of data is missing.

3. **REP Tree:** Reduced Error Pruning Tree uses the concept of regression tree and creates multiple trees in different iterations. Afterwards, the best one is chosen among all the available trees. REP Tree is the fast version of the decision tree that uses information gain as the splitting criteria and prunes the tree according to mean square error.

Feature Extraction

In order to develop an accurate, scalable and real-time machine learning model, it is very important to use feature selection techniques on high-dimensional data. Selection of the right set of features reduces the complexity, increases the accuracy and reduces the time.

Feature selection techniques can be broadly classified into two categories: wrapper and filter.

In case of wrapper method, subsets of features are selected on the basis of the classifier that is being used for performance evaluation i.e. effectiveness of features is determined from the performance of the classifier. Therefore, the performance of a particular classifier is evaluated using the different subset of features and set of features with which classifier performs best is selected as the final output.

Filter method chooses a subset of features regardless of any particular classifier. It evaluates the utility of features and assigns rank according to their relevance in performance evaluation. Their performance is independent of any classifier.

This chapter uses correlation feature selection (CFS) as filter method and WrapperSubsetEval as wrapper method. Best First Search will be used to identify the best set of features with the help of above-mentioned feature selection approaches.

RESULTS

In order to determine the performance of classifiers, WEKA machine learning framework is used in this chapter. To extract and export important features from a given pcap file, nfcapd and nfdump are used. Cross-validation method is used to evaluate the performance and effectiveness of evaluated models. During the assessment, the dataset was distributed into 10 sub-datasets, out of which 9 are used for training purpose and 1 is used for testing purpose. The same phenomenon is repeated again and again until all the subsets are used for testing purpose precisely once.

Different performance measures such as detection rate (DR), false positive rate (FPR), Accuracy are used to assess the performance of various classifiers. DR defines the ratio of intrusions detected out of a total number of intrusions in network traffic. FPR specifies the percentage of normal traffic identified as intrusions. Accuracy determines the percentage of traffic classifier is able to distinguish properly as the botnet and normal traffic. The objective of this chapter is to achieve high DR and Accuracy and low FPR.

The above-mentioned are determined with the help of following formulas:

$$DR = \frac{TP}{TP + FN}$$

$$FPR = \frac{FP}{TN + FP}$$

$$Accuracy = \frac{TP + TN}{TP + TN + FP + FN} * 100$$

where, True Positive (TP) is the ratio of intrusions that are correctly identified as intrusions, True Negative (TN) is the number of normal traffic instances that are correctly classified as normal traffic instances. False Positives (FP) defines the number of normal traffic instances that are incorrectly classified as botnet type. False Negative (FN) defines the number of instances of botnet traffic incorrectly classified as normal traffic.

The DR, FPR, and Accuracy for SVM, Random Tree, and REP Tree are listed in Table 1. These values are an average of results of 10 simulations.

Table 1. Performance of algorithms on different performance metrics with full feature set

	DR	FPR	Accuracy
SVM	0.9651	0.00016	99.9411
RandomTree	0.9902	0.00007	99.981
REPTree	0.9932	0.00012	99.982

It became clear from Table 1 that all the algorithms performed really well in terms of accuracy, more than 99%. Further, they possess a detection rate of more than 96%. It is clear from the table that Random Tree and REP Tree outperform SVM in terms of accuracy and performance of REP Tree is marginally better than Random Tree. Further, the detection rate is above 99% in case of Random Tree and REP Tree so they only less than 1% of the botnet instances will remain undetected.

Table 1 results make it more evident that botnets possess certain unique features in comparison to normal network traffic.

Figure 1 demonstrates the performance of different algorithms: SVM, Random Tree, and REPTree in terms of accuracy. Out of all the 3 algorithms, REP Tree and Random Tree are more accurate than SVM, classifying more than 99.98% instances accurately while inaccurately classifying less than .02% instances.

Figure 2 demonstrates model performances in terms of DR. Detection rate is highest in REP Tree followed by Random Tree. Performance of SVM is not up to the mark when compared with Random Tree and REP Tree.

Figure 3 demonstrates model performances in terms of FPR. The false positive rate should be minimum for a good classifier. During analysis, it was determined that SVM possess highest FPR in comparison to other two. FPR is minimum in case of Random Tree.

During the overall assessment, the author concludes that Random Tree is best among all the classifiers because while achieving the similar level of detection rate and accuracy with REP Tree it offers the minimum amount of false positive rate. False positive rate is an important parameter while assessing the performance of a classifier in botnet because a large number of false positives will interrupt the normal functioning of a user and hence not desired.

In order to determine some of the crucial discriminating attributes and the effectiveness of above-mentioned algorithms on a subset of features, ML algorithms are then re-evaluated (Table 2 and Table 3) using wrapper and filter feature selection methods: CFSSubsetEval (Filter) and Wrapper method.

Figure 1. Accuracy of SVM, Random Tree, and REP Tree

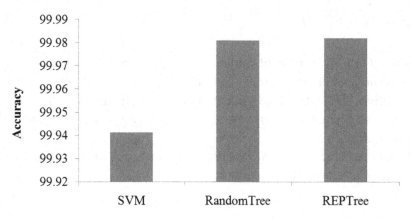

Figure 2. DR of SVM, Random Tree, and REP Tree

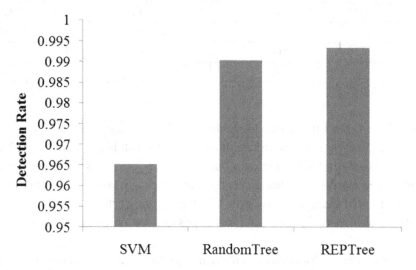

Figure 3. FPR of SVM, Random Tree, and REP Tree

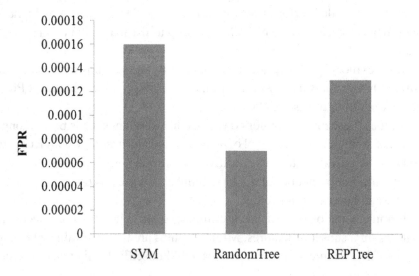

Table 2 depicts the performance of different models when a subset of features was selected using CFS algorithm (correlation based attribute evaluation). In case of CFSSubsetEval, each feature is evaluated or ranked w.r.t information gain. If information gain is high, the feature will have the lowest rank and so on. It is clear from the Table 2 that, in general, the performance of SVM, Random Tree, and REP Tree decreases when evaluated with a subset of features determined by CFSSubsetEval in comparison to the evaluation with the entire feature set.

Table 2. Performance of algorithms on different performance metrics with CFS feature set

	DR	FPR	Accuracy
SVM	0.9641	0.00018	99.9339
RandomTree	0.9882	0.00011	99.9712
REPTree	0.9945	0.00017	99.975

Table 3 shows the performance of models when a subset of features was selected using Wrapper algorithm. In case of wrapper method, the subset of features was different for different classifiers. Although DR of REP Tree increases when evaluated with feature set generated by wrapper method but wrapper method doesn't increase the performance of other algorithms.

Table 3. Performance of algorithms on different performance metrics with Wrapper feature set

	DR	FPR	Accuracy
SVM	0.9646	0.00016	99.94
RandomTree	0.9889	0.00011	99.9756
REPTree	0.9964	0.00017	99.9803

CONCLUSION

This chapter proposed a botnet detection model that can detect bots with high accuracy and minimum false positive rate on the basis of network flow characteristics. To train and test the models, the author generated real-world botnet and normal traffic as well as utilized existing datasets. Since machine learning algorithms cannot be directly applied to network traffic so Flow collector (softflowd) and exporter (nfdump) are used for extracting important features vectors. Thereafter, machine learning algorithms (Random tree, REP Tree, and SVM) are used to analyze these feature vectors and to differentiate between the botnet traffic and normal traffic. Further, feature selection is applied to extract important features and discard the irrelevant features. After analyzing the performance of various models on different metrics with the full feature set and with a subset of features, the author concluded that Random Tree and REP Tree performed much better than SVM. In case of the real-world scenario, the author recommended Random Tree over REP Tree because it possesses minimum FPR while DR, Accuracy is quite comparable with REP Tree. FPR is very important metric while designing real-life botnet prevention solutions because high FPR will generate a large number of false alarms and create a really annoying solution for the user.

REFERENCES

Alexa. (2017) Retrieved March 1, 2017, from https://www.alexa.com/topsites

Alpaydin, E. (2004). *Introduction to Machine Learning.* MIT Press.

Arshad, S., Abbaspour, M., Kharrazi, M., & Sanatkar, H. (2011). An anomaly based botnet detection approach for identifying stealthy botnets. in *Proceedings of the IEEE International Conference on Computer Applications and Industrial Electronics,* Penang, Malaysia (pp. 564–569).

Cisco. (n.d.). IOS NetFlow. Retrieved March 1, 2017 from http://www.cisco.com/en/US/products/ps6601/products_ios_protocol_group_home.html

Cox, O. (2013). Citadel's defences breached. *Symantec.* Rederived March 13, 2017, from http://www.symantec.com/connect/blogs/citadel-s-defenses-breached

David. (2012). Open DNS Security Talk: The Role of DNS in Botnet Command & Control. *Open DNS Inc.* Rederived March 13, 2017, from info.opendns.com/rs/opendns/images/WB-Security-Talk-Role-Of-DNS-Slides.pdf

Denning, D. E. (1987). An intrusion-detection model. *IEEE Transactions on Software Engineering, 13*(2), 222–232. doi:10.1109/TSE.1987.232894

Eslahi, M., Rohmad, M., Nilsaz, H., Naseri, M., Tahir, N., & Hashim, H. (2015). Periodicity classification of http traffic to detect http botnets. In *Proceedings of the IEEE Symposium on Computer Applications Industrial Electronics,* Langkawi, Malaysia (pp. 119–123). 10.1109/ISCAIE.2015.7298339

García, S., Grill, M., Stiborek, J., & Zunino, A. (2014). An empirical comparison of botnet detection methods. *Computer Security Journal, 45,* 100–123. doi:10.1016/j.cose.2014.05.011

Giroire, F., Chandrashekar, J., Taft, N., Schooler, E., & Papagiannaki, D. (2009) Exploiting Temporal Persistence to Detect Covert Botnet Channels. In: E. Kirda, S. Jha, & D. Balzarotti (Eds.), *International Workshop on Recent Advances in Intrusion Detection: Recent Advances in Intrusion Detection,* LNCS (Vol. 5758, pp. 326-345). Springer, Berlin, Heidelberg 10.1007/978-3-642-04342-0_17

Gu, G., Perdisci, R., Zhang, J., & Lee, W. (2008). BotMiner: clustering analysisof network traffic for protocol- and structure- independent botnet detection. In *Proceedings of the 17th conference on Security symposium,* San Jose, CA (pp. 139-154).

Gu, G., Porras, P., Yegneswaran, V., & Fong, M. (2007). BotHunter: Detecting malware infection through IDS-driven dialogcorrelation. In *Proceedings of 16th USENIX Security Symposium on USENIX Security Symposium,* Boston, MA (pp. 167–182).

Gu, G., Zhang, J., & Lee, W. (2008). BotSniffer: Detecting botnet commandand control channels in network traffic. In *Proceedings of the Network and Distributed System Security Symposium,* San Diego, CA.

Guntuku, S. C., Hota, C., Singh, K., & Thakur, A. (2014). Big data analytics framework for peer-to-peer botnet detection using random forests. *Information Sciences, 278,* 488–497. doi:10.1016/j.ins.2014.03.066

Haddadi, F., Phan, D. T., & Zincir-Heywood, A. N. (2016). How to choose from different botnet detection systems? In *Proceedings of the IEEE/IFIP Network Operations and Management Symposium,* Istanbul, Turkey (pp. 1079–1084). 10.1109/NOMS.2016.7502964

Huang, C. T., & Sakib, M. N. (2016). Using anomaly detection based techniques to detect HTTP-based botnet C&C traffic. In *Proceedings of the IEEE International Conference on Communications*, Kuala Lumpur, Malaysia.

Khari, M., & Karar, A. (2013). Preventing SQL-Based Attacks Using Intrusion Detection System. *International Journal of Science and Engineering Applications*, 2(6), 145–150. doi:10.7753/IJSEA0206.1006

Khari, M., & Kumar, M. (2016). Comprehensive study of web application attacks and classification. In *3rd International Conference on Computing for Sustainable Global Development*, New Delhi, India (pp. 2159-2164).

Khari, M., & Kumar, N. (2013). User Authentication Method against SQL Injection Attack. *International Journal of Scientific & Engineering Research.*, 4(6), 1649–1653.

Khari, M., & Sangwan, P. (2016). Web-application attacks: A survey. In *Proceedings of the 3rd International Conference on Computing for Sustainable Global Development*, New Delhi, India (pp. 2187-2191).

Kimbahune, V. V., Deshpande, A. V., & Mahalle, P. N. (2017). Lightweight Key Management for Adaptive Addressing in Next Generation Internet. *International Journal of Ambient Computing and Intelligence*, 8(1), 50–69. doi:10.4018/IJACI.2017010103

Kirubavathi, G., & Anitha, R. (2016). Botnet detection via mining of traffic flow characteristics. *Computers & Electrical Engineering*, 50, 91–101. doi:10.1016/j.compeleceng.2016.01.012

Ma, X., Zhang, J., Li, Z., Li, J., Tao, J., Guan, X., ... Towsley, D. (2015). Accurate DNS query characteristics estimation via active probing. *Journal of Network and Computer Applications*, 47, 72–84. doi:10.1016/j.jnca.2014.09.016

Matallah, H., Belalem, G., & Bouamrane, K. (2017). Towards a New Model of Storage and Access to Data in Big Data and Cloud Computing. *International Journal of Ambient Computing and Intelligence*, 8(4), 31–44. doi:10.4018/IJACI.2017100103

Miglani, A., Bhatia, T., Sharma, G., & Shrivastava, G. (2017). An Energy Efficient and Trust Aware Framework for Secure Routing in LEACH for Wireless Sensor Networks. Scalable Computing. *Practice and Experience*, 18(3), 207–218.

NfDump. (2017). Retrieved March 1, 2017 from http://nfdump.sourceforge.net/

Roesch, M. (1999). Snort—Lightweight intrusion detection for networks. In *Proceedings of the 13th USENIX conference on System administration*, Seattle, WA (pp. 229-238).

Saad, S., Traore, I., Ghorbani, A., Sayed, B., Zhao, D., & Lu, W. et al. (2011). Detecting P2P botnets through network behavior analysis and machine learning. In Proceedings of ninth annual international conference on privacy, security and trust, Montreal, Canada (pp. 174–80).

Saini, R., & Khari, M. (2011). An Algorithm to detect attacks in mobile ad hoc network. In *International Conference on Software Engineering and Computer Systems* (pp. 336-341). Springer, Berlin, Heidelberg 10.1007/978-3-642-22203-0_30

Shrivastava, G. (2016, March). Network forensics: Methodical literature review. In *Proceedings of the 2016 3rd International Conference on Computing for Sustainable Global Development (INDIACom)* (pp. 2203-2208). IEEE.

Shrivastava, G. (2017). Approaches of network forensic model for investigation. *International Journal of Forensic Engineering, 3*(3), 195–215. doi:10.1504/IJFE.2017.082977

Shrivastava, G., Sharma, K., & Kumari, R. (2016, March). Network forensics: Today and tomorrow. In *Proceedings of the 2016 3rd International Conference on Computing for Sustainable Global Development (INDIACom)* (pp. 2234-2238). IEEE.

Shrivastava, G., Sharma, K., & Rai, S. (2010, December). The Detection & Defense of DoS & DDoS Attack: A Technical Overview. In *Proceeding of ICC* (Vol. 27, p. 28).

Softflowd. (n.d.). Retrieved March 1, 2017 from http://www.mindrot.org/projects/softflowd/

Strayer, W. T., Lapsely, D., Walsh, R., & Livadas, C. (2008). Botnet Detection Based on Network Behavior. In W. Lee, C. Wang, & D. Dagon (Eds.), *Botnet Detection. Advances in Information Security* (Vol. 36, pp. 1–24). Boston, MA: Springer. doi:10.1007/978-0-387-68768-1_1

Supriya, K. M. (2012). Mobile Ad Hoc Netwoks Security Attacks and Secured Routing Protocols: A Survey. In N. Meghanathan, N. Chaki, & D. Nagamalai (Eds.), *Advances in Computer Science and Information Technology, Networks and Communications* (Vol. 84, pp. 119–124). Berlin, Heidelberg: Springer. doi:10.1007/978-3-642-27299-8_14

Wurzinger, P., Bilge, L., Holz, T., Goebel, J., Kruegel, C., & Kirda, E. (2009) Automatically Generating Models for Botnet Detection. In M. Backes & P. Ning (Eds.), *Computer Security – European Symposium on Research in Computer Security, LNCS* (Vol 5789, pp. 232-249). Springer, Berlin, Heidelberg 10.1007/978-3-642-04444-1_15

Zeidanloo, H. R., Manaf, A. B., Vahdani, P., Tabatabaei, F., & Zamani, M. (2010). Botnet detection based on traffic monitoring. In *Proceedings of the International Conference on Networking and Information Technology*, Manila, Philippines (pp. 97-101).

Zeidanloo, H. R., & Rouhani, S. (2012). *Botnet detection by monitoring common network behaviors.* Lambert Academic Publishing.

Zhang, J., & Zulkernine, M. (2005). Network intrusion detection using random forests. In *Proceedings of the Third Annual Conference on Privacy, Security and Trust,* St. Andrews, Canada (pp. 53–61).

Zhao, D., Traore, I., Ghorbani, A., Sayed, B., Saad, S., & Lu, W. (2012). Peer to Peer Botnet Detection Based on Flow Intervals. In D. Gritzalis, S. Furnell, & M. Theoharidou (Eds.), *Information Security and Privacy Research: IFIP Advances in Information and Communication Technology* (Vol. 376, pp. 87–102). Berlin, Heidelberg: Springer. doi:10.1007/978-3-642-30436-1_8

This research was previously published in the Handbook of Research on Network Forensics and Analysis Techniques edited by Gulshan Shrivastava, Prabhat Kumar, B. B. Gupta, Suman Bala and Nilanjan Dey; pages 101-116, copyright year 2018 by Information Science Reference (an imprint of IGI Global).

Chapter 5
Detecting DDoS Attacks on Multiple Network Hosts:
Advanced Pattern Detection Method for the Identification of Intelligent Botnet Attacks

Konstantinos F. Xylogiannopoulos
https://orcid.org/0000-0003-2376-898X
University of Calgary, Canada

Panagiotis Karampelas
https://orcid.org/0000-0003-1684-7612
Hellenic Air Force Academy, Greece

Reda Alhajj
University of Calgary, Canada and Global University, Lebanon

ABSTRACT

The proliferation of low security internet of things devices has widened the range of weapons that malevolent users can utilize in order to attack legitimate services in new ways. In the recent years, apart from very large volumetric distributed denial of service attacks, low and slow attacks initiated from intelligent bot networks have been detected to target multiple hosts in a network in a timely fashion. However, even if the attacks seem to be "innocent" at the beginning, they generate huge traffic in the network without practically been detected by the traditional DDoS attack detection methods. In this chapter, an advanced pattern detection method is presented that is able to collect and classify in real time all the incoming traffic and detect a developing slow and low DDoS attack by monitoring the traffic in all the hosts of the network. The experimental analysis on a real dataset provides useful insights about the effectiveness of the method by identifying not only the main source of attack but also secondary sources that produce low traffic, targeting though multiple hosts.

DOI: 10.4018/978-1-7998-5348-0.ch005

INTRODUCTION

Distributed Denial of Service (DDoS) attacks tend to be one of the major security threats against information system infrastructure. In the first half of 2018 according to Netscout took place more than 2.8 billion attacks with escalated metrics such as volume and maximum size (Modi, 2018). This is mainly attributed to the rapid deployment of Internet of Things (IoT) devices in various application fields such as automotive applications, industrial sites, consumer places, smart cities, etc. The latest reports estimate the active IoT devices to 27 billion in 2018 and project them to 125 billion by 2030 (HIS Markit, 2017). These devices can be smart TVs, watches, security cameras, printers, washing machines, smart vehicles, autonomous sensors, etc. which most of the times are connected directly to the Internet. According to security experts (Bhattacharya, 2018 and OWASP, 2016), there is a large number of potential vulnerabilities in IoT devices ranging from insecure or misconfigured web servers, insufficient authentication mechanisms that communicate the user credentials in text to insufficient configuration with default passwords, etc. As a result, while the number of the devices is increasing and as more and more types of devices are Internet-connected, the possibility of a device high jacking is also increasing. From 2014, there are reports of exploiting vulnerabilities in routers, VoIP gateways, network printers and surveillance cameras in order to realize DDoS attacks against legitimate services (Kührer et al., 2014). The following years, several DDoS attacks were reported to have been initiated by bot networks constituted by IoT devices. On September 2016, an attack that created traffic of over 600 Gbps and was attributed to an IoT botnet created by Mirai malware was unleashed against Brian Krebs's security blog (Bertino and Islam, 2017). At the same time, another attack was reported against a French webhost called OVH at 1.1 or more Tbps (US CERT, 2017). Later in the same year, Dyn Service Provider in the US experienced a very large DDoS attack of more than 1 Tbps which again is attributed to the infected from Mirai malware IoT devices (Arbor Networks, 2016). In 2017, several more DDoS attacks took place in companies from different business domains interrupting their services for several hours. In August 2017, Dreamhost one of the biggest web hosting companies suffered a DDoS attack targeting their DNS servers making the hosted by the company websites inaccessible for four hours (Blake, 2017) while in October 2017 a DDoS attack put offline the UK National Lottery's website during the Saturday's draws when a lot of people were ready to play in the lottery (Cluley, 2017). Another victim, on November 2017, was the US newspaper Boston Globe that suffered from a two-day DDoS attack which made their websites inaccessible for most of the period of both days (Bray, 2017). The DDoS attacks have continued in 2018 culminating with the largest known so far DDoS attack against GitHub with peak at 1.35Tbps which was successfully mitigated after 10 minutes of service unavailability moving the traffic to the infrastructure of an edge computing provider Akamai (Kottler, 2018). The consequences of such attacks in the cloud infrastructure are not only catastrophic to the attacked services but they may also affect other services that are not in the spot due to the possible migrations of the virtual machines of these other services during the attack (Somani, Gaur and Sanghi, 2015). In GitHub, for example, the intermission of operation affected several other companies that use GitHub as their code repository and thus during the attack they were not able to run their businesses. Apart from individual companies, several governmental services have also been targeted by DDoS attacks. Several such incidents have been reported in the past in several countries such as Georgia, Estonia, Ukraine, Syria, UK, USA, etc. (Loukas and Oke, 2010) where multiple governmental services become unavailable during the DDoS attacks. A more recent attack on November 2016 in Liberia targeted two Internet Service Providers that operate the only fiber Internet cable that connects the country to the Internet (Kolkman, 2016). The specific attack which interrupted country's connection to the Internet was attributed to a mirai enabled botnet that was tested by its creators (Whittaker, 2016). According to security researchers (Zeifman and Saeed, 2015), online game servers are frequently the target of DDoS attacks mainly because some players get emotionally involved when frustrated and see DDoS attack as a means for revenge or to hinder other players to continue their play. Such attacks have been recorded over the years as for example in 2015 against Blizzard WoW.

The effects of the aforementioned DDoS attacks, apart from the unavailability of service of the target, are also extended to everyone using the Internet. It has been monitored that due to the increasing number of DDoS attacks the Internet traffic has been increased correspondingly (Wang, Yufu and Jie, 2015) and thus it has become harder and more sophisticated to be able to monitor and detect DDoS on complex infrastructure such as server farms or cloud infrastructure. Moreover, the bot networks that are employed to initiate and carry out the attack nowadays utilize a very long list of different techniques to mitigate different protocols such as TCP SYN, TCP RST, TCP NULL, UDP, ICMP, DNS, SSDP, NTP or a combination of the aforementioned techniques as a hybrid attack in an effort to evade detection by the intrusion detection systems in place (nexusguard, 2016).

On the other side, security researchers and experts are trying to develop novel techniques that will enable them to detect as early as possible the DDoS attacks and either stop them immediately or reduce their impact on the information systems. In this context, several different techniques can be found in the literature; they attempt to either detect or to stop a DDoS attack something which is very difficult due to the diverse characteristics of each attack. These difficulties derive from the number of the zombie computers that are used in botnets coming from different countries around the world (Mirkovic, 2002), the availability of sophisticated attack tools such as LOIC (Low Orbit Ion Canon), HULK (HTTP Unbearable Load King), Tor's Hammer, PyLoris, Trinoo, Stacheldraht, (Infosec Institute, 2013), and the contemporary tools that capture IoT devices and create botnets such as mirai or leet (Zawoznik and Bekerman, 2016). Other factors that affect directly or indirectly the success of DDoS rate are attributed to human factors. The illiteracy of information systems' users who e.g., fail to update their operating system or install antivirus software leave the information systems vulnerable to various exploits that are found by malicious users and exploit security weakness that are inherent to most of the systems. Especially for IoT devices, Bertino and Islam attributed their security weaknesses to the heterogeneity of protocols, devices and platforms used by the manufacturers and the fact that this type of devices can be moved in less secure environments e.g. outside a firewall or to be connected in less secure networks that are usually unmonitored (Bertino and Islam, 2017). Moreover, sometimes it is impractical, costly or impossible to update a very large number of such devices found e.g. in a surveillance network in order to patch a security vulnerability and thus they may remain exposed to security threats for a long time. Ideally, the manufacturers should improve the security standards of the IoT devices and assess their behavior in diverse networks. However, security flaws usually are found after the deployment of the devices and thus proactive measures may not enough to ensure that the specific devices will not be exploited and used to attack legitimate services. Thus, apart from preemptive measures, it is necessary to develop the appropriate techniques and methods to protect complex infrastructure by being able to early detect very large DDoS attacks from any source such as those currently reported by using advanced detection methods in real time that can identify the source of attack in multiple hosts as the method proposed in this paper.

The rest of the chapter is organized as follows: Section 2 presents a brief review of the most important DDoS detection methods. Section 3 presents the proposed method to mitigate DDoS attacks on multiple hosts. Section 4 presents the experimental analysis on an existing publicly available dataset with DDoS attack data. Finally, the conclusions and future work is presented.

Related Work

Security researchers have mainly focused in two types of methods to alleviate the catastrophic results of DDoS attacks (Mirkovic and Reiher, 2004). The first type is based on the invention of preventive mechanisms that will increase the immunity of the information systems against the DDoS attacks. Such methods entail the application of strict security policies on the information systems by hardening the security of the software and hardware components. At hardware level, this can be achieved by installing firewalls in the network, honeypots to deceive the attackers, intrusion detection systems that will detect the attack and block either the attacker or the resources under attack. Correspondingly, automatic software update policies are enforced upon all the systems of the company, constant user monitoring is implemented in order to detect suspicious use of resources, complex access rules are devised in order to avoid infection by random visits in malicious websites, etc. Another type in this category aims to alleviate the consequences of a DDoS attack by balancing the payload of the attack intelligently to either more resources if they are available or to resources that are not actually used or to edge network services such as Akamai or Cloudflare and thus limit the effects of the attack to their active infrastructure. In terms of cost, while the software hardening of the systems and the revision of security policies and processes may be affordable, the installation of sophisticated firewalls, honeypots and intrusion detection systems is more expensive and difficult to configure and maintain especially for small or medium companies since highly-paid specialized personnel is required. However, when it comes to the increase of the available resources, the expansion of the available infrastructure may not be affordable while the solution of transferring the traffic to an edge network provider will deflect the attack and absorb the excessive traffic of the DDoS charging though the respective cost.

The second type of methods used to mitigate DDoS attacks aims at detecting traffic anomalies throughout the network infrastructure. Usually, these methods monitor network traffic in order to recognize known DDoS attack patterns by comparing the incoming datagrams to those of known signatures of DDoS attacks that are stored in their database. When known DDoS attack patterns are detected, the monitoring system either attempts to mitigate the attack by blocking the IPs of the attackers or notifies the network administrator to decide how the attack will be mitigated. The attack patterns appear as spikes in the normal traffic of the network however it is not easy to identify them since the attackers usually customize the intensity of the attack or the time intervals of the payloads sent to their target. As a result, anomaly detection may not immediately recognize an attack as it is developed usually with catastrophic consequences. Thus, it is very important to early detect the DDoS attack in order to provide time to the network administrator to develop and implement a defensive plan that will block the attack. The anomaly detection methods as it is mentioned may address two or three stages in the DDoS attack mitigation lifecycle. The first phase starts with the successful detection of the attack, the second phase then takes place where the DDoS attack is classified according to its characteristics and finally the response or mitigation phase takes place (Oke, Loukas and Gelenbe, 2007). Some methods focus on detecting and classifying the attack and leave the mitigation of the attack to the network administrators who will decide what is the most appropriate way to respond according to the normal traffic and the available resources. Most of the times, the response to an attack is trivial and it is adequate for mitigating the attack to block the malicious IPs or IP ranges or redirecting the normal traffic through alternative routes to resources that are not under attack.

Thus, the majority of detection methods focus on the first two stages, using various techniques for pattern or signature detection such as artificial neural networks, data mining, statistical analysis and hybrid techniques. Artificial neural network methods apply machine learning techniques using patterns or signatures that have already been detected from previous DDoS attacks in order to predict whether the incoming network traffic resembles those patterns and thus classified as DDoS attack. These methods usually monitor various network metrics of the traffic and then feed the artificial network which on its turn decide whether the current traffic resembles to a DDoS attack or not (Öke and Loukas, 2007). The accuracy of such a method depends on various factors, such as the previous patterns that have been used to train the artificial neural network. If for example, the new DDoS attack datagram does not resemble the one that have been used for training may not be classified correctly as an attack or if the intensity or periodicity of the attack has been modified by the attacker again it may not be classified correctly by the artificial neural network.

Other detection methods utilize data mining techniques in order to analyze the arriving datagrams and detect anomalies in the incoming traffic. The malicious traffic may consist of specific features or come in a specific time pattern which can both identified by a data mining technique and classified as a DDoS attack. The most popular data mining technique for this purpose that appear in the literature are feature selection and classification (Kim et al., 2004). The specific technique devises the use of specific attributes of the network traffic to be analyzed and then a classification algorithm is used to decide whether the specific datagram is part of DDoS attack or not. Other data mining techniques that are used for the specific purpose is a combination of classification and association rule mining algorithms in which a classification technique, such as C4.5 can be applied to develop a learning model for known attack types. Then the association rule learning algorithm analyzes the traffic and recognizes relationships between the classes created and the learning model (Yu et al., 2013). Data mining detection techniques may also attempt to understand the behaviour and characteristics of a botnet which creates the DDoS attack traffic, by using different classification techniques such as Boosted Decision Trees, Naïve Bayesian Classification, Support Vector Machine (Kirubavathi & Anitha, 2016), Expectation-Maximization Clustering (Garcia et al, 2014) and Hidden Markov model for pattern matching (Kim et al, 2012).

Another category of anomaly detection methods use statistical analysis techniques. These techniques also monitor and model the network traffic and when the traffic deviates from a predetermined threshold this will be considered suspicious and potentially a DDoS attack (Thapngam et al., 2012). However, a deviation from the normal network traffic can happen due to several reasons and not only by a DDoS attack and thus it is very difficult to select the appropriate threshold that will be able to correctly detect a DDoS attack and not provide false alarms frequently. The specific methods are also susceptible to low and slow attacks since the predefined threshold may be set higher than the under-development DDoS attack and thus the detection method may fail to timely notify the network administrator.

Another approach in detection techniques utilize a hybrid approach combining features of the other categories in order to improve the success rate of the detection. For example, a detection method that combines Markov's prediction and wavelet singularity detection is proposed to detect DDoS attacks (Wang et al., 2012) while Hwang et al proposed a detection method that combines anomaly detection with weighted association rules to produce attacks' signatures that could be used in a future DDoS attack. As it is reported by the authors, the hybrid method is more successful than the individual detection methods (Hwang et al., 2007).

Problem Statement

As DDoS attacks become more complex and sophisticated utilizing new devices and employing novel attack methods, there is a constant need for novel detection techniques that will be able either to detect an attack at its early stage or to deflate and absorb the attack in an affordable way without the use of disproportionate large infrastructure. Provided the size of the latest attacks, the available infrastructure of the edge network solution providers may not be sufficient in case such an attack is initiated across multiple targets. In this context, we propose an affordable DDoS attack detection technique that utilizes an advanced pattern detection method to identify excessive network traffic and early detect a developing attack.

The main advantages of the proposed method are summarized as follows:

- The method is based on an established pattern detection methodology that performs very well against very big datasets and thus can detect from a low and slow attack to large volumetric attacks.
- The proposed method can take advantage of all the resources of the computing environment that is installed and as a result raises alerts in real time even in extreme cases when very large attacks are in progress.
- Based on the fundamental features of the utilized pattern detection technique, the method is able to detect all the repeated patterns without using any confidence and thus it is able to detect an attack in a very early stage.
- The method can find application either to protect a single server or very complex computing infrastructures comprising several hosts.

The proposed detection method focuses on the two first stages of the DDoS attack detection and leaves the mitigation of the attack to the networks administration. However, since the method detects a potential DDoS attack at an early stage, it provides them with plenty of time to respond especially at a point when the full DDoS attack has not been escalated.

Our Methodology

The proposed method is an advanced expansion of the methodology described in [Xylogiannopoulos et al. 2017]. The original method as described in [Xylogiannopoulos et al. 2017] allows us to detect in real time a potential DDoS attack by performing pattern detection on the incoming IP traffic. The pattern detection is based on the IP octets and, therefore, it is possible to detect not only single hosts that are trying to consume a server resources but also subnets and domains of the incoming IP addresses. This allows to identify potential attacks from multiple hosts that have the same geolocation characteristics and similar metadata information such as common time zone, etc. In order to perform such a pattern detection, the Longest Expected Repeated Pattern Reduced Suffix Array (LERP-RSA) data structure has been used that allows the All Repeated Patterns Detection (ARPaD) algorithm to be executed so as to detect repeated patterns in IP addresses [Xylogiannopoulos et al. 2014, 2016; Xylogiannopoulos 2017].

However, in more sophisticated attacks multiple hosts can be used against single client computers of big organizations that could be distributed around the globe. Furthermore, this kind of attack can be executed by multiple sources repeated in cycles that could have random behavior and, thus, the direct identification of such attack could be very difficult if not impossible. The advanced methodology presented here, allows us to apply pattern detection on multiple datasets that are produced from the traffic load of multiple servers as it is depicted in Figure 1. The traffic loads are combined together and classified in order to perform threat analysis. However, the identification of such malicious activity requires a more advanced version of the LERP-RSA data structure and more specifically the Multivariate LERP-RSA [Xylogiannopoulos 2017]. With the use of the multivariate LERP-RSA, it is possible to merge multiple LERP-RSA data structures that are created from different servers and then execute the ARPaD algorithm on the LERP-RSA which represents the full traffic load. Therefore, this process detects not only patterns that exist on single server datasets but furthermore and most important detect patterns that exist among different datasets from multiple hosts. As a result, we are able to identify a more sophisticated DDoS attack where multiple sources are used to repeatedly attack several hosts by consuming each one a small amount of host resources, yet, in total could lead to system unavailability since they maximize the consumption of total resources.

Figure 1. Process diagram

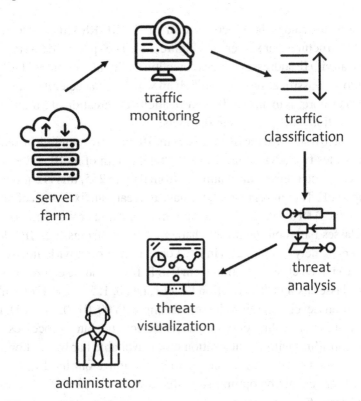

The proposed methodology is divided in three phases as it can be seen in Figure 2. In the first phase, the LERP-RSA is constructed from combined IP information from all servers (hosts) (Figure 2.b to Figure 2.d). The next phase is the pattern detection with the execution of the ARPaD (Figure 2.e). Finally, meta analyses are performed for further investigation of the data and the detection of potential threats (Figure 2.f).

Figure 2. Methodology execution phases

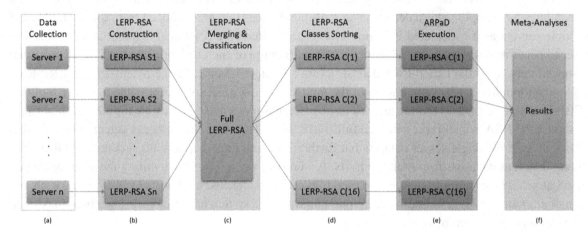

LERP-RSA Data Structure

The first phase of the methodology is the creation of the LERP-RSA data structure by constructing partial LERP-RSA data structures per server (see Figure 2.b). The specific data structure has significant advantages when we deal with IP addresses pattern detection [Xylogiannopoulos 2017; Xylogiannopoulos et al. 2017] since it allows classification and parallelism which can accelerates significantly the pattern detection process. Furthermore, as mentioned before, it allows the creation of a multivariate data structure that enables pattern detection among different data sets.

Initially it is important to transform the IP addresses into their corresponding hexadecimal form in case of IPv4 format. This creates two advantages. First, the total length of an IP address is reduced from 12 characters to 8. Since each octet represents a number from 0 up to 255, this is equivalent in hexadecimal to a number from 0 up to FF. Therefore, in total, we have to create suffix strings of length 8 instead of 12 and as a result improve the ARPaD algorithm execution time. Another very important advantage is that we can create more classes based on the initial characters of the strings (i.e., IP addresses). Instead of having only 3 characters namely 0, 1 and 2 as in IPv4 octet numbering, with the use of the hexadecimal transformation we have sixteen classes starting from 0 to F. If we assume equidistribution of the strings, then we can create 16 classes using Classification Level 1, i.e., 0, 1, 2, ..., E, F or multiples of 16, using, for example, Classification Level 2 creating classes starting with 00, 01, 02, ..., FD, FE, FF. This allows considerably faster execution on sorting or other pattern detection related processes (such as the parallel execution of ARPaD algorithm) with the utilization of the available hardware. For example, if we have an 8 core CPU, we can execute two classes per core and maximize our hardware resources while with only 3 classes our hardware cannot be optimized in this way. In the case of IPv6 format, addresses are already in the desired format and no action is required except minor modifications such as inserting double zeros "00" when the double column is used "::".

The next step of the first phase is to combine together the IP addresses datasets from different sources (Figure 2.c). By merging the datasets, we transform the partial servers traffic of a big organization to a single traffic channel. For example, if an organization has in each continent a server, by combining the traffic from all servers, we create a LERP-RSA data structure representing the global traffic. The simplest way to do this is to directly merge the datasets of the IP strings. However, we can create a more advanced version of the LERP-RSA by storing additional information such as the source (server in our case) and the IP position in the traffic (time parameter in our case). These two attributes can significantly contribute in our work because we can use the information for further meta analyses of the traffic from specific IPs. For example, we can identify patterns or periodicities in IP occurrences which in other DDoS detection methods could appear completely random and thus they would not raise any suspicion. This can further help us in our method to classify an IP address as a potential malicious source.

The first phase is concluded with the last step which is the lexicographically sorting of the LERP-RSA classes (Figure 2.d). This is the most time-consuming part of this phase since Merge-Sort algorithm has O(nlogn) time complexity. Furthermore, this step is the only step of the first phase that happens synchronously, i.e., we have to execute it after the collection and transformation of all IP address strings. However, with the use of classification, we can sort in parallel many classes, something that accelerates the process. Furthermore, the worst-case input size for the sorting algorithm is not that of the full LERP-RSA, rather than the size of the largest class which yet it can be multiple times smaller than the full LERP-RSA.

ARPaD Algorithm

After the creation and sorting of the LERP-RSA data structure as a single data structure or with the use of classification, we use ARPaD to detect all repeated patterns (Figure 2.e). In this case though, instead of detecting patterns that exist in a single sequence (string), we detect patterns that exist in multiple sequences (IP strings). More specifically, the algorithm will detect all domains, subdomains, subnets and hosts that exist based on the octets of the IP addresses. Therefore, the algorithm will detect only patterns of length which is multiple of 2, i.e., the first two characters representing the domain, the first four characters representing the subdomain, etc. This means that the algorithm does not need to run on the entire string (8 characters, 8 steps) but only run per second character which represents 4 steps. For example, if the input IPs are C0A80A05 and C0A80A06, the algorithm will identify as repeated patterns the strings C0, C0A8, C0A80A representing domain, subdomain and subnets respectively. However, the algorithm will skip strings C, C0A, C0A80, C0A80A0 which does not represent any IP exploitable information. The specific customization in the ARPaD algorithm dramatically improves its performance by approximately 50%. The same applies for IPv6 where instead of 32 steps (32 characters), we have only 16 steps.

Meta Analyses

The final phase of the methodology is the meta analyses that can be performed on the repeated patterns detected by ARPaD algorithm (Figure 2.f). Such analyses can include, for example, geolocation detection of IP traffic (domain, subdomain, subnet and host), time intervals, potential periodicities of the packets, etc. However, the most important outcome of these analyses based on the problem definition is the detection of IP addresses which although produce very low traffic per host (or individual server), they have a total impact in traffic that is significantly larger and spread among different hosts (servers). Additionally, they may also have other characteristics such as periodicity in their repetitions (slow rate of appearance). Moreover, we can identify patterns in the traffic based on multiple sources. For example, we may have three IPs that consume our resources (e.g., C0A80A05, C0A80A06 and C0A80A07) and we furthermore can observe that the packets are sent in the same order C0A80A05, C0A80A06 and C0A80A07 repeatedly. On top of this, we can further observe that this pattern occurs on all our servers across the globe, which is an extremely unusual case and can raise an alert of a potential DDoS attack.

Experimental Analysis

For the experimental analysis of the proposed methodology, a laptop with an Intel i7 CPU has been used. The CPU has 4 cores and 8 logical processors. Furthermore, the hardware includes 16GB of RAM and a solid state 500GBs disk. The code is written in Microsoft C# and Microsoft SQL Server 2016 has been used to store the results and metadata.

The dataset used to simulate a multiple DDoS attack is the Friday-WorkingHours-Afternoon-DDos. pcap_ISCX from the CICIDS 2017 [Sharafaldin et al. 2018]. The specific dataset although it is very small, 225,745 packets, yet, it serves perfectly our scope since it includes traffic from 2,067 source IPs towards 2,554 destination IPs. For simulation purposes, source IPs are considered to be the attackers (incoming IPs) while destination IPs are considered to be the organization host computers. It has to be mentioned that the analysis of the specific dataset takes approximately 50 milliseconds on the afore-mentioned computer system, which also serves very well our purposes from performance point of view since it is equivalent to approximately 4.5 million incoming IPs per second. Moreover, the performance of the LERP-RSA and ARPaD has been measured and described extensively in [Xylogiannopoulos et al. 2017] where we were able to analyze more than 12 million IPs per second using more advanced computer system with dual CPUs.

In order to simulate traffic across multiple hosts, the dataset has been split into smaller datasets per destination IP. For each one of these smaller datasets the LERP-RSA data structure has been created and then all of them are merged together and sorted. After that, ARPaD algorithm is executed and all repeated patterns in IP address strings are being detected. From the second phase of the methodology execution, some initial results are collected. More specifically, there is an incoming IP "AC100001" which completely dominates the traffic with 128,181 packets or approximately 57% of the total traffic. This traffic is directed towards a single host with IP "C0A80A32" sending 128,024 packets which is the full traffic of the specific host. Such abnormal high traffic can be detected easily and identified as a potential direct DDoS attack by not only our method but also from most of the already published methods.

However, in the specific research work, we want to identify rather low and slow traffic from many source IPs that have targeted many host IPs in different servers. This is very difficult if not impossible to be detected, yet, with the presented methodology we have managed to identify such behavior in the simulated dataset. One characteristic example is the host IP "C0A80A03" with a total traffic of 24,165 packets. The specific traffic can be broken down to the incoming IPs, which are 19 in total. In Table 1, we can observe that there are 19 IPs sending traffic from 1 up to 6,034 packets. We have no reason to label this traffic from the specific IPs as not legitimate.

However, by detecting repeated patterns with the use of the ARPaD algorithm, we have observed that 24,150 packets or 99% of the total traffic come from the same subnet, i.e., "C0A80Axx" (Figure 3). Moreover, by applying a reverse check on the source IP patterns, we can see that, for example, although the source IP "C0A80A08" has sent only 1,025 packets to "C0A80A03", yet, in total has established communication with other 215 hosts in completely different domains (i.e., servers and geolocations) as it is reported in Table 2. A more in-depth look can reveal something very interesting as it can be seen in Figure 4. All 19 source IPs that have sent packets to host with IP "C0A80A03", have in total communicated with almost every other one of the 2,554 hosts in the dataset and they have sent in total 80,243 packets to them meaning that they are responsible for approximately 35% of the total traffic of the whole network.

Table 1. Incoming traffic example for host C0A80A03

Index	Source	Packets	%Traffic
1	C0A80A0C	6,034	24.99%
2	C0A80A0F	4,304	17.82%
3	C0A80A05	2,929	12.13%
4	C0A80A09	2,465	10.21%
5	C0A80A0E	1,870	7.74%
6	C0A80A10	1,792	7.42%
7	C0A80A11	1,637	6.78%
8	C0A80A08	1,025	4.24%
9	C0A80A32	967	4.00%
10	C0A80A13	834	3.45%
11	C0A80A19	234	0.97%
12	C0A80A33	59	0.24%
13	400436FE	3	0.01%
14	0D4EBC93	3	0.01%
15	17D36689	3	0.01%
16	400436FD	2	0.01%
17	17C28D8F	2	0.01%
18	2850911B	1	0.00%
19	41372C6D	1	0.00%

Figure 3. Percentage distribution of incoming IPs for host C0A80A03

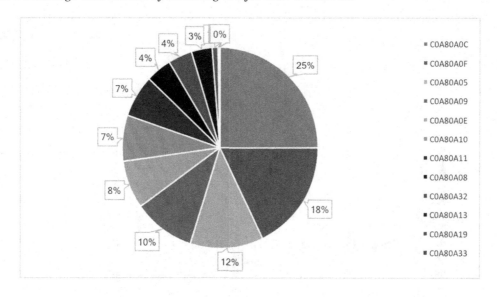

Table 2. Traffic load of incoming IPs of host C0A80A03

Index	Source	Hosts	Packets	Packets/Host
1	C0A80A0C	250	9,216	36.86
2	C0A80A0F	744	9,278	12.47
3	C0A80A05	599	5,884	9.82
4	C0A80A09	545	5,107	9.37
5	C0A80A0E	413	3,947	9.56
6	C0A80A10	495	4,571	9.23
7	C0A80A11	278	3,299	11.87
8	C0A80A08	216	2,128	9.85
9	C0A80A32	19	32,896	1731.37
10	C0A80A13	215	1,885	8.77
11	C0A80A19	118	1,584	13.42
12	C0A80A33	3	414	138.00
13	400436FE	3	13	4.33
14	0D4EBC93	3	7	2.33
15	17D36689	1	3	3.00
16	400436FD	3	5	1.67
17	17C28D8F	1	2	2.00
18	2850911B	1	1	1.00
19	41372C6D	3	3	1.00

Figure 4. Traffic load of incoming IPs of host C0A80A03

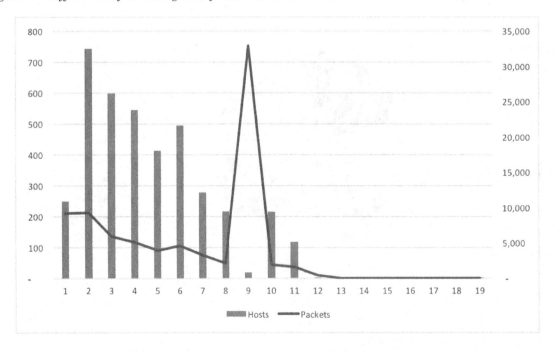

CONCLUSION

In this chapter, an innovative method has proposed that allows the detection of DDoS low and slow attacks on multiple network hosts. The data structure and algorithm that were used, proved to be very efficient and effective using commodity computers while analyzing traffic from multiple sources. The advantage of the proposed methodology allows more efficient hardware utilization and therefore is able to perform real time data analytics.

The methodology used on the simulated dataset was able to detect not only high volume traffic from individual sources but also it was able to identify simultaneously repeated multi source traffic to single hosts which is characteristic of slow and low DDoS attacks. Furthermore, significant metadata results of the attack have been revealed based on the domain, subdomain information collected showing significant traffic from specific domains, subdomains and not only hosts as typically other DDoS attack detection methods can identify. The competitive advantage of the methodology is that it uses pure pattern detection and data analytics methods which have very good performance with big datasets and maximize hardware utilization. Concluding, the method proved that it can protect from individual servers up to very complex computing infrastructures comprising several hosts in different geolocations.

REFERENCES

Arbor Networks. (2016). *IoT DDoS attacks show the stakes have changed. Quick take: poor planning, not an IoT Botnet, disrupted the internet.* Author.

Bertino, E., & Islam, N. (2017). Botnets and Internet of Things Security. *Computer, 50*(2), 76–79. doi:10.1109/MC.2017.62

Bhattacharya, S. (2018). *The Top Ten IoT Vulnerabilities*. Retrieved from https://resources.infosecinstitute.com/the-top-ten-iot-vulnerabilities

Blake, A. (2017). *DreamHost, web hosting company, blames powerful DDoS attack for online outages.* Retrieved from https://www.washingtontimes.com/news/2017/aug/24/dreamhost-web-hosting-company-blames-powerful-ddos/

Bray, H. (2017). *Boston Globe hit by denial of service attacks*. Retrieved from https://www.bostonglobe.com/business/2017/11/09/boston-globe-hit-denial-service-attacks/yS2mI5DJwDAuRnzxqzVKsI/story.html

Cluley, G. (2017). *UK National Lottery knocked offline by DDoS attack*. Retrieved from https://www.welivesecurity.com/2017/10/02/uk-national-lottery-ddos-attack/

Garcia, S., Grill, M., Stiborek, J., & Zunino, A. (2014). An empirical comparison of botnet detection methods. *Computers & Security, 45*, 100-123.

HIS Markit. (2017). *The Internet of Things: a movement, not a market*. Retrieved from https://cdn.ihs.com/www/pdf/IoT_ebook.pdf

Hwang, K., Cai, M., Chen, Y., & Qin, M. (2007). Hybrid Intrusion Detection with Weighted Signature Generation over Anomalous Internet Episodes. *Dependable and Secure Computing IEEE Transactions*, *4*(1), 41–55.

Infosec Institute. (2013). *DOS Attacks and Free DOS Attacking Tools*. Retrieved from http://resources.infosecinstitute.com/dos-attacks-free-dos-attacking-tools

Kim, D. H., Lee, T., Kang, J., Jeong, H., & In, H. P. (2012). Adaptive pattern mining model for early detection of botnet-propagation scale. *Security and Communication Networks*, *5*(8), 917–927. doi:10.1002ec.366

Kim, M., Na, H., Chae, K., Bang, H., & Na, J. (2004). A combined data mining approach for DDoS attack detection. In Networking Technologies for Broadband and Mobile Networks (pp. 943-950). Springer Berlin Heidelberg. doi:10.1007/978-3-540-25978-7_95

Kirubavathi, G., & Anitha, R. (2016). Botnet detection via mining of traffic flow characteristics. *Computers & Electrical Engineering*, *50*, 91–101. doi:10.1016/j.compeleceng.2016.01.012

Kolkman, O. (2016). *The DDoS Attack Against Liberia - we must take collective action for the future of the Open Internet*. Retrieved from https://www.internetsociety.org/blog/2016/11/the-ddos-attack-against-liberia-we-must-take-collective-action-for-the-future-of-the-open-internet/

Kottler, S. (2018). *February 28th DDoS Incident Report*. Retrieved from https://githubengineering.com/ddos-incident-report/

Kührer, M., Hupperich, T., Rossow, C., & Holz, T. (2014). Hell of a handshake: Abusing TCP for reflective amplification DDoS attacks. *USENIX Workshop on Offensive Technologies (WOOT)*.

Loukas, G., & Oke, G. (2010). Protection against denial of service attacks: A survey. *Computer J. British Computer Society*, *53*, 1020–1037.

Mirkovic, J. (2002). *D-WARD: DDoS network attack recognition and defense* (PhD dissertation prospectus). UCLA.

Modi, H. (2017). *Introducing NETSCOUT's Threat Intelligence Report*. Retrieved from https://asert.arbornetworks.com/introducing-netscouts-threat-intelligence-report/

NexusGuard. (2016). *Distributed Denial of Service (DDoS) Threat Report Q4 2016*. Author.

Öke, G., & Loukas, G. (2007). A Denial of Service Detector based on Maximum Likelihood Detection and the Random Neural Network. *The Computer Journal*, *50*(6), 717–727. doi:10.1093/comjnl/bxm066

Oke, G., Loukas, G., & Gelenbe, E. (2007) Detecting denial of service attacks with bayesian classifiers and the random neural network. In *Fuzzy Systems Conference, FUZZ-IEEE 2007*. IEEE International. 10.1109/FUZZY.2007.4295666

OWASP. (2016). *Top IoT Vulnerabilities*. Retrieved from https://www.owasp.org/index.php/Top_IoT_Vulnerabilities

Sharafaldin, I., Lashkari, A. H., & Ghorbani, A. A. (2018). Toward Generating a New Intrusion Detection Dataset and Intrusion Traffic Characterization. *4th International Conference on Information Systems Security and Privacy (ICISSP)*. Retrieved from http://www.unb.ca/cic/datasets/ids-2017.html

Somani, G., Gaur, M. S., & Sanghi, D. (2015). DDoS/EDoS attack in cloud: affecting everyone out there! *Proceedings of the 8th International Conference on Security of Information and Networks (SIN '15)*, 169-176. 10.1145/2799979.2800005

Thapngam, T., Yu, S., Zhou, W., & Makki, S. K. (2012). Distributed Denial of Service (DDoS) detection by traffic pattern analysis. *Peer-to-Peer Networking and Applications*, 1–13.

US-CERT. (2017). *Heightened DDoS Threat Posed by Mirai and Other Botnets*. Retrieved from http://www.us-cert.gov/ncas/alerts/TA16-288A

Wang, D., Yufu, Z., & Jie, J. (2010). A multi-core based DDoS detection method. *Computer Science and Information Technology (ICCSIT), 2010 3rd IEEE International Conference, 4*, 115-118.

Wang, F., Wang, H., Wang, X., & Su, J. (2012). A new multistage approach to detect subtle DDoS attacks. *Mathematical and Computer Modelling, 55*(1), 198–213. doi:10.1016/j.mcm.2011.02.025

Whittaker, Z. (2016). *Mirai botnet attackers are trying to knock an entire country offline*. Retrieved from https://www.zdnet.com/article/mirai-botnet-attack-briefly-knocked-an-entire-country-offline/

Xylogiannopoulos, K. F. (2017). *Data structures, algorithms and applications for big data analytics: single, multiple and all repeated patterns detection in discrete sequences*. PhD thesis.

Xylogiannopoulos, K. F., Karampelas, P., & Alhajj, R. (2014). Analyzing very large time series using suffix arrays. *Applied Intelligence, 41*(3), 941–955. doi:10.100710489-014-0553-x

Xylogiannopoulos, K. F., Karampelas, P., & Alhajj, R. (2016). Repeated patterns detection in big data using classification and parallelism on LERP reduced suffix arrays. *Applied Intelligence, 45*(3), 567–597. doi:10.100710489-016-0766-2

Xylogiannopoulos, K. F., Karampelas, P., & Alhajj, R. (2017). Advanced Network Data Analytics for Large-scale DDoS Attack Detection. *International Journal of Cyber Warfare & Terrorism, 7*(3), 44–54. doi:10.4018/IJCWT.2017070104

Yu, J., Kang, H., Park, D., Bang, H.-C., & Kang, D. W. (2013). An in-depth analysis on traffic flooding attacks detection and system using data mining techniques. *Journal of Systems Architecture, 59*(10), 1005-1012.

Zawoznik, A., & Bekerman, D. (2016). *650Gbps DDoS Attack from the Leet Botnet*. Incapsula. Retrieved from https://www.incapsula.com/blog/650gbps-ddos-attack-leet-botnet.html

Zeifman, I., & Saeed, N. H. (2015). *It's Not a Game: The Ever-Growing Risk of DDoS Attacks on Online Games*. Retrieved from https://www.incapsula.com/blog/ddos-attacks-on-online-gaming-servers.html

This research was previously published in Developments in Information Security and Cybernetic Wars edited by Muhammad Sarfraz; pages 121-139, copyright year 2019 by Information Science Reference (an imprint of IGI Global).

Chapter 6
Botnet Threats to E–Commerce Web Applications and Their Detection

Rizwan Ur Rahman
Maulana Azad National Institute of Technology, India

Deepak Singh Tomar
Maulana Azad National Institute of Technology, India

ABSTRACT

Security issues in e-commerce web applications are still exploratory, and in spite of an increase in e-commerce application research and development, lots of security challenges remain unanswered. Botnets are the most malicious threats to web applications, especially the e-commerce applications. Botnet is a network of BOTs. It executes automated scripts to launch different types of attack on web applications. Botnets are typically controlled by one or more hackers known as Bot masters and are exploited for different types of attacks including Dos (denial of service), DDos (distributed denial of service), phishing, spreading of malware, adware, Spyware, identity fraud, and logic bombs. The aim of this chapter is to scrutinize to what degree botnets can cause a threat to e-commerce security. In the first section, an adequate overview of botnets in the context of e-commerce security is presented in order to provide the reader with an understanding of the background for the remaining sections.

INTRODUCTION

Electronic Commerce is a transaction of purchasing, selling and marketing online. E-commerce makes use of computer technologies such as Internet, World Wide Web, EFT (Electronic Funds Transfer), Internet marketing, and online transaction. Current electronic commerce usually uses the World Wide Web for one part of the life cycle of transaction even though it could also use e-mail systems (O'Leary, 2000).

DOI: 10.4018/978-1-7998-5348-0.ch006

E-Commerce uses different Business models such as B2B (Business - to - Business), C2C (Consumer - to - Consumer), C2B (Consumer - to - Business), B2C (Business - to - Consumer). The main objective of this chapter is to study the perception of security in different business models of e-commerce such as B2B, B2C, C2B, and C2C web application from both organizational and consumer viewpoint (Combe, 2012).

Security is one of the principal and ongoing concerns that limit clients and organizations engaging with e-commerce. E-commerce Security is a part of the Computer Security and is particularly applied to the components that concern e-commerce applications including Information Security and Data security. This chapter addresses the vulnerabilities, threats, and detection methods in the context of e-commerce applications. This chapter explores the perception of security in e-commerce websites from Bot and Botnet attacks viewpoint.

E-Commerce applications have numerous components including web server, database server, and payment gateway for online transaction. In Cyber world each component of e-commerce application is targeted by different attacks. According to numbers of survey reports, almost ninety percent (90%) of the attack comes from either Bot or Botnet. The given figure (Figure 1) shows the typical components involved in simple life cycle of e-commerce with different attacks on each component (Wokosin, 2002). For instance, attacks particularly targets customers are account takeover and account lockout. Similarly, the attacks that target the application are price scraping, content scraping, and database scraping.

The first section introduces the overview of Bots including basic and advanced Bots, good and bad Bots, generalized and specialized Bots. Further, this section elaborates the attacks on different components of e-commerce application such as Price Scarping, Content Scrapping, and Man in the Browser attack on e-commerce transaction.

Figure 1. E-commerce components and cycle

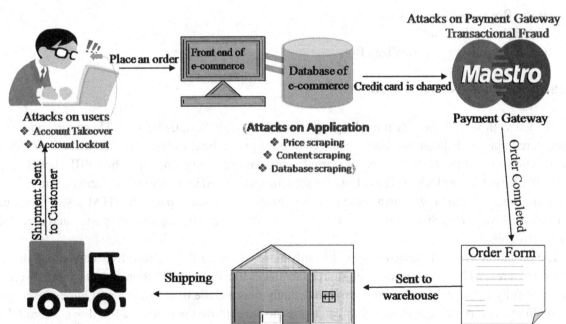

The next section presents the more malicious form of Bot known as Botnet i.e., network of Bots. In this section technologies related to Botnet are explored and different architecture of Botnet including centralized and decentralized architectures is presented. Additionally, this section explores the taxonomy of attacks which are executed by Botnets including, Malware, DoS, Phishing, Injection attacks.

The last section presents the taxonomy of detection and prevention methods such as various forms of CAPTCHA, Honeypot, and Firewalls. It also explores the Data mining techniques including anomaly and rule base detection. Finally, it introduces briefly the Big Data Approach such as Security Analytics. At last conclusion of the chapter is presented.

OVERVIEW AND INTRODUCTION OF BOT

The term Bot has come from the word robot. Fundamentally, the Bot is a software program which is used to execute fully automated, well-defined, repetitive task over a network. Bots can interact with any web application that has an API (Application Programming Interface). The tasks usually performed by Bots could vary from making lunch reservation in a restaurant, booking a ticket, giving an email reply and, checking product's price on their e-commerce websites (Geer, 2005).

Taxonomy of Bots

There is huge number of Bots and every single day new Bots are coming with many different reasons. According to Global Bot Traffic Report (Bariso, 2016) more than fifty percent (50%) of the internet traffic is from the Bots. In literature, different categorizations are proposed by different scholars. In this section, taxonomy of Bots is presented in three different headings.

- Basic Bot vs. Advanced Bots.
- Good Bot vs. Bad Bots.
- Generalized Bot vs. Specialized Bot.

Basic Bot vs. Advanced Bots

Bot started with very simple scripting languages like w-get, VB Script, and Perl. These scripting languages are light weight languages and they are easy to script, can be easily uploaded on to the web server and simple to parse the HTML. Then, it started using web scripting languages like PHP, JavaScript, and ASP (Active Server Pages). These Bots are sometimes referred as a basic Bots. Fundamentally, it is different from real web browser in a sense that they are easy to execute, parse the HTML, store cookies and execute Java Script. Since, the basic Bots are very simple scripts they can be spotted and detected with no troubles.

The programmers then, started moving towards more advanced Bots. These Bots can embed themselves into a real web browser using open source languages like Ruby and Python and custom malwares. They can fully automate the web browsers can actually masquerade that; Bot is a real human user can do anything a real person can do. So, they can move the page, move the mouse, scroll down, submit the information on web server, and extract the information from server (Jeong et al., 2010). Unlike basic Bots, they are difficult to spot and detect.

Good Bots vs. Bad Bots

The purpose and the behavior categorized the Bot to be either good or bad bot. Good bots are useful for all e-commerce application. These Bots assist in making the required visibility of the e-commerce application on the internet, and in addition assist these businesses attain an online visibility. When customer searches for an e-commerce website or key-word related to the products in website, the result is the relevant list of products on the search page. This can be achieved only with the help of search engine Bots also known as spiders, or web crawler Bots.

On the other hand, bad Bots are created to execute a variety of malicious tasks. Their behavior and pattern are malicious and generally unregulated. Generally, they do not follow the rules. If huge number of web page requests are originating from a particular IP address in a very short duration. This type of malicious activity burden or exhaust e-commerce web application, and block the available network bandwidth. These malicious activities directly affect those legitimate users on e-commerce application, trying to search a product or doing a transaction (Dunham et al., 2008).

One more example of bad Bot is that, it can exploit third party web scrapers to take contents from website. The contents can be unique to website or e-commerce web application. For instance, the contents could be reviews of product, information related to dynamic pricing of products available on e-commerce website, product list, and so on.

The good Bot are further categorized as given below.

- Web Crawler
- Social Media Bot
- Chatbot
- Informational Bot

Web Crawler

This is specialized Internet Bot also known as a spider, which thoroughly browses the WWW (World Wide Web), usually for indexing the websites. These Bots run constantly mainly obtain data from websites, and are obedient in a sense that they follow directions define in (robots.txt) file.

For instance, the entire website or web service from search engine Bots can be hidden by stopping search engine Bots in (robots.txt) file of website. This will keep the contents of website out of search engines (Markov et al., 2007).

These Bots extract URLs (Hyperlinks) from HTML Pages, and fetch all the contents from each URL, and then it passes the contents to search engines system for building the searchable index. Googlebot from Google and Bingbot from Microsoft are the two most familiar examples of spiders or search engine Bots.

Social Media Bot

Social Media Bot also known as socialbot or social networking Bot is s a type of Bot that runs automatically accounts of social media websites. It has the capability to perform essential activities for instance, message posting, send a request for joining a group, and posting updated weather forecasts. Since social media Bot penetrates a targeted social media websites, additionally they are able to steal user data for instance, phone numbers, emails, and other private data that could have monetary value (Sharma et al., 2017). Facebook Bot and Twitter Bot are the two most common examples of social media Bots

Chatbot

A chatbot sometimes referred as a Chatterbot, Chatterbox, and Talkbot is an automated computer programs that can be used with users in natural communication. The first Chabot program was made in 1960s; the goal was to determine whether Chatbots could convince users that they are really human beings (Shawar et al., 2003). Chatbots are not only built to imitate human communication and to provide users an entertainment but also useful in education and e-commerce applications.

Chatterbot Assistants in E-Commerce Applications

Shopping assistant is the most useful things in conventional commerce. Shopping assistant supports in a store, by giving further information on products and make things easier for decision making process helping to find a best product that makes customer happy (Bog-danovych et al., 2005).

Happy Assistant is a natural language based system that assists users accessing e-commerce application to find appropriate information about products and services (Chai et al., 2000). The system is composed of three main modules: the Action Manager, the dialog Manager, and the presentation manager.

Informational Bot

Bots in this group assists in information related things; include breaking news and push notifications. A number of informational Bots transmit data as soon as it becomes available.

Similarly, the bad Bot are also further categorized as follows

- Web Scrapper
- Spammer
- Vulnerability Scanner
- Impersonator

Generalized Bot vs. Specialized Bot

The Bots can be categorized as "General Bot" and "Special Bot. The general Bots are created for general tasks. For instance, the attacker can create a Bot which searches for website vulnerabilities and loopholes. As soon as it finds any vulnerability it attacks the website by injecting malicious code. On the other hand, "Special Bot" is created by attacker to attack a particular website.

Bot Traffic

When examining website traffic, it is imperative to distinguish between human and Bot. Further, it is also required to make a distinction between good and bad Bots. According to global Bot traffic report (Figure 2) (2016) almost report fifty percent (50%) of the web traffic is coming from web Bots.

Figure 2. Bot traffic by type

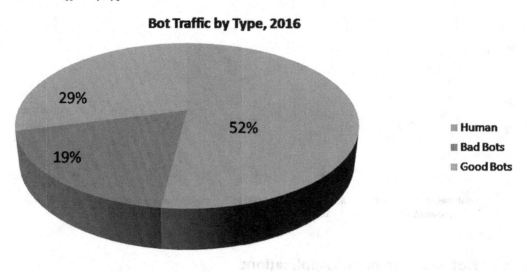

Out of fifty percent (50%) about thirty percent (30%) constitute good Bot traffic and rest of the twenty percent (20%) is from bad Bots. The year wise distribution of the Bot traffic from the year 2012 to 2014 is shown in figure (Figure 3). It shows that human traffic drops in year 2013 and then it increases to five percent (5%). The important point to be noticed is that, the bad Bot traffic is almost constant (30%).

Figure 3. Year wise bot traffic

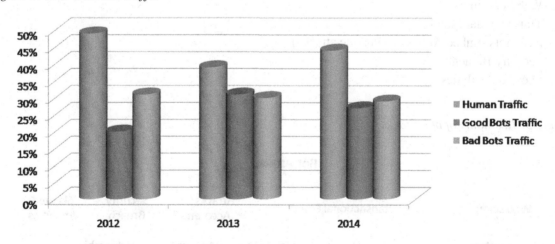

Analyzing deeper, the report shows whether particular sized websites were further exposed to cyber attacks using Bots in the year 2014. As it comes up, bad Bots attacked categorically to all the websites, regardless of their size.

As shown in the next graph (Figure 4), the percentage of bad Bots traffic comparing to total visits is constantly thirty percent (30%), regardless of website popularity or size. The larger sites are attacked by a huge number of malicious Bots; on the whole, risk factor is the identical for every website administrator that is approximately one in three requests is a malicious Bots.

Figure 4. Bot traffic according to size of applications

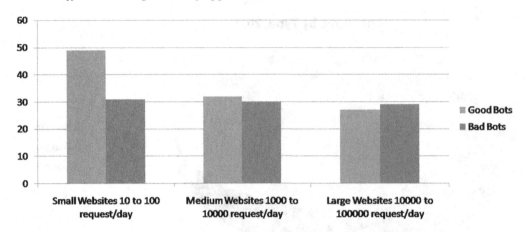

Threats of Bot to E-Commerce Applications

In this section, Bot threats to e-commerce application are explored in detail. As mention in the previous section, Bot traffic survey report from the year 2012 to 2014 bad Bot traffic is continuously about 30%. The bad Bots causes the majority of website attacks. These attacks are ranging from minor cyber crimes like spamming, click fraud to big crimes credential stuffing. These attacks can be classified into five major categories and their taxonomy is shown in figure (Figure 5).

- Web Scraping
- Transactional Fraud
- Accounts -linked Attacks (Semantic attacks)
- Security Breach
- Skewed Analytics

Figure 5. Taxonomy of bot attacks

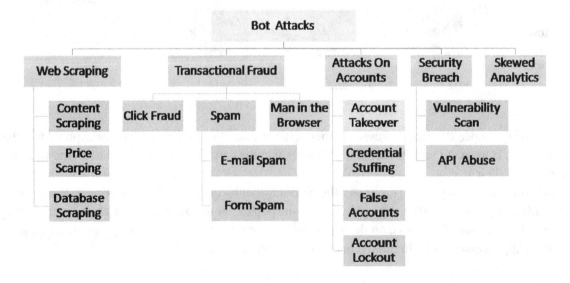

Web Scraping

Web Scrapping is further categorized into Content Scraping, Price Scarping, and Database Scraping.

Content scraping sometimes also known as data scraping is stealing original and unique content from websites and publishing or pasting it in another website. This method is illicit as it is done without permission of the original website owner. Content scraping usually copy the complete content and passed it to its own website.

These contents can be product reviews, product prices, news, opinion pieces, and list of classifieds. This is different from web crawler Bots, scraper Bots do not obey with the set of rules set in the (robots.txt) file. The aim is to take information and distribute it elsewhere, or trade it in black market. This sort of fraudulent scraping affects e-commerce in a number of ways, including declining SEO (Search engine optimization) rankings, growing server bandwidth, impact on customers, and finally the most important revenue loss (Salerno et al., 2006).

Price Scarping is when a competitor indexes an entire e-commerce website inventory and identifies what is in stock inventory, price of the products and all the details related to the cost of products. Then, it creates an automated strategy to adjust their pricing based on the inventory and prices this makes you less competitive and gives them a competitive advantage.

Competitors exploit this tactic to take over the dynamic price. Dynamic pricing is an important tactic used by e-commerce application to attract customer buying decisions and optimize profits in real-time, so that they can draw attention of customers by putting their prices lower than baseline prices in the e-commerce market.

Database Scraping, in this type of scraping in which the Bot master uses programming scripts to lift off the entire database of e-commerce portals.

Transactional Fraud

The transactional fraud or fraudulent transactions attacks specifically target transactional data on the e-commerce applications. These types of fraud include Click Fraud, E-Mail Spam, Form Spam, and Man in the browser attack.

Click Fraud

Click fraud is a type of cybercrime in which an attacker continuously clicks on the websites having advertisements of pay per click. This is special kind of digital advertising; where administrators of websites that publish the ads are remunerated a sum of money decided by how many website visitors click on the advertisements. Fraud takes place when an attacker, makes a Bot which mimics a genuine user of a web browser, clicking on an advertisement (Wilbur et al., 2009).

E-Mail Spamming

Email spamming sometimes also referred as, junk mailing, is a type of digital spam where unwanted email messages are sent by an attacker. A lot of email spam messages are viable in nature but may also contain masked hyperlinks that seem to be well-known websites but in reality, they redirect to phishing websites. An email spammer usually, sends an email to lacks of mailing addresses, with the probability that only a few numbers will answer. Spammers make use specialized Bot known as spambot to generate mass email list (Mijatovic, 2004).

These spambots steal e-mail addresses from contents found on the World Wide Web in order to construct mailing lists for sending unwanted e-mail. These spambots works as crawlers that can collect e-mail addresses from blogs, news-groups, and Social media sites. Since, e-mail addresses have a typical format; such Bots are easy to script using simple scripting languages.

Man in the Browser Attack

Most important category where Bots are used in transactional fraud is the Man in the browser attack. These types of attacks infects a browser by exploiting the vulnerabilities in web browser for instance, change the web pages, hijacking sessions, modify transactions, all in a entirely hidden way undetectable to both the end user and the hosting websites. It is also represented by MitB, MiB, MIB, and MITB.

A Man in the browser attack works by exploiting general services provided to increase the browser facilities for instance, browser extensions such as Flash, Browser Helper Objects only in Microsoft's Internet Explorer, and browser scripts such as JavaScript.

An associated, but simpler attack is the Boy in the browser attack sometimes represented by BITB, BitB. The mainstream banking service employees believed that Man in the browser attack is the biggest threat to banking systems (Weigold et al., 2008).

Security Breaches

A security breach is an event that results in illegal access of applications, network data, web services, network devices by bypassing their fundamental security mechanisms. Generally, security violation is used for the term security breach. These types of Bot attacks can be further classified as Vulnerability Scanning and API Abuse.

Vulnerability Scanning

The Vulnerability Scanning is an automated process of constantly identifying security weakness of websites in a network in order to exploit, threaten, and attack the websites. Vulnerability scanning makes use of Bots that search for security flaws and compare in a database with identified flaws (Fonseca et al., 2007).

API Abuse

The problem of API abuse is a growing one, as attackers are taking interest to the mobile application as a way of targeting APIs (Application Programming Interface) to steal sensitive information. An API Abuse is illegal or unauthorized access to the servers API through mobile applications or web applications. This may result in stealing of precious intellectual property application codes. Mobile application development is a vital area, where the applications are becoming a growing target for the attackers. It is important for both end users and application programmers to ensure that APIs are protected against attacks, and an important measure is ensuring that the application use to access the servers API is recognized and well-known (Tsipenyuk et al., 2005).

Skewed Analytics

Web behavior analytical systems are developed to assist traffic patterns analysis and end user behavior on a web site or web service. As discussed in the previous section about fifty percent (50%) of all the traffic on the website and web services are generated by Bots. An efficient web behavior analytical systems need to distinguish between the legitimate human traffic and the Bot the traffic and provide particulars of both categories of traffic individually.

OVERVIEW AND INTRODUCTION OF BOTNET

The word Botnet is used to define an interconnected network of infected (infected with viruses without the user's information) computers known as Bot, are under the command and control of a computer programmer usually known as the Bot-Master. The Botnet make use of vulnerable computers by using techniques such as Malware, Viruses Trojans, exploiting software vulnerabilities and social engineering to connect Bots to their Bot-Masters. The Bot-Master could control the Botnet using C&C (command and control) application. The term Botnet is a combination of the two words Bot and network (Rodríguez et al., 2013).

They are generally used to send spam emails, performing DDoS (Distributed Denial of Service) attack, transmit malwares and employed in other work of cybercrime. Botnet is also known as a zombie army and they are considered as the biggest threats on web security today. The given figure (Figure 6) shows the typical structure of Botnet.

Figure 6. Structure of botnet

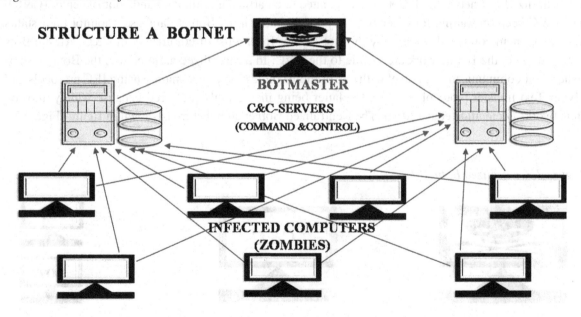

The Bot-Master uses command and control servers, first to infect the computers and then, to form a network of infected computers (zombies). This network can be used launch an attack to target a system using a variety of attacks such as DDos.

Evolution of Botnet

The earliest Botnet were exclusively based on IRC (Internet Relay Chat) and during those days IRC was the most frequent protocol used for communication. IRC is a protocol that facilitates many users to communicate in real time via the internet. This protocol was developed by Jarkko Oikarinen in the year 1988. Oikarinen defines: "The key idea is to allow discussion on news and create groups on a Bulletin Board Service in real time discussions and other Bulletin Board Service associated stuff". IRC end users have an application client on their terminal that facilitates them to make a connection to an IRC server. Different users can make a connection to channels and converse to other users. The server of IRC makes connections simultaneously to all the IRC clients. Bots invented from the condition for automated administrative tasks on servers. The Bot can reside on an IRC channel and carry out tasks as set by an owner of channel (Tyagi et al., 2011).

Botnet Classification According to Their Architectures

Botnet can be classified according to their architectures into two categories namely, centralized Botnet and decentralized Botnet.

Centralized Botnet Architecture

In Centralized Bot network, all Bots are associated to a particular command and control center (C&C). The C&C keep on waiting for other Bots to join, list them in its Botnet database, monitor their status and sends them commands chosen by the Bot-Master from a list of commands in C&C. All the Bots (computers) in the Bot network are visible to the C&C. In a centralized architecture, the Botnet establishes their communication channel with one or more connection points mainly using IRC protocols and Hyper Text transfer protocol (HTTP), the latter being increasingly preferred because widely allowed in networks (Zeidanloo et al., 2010). The Centralized Botnet architecture is shown in figure (Figure 7).

Figure 7. Centralized Botnet

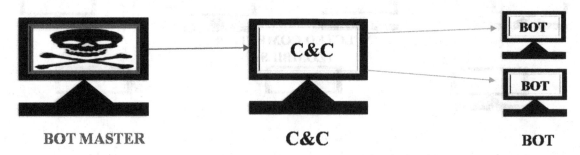

Decentralized Botnet Architecture

In this type of Botnet architecture, infected computers are connected to a number of Bot on a Botnet (network) instead of command and control center. Instructions are move from one Bot to other Bot. Every Bot maintains a list of a number of neighboring Bots, and any instruction received by a Bot from its neighboring Bot will be passed on to the other Bots, finally making the zombie network. In decentralized Botnet, an attacker must have an access to at least one Bot on the Bot network in order to control the entire Botnet (Studer et al., 2011).

A decentralized architecture enables the point of intrinsic failure of a centralized architecture. This is done to peer-to peer networks, each Bot contributing according to its capacities to the whole command and control systems. The Decentralized Botnet architecture is shown in figure (Figure 8).

Figure 8. Decentralized Botnet

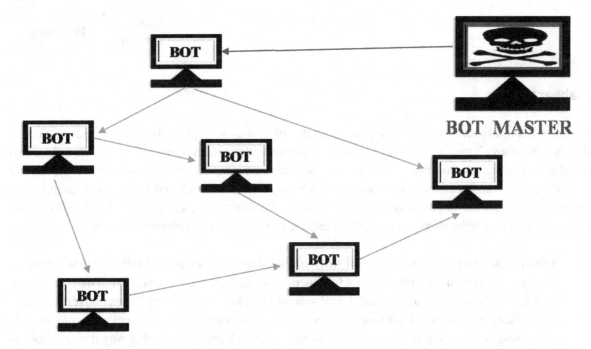

It should be noted that the HTTP communication protocol can be used in centralized as well in decentralized architectures. In particular, it is often used because it allows communications to cross private networks protected by a firewall.

Taxonomy of Botnet Attacks

Once the network of infected computers that is Botnet is formed, then the Bot-master is used to launch numerous types of attacks on web applications. These attacks are classified into four categories including Malwares, Denial of Service, Injection Attacks, Phishing, and their taxonomy is shown in figure (Figure 9).

Figure 9. Taxonomy of Botnet attacks

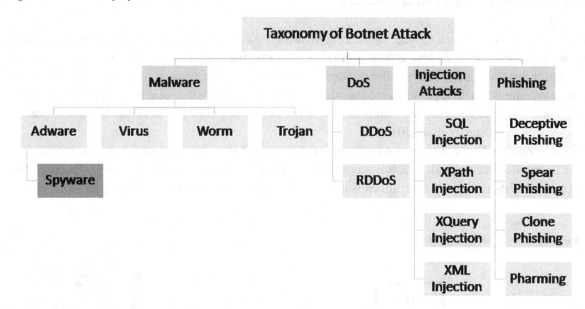

Malware

Malware is the broader term including all the types of threats to web application protection such as Adware, Spyware, Virus, Trojans, and Worms. Malware is short form of malicious software programs developed to penetrate and harm software without the users consent. Malicious software is software program either directly executable or in some interpreted language inserted in a system, usually in a discreet manner, with the intention of compromising Confidentiality, Integrity or Availability of the victim's Data, its Applications, Operating system and to try to annoy or disturb the victim.

- **Adware:** An Adware is ad-supported software or advertising-supported software that automatically put advertisements on websites to generate an income for its developer. These terms are used for any software program that downloads and displays unnecessary banner advertisements. They often comes bundled with some software that someone downloads, developers may include advertising- component in their software to recover development costs this way they are able to provide the product for free or in discounted price. An adware can be designed to collect user's data for instance, it can monitor the websites visited by the user then sent back to the company so that it can deliver advertisement based on the collected information. The advertisements produced by Adware could be seen as an interruption and attack on privacy. In return the developer receives profits from the advertisers he may use it to maintain upgrade and hence continue to develop more software. Generally users are given the option to purchase a registered or licensed version that would remove the ads the adware free version may also offer more functionality (Dai et al., 2007).
- **Spyware:** The adware may also contain a spying component; in this case the malware would be classified as spyware. The Spyware could steal user's information and may also corrupt system files. This is the reason the software companies usually state the privacy policy, saying no sensitive information will be collected. However, there is no way to be one hundred percent sure that

no spying is taking place. Therefore because of privacy concerns most antivirus software today detects and removes both the adware and spyware (Kirda et al., 2006).

- **Virus:** A virus is self replicating computer program that attaches itself to the host program and only exists in on the infected host computer. Computer Virus attacker use security vulnerabilities exploits and social engineering to gain access to their host computer and resources.
- **Worm:** A Worm is self replicating and stand alone software program that replicates itself over the network connections. Generally, it makes use of network to spread itself, rely on system weakness on the target machine to gain access in it. As a minimum Worms always cause harm to the network, albeit only by consuming network bandwidth, while viruses damage or modify the files on a targeted machine.
- **Trojan:** A Trojan is software program performing unidentified and unwanted actions for the user while posing as genuine program. Trojans are usually propagated by various types of social engineering, for instance where an end user is tricked into opening an e-mail attachment containing malicious files or by drive by download. Even though their payload could be anything, a lot of current type operates as a backdoor, having a controller which could then have illegal access to the affected machine.

Denial of Service

During Denial of Service a mostly single computer is used by the Bot to exploit the vulnerabilities of application. It could be done in number of ways for instance, flooding a network by redundant traffic their by preventing legitimate user request, twisting the connection information for instance, resetting a TCP session, blocking the access by disrupting the connection among the communicating systems. A typical DoS Attack is shown in figure (Figure 10).

Figure 10. Typical DoS attack

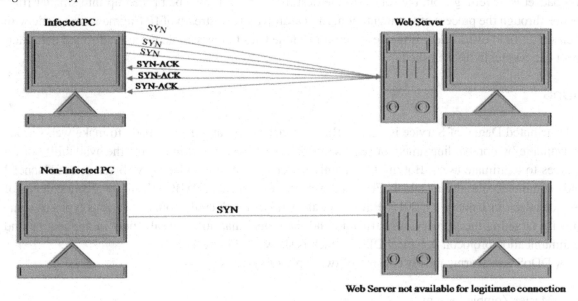

Flooding

In Flooding Denial of Services attack, continuous and particular types of data frames are sent into the computer network. In flood attack, Botnet floods victim with unbounded number of request but does not respond with Acknowledgment packet when a packet is received from the server their by making half open connection with the server. As the number of pending request increases the server resource get consumed and fails to provide service to other genuine clients. Flooding in networks can be of two types Authentication flooding and De-Authentication flooding.

Ping of Death Attack

Ping is used to check the reachability of a client on a network. Ping sends ICMP echo request packets and waits for ICMP echo reply. Ping of Death attack is performed by sending packets of size larger as large as 65535 bytes. A ping packet is of size 56 bytes if it is correctly formed. If a packet is of size larger than the allowed limit packet gets divided into multiple packets. Victim system crashes when it performs reassembling of these malformed packets.

Smurf Attack

Smurf attacks are those attacks caused because of misconfiguration of network devices. Spoofed packets are sent to the broadcast address of the network. Source IP is spoofed to victim IP address by the attacker. Each host receiving the broadcasted packet try to reply the spoofed IP address their by exhausting victim resources.

Teardrop Attack

If a packet is travelling from the source to the destination host, it may be broken up into smaller fragments, through the process of fragmentation. In Teardrop attack a stream of IP fragments are made with their offset field overloaded. If the destination machine tries to reassemble these malformed data fragments, it eventually gets crashed.

DDoS

A Distributed Denial of Service is type of Botnet attack where an effort is made to make web service unavailable by bombarding ample of requests from several sources. It interrupts the availability of resources to legitimate users. Bot masters mainly targets services provided by web servers of financial and ecommerce sites during attack. Financial websites for instance, HSBC UK hit by gigantic denial of service attack in January 29, 2016 (Bawany et al., 2017). Attack could come in various types as some directly targeting the primary infrastructure and the others that utilize weak spots in application and communication protocol. A typical DDoS attack is shown in Figure 11.

A DDoS attack army mostly consists of two types of systems

- Master Zombie System
- Slave Zombie System

Figure 11. Distributed Denial of Service attack

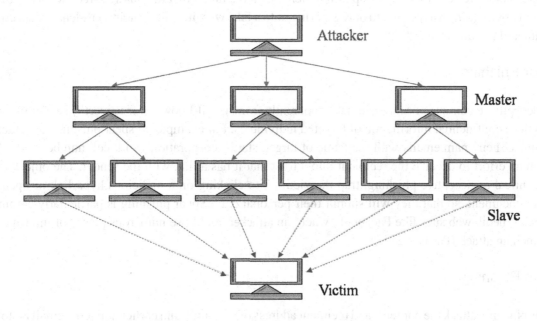

Systems of both these categories are compromised systems which are employed at the time of scanning process and are infected with malicious code. Various processes which happen during a typical DDoS attack include.

- The Bot master controls and coordinates master machine which then coordinates and starts slave systems.
- Bot master then commands master zombies to start all the attack commands present on that system.
- Bot master using those processes, launch attack instructions to slave systems, instructing them to initiate a DDoS attack against the victim system.
- Slave systems then start sending an enormous amount of traffic to the victim system, flooding it with bogus traffic and overwhelming its resources.

Phishing

Phishing is the technique to achieve confidential information such as credentials (username and password, and bank card details (debit card and credit card) regularly for malicious cause, by acting as an honest entity in network communication. The most common types of phishing are Deceptive Phishing, Spear Phishing, Clone Phishing, and Pharming.

Deceptive Phishing

The word "phishing" initially used for account credential theft using instant messaging services but today, the most common technique is a deceptive email message (spam). Emails which ask for verification of account information, system breakdown users need to re enter their username and password, false account charges, unwanted changes in account, fresh free services requiring rapid action, and a lot of other scams are send to a big group of recipients with the target that the unaware recipients (victims) will reply by clicking a hyperlink to or registering onto a fake website where their confidential data could be gathered (Huang et al., 2009).

Spear Phishing

The deceptive technique of sending emails apparently from a well-known or trustworthy sender in order to disclose confidential information of targeted individuals. For example, in spear phishing, an attacker customize their spam emails with the name of target, status, corporation, work cell number and other data in an effort to deceive the recipient into a trust that it has a link with the sender. The objective is the identical as deceptive phishing, trap the victim into clicking on a malicious hyperlink or open an email attachment, so that they will submit their personal data. Spear phishing is particularly common on social media web sites like Facebook, where an attacker could use numerous places of information to launch an attack (Parmar, 2012).

Clone Phishing

In this phishing attack the contents and recipient address of a genuine and earlier delivered email is stolen and used to make a cloned email or nearly identical email. The hyperlink or the attachment files inside the email is replaced with malicious files and contents and then resend from a spoofed email address; seems like it has come from the legitimate sender. The Clone Phishing email could ask to resend the updated information (Khan, 2013).

Pharming

This type of Pharming attack also known as DNS cache poisoning or DNS spoofing. In this attack a fraudulent Domain Name System data is inserted into the DNS cache resolver, as a result the domain name server returns a false IP address. At the end, the attackers are able to divert the HTTP traffic to their system or any other system. The World Wide Web naming system makes use of DNS servers to convert website URLs, such as "www.flipkart.com," to particular format of IP addresses used to locate computer devices. In DNS spoofing attack, a pharmer attacks a Domain Name Server and modifies the IP address related with URL of website. This means pharmer may redirect end users to a malicious website even though the users typed the correct URL of website (Karlof et al., 2007).

XML Injection

In XML Injection attack, the attacker attempt to alter or modify XML document, particularly SOAP message structure by placing parameters having XML tags such as "<" ">" characters. These attacks are only possible if the special characters are not escaped properly. This content is considered as an element of SOAP message and can cause damage at web service provider side.

Different security goals could be violated depending on the executed code. For example, modification of sensitive payment data, here the integrity of payment data has been violated. Another example is the unauthorized login; here the authentication has been violated. For instance, the following code (Figure 12) snippet is an XML injection attack.

Figure 12. XML injection attack

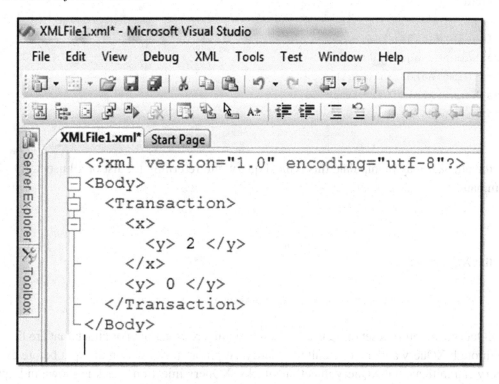

This type of an XML message might result in xml injection attack because <y> 2 </y> is inserted without escaping the special characters "<",">". The resultant variable values within the application for this particular service request were: x = 2, y = 0. As a result, the attacker is able to modify the value of y just by changing the content of x.

An important check in identification of XML injection attack is a strict validation of schema on the XML message, for instance, in given code data type validation should be applied. This validation will reject the message from the given attack.

XQuery Injection

The idea of XQuery Injection attack is borrowed from the SQL injection attack. In this attack, the attacker exploits the XML XQuery Language instead of structured query language through invalidated data that is given to XQuery commands.

XQuery injection could be used to inject XQuery commands to the service provider, enumerate XML elements of document on the victim's end, or execute XQuery to remote servers and XML data sources. Very similar to SQL injection attacks, the attacker exploits the application entry point to attack the XML data resource. For instance, consider the following code snippet shown in figure (Figure 8).

The XQuery of this XML document for the User Aakash

```
doc("XMLFile1.xml")/UserList/user[UserName ="Manager"]
```

Would return:

```
<user level="Manager">
    <UserName>Manager</UserName>
    <FirstName>Aakash</FirstName>
    <LastName>Patel</LastName>
    <Status>good</Status>
</user>
```

Now, the attacker may manipulate this typical query into returning the list of all users. By give the input command

```
Username or "1" = "1"
```

Now, the XQuery is:

```
doc("XMLFile1.xml ")/ UserList /user[UserName =" Username " or "1" = "1"]
```

This XQuery will return a set of all users. There are numerous variants of attack that are likely to be possible through XQuery and are difficult to identify. Appropriate validation of input before executing the XQuery can mitigate the XQuery injection attacks. XQuery injection attack is shown in Figure 13.

Figure 13. XQuery injection attack

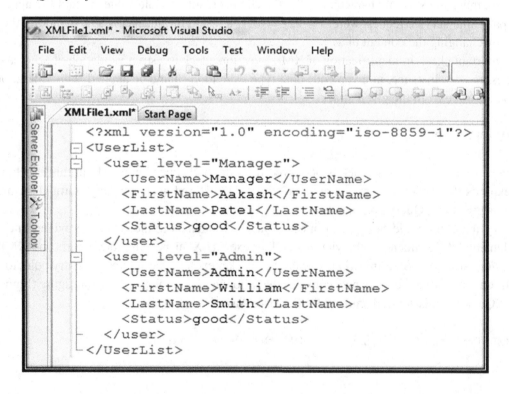

XPath Injection

XPath Injection is also related to XQuery Injection, XPath Injection attacks happen when a web application takes information supplied by user to construct an XPath query for XML document. By supplying deliberately twisted information into the web application, an attacker could expose how the XML document is made, or could gain the document access.

Coercive Parsing

The concept of Coercive Parsing is borrowed from denial of service attack (DoS). The very first step in processing a request of Web Service is to parse the SOAP message and converting the message content to make it available for the application. In particular while using XML namespaces, it may become complex and deadly in parsing, contrast to other message parsing. As a result, the XML parsing permits s possibilities for a particular type of Denial-of- Service attacks, which is known as Coercive Parsing attacks.

The goal of Coercive Parsing attacks is to exhaust the system resources of the victim web service. The attacker sends indefinite number of opening tags in the SOAP Body of SOAP message. That is the attacker sends an intensely nested XML document to the victim web service. Coercive Parsing attack might results in a hundred present utilization of CPU; when the SOAP message is processed. Typical Coercive Parsing attack is shown in Figure (Figure 14)

Figure 14. Coercive Parsing attack

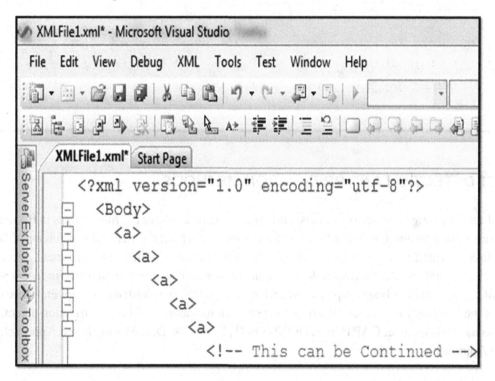

Oversized XML Attack

Typical SOAP message components inside an XML tag generally have a length of a small number of characters. The Namespace declarations can have hardly hundred characters but that generally doesn't cause any problem to XML parser.

On the other hand, if it is used in a malicious means the components inside an XML tag may be exploit to launch Oversized XML attack. For instance, by using excessively long names of attribute, a parser could break down due to memory exhaustion. Oversized XML attack is achievable since the standard of XML does not restrict the number of characters in XML tags. For instance the following code snippet shows the Oversized XML attack. Here, the name of element continued till it a size becomes in MBs. This attack is shown in Figure (Figure 15)

Figure 15. Oversized XML attack

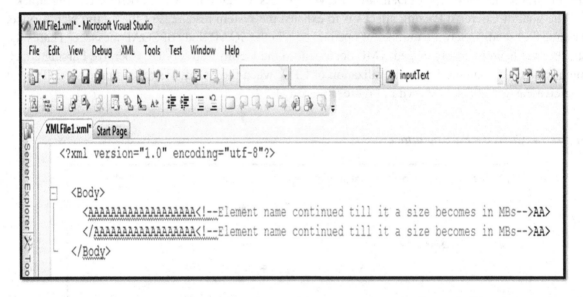

BOTNET DETECTION AND PREVENTION METHODS

In spite of the very long presence of Botnets, numerous researchers have put their efforts in Botnet detection and prevention techniques. Up till now, little is identified about the malicious behavior of Botnets. Nevertheless, research is in progress to counter the Botnet attacks, detection of Botnets, and defense mechanism against their attacks. Botnet detection and prevention is main research area in recent years. A number of techniques have been proposed in academia as well as in industries. The given figure (Figure 16) shows the taxonomy of Botnet detection and preventions methods. The classification detection and prevention methods include, CAPTCHA, HONEYPOT, Firewalls, Data Mining based Approaches, and Big Data Approaches.

Figure 16. Taxonomy of Botnet detection and prevention methods

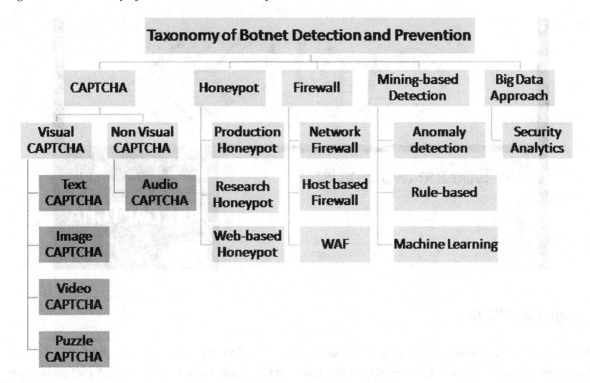

CAPTCHA

CAPTCHA is security mechanism against specialized Bot attacks known as Form Spamming. This system is developed a security mechanism to differentiate between legitimate human users and illegitimate Bots particularly in online registration. A typical security mechanism used at this time to address the problem is CAPTCHA Acronym of Completely Automated Public Turing Test to Tell Computers and Humans Apart. The notion of CAPTCHA is based on the capability of human beings to accomplish some tasks which software programs cannot accomplish for instance, asking end users to type alphabets in a distorted image of text or select a particular image from a number of displayed images. For instance, humans could read the distorted text shown in figure (Figure 17) however, present computer Bots cannot read (Von Ahn et al., 2003).

The CAPTCHA systems can be categorized into two types visual and non-visual. Visual CAPTCHA systems are further categorized as Text CAPTCHA, Image CAPTCHA, Video CAPTCHA, and Puzzle CAPTCHA. Non visual CAPTCHA systems are based only on audio.

Text CAPTCH

Text CAPTCHA systems are easy to implement in which a sequence of alphabets and numeric digits are given to the end user with adding a little alteration to the characters for instance, noise, rotation, drawing, or alphabets in 3D form. These alterations added to stop computer Bot programs from identifying the real characters. Humans can identify easily these characters. Figure (Figure 13) shows the Text CAPTCHA.

Figure 17. Text CAPTCHA

Image CAPTCHA

In this CAPTCHA system end user is ask to select an image. ESP Pix is an earliest CAPTCHA system based on images and it was first developed and tested at Carnegie Mellon University. A picture of ESP Pix is shown in Figure (Figure 18). In ESP Pix CAPTCHA four pictures are shown and in order to pass Turing test the end user has to choose word associated with those four pictures from a drop-down list having seventy two (72) choices.

Figure 18. Image CAPTCHA

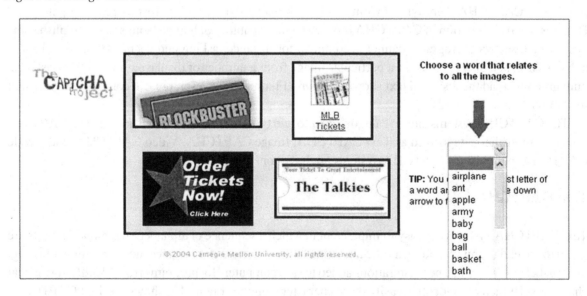

Puzzle CAPTCHA

In puzzle CAPTCHA, a little mathematical puzzle is created according to a number of predefined rules. The puzzle then displayed by system is and user has to solved the puzzle. Answering of this puzzle requires an ability of comprehending text of puzzle, only a human user can solve it (Gao et al., 2010). Figure shows the puzzle CAPTCHA System. (Figure 19).

Figure 19. Puzzle CAPTCHA

Audio CAPTCHA

In Audio CAPTCHA system, am end user is ask to pass typical audio or voice recognition task. A particular audio CAPTCHA system is shown in Figure 20 (Gao et al., 2010).

Figure 20. Audio CAPTCHA

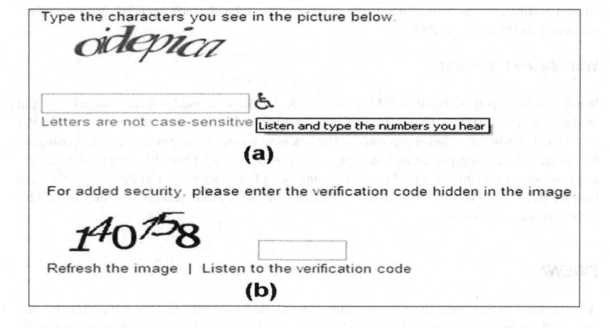

HONEYPOT

In web environment, a Honeypot is a security method use to detect, repel, and counter attempts of illegal use of information systems. Honeypot are trap systems setup to collect the data of an intruder and attacker who are penetrating into the information system. Usually, a honeypot system having data for instance, in a website that seems to be a genuine data of the website, however it is in fact and isolated and under monitoring, and it gathers the information of an attackers, which are then blocked. It should be noted that Honeypots cannot substitute the other conventional computer security systems. They are installed as an additional security level to the system. Honeypots are categorized as production honeypots, research honeypots, web based honeypots.

Production Honeypot

These types of honeypots are easy to developed, gather only limited amount of data, and are mainly used in IT companies. They are installed inside the network with other different servers such as web servers and Database servers by a software organization to attain the overall security. Generally, production honeypots are little interactive honeypots, which can simply be deployed. They provide a lesser amount of information about the intruders or attackers as compared to the research honeypots (Zhang et al., 2003).

Research Honeypots

These Types of honeypots are developed to collect massive information about the strategies and motives and of the attackers and intruders targeting different systems. These Research honeypots do not put the direct value to a particular user or network; rather, they are used to investigate and explore the attacks and threats that companies are facing and to examine how to better guard against those attacks and threats. Research honeypots are difficult to develop and their maintenance is high. They gather extensive amount of data, and mainly used in research and development, Intelligence Agencies, and government organizations (Abbasi et al., 2009).

Web-Based Honeypot

Web-based honeypots are based on HTML and Java Script. They use hidden links, hidden forms, and hidden elements of HTML. Legitimate user will not click on hidden link or hidden button. If a Bot clicks on hidden button or link it gets caught. The Key in web-based honeypot is its constant changing. For instance, Form honeypot is based on giving a fixed single or several invisible form fields rendering as a honeypot. If invisible form field is filled out, in case of Bots, they will typically fill in a value, and then the HTML form will give back an error. The fields are not visible to real users, so they will not fill it out (Watson et al., 2008).

FIREWALL

A firewall is a security mechanism in computer networks that constantly monitor and manage the network traffic both the incoming and outgoing based on predefined security policies. A firewall normally set up a boundary between a genuine, protected internal network and outside network, for instance, the Internet. Firewalls could be made in hardware as well as software or sometimes a mixture of both. Firewalls are often used to check illegal users from gain an access to private network of some organization linked to the Internet, particularly the Intranet. Every incoming or outgoing message of intranet goes through the firewall, which monitors a message and stops those that do not qualify the security criteria (Zaliva et al., 2008).

Firewalls are generally categorized as network firewalls, host based firewalls, web application firewall. Network firewalls set up a boundary between two networks. Host based firewalls give an extra layer of software on the system that monitors network incoming and outgoing of that single machine. A third category is specifically made for the web application is Web Application Firewall (WAF).

A web application firewall constantly monitors HTTP (Hyper Text Transfer Protocol) traffic and apply rules to communication using HTTP and HTTPs. Mostly, these rules used to check whether the HTTP traffic containing Injection attacks, DoS, DDOS, cross site scripting (XSS) or any other attack on web application. Proxy sites typically guard clients, while web application firewall guards application servers. A web application firewall can be installed to protect a particular website or web applications. A web application firewall can be thought as a reverse proxy (Rahimi, 2006).

The web application firewall secures the web server by examining every HTTP or HTTPS request. It inspects through the deep packet inspection and the web traffic analysis of patterns. If found any sort of security breach or threat not according to the security policy, then the web application firewall stops the attack by blocking the particular HTTP request or session or, user agent or by IP.

Mining-Based Detection

Numerous data mining and machine learning techniques, such as Supervised Learning, Unsupervised Learning, Rule based Classification, and Anomaly based Detection using clustering can be used effectively and efficiently to detect HTTP Botnet traffic and C&C Botnet traffic.

Anomaly Detection Methods

In Anomaly detection methods, they try to distinguish Botnet traffic from genuine traffic based on a number of network traffic variance i.e., anomalies for instance, large volume traffic, high latency of network, traffic of unusual ports, and abnormal behavior of system that may specify presence of system Botnet in the network. The effective method for Botnet detection is to find out the Botnet HTTP traffic and C&C traffic. Although, the Botnet HTTP traffic is not easy to detect, however, Botnet make use of normal HTTP traffic communications, the HTTP Bot traffic is similar to normal HTTP traffic. In addition to that, the HTTP traffic is not a large volume and not causes high latency of network. Consequently, anomaly based methods cannot be used to identify HTTP Botnet traffic (Bhuyan et al., 2014).

Rule-Based Detection

Information of patterns and behavior of existing Bots is useful for Bot detection and identification. For instance, SNORT is the most common IDS (Intrusion Detection System) that monitors traffic of network to identify the patterns of Bots and intrusions. Similar to all the Intrusion Detection System, Snort can be configured with signatures or patterns or a set of rules or to keep a record of traffic which is considered as suspicious. On the other hand, rule-based detection techniques mostly, could be used for identification and detection of known Bots. As a result, this technique is not helpful for detecting the unknown Bots.

Supervised Learning and Unsupervised Learning

Supervised Learning and Unsupervised Learning techniques are based on Machine Learning Algorithms such as Classification including Decision Trees, Random Forest, K-Nearest Neighbor, and Clustering Techniques including Flat and Hierarchical Clustering.

The well-known system based on supervised learning and unsupervised learning is Botminer approach which implements Hierarchical and K-Means Clustering algorithm for HTTP Botnet traffic and C&C traffic detection.

The Botminer (Perdisci et al., 2008) is an enhancement of Botsniffer. It groups the similar legitimate HTTP traffic in one group and similar malicious Bot traffic in other group. After that, it carries out cross correlation on different clusters to classify the users that has both similar normal communication patterns and similar abnormal communication patterns. The Botminer tool is a sophisticated Bot detection system which is not dependent on communication protocol and its structure. Botminer is able to detect actual Botnets including HTTP based Botnet, and Peer to Peer Botnets with quite high accuracy.

Big Data Approach

In a last decade, numerous researchers have proposed solutions for mitigating security threats through machine learning techniques. Lot of packet processing tools are used for web traffic analysis such as Wireshark, Nmap, netsniff-ng, tcpdump and wireshark, and snort. In general, these packet-processing tools have limitations that they run on a single machine with limited amount of storage and computing resources. Furthermore, with a single machine, it is hard to give fault tolerant analysis services against a node failure, which over and over again happens when read/write jobs are repeatedly performed on disks. Researchers have steadily shifting from SIEM based methods to Big Data approaches like in (Lee et al., 2011) developing DDoS attack detection system based on Hadoop using large network traffic for mitigation of security threats. In (Suryawanshi et al., 2014), authors devise the first packet processing technique for Hadoop that examines packet trace files using map reduce by analyzing packets across multiple HDFS blocks. Researchers (Lee et al., 2013) report their work on developing a novel traffic monitoring system that carry out flow analysis on terabytes of web traffic in a scalable manner. They developed Map Reduce algorithm with a new format able to handle libpcap files in parallel manner. But there is limitation associated with this method. They hardcode the features that are extracted from the libpcap files and thereby the user is not allow to decide the feature set based on the problem instance.

In (Yen et al., 2010) authors made a distinction based on certain features related to traffic volume and classify them as benign and malicious in network flow records. Authors in (Guntuku et al., 2013) developed Bayesian Regularized Neural Network based Botnet detection method which achieved high precision. Researchers in (Singh et al., 2010) build up scalable quasi-real-time intrusion detection system. It is used to detect Peer-to-Peer Bot net attacks using machine-learning approach. This is based on distributed framework using Hive and Mahout. Francois, et al., (2010) describes a scalable method for detecting P2P Bot net regarding the relationships between hosts and it based on a Hadoop cluster. Their evaluation illustrates reasonably high detection accuracy and a good efficiency.

Cheon et al., (2013) developed a distributed Snort system that assembles warning messages from numerous Snort processes, which execute warning messages on different machines in a parallel manner using MapReduce functionality by Hadoop. Their experiment shows that using two or more slave nodes has enhanced performance than a single node system, also system with eight slave nodes shows almost four times faster speed than that of a single node system. However, it is not capable of real-time analytics.

Kumar and Hanumanthappa (2013) proposed scalable NIDS (Network Intrusion Detection System) log analysis system based on cloud computing. The main purpose is to efficiently handle large volume of NIDS logs from server's machines using Mapreduce and cloud computing. Analysis is carried out on Snort log report with file size of 4 GB. The running time for log analysis is found by evaluating with Hadoop based system and with a single node without Hadoop. As number of nodes increases, the system performance increases as compared to the single system. When number of nodes in the system is five, performance of the system is almost double than that of the single node.

Prathibha and Dileesh (2013) developed Hybrid intrusion detection system, analysis is performed using Hadoop Hive ecosystem. Hive is used as data warehousing tool, which efficiently analyses large size of data. Hadoop configured with Hive makes IDS very scalable by giving packet analysis with language HiveQL similar to SQL. Another Network Intrusion Detection System (Bandr et al., 2015) is able to perform analytics over the behavior of intrusion and their patterns on the network, which assists administrator to configure policies and settings for network security. Analytics over intrusion is performed by using a Score-Weight approach known as Pattern Frequency Inverse Cluster Frequency (PF-ICF).

Earlier most of the attempt from researcher was focused on detecting a specific activity and specific attack and their solutions were not described to be successful in identifying general malicious behavior and attacks, whose features were not used in the training data set. Indeed, it can be observed that using a machine learning techniques for the detection of malicious behavior is far better than conventional signature based approach as the attackers redesign the scripts frequently and the behavior and functionality of attacks varies quite extensively with each version release of the virus. Signature based techniques depends a lot upon the existing virus signatures to identify any activity.

In particular when handling zero-day attacks, signature based technique fall short completely as there is no account of prior activity for that attack. As a result, a machine learning technique is preferred to identify suspicious activity based on the anomalous behavior of the request.

On the other hand, SIEM (Security Information and Event Management) based tools provide real time analysis of security alerts generated by network hardware and applications (Miller et al., 2010).

SIEM has been a foundational tool for long time on the market place and it is the core data repository for security events about most organizations. However, it has number of limitations, which causes researches to move from SIEM based tools to Security analytics. Limitations of SIEM based tools are briefly given as follows.

- SIEM does the limited analysis mainly based on correlating and normalization of alerts.
- SIEM only understands those events inside of its defined rules or policies because it is primarily rules based, policy-based and trigger-based.
- SIEM does not understand application specific activity and behaviour or pattern (anomaly detection) to find out how a number of activities raise threat level.
- SIEM only understands log entries and network information to compare events at network level and find out network alerts.
- For advanced security notification, SIEM requires manual investigation.

Consequently, the existing correlation capabilities of SIEM tools, primarily based on a single machine in centralized servers, have confirmed to be inadequate to process large volume of events and data.

Due to these limitations, the scenario has been shifted from SIEM base approach to security analytics, which can analyze security intelligence in real time. It incorporates current data being generated and the massive volumes of event data and existing logs.

By applying this it is possible to stop and distinguish advanced threats as they occur, for that parallel processing is necessary; the tools should have the intelligence to evaluate anomalies and make a decision whether they are true threats or not, to keep away from troubles and damage to the productivity. Salient features of Security analytics are as follows (Cybenko & Landwehr, 2012).

- The ability to analyze and process huge volumes of security related data (offline and online) in real time.
- Reduce false positives and alert volumes.
- Provide better prioritization and enhanced visualization.
- Increased ability to easily aggregate and cross analyze data from non-security sources for instance web access logs and server logs.
- Sophisticated process engine for correlating the information from different sources.
- Advanced automated response capabilities.
- Ability to use of data from outside sources to give information on the new categories of threat that have been observed somewhere else.

CONCLUSION

As described in the chapter, although there are tremendous advantages of using e-commerce applications but there are lot of practical issues related to e-commerce security needs to be solved. Similar to any technology, several security issues confront e-commerce applications. In this chapter security mechanism of (Detection methods and prevention methods) e-commerce web applications from Bot and Botnets are reviewed, and the primary characteristics and elements of Botnets are also discussed. It is revealed that these attacks have a severe impact on e-commerce applications and the attacks may lead to the serious problem for e-commerce. Nearly all central attacks of Botnets in e-commerce along with the possible impacts and the available countermeasures have been described.

REFERENCES

Abbasi, F. H., & Harris, R. J. (2009, November). Experiences with a Generation III virtual Honeynet. In *Telecommunication Networks and Applications Conference (ATNAC), 2009 Australasian* (pp. 1-6). IEEE. 10.1109/ATNAC.2009.5464785

Ashley, P., Hinton, H., & Vandenwauver, M. (2001, December). Wired versus wireless security: The Internet, WAP and iMode for e-commerce. In *Computer Security Applications Conference, 2001. ACSAC 2001. Proceedings 17th Annual* (pp. 296-306). IEEE. 10.1109/ACSAC.2001.991545

Bandre, S. R., & Nandimath, J. N. (2015, January). Design consideration of network intrusion detection system using Hadoop and GPGPU. In *Pervasive Computing (ICPC), 2015 International Conference on* (pp. 1-6). IEEE. 10.1109/PERVASIVE.2015.7087201

Bariso, P. F., III. (2016). *No Need to Fear Robots: Online "Bot" Use under the Computer Fraud and Abuse Act*. Academic Press.

Bawany, N. Z., Shamsi, J. A., & Salah, K. (2017). DDoS Attack Detection and Mitigation Using SDN: Methods, Practices, and Solutions. *Arabian Journal for Science and Engineering*, *42*(2), 425–441. doi:10.100713369-017-2414-5

Bherde, G. P., & Pund, M. A. (2016, September). Recent attack prevention techniques in web service applications. In *Automatic Control and Dynamic Optimization Techniques (ICACDOT), International Conference on* (pp. 1174-1180). IEEE. 10.1109/ICACDOT.2016.7877771

Bhuyan, M. H., Bhattacharyya, D. K., & Kalita, J. K. (2014). Network anomaly detection: Methods, systems and tools. *IEEE Communications Surveys and Tutorials*, *16*(1), 303–336. doi:10.1109/SURV.2013.052213.00046

Cheon, J., & Choe, T. Y. (2013). Distributed processing of snort alert log using hadoop. *IACSIT International Journal of Engineering and Technology*, *5*(3), 2685–2690.

Chonka, A., Xiang, Y., Zhou, W., & Bonti, A. (2011). Cloud security defence to protect cloud computing against HTTP-DoS and XML-DoS attacks. *Journal of Network and Computer Applications*, *34*(4), 1097–1107. doi:10.1016/j.jnca.2010.06.004

Combe, C. (2012). Introduction to *e*-business. Routledge. doi:10.1017/CBO9780511805936

Cybenko, G., & Landwehr, C. E. (2012). Security analytics and measurements. *IEEE Security and Privacy*, *3*(10), 5–8. doi:10.1109/MSP.2012.75

Dai, S. Y., & Kuo, S. Y. (2007, December). Mapmon: A host-based malware detection tool. In *Dependable Computing, 2007. PRDC 2007. 13th Pacific Rim International Symposium on* (pp. 349-356). IEEE. 10.1109/PRDC.2007.23

Dunham, K., & Melnick, J. (2008). *Malicious bots: an inside look into the cyber-criminal underground of the internet*. CRC Press. doi:10.1201/9781420069068

Fonseca, J., Vieira, M., & Madeira, H. (2007, December). Testing and comparing web vulnerability scanning tools for SQL injection and XSS attacks. In *Dependable Computing, 2007. PRDC 2007. 13th Pacific Rim International Symposium on* (pp. 365-372). IEEE. 10.1109/PRDC.2007.55

Francois, J., Wang, S., Bronzi, W., State, R., & Engel, T. (2014, November). Botcloud: Detecting botnets using mapreduce. In *2014 IEEE International Workshop on Information Forensics and Security* (pp. 1-6). IEEE.

Furnell, S. (2006). E-commerce security. In Enterprise Information Systems Assurance and System Security: Managerial and Technical Issues (pp. 131-149). IGI Global. doi:10.4018/978-1-59140-911-3.ch009

Gadge, J. (2008, December). Comprehensive test mechanism to detect attack on Web Services. In *Networks, 2008. ICON 2008. 16th IEEE International Conference on* (pp. 1-6). IEEE.

Gao, H., Liu, H., Yao, D., Liu, X., & Aickelin, U. (2010, July). An audio CAPTCHA to distinguish humans from computers. In *Electronic Commerce and Security (ISECS), 2010 Third International Symposium on* (pp. 265-269). IEEE. 10.1109/ISECS.2010.65

Gao, H., Yao, D., Liu, H., Liu, X., & Wang, L. (2010, December). A novel image based CAPTCHA using jigsaw puzzle. In *Computational Science and Engineering (CSE), 2010 IEEE 13th International Conference on* (pp. 351-356). IEEE. 10.1109/CSE.2010.53

Geer, D. (2005). Malicious bots threaten network security. *Computer, 38*(1), 18–20. doi:10.1109/MC.2005.26

Gordeychik, S., Grossman, J., Khera, M., Lantinga, M., Wysopal, C., Eng, C., & Evteev, D. (2010). *Web application security statistics*. The Web Application Security Consortium.

Gu, G., Perdisci, R., Zhang, J., & Lee, W. (2008, July). BotMiner: Clustering Analysis of Network Traffic for Protocol-and Structure-Independent Botnet Detection. In *USENIX Security Symposium (Vol. 5, No. 2, pp. 139-154)*. Academic Press.

Guntuku, S. C., Narang, P., & Hota, C. (2013). *Real-time Peer-to-Peer Botnet Detection Framework based on Bayesian Regularized Neural Network*. Academic Press.

Gupta, A. N., & Thilagam, P. S. (2013). Attacks on web services need to secure xml on web. *Computing in Science & Engineering, 3*(5), 1.

Gupta, A. N., & Thilagam, P. S. (2013). Attacks on web services need to secure xml on web. *Computing in Science & Engineering, 3*(5), 1.

Huang, H., Zhong, S., & Tan, J. (2009, August). Browser-side countermeasures for deceptive phishing attack. In *Information Assurance and Security, 2009. IAS'09. Fifth International Conference on* (Vol. 1, pp. 352-355). IEEE. 10.1109/IAS.2009.12

Karlof, C., Shankar, U., Tygar, J. D., & Wagner, D. (2007, October). Dynamic pharming attacks and locked same-origin policies for web browsers. In *Proceedings of the 14th ACM conference on Computer and communications security* (pp. 58-71). ACM. 10.1145/1315245.1315254

Khan, A. A. (2013). *Preventing phishing attacks using one time password and user machine identification*. arXiv preprint arXiv:1305.2704

Kirda, E., Kruegel, C., Banks, G., Vigna, G., & Kemmerer, R. (2006, August). Behavior-based Spyware Detection. *Usenix Security, 6*.

Kumar, M., & Hanumanthappa, M. (2013, December). Scalable intrusion detection systems log analysis using cloud computing infrastructure. In *Computational Intelligence and Computing Research (ICCIC), 2013 IEEE International Conference on* (pp. 1-4). IEEE. 10.1109/ICCIC.2013.6724158

Kumar, S. (2007, July). Smurf-based distributed denial of service (ddos) attack amplification in internet. In *Internet Monitoring and Protection, 2007. ICIMP 2007. Second International Conference on* (pp. 25-25). IEEE.

Lau, F., Rubin, S. H., Smith, M. H., & Trajkovic, L. (2000). Distributed denial of service attacks. In *Systems, Man, and Cybernetics, 2000 IEEE International Conference on* (Vol. 3, pp. 2275-2280). IEEE. 10.1109/ICSMC.2000.886455

Lee, Y., & Lee, Y. (2013). Toward scalable internet traffic measurement and analysis with hadoop. *Computer Communication Review, 43*(1), 5–13. doi:10.1145/2427036.2427038

Markov, Z., & Larose, D. T. (2007). *Data Mining the Web: Uncovering Patterns in Web Content*. Academic Press.

Mijatovic, V. (2004). Mechanisms for Detection and Prevention of Email Spamming. P*eer to Peer and SPAM in the Internet, 135*.

Miller, D., Harris, S., Harper, A., VanDyke, S., & Blask, C. (2010). *Security information and event management (SIEM) implementation*. McGraw Hill Professional.

O'Leary, D. E. (2000). *Enterprise resource planning systems: Systems, life cycle, electronic commerce, and risk*. Cambridge University Press.

Oh, J., Im, C., & Jeong, H. (2010, March). A system for analyzing advance bot behavior. In *International Conference on Information Systems, Technology and Management* (pp. 56-63). Springer Berlin Heidelberg. 10.1007/978-3-642-12035-0_7

Orrin, S. (2007). The SOA/XML Threat Model and New XML/SOA/Web 2.0 Attacks & Threats. In Security conference DEFCON (Vol. 15). Academic Press.

Parmar, B. (2012). Protecting against spear-phishing. *Computer Fraud & Security, 2012*(1), 8–11. doi:10.1016/S1361-3723(12)70007-6

Prathibha, P. G., & Dileesh, E. D. (2013). Design of a hybrid intrusion detection system using snort and hadoop. *International Journal of Computers and Applications, 73*(10).

Rahimi, M. I. (2006). *Web application firewall*. University Technology, Mara.

Richards, K. (1999). Network based intrusion detection: A review of technologies. *Computers & Security, 18*(8), 671–682. doi:10.1016/S0167-4048(99)80131-X

Rodríguez-Gómez, R. A., Maciá-Fernández, G., & García-Teodoro, P. (2013). Survey and taxonomy of botnet research through life-cycle. *ACM Computing Surveys, 45*(4), 45. doi:10.1145/2501654.2501659

Salerno, J. J., & Boulware, D. M. (2006). *U.S. Patent No. 7,072,890*. Washington, DC: U.S. Patent and Trademark Office.

Sharma, M., Yadav, K., Yadav, N., & Ferdinand, K. C. (2017). Zika virus pandemic—analysis of Facebook as a social media health information platform. *American Journal of Infection Control, 45*(3), 301–302. doi:10.1016/j.ajic.2016.08.022 PMID:27776823

Shawar, B. A., & Atwell, E. (2003). Using dialogue corpora to train a chatbot. *Proceedings of the Corpus Linguistics 2003 conference*, 681-690.

Shawar, B. A., & Atwell, E. (2007). Chatbots: are they really useful? In *LDV Forum* (Vol. 22, No. 1, pp. 29-49). Academic Press.

Singh, K., Guntuku, S. C., Thakur, A., & Hota, C. (2014). Big data analytics framework for peer-to-peer botnet detection using random forests. *Information Sciences, 278*, 488–497. doi:10.1016/j.ins.2014.03.066

Studer, R. (2011). Economic and technical analysis of botnets and denial-of-service attacks. *Communication Systems, 4*, 19.

Su, Z., & Wassermann, G. (2006, January). The essence of command injection attacks in web applications. *ACM SIGPLAN Notices, 41*(1), 372–382. doi:10.1145/1111320.1111070

Suryawanshi, D. J., & Mande, U. A (2014). *Parallel Processing of Internet Traffic Measurement and Analysis Using Hadoop*. Academic Press.

Tan, Z., Jamdagni, A., He, X., Nanda, P., & Liu, R. P. (2014). A system for denial-of-service attack detection based on multivariate correlation analysis. *IEEE Transactions on Parallel and Distributed Systems, 25*(2), 447–456. doi:10.1109/TPDS.2013.146

Tao, Z. (2013, August). Detection and service security mechanism of xml injection attacks. In *International Conference on Information Computing and Applications* (pp. 67-75). Springer. 10.1007/978-3-642-53703-5_8

Tsipenyuk, K., Chess, B., & McGraw, G. (2005). Seven pernicious kingdoms: A taxonomy of software security errors. *IEEE Security and Privacy, 3*(6), 81–84. doi:10.1109/MSP.2005.159

Tyagi, A. K., & Aghila, G. (2011). A wide scale survey on botnet. *International Journal of Computers and Applications, 34*(9), 9–22.

Vargiu, E., & Urru, M. (2012). Exploiting web scraping in a collaborative filtering-based approach to web advertising. *Artificial Intelligence Review, 2*(1), 44.

Vieira, M., Antunes, N., & Madeira, H. (2009, June). Using web security scanners to detect vulnerabilities in web services. In *Dependable Systems & Networks, 2009. DSN'09. IEEE/IFIP International Conference on* (pp. 566-571). IEEE. 10.1109/DSN.2009.5270294

Von Ahn, L., Blum, M., Hopper, N. J., & Langford, J. (2003, May). CAPTCHA: Using hard AI problems for security. In *International Conference on the Theory and Applications of Cryptographic Techniques* (pp. 294-311). Springer Berlin Heidelberg. 10.1007/3-540-39200-9_18

Wang, X., Kohno, T., & Blakley, B. (2014, June). Polymorphism as a defense for automated attack of websites. In *International Conference on Applied Cryptography and Network Security* (pp. 513-530). Springer International Publishing. 10.1007/978-3-319-07536-5_30

Watson, D., & Riden, J. (2008, April). The honeynet project: Data collection tools, infrastructure, archives and analysis. In *Information Security Threats Data Collection and Sharing, 2008. WISTDCS'08. WOMBAT Workshop on* (pp. 24-30). IEEE.

Weigold, T., Kramp, T., Hermann, R., Höring, F., Buhler, P., & Baentsch, M. (2008, March). The Zurich Trusted Information Channel–an efficient defence against man-in-the-middle and malicious software attacks. In *International Conference on Trusted Computing* (pp. 75-91). Springer Berlin Heidelberg. 10.1007/978-3-540-68979-9_6

Wilbur, K. C., & Zhu, Y. (2009). Click fraud. *Marketing Science, 28*(2), 293–308. doi:10.1287/mksc.1080.0397

Wokosin, L. (2002). Components of E-Commerce. *Annual Conference-Society for Technical Communication, 49*, 172–175.

Yee, C. G., Shin, W. H., & Rao, G. S. V. R. K. (2007, November). An adaptive intrusion detection and prevention (ID/IP) framework for web services. In *Convergence Information Technology, 2007. International Conference on* (pp. 528-534). IEEE.

Yen, T. F., & Reiter, M. K. (2010, June). Are your hosts trading or plotting? Telling P2P file-sharing and bots apart. In *Distributed Computing Systems (ICDCS), 2010 IEEE 30th International Conference on* (pp. 241-252). IEEE.

Zaliva, V. (2008). *Firewall policy modeling, analysis and simulation: a survey*. Source-Forge, Tech. Rep.

Zeidanloo, H. R., Shooshtari, M. J. Z., Amoli, P. V., Safari, M., & Zamani, M. (2010, July). A taxonomy of botnet detection techniques. In *Computer Science and Information Technology (ICCSIT), 2010 3rd IEEE International Conference on* (Vol. 2, pp. 158-162). IEEE. 10.1109/ICCSIT.2010.5563555

Zhang, F., Zhou, S., Qin, Z., & Liu, J. (2003, August). Honeypot: a supplemented active defense system for network security. In *Parallel and Distributed Computing, Applications and Technologies, 2003. PDCAT'2003. Proceedings of the Fourth International Conference on* (pp. 231-235). IEEE. 10.1109/PDCAT.2003.1236295

This research was previously published in Improving E-Commerce Web Applications Through Business Intelligence Techniques edited by G. Sreedhar; pages 48-81, copyright year 2018 by Business Science Reference (an imprint of IGI Global).

Chapter 7
Botnet and Internet of Things (IoTs):
A Definition, Taxonomy, Challenges, and Future Directions

Kamal Alieyan
Universiti Sains Malaysia, Malaysia

Rosni Abdullah
Universiti Sains Malaysia, Malaysia

Ammar Almomani
ⓘ https://orcid.org/0000-0002-8808-6114
Al-Balqa Applied University, Jordan

Badr Almutairi
Majmaah University, Saudi Arabia

Mohammad Alauthman
ⓘ https://orcid.org/0000-0003-0319-1968
Zarqa University, Jordan

ABSTRACT

In today's internet world the internet of things (IoT) is becoming the most significant and developing technology. The primary goal behind the IoT is enabling more secure existence along with the improvement of risks at various life levels. With the arrival of IoT botnets, the perspective towards IoT products has transformed from enhanced living enabler into the internet of vulnerabilities for cybercriminals. Of all the several types of malware, botnet is considered as really a serious risk that often happens in cybercrimes and cyber-attacks. Botnet performs some predefined jobs and that too in some automated fashion. These attacks mostly occur in situations like phishing against any critical targets. Files sharing channel information are moved to DDoS attacks. IoT botnets have subjected two distinct problems, firstly, on the public internet. Most of the IoT devices are easily accessible. Secondly, in the architecture of most of the IoT units, security is usually a reconsideration. This particular chapter discusses IoT, botnet in IoT, and various botnet detection techniques available in IoT.

DOI: 10.4018/978-1-7998-5348-0.ch007

INTRODUCTION

In this digital world where everything is connected through the internet, the Internet of Things (IoT) plays a major role. Most of the people get attracted towards this innovative approach which helps the people to enjoy their life in their hectic routine. For instance, just imagine if refrigerators will be able to monitor their content and can place the order to a retailer shop if any food item is running out or imagine if you would be able to order your Sunday breakfast from your bed through a gesture or a voice command like the intelligent assistants Google Assistant, Apple Siri or Amazon Alexa. All these thoughts are not only some science fiction story but is now becoming a reality just because with use of smart devices such as Google Home, Amazon echoes with Alexa, etc., smart television, smart phones, etc. (Engrish, 2017).

In 1999, the concept of IoT was proposed by Kevin Ashton. IoT was refereed as the objects that are interoperable and exclusively identifiable and are connected with radio-frequency identification technology. Though, IoT is defined by in many forms by the various researchers as (Ray, 2018):

- ''A global infrastructure for the information society enabling advanced services by interconnecting (physical and virtual) things based on, existing and evolving, interoperable information and communication technologies'' (ICTP Workshop, 2015).
- ''3A concept: anytime, anywhere and any media, resulting into sustained ratio between radio and man around 1:1'' (Srivastava, 2006).
- ''a dynamic global network infrastructure with self-configuring capabilities based on standard and interoperable communication protocols where physical and virtual 'Things' have identities, physical attributes, and virtual personalities and use intelligent interfaces, and are seamlessly integrated into the information network'' (Kranenburg, 2008).

Evolution of Internet of Things (IoT)

As shown in Figure 1 that is how the Internet of Things actually evolved with the advent of time. At the era of pre-internet, which is also known as "H2H" or "Human-to-Human" era, people had the fixed or mobile telephony. Except that one of the primary ways of communication was through SMS services. After that with the incorporation of smart networks when the internet came into existence, the "www" or "world wide web" era the communication as well as information and entertainment etc. gets better through the internet. Furthermore, smart IT platforms and services were added to "www" that results in "web 2.0" era that totally converts everything into digital transformation like e-productivity, e-commerce, etc.

Figure 1. Evolution of IoT

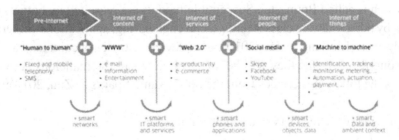

Next era is considered to bean era of "social media" that is Skype, Facebook, YouTube, etc. which involves the smart phones and applications. Moreover, currently, we live in "M2M" or "Machine-to-Machine" era that is possible because of the Internet of Things and with smart devices, objects, and data. Here we can easily identify, trace, monitor things with smart devices as well as automation, actuation and payment are also possible through IoT.

Generic Architecture of IoT

Basically, the Internet of Things architecture consists of smart things that may be devices, objects or data that are connected to one another through internet and all the data that is shared among them is stored at a cloud with the help of Big Data and these things are further managed, analyzed and visualized by the various units that are used to provide the services to a cloud.

The simplest architecture of the Internet of Things is shown in Figure 2. Where things may be any smart device, data or object and all these things are connected to the cloud through a gateway mostly internet. Many individual units like device management, analytics, visualization, etc. are used for managing the data with the help of Big Data that is used to store this data.

Figure 2. Generic architecture of IoT

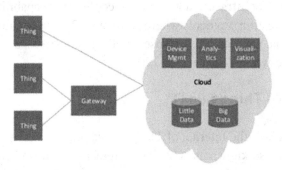

BOTNETS WITH IOT

The risks to the IoT units are an essential problem since they are difficult to repair and resolve. These can be easily affected by the attackers. The presence of IoT botnets was recognized after 2008. Nevertheless, the scope of risk presented by them was not recognized until 2016 (Engrish, 2017). Generally, the infected end-hosts (called bots) network is defined by the botnets, and these networks are actually controlled by a human being which is called Botmaster. Susceptible models are recruited by botnets using strategies that are employed by other malware classes (e.g., social engineering, applications vulnerabilities that are exploited remotely, etc.) (Li, Jiang & Zou, 2010), such devices establish a command and control (C&C) infrastructure among them so that they will be able to implement the malicious activities. Therefore, Botmaster receives the following services from the bots (Wang, Sparks & Zou, 2010):

- Botmaster provides easy recovery and monitoring

- Each bot has limited botnet exposure
- Distinct control traffic dispersion as well as encryption
- Robust network connectivity

Components of Botnet

Command and Control (C&C) Server

It is a centralized system which can receive the information and sends the instructions to the bots residing in that particular network. This infrastructure comprises of many technical parts along with many servers. Many botnets make use of a client server-structure, but several botnets use peer-to-peer (P2P) architecture consisting of botnets that are having the C&C functionality.

Peer-to-Peer (P2P) Botnet

For providing additional security against the takedowns a decentralized bot network is used that is called P2P botnet. While P2P botnets can have a C&C server, they might additionally run without this and also be organized arbitrarily to additional obscure the botnet and its goal. While P2P botnets are not as likely being revealed, the botmaster cannot quickly supervise command distribution as well as there exist complex implementation of it.

Botmaster

It is also known as a bot herder or botnet controller, the botmaster performs the botnets operator function. A botnet is regulated by issuing the commands to specific botnets as well as C&C server within the system by the remote botmaster. To prevent the law enforcement prosecution and identification of botmaster, the location, and name of botmaster are kept obscured.

Bot

It is defined as the device that is connected to the internet within a botnet network. Mostly computer system is used as a bot, but with the advent of the technology an IoT device, a smartphone can also be used as botnet part. Operational instruction is sent to the botnets either from the bots of the same network or from the botmaster directly or from a C&C server.

Zombie

Zombie is nothing just another synonym for a bot. As an external person or a computing device is used to control the bot; therefore, a bot is called as 'zombie' and botnet is called a "zombie army."

Botnet Attack

- A botmaster gets a botnet by distributing bot malware to infect PCs and additional systems. He might also lease a current botnet from an additional criminal.

- The botnet's C&C is reported by a newly harvested bot or "zombies."
- These bots are now controlled by C&C, and potential victim address lists, email templates, and executable malware files are distributed by the bots as per C&C instructions.
- Many potential victims then receive the malware containing email messages from the infected bots on the order of botmaster.

BOTNET DETECTION TECHNIQUES BASED ON IOT ENVIRONMENT

Typically, Botnet detection, as well as monitoring, is a significant investigation subject in recent years as a result of a boost in the malicious activity. Because of the existence of malicious activity (Botnet) from a while, till currently few proper researches has analyzed the Botnet issue. Therefore, various bot detection methods were proposed by researchers as discussed in the next section.

Related Work and Taxonomy of Botnet Detection Techniques

Figure 3 shows the taxonomy of botnet detection techniques. There are two main categories of botnet detection techniques (Liu et al., 2008), Intrusion Detection Systems (IDSs) and HoneyNets (Stinson & Mitchell, 2007; Provos, 2004).

Figure 3. Botnet detection technique taxonomy (Ahmad et al., 2014)

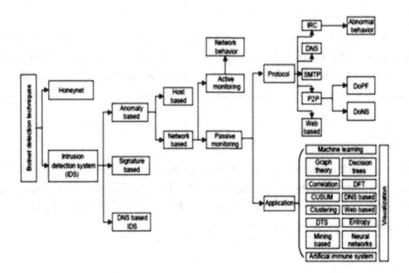

Honeynet

Usually Honeypot and Honeywell collectively make the Honeynet based method (Zang et al., 2011). In terms of security, Honeypot is considered as a computer system which helps to lure the attackers so that the attacker will attack on a specific computer system. This honeypot is supposed to be an end host. It can be compromised in a small time and is much more susceptible to malicious attacks whereas honeywall consists of software through which the traffic through the honeypot is monitored, collected, controlled as well as modified, e.g., Snort (Schaffer, 2006). The computer systems that are used as Honeypots do not possess any kind of production value. Based on this particular principle, most interactions among other systems and honeypot are distrustful or suspicious and should be examined. For instance, in your network, you could install a honeypot web server in a particular location. Since it is a honeypot and it does not have some productive tasks, therefore any interaction with this particular web server is actually an unauthorized entry or a malicious task. A comparable Honeynet was built (Zeidanloo et al., 2010), where Honeywell component shall be in a position to examine as well as capture all of the site traffic payloads to access information related to Botnet like the DNS/IP address of the C&C server with the corresponding port number as well as the authentically data required to sign up for the C&C channel and also able to isolating the Honeypots from various other devices in the area community by obstructing outgoing contacts that contain distrustful key phrases connected to potential malicious pursuits.

Therefore in order to record the detailed steps of the Botnets, Rajab et al. (2006) have built a distributed and multifaceted measurement infrastructure by merging Honeynets with an altered version of the nepenthes platform.

IDS

IDSs are used to report the managing website when system policies are violated, system services are monitored for malicious activities or there are any other violations. These IDS can be either a hardware machine or a software application. The benefit of an IDS detection feature (Wurzinger et al., 2009; Kugisaki et al., 2007; Goebel & Holz, 2007) is that it has signatures of a selection of recognized botnets. Nevertheless, the main disadvantages of such methods are: firstly, the primary reason why there is an increase in anomaly is because of the small refresh rate of IDS signature updates. Secondly, for detecting the freshly activated botnets, the signature knowledge base repository needs to be refreshed frequently (Kugisaki et al., 2007). Further, these detection methods are categorized into signature based, anomaly based and DNS-based IDSs (Stalmans & Irwin, 2011).

Signature-Based Detection

In this particular method according to the accessible information as well as the signature of the current bot is adequate to trap the bots. To identify the botnets, a library of particular Botnet function names as well as instructions is collected that may be included and summarized in the IDS that are proposed by various researchers. After the IDS located corresponding search phrases while examining the content of payload, it can cause the alert and take additional steps from the Botnet though this particular method is restricted to identify just the recognized Botnets. For instance, Snort (Roesch, 1999) is a wide open source IDS which monitors network traffic to locate indications of intrusion by looking matches depending on the predefined set of signature as well as guidelines.

Anomaly-Based Detection

This method detects risk, malicious risk by looking for irregular or abnormal actions of the system. Here "abnormal" action usually means bots detection as a variation from "normal" action that is already defined appropriately by some guidelines. Sigh and Binkley (2006) proposed a good TCP based anomaly detection method with IRC tokenization as well as IRC message statistics to identify Botnet customers and also expose Botnet servers. Initially, an IRC parsing component is implemented in this particular anomaly based method that collects the TCP packet information as well as determines the IRC channel. Further, the scanning activities are performed on a large sampled data set which is correlated with the IRC channel traffics (Dagon et al., 2007). Moreover, finally, the IRC routes with good checking matter will be stamped as the attainable Botnet stations. A 3-metrics based measurement is proposed by Akiyama et al. (2007) that helps in detecting the behaviors of abnormal Botnets. It was assumed that all the bots would show some similar synchronization, response, and relationship that belongs to the same Botnet. BotHunter, a Botnet detection system was proposed by Gu et al. (2007). This detection system by using user-defined bot infection life cycle model runs a correlation algorithm that helps in recognizing the bot infection phase.

DNS-Based Detection

This detection method is a hybrid of data-mining based and behavior based methods that are used on the DNS traffic. In general, a Botmaster can easily hide and maintain its bots, therefore, think about the factors DNS queries are applied in several Botnet phases, like C&C server update, malicious attack initiation, and rallying process after infection that is a benefit of the strategy.

Bot Net Attacks

Attacking BotNet occurs when a bot is infected with an internet-connected device. A botnet is therefore also part of an infected device web which is monitored by a single attacker or group. Often Botnets are called Computer Worms or Zombie Armies, and bot masters or bot herders are their owners.

Command and Control (C&C)

Botnet C&Cs are unique and will probably not change between botnets and variants. In addition to supporting an operating, efficient botnet the botnet C&C is essential. The C&Cs are also believed to be the weakest link in the operational dimension of botnets-if we manage to disrupt an active C&C or simply cause communication disruption-botmasters cannot connect too many bots or initiate large, coordinated attacks. In order to combat botnets, therefore, it is important to understand the C&C function in botnets. This is how C&C operates a C&C server. Usually, an IRC server is created by Botmaster. If a host is infected by a bot virus, it will return to a server in C&C to wait on command of the botmaster. The bot joins a specific IRC channel in a typical IRC botnet to read messages from its master.

Rallying Mechanisms

The rallying mechanisms for botnets are another feature studied. Mechanisms for rallying botnets to find and rally new bots under their botmasters are crucial. Following are discussed the most commonly used rallying mechanisms.

Hard-Coded IP Address

This is the most common procedure used to rally new bots: A bot has C&C server IP addresses that are hard-coded in its database. If the bot initially infects a computer, the IP address of the hardcoded server contained within the binary code can be used to connect back to the C&C server.

Dynamic DNS Domain Name

Hard-coded domain names are frequently given by dynamic DNS providers in the bots today. The benefit of dynamic DNS is to allow botmasters to easily resume control by creating a new C&C server and by updating the IP address in the corresponded dynamic DNS input if a C&C server is shut down by authorities. The bots will make DNS queries and be sent back to the new C&C server when connections to the old C&C server fail.

Distributed DNS Service

Many of the newest botnet breeds operate in locations outside the reach of the law enforcement authorities their own distributed DNS service. Bots include the DNS server's addresses and communicate with them to solve the C&C server's IP addresses. In order to avoid detection by security devices on gateways, these services are often used at large port numbers.

Communication Protocols

The communication protocols used in botnets are among the main botnet characteristics. In this respect, as with many other software tools that rely on a network to communicate, bots communicate in certain well-defined network protocols with each other and their botmasters. Botnets generally do not create new communication network protocols. They use existing communication protocols that are implemented by software tools that are publicly available.

DISCUSSION AND OPEN CHALLENGE

The standard botnet is made up of computers that have been remotely accessed without knowledge of the owner and set up to forward transmissions to other computers on the Internet. The IoT is generally consisted of not only dedicated computers but also mechanical sensors, automobiles, industrial and household appliances, cardiac implant monitors and various other devices that are equipped by IP addresses and can also transmit data over a network. In the IoT context, these are known as things. Generally, the infected end-hosts (called bots) network is defined by the botnets, and these networks are actually controlled by a human being which is called Botmaster. Susceptible models are recruited by botnets using strategies that are employed by other malware groups.

Botnets have turned out to be a worldwide phenomenon as well as the botmaster is responsible for recording a huge number of insecure hosts that are present in domains throughout the world. There are many issues which encircle the analysis of botnets as well as detection of a botnet. The primary issues regarding botnet detection over a broad scale are as follows:

Among the key elements in finally identifying the intensity of botnet, risks are assessing the impacted botnet span. Pre-existing detection techniques typically do not have precision in computing the dimensions of botnets, and also the figures produced are appropriate only for a small range.

The applicability of assured detection, as well as mitigation techniques, is restricted through particular conflicts involving the laws that provide secure IT services operation as well as some data protection laws (Plohmann, Gerhard-Padilla & Leder, 2011). Researchers face difficulty in evaluating the outcomes of theirs with earlier published benchmarks, as the datasets to a complete level are not readily available for the researcher group. It is tough to get actual traces, whereas scientists need contents for analyzing the functionality of the methods of theirs on small data traces sets that is a difficult job since heterogeneity (differences in hardware, software, architectural design, etc.) on the web is not clearly identified for many datasets. Another threat that is becoming extremely terrifying in this particular area may be the botnet phenomenon in devices that are mobile and the detection of its that is caused due to the increasing expansion of Internet use and computing proficiencies (e.g., GPRS, 3G, and Wi-Fi) for mobile devices like hand-held devices and smartphones. Further, there are many restrictions in botnet detection mechanism that are caused by various factors namely; (i) private IP addresses (ii) tracking other mobile devices (iii) SMS messages (iv) GPS data (v) saturated phone service (vi) limited bandwidth (vii) limited battery power.

When it is decided to use a botnet with hundreds or perhaps thousands of products, most with their very own unique IP addresses, the hacker causes it to be nearly impossible to quit the attack or even differentiate genuine owners from a bunch of fake ones. Today, botnets are not brand new. Since as earlier as 2000, hackers have already been by using botnets by increasing entry to unsecured products (usually computer systems then) to be able to produce the DDoS attacks. Though the Internet of Things makes the issue significantly more terrible. The market place was flooded with affordable products - webcams, baby monitors, thermostats, moreover, of course, even yoga mats as well as fry pans - that connects on the Internet, each one of that has the own IP address of its. Though the gadgets have minimal or maybe no integrated protection, and also whenever they do, subscribers frequently fail to actually consider the fundamental stage of setting a password for them. Which permits them to be very easy goals for online hackers desiring to develop as well as make use of a botnet.

An integral Internet infrastructure supplier, Dyn, was partly offline with a botnet of approximately 100,000 unsecured IoT devices in 2016. This led to a short period of departure from the Internet for many high profile and traffic websites. This botnet was made with Mirai malware which automates the co-opting of these unsecured devices— and it is available to the public. In other words, it was not a genius hacker who wrote new and innovative code, but someone who puts what is existing in new ways. Such DDoS attacks are not the only way hackers can use botnets. They can be used for clicking fraud, avoiding spam filters, speeding up password guessing, anything else, which would require a huge network of computers working together. They can be used to perpetrate fraudulent clicks. It is actually an open secret for criminal organizations to rent time on a botnet for any task they want.

The best solution would be to make sure all IoT devices work with safe software, but the probability is slim. Most IoT devices are not security-constructed, and no way to add additional security is patched. Moreover, millions of devices are already in use, produced and sold. The problem of botnets is also likely to grow since the use and fabrication of IoT devices is expected to exponentially increase over the next few years. Moreover, the security measures we have against the attackers will soon be overwritten and outmoded, or at least somewhat effective.

CONCLUSION AND FUTURE WORK

As in 2007, the first Botnet workshop was organized and after that various researchers proposed the different Botnet detection techniques and depending on some of these techniques some systems were implemented with actual bot detection methods. One of the most difficult issues is the Botnet detection. Therefore, this particular paper described a total Botnet detection methods survey. Further, Botnet detection strategies are classified in 2 primary types: establishing honeynets as well as Intrusion Detection System (IDS), and also other detection techniques in particular category are discussed.

The future directions hope for the innovation of new technologies for IoT because if in the coming years there is similar development in technology then it is obvious that the IoT will not be able to provide the same services in terms of addressability, scalability, concurrency, interoperability, and flexibility. Because of such issues the botnets may also become more prominent in such networks and may harm users. So there will be a need for some techniques that will help in overcoming these issues.

REFERENCES

Akiyama, M., Kawamoto, T., Shimamura, M., Yokoyama, T., Kadobayashi, Y., & Yamaguchi, S. (2007). A proposal of metrics for botnet detection based on its cooperative behaviour. *Applications and the Internet Workshops, 2007. SAINT Workshops in 2007. International Symposium on*, 82–82.

Bailey, M., Cooke, E., Jahanian, F., Xu, Y., & Karir, M. (2009). *A survey of botnet technology and defenses*. IEEE Cybersecurity Applications & Technology Conf. for Homeland Security. doi:10.1109/CATCH.2009.40

Bailey, M., Cooke, E., Jahanian, F., Xu, Y., & Karir, M. (2009). A survey of botnet technology and defenses. In *Proceedings of the 2009 Cybersecurity Applications & Technology Conference for Homeland Security*. Washington, DC: IEEE Computer Society. 10.1109/CATCH.2009.40

Barford, P., & Yagneswaran, V. (2006). An Inside Look at Botnets. In *Special Workshop on Malware Detection, Advances in Information Security*. Springer.

Binkley, J., & Singh, S. (2006). An algorithm for anomaly-based botnet detection. *Proceedings of USENIX Steps to Reducing Unwanted Traffic on the Internet Workshop (SRUTI)*, 43–48.

Binkley, J. R., & Singh, S. (2006). An algorithm for anomaly based botnet detection. *Proc. USENIX Steps to Reducing Unwanted Traffic on the Internet Workshop*, 43-48.

Cai, T., & Zou, F. (2012). Detecting HTTP botnet with clustering network traffic. *IEEE 8th Int. Conf. on Wireless Communications, Networking and Mobile Computing*, 1-7. 10.1109/WiCOM.2012.6478491

Chang, S., & Daniels, T. E. (2009). P2P botnet detection using behavior clustering & statistical tests. *Proc. 2nd ACM Workshop on Security and Artificial Intelligence*, 23-30. doi:10.1145/1654988.1654996

Choo, K. K. R. (2007). *Zombies and Botnets. Trends and issues in crime and criminal justice, no.333*. Canberra: Australian Institute of Criminology.

Coskun, B., Dietrich, S., & Memon, N. (2010). Friends of an enemy: identifying local members of peer-to-peer botnets using mutual contacts. *Proc. 26th Annual Computer Security Applications Conf.*, 131-140. 10.1145/1920261.1920283

Cremonini, M., & Riccardi, M. (2009). The Dorothy project: an open botnet analysis framework for automatic tracking and activity visualization. *IEEE European Conf. on Computer Network Defense*, 52-54. 10.1109/EC2ND.2009.15

Dagon, D., Gu, G., Lee, C. P., & Lee, W. (2007). A Taxonomy of Botnet Structures. *Proc. 23rd Annual Computer Security Applications Conference (ACSAC 2007)*, 325-339.

Dagon, D., Gu, G., Lee, C. P., & Lee, W. (2007). A taxonomy of botnet structures. *IEEE 23rd Annual Computer Security Applications Conf.*, 325-339. 10.1109/ACSAC.2007.44

Engrish, K. (2017). *Turning internet of things (not) into the internet of vulnerabilities (Nov): It botnets.* Retrieved from: https://arxiv.org/pdf/1702.03681.pdf

Ezhilarasi, M., & Krishnaveni, V. (2018). *A Survey on Wireless Sensor Network: Energy and Lifetime Perspective* (Vol. 14). Taga Journal of Graphic Technology.

Ezhilarasi, M., & Krishnaveni, V. (2019). An evolutionary multipath energy-efficient routing protocol (EMEER) for network lifetime enhancement in wireless sensor networks. *Soft Computing*, 1–11. doi:10.100700500-019-03928-1

Feily, M., Shahrestani, A., & Ramadass, S. (2009). A survey of the botnet and botnet detection. *3rd Int. Conf. on Emerging Security Information, Systems, and Technologies*, 268-273. 10.1109/SECUR-WARE.2009.48

Freiling, F., Holz, T., & Wicherski, G. (2005). Botnet Tracking: Exploring a Root-cause Methodology to Prevent Denial of Service Attacks. *Proceedings of 10th European Symposium on Research in Computer Security (ESORICS'05)*. 10.1007/11555827_19

Ge, L., Liu, H., & Zhang, D. (2012). On effective sampling techniques for host-based Intrusion detection in MANET. *IEEE Military Communications Conf.*, 1-6. 10.1109/MILCOM.2012.6415605

Goebel, J., & Holz, T. (2007). Rishi: identify contaminated bot hosts by IRC nickname evaluation. *Proc. 1st Conf. on 1st Workshop on Hot Topics in Understanding Botnets*, 1-12.

Gu, G., Porras, P., Yegneswaran, V., Fong, M., & Lee, W. (2007). BotHunter: Detecting malware infection through ids-driven dialog correlation. *Proceedings of the 16th USENIX Security Symposium*, 167–182.

Gu, G., Porras, P., Yegneswaran, V., Fong, M., & Lee, W. (2007). BotHunter: Detecting Malware Infection through ids-driven dialog correlation. *Proceedings of the 16th USENIX Security Symposium (Security'07)*.

Jian, G., Zheng, K., Yang, Y., & Niu, X. (2012). An evaluation model of botnet based on peer to peer. *IEEE 4th Int. Conf. on Computational Intelligence and Communication Networks*, 925-929. 10.1109/CICN.2012.46

Karim, A., Bin Salleh, R., Shiraz, M., Shah, S. A. A., Awan, I., & Anuar, N. B. (2014). Botnet detection techniques: Review, future trends, and issues. *Journal of Zhejiang University Science C*, *15*(11), 943–983. doi:10.1631/jzus.C1300242

Kranenburg, R.V. (2008). The Internet of Things: A Critique of Ambient Technology and the All-Seeing Network of RFID, Institute of Network Cultures. ITU work on Internet of things, 2015. *ICTP Workshop.*

Kugisaki, Y., Kasahara, Y., Hori, Y., & Sarkurai, K. (2007). Bot detection based on traffic analysis. *IEEE Int. Conf. on Intelligent Pervasive Computing*, 303-306.

Li, C., Jiang, W., & Zou, X. (2009). Botnet: Survey and case study. *4th International Conference on Innovative Computing, Information and Control.*

Liu, L., Chen, S., Yan, G., & Zhang, Z. (2008) BotTracer: execution based bot-like malware detection. *International Conference on Information Security*, 97-113. 10.1007/978-3-540-85886-7_7

Nagarajan, M., & Karthikeyan, S. (2012) *A New Approach to Increase the Life Time and Efficiency of Wireless Sensor Network.* IEEE. doi:10.1109/ICPRIME.2012.6208349

Plohmann, D., Gerhard-Padilla, E., & Leder, F. (2011). *Botnets: Detection, Measurement, Disinfection & Defence.* ENISA.

Provos, N. (2004). A virtual honeypot framework. *USENIX Security Symp.*

Rajab, M., Zarfoss, J., Monrose, F., & Terzis, A. (2006). *A multifaceted approach to understanding the botnet phenomenon.* Retrieved October 31, 2009, from http://www.imconf.net/imc- 2006/papers/ p4-rajab.pdf

Rajab, M., Zarfoss, J., Monrose, F., & Terzis, A. (2007). My botnet is bigger than yours (maybe, better than yours): Why size estimates remain challenging. *USENIX Workshop on Hot Topics in Understanding Botnet.*

Rajab, M. A., Zarfoss, J., Monrose, F., & Terzis, A. (2007). My Botnet is Bigger than Yours (Maybe, Better than Yours): why size estimates remain challenging. *First Workshop on Hot Topics in Understanding Botnets (HotBots'07).*

Ray, P. P. (2018). A survey on the Internet of Things architectures. *Journal of King Saud University-Computer and Information Sciences*, *30*(3), 291–319. doi:10.1016/j.jksuci.2016.10.003

Roesch, M. (1999). Snort-lightweight intrusion detection for networks. *Proceedings of the 13th USENIX conference on System administration*, 229–238.

Sable, N. A., & Datar, D. S. (2013). A review-botnet detection and suppression in clouds. *Journal of Information Engineering and Applications*, *3*(12), 1–7.

Saha, B., & Gairola, A. (2005). *Botnet: An overview.* CERT-In White PaperCIWP-2005-05.

Schaffer, G. (2006). Worms and Viruses and Botnets, Oh My: Rational Responses to Emerging Internet Threats. *IEEE Security and Privacy*, *4*(3), 52–58. doi:10.1109/MSP.2006.83

Shanmughapriya, M., Sumathi, G., & Aarthi, K. C. (2018). Bot Net of Things – A Survey. *International Journal of Engineering and Computer Science*, *7*(5), 23926–23930.

Srivastava, L. (2006). Pervasive, ambient, ubiquitous: the magic of radio. *Proceedings of European Commission Conference From RFID to the Internet of Things*.

Stalmans, E., & Irwin, B. (2011). *A framework for DNS based detection and mitigation of malware infections on a network*. IEEE Information Security South Africa. doi:10.1109/ISSA.2011.6027531

Stevanovic, M., & Pedersen, J. (2014). An efficient flow-based botnet detection using supervised machine learning. *International Conference on Computing, Networking, and Communications (ICNC)*, 797 – 801. 10.1109/ICCNC.2014.6785439

Stinson, E., & Mitchell, J. C. (2007). Characterizing bots' remote control behavior. In *Detection of Intrusions and Malware, and Vulnerability Assessment* (pp. 89–108). Springer. doi:10.1007/978-3-540-73614-1_6

Stinson, E., & Mitchell, J. C. (2007). Characterizing bots' remote control behaviour. *Proceedings of the 4th GI International Conference on Detection of Intrusions and Malware, and Vulnerability Assessment (DMV A'07)*.

Tyagi, A. K., & Aghila, G. (2011). A wide-scale survey on a botnet. *International Journal of Computers and Applications*, *34*(9), 10–23.

Villamarin-Salomon, R., & Brustoloni, J. C. (2008). Identifying Botnets Using Anomaly Detection Techniques Applied to DNS Traffic. *Proc. 5th IEEE Consumer Communications and Networking Conference (CCNC2008)*, 476-481. 10.1109/ccnc08.2007.112

Wang, P., Sparks, S., & Zou, C. C. (2010). An advanced hybrid peer-to-peer botnet. *Proc. in Workshop on Hot Topics in Understanding Botnets*.

Whitmore, A., Agarwal, A., & Xu, L. D. (2015). The Internet of Things—A survey of topics and trends. *Information Systems Frontiers*, *17*(2), 261–274. doi:10.100710796-014-9489-2

Wurzinger, P., Bilge, L., Holz, T., Goebel, J., Kruegel, C., & Kirda, E. (2009). *Automatically generating models for botnet detection*. Computer Security ESORICS.

Zang, X., Tangpong, A., Kesidis, G., & Miller, D.J. (2011). *CSE Dept Technical Report on "Botnet Detection through Fine Flow Classification."* Report No. CSE11-001.

Zeidanloo, H. R., & Manaf, A. A. (2010). Botnet Detection by Monitoring Similar Communication Patterns. *International Journal of Computer Science and Information Security, 7*(3).

Zeidanloo, H.R., Manaf, A.B., Vahdani, P., Tabatabaei, F., & Zamani, M. (2010). Botnet Detection Based on Traffic Monitoring. *IEEE Transaction*.

This research was previously published in Security, Privacy, and Forensics Issues in Big Data edited by Ramesh C. Joshi and Brij B. Gupta; pages 304-316, copyright year 2020 by Information Science Reference (an imprint of IGI Global).

Chapter 8
Successful Computer Forensics Analysis on the Cyber Attack Botnet

Kavisankar Leelasankar
Hindustan Institute of Technology and Science, India

Chellappan C.
GKM College of Engineering and Technology, India

Sivasankar P.
National Institute of Technical Teachers Training and Research, India

ABSTRACT

The success of computer forensics lies in the complete analysis of the evidence that is available. This is done by not only analyzing the evidence which is available but also searching for new concrete evidence. The evidence is obtained through the logs of the data during the cyberattack. When performing analysis of the cyberattack especially the botnet attacks, there are many challenges. First and the foremost is that it hides the identity of the mastermind, the botmaster. It issues the command to be executed using its subordinate, the command and control (C&C). The traceback of C&C itself is a complex task. Secondly, it victimizes the innocent compromised device zombies. This chapter discusses the analysis done in both proactive and reactive ways to resolve these challenges. The chapter ends by discussing the analysis to find the real mastermind to protect the innocent compromised system and to protect the victim system/ organization affected by the botnet cyberattack.

INTRODUCTION

Successful prosecution of computer-based crime is dependent upon the investigation. The investigator should be asking all these questions like who, what, how and when a criminal event occurred. It depends upon how the evidence is examined. The general public will not understand or even know that they are

DOI: 10.4018/978-1-7998-5348-0.ch008

under some kind of cyber attack. Victim of these attacks is not only the large corporations but also the unaware public. The hackers come with the number of ways to bypass or intrude the network using the number of methods. First and foremost thing they do is that they hide their identity or they use the trusted source identity to intrude the network. They try to compromise the number of cyber devices, where these cyber devices become the compromised zombies. These compromised zombies cyber devices belong to the unaware public. The hackers use the internet which provides them the borderless environment. The internet, compromised zombies are used and they are brought into a network. This network is very powerful and it can be used to launch the intended attack on the intended victim.

Botnets are networks of robots or robot net. A software program bot obeys the instructions of command-and-control (C&C). They act as remotely located, a single coordinated central collection point of the bots. They would be taking over a remote machine (victim 1) and using that, attack another machine (victim 2). Botnets are compromised hosts under a common C&C (command and control) server. Their purpose is to produce Denial of Service attacks (DOSs), id theft, flood the user with spams, and many more.

A large number of the system is compromised using Active worms. These compromised systems are the bots or zombies. The botnet is formed by these large number bot or zombies when networked together with help of the C&C. The number of destruction done using botnet: (i) large-scale distributed voluntary advertisement through emails spam or malware. (ii) large scale sniffing of traffic which gives access to critical information that can be misused. (iii)The network components are destroyed by launching the massive DDoS attack.

Botnet when comparing with customary malware is more dangerous because of the C&C channel. It is one of the high-risk security threats. Where the malware used for fun is now turning to be malware used for financial benefit.

The detailed analysis and discussion are made on onetime request flooding using a Botnet are generally detected and defended against, using a number of schemes. The detection schemes provide the detection of three major components of Botnet architecture, namely, Bot, C&C, and Botmaster. These detection schemes are in two modes, active and passive. First, the passive detection of Bot is done by two major ways i.e. Correlation and Behavioral analysis.

There are various Botnet Detection Schemes; a few botnet detection schemes developed are Mining-based Detection, Signature-based Detection, and Anomaly-based detection techniques. Most importantly the detection scheme like Host-based detection is a detected scheme built on the host system. Some of the Host-based detection is a detected schemes are HoneyPots / Virtual HoneyPots, DNS- based detection techniques, Infiltration, Filtering, Packet Filtering, Remedial measure and Index Poisoning Attack.

For performing the forensic analysis the trace back to botmaster is required. Packet marking Techniques is used to Traceback of Botmaster, similarly Probabilistic Packet Marking Schemes is also used in Traceback of Botmaster, Other Schemes like Deterministic Packet Marking Schemes, and Probabilistic Packet Marking Schemes.

Even using all these techniques one of the most challenging tasks of the botnet network is that the identity of the botnet master is hidden, Traceback to command and control is also very difficult, since the attack is from the compromised zombies, these compromised zombies are the unaware public who get victimized by the crime they haven't done. A proper computer forensics investigation is required here. In the first instance, you will criminalize the compromised zombies. But when you criminalize you have to criminalize a huge number of compromised system that is legally impossible adding to that point they are totally unaware what is happening. It is the part of the security experts to build all the cyber devices with additional security features.

There is the number of methods that perform the forensic analysis of the cyber attack which has taken place. The scenario discussed here is the Distributed Denial of Service (DDoS) attack performed using the botnet network. Now when the forensics investigation happens the first step is to analyze the intensity of the attack. It needs to validate that the cyber crime has happened using the botnet. In case of botnet attack, it would have come from the number of compromised systems. The attack is traced back using the traceback mechanism. The honeypot installed in the compromised zombies operates like a computer forensics analyst provides a concrete evidence to find the real source of cyber attack (Shrivastava et al., 2010).

DDoS Attacks by Botnet

Botnets are networks of robots or robot net. A software program bot obeys the commands of command-and-control (C&C). The C&C is remotely located and they act as a single coordinated central collection point of the bots. They would be taking over a remote machine (victim 1) and using that, attack another machine (victim 2). Botnets are compromised hosts under a common C&C (command and control) server. Their purpose is to produce Denial of Service attacks (DOSs), id theft, flood the user with spams, and many more.

A large number of the system is compromised using Active worms. These compromised systems are the bots or zombies. The botnet is formed by these large number bot or zombies when networked together with help of the C&C. The number of destruction done using botnet: (i) Large-scale distributed voluntary advertisement through emails spam or malware. (ii) Large-scale sniffing of traffic which gives access to critical information that can be misused. (iii)The network components are destroyed by launching the massive DDoS attack.

Figure 1 represents the Botnet Architecture. Botnet when comparing with customary malware is more dangerous because of the C&C channel. It is one of the high-risk security threats. Where the malware used for fun is now turning to be malware used for financial benefit.

Figure 1. Botnet architecture

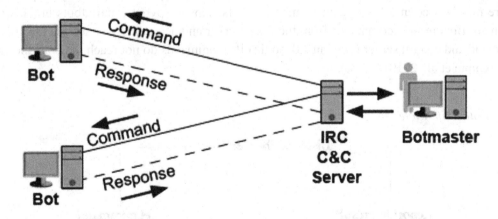

Botnet Life-Cycle

- **Initial Infection Phase:** In the initial phase vulnerabilities are exploited by scanning. This scanning is done on the entire targeted subnet. The scan is followed by infection of the target victim using the discovered vulnerabilities. For infection of the target, the number of exploitation methods is used.
- **Secondary Injection Phase:** Once the infection is done. The shell code is executed. This Shell code/ script using FTP, HTTP, or P2P from the particular location get the image of the actual binary. Target machine is installed with the bot program and it is made has "Zombie". Whenever the compromised zombie system is booted the bot application is started automatically.
- **Connection Phase:** Channel between Command-and-Control (C&C) is established using bot binary. By establishing the connection with C&C channel, the zombies are attached to attacking botnet group.
- **Malicious Command-and-Control (C&C):** The C&C channel are used by the Botmaster to broadcast the commands to the bot army. Botmaster commands are followed by the compromised zombies.
- **Update and Maintenance:** The update is done mainly by C&C to avoid detection techniques and maintain the botnet network. It is also used to append new functionality, the feature to the bot.

Figures 2 and 3 represent the life cycle of the botnet.

There are various botnet taxonomies given by Hachem et al. (2011). Botnets are classified, based upon their structure, as centralized and decentralized bots; they are the based on their language as compilers (C, C++) and as interpreted (Perl, PHP, JavaScript), and lastly they are also classified based on their features as attacks (DDOS, Exploit), server (HTTP, FTP, RLOGIN) and as proxy (socks4, socks5, HTTP). Botnets have so many taxonomies because bots are multifaceted and complex beasts. Bots in malware taxonomy have worm characteristics and spyware components. Bots spread along the network through emails as Trojans, or attach mentors installed by explicit tools, as link spams, websites, or by even by explicit attacks on hosts. We have different types of bots because of their pride, purpose, different languages and their actions on different platforms. The Bot family is very vast; they are pBot, Kaiten which are mostly used in a Linux environment, agobots, sdbots, spybots, and gtbots in the windows environment. Bots receive commands from the C&C server and accordingly attack the target hosts. If the command and control server is corrupted, so that the commands do not reach the bots, they remain dormant (Gupta et al., 2010).

Figure 2. Botnet life-cycle

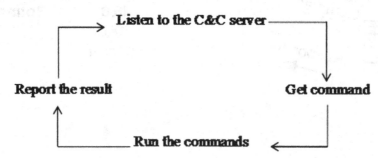

Figure 3. Detailed Botnet life cycle

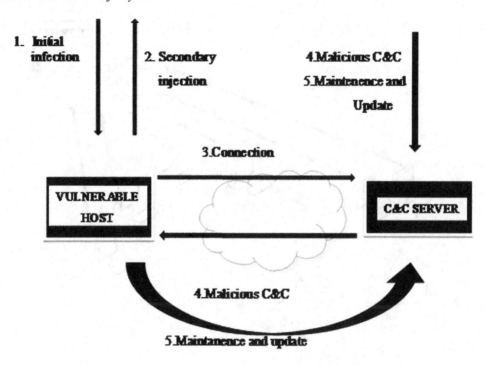

Figure 4 shows the example scenario of DDoS attack generation using Botnet.

ONE TIME REQUEST FLOODING (BOTNET) DDOS ATTACK DETECTION

Distributed Denial-of-Service (DDoS) attacks are generated by large number of the request at one instance. It consumes large volume of server resources using malicious traffic or utilizing the large-scale botnet to mimic the average request rate of the normal users and produce the low rate attack flows. These aspects contribute to the factors in difficult in identifying the botnet. Now, in order to concentrate more on the basic methodologies used in the proposed approach, we shall discuss the existing models to detect the botnets and their respective C&Cs.

Onetime request flooding using a Botnet is generally detected and defended against, using a number of schemes as given in Figure 5. The detection schemes provide the detection of three major components of Botnet architecture, namely, Bot, C&C, and Botmaster. These detection schemes are in two modes, active and passive. First, the passive detection of Bot is done by two major ways i.e. correlation and Behavioral analysis.

Botnet Detection Schemes

A Few botnet detection schemes developed are discussed below.

Figure 4. DDoS attack generation using Botnet

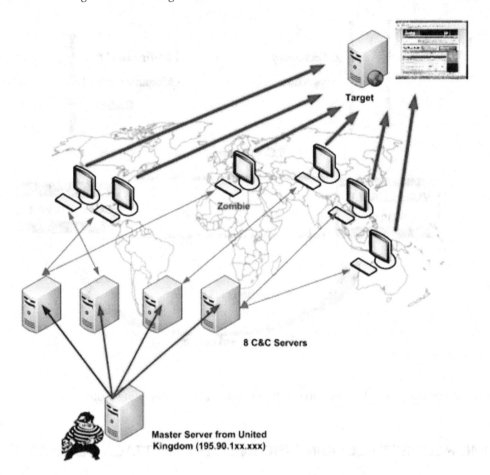

- **Anomaly-Based Detection Techniques:** Anomaly detection on network traffic based on several network traffic anomalies that could point out the existence of malicious bots in the network is huge volumes of traffic, towering network latency, unusual system behavior and unusual ports used with sudden increase in traffic. Gu et al. (2007) BotHunter uses dialog trace of Intrusion Detection System in that network and a novel system, botfinder, by Tegeler et al. (2012) analyses bot's network traffic using the properties of high-level to detect compromised zombie machines. It works based on machine learning so it has two phases, first phase is training and second phase is detection. The first training phase requires a trace file to be maintained; hence, this needs a higher space complexity. The main drawback is that it needs a history to be maintained.

Pratik Narang et al. (2013) discussed algorithms of feature selection like Correlation-based feature selection; Consistency based subset evaluation, and Principal component analysis using Machine learning techniques. The merit is that problem of detecting unknown botnets is solved by anomaly detection techniques. The drawback is that if no anomaly is found it cannot detect bot. It cannot detect encrypted bot and has no real-time detection.

Figure 5. One time request flooding Botnet taxonomy

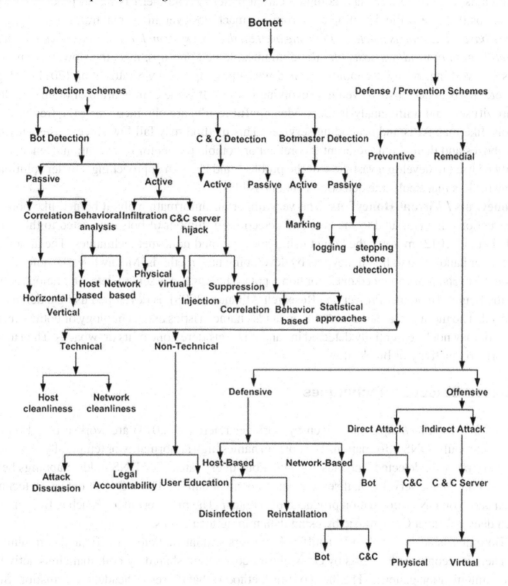

- **Signature-Based Detection:** Intrusion detection systems (IDS) find signs of intrusion. This is done by the real-time log of network traffic Snort (2009) an open source intrusion detection system (IDS) is the best example. The spatial-temporal behavioral similarity is used in BotSniffer Gu et al. (2008a) to identify botnets. The merit is that detection of known botnets is done by using signature-based detection techniques. There are low false positives as long as attacks are clearly defined in advance. The drawback is that unknown bots cannot be detected using this method. Another drawback is that the Antisignature techniques make the malware evade these techniques.
- *Mining-Based detection is* based on characteristics of the flow, like pushed packets, bytes per packet, TCP flags, bits per second, and duration. It is done to classify network flows using Bayesian net algorithms, Naive Bayes, and decision trees. The BotMiner Gu et al. (2008b) is independent of both structure and protocol. The flows in the BotMiner are classified into groups based on alike

malicious activity patterns and communication patterns. The merit is that it produces very low false positive rate while detecting compromised machines even in normal traffic.

- *Host-based detection is a detected scheme built on the host system. It is done based on the symptom modification of windows hosts file,* Random unexplained pop-ups, machine slowness, and antivirus not working. A new technology, called mashups proposed by Santos et al. (2011), integrates several tools to detect such even new evolving botnets. It is the combination of online sandboxes, anti-viruses, and traffic analysis tools. Meaningful results are obtained using the free web-based tools, like map APIs and geocoding services. This method may fall low since it uses only online toolboxes and there are no relevant theoretical or notable proofs for its execution. Hence, this can only be used to develop a vast view of the problem and helps in approaching a better solution. The drawback is that Real-time detection is not possible.

- **HoneyPots / Virtual HoneyPots:** The very important information about botnet, like botmasters instructions that is issued to the bots and detection of number of bots connected to the network. Choi et al. (2012) monitor the botnet using honeypot and honeynet techniques. The attackers, on the other hand, tried to find honeypots by developing new methods. Meanwhile, the defenders provide the even more enhanced mask for honeypots. The Spy bot is sent to detect malicious activities in the botnet. Honeynet Project and Research Alliance (2008), is developed using a defender employed. The merit is that honeynets understands characteristics and technology of botnet. Infection may or may not be essentially detected in sand it is considered one of its drawbacks. The Honeypot resorts to inactivity or breaks down.

DNS-Based Detection Techniques

DNS-based detection techniques are given by Springer reference (2014) are worked based on botnet generating particular DNS information. The domain names high abnormality or temporally concentrated DDNS query rates are detected, and classify analogous query rates. The DNS holds mappings between IP addresses and name servers, mail servers, and canonical names. These Botnet detection techniques identified based on DNS information produced by a botnet. The most recent approach is Botminer. This approach detects Botnet C&C traffic by using data mining techniques.

The Botminer is advanced than Botsniffer. It clusters similar malicious traffic and communication traffic. Then, it recognizes the hosts by cross-cluster correlation shared by both malicious activity and similar communication patterns. The merit of this method is that it uses IP headers information. So, that it can even find the botnets with encrypted channels. The drawback is that only HTTP and IRC traffics are analyzed. Techniques have the same weakness that when the bogus DNS queries are used it could be easily avoided. Misclassification of legitimate or well-known domains occurs while DNS with short time-to-live (TTL) is encountered and it, in turn, increases the false positives.

Infiltration

Infiltration is done by penetration testing the bot system. The probes are made to C&C and other bots by changing its identity to an actual bot. The replay attack is used by Nappa et al. (2010) on a Skype-based botnet. Crafted bogus messages are issued by the defenders to gain information about the bots.

Timing Analysis

Using Probabilistic Context-Free Grammars by Chen and Richard (2012) automated network processes generally carry timing signatures. The fastflux creates moving targets and resilient to detection. The merit is that it improves the True Positive rate. The demerit is that decreases the False Positive rate, which can be further reduced. If the timing signatures are not considered, the system performance degrades.

Filtering

Saliva (2008) describes in RFC 2827 the filtering techniques is the most basic network level defense. An ISP is used in ingress filter blocks based on IP sources not belong to that end site. It works very effectively on spoofed IP packet along with SYN flooding.

Packet Filtering

Kolias et al. (2011) discusses about Packet Score filtering uses some attributes in the TCP and IP headers, and the Bayes Theorem to score packets. This method is not suitable for handling large amounts of attack traffic. Based on a set of rules, the firewall makes a decision whether to accept or drop the packet. The drawback is that ingress filtering provides low security due to two reasons; it is not universally deployed and wholly ineffective against the policies employed by ISPs.

HTTP Flooding Attack

In case of HTTP flooding attack, The HTTP request to the server is of many types the two main types are GET and POST. GET normally used for the static pages and data. The POST is used with forms. In most of the cases GET is used by the attackers since it is easier for the attackers to execute. Whereas in the case of POST it consumes relatively lot of resources it performs relatively complex process. When the attacker wants to be more successful they try to immerse the entire target with the method that allocates a lot of resources. It basically spams the server with requests, like refreshing a page. With enough people participating in the DDoS attack, the server might not be able to handle all the requests simultaneously, and hence, crashes. Choi et al. (2012) detected the DDoS attack based on Time Slot (TS) and Monitoring Period (MP). It is observed more HTTP requests in MP and TS during attack than normal traffic. The drawback is that parameters should be analyzed for accurate detection.

One of the Remedial Measure is given below:

- Index Poisoning Attack
  Wang et al. (2010) proposed copyright content protection with help of Index poisoning attack. In a P2P network, peers try to get a file search for the target file while the target file is poisoned with the bogus record is redirected and return the bogus result in a way that the bogus result is downloaded. It is used to defend the P2P botnet where the communication between zombies and botmaster in the P2P protocol employs pull-based C&C communication mechanism the file index is used.

The detection schemes discussed in the above is helpful in the forensic analysis of the botnet attack. The above schemes try to analyze the behavior of the botnet network especially the compromised zombie devices.

Flow-Based Techniques

There are a number of techniques used for DoS detection, using only the flow information. A sketches data structure is used to collect the aggregate of the flow measures. This approach was proposed by Gao et al. (2006). However, they lack the ability to differentiate between different types of attacks. Another approach proposed by Munz et al. (2007), is TOPAS (Traffic flow and Packet Analysis System). However, it runs based on the requirements given by the network administrator. Banks et al. (2007) provided a review of particle swarm optimization, a natural computing technique. The proposed system uses an ACO technique to traceback the victim of the DoS/DDoS attack to the zombie system. This is done by using the incoming flow information of the routers. Based on the flow and pheromone intensity, the probability is calculated and the path with high probability is taken by the ants.

The detection schemes discussed in the above is helpful in the forensic analysis of the botnet attack. The above schemes try to analyze the traffic behavior of the botnet network especially to traceback to the origin of the attack. The scheme helps in finding out the attack source with the path traveled frequently. It may lead to traceback of two sources first is compromised zombies and the command and control.

Traceback of Botmaster

An Ant algorithm by Kolias et al. (2011) is used for resource scheduling and vehicle routing associated with discrete optimization problem. The Ant colony algorithm was biologically inspired by ants and works based on how the natural ants work. In case of the botnet, the Ant colony algorithm has always been successful in finding the path of attack launch of DOS, though it lagged in finding the C&Cs and tracing back their IP address. The execution of the ant colony algorithm does not even require the complete information about the routers and their route. Swarm intelligence has many different algorithms in it, but among them, the ACO overcomes others with a high performance in source detection.

Figure 6, gives us an overview of the different existing flow based, packet marking, and hybrid IP traceback techniques available.

- Packet Marking Techniques
  Probabilistic Packet Marking (PPM) is a scheme proposed by Savage et al. (2000) packets are marked by the router. The spoofing of IP address is detected, even though spoofed IP address is used the full path is reconstructed. Similarly, Deterministic Packet Marking was proposed by Belenky and Ansari (2003a, 2003b) where each packet entering a router is marked. The incoming packets are marked with the address information of the interface in the packets identification field and the reserved flag bit is used for marking which part of the address the ID field contains. The received information from this is the address of the ingress routers. Deterministic Packet Marking engages the marking of each and every packet entering the network, which leads to computation delay. The Probabilistic packet marking scheme is similar to this scheme; only the marking is not done based on probability. Both the schemes require a large number of incoming packets for path reconstruction.

Figure 6. IP traceback taxonomy

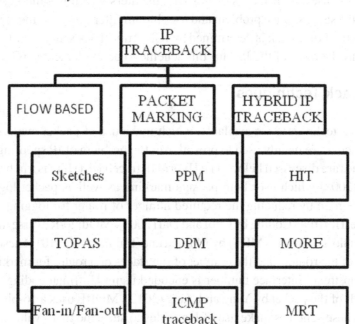

- Probabilistic Packet Marking Schemes
  It was developed by the Computer Security Institute and Federal Bureau of Investigation (1999). Goodrich (2008) proposed Probabilistic packet marking for large-scale IP traceback. The drawback is that high computational work is required for the path reconstruction process, in particular when there is the number of sources and also creates high false positives the possible rebuilt path branches are actually becoming useless according to Dean et al. (2001).

- Other Probabilistic Packet Marking Schemes
  The PPM method proposed by Song and Perrig (2001), and Govindan and Tangmunarunkit (2000) reduce the overhead of reconstruction. Adler et al. (1996) examined on the middle ground between the mark bits required in the IP header and the number of packets required to reconstruct the paths. On the other hand, Savage et al. (2000) used edge sampling PPM scheme, which is known as FMS. Gong and Sarac (2009), Yaar et al. (2005), Al-Duwari and Govindarasu (2006), Lee et al. (2004), and Li et al. (2004) are the other probabilistic packet marking schemes.

- Deterministic Packet Marking Schemes
  Belenky and Ansari (2003a) proposed Deterministic Packet Marking (DPM). DPM as by Howard (1998), and Kam and Simpson (1999). Recently, in "A Formal Framework and Evaluation Method for Network Denial of Service," by Meadows, (1999) false positive rates are reduced by marking fields with adding redundant information. The drawback is that repeated spoofing with the different value of the source address may bypass the successful mitigation of DPM. Another efficient scheme named TOPO was proposed by Zhang et al. (2006). Source Path Isolation Engine (SPIE) by Ehrenkranz and Li (2009) is an IP traceback scheme which stores the packet digests alone and

not the packets themselves. It makes use of Bloom filters which has the false positive problem. TOPO also has the same storage problem and uses bloom filters with has the same the false positive problem. Full path of the attack is determined by ICMP traceback scheme by Bellovin et al. (2003). It requires the involvement of the ISP for this scheme to be implemented (Gong & Sarac, 2008).

Hybrid IP Traceback Techniques

Many hybrid traceback techniques are available, which make use of packet marking as well as packet logging. These techniques are mainly used to prevail over the problem of IP spoofing. Few of the hybrid IP traceback techniques are discussed below. The Hybrid IP traceback (HIT) is a hybrid scheme proposed by Gong and Sarac (2008) which uses both packets marking as well as packet logging. Packet marking reduces logging burden by reducing the required number of router for logging. A few more hybrid schemes proposed are, Huffman Coding by Choi and Dai (2004), MOdulo/REverse modulo (MORE) and Modulo/Reverse modulo Technique (MRT) by Malliga and Tamilarasi (2010). These schemes make use of interface numbers of the routers and the number of interfaces of a router for marking. In the Huffman coding scheme, the upstream interface number is encoded using Huffman coding, and this is inserted into the marking fields of the packet by Yang and Yang (2012). MORE uses a 16-bit field and MRT uses a 32-marking field. These schemes make use of log tables to store the mark value in the routers, which demands a high storage space. It also requires doing an exhaustive search on the log tables during path reconstruction. During path reconstruction it encounters inefficient search and false positive problem due to big size of the log table and digest in a log table might have a collision.

Since the Distributed Denial of service (DDoS) attacks are on the increase, we propose an efficient approach to detect and defend the botnet from performing DDoS attacks. The solutions to the problem statement can detect, mitigate and filter the DDoS attacks.

The detection scheme discussed in the above scheme is helpful in the forensic analysis of the botnet attack (Shrivastava, 2017). The above schemes try to analyze the traffic behavior of the botnet network especially to traceback to the source of the attack. The scheme helps in finding out the attack origin with help of the marking scheme. It is helpful in finding the ultimate mastermind the botmaster.

Table 1 provides the performance comparison of the existing one Time Request Flooding (BOTNET) detection schemes with various parameters.

Table 1. Performance comparison of the existing detection one Time Request Flooding (BOTNET) detection schemes

Schemes		Bot Miner (2008)	Bot Hunter (2008)	Bot Sniffer (2008)	Heuristic (2012)	Feature (2013)	Timing Based (2013)
Deployment		Not universally Deployed	Easily Deployed	Easily Deployed	Easily Deployed	Router level deployment	Not universally Deployed
Detection rate		74.7%	69.81%	70.23%	80% to 95%	98%	96.7%
False alarm rate		23%	29%	29%	1%	2%	1.6%
Type of attack	Multiple Flooding		√	√	√	√	
	Spoofed Flooding	√	√	√			
	One Time Request Flooding		√	√			

From the detailed analysis of the various detection and defense schemes which are discussed above gives us the clear picture that they do not collect all the evidence required for the complete analysis of the various components of the botnet network. Either the compromised zombies or command and control are detected. The detection of the botmaster is even more difficult. It requires special marking scheme to traceback to the botmaster. This kind of special marking scheme is hard to be implemented in ever network. But there is a need for some pro-active measure to be taken to find the real origin of the attack.

The state-of-art works like Alieyan et al. (2017) discusses the botnet hidden identities using the DNS services and the botnet detection techniques depend on DNS traffic analysis. Al et al. (2016) discuss the about detection of the botnet using machine-learning models. Garg et al. (2017) filters and classifies on data received by Botflex and detects botnet based on this method.

The two important challenges in the trackback of cyber attack botnet are

- The attack is the number of compromised zombies systems they tend to be legitimate.
- The difference between the request from the compromised zombies and the legitimate device is very difficult to identify.
- Since there is the number of compromised zombies system it is difficult to defend by adding the entire compromised zombie's list to the firewall.

The steps taken to identify the Origin of the botnet botmaster (Shrivastava, 2016).

- The cyber forensic analysis is to be done on the behavior of compromised zombies and the comparison is made with the existing behavior of the compromised zombies.
- With the comparison, concrete evidence is taken and the compromised zombies are identified.
- The cyber forensic analysis is to be done on the network traffic and based on the frequent path traversed the command and control are identified.
- The comparisons are made with the existing identified command and control the network traffic behavior and the host behavior of command and control.
- With the comparison, concrete evidence is taken and the real command and control are identified.
- The cyber forensic analysis is to be done based on the special marking scheme applied it is used to uncover the actual origin of the attack.
- The special marking scheme provides us the concrete evidence to identify the real originator of the attack.
- To identify botmaster (origin of the attack) it is necessary to follow these stepwise evidence gathering.
- First the compromised zombies, then the command and control, and then the big fish botmaster.

The ultimate target of the forensics expects is to find the real origin of the attack the mastermind the botmaster. The traceback of the compromised zombies and the command and control is essential. The successful computer forensics analysis on the cyber attack botnet can be fulfilled only when the traceback of the real origin of the attack botmaster is found successful. Since if the identity of the real botmaster is revealed then the attack from that origin can be mitigated easily. It can be used for the future to defend against these kinds of attacks by the cybersecurity professionals. It is helpful in making the entire botnet network becomes inactive.

CONCLUSION

One of the most challenging tasks of the botnet network forensics analysis is that the identity of the botnet hidden master, Traceback to command and control is also very difficult, since the attack is from the compromised zombies, these compromised zombies are the unaware public who get victimized for the crime they haven't done. A proper computer forensics investigation is required here to provide the concrete evidence. This chapter discussed the existing works related to botnet attack and the forensics method to discover the real source of the attack. It not only finds evidence that the botnet attack has taken place. It also finds the evidence that the botnet attack has taken place especially using compromised zombies. It also collects the evidence to justify that the compromised zombies are not the real source of attack. It identifies and collects the evidence that, the Command and Control (C&C) work under the control of botmaster. Forensic analysis does not stop with this it also find evidence to identify the real source of the attack the botmaster, with help of special marking scheme the mastermind botmaster is identified. The real origin of the attack is identified with concrete evidence then the effect of the botnet could be mitigated very easily.

REFERENCES

Al-Jarrah, O. Y., Alhussein, O., Yoo, P. D., Muhaidat, S., Taha, K., & Kim, K. (2016). Data randomization and cluster-based partitioning for botnet intrusion detection. *IEEE Transactions on Cybernetics*, *46*(8), 1796–1806. doi:10.1109/TCYB.2015.2490802 PMID:26540724

Alieyan, K., ALmomani, A., Manasrah, A., & Kadhum, M. M. (2017). A survey of botnet detection based on DNS. *Neural Computing & Applications*, *28*(7), 1541–1558. doi:10.100700521-015-2128-0

Banks, A., Vincent, J., & Anyakoha, C. (2007). A review of particle swarm optimization. Part I: Background and development. *Natural Computing*, *6*(4), 467–484. doi:10.100711047-007-9049-5

Belenky, A., & Ansari, N. (2003a). IP traceback with deterministic packet marking. *IEEE Communications Letters*, *7*(4), 162–164. doi:10.1109/LCOMM.2003.811200

Belenky, A., & Ansari, N. (2003b). On IP traceback. *IEEE Communications Magazine*, *41*(7), 142–153. doi:10.1109/MCOM.2003.1215651

Bellovin, S. M., Leech, M., & Taylor, T. (2003). *ICMP traceback messages*. Marina del Ray, CA: Internet Engineering Task Force; doi:10.7916/D8FF406R

Choi, K. H., & Dai, H. K. (2004, May). A marking scheme using Huffman codes for IP traceback. In *Parallel Architectures, Algorithms and Networks, 2004. Proceedings. 7th International Symposium on* (pp. 421-428). IEEE. 10.1109/ISPAN.2004.1300516

Choi, Y. S., Kim, I. K., Oh, J. T., & Jang, J. S. (2012). Aigg threshold based http get flooding attack detection. *Information Security Applications*, 270-284.

Dos Santos, C. R. P., Bezerra, R. S., Ceron, J. M., Granville, L. Z., & Tarouco, L. M. (2011, October). Identifying botnet communications using a mashup-based approach. In *Network Operations and Management Symposium (LANOMS), 2011 7th Latin American* (pp. 1-6). IEEE. 10.1109/LANOMS.2011.6102273

Ehrenkranz, T., & Li, J. (2009). On the state of IP spoofing defense. *ACM Transactions on Internet Technology*, *9*(2), 6. doi:10.1145/1516539.1516541

Garg, S., & Sharma, R. M. (2017). Classification Based Network Layer Botnet Detection. In *Advanced Informatics for Computing Research* (pp. 332–342). Singapore: Springer. doi:10.1007/978-981-10-5780-9_30

Gong, C., & Sarac, K. (2008). A more practical approach for single-packet IP traceback using packet logging and marking. *IEEE Transactions on Parallel and Distributed Systems*, *19*(10), 1310–1324. doi:10.1109/TPDS.2007.70817

Goodrich, M. T. (2008). Probabilistic packet marking for large-scale IP traceback. *IEEE/ACM Transactions on Networking*, *16*(1), 15–24. doi:10.1109/TNET.2007.910594

Gu, G., Perdisci, R., Zhang, J., & Lee, W. (2008, July). BotMiner: Clustering Analysis of Network Traffic for Protocol-and Structure-Independent Botnet Detection. In *USENIX security symposium* (Vol. 5, No. 2, pp. 139-154). Academic Press.

Gu, G., Zhang, J., & Lee, W. (2008, February). BotSniffer: Detecting Botnet Command and Control Channels in Network Traffic. In *NDSS* (Vol. 8, pp. 1-18). Academic Press.

Gupta, B. B., Joshi, R. C., Misra, M., Meena, D. L., Shrivastava, G., & Sharma, K. (2010). Detecting a Wide Range of Flooding DDoS Attacks using Linear Prediction Model. In *2nd International Conference on Information and Multimedia Technology* (pp. 535-539). IEEE.

Hachem, N., Mustapha, Y. B., Granadillo, G. G., & Debar, H. (2011, May). Botnets: lifecycle and taxonomy. In *Network and Information Systems Security (SAR-SSI), 2011 Conference on* (pp. 1-8). IEEE. 10.1109/SAR-SSI.2011.5931395

Honeynet Project and Research Alliance. (2008). *Know your enemy: Tracking Botnets*. Retrieved October 8, 2008, from http:// www. honeynet. org/papers/bots

Kolias, C., Kambourakis, G., & Maragoudakis, M. (2011). Swarm intelligence in intrusion detection: A survey. *Computers & Security*, *30*(8), 625–642. doi:10.1016/j.cose.2011.08.009

Malliga, S., & Tamilarasi, A. (2010). A hybrid scheme using packet marking and logging for IP traceback. *International Journal of Internet Protocol Technology*, *5*(1-2), 81–91. doi:10.1504/IJIPT.2010.032617

Savage, S., Wetherall, D., Karlin, A., & Anderson, T. (2000, August). Practical network support for IP traceback. *Computer Communication Review*, *30*(4), 295–306. doi:10.1145/347057.347560

Shrivastava, G. (2016, March). Network forensics: Methodical literature review. In *Computing for Sustainable Global Development (INDIACom), 2016 3rd International Conference on* (pp. 2203-2208). IEEE.

Shrivastava, G. (2017). Approaches of network forensic model for investigation. *International Journal of Forensic Engineering*, *3*(3), 195–215. doi:10.1504/IJFE.2017.082977

Shrivastava, G., Sharma, K., & Rai, S. (2010, December). The Detection & Defense of DoS & DDoS Attack: A Technical Overview. In *Proceeding of ICC* (Vol. 27, p. 28). Academic Press.

Snort I. D. S. (2009). *Snort IDS*. Retrieved January 5, 2009, from http://www.snort.org

Springer reference. (2014). *DNS based botnet detection*. Retrieved July 15, 2014, from http://www.springerreference.com/docs/html/chapterdbid/317753.html

Tegeler, F., Fu, X., Vigna, G., & Kruegel, C. (2012, December). Botfinder: Finding bots in network traffic without deep packet inspection. In *Proceedings of the 8th international conference on Emerging networking experiments and technologies* (pp. 349-360). ACM. 10.1145/2413176.2413217

Wang, P., Sparks, S., & Zou, C. C. (2010). An advanced hybrid peer-to-peer botnet. *IEEE Transactions on Dependable and Secure Computing, 7*(2), 113–127. doi:10.1109/TDSC.2008.35

Yaar, A., Perrig, A., & Song, D. (2006). StackPi: New packet marking and filtering mechanisms for DDoS and IP spoofing defense. *IEEE Journal on Selected Areas in Communications, 24*(10), 1853–1863. doi:10.1109/JSAC.2006.877138

Yang, M. H., & Yang, M. C. (2012). RIHT: A novel hybrid IP traceback scheme. *IEEE Transactions on Information Forensics and Security, 7*(2), 789–797. doi:10.1109/TIFS.2011.2169960

Zhang, L., & Guan, Y. (2006, August). TOPO: A topology-aware single packet attack traceback scheme. In Securecomm and Workshops, 2006 (pp. 1-10). IEEE. doi:10.1109/SECCOMW.2006.359556

This research was previously published in the Handbook of Research on Network Forensics and Analysis Techniques edited by Gulshan Shrivastava, Prabhat Kumar, B. B. Gupta, Suman Bala and Nilanjan Dey; pages 266-281, copyright year 2018 by Information Science Reference (an imprint of IGI Global).

Section 2

Detection and Prevention: Intrusion Detection Systems and General Strategies

Chapter 9
Visualization Technique for Intrusion Detection

Mohamed Cheikh
Constantine 2 University, Algeria

Salima Hacini
Constantine 2 University, Algeria

Zizette Boufaida
Constantine 2 University, Algeria

ABSTRACT

Intrusion detection system (IDS) plays a vital and crucial role in a computer security. However, they suffer from a number of problems such as low detection of DoS (denial-of-service)/DDoS (distributed denial-of-service) attacks with a high rate of false alarms. In this chapter, a new technique for detecting DoS attacks is proposed; it detects DOS attacks using a set of classifiers and visualizes them in real time. This technique is based on the collection of network parameter values (data packets), which are automatically represented by simple geometric graphs in order to highlight relevant elements. Two implementations for this technique are performed. The first is based on the Euclidian distance while the second is based on KNN algorithm. The effectiveness of the proposed technique has been proven through a simulation of network traffic drawn from the 10% KDD and a comparison with other classification techniques for intrusion detection.

INTRODUCTION

Intrusion Detection Systems (IDSs) were introduced by Anderson (Anderson.J,1980). Denning (Denning.D,1987) designed then an intrusion detection model which marked a real impetus of the field. IDSs are essential complements to the preventive security mechanisms provided for computing systems and networks. They are used in the monitoring control process for the detection of potential intrusions and infections (Zanero, 2004).

DOI: 10.4018/978-1-7998-5348-0.ch009

IDS is based on two basic approaches, the behavioral approach and the scenario approach. The scenario approach, often called misuse detection approach defines the user actions that constitute abuse. It uses rules defined to encode and detect known intrusions. The behavioral approach, on its side, can detect unknown intrusions, and does not require any prior knowledge of intrusions (Boudaoud.K,2000). This approach is based on the fact that an intruder does not behave the same way as a regular user. Contrary to the user, who has a normal behavior, the intruder has an abnormal behavior. Thus, all intrusive activities are necessarily abnormal (Sundaram.A,2000).

Classification techniques in IDS intended to classify network traffic into two classes: "normal" and "intrusion". Classification requires learning. The accuracy of this learning provides lower false positive rate and false negative rate (Maxime DUMAS,2011).

Among the techniques commonly used for classification in IDS, we find the ANN, SVM and often the K-means and others (see section 2).

This chapter presents a new technique for classifying DoS attacks based on a visual representation of the network traffic. This representation is based on simple geometric forms and has two objectives:

1. Find models of DoS attacks and in particular be able to distinguish between them and the normal traffic. These models are later used in the classifiers. Seven models were identified to recognize six types of DoS attacks (Neptune, Smurf, Teardrop, Land, Pack, Pod) to which is added the normal case.
2. Improve the detection rate, which presents a great challenge for IDS.

The effectiveness of this technique has been proved through simulation of network traffic drawn from the 10% KDD. The proposed technique treats DoS attacks. However, it can also be applied to other types of attacks with the integration of their geometric forms in the detection system.

The remaining of this chapter is organized as follows: Section 2 presents some works dealing with the classification in IDS, Section 3 describes the proposed detection technique. Finally, Section 4 concludes the chapter and suggests some perspectives.

RELATED WORK

There are several techniques used for classification in IDS, the most frequently are ANN, SVM and K-means as well as others.

The k-means classifier, originally an algorithm for pattern recognition that has proven its effectiveness against the text processing (Yang Y,1997) represents a simple and popular classification that uses statistics properties (Kaplantzis.S & N. Mani,2006). It allows the partition of a collection of objects into K classes (K is a number set by the user). In the context of intrusion detection, there are generally two groups (classes), one for attack and another for normal cases. The classification is then performed by taking each individual point in a test set and associating it with the nearest class. At the end, each point is assigned to a class "attack" or "normal." Most distance measures used in this category of classification algorithms are Euclidean and Manhattan distances.

Neural networks are also used for ANN classification in IDS (Kevin L et al,1990), (Herve Debar et al,1992), (Jake Ryan et al,1998), (James Cannady,1998), (B. Subba, 2016). In the work of Fox et al. (Kevin L et al,1990), the authors propose the use of artificial neural networks to detect intrusions. The input network is actually a collection of URLs elements that often appear together to refine the recognition of simultaneous occurrence of different elements. (Herve Debar et al,1992) Proposed to learn the next commands predict using the history of previous commands of the user. In this case, a window offset **w** recent orders is used. The predicted command of the user is compared with the current command of the user and each deviation is shown as an intrusion. The size of the window **w** plays an important role, because if **w** is too small, there will be many false positives and it is too attacks will not be detected (Fady HAMOUI,2007).

The neural network intrusion detector NNID (Neural Network Intrusion Detector) (Jake Ryan et al,1998) identifies intrusions based on the distribution of commands used by a user. This approach is based on three phases. Firstly, the training data are derived from audit files for each user. A vector represents the distribution of the execution of a command for each user. In the second phase, the neural network is trained to identify the user based on these vectors control distribution. In the last phase, the network identifies the user for each new vector control distribution. If it identifies a user as different from the current user, an intrusion is reported.

In this context, the neuron networks are also proving effective in the case of noisy data (Fady HAMOUI,2007). However, the main problem with this approach lies in the training of neural networks where the training phase requires a very large amount of data and also an important time.

The technique of SVM (Support Vector Machines) has been used in (Srinivas Mukkamala et al,2003) (Kim, D.S,2003). This technique belongs to the class of supervised learning, developed in 1998 by Vapnik (Vapnik.V.N,1998). SVM learning is machines that project the vector drive space properties labeling each vector by its class. SVM classify the data by determining a set of support vectors, which are members of the inputs of the learning set which generates a surface in space hyper property. This type of approach has proven they can be a good solution for intrusion detection because of their speed (Fady HAMOUI,2007).

An interesting comparative study of Kaplantzis and Mani (Kaplantzis.S & N. Mani, 2006) on the three classification techniques (K-Means, ANN, SVM) for intrusion detection showed that the SVM is learning in the shortest amount of time with acceptable accuracy while the ANN provides high accuracy through long hours of learning.

Other classification techniques were used in Cohen.W. W,(1995), Wenke Lee et al,(1999), Giordana.A et al, (1995), Chittur.A, (2001), Chris Sinclair et al,(1999), Dickerson.J.E. and Dickerson.J.A, (2000), and Lue.J, (1999). They are based on the generation of inductive rules, genetic algorithms, fuzzy logic, etc.

We begin with the RIPPER system (Cohen.W. W,1995) which uses the "generation of inductive rules" classification (Wenke Lee et al,1999; Wenke Lee & Salvatore Stolfol,1998; Wenke Lee & Salvatore Stolfol, 2000; Wenke Lee et al,2000). It is effective to classify cases in the normal category and in various cases of intrusions (n-ary classification). RIPPER has two characteristics (Saneifar. H,1999):

- Generated rules are easy to understand.
- Possibility to generate multiple sets of rules.

REGAL (Giordana.A et al,1995) is another system using IDS classification techniques based on genetic algorithms (Filippo Neri,2000). It looks like approaches based on inductive rules but the author does not clarify the effectiveness of the approach (Saneifar. H,1999). Generally, this approach which uses the concept of natural selection is applied to a population of potential solutions to a difficult problem (which is not the optimal solution) to find an approximate solution in a reasonable time. In the case of

IDS, the initial population can be basic detection rules. Through the genetic algorithm, other rules that cover the best case of abnormal flows are generated.

The decision tree is also used as a classification technique in Chittur's work (Chittur.A,2001). Each node of the tree represents an attribute in the data set. Attributes are weighted and the final decision on the type of connection depends on the weight of attributes. By traversing the tree from the root to the leaves, there are decision rules (consisting of attributes and values present on the corresponding nodes) that enable classification of new instances.

In Chris Sinclair et al (1999), the authors convert attributes of network connections in the form of a gene sequence. Each connection is compared to all chromosomes. If there is no match, the connection is labeled as an anomaly.

In Dickerson.J.E. and Dickerson.J.A (2000), a combination of fuzzy logic and classification has been proposed to address portions of the data to be classified into two categories: "general" and "intrusion". This approach is effective in detecting intrusions type SCAN: the network is scanned to determine the architecture and to discover vulnerabilities. A user connects to multiple hosts sequentially for a short time. Because the classification is done on portions connected temporally, this approach has good results for detecting scans. The disadvantage is the difficult task of generating rules and definition of a good constraint (Time-Window) to determine the portions.

Lue (Lue.J,1999) developed the work of Wenke Lee et al,(1999), Wenke Lee and Salvatore Stolfol,(1998) by adding the concept of fuzzy logic. Its work scored more flexible. According to him, the intrusion detection is a natural application of fuzzy logic for determining an absolute given that a connection is an intrusion or not is not possible, but with fuzzy logic, we can give the probability of an intrusion.

Despite the development marked by the application of these techniques known as classification, many problems still arise. Many researches have inspired works based on neural networks. While they may be effective in the context of detection and provide better accuracy, they have a major shortcoming; it is not possible to know the reasons for the output algorithm. In other words, the end user does not have a clear definition of what characterizes an attack of non-attack. Moreover, the high rate of false alarms remains the black point of IDS. Fortunately, it is possible to limit the scope of most of the problems mentioned above using some visualization techniques. Latter is to represent graphically complex sets of information in order to highlight relevant elements (Maxime DUMAS,2011).

THE PROPOSED DETECTION TECHNIQUE

The proposed detection technique is based on a visual representation of network traffic after normalization of some parameters in the KDD. This representation aims to find visual models of DoS attacks and be able to distinguish between them and normal traffic. These models are subsequently used in the classifiers for intrusion detection. Seven models were identified to recognize six types of DoS attacks (Neptune, Smurf, Teardrop, Land, Pack, Pod) to which is added the normal case.

We can therefore consider the problem of intrusion detection as a pattern recognition problem. Thus, the classification is not made on the basis of parameters often complex, but rather on the basis of forms from a geometric transformation.

The Visualization

The Choice of Visualization Parameters

We focus in this work the application of our technique on DoS attacks. The choice of parameters based KDD derives from several tests and some work (Kayacık.H. G et al, 2005;Aikaterini M et al,2005), which cover both better visual classification of attacks and a small number of parameters. For this, the 41 KDD parameters are taken and a representation of the parameters as geometric forms is applied. The used parameters are those that give a better discrimination of forms. Our study has highlighted ten parameters (*Cf.* Table 1).

Table 1. Detection parameters

	Parameters	Description
1	Pr(1)	duration
2	Pr(23)	Count
3	Pr(24)	srv count
4	Pr(13)	compromised
5	Pr(25)	serror rate
6	Pr(26)	srv serror rate
7	Pr(29)	same srv rate
8	Pr(34)	dst host same srv rate
9	Pr(38)	dst host serror rate
10	Pr(39)	dst host srv serror rate

The transformation of collected values for these parameters has highlighted seven geometric forms leading to the classification of the six attacks (Smurf, Neptune, Teardrop, Land, Back, Pod) and the normal case.

The Representation Graph

Our technique is based on a graphical representation of the attacks which performs a transformation of parameters values by using the polar system. Each parameter value is well represented by polar coordinates, which are the radial coordinate r and the angular coordinate θ. Thereafter, each packet is represented by all ten descriptors di(i= 1, .. 10) corresponding to the ten parameters of detection. For example, a normal packet is represented as follows:

Normal Packet = {d1(1,0), d2(0, $\frac{\pi}{5}$), d3(0, $\frac{2\pi}{5}$), d4(1, $\frac{3\pi}{5}$), d5(1, $\frac{4\pi}{5}$), d6(0, π), d7(0, $\frac{6\pi}{5}$), d8(0, $\frac{7\pi}{5}$), d9(0, $\frac{8\pi}{5}$), d10(0, $\frac{9\pi}{5}$)}.

The result of this transformation is similar to a radar graph. Figure 1 shows the geometric form of a normal packet.

Practically, if we take all normal packets, the graph keeps the same pace with some insignificant changes (form remains invariant in space). This experiment was repeated using packet DoS attacks taken from 10% KDD. Each type of attack (Smurf, Neptune, Teardrop, Land, Back, Pod) has its own geometric form (see Figure 2) (for better visualization, the forms are displayed with a rotation of 90 °).

Figure 1. Representation of a normal packet

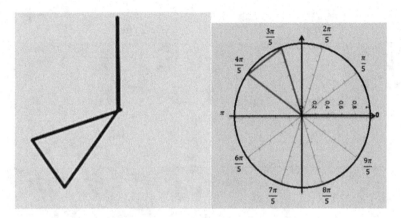

It can be noted from Figures 2 and 3 that the detection of DoS attacks will be greatly simplified through representation by means of the simple geometric forms.

Classification of Packets

For the packets classification we used two techniques, the first one is based on Euclidean distance, and the second one is at the base of Kppv algorithm.

Minimum Distance Classification

Pattern recognition (Kumar.S & Spafford.E. G,1995) is to encode the signatures of known intrusions into forms that can be recognized in the audit data in the model, based on the notion of event. In our case, we used the calculation of the Euclidean distance between the vector form of the unknown object (new packet) and the vector form of the reference object (the attack model / Normal). To determine the form vector of the reference object, we used a mean vector of a set of vectors according to the following formula:

$$Mj = \frac{1}{Nj} \sum_{X \in \omega j} Xj \qquad j = 1, 2, 3, \ldots, W \tag{1}$$

where Nj is the number of form vectors in the class ωj, and Mj the reference vector. We distinguish seven classes: $\omega1, \omega2, \omega3, \omega4, \omega5, \omega6, \omega7$ and each class of attack is evaluated by ten descriptors (d1, d2, d3, d4, d5, d6, d7, d8, d9, d10) where each descriptor represents a detection parameter characterized by two arguments: r (module) and θ (angle) (we use only the argument r to calculate the Euclidean distance). For example, the Smurf attack shown in Figure 3 represents a model (reference vector) graphic of Smurf Attack, taken randomly from a sample of 1000 Smurf packets.

Figure 2. Forms representing DoS Attacks

	Form	Type
1		Back
3		Land
3		Teardrop
4		Neptune
5		Pod
6		Smurf

Thus, at each occurrence of new packet, the Euclidean distance between the vector form of the unknown packet and the reference vector of Smurf attack (Smurf attack model) is estimated:

IF the Euclidian distance is minimal **Then** This packet denotes a Smurf attack

ELSE this packet is not a Smurf attack.

Similar processing is applied to other DoS attacks and also to normal packet.

Detection System Architecture

The intrusion detection system proposed is applicable to network traffic, so the parameters observed concern the detection during the routed packets in the network. They were, in this case, taken from KDD10%. A set of classifiers is used to distribute the task of detection. Seven classifiers are adopted

Figure 3. Form of the Smurf attack

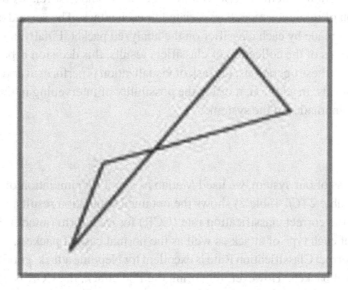

to detect DOS attacks and normal packets. Each classifier is identified by a reference vector (model) created during the learning phase. Thus, with each occurrence of a new packet, each classifier computes the Euclidean distance between the input vector (parameters of packet) and the reference model. The results of these classifiers are subsequently used in the overall decision algorithm. The classifier that has the minimal distance value is the one whose class corresponds to the final decision. Figure 4 shows the overall architecture of the proposed detection system.

Figure 4. The detection System architecture

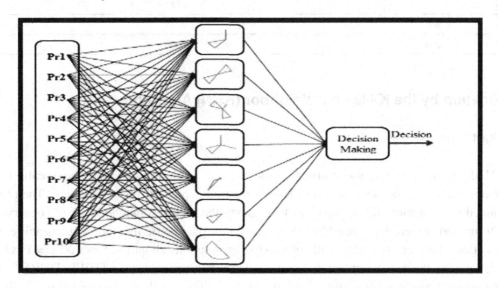

The task of the detection system is divided into three steps. The first relates to learning phase and deals with the creation of reference models associated to each attack. The second step is to manage the task of partial decision made by each classifier on the analyzed packet. Finally, the third step generates the final decision on basis of the collection of classifiers results, this decision is based on the minimum distance. In parallel with these operations, the task of visualization is performed to recognize DoS attacks by simple geometric forms. In addition, it offers the possibility of intervening in the detection system to correct any detection anomalies in the system.

Experimentation

To test the effectiveness of our system, we used Matlab as a tool for simulation of network traffic from the 10% KDD base. Table 2 (*Cf.* Table 2) shows the obtained simulation results.

We will calculate the correct classification rate (CCR) for each form (attack). For this we will randomly take samples of each type of attack as well as the normal case of packets.

We note that the Correct Classification Rate is excellent for Neptune attack, good for Smurf, Teardrop, Back, Land and normal packets. However, regarding the Pod attack, the CCR is a bit low compared to the other attacks, since the forms of Pod attacks are very varied.

Table 2. Experimental results

	Type	Correct Classification Rate %
01	**Normal**	**97%**
02	Smurf	99.8%
03	TearDrop	99.8%
04	Back	96.6%
05	Pod	68.6%
06	Land	90.5%
07	Neptune	100%

Classification by the K-Nearest Neighbor (KNN) Algorithm

KNN Algorithm

The KNN algorithm is among the simplest artificial learning algorithms. In a classification context of a new observation x, the basic idea is to vote nearest neighbors of this observation. The class of x is determined as a function of the majority class among the k closest neighbors of the observation x. The KNN method is therefore a neighborhood-based, non-parametric method; This meaning that the algorithm allows for a classification without making assumptions about the function $y = f(x1, x2, ... xp)$ which connects the dependent variable to the independent variables (MATHIEU-DUPAS, 2010).

The k-neighrest neighbors algorithm is an intuitive algorithm, easily parameterized to handle a classification problem with any number of labels. The principle of the algorithm is particularly simple: for each new point x we start by determining the set of its k-nearest neighbors among the learning points that we denote by Vk (x) (of course we must choose $1 \leq k \leq n$ to make sense). The class which is assigned to the new point x is then the majority class in the set Vk (x). An illustration of the method is given in Figure 5 for the case of three classes (Anne Sabourin, 2015).

The Distance

In order to find the K closest to a given datum, we have chosen the Euclidean distance. Let two data represented by two vectors xi and xj, the distance between these two data is given by (MATHIEU-DUPAS, 2010):

$$d(x_i, x_j) = \sqrt{\sum_{k=1}^{d}(x_{ik} - x_{jk})^2} \tag{2}$$

Figure 5. Example of the k-nearest neighbor's method for parameter values k = 5 and k = 11 (Anne Sabourin, 2015)

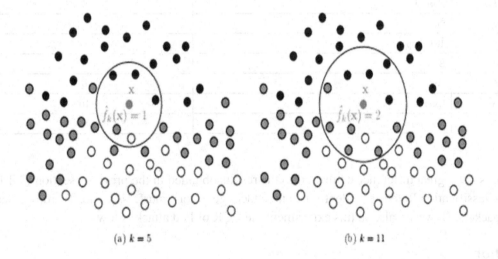

(a) $k = 5$ (b) $k = 11$

Implementation

It involves implementing in the JAVA language the algorithm of the K-nearest neighbors to predict the classes of new data (Packets) from learning data labeled (the attack/normal model (see Section 3.2 .1)).

These are the same learning data as in the previous section, but this time we take the models (attacks / normal) (see Figure 6) as an image.

By the following we applied the different binarization and projection steps (vertical and horizontal), to obtain the global vector of the image.

At the end of the training data construction, the detection can be applied by the KNN algorithm.

The following table shows the results of the experiment (Table 3).

Figure 6. Images show the attack patterns

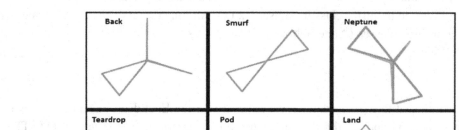

Table 3. Experimental results

	Type	Correct Classification Rate %
01	Normal	95.5%
02	Smurf	99.9%
03	Tear drop	94%
04	Back	97%
05	Pod	64%
06	Land	100%
07	Neptune	98.3%

There is not a great difference compared to the results obtained in the previous section (3.2.1). The Correct Classification Rate is excellent for Land attack, good for Smurf, Neptune, Teardrop, Back and normal packets. However, also in this experiment the CCR of Pod attack is low.

Validation

To validate the results, it was deemed necessary to make comparisons with other works; particularly those based on neural networks (Naoum.R.S et al, 2012;Sammany.M et al,2007; Chaivat Jirapummin et al,2002) and others, because they can be effective in the context detection and provide better accuracy. Table 4 shows the correct classification rate outcome of our technique in comparison with other techniques.

Table 4 proves the effectiveness of our technique with the two methods used. However, there are many algorithms and methods of classification developed by the scientific community. Their performances are evaluated on the datasets indexed (such as KDD'99). Applied to the same set of data, some methods provide good results, that is to say, the results are conform to our expectations of good classification such a good packet classification between different types of attack and the normal case, while others provide results generally less efficient. However, a less efficient method results can highlight links that have not been seen by the most effective (Maxime DUMAS,2011) and also can provide more efficient results against some types of attacks. The basic idea is that the information provided by the different

Table 4. Comparison Results

	Type	Our Technique (Minimum Distance)	Our Technique (KNN algorithm	(Jiang.S, Song. X, 2006)	(Gunes Kayacik, H., 2006)	ERBP (Naoum, R.S., 2012)	(Sammany, M., 2007)	(Chaivat Jirapummin, 2002)
01	Normal	97%	95.5%			84.3%	96.3%	-
02	Smurf	99.8%	99.9%	99.96%	99.9%	-	-	-
03	TearDrop	99.8%	94%	26%	16.7%	-	-	-
04	Back	96.6%	97%	0.32%	50%	-	-	-
05	Pod	68.6%	64%	3.79%	6.9%	-	-	-
06	Land	90.5%	100%	100%	100%	-	-	-
07	Neptune	100%	98.3%	99.99%	96.4%	-	92.4%	99.7%

classifiers or different methods are complementary, and therefore the combination of different classification methods such as ANN, SVM, minimum distance, and others can increase their effectiveness and their accuracy. (Projet Pari, 2013) One classification is performed based on the results of methods with different viewpoints: all decisions of individual classifiers are used to obtain a consensus decision. (Yang Y,1997) The challenge is how to improve the overall performance by combining the advantages and without keeping disadvantages.

CONCLUSION

In this chapter, we present a new technique for intrusion detection, that can detect, classify and visualize attacks in real time. Packets related to traffic represented by our graphs as images with simple geometric forms, to find models of visual DoS attacks and be able to distinguish between them and the normal traffic. These models are used in classifiers for intrusion detection.

So we can consider the problem of intrusion detection as a pattern recognition problem where the classification is not made on the basis of often complex arithmetic parameters, but rather on the basis of forms derived from a geometric transformation.

Finally, simulation results with KDD10% illustrate the effectiveness of this technique with a high rate of correct classification. To improve the detection rate, the combination of different classification methods using a Multi-Agents System is considered. Its aim is to obtain a consensus classification that can improve the detection rate and reduce the false alarm rate.

REFERENCES

Aikaterini, M., & Christos, D. (2005). Detecting Denial of Service Attacks Using Emergent Self-Organizing Maps. *2005 IEEE International Symposium on Signal Processing and Information Technology.*

Anderson, J. (1980). *Computer security threat monitoring and surveillance.* Academic Press.

Anne Sabourin, J. S. (2015). *Méthodes des k-plus proches voisins*. Paris: Travaux Pratiques, Telecom Paristech.

Boudaoud, K. (2000). *Détection d'intrusions: Une nouvelle approche par systèmes multi-agents* (Thèse de doctorat). l'école Polytechnique Fédérale de Lausanne.

Cannady, J. (1998). Articial neural networks for misuse detection. *Proceedings of the 1998 National Information Systems Security Conference (NISSC'98)*, 443-456.

Chittur, A. (2001). *Model generation for an intrusion detection system using genetic algorithms* (PhD thesis). Ossining High School in cooperation with Columbia Univ.

Cohen, W. W. (1995). Fast effective rule induction. In *Machine Learning: the 12th International Conference*. Morgan Kaufmann. 10.1016/B978-1-55860-377-6.50023-2

Debar, H., Becker, M., & Siboni, D. (1992). A neural network component for an intrusion detection system. In *SP '92: Proceedings of the 1992 IEEE Symposium on Security and Privacy*. IEEE Computer Society. 10.1109/RISP.1992.213257

Denning, D. (1987). An intrusion-detection model. *IEEE Transactions on Software Engineering, 13*, 222–232.

Dickerson, J. E., & Dickerson, J. A. (2000). Fuzzy network proling for intrusion detection. In *Proc. of NAFIPS 19th International Conference of the North American Fuzzy Information Processing Society* (pp. 301-306). North American Fuzzy Information Processing Society (NAFIPS).

Dumas, M. (2011). *Alertwheel: Visualisation radiale de graphes bipartis appliquée aux systèmes de détection d'intrusions sur des réseaux informatiques*. Mémoire de l'école de technologie supérieure, université du Québec.

Fady, H. (2007). *Détection de fraudes et Extraction de Connaissances* (Master's thesis). Montpellier 2 Univ.

Fox, Henning, Reed, & Simonian. (1990). A neural network approach towards intrusion detection. *Proceedings of the 13th national computer security conference*, 125-34.

Giordana, A., Neri, F., & Saitta, L. (1995). Search-intensive concept induction. *Evolutionary Computation, 3*(4), 375-416.

Jiang, S., Song, X., Wang, H., Han, J.-J., & Li, Q.-H. (2006). A clustering-based method for unsupervised intrusion detections. *Pattern Recognition Letters, 27*(7), 802–810. doi:10.1016/j.patrec.2005.11.007

Jirapummin, C., Wattanapongsakorn, N., & Kanthamanon, P. (2002). Hybrid neural networks for intrusion detection system. *2002 International Technical Conference on Circuits/Systems,Computers and Communications (ITC-CSCC 2002)*, 928–931.

Kaplantzis, S., & Mani, N. (2006). A study on classification techniques for network intrusion detection. *IASTED Conference on Networks and Communication Systems (NCS 2006)*.

Kayacik, G. (2006). A hierarchal SOM-based intrusion detection system. *Engineering Applications of Artificial Intelligence*. doi:10.1016/j.engappai.2006.09.005

Kayacık, H. G., Zincir-Heywood, A. N., & Heywood, M. I. (2005). Selecting Features for Intrusion Detection: A Feature Relevance Analysis on KDD 99 Intrusion Detection Datasets. *Third Annual Conference on Privacy, Security and Trust.*

Kim, D. S., & Park, J. S. (2003). Lecture Notes in Computer Science: Vol. 2662. *Network-based Intrusion Detection with Support Vector Machines.* Berlin: Springer-Verlag. doi:10.1007/978-3-540-45235-5_73

Kumar, S., & Spafford, E. G. (1995). *A Software Architecture to support Misuse Intrusion Detection.* Technical Report CSD-TR-95-009, Purdue University.

Lee, W., Stolfo, S. J., & Mok, K. W. (1999). A data mining framework for building intrusion detection models. *IEEE Symposium on Security and Privacy*, 120-132.

Lee, W., & Stolfo, S. (1998). Data mining approaches for intrusion detection. *Proceedings of the 7th USENIX Security Symposium.*

Lee, W., & Stolfo, S. J. (2000). A framework for constructing features and models for intrusion detection systems. *Information and System Security*, *3*(4), 227261.

Lee, W., Stolfo, S. J., & Mok, K. W. (2000). Adaptive intrusion detection, a data mining approach. *Artificial Intelligence Review*, *14*(6), 533567. doi:10.1023/A:1006624031083

Lue, J. (1999). *Integrating fuzzy logic with data mining methods for intrusion detection* (Master's thesis). Mississippi State Univ.

Mathieu-Dupas, E. (2010). *Algorithme des K plus proches voisins pondérés (WKNN) et Application en diagnostic.* Montpellier: SysDiag, Unité Mixte de Recherche CNRS-BIO-RAD.

Mukkamala, Sung, & Abraham. (2003). *Intrusion detection using ensemble of soft computing paradigms.* Academic Press.

Naoum, R.S.. Abdula Abid, N., & Namh Al-Sultani, Z. (2012). An Enhanced Resilient Backpropagation Artificial Neural Network for Intrusion Detection System. *International Journal of Computer Science and Network Security, 12*(3).

Neri, F. (2000). Comparing local search with respect to genetic evolution to detect in-trusion in computer networks. In *Proceedings of the 2000 Congress on Evolutionary Computation CEC00* (pp. 238-243). IEEE Press.

Pari, P. (2011-2013). *Classification consensuelle.* Retrieved from http://pari.ai.univ-paris8.fr/?author=1

Ryan, J., Lin, M.-J., & Miikkulainen, R. (1998). Intrusion detection with neural networks. In M. I. Jordan, M. J. Kearns, & S. A. Solla (Eds.), Advances in Neural Information Processing Systems: Vol. 10. *The MIT Press.*

Sammany, M., Sharawi, M., El-Beltagy, M., & Saroit, I. (2007). Artificial Neural Networks Architecture for Intrusion Detection Systems and Classification of Attacks. *Fifth international conference- INFO 2007.*

Saneifar, H. (2008). *Clustering de motifs séquentiels Application à la détection d'intrusions* (Master's thesis). Montpellier 2 Univ.

Sinclair, C., Pierce, L., & Matzner, S. (1999). An application of machine learning to network intrusion detection. In *ACSAC '99: Proceedings of the 15th Annual Computer Security Applications Conference*. Washington, DC: IEEE Computer Society. 10.1109/CSAC.1999.816048

Subba, B., Biswas, S., & Karmakar, S. (2016). A Neural Network based system for Intrusion Detection and attack classification. In *Communication (NCC), 2016 Twenty Second National Conference on* (pp. 1-6). IEEE.

Sundaram, A. (1996). An Introduction to Intrusion Detection. Technical Report, Purdue University.

Vapnik, V. N. (1998). *Statistical learning theory. Adaptive and learning systems for signal processing, communications, and control*. New York: Wiley.

Yang, Y. (1997). *An evaluation of statistical approach to text categorization*. Rapport interne Technichal Report CMU-CS-97-127, Carnegie Mellon University.

Zanero, S. (2004). Behavioural intrusion detection. In *Proceedings of the 19th ISCIS Symposium* (pp. 657-666). Springer-Verlag.

This research was previously published in Security and Privacy Management, Techniques, and Protocols edited by Yassine Maleh; pages 276-290, copyright year 2018 by Information Science Reference (an imprint of IGI Global).

Chapter 10
Association Rule–Mining–Based Intrusion Detection System With Entropy–Based Feature Selection:
Intrusion Detection System

Devaraju Sellappan

 https://orcid.org/0000-0003-3116-4772

Sri Krishna Arts and Science College, Coimbatore, India

Ramakrishnan Srinivasan

 https://orcid.org/0000-0002-8224-4812

Dr. Mahalingam College of Engineering and Technology, Pollachi, India

ABSTRACT

Intrusion detection system (IDSs) are important to industries and organizations to solve the problems of networks, and various classifiers are used to classify the activity as malicious or normal. Today, the security has become a decisive part of any industrial and organizational information system. This chapter demonstrates an association rule-mining algorithm for detecting various network intrusions. The KDD dataset is used for experimentation. There are three input features classified as basic features, content features, and traffic features. There are several attacks are present in the dataset which are classified into Denial of Service (DoS), Probe, Remote to Local (R2L), and User to Root (U2R). The proposed method gives significant improvement in the detection rates compared with other methods. Association rule mining algorithm is proposed to evaluate the KDD dataset and dynamic data to improve the efficiency, reduce the false positive rate (FPR) and provides less time for processing.

DOI: 10.4018/978-1-7998-5348-0.ch010

INTRODUCTION

Today many people have connected with internet for their business purpose and other related purpose. So, the intrusion detection system (IDSs) is important for any industry to protect their information from intruders. Industries are using software and hardware devices to secure the information, even though many intruders were not identified. Today the information is most important role in our life. So, need to protect the data from intruders because many malicious users are using various techniques to exploit the systems vulnerabilities. While the information is sent from one system to another, there is no protection from intruders. In these aspects, need to protect the information more securely.

Intrusion Detection Systems (IDS) are typically classified into two groups: Anomaly based IDS and Signature based IDS. The anomaly-based IDS which is observed from network when it behavior deviates from the normal attacks. The signature-based IDS detects the intrusion by comparing with its existing signatures in the log files. Intrusion Detection System is classified as Host based IDS and Network based IDS. The host-based IDS is a system which monitor and analyze the computer system if there is any misbehavior. The network-based IDS is a system which detect the misbehavior whenever the system can able to communicate with each other over the network (Devaraju & Ramakrishnan, 2013).

Data mining technique is used to process the large volume of raw data easily. The various techniques are Association Rule, Clustering, Decision Trees and Neural Networks. The various authors have tried to improve the performance and reduce the false positive rate of intrusion detection system. Even though there are some misbehavior happening in IDS and could not be improve the performance and reduce the false positive rate due to the dataset contains large volume of data. The data contains many features and the authors were used all the features for processing but some features are not important.

In this paper, try to create a new set of rulesets based on the protocol features which will help us to improve the performance, reduce the false positive rate and less processing time. There are three types of protocol feature are considered such as TCP, UDP and ICMP. Mainly attacks are depending on any one of the protocol features so need to category the data based on the protocol features to reduce the feature as well. The purpose of the systems is i) to generate association rules to improve the detection rate and ii) to refine the association rules correctly to reduce the false alarm. The association rule-based systems are developed using Java Development Kit (JDK) for better performance applied to KDD dataset and dynamic data using Association Rule-Mining Algorithm.

The paper is organized as follows: In Section 2, discusses the related work, Section 3, discusses KDD Dataset Description, Section 4, discussing Entropy based Feature Selection, Section 5, describes the Methodology. Section 6 gives the results and discussion and Section 7 deals with conclusion of the research work.

RELATED WORK

There are various techniques have been proposed. They are statistical methods, neural network, data mining etc. In this section, the various techniques used for intrusion detection systems are discussed.

C-Means Clustering was applied for intrusion detection which uses minimum testing dataset and reducing the features by using reduction algorithm to improve the detection time (Minjie & Anqing, 2012). A novel twin support vector machine and SVM were used to overcome the normal traffic patterns and classification accuracy (Nie & He, 2010; Srinivas, Andrew & Ajith, 2004; Sumaiya & Aswani, 2017).

Hidden Markov Model was used to implement and determine the system call based anomaly intrusion detection system (Jiankun, Xinghuo, Qiu & Chen, 2009; Xie & Yu, 2008). Conditional Random Fields and Layered Approach were demonstrated the attack detection accuracy by KDD cup '99 dataset (Gupta & Kotagiri, 2010). The Genetic Algorithm was used to detect the intrusion which considers both temporal and spatial information of network connections during the encoding of the problem (Wei, 2004; Jiang & Junhu, 2009).

Hierarchical Gaussian Mixture Model was used to detect network-based attacks as anomalies using statistical classification techniques using KDD99 dataset. Also, it was used to reduce the missing alarm and accuracy of the attacks (Suseela, Zhu & Julie, 2005; Kabir, Jiankun, Wang & Zhuo, 2018). The various Neural Network approaches were used to improve the performance of the intrusion detection system. The KDDCup'99 dataset was used as testing data and gives the robust result (Devaraju & Ramakrishnan, 2011; Ran, Steren, Nameri, Roytman, Porgador & Yuval, 2019) (Neveen, 2009). The SVM and GA were used for classification purpose and these methods minimize the features for increase the detection rate (Iftikhar, Azween, Abdullah & Muhammad, 2011). The correlation coefficient and data mining techniques were used to improve the detection of new types of anomaly using KDD cup'99 dataset (Ning, Chen, Xiong & Hong-Wei, 2009; Anbalagan, Puttamadappa, Mohan, Jayaraman & Srinivasarao, 2008). Association rule mining algorithm was used to detect the attacks for intrusion detection system. It was considered only individual attacks to frame the rulesets applied with KDD dataset (Zhiwen, Salim & Pacheco, 2019; Devaraju & Ramakrishnan, 2015).

Recurrent Neural Network was used to improve the classification rates, especially for R2L attack. Decision trees and support vector machines were used to improve the detection accuracy and minimize the computational complexity (Mansour, Zahra & Ali, 2010; Sandhya, Ajith, Crina & Johnson, 2005; Akashdeep, Ishfaq & Neeraj, 2017; Alex, David & Aladdin, 2018). Data mining clustering technique was used for detection of intrusion and reduction algorithm was used to cancel the redundant attribute set (Nadiammai & Hemalatha, 2014; Srinivas, Andrew & Ajith, 2007; Vajiheh & Shahram, 2018). Rule-based classification, decision tree methods and novel fuzzy class association rule-mining method were used for detecting network intrusions (Anuar, Hasimi, Abdullah & Omar, 2008; Shingo, Chen, Nannan, Shimada & Hirasawa, 2011; Adnan & Cameron, 2017; Ashfaq, Wang, Huang, Abbas & Yu-Lin, 2017).

The various techniques are discussed and finding some difficulties to improve the detection rate and false positive rate. The data mining techniques is better choices to define the ruleset depends on the selected features. In order to address the limitations, in this paper, proposed a new set of association rule-mining algorithm. This proposed algorithm improves the detection rate, reduces the FPR and minimizes the processing speed. Data mining techniques are grouped into four levels, namely Mining Data Streams, Clustering, Classification and Pattern Mining. Figure 1 has shown the various techniques in data mining.

Motivation

Most of the organizations and industry are struggling with more vulnerable to threats. The intrusion detection system is used to compromise the integrity and confidentiality of the resources. In recent years, intrusion detection is the highest priorities and challenging tasks for administrators to detect the emerging threats.

Figure 1. Comparison of various data mining techniques

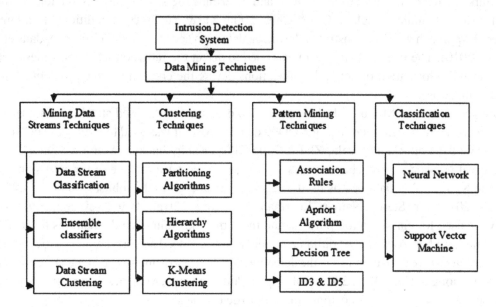

Problem Statement

In intrusion detection system, there are several methods employed like data mining techniques (Devaraju & Ramakrishnan, 2013; Minjie & Anqing, 2012; Nadiammai & Hemalatha, 2014; Anuar, Hasimi, Abdullah & Omar, 2008; Muniyandi, Rajeswari & Rajaram, 2012), probability approach and support vector machine (Nie & He, 2010), neural network (Devaraju & Ramakrishnan, 2011), Fuzzy C-Means (Shingo, Chen, Nannan, Shimada & Hirasawa, 2011), genetic algorithm (Wei, 2004) (Jiang & Junhu, 2009), Hidden Markov Model (Jiankun, Xinghuo, Qiu & Chen, 2009; Xie & Yu, 2008), etc. The existing systems do not provide data security. The Data Mining Technique is employed to overcome the existing problem, reduce the false alarm and improve their attack detection accuracy.

KDD DATASET DESCRIPTION

The KDD dataset is the benchmarking dataset which is used to evaluate the Intrusion Detection System (Mansour, Zahra & Ali, 2010). There are categories of attacks in KDD dataset: DoS, Probe, R2L, and U2R. The dataset consists of three components which are "10% KDD Dataset", "Corrected KDD Dataset" and "Full KDD Dataset". Dataset which contains millions of records and each record contains 41 features and labeled as either normal or an attack, with exactly one specific attack type. Table 1 shows the training and testing data in KDD Dataset (Srinivas, Andrew & Ajith, 2004).

The "10% KDD Dataset" is used for training data, "corrected KDD Dataset" and "Full Dataset "is used for testing data.

KDD dataset has different types of attacks: guess_passwd, buffer_overflow, back, ftp_write, ipsweep, land, imap, multihop, loadmodule, neptune, nmap, phf, perl, pod, rootkit, portsweep, satan, smurf, spy, warezclient, teardrop, warezmaster. These attacks can be divided into following groups (Nie & He, 2010).

- **Denial of Service (DoS) Attacks:** Which can deny legitimate requests to a system, example. Flood.
- **User-to-Root (U2R) Attacks:** Which is an unauthorized access to local super user (root) privileges, example. Buffer overflow attacks.
- **Remote-to-Local (R2L) Attacks:** Which is an unauthorized access from a remote machine, example. Guesses a different password.
- **Probing:** Probing is a surveillance and other probing attacks, example. Port scanning.

KDD Dataset contains 41 features that are categorized into continuous and discrete type. The features are assigned the label as c0, c1, c2, ..., c40. Table 2 shows the Description of Variable in KDD dataset.

Table 1. Training and testing data

Dataset	Normal	DoS	Probe	R2L	U2R	Total
Training Data						
10% KDD	97278	391458	4107	1126	52	494021
Testing Data						
Corrected KDD	60593	229853	4166	16347	70	311029
Whole KDD	972781	3883370	41102	1126	52	4898431

The association rule-mining algorithm derives from the important features based on the protocol types (tcp, udp and icmp). Table 4 shows the important features that improve the performance, reduce the False Positive Rate and also reduce the evaluation time (Jiankun, Xinghuo, Qiu & Chen, 2009). The proposed system uses selected important features (Srilatha, Ajith & Johnson, 2005). The feature is selected based on the variable which is filtered if the probability of the variable is closer to minimum by the calculation of mean value.

In KDD Dataset, the normal record and snmpgetattack record of all 41 feature values are same. Due to this kind of problem the false correlation may be increased. The table 3 shows the sample records of normal and snmpgetattack.

ENTROPY BASED FEATURE SELECTION

Feature Selection

The KDD Dataset contains a millions of records and each record which contains 41 attributes. When designing a network intrusion detection system, all 41 features are not necessary. The KDD dataset may contain redundant data in which the additional features can increase the computation time and which declines the accuracy of intrusion detection system and increase the false positive rate. The feature selection is more important to improve the performance and reduce the false positive rate. Though, apply the entropy based feature selection for improving their efficiency and false positive rate. The following steps are used for feature selection:

Table 2. Description of variable in KDD dataset

Var. No.	Variable Name	Variable Type	Label Name	Var. No.	Variable Name	Variable Type	Label Name
1	duration	continuous	c0	22	is_guest_login	discrete	c21
2	protocol_type	discrete	c1	23	count	continuous	c22
3	service	discrete	c2	24	srv_count	continuous	c23
4	flag	discrete	c3	25	serror_rate	continuous	c24
5	src_bytes	continuous	c4	26	srv_serror_rate	continuous	c25
6	dst_bytes	continuous	c5	27	rerror_rate	continuous	c26
7	land	discrete	c6	28	srv_rerror_rate	continuous	c27
8	wrong_fragment	continuous	c7	29	same_srv_rate	continuous	c28
9	urgent	continuous	c8	30	diff_srv_rate	continuous	c29
10	hot	continuous	c9	31	srv_diff_host_rate	continuous	c30
11	num_failed_logins	continuous	c10	32	dst_host_count	continuous	c31
12	logged_in	discrete	c11	33	dst_host_srv_count	continuous	c32
13	num_compromised	continuous	c12	34	dst_host_same_srv_rate	continuous	c33
14	root_shell	continuous	c13	35	dst_host_di_srv_rate	continuous	c34
15	su_attempted	continuous	c14	36	dst_host_same_src_port_rate	continuous	c35
16	num_root	continuous	c15	37	dst_host_srv_diff_host_rate	continuous	c36
17	num_file_creations	continuous	c16	38	dst_host_serror_rate	continuous	c37
18	num_shells	continuous	c17	39	dst_host_srv_serror_rate	continuous	c38
19	num_access_files	continuous	c18	40	dst_host_rerror_rate	continuous	c39
20	num_outbound_cmds	continuous	c19	41	dst_host_srv_rerror_rate	continuous	c40
21	is_host_login	discrete	c20				

Table 3. Sample records of normal and snmpgetattack

Sample Records
0 udp private SF 105 146 0 0 0 0 0 0 0 0 0 0 0 0 0 0 0 0 0 2 2 0.00 0.00 0.00 0.00 1.00 0.00 0.00 255 254 1.00 0.01 0.00 0.00 0.00 0.00 0.00 0.00 normal.
0 udp private SF 105 146 0 0 0 0 0 0 0 0 0 0 0 0 0 0 0 0 0 2 2 0.00 0.00 0.00 0.00 1.00 0.00 0.00 255 254 1.00 0.01 0.00 0.00 0.00 0.00 0.00 0.00 snmpgetattack.
0 udp private SF 105 146 0 0 0 0 0 0 0 0 0 0 0 0 0 0 0 0 0 1 1 0.00 0.00 0.00 0.00 1.00 0.00 0.00 255 254 1.00 0.01 0.00 0.00 0.00 0.00 0.00 0.00 normal.
0 udp private SF 105 146 0 0 0 0 0 0 0 0 0 0 0 0 0 0 0 0 0 1 1 0.00 0.00 0.00 0.00 1.00 0.00 0.00 255 254 1.00 0.01 0.00 0.00 0.00 0.00 0.00 0.00 snmpgetattack.

Step 1: Before feature selection, normalization of data to the scale of [0,1] is done through the following formula:

$$Res_m[n] = \left(Res_m[n] - Res_{c\_min}[n]\right) \big/ \left(Res_{c\_max}[n] - Res_{c\_min}[n]\right) \tag{1}$$

where,

Res$_m$[n] is the value of mth data instance from nth attribute.

Res$_{c\_min}$[n] is the minimum value of attribute 'n' among the dataset Res,

Res$_{c\_max}$[n] is the maximum value among all the data instances.

Step 2: There are four classes (DoS, Probe, R2L and U2R) used for feature selection based on the within-class entropy and between-class entropy for all the 41 features. The 10% KDD Dataset is used for training. The within-class and between-class entropy is calculated using the entropy formula for normalized data.

$$Entropy = -\sum_{i=1}^{k} P(value_i).\log_2(P(value_i))$$

(2)

where, P(value$_i$) is the probability of getting ith value.

Step 3: Using calculated value of within-class entropy and between-class entropy, grouping of the classes based on the entropy value is done (very low, low, high or very high), after computed the between-class entropy and within-class entropy for 41 features.

Step 4: After categorizing, select the features and rank the features for the following condition:

RANK 1: Between-entropy is very high and within-class entropy is very low, then the feature is selected.

RANK 2: Between-entropy is very high and within-class entropy is low, then the feature is selected.

RANK 3: Between-entropy is high and within-class entropy is very low, then the feature is selected.

Step 5: Based on the ranking, the features are ranked in Feature Rank Matrix.

Step 6: Identify number of features by considering Detection Rate and Computational Time. If Detection Rate is high and Computational Time is low, the feature is selected. Calculate the Detection Rate and Computational Time based on the selected features, which will help to select number of feature and then calculate the overall within-class entropy for only selected features.

As a result, only selected feature is used for each class. However, when performed the experiments on the selected features and compared the results, there is significant improvement in the detection rate and False Positive Rate. The feature selection is shown in table 4.

Table 4. Selected features

Class No.	Class Name	Important Features (Label Name Is Listed)		
		tcp (c1)	udp (c1)	icmp (c1)
1	DoS	c0, c2, c3, c4, c5, c6, c9, c11, c12, c22, c24, c25, c28, c29, c31, c32, c33, c37, c38, c39, c40	c0, c2, c3, c4, c5, c7	c0, c2, c3, c4, c5
2	Probe	c0, c2, c3, c4, c5, c22, c23, c24, c25,26, c27, c28, c29, c31, c32, c34, c35, c37, c38, c39, c40	c0, c2, c3, c4, c5, c23, c31, c32, c34, c35	c0, c2, c3, c4, c5, c22, c23, c28, c31, c33, c35
3	R2L	c0, c2, c3, c4, c5, c9, c10, c11, c21, c22, c23, c28, c31, c33, c35	c0, c2, c3, c4, c5, c22, c23, c28, c34	c0, c2, c3, c4, c5, c22, c23, c28, c31, c32, c34, c39
4	U2R	c0, c2, c3, c4, c5, c12, c16, c20, c21, c23, c28, c31, c32, c33, c34, c35, c36, c39, c40	-	-

Discrimination Capability of the Proposed Method

In this paper, the box plot and whisker chart are presented to exhibit the unfairness capability and represent the different distribution of data into ranges within the different classes. X-axis shows the number of classes and Y-axis shows the variation. The median of before feature selection is high when compare with the after feature selection is considered. Hence the variation is better than the box plot and whisker chart are well suited. The variables are randomly selected for finding the variations. The variation between before feature selection and after feature selection for the classes has been shown in figure 2.

Figure 2. Box plot and whisker chart for the classes

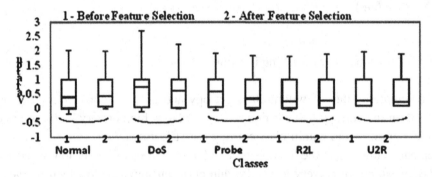

In this paper, average between-class and within-class entropies are computed, before and after the feature selection method which demonstrate the effectiveness. Between-class entropy for before feature selection is low and after feature selection is high. Within-class entropy for before feature selection is high and after feature selection is low for the classes. The rulesets are applied to the Association Rule-Mining Algorithm for verifying the consistency. The selection of features and rulesets are well suitable to employ this system. Figure 3 shows the average of between-class and within-class entropy.

Figure 3. Average of between-class and within-class entropy

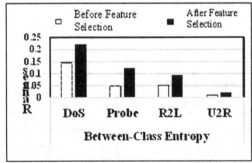
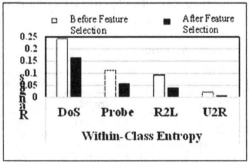

(a) Average of Between-Class Entropy   *(b) Average of Within-Class Entropy*

In this paper, a scatter plot is employed to demonstrate the discrimination capability of the proposed feature selection method which represents the relationship between the different classes. A scatter plot for the variables same_srv_rate vs diff_srv_rate is presented from the corrected dataset for the classes DoS, Probe, R2L, U2R and Normal. Six samples are selected randomly for finding the relationships. Each class in the scatter plot is shown in the figure 4. It is observed that the scatter plot for the proposed feature selection method is performing in a better way.

Figure 4. Scatter plot for different features

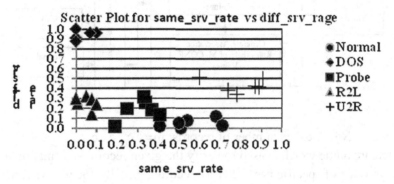

METHODOLOGY

Association Rule-Mining Algorithm

Association Rule-Mining Algorithm is utilized to create the ruleset which is different from other algorithms with larger datasets. The ruleset is performed with the help of generating rulesets step by step using support and confidence. The ruleset is generated based on the feature selection. When the numbers of samples are too big, Data Mining algorithms like decision tree and rule based can be used. It is vitally utilized to generate rulesets which consist of unordered collections of IF-THEN rules. The rulesets are generally easier to understand when compared with other algorithms. Each rule from rulesets describes a specific context associated with a class or an attribute. This approach is designed to improve the performance based on the type of classes such as Normal, DoS, Probe, R2L and U2R (Anuar, Hasimi, Abdullah & Omar, 2008) (Selvakani & Rajesh, 2011).

The data mining algorithm is modified from the apriori association rules algorithm (Hanguang & Ni Yu, 2012). Rules can be viewed simply as [If Then Else] structure (Jiang, Xindan, Wang & Zhuo, 2011). A new association rule-mining algorithm is proposed for classifying and predicting uncertain datasets. In this study, the Dataset consists of 41 features which process selected features to classify the dataset based on their protocol. The protocol may be 'tcp', 'udp' or 'icmp'. Each protocol is exemplified by the uses of services and flags [Refer Table 4]. If the protocol is 'tcp' || 'udp' || 'icmp' then the various parameters are checked then declared as Normal, DoS, Probe, R2L or U2R (Muniyandi, Rajeswari & Rajaram, 2012). Figure 5 shows the architecture for association rule-mining classifier.

Figure 5. Architecture for association rule mining classifier

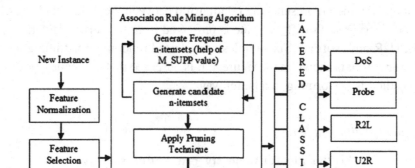

Suppose, n={N1,N2,N3,....∞} is number of records; m={ c_0, c_1, c_2, c_3, c_4 .... c_{40} } is number of features; c_j is the feature name which is used to verify the given record is normal or attack; d is the numeric value or string value of specific parameter for records. Initially, the features are compared with d and continued with number of records until the number of records turned to be empty. The Association Rule-Mining Algorithm is shown as

$$R = \sum_{i=1}^{n} \sum_{j=0}^{m} if((c_j >= d) \,||\, (c_j <= d)) \tag{3}$$

where, R is the Result variable; i,j is the initial variable; n= number of records; m=number of features used (Refer Table 4); c_j is the feature name; d is the numeric value or string value.

Calculation of χ^2 value of rule X ⇒ Y is shown as follows.

Assume support(X) = x, support(Y) = y, support(X ∪ Y) = z, and the total number of records is N. It calculates χ^2 as

$$\chi^2 = \frac{N\left(z - xy\right)^2}{xy\left(1 - x\right)\left(1 - y\right)} \tag{4}$$

If χ^2 is greater than a cutoff value, may reject the assumption that X and Y are independent.

Let A_i be an attribute in a database with value 1 or 0, and k be class labels. Then, association rule can be represented by

$$\left(A_p = 1\right) \wedge \cdots \wedge \left(A_q = 1\right) \Rightarrow \left(C = k\right) k \in \left\{0,1\right\} \tag{5}$$

as a special case of the association rule X ⇒ Y with fixed consequent C.

In this paper, association rules satisfying the following are defined as important rules:

$$\chi^2 > \chi^2_{min} \tag{6}$$

$$support \geq sup_{min} \tag{7}$$

$$confidence \geq conf_{min} \tag{8}$$

where χ^2_{min}, sup_{min} and $conf_{min}$ are the minimum χ^2, minimum support, and minimum confidence, respectively given in advance.

Support

The rule $X \Rightarrow Y$ holds with SUPPORT if SUPPORT % of records in KDD Dataset contains $X \bigcup Y$. Minimum support (M_SUPP) is the rules that have a SUPPORT greater than a user-specified support.

$$SUPPORT = \frac{No.\,of\,Occurrences}{Total\,Records} \tag{9}$$

Confidence

The rule $X \Rightarrow Y$ holds with CONFIDENCE if CONFIDENCE % of the records in KDD Dataset that contain X and Y. The rules have a CONFIDENCE which is greater than a user-specified confidence is called as minimum confidence (M_CONF). Table 5 shown the support and confidence measures for KDD Dataset.

$$CONFIDENCE = \frac{Occurrence\left[Y\right]}{Occurrence\left[X\right]} \tag{10}$$

Table 5. Support and confidence measures for KDD dataset

Dataset	Total Records	SUPPORT	CONFIDENCE
10% KDD	494021	3.53%	88.58%
Corrected KDD	311029	3.30%	95.39%
Whole KDD	4898431	3.43%	76.57%

Summary

Intrusion Detection System is used to classify the attacks as either normal or malicious activity. Numbers of methods are available to classify the attacks. These attacks are having features with different natures. In this paper, proposed the Association Rule-Mining Algorithm to classify the attacks with the help of support and confidence. KDD dataset is used for experimentation and several attacks are grouped into Denial of Service (DoS), Probe, Remote to Local (R2L), and User to Root (U2R). The KDD dataset may contain redundant data which declines the accuracy of intrusion detection system and increase the false positive rate. The feature selection is important to improve the performance and reduce the false positive rate. In this paper, apply the entropy-based feature selection for improving their efficiency and false positive rate. Entropy based feature selection and Association rule mining algorithm are proposed to evaluate the KDD Dataset and dynamic data to improve the efficiency, reduce the False Positive Rate (FPR) and less time for processing. In future, Entropy based feature selection and Association Rule-Mining algorithm can be regenerating the rules with the help of support and confidence then apply the modified algorithm into Cloud based Intrusion Detection and Internet of Things based Intrusion Detection for improving the detection rate, reducing False Positive Rate and minimize the time.

RESULTS AND DISCUSSION

Two different metrics are used to measure the performance namely Attack Detection Rate (ADR) and False Positive Rate (FPR) by using confusion matrix (Lidio, Roberto & Mauro, 2012) (Devaraju & Ramakrishnan, 2014).

Table 6. Confusion Matrix

	Classified as Normal	**Classified as Attack**
Normal	TN	FP
Attack	FN	TP

TN – denotes the number of connections classified as normal while they actually were normal.

FP – denotes the number of connections classified as attack while they actually were normal.

FN – denotes the number of connections classified as normal while they actually were attack.

TP - denotes the number of connections classified as attack while they actually were attack.

Attack Detection Rate (ADR): It is the ratio between total numbers of attacks detected by the system to the total number of attacks present in the dataset.

$$ADR = \frac{total\ detected\ attack}{total\ attacks} * 100 \qquad (11)$$

False Positive Rate (FPR): It is the ratio between total numbers of misclassified instances to the total number of normal instances.

$$FPR = \frac{total\ misclassified\ instances}{total\ normal\ instances} * 100 \tag{12}$$

The association rule-mining algorithm is used to generate the rulesets and applied with KDD dataset. The system configuration for applying the dataset is Intel(R) Core2 Duo @ 2.20GHz, 2.00GB RAM and 32-bit OS. The open source application is used to apply the dataset and improve the detection rate (Nie & He, 2010) (Lin, Ying, Lee & Zne-Jung, 2012) (Ramakrishnan & Devaraju, 2017).

The rules have been generated for each category depending on the support and confidence value. The process functions aptly by choosing minimum support and minimum confidence value. The following steps are used to generating the rules and table 6 shows the classwise rules.

Step 1: Select the frequent dataset FRQ with M_SUPP and M_CONF value.
Step 2: Generate all possible datasets of FRQ and store it in SUBSTITUTE.
Step 3: Count SUPPORT and CONFIDENCE value for each elements of SUBSTITUTE.
Step 4: If (SUPPORT>=M_SUPP && CONFIDENCE>=M_CONF) then
    Step 4.1:   Choose the particular elements of SUBSTITUTE and store in RULE_GEN.
    Step 4.2:   Generate various rules and store in RULE_GEN.
Step 5: Else reject the particular element of SUBSTITUTE and go to step 3.
Step 6: Return RULE_GEN.
Step 7: Terminate.

where,

FRQ – frequent dataset.
M_SUPP - user define support
M_CONF - user define confidence
RULE_GEN – rules generated from dataset

Using 10% KDD Dataset (Training Data)

Table 8 contains the Training Results for five types of classes and the efficiency is measured using open source application. Confusion Matrix and Training Results for 10% KDD Dataset when Support and Confidence are 3.53% and 88.58%

Depends on the training result, the pictorial representation is given in figure 6. Figure 6 has shown the training result for 10% KDD Dataset.

The performance of association rule-mining algorithm is applied for 10% KDD dataset. The percentage of detection rate for five classes is listed in Table 7. Here detection rate of Normal is 90.51%; detection rate of DoS attack is 99.43%; detection rate of Probe attack is 76.80%; detection rate of R2L attack is 54.44%; detection rate of U2R attack is 78.85%. The algorithm has improved the detection rate and has taken less time for processing.

The False Positive Rate for 10% KDD dataset is also discussed. The False Positive Rate for Normal is 2.87%; False Positive Rate for DoS is 0.04%; False Positive Rate for Probe is 7.69%; False Positive Rate for R2L is 23.45% and False Positive Rate for U2R is 1.92%. The False Positive Rate for R2L is

Table 7. Classwise rule generation

Number	Protocol	Rule	Class
1	tcp	c1=tcp and c0 <=800 and (c2=http or c2=smtp or c2=ftp or c2=ftp_data) and c3=sf and c4 <=400 and c11=1 and c22<=30 and c23<=8 and c31<=254 and c28>=0.01 and c32>=1 and c33>=0.01and (c34>=0.01 or c35>=0.01)	Normal
2	udp	c1=udp and c0<=20750 and (c2=domain_u or c2=other or c2=private) and c3=sf and c4>=1 and c7<=3 and c11=0 and c22<=20 and c23>=2 and c28<=1.00 and c33>=0.01 and c34>=0.01	Normal
3	icmp	c1=icmp and c0=0 and (c2=ecr_i or c2=eco_i or c2=urp_i) and c3=sf and c4>=30 and c5=0 and c7=0 and c11=0 and c22<=6 and c23<=6 and c28>=0.01 and c32>=1 and c33>=0.01 and c34>=0.01	Normal
4	tcp	c1=tcp and c0=0 and (c2=http or c2=finger or c2=smtp) and (c3=s0 or c3=sf) and c9<=3 and c11=1 and c12<=1 and c28=1.00 and c31=255and c33>=0.50 and c40>=0.01	DoS
5	udp	c1=udp and c0=0 and c2=private and c3=sf and c4=28 and c5=0 and c7<=3	DoS
6	icmp	c1=icmp and c0=0 and c2=ecr_i and c3=sf and (c4>=520 or c4<=1480) and c5=0	DoS
7	tcp	c1=tcp and c0=0 and (c2=private or c2=other) and (c3=rej or c3=s0 or c3=rstr) and c4=0 and c22>=1 and c23>=0.50 and c27=1 and c29>=0.97 and c31=255 and c38=1.00 and c39>=0.50 and c40=1.00	Probe
8	udp	c1=udp and c0=0 and (c2=other or c2=domain_u or c2=private) and c3=sf and c4=1 and c5<=1 and c22>=20 and c23<=2 and c31=255 and c32<=22 and c34>=0.01 and c35>=0.01	Probe
9	icmp	c1=icmp and c0=0 and (c2=ecr_i or c2=eco_i or c2=urp_i) and c3=sf and (c4>=37 or c4<=1032) and c5=0 and c22<=2 and c23<=50 and c28=1.00 and c31<=255 and c33>=0.01 and c35>=0.01	Probe
10	tcp	c1=tcp and c0 <=20 and (c2=pop_3 or c2=ftp_data or c2=ftp) and (c3=sf or c3=rsto) and (c4 >=20 or c4<=28) and (c5>=90 or c5<=250) and c11=1 and c22<=8 and c28>=0.12 and c31>=1 and c33>=0.01 and c35>=0.01	R2L
11	udp	c1=udp and c0=0 and c2=other and c3=sf and (c4>=23 or c4<=516) and c5=0 and c22<=6 and c23<=6 and c28=1.00 and c34>=0.02	R2L
12	icmp	c1=icmp and c0=0 and c2=urp_i and c3=sf and c4=552 and c5=0 and c22=1 and c23=1 and c28=1.00 and c31=255 and c32=1 and c34=0.02 and c39=0.03	R2L
13	tcp	c1=tcp and c0=0 and (c2=ftp_data or c2=telnet or c2=ftp) and c3=sf and ((c4=0 and c5 !=0) or(c4!=0 and c5 =0)) and c23<=3 and c32<=52 and c33>=0.01 and c34>=0.01and (c36>=0.20 or c39<=0.05)	U2R

Table 8. Confusion matrix and training results for 10 percent dataset

	Normal	DoS	Probe	R2L	U2R	Detection Rate %	False Positive Rate %	Total Time Taken (seconds)
Normal	88047	374	0	2357	58	90.51	2.87	
DoS	176	389232	0	0	0	99.43	0.04	
Probe	316	1	3154	0	0	76.80	7.69	10
R2L	264	0	0	613	17	54.44	23.45	
U2R	1	0	0	2	41	78.85	1.92	

Figure 6. Detection Rate for 10% KDD Dataset

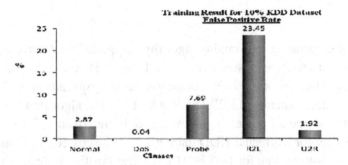

Figure 7. False Positive Rate for 10% KDD Dataset

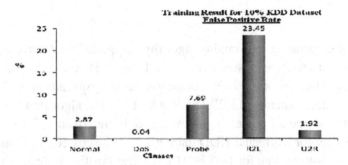

high because normal and snmpgetattack of all 41 feature values are the same (refer table 3). Figure 7 has shown the False Positive Rate for 10% KDD Dataset.

Using Corrected KDD Dataset (Testing Data)

Table 9 contains the Testing Results for five types of classes and the efficiency is measured using open source application. Confusion Matrix and Testing Results for Corrected KDD Dataset when Support and Confidence are 3.30% and 95.39%

Table 9. Confusion matrix and testing results for corrected dataset

	Normal	DoS	Probe	R2L	U2R	Detection Rate %	False Positive Rate %	Total Time Taken (seconds)
Normal	58792	233	0	1033	28	97.03	2.14	
DoS	26	228308	0	252	0	99.33	0.01	
Probe	21	3	2818	15	0	67.64	0.50	12
R2L	3087	0	0	5404	13	33.06	18.88	
U2R	0	0	0	9	61	87.14	0.00	

Depends on the testing result, the pictorial representation is given in figure 8. Figure 8 has shown the testing result for Corrected KDD Dataset.

Figure 8. Detection Rate for Corrected KDD Dataset

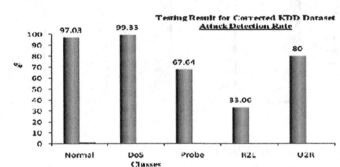

The performance of association rule-mining algorithm is applied for Corrected KDD dataset. The percentage of detection rate for five classes is listed in Table 8. Here the detection rate of Normal is 97.03%; detection rate of DoS attack is 99.33%; detection rate of Probe attack is 67.64%; detection rate of R2L attack is 33.06%; detection rate of U2R attack is 87.14%. The algorithm has improved the detection rate and has taken less time for processing (Devaraju & Ramakrishnan, 2014).

The False Positive Rate for Corrected KDD dataset is also discussed. The False Positive Rate for Normal is 2.14%; False Positive Rate for DoS is 0.01%; False Positive Rate for Probe is 0.50%; False Positive Rate for R2L is 18.88% and False Positive Rate for U2R is 0.00%. The False Positive Rate for R2L is high because normal and snmpgetattack of all 41 feature values are the same (refer table 3). Figure 9 has shown the False Positive Rate for Corrected KDD Dataset.

Figure 9. False positive rate for corrected KDD dataset

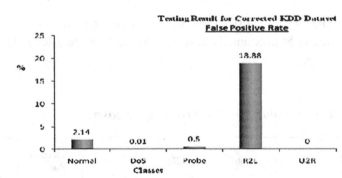

Using Full KDD Dataset (Testing Data)

Table 10 contains the Testing Results for five types of classes and the efficiency is measured using open source application. Confusion Matrix and Testing Results for Full KDD Dataset when Support and Confidence are 3.43% and 76.57%

Table 10. Confusion matrix and testing results for full dataset

	Normal	DoS	Probe	R2L	U2R	Detection Rate %	False Positive Rate %	Total Time Taken (seconds)
Normal	879458	3247	0	27704	627	90.41	3.25	
DoS	1017	3873237	0	0	0	99.74	0.03	
Probe	4089	15	31356	2	1	76.29	9.95	72
R2L	264	0	0	613	17	54.44	23.45	
U2R	1	0	0	2	41	78.85	1.92	

Depends on the testing result, the pictorial representation is given in figure 10. Figure 10 has shown the testing result for Full KDD Dataset.

Figure 10. Detection rate for full KDD dataset

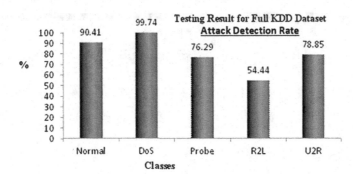

The performance of association rule-mining algorithm is applied for Full KDD dataset. The percentage of detection rate for five classes is listed in Table 9. Here detection rate of Normal is 90.41%; detection rate of DoS attack is 99.74%; detection rate of Probe attack is 76.29%; detection rate of R2L attack is 54.44%; detection rate of U2R attack is 78.85%. The algorithm has improved the detection rate and has taken less time for processing.

The False Positive Rate for Full KDD dataset is also discussed. The False Positive Rate for Normal is 3.25%; False Positive Rate for DoS is 0.03%; False Positive Rate for Probe is 9.95%; False Positive Rate for R2L is 23.45% and False Positive Rate for U2R is 1.92%. The False Positive Rate for R2L is high because normal and snmpgetattack of all 41 feature values are the same (refer table 3). Figure 11 has shown the result for Full KDD Dataset.

Figure 11. False positive rate for full KDD dataset

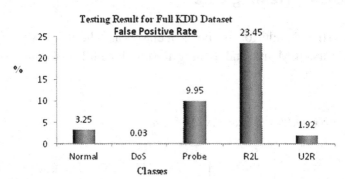

Evaluation of Dynamic Data

In this paper consider the dynamic data to be evaluated using association rule mining algorithm. The wireshark tool is used to get the dynamic data. The system is connected with local area network and internet. The wireshark tool is detected as normal as well as intruder. The Association rule mining algorithm is used to employ the dynamic data with vital use of 2500 TCP samples in which 1500 are reported to be normal and 1000 are reported to be attacks. Figure 12 shows that to trace the real-time dynamic data through wireshark.

Figure 12. Generation of dynamic data using wireshark

Table 11. Results for dynamic data

Real-Time Data (TCP) With Total Records	Normal	Attacks	Detection Rate %	False Positive Rate %
Normal (1500)	1373	78	91.53	5.2
Attacks (1000)	39	926	92.60	3.9

Figure 13. ROC curves on detection rates and false positive rates

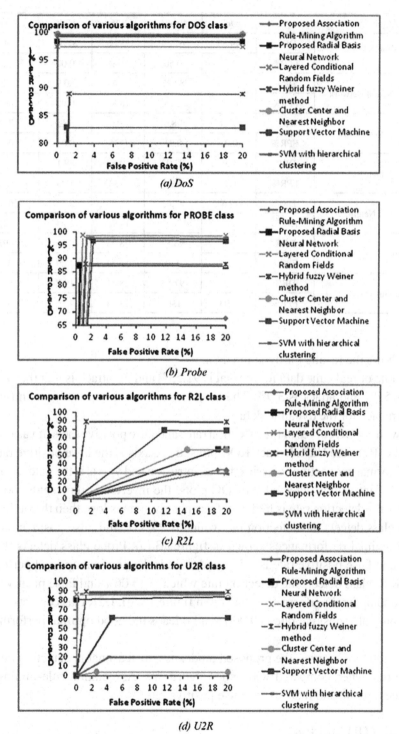

(a) DoS

(b) Probe

(c) R2L

(d) U2R

Table 12. Performance comparison of various algorithms

Algorithm		DoS	Probe	R2L	U2R	Average	CT (sec.)
Proposed Association Rule-Mining Algorithm	DR%	99.33	67.64	33.06	87.14	71.79	126
	FPR%	0.01	0.50	18.88	0.00	4.84	
Proposed Radial Basis Neural Network	DR%	98.38	87.27	57.43	80.9	80.99	129
	FPR%	0.01	0.55	18.88	0.00	04.86	
Layered Conditional Random Fields	DR%	97.4	98.6	29.6	86.3	77.97	156
	FPR%	0.07	0.91	0.35	0.05	00.35	
Hybrid fuzzy Weiner method	DR%	88.92	87.92	89.12	89.1	88.76	343
	FPR%	1.34	1.34	1.38	1.29	01.34	
Cluster Center and Nearest Neighbor	DR%	99.68	97.61	57.02	3.85	64.54	1570
	FPR%	0.09	2.08	14.78	2.64	04.89	
Support Vector Machine	DR%	82.85	96.59	78.95	61.5	79.97	189
	FPR%	1.05	2.31	11.74	4.69	04.95	
SVM with hierarchical clustering	DR%	99.53	97.55	28.81	19.7	61.39	193
	FPR%	0.04	1.41	13.54	4.16	04.78	

The table 11 shows the results for dynamic data.

The detection rate of real-time data for normal is 91.53% and for attack is 92.60%. The false positive rate for normal is 5.2% and attack is 3.9%. The association rule-mining is also significantly achieving the overall performance for the dynamic data.

Figure 13 shows the ROC curves of the detection rates and false positive rates of various attack classes, namely DoS, Probe, R2L and U2R. In each ROC plots, the x-axis is the false positive rate, calculated as the percentage of normal connections classified as an intrusion and y-axis is the detection rate, calculated as the percentage of intrusions detected. In ROC plots, the inverted L represents the optimal performances. Whenever the detection rate is high and false positive rate is low, then the optimal performance is achieved. DoS class detects the detection rate which is 99.33% and false positive rate is 0.01%, and it leads the good optimal performances shown in figure 13 (a). Probe class detects the detection rate which is 67.64% and false positive rate is 0.5%, and it leads the nominal optimal performances shown in figure 13 (b). R2L class detects the detection rate which is 33.06% and false positive rate is 18.88%, and it leads the good optimal performances shown in figure 13 (c). U2R class detects the detection rate which is 80.00% and false positive rate is 0.00%, and it leads the good optimal performances shown in figure 13 (d).

However, from the ROC curves, the proposed model has the reasonable detection rate and it reduces the false positive rate when compared with other algorithms. Association rule-mining algorithm has improved the detection rate and reduces the false positive rate.

Comparison of KDD Dataset

It is considerably evident that the Association Rule-Mining Algorithm can be awfully effective in detecting the DoS and R2L attacks and minimizing the FPR and also reducing the time (Gupta & Kotagiri,

2010) (Devaraju & Ramakrishnan, 2014). In this comparison, the corrected dataset is used for testing and compared with various algorithms which improve the detection rate and False Positive Rate. The full dataset is also used for testing the dataset which improves the detection rate and False Positive Rate shown in table 9. In table 12, corrected dataset is used for comparing the performance and False Positive Rate.

CONCLUSION

The Association Rule-Mining algorithm is applied for network intrusion detection system. Feature reduction is applied to eliminate the unwanted features. The Entropy based feature selection algorithm is used to reduce the number of features and these features do not affect the overall performance of the system. The Association Rule-Mining algorithm is successfully applied in different benchmarking KDD Dataset (10%, Corrected and Full Dataset). Compared with various algorithms, the testing dataset (corrected dataset) is used to compare and the detection rate of Association Rule-Mining algorithm has improved for class DoS as 99.33% and R2L as 33.06%. It is observed that the False Positive Rate has reduced as well as the time taken for processing has become less. The dynamic data is generated using wireshark tool which is employed in this paper. The significant detection rate and false positive rate is achieved through dynamic data. The overall results for detection rate, False Positive Rate and time taken for processing are significant comparing with other algorithms. The Entropy based feature selection and Association rule-Mining algorithm are applied both known and unknown attacks to improve the detection rate, reduce the false positive rate, minimize the computational time and also improve the overall performance of the Intrusion Detection System.

For future enhancements, Association Rule-Mining algorithm can be modified or rules can be refined then apply the modified algorithm into Cloud based Intrusion Detection and Internet of Things based Intrusion Detection. Further the support and confidence will helps to identify the various attacks with regenerating the rules for improving the detection rate, reducing False Positive Rate and minimize the time.

REFERENCES

Ahmad, I., Abdullah, A., Alghamdi, A., & Hussain, M. (2013). Optimized intrusion detection mechanism using soft computing techniques. *Telecommunication Systems*, *52*(4), 2187–2195.

Akashdeep, I. M., & Kumar, N. (2017). A Feature Reduced Intrusion Detection System using ANN Classifier, Elsevier -. *Expert Systems with Applications*, *88*, 249–257. doi:10.1016/j.eswa.2017.07.005

Anuar, N. B., Sallehudin, H., Gani, A., & Zakari, O. (2008). Identifying False Alarm for Network Intrusion Detection System using Hybrid Data Mining and Decision Tree. *Malaysian Journal of Computer Science*, *21*(2), 101–115. doi:10.22452/mjcs.vol21no2.3

Chebrolu, S., Abraham, A., & Thomas, J. P. (2005). Feature deduction and ensemble design of intrusion detection systems. *Computers & Security*, *24*(4), 295–307. doi:10.1016/j.cose.2004.09.008

Chen, N., Chen, X. S., Xiong, B., & Lu, H. W. (2009, September). An anomaly detection and analysis method for network traffic based on correlation coefficient matrix. *Proceedings of the 2009 International Conference on Scalable Computing and Communications; Eighth International Conference on Embedded Computing* (pp. 238-244). IEEE.

KDD Cup 1999 Intrusion Detection Data. (2010). Retrieved from http://kdd.ics.uci.edu/databases/kddcup99/kddcup99.html

Anbalagan, E., Puttamadappa, C., Mohan, E., Jayaraman, B., & Madane, S. (2008). Datamining and Intrusion Detection Using Back-Propagation Algorithm for Intrusion Detection. *International Journal of Soft Computing*, *3*(4), 264–270.

de Campos, L. M. L., de Oliveira, R. C. L., & Roisenberg, M. (2012, September). Network intrusion detection system using data mining. *Proceedings of the International Conference on Engineering Applications of Neural Networks* (pp. 104-113). Springer. doi:10.1007/978-3-642-32909-8_11

Devaraju, S., & Ramakrishnan, S. (2011). Performance Analysis of Intrusion Detection System Using Various Neural Network Classifiers. *IEEE Proceedings of the International Conference on International Conference on Recent Trends in Information Technology (ICRTIT 2011)*, Madras Institute of Technology, Anna University, Chennai, India (pp. 1033-1038). IEEE.

Devaraju, S., & Ramakrishnan, S. (2013). Performance Comparison of Intrusion Detection System using Various Techniques – A Review. *ICTACT Journal on Communication Technology*, *4*(3), 802–812. doi:10.21917/ijct.2013.0114

Devaraju, S., & Ramakrishnan, S. (2014). Performance Comparison for Intrusion Detection System using Neural Network with KDD Dataset. *ICTACT Journal on Soft Computing*, *4*(3), 743–752. doi:10.21917/ijsc.2014.0106

Devaraju S. & Ramakrishnan S. (2015). Detection of Attacks for IDS using Association Rule Mining Algorithm. *IETE Journal of Research*, *61*(6), 624-633.

Ghali, N. I. (2009). Feature Selection for Effective Anomaly-Based Intrusion Detection. *International Journal of Computer Science and Network Security*, *9*(3), 285–289.

Gupta, K. K., Nath, B., & Kotagiri, R. (2010). Layered Approach Using Conditional Random Fields for Intrusion Detection. *IEEE Transactions on Dependable and Secure Computing*, *7*(1), 35–49. doi:10.1109/TDSC.2008.20

Hajisalem, V., & Babaie, S. (2018). A hybrid intrusion detection system based on ABC-AFS algorithm for misuse and anomaly detection. *Computer Networks*, *136*, 37–50. doi:10.1016/j.comnet.2018.02.028

Hanguang, L., & Yu, N. (2012). Intrusion detection technology research based on apriori algorithm. *Physics Procedia*, *24*, 1615–1620.

Hu, J., Yu, X., Qiu, D., & Chen, H.-H. (2009). A simple and efficient hidden Markov model scheme for host- based anomaly intrusion detection. *Journal IEEE Network*, *23*(1), 42–47. doi:10.1109/MNET.2009.4804323

Jiang, H., & Ruan, J. (2009). The Application of Genetic Neural Network in Network Intrusion Detection. *Journal of Computers*, *4*(12), 1223–1230. doi:10.4304/jcp.4.12.1223-1230

Jiang, M., Gan, X., Wang, C., & Wang, Z. (2011). Research of the Intrusion Detection Model Based on Data Mining, Elsevier. *Energy Procedia*, *13*, 855–863.

Kabir, E., Hu, J., Wang, H., & Zhuo, G. (2018). A novel statistical technique for intrusion detection systems, Elsevier-. *Future Generation Computer Systems*, *79*, 303–318. doi:10.1016/j.future.2017.01.029

Li, W. (2004). Using Genetic Algorithm for network intrusion detection. *Proceedings of the United States Department of Energy Cyber Security Group 2004 Training Conference*. Academic Press.

Lin, S.-W., Ying, K.-C., Lee, C.-Y., & Lee, Z.-J. (2012). An intelligent algorithm with feature selection and decision rules applied to anomaly intrusion detection. *Applied Soft Computing*, *12*(10), 3285–3290. doi:10.1016/j.asoc.2012.05.004

Mabu, S., Chen, C., Lu, N., Shimada, K., & Hirasawa, K. (2011). An Intrusion-Detection Model Based on Fuzzy Class-Association-Rule Mining Using Genetic Network Programming. *IEEE Transactions on Systems, Man and Cybernetics. Part C, Applications and Reviews*, *41*(1), 130–139. doi:10.1109/TSMCC.2010.2050685

Mukkamala, S., Sung, A. H., & Abraham, A. (2005). Intrusion detection using an ensemble of intelligent paradigms. *Journal of Network and Computer Applications*, *28*(2), 167–182.

Mukkamala, S., Sung, A. H., & Abraham, A. (2007). Hybrid multi-agent framework for detection of stealthy probes. *Applied Soft Computing*, *7*(3), 631–641. doi:10.1016/j.asoc.2005.12.002

Muniyandi, A. P., Rajeswari, R., & Rajaram, R. (2012). Network Anomaly Detection by Cascasding K-Means Clustering and C4.5 Decision Tree Algorithm. *Procedia Engineering*, *30*, 174-182.

Nadiammai, G. V., & Hemalatha, M. (2014). Effective Approach toward Intrusion Detection System using Data Mining Techniques. *Elsevier Egyptian Informatics Journal*, *15*(1), 37–50. doi:10.1016/j.eij.2013.10.003

Nie, W., & He, D. (2010). A probability approach to anomaly detection with twin support vector machines. *Journal of Shanghai Jiaotong University (Science)*, *15*(4), 385–391.

Pan, Z., Hariri, S., & Pacheco, J. (2019). Context Aware Intrusion Detection of Building Automation Systems. *Computers & Security*, *85*, 181–201. doi:10.1016/j.cose.2019.04.011

Peddabachigari, S., Abraham, A., Grosan, C., & Thomas, J. (2007). Modeling intrusion detection system using hybrid intelligent systems. *Journal of Network and Computer Applications*, *30*(1), 114–132.

Ramakrishnan, S., & Devaraju, S. (2017). Attack's Feature Selection-Based Network Intrusion Detection System Using Fuzzy Control Language, Springer-. *International Journal of Fuzzy Systems*, *19*(2), 316–328. doi:10.100740815-016-0160-6

Rana, A. R. A., Wang, X.-Z., Huang, J. Z., Abbas, H., & He, Y.-L. (2017). Fuzziness based semi-supervised learning approach for intrusion detection system. *Information Sciences*, *378*, 484–497. doi:10.1016/j.ins.2016.04.019

Sarasamma, S. T., Zhu, Q. A., & Huff, J. (2005). Hierarchical Kohonen Net for Anomaly Detection in Network Security. *IEEE Transactions on Systems, Man, and Cybernetics, 35*(2), 2, 302–312. PMID:15828658

Selvakani Kandeeban, S. & Dr. R.S. Rajesh. (2011). A Genetic Algorithm Based elucidation for improving Intrusion Detection through condensed feature set by KDD 99 data set. *Information and Knowledge Management, 1*(1), 1–9.

Shaout, A., & Smyth, C. (2017). Fuzzy zero day exploits detector system. *International Journal of Advanced Computer Research, 7*(31), 154–163. doi:10.19101/IJACR.2017.730022

Sheikhan, M., Jadidi, Z., & Farrokhi, A. (2010). Intrusion detection using reduced-size RNN based on feature grouping, Springer-Verlag London Limited. *Neural Computing & Applications, 21*(6), 1185–1190. doi:10.100700521-010-0487-0

Shenfield, A., Day, D., & Ayesh, A. (2018). Intelligent intrusion detection systems using artificial neural networks. *ICT Express, 4*(2), 95–99. doi:10.1016/j.icte.2018.04.003

Thaseen, I. S., & Kumar, C. A. (2017). Intrusion detection model using fusion of chi-square feature selection and multi class SVM. *Journal of King Saud University-Computer and Information Sciences, 29*(4), 462–472.

Wang, M., & Zhao, A. (2012). Investigations of Intrusion Detection Based on Data Mining. *Springer Recent Advances in Computer Science and Information Engineering Lecture Notes in Electrical Engineering, 124*, 275–279.

Xie, Y., & Yu, S.-Z. (2008). A Large Scale Hidden Semi-Markov model for Anomaly Detection on User Browsing Behaviors. *IEEE/ACM Transactions on Networking, 17*(1), 1–14.

Yahalom, R., Steren, A., Nameri, Y., Roytman, M., Porgador, A., & Elovici, Y. (2019). Improving the effectiveness of intrusion detection systems for hierarchical data. *Knowledge-Based Systems, 168*, 59–69. doi:10.1016/j.knosys.2019.01.002

This research was previously published in the Handbook of Research on Intelligent Data Processing and Information Security Systems edited by Stepan Mykolayovych Bilan and Saleem Issa Al-Zoubi ; pages 1-24, copyright year 2020 by Engineering Science Reference (an imprint of IGI Global).

Chapter 11
Security Integration in DDoS Attack Mitigation Using Access Control Lists

Sumit Kumar Yadav
Indira Gandhi Delhi Technical University for Women, Delhi, India

Kavita Sharma
National Institute of Technology Kurukshetra, India

Arushi Arora
Indira Gandhi Delhi Technical University for Women, Delhi, India

ABSTRACT

In this article, the authors propose a DDoS mitigation system through access list-based configurations, which are deployed at the ISP (Internet Service Provider's) edge routers to prohibit DDoS attacks over ISPs' networks traffic. The effectiveness of the proposed system relies heavily on the willingness of ISPs in implementing the system. Once each ISP implements the system, most attacks can easily be stopped close to their point of origin. The main challenge is to implement such a system with the fixed amount of memory and available processing power with routers. A coordinated effort by participating ISPs filters out attacks close to their source, reducing the load on other routers. The suspicious traffic is first filtered out based on their source IP address. The authors also implemented the WRED algorithm for their case and conduct GNS3 experiments in a simulated environment.

INTRODUCTION

Denial of Service Attacks[1] aimed at various targets which led to the production of new challenges in the Internet within the network security communities and Internet Service Provider (ISP), to look for innovative and ingenious methods to secure our systems from these types of attacks. Denial of Service (DoS) attacks is mainly done in order to disrupt services. Hundreds or even thousands of compromised

DOI: 10.4018/978-1-7998-5348-0.ch011

hosts, called "zombies", are used to direct attacks to a particular host, in a Distributed Denial of Service (DDoS). These zombie hosts are usually unprotected computers connected to the internet through high bandwidth or always-on connection. Attackers recruit such hosts from millions of such computers by exploiting its vulnerabilities and planting sleeper codes that can quickly be activated with a command to launch DDoS attacks. The user or owner of such zombie hosts may not be aware that their system/computer is participating in such activities. By overloading servers, DDoS attacks incapacitate network links, internet systems and connected devices with malicious or bogus traffic, unlike other attacks that are focused on stealing information penetrating security perimeters. With the growing dependence on internet, the impact of successful DDoS attacks on important installations can be devastating. Many websites have fallen victim to DoS attacks resulting in inconvenience and millions of dollars in damage[2]. The DDoS attacks have also caused a less severe but measurable consequences for the Composite Block List (CBL) as well as Project Honey Pot.

Many approaches and techniques have been proposed in the past years that help to prevent DDoS attacks (Kumar & Kumar, 2016; Shrivastava, Sharma & Rai, 2010; Sharma & Gupta, 2018). A structural approach to the DDoS problem was presented by developing a classification of DDoS attacks and DDoS defense mechanisms which placed some order in the existing approaches and defense mechanisms (Douligeris & Mitrokotsa, 2004; Rajkumar, 2013; Arora & Yadav, in press a; Arora & Yadav, in press b). Other approaches to prevent the DDoS attack that were proposed include techniques like web referrals (Desai, Patel, Somaiya & Vishwanathan, 2016) and linear prediction model (Gupta et al., 2010; Ahuja & Yadav, 2012, Al-Anzi, Yadav & Soni, 2014). In one approach multivariate data analysis was used to measure low and high rate DDoS attack (Hoque, Bhattacharyya & Kalita, 2016; Arora, Yadav & Sharma, 2018; Bhushan, Banerjea & Yadav, 2014; Dhingra & Yadav, 2017). In his paper, a DDoS mitigation system is proposed which uses access list-based configurations. These are deployed at the Internet Service Provider's (ISP) edge routers to prohibit DDoS attacks into and from the ISPs' networks. The effectiveness of the proposed system will rely heavily on the willingness of the ISPs in implementing the system. The following section discusses the problem identification and further the approach and mechanism of the proposed work and the implementation on the test environment are discussed.

TYPES OF ATTACKS

In this section, the two categories of DDoS attacks are explained in addition to DDoS attack taxonomy and well-known attacks.

Bandwidth Attacks

When a large amount of traffic is sent to the host or target network, an attack is carried out. This attack causes overuse of network bandwidth, memory or processing resources. If such traffic is left uncontrolled, devices in the target path such as routers, servers and firewalls can fail. In packet-flooding attack (a type of bandwidth attack) a large number of seemingly legitimate - UDP (User Datagram Protocol) or TCP (Transmission Control Protocol), ICMP (Internet Control Message Protocol) - packets are sent to a specific destination. These packets may misrepresent their source IP (Internet Protocol) address to make detection even more difficult and lead to "spoofing". An approach MULTOPS (MUlti-Level Tree for Online Packet Statistics) was proposed for bandwidth attack detection (Gil & Poletto, 2001).

A framework based on header count, ramp-up behaviour and other techniques are used to classify DoS attacks (Hussain, Heidemann & Papadopoulos, 2003).

Application Attacks

This type of attack uses legitimate packets with specially crafted to consume computational resources and preventing the target host/application from processing other transactions or requests. An example of such attack can be the famous TCP half-open or SYN flood attack. A high volume of TCP SYN request is sent to the target host to initiate a three-way TCP connection handshake. The packets are crafted so as not to complete the handshake sequence. Thus, the target host is busy replying to the SYN and waiting for the connection to be completed. Some proposals for defending against include defense and offense wall which combats against application layer attacks (Yu, Chen & Chen, 2007; Khari & Kumar, 2016; Khari & Sangwan, 2016) and DDoS resilient scheduling (Ranjan et al., 2006). Methods have also been proposed to monitor the application attacks (Xie & Yu, 2009).

DDoS Attack Taxonomy

As previously stated, a DDoS attack exhausts victim's resources and forces it to deny service to legitimate visitors or clients. The coordinated and simultaneous act of compromised hosts that are infected by the malicious code, results in break into the victim's system causing a DDoS attack. The two types of DDoS attacks, (Peng, Leckie & Ramamohanrao, 2004; Mirkovic & Reiher, 2004) *DoS* attack and distributed reflector typical DDoS attack i.e. Distributed Reflection Denial of Service attack (Patrikakis, Masikos & Zouraraki, 2004) are explained with their analytical description in the sections below.

Typical DDoS Attacks

One or multiple master zombies are controlled by the attacker which, in turn, controls multiple slave zombies. The compromised machines, master and slave zombies have been created for this purpose and are infected by malicious code. Slave zombies carry out the coordinated attack and are triggered by the attacker's coordinated orders to master zombies. Unless master zombies receive attack commands from the attacker with activated attack processes on those machines, those machines are idle and stay in hibernation. To start attacking, the attacker has to just send the wake-up command. On receiving the command relays, master zombies attack commands to slave zombies. A DDoS attack is then mounted by the slave zombies who send a large amount of packets to the victim, flooding the system and exhausting the resources. This kind of DDoS attack is shown in Figure 1.

In the packets of the attack traffic, spoofed source IP (Internet Protocol) addresses are mostly used. Such counterfeit source IP addresses are preferred by the attackers for two major reasons: first, using spoofed IP addresses, the identity of the zombies can be hidden by the attackers, so that it becomes impossible to trace packets back to their source. The second reason is that the performance of the attack improves when the victim is incapable of filtering the attacker's traffic due to lack of identifying its source. Filtering suspicious IP addresses could result in denying services to legitimate clients. Various approaches were proposed to detect DDoS attacks including detection using NOX/OpenFlow (Braga, Mota & Passito, 2010), cluster analysis (Lee, Kim, Kwon, Han & Kim, 2008) and covariance analysis (Jin & Yeung, 2004).

Figure 1. A DDoS Attack

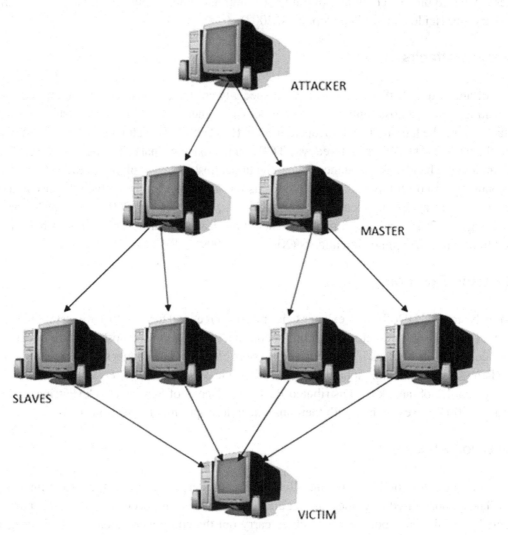

DRDoS (Distributed Reflection Denial of Service) Attacks

In DRDoS attacks (Gibson, 2002), master zombies are controlled by the attacker, which in turn, masters the slave zombies by sending a number of packets that contain the victim's IP address as the source IP address to reflectors, with spoofed IP address. These packets can either be the infected or an uninfected host, exhorting these machines to either send replies to the victim or to connect. As a reply to the connection request initiated by the spoofed packets, they contain requests that result with the reflectors sending a larger volume of traffic to the victim. Such attacks are also called DoS amplification attacks. An example scenario is when a DNS (Domain Name System) request is sent by the attacker using a spoofed IP address. The DNS server would then reply with the information requested, whose packet size is much larger than the size of the request packet. This reply packet goes to the victim that has a spoofed IP address. What makes the DRDoS attack is more distributed is that they have more machines to share the attack. Also, the reflected packet generated by the reflector hosts may be much larger in size than the original packet thus creating a greater volume of traffic. The distributed feature along with the amplification factor caused by the reflected packet can cause a huge amount of damage to the victim network. Since both attacks are distributed in nature, one cannot differentiate both attacks and consider both types of attacks generally as DDoS. Figure 2 graphically depicts a DRDoS attack. The detection of DDoS attacks is discussed in the section below.

DDOS ATTACK DETECTION

A key problem is detection when addressing DDoS attacks. The two common methods to detect DDoS attacks are discussed in the following sections.

Figure 2. A DRDoS Attack

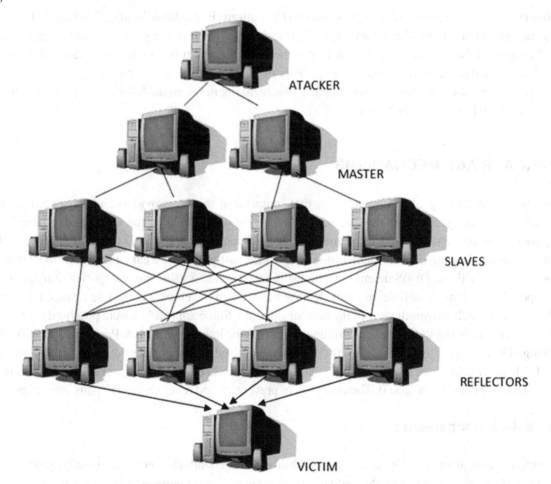

Detection by Traffic Patterns

Each network has a specific network traffic pattern. With normal traffic, this general pattern will repeat itself on and on with little deviation from time to time. Studying this regular traffic pattern can tell us how to distinguish between non-regular traffic from the standard normal pattern. Also, another approach was to detect LRD traffic time series which is based on identifying abnormal variations (Li, 2004). Historical traffic pattern can be used significantly whether abnormal traffic or normal traffic is being dealt with. Triggers can be set to enforce human interference or to notify other systems or when there occurs a huge difference in the pattern. The optimal setting for early detection mechanisms can be determined from the information based on the regular traffic pattern.

DETECTION BY (SUDDEN) TRAFFIC INCREASE

A simple, yet effective mechanism is to monitor traffic pattern (Bencsáth & Vajda, 2004) and to look out for a sudden increase in traffic. When a specific threshold is overrun, a trigger can be configured. The possibility of a false positive is very high in this method although it is effective. A sudden increase in traffic might be caused by an increase in popularity of the site. For example, an online news site might suddenly attract a lot of visitors because of particular breaking news. In the following section, the effective proposed approaches have been discussed.

APPROACH AND MECHANISMS

From the very beginning, all legitimate users that comprise of service providers and concerned groups have tried to react against these threats. Several countermeasures against the DDoS threat have been proposed by the university, research communities and software corporations. Despite all the efforts, the ultimate solution has still not been achieved. The attackers easily find out weaknesses in the mechanism. In order to clarify them, DDoS defense mechanisms have been classified into categories (Zargar, Joshi & Tipper, 2013). This classification helps defense mechanism developers cooperate against the threat and provides us with an overall view of the current situation. Some approaches were proposed to counter DDoS attacks. These methods include coordinating across the internet (Zhang & Parashar, 2006), Botnet tracking (Freiling, Holz & Wicherski, 2005), perimeter-based defence (Chen & Song, 2005), router-based defense (Ioannidis & Bellovin, 2002) and IP traceback-based intelligent packet filtering (Sung & Xu, 2003; Aljifri & Hassan, 2003). The overview of preventive and reactive mechanisms is given below.

Preventive Mechanisms

Preventive mechanisms can decrease the probability of DDoS attacks. For this, modification of the system configuration is required. Preventive measures should be implemented by each network against illegitimate traffic from or toward the network. The chance of computers becoming zombies can be reduced by ensuring that latest standard protocols are followed and software applications are updated. It is also necessary to regularly scan the machines to detect any abnormal behaviour. The client is informed in case of attack detection by guarding the network, to take defending measures by the modern security companies. Network strength is determined by several sensors checking the network traffic after which the information is sent to a server. The probability of becoming not only a victim or a zombie is reduced by securing computers and network. It is very important to prevent a computer from becoming a zombie as it reduces the chance of them becoming attacker's army. Such preventive measures against the DDoS attacks can certainly decrease their occurrence or strength, though they can never guarantee a hundred-percent effectiveness.

Analysing the methods of attack can help us recognize the weaknesses in protocols. For example, in order to filter I/O traffic, network gateways can be adjusted by their respective administrators. By doing this, the traffic can be reduced with spoofed IP addresses on the network[1]. If the filtering is applied close to the attacker, it would be more effective. This is because the network is already flooded when traffic is filtered by victims, though the victim may "survive". To filter traffic on the source would be the best solution. Concerning criteria for filters, three filtering possibilities have been reported to date. The first possibility uses filtering on the source address. If each time the attacker is known, only then this would be effective. This is not always possible as spoofed IP addresses are usually used by the attacker. In most DDoS attacks, they use a large number of zombies. Implementation of a filter is practically impossible here. Filtering on the service is suggested by the second filtering possibility. In this tactic, it is presumed that the attack mechanism and what all services will be affected by this are known. In such a scenario, the traffic can be filtered. Rejecting every packet is similar to denying services to everybody. Filtering on the destination address is another possibility. A technique called *Ingress Filtering*[3] was developed by Paul Ferguson and Fred Baker for mitigating DoS attacks (Ferguson & Senie, 1997). Router-based approach was proposed (David, Sood & Kajla, 2011) to Mitigate DoS attacks on the wireless networks, Smurf attacks and where SYN Flood attacks were successfully traced and mitigated. In this paper, a mechanism is proposed to apply both concepts together thereby allowing us to properly mitigate DDoS. In order to make attackers more traceable and to prohibit the use of spoofed addresses, this filtering should be implemented at multiple levels even if asymmetric/ multihomed networks are presented. A method for mitigating high volume attacks is also presented. Some techniques were proposed to prevent DDoS attacks that based on Software Defined Networking (SDN) using thorough packet inspection (Hyun, Kim, Hong & Jeong, 2017) (Bhushan & Gupta, 2018).

Reactive Mechanisms

Besides detecting a DDoS attack and mitigating it, identifying the cause/origin of the attack and the actual culprit apart from diagnosing which part of the network is under attack. This can be very difficult. An independent system or software may be delegated within the network to log and collect records of traffic passing through the network. Relying on the traffic logging capabilities of the routers will just put more load on them and degrade performance. A dedicated system for this purpose will enable us to have access to essential information on network activity while taking the load off the routers. Based on this information, it can be determined if an attack is carried out by many compromised hosts or just a single one. The provider of the network/internet service or local law enforcement agencies can be alerted regarding the malicious activities being carried out against the network if the origin(s) of the attack can be traced. But in most cases, attackers use spoofed IP addresses to protect themselves from being caught. Keeping a record of such traffic pattern will serve as evidence that the network is under attack and will help in creating better mitigation tools and techniques in the future. In the next section, the test setup mechanism is discussed.

TEST ENVIRONMENT

In this Section we will be discuss the test setup which is used to prove the concept of DDoS mitigation mechanism. The logical overview of this setup is shown below. Each part of the network is discussed by explaining its function.

R1 represents the edge router on which the target hosts are located.

S1 represents the target host.

C1, C2 & C3 represents any other host within their individual subnet.

R2 & R3 represent remote routers on which DDoS generator hosts are located.

PC1 & PC2 represent attacker's hosts

SW1 & SW2 represent the switches on which hosts are connected to their respective routers.

The whole setup is implemented through a simulated network environment using GNS3 (Graphical Network Simulator). An intuitive graphical user interface is also provided by GNS3, to design and configure virtual networks. Routers R1, R2 and R3 use Cisco 3745 image for emulating a Cisco 3745 router. These are the routers where rules will be set up to mitigate DDoS traffic. Router R1 is the edge router of the network that is to be protected. A server running web services accessible to the public is running on S1 which is connected to R1. C1 represents any other host or server within the subnet connected to R1. S1 is the only publicly accessible router within the subnet.R1 is connected to external networks. R2 and R3 represent the edge routers of the external networks. Traffic coming through these two routers has to pass through R1 to reach S1 and the other internal hosts. Traffic is generated using PC1 which is connected to a Windows host and PC2 which is connected to a Linux host. PC1 and PC2 are used to generate traffic for the simulation. The whole network setup is prepared for simulation on GNS3 as given Figure 3.

The following assumptions have been made concerning the proposed work:

- All router units are initially configured to run with factory default settings.
- Proper security settings have been implemented and configured on the routers to restrict access to the configuration interface from a remote location as well as local management consoles.
- All internal hosts with private addresses are managed through a gateway router and access to the internet is provided through proper port forwarding.
- All logs and traffic flow information passing through each router is recorded using a dedicated flow collector or traffic logging system.

Generating Dos Traffic

To test the setup, DDoS traffic is required to be generated. To generate a lot of traffic to the attacked host, two different techniques were used. The main tool used for the purpose is hping2. Hping[4] is a TCP/IP packet crafter which is command-line oriented. It can be used for creating IP packets containing UDP, TCP or ICMP payloads. Using the command line, all header fields can be controlled and modified. The first technique was to generate as much traffic with different a spoofed IP addresses as possible. The bulk of this traffic will be filtered out as close to their source as possible as the egress filtering rules wouldn't allow traffic from spoofed IP address to go through their edge router and reach a remote host.

Figure 3. Logical Overview of Simulated Network

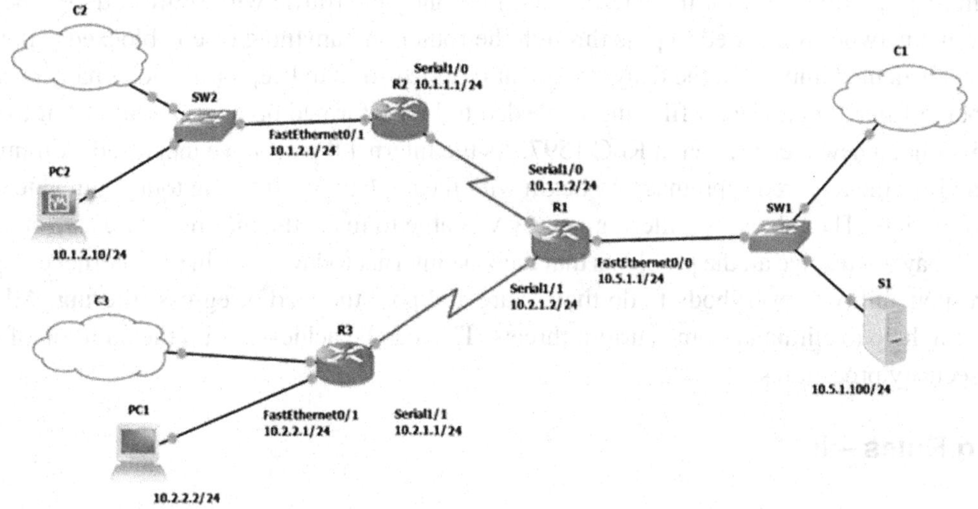

The second was to generate as much traffic without spoofed IP addresses as possible. This traffic would reach their destination network, but the WRED (Weighted Random Early Detection) configuration would try to filter out bad traffic and minimize the load on the target network and also to the target host.

Filtering Rules – I

Only traffic with a source addresses belonging to the customer network should be accepted by the ISP edge router. Any source address outside of the customer's network is readily a spoofed IP address. This is required to be implemented on the part of the ISP to prevent customers from participating in such malicious activities. Only traffic with source addresses other than the customer network address-block should be accepted by customer network. ACL (Access Control List) for an ISP (Internet Service Provider) edge router to enable this filtering can be implemented as shown in Figure 4.

Figure 4. Implementation of filtering rules-I

> *access–list 111 permit ip {customer network} {customer network mask} any*
>
> *access–list 111 deny ip any any [log]*
>
> *interface {internal interface} {interface #}*
>
> *ip access–group 111 in*

These are called egress filtering because traffic with invalid sources from passing through the router to the external interface is denied. To the internal interface of the router, these rules are applied. In Cisco access-list implementation, on an interface, once an access-list is activated, any traffic which is not explicitly permitted is denied. So, once access–list 111 permit ip {customer network} {customer network mask} any rule is set for the internal interface and only traffic with source address belonging to the internal network is allowed to pass through the router and anything else is blocked. Though any other packet is denied implicitly, the deny statement is added so as to keep tab of how many packets are actually being filtered out. Egress filtering is needed to be performed on a large scale for it to be efficient. This is not a new idea as seen in RFC 1597. As the internet threats have increased, administrators have been given the required supremacy, to begin with the applying of filtering total aggregate network nodes and borders. Though egress filtering is very valuable to make the internet more safe and secure, however, it may not resolve all the problems that face the internet today. Also, in the internet community, it is the responsibility of everybody to do their share and pool the load of egress filtering. All service providers can help to eliminate some current threats. This can be achieved with the addition of steps to network security procedures.

Filtering Rules – II

Figure 5. Implementation of filtering rules-II

access–list 110 permit {protocol} any host {host address} [packet type |eq {port #}]

access–list 110 deny ip any any [log]

interface {external interface} {interface #}

ip access–group 110 in

As mentioned earlier, access-list implicitly denies any traffic that is not explicitly permitted. So, the best strategy is to allow only that traffic related to services provided by the publicly accessible servers. So, services like FTP (File Transfer Protocol), SMTP (Simple Mail Transfer Protocol), POP (Point Of Presence) and other network service that needs to be accessed by the external hosts may be explicitly allowed through the network and only to those servers that provide the service. ACL for an ISP edge router to enable this filtering can be implemented as shown in Figure 5. As opposed to the previous filtering where the source address is filtered, the destination address or port is checked and filtered for filtering. Whatever is not included in the permit list will be rejected. Most of the time ICMP echo and echo-reply packets are allowed to pass through the network as it is an important tool for network troubleshooting and also for checking connectivity. But care must be taken when allowing ICMP traffic coming from the external networks. Although it has been a recommended practice to block known malware ports to prevent misuse of the network through such programs and to reduce the chances of individual computers participating in such activities as zombies, this system of ingress-filtering implicitly blocks any traffic targeted at ports not utilized by the publicly accessible server and thus effectively prevents unused ports from being manipulated. Emsisoft, an anti-malware vendor, has a publicly viewable list of such malware ports[5]. It can be seen from the list that even some well-known ports have been exploited and used to run malicious activities. So, by explicitly allowing access only to specific ports where verified services are being provided is the most effective way to prevent networked systems from being manipulated.

WRED (Weighted Random Early Detection)

Sally Floyd and Van Jacobson proposed the RED mechanism in the 1990s. This detects the Congestion Avoidance (CA). The main functional idea of the RED mechanism is to detect the load on data transport layer. The network may slow down itself if such important traffic drops. In WRED IP Precedence feature is used to provide special traffic handling in consideration with high priority data. When congestion takes place, lower priority traffic is discarded. WRED differentiate itself from other CA techniques by using its anticipating strategy. The packet source is told to lower down its transmission rate, by WRED. This will happen if the packet source is using TCP and is done by dropping packets before high congestion. Based on IP precedence, WRED selectively drops packets. It is less likely that the packets with a higher IP precedence will be dropped. The delivery of the packet is done on the basis of its priority. By selectively dropping packets, WRED decreases the chances of tail drop. This happens after the output interface signals congestion. In order to avoid congestion, tail drop is a means that does not differentiate between classes of service and treats all traffic equally. Queues fill when there is high congestion. The packets are then dropped. This is achieved to eliminate the congestion. The queue then is no more full. WRED lowers the chances of global synchronization and dodges dropping large numbers of packets together. Some packets are dropped early, instead of waiting for the queue to be full. Therefore, at all times, usage of a transmission line is allowed by WRED. When statistically seen, WRED drops more packets from large sources and hence, these traffic sources are likely to be slowed down. Tail drop causes certain globalization problems occur and are avoided by WRED. When a number of TCP hosts decrease their respective transmission rates because of packet dropping, global synchronization manifests. When the congestion is reduced transmission rates increase again. Only in the case of TCP/IP traffic, WRED is useful. Packet sources may not respond to other protocols, like ICMP and UDP. Therefore, congestion is not reduced by dropping packets. According to WRED, the precedence of non-IP traffic is 0, which is the lowest precedence, therefore they are more likely to be dropped. Parameters are automatically determined by the router that is to be used in the WRED calculations. The formula 1 of average queue size is as shown below:

$$Avg = (previous\_avg*(1-2^{-n})) + (present\_queue\_size* 2^{-n}) \tag{1}$$

here, n is the exponential weight factor. The following command is used to change the exponential weight factor:

random-detect exponential-weighting-constant exponent

The experimental test set-up is elaborated in the next section explaining this model's implementation in addition to network setup, configuration and test traffic analysis.

Deployment Within the Simulated Network

This section will explain in detail about the simulation process as well as the step by step procedure of the experimental set-up.

Network Setup and Configuration

Configurations of each router and connected hosts or devices are shown in Figure 6, Figure 7, Figure 8 and Figure 9.

Figure 6. Configuration of R1 first

Configuration of R1

```
interface Serial1/0
ip address 10.1.1.2 255.255.255.0
ip access-group 110 in
ip flow ingress
* ip flow egress
random-detect

interface Serial1/1
ip address 10.2.1.2 255.255.255.0
ip access-group 110 in
ip flow ingress
ip flow egress
random-detect

interface FastEthernet0/0
ip address 10.5.1.1 255.255.255.0
ip access-group 111 in
ip flow ingress
ip flow egress

access-list 110 deny   icmp any any fragments
access-list 110 permit icmp any any echo
access-list 110 permit icmp any any echo-reply
access-list 110 permit icmp any any packet-too-big
access-list 110 permit icmp any any time-exceeded
```

Figure 7. Configuration of R1 second

```
access-list 110 permit icmp any any traceroute
access-list 110 permit icmp any any log-input
access-list 110 deny  icmp any any
access-list 110 permit udp any any eq echo
access-list 110 permit udp any eq echo any
access-list 110 permit tcp any any established
access-list 110 permit tcp any host 10.5.1.100 eq www
access-list 110 permit tcp any host 10.5.1.100 eq 443
access-list 110 permit tcp any gt 1023 host 10.5.1.100 eq ftp
access-list 110 permit tcp any gt 1023 host 10.5.1.100 eq ftp-data
access-list 110 permit tcp any gt 1023 host 10.5.1.100 gt 1023
access-list 110 deny  ip any any
access-list 111 permit ip 10.5.1.0 0.0.0.255 any
access-list 111 deny  ip any any
```

Figure 8. Configuration of R2

Configuration of R2

```
interface FastEthernet0/1
 ip address 10.1.2.1 255.255.255.0
 ip access-group 111 in
 ip flow ingress
 ip flow egress

interface Serial1/0
 ip address 10.1.1.1 255.255.255.0
 ip flow ingress
 ip flow egress

access-list 111 permit ip 10.1.2.0 0.0.0.255 any
access-list 111 deny  ip any any
```

Figure 9. Configuration of R3

Configuration of R3

```
interface FastEthernet0/1
ip address 10.2.2.1 255.255.255.0
ip access-group 111 in
ip flow ingress
ip flow egress


interface Serial1/1
ip address 10.2.1.1 255.255.255.0
ip flow ingress
ip flow egress


access-list 111 permit ip 10.2.1.0 0.0.0.255 any
access-list 111 deny  ip any any
```

Fast Ethernet interface is used as the internal interface for connecting to hosts within the network. R1 is connected to external routers R2 and R3 using Serial interfaces. Egress filtering is done on the Fast Ethernet interface using access-list 111 so that packets with invalid source IP addresses would not be allowed through the network and ultimately blocking them from reaching any external hosts. WRED is activated only on the interfaces that are connected to the external network. Ingress filtering is applied to the external interfaces so that only legitimate traffic passes through the network. Since the focus is on the security of the network within the subnet of R1, Ingress filtering is used only on this router. R2 and R3 are remote networks and the concern is not about the security configurations and policy required at their respective end. The only concern is that they have proper Egress filtering so that malicious packet may be blocked within their respective subnet. A host with IP address 10.5.1.100/24 within the subnet provides various internet services which are publicly accessible.

R2 and R3 are remote networks where the source of legitimate or illegitimate traffic is located. For egress filtering, the access-list will drop packets. These are dropped at those routers that do not belong to their respective networks (with spoofed IP addresses).

Test Traffic and Analysis

A set of tests were performed to confirm whether the access-list entries were effective. The tools used to generate test internet traffic packets include hping2, ping, web browsers and an ftp client. Our target host is the host **S1** with IP address 10.5.1.100. It is a Linux server running http, https and ftp on standard ports. **S1** is configured to respond to common network diagnostic requests such as trace route and ICMP echo requests.

Firstly, since the bulk of DDoS attacks comprised of Spoofed IP packets, to generate spoofed IP packets, hping2 is used with the *"—rand-source"* option. In the test setup the hping2 command is as below:

hping2 –rand-source 10.5.1.100 –icmp –i u100

This generates ICMP packets. They are created with spoofed IP addresses and are sent to the target host, which is **S1**(10.5.1.100). The *"—icmp"* option is supplied because hping2 uses TCP as the default protocol. Since the source IP address does not belong to the attacker, no ICMP echo-reply packets are received by the attacker. The default interval for sending packets to the host is one second, but this can be changed by using the interval option *"-i"* with the required interval value. An interval of 100 microseconds is used to emulate a real attack scenario. Several instances of this command are executed from different hosts connected to the network.

Since most of the packets generated this way have IP addresses that do not belong to the subnet most of these packets are filtered out by the router closest to the attacker. A check on the access-list entry confirms that most of the packets were blocked by the access-list.

Figure 10, Figure 11 and Figure 12 show access-list entries that belong to egress filters at the attacker's ISPs. Apart from ARP packets released by the routers, most of the packets shown above are generated by the previous hping2 command. It can be seen that more than seventy percent of the packets are successfully filtered out by the access-list. A Smurf and Land attacks are examples of DoS attack that uses IP spoofing. Cisco routers came with a default setting that restricts redirection of broadcast packets, and unless enabled explicitly, it denies retransmission of broadcast packets. The routers used in this setup are used with the default broadcast redirect disabled. Egress filtering at remote ISP edge routers prohibits this from happening by denying packets from invalid source, i.e. packets with source IP address outside of its subnet, from reaching the target. Secondly, to test the effectiveness of the WRED implementation, the network is subjected to a lot of traffic from different sources. This time the traffic consists of different types of packets using different protocols and targeted to different services running on the target host. The hping2 tool is used again here for this purpose, but with different instances using different protocol options – icmp, tcp, udp. Additionally, ping flood, i.e. ping with the *"-f"* option is used to generate more traffic reaching the target host network. At the same time, the responsiveness of the web server is tested through a web browser by requesting a webpage every second. Access to the ftp service is also regularly tested during the session using ftp client. Summary of the traffic through the target host router is shown in Figure 13.

The target host router is allowed to permit only a specific subset of IP traffic. Any packet that does not match the explicitly declared permit rules are denied and dropped by the router. WRED is activated on the interfaces of the target host router and as specified above, when the amount of traffic reaches a certain limit DWRED (Distributed Weighted Random Early Detection) algorithm takes over the queuing of traffic for congestion control. Using the *"show queue {interface name}"* command, the details of packets that are currently in the queue can be seen. The packets are placed in this queue from all IP precedence. To show only nine of the one hundred and fifty-four packets, the output has been truncated in Figure 14 and Figure 15.

The contents of the queue and queue size changes with the amount of traffic and type of traffic[6]. WRED controls the average depth of Layer 3 queues. The contents of the queue and queue size changes with the amount of traffic and type of traffic.

Figure 10. Access-list entries (R1) belonging to egress filters at the attacker's ISPs

```
R1#sh access-list
Extended IP access list 110
    10 deny icmp any any fragments
    20 permit icmp any any echo (84774 matches)
    30 permit icmp any any echo-reply (769 matches)
    40 permit icmp any any packet-too-big
    50 permit icmp any any time-exceeded (515 matches)
```

Figure 11. Access-list entries (R2) belonging to egress filters at the attacker's ISPs

```
R2#sh access-list
Extended IP access list 111
    10 permit ip 10.1.2.0 0.0.0.255 any (989128 matches)
    20 deny ip any any (8779623 matches)
```

Figure 12. Access-list entries (R3) belonging to egress filters at the attacker's ISPs

```
R3#sh access-list
Extended IP access list 111
    10 permit ip 10.2.2.0 0.0.0.255 any (714662 matches)
    20 deny ip any any (1456632 matches)
```

CONCLUSION

On the basis of the proposed mechanism, it can be seen that proper filtering of packets at the point of origin can greatly reduce the amount of malicious traffic going through a network. Once such packets are filtered they do not reach their intended destination. A coordinated effort across all ISPs would reduce such malicious packets and ultimately reduce the load on targeted hosts and the target network. This also prevents the individual internet users from participating in such activities. As soon as the first packet is received, the mean queue size is calculated with WRED and is then compared with maximum queue size. Based on these packets are either queued or dropped. Thus, packets are not abruptly dropped due

Figure 13. Summary of the traffic through the target host router

```
60 permit icmp any any traceroute
70 permit icmp any any log-input (41116 matches)
80 deny icmp any any
90 permit udp any any eq echo
100 permit udp any eq echo any
110 permit tcp any any established (5201 matches)
120 permit tcp any host 10.5.1.100 eq www (81141 matches)
130 permit tcp any host 10.5.1.100 eq 443 (16125 matches)
140 permit tcp any gt 1023 host 10.5.1.100 eq ftp (41120 matches)
150 permit tcp any gt 1023 host 10.5.1.100 eq ftp-data (41121 matches)
160 permit tcp any gt 1023 host 10.5.1.100 gt 1023 (2146317 matches)
170 deny ip any any (7143704 matches)
Extended IP access list 111
10 permit ip 10.5.1.0 0.0.0.255 any (8526960 matches)

20 deny ip any any
```

to a sudden surge in the amount of traffic. As mentioned earlier WRED is slow to start dropping packets and also slow to stop dropping packets. Analysis of the volume of traffic passing through the victim's network shows that DWRED is highly effective in reducing the load on the network by queuing and dropping low priority packages. Figure 16 shows the volume of traffic passing through the network per minute for a total duration of one hour during a test run of attacks on the simulated network. It should be noted that most of the packets with spoofed IP addresses have been filtered at their source and didn't reach the victim's network. The packets that are dropped at the victim's edge router do not contribute to the analysed volume of traffic as they are dropped by the router at the source and do not reach the target host or network. Packets that reach the target network are again filtered by the access-list entries and only those packets allowed by the access-list rules are allowed through the router.

It is seen that the bulk of malicious DDoS traffic can be effectively filtered out using proper configuration and filtering rules on the routers. Summary of the traffic through the target host router is shown in Figure 16. This mechanism efficiently eliminates bogus traffic from their source and based on the type of packet and the volume of traffic at that instance, it is either allowed to pass through the network to the targeted host or queued or completely dropped at the destination. This ensures high priority packets to pass through the network and reach the destination and such services are not denied to the clients. This hybrid mechanism proposed in the paper is a two-way approach. Hence, it is better than other techniques used like web referrals and linear prediction model and is, therefore, more secure. Moreover, Access Control Lists provide packet filtering which provides security by restricting user and device access to the network. It, therefore, limits access of traffic into the network.

Figure 14. Output queue of nine of the one hundred and fifty-four packets (first)

```
R1# show queueFastEthernet0/0
Output queue for FastEthernet0/0 is 154/0

Packet 1, linktype: ip, length: 42, flags: 0x88
  source: 10.1.2.10, destination: 10.5.1.100, id: 0xF915, ttl: 62, prot: 1
   data: 0x0800 0x0E25 0x3E05 0xABD5 0x4500 0x041C 0xEF3A
       0x0000 0x3F01 0x6C0B 0x1FC3 0xF16F 0x0A05 0x0164

Packet 2, linktype: ip, length: 42, flags: 0x88
  source: 10.1.2.10, destination: 10.5.1.100, id: 0xAA5E, ttl: 62, prot: 1
   data: 0x0800 0xE424 0x3E05 0xD5D5 0x4500 0x041C 0x4206
       0x0000 0x3F01 0x6410 0x7DA5 0x48BD 0x0A05 0x0164

Packet 3, linktype: ip, length: 42, flags: 0x88
  source: 10.1.2.10, destination: 10.5.1.100, id: 0x9221, ttl: 62, prot: 1
   data: 0x0800 0xE324 0x3E05 0xD6D5 0x4500 0x041C 0x8A75
       0x0000 0x3F01 0x86E8 0x841C 0xD6FE 0x0A05 0x0164
```

Figure 15. Output queue of nine of the one hundred and fifty-four packets (second)

```
Packet 4, linktype: ip, length: 42, flags: 0x88
  source: 10.1.2.10, destination: 10.5.1.100, id: 0xDF12, ttl: 62, prot: 1
   data: 0x0800 0xA924 0x3E05 0x10D6 0x4500 0x041C 0x3EF9
       0x0000 0x3F01 0x3AB0 0x5E84 0x944B 0x0A05 0x0164

Packet 5, linktype: ip, length: 42, flags: 0x88
  source: 10.1.2.10, destination: 10.5.1.100, id: 0x2DF4, ttl: 62, prot: 1
   data: 0x0800 0xA824 0x3E05 0x11D6 0x4500 0x041C 0xEBEB
       0x0000 0x3F01 0xF95E 0xD47B 0xB2B2 0x0A05 0x0164

Packet 6, linktype: ip, length: 42, flags: 0x88
  source: 10.1.2.10, destination: 10.5.1.100, id: 0xF473, ttl: 62, prot: 1
   data: 0x0800 0xA724 0x3E05 0x12D6 0x4500 0x041C 0x2986
       0x0000 0x3F01 0x2861 0x5725 0xC36C 0x0A05 0x0164

Packet 7, linktype: ip, length: 42, flags: 0x88
  source: 10.1.2.10, destination: 10.5.1.100, id: 0x002C, ttl: 62, prot: 1
   data: 0x0800 0xA624 0x3E05 0x13D6 0x4500 0x041C 0x2BA8
       0x0000 0x3F01 0x70A2 0x3DA5 0x9289 0x0A05 0x0164
```

Figure 16. Traffic Analysis

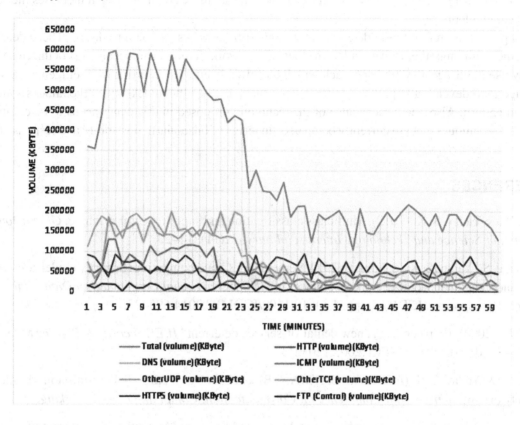

FUTURE WORK

The two characteristics of DDoS attacks that impose a challenge are: that they are denial-of-service attacks, an attack that is not targeted at gaining unauthorized access to a service or system, and that they are distributed attacks. Since they are distributed, large-scale attacks can be caused, which can, in turn, cause a great impact on the victims. Access to a service or a resource by the victim or others' access to the victim's services is denied by them. The results of these attacks are disastrous. This is not too difficult for an attacker as the internet is designed with connectivity in mind, and from the beginning, it is not designed with security.

One of the results that the attackers try to achieve at first is overloading *bandwidth*. For example, when useless packets flood the network, legitimate ICMP echo packets are prevented from reaching its destination. Secondly, attackers try to overload the processing power of the target. Attackers manage to use up the memory and process tables to full extent, when a lot of useless requests to the victim's system are generated. This results in the inability of the victim's system to create new processes to respond to legitimate requests and may eventually cause the system to crash. Accessing the victim's services for its clients can be successfully prevented by the attacker. Finally, to avoid anyone else's access to the victim's services, the attackers try to use up all of them. DDoS attacks can prevent victims either from being reached by other people or using the Internet services. For Internet Service Providers (ISP), the result of such attacks is far more severe when access to the services is denied for the client. Also, for providing goods and services, companies rely on the internet more and more which increases the severity of such incidents.

As a part of the future work, detectors in various sub-networks can be introduced. These detectors communicate amongst themselves and warn other sub-networks if they are under attack. For this, researchers may use multi-agent system approach which has often been used in artificial intelligence. Another challenge is to develop a hypothesis to trace back the source of the attacks since the attacks follow a common pattern. Also, the performance of the technique proposed in this paper needs to be compared with other techniques that are currently being used in terms of false-alarm possibility and response time.

REFERENCES

Ahuja, Y., & Yadav, S. K. (2012). Multiclass classification and support vector machine. *Global Journal of Computer Science and Technology Interdisciplinary, 12*(11), 14–20.

Al-Anzi, F. S., Yadav, S. K., & Soni, J. (2014, September). Cloud computing: Security model comprising governance, risk management and compliance. In *2014 International Conference on Data Mining and Intelligent Computing (ICDMIC)* (pp. 1-6). 10.1109/ICDMIC.2014.6954232

Aljifri, H. (2003). IP traceback: A new denial-of-service deterrent? *IEEE Security & Privacy Magazine, 1*(3), 24–31. doi:10.1109/MSECP.2003.1203219

Arora, A., & Yadav, S. K. (in press a). BATMAN: Blockchain based Aircraft Transmission Mobile Ad-hoc Network. In *International Conference on Communication, Computing and Networking.*

Arora, A., & Yadav, S. K. (in press b). Blockchain based Security Mechanism for Internet of Vehicles (IoV). In *International Conference on Internet of Things and Connected Technologies.*

Arora, A., Yadav, S. K., & Sharma, K. (2018). Denial-of-Service (DoS) Attack and Botnet. In Handbook of Research on Network Forensics and Analysis Techniques (pp. 117-141).

Bencsáth, B., & Vajda, I. (2004, January). Protection against DDoS attacks based on traffic level measurements. In *2004 International Symposium on Collaborative Technologies and Systems*, 22-28.

Bhushan, K., & Gupta, B. B. (2018). Distributed denial of service (DDoS) attack mitigation in software defined network (SDN)-based cloud computing environment. *Journal of Ambient Intelligence and Humanized Computing*, 1–13.

Bhushan, M., Banerjea, S., & Yadav, S. K. (2014, September). Bloom filter based optimization on HBase with MapReduce. In *2014 International Conference on Data Mining and Intelligent Computing (ICDMIC)* (pp. 1-5). 10.1109/ICDMIC.2014.6954230

Braga, R., Mota, E., & Passito, A. (2010, October). Lightweight DDoS flooding attack detection using NOX/OpenFlow. In *Conference on Local Computer Networks (LCN)* (pp. 408-415).

Chen, S., & Song, Q. (2005). Perimeter-based defense against high bandwidth DDoS attacks. *IEEE Transactions on Parallel and Distributed Systems, 16*(6), 526–537. doi:10.1109/TPDS.2005.74

David, L., Sood, M., & Kajla, M. K. (2011, February). Router based approach to mitigate DOS attacks on the wireless networks. In *Proceedings of the 2011 International Conference on Communication, Computing & Security* (pp. 569-572). 10.1145/1947940.1948058

Desai, M., Patel, S., Somaiya, P., & Vishwanathan, V. (2016). Prevention of Distributed Denial of Service Attack using Web Referrals. *RE:view*.

Dhingra, K., & Yadav, S. K. (2017). Spam analysis of big reviews dataset using Fuzzy Ranking Evaluation Algorithm and Hadoop. *International Journal of Machine Learning and Cybernetics*, 1–20.

Douligeris, C., & Mitrokotsa, A. (2004). DDoS attacks and defense mechanisms: Classification and state-of-the-art. *Computer Networks*, *44*(5), 643–666. doi:10.1016/j.comnet.2003.10.003

Ferguson, P., & Senie, D. (1997). *Network ingress filtering: Defeating denial of service attacks which employ IP source address spoofing* (No. RFC 2267).

Freiling, F. C., Holz, T., & Wicherski, G. (2005, September). Botnet tracking: Exploring a root-cause methodology to prevent distributed denial-of-service attacks. In *European Symposium on Research in Computer Security* (pp. 319-335). 10.1007/11555827_19

Gibson, S. (2002). *Distributed reflection denial of service: description and analysis of a potent, increasingly prevalent, and worrisome Internet attack*. Gibson Research Corporation.

Gil, T. M., & Poletto, M. (2001, August). MULTOPS: A Data-Structure for Bandwidth Attack Detection. In *USENIX Security Symposium* (pp. 23-38). 10.21236/ADA401819

Gupta, B. B., Joshi, R. C., Misra, M., Meena, D. L., Shrivastava, G., & Sharma, K. (2010). Detecting a Wide Range of Flooding DDoS Attacks using Linear Prediction Model. In *IEEE 2nd International Conference on Information and Multimedia Technology (ICIMT 2010)* (Vol. 2, pp. 535-539).

Hoque, N., Bhattacharyya, D. K., & Kalita, J. K. (2016, January). A novel measure for low-rate and high-rate DDoS attack detection using multivariate data analysis. In *2016 8th International Conference on Communication Systems and Networks (COMSNETS)*. 10.1109/COMSNETS.2016.7439939

Hussain, A., Heidemann, J., & Papadopoulos, C. (2003, August). A framework for classifying denial of service attacks. In *Proceedings of the 2003 conference on Applications, technologies, architectures, and protocols for computer communications* (pp. 99-110). 10.1145/863955.863968

Hyun, D., Kim, J., Hong, D., & Jeong, J. P. (2017, October). SDN-based network security functions for effective DDoS attack mitigation. In *2017 International Conference on Information and Communication Technology Convergence (ICTC)* (pp. 834-839). 10.1109/ICTC.2017.8190794

Ioannidis, J., & Bellovin, S. M. (2002, February). Implementing Pushback: Router-Based Defense Against DDoS Attacks. In NDSS.

Jin, S., & Yeung, D. S. (2004, June). A covariance analysis model for DDoS attack detection. In *IEEE International Conference on Communications* (Vol. 4, pp. 1882-1886).

Khari, M., & Kumar, M. (2016, March). Comprehensive study of web application attacks and classification. In *3rd International Conference on Computing for Sustainable Global Development (INDIACom)* (pp. 2159-2164).

Khari, M., & Sangwan, P. (2016, March). Web-application attacks: A survey. In *3rd International Conference on Computing for Sustainable Global Development (INDIACom)* (pp. 2187-2191).

Kumar, V., & Kumar, K. (2016, September). Classification of DDoS attack tools and its handling techniques and strategy at application layer. In *International Conference on Advances in Computing, Communication, & Automation (ICACCA)(Fall)* (pp. 1-6).

Lee, K., Kim, J., Kwon, K. H., Han, Y., & Kim, S. (2008). DDoS attack detection method using cluster analysis. *Expert Systems with Applications, 34*(3), 1659–1665. doi:10.1016/j.eswa.2007.01.040

Li, M. (2004). An approach to reliably identifying signs of DDOS flood attacks based on LRD traffic pattern recognition. *Computers & Security, 23*(7), 549–558. doi:10.1016/j.cose.2004.04.005

Mirkovic, J., & Reiher, P. (2004). A taxonomy of DDoS attack and DDoS defense mechanisms. *Computer Communication Review, 34*(2), 39–53. doi:10.1145/997150.997156

Patrikakis, C., Masikos, M., & Zouraraki, O. (2004). Distributed denial of service attacks. *The Internet Protocol Journal, 7*(4), 13–35.

Peng, T., Leckie, C., & Ramamohanarao, K. (2004, May). Proactively detecting distributed denial of service attacks using source IP address monitoring. In *International Conference on Research in Networking* (pp. 771-782). 10.1007/978-3-540-24693-0_63

Rajkumar, M. J. N. (2013). A Survey on Latest DoS Attacks: Classification and Defense Mechanisms. *IJIRCCE, 1*(8).

Sharma, K., & Gupta, B. B. (2018). Taxonomy of Distributed Denial of Service (DDoS) Attacks and Defense Mechanisms in Present Era of Smartphone Devices. *International Journal of E-Services and Mobile Applications, 10*(2), 58–74. doi:10.4018/IJESMA.2018040104

Shrivastava, G., Sharma, K., & Rai, S. (2010, December). The Detection & Defense of DoS & DDos Attack: A Technical Overview. In *Proceeding of ICC (Vol. 27, p. 28).*

Sung, M., & Xu, J. (2003). IP traceback-based intelligent packet filtering: A novel technique for defending against Internet DDoS attacks. *IEEE Transactions on Parallel and Distributed Systems, 14*(9), 861–872. doi:10.1109/TPDS.2003.1233709

Xie, Y., & Yu, S. Z. (2009). Monitoring the application-layer DDoS attacks for popular websites. *IEEE/ACM Transactions on Networking, 17*(1), 15–25. doi:10.1109/TNET.2008.925628

Yu, J., Li, Z., Chen, H., & Chen, X. (2007, June). A detection and offense mechanism to defend against application layer DDoS attacks. In *Third International Conference on Networking and Services* (pp. 54-54). 10.1109/ICNS.2007.5

Zargar, S. T., Joshi, J., & Tipper, D. (2013). A survey of defense mechanisms against distributed denial of service (DDoS) flooding attacks. *IEEE Communications Surveys and Tutorials, 15*(4), 2046–2069. doi:10.1109/SURV.2013.031413.00127

Zhang, G., & Parashar, M. (2006). Cooperative defence against ddos attacks. *Journal of Research and Practice in Information Technology, 38*(1), 69–84.

ENDNOTES

[1]   CERT® Advisory CA-1996-21 TCP SYN Flooding and IP Spoofing Attacks http://www.cert.org/advisories/CA-1996-21.html

[2]   http://www.cnn.com/2000/TECH/computing/02/09/-cyber.attacks.01/index.html

[3]   Network Ingress Filtering: Defeating Denial of Service Attacks which employ IP Source Address Spoofing [RFC 2827]

[4]   http://www.hping.org

[5]   http://www.emsisoft.com/en/kb/portlist/

[6]   "Implementing Quality of Service Policies with DSCP", Cisco Press, Document-ID: 10103

This research was previously published in the International Journal of Information System Modeling and Design (IJISMD), 9(1); edited by Remigijus Gustas; pages 56-76, copyright year 2018 by IGI Publishing (an imprint of IGI Global).

Chapter 12
A Survey on Denial of Service Attacks and Preclusions

Nagesh K.

Pondicherry Engineering College, Department of Computer Science and Engineering, Puducherry, India

Sumathy R.

Pondicherry Engineering College, Department of Computer Science and Engineering, Puducherry, India

Devakumar P.

Pondicherry Engineering College, Department of Computer Science and Engineering, Puducherry, India

Sathiyamurthy K.

Pondicherry Engineering College, Department of Computer Science and Engineering, Puducherry, India

ABSTRACT

Security is concerned with protecting assets. The aspects of security can be applied to any situation-defense, detection and deterrence. Network security plays important role of protecting information, hardware and software on a computer network. Denial of service (DOS) attacks causes great impacts on the internet world. These attacks attempt to disrupt legitimate user's access to services. By exploiting computer's vulnerabilities, attackers easily consume victim's resources. Many special techniques have been developed to protest against DOS attacks. Some organizations constitute several defense mechanism tools to tackle the security problems. This paper has proposed various types of attacks and solutions associated with each layers of OSI model. These attacks and solutions have different impacts on the different environment. Thus the rapid growth of new technologies may constitute still worse impacts of attacks in the future.

DOI: 10.4018/978-1-7998-5348-0.ch012

INTRODUCTION

The main objectives of network security are to attain availability, integrity, and confidentiality of computer system resources (includes hardware, software, firmware, data and telecommunications) (Kumar, 2004). Security protocol acts as an important component of network security. Ahead data communications between any network entities, security protocols is implemented for entity authentication, key agreement and secure associations formed. For example, Internet Key Exchange (IKE) protocol uses public key schemes to authenticate the protocol initiator to prevent unwanted traffics flooding (Jain, 2011). Sometimes security protocols may have DOS vulnerability, because some of the stages of verification process may involve resource consuming executions which may cause the attackers to invoke legitimate user's resources. Consequently, protocol designers should ensure about this problem and develop secure protocol to handle DOS attacks. Thus, security protocols can be used to provide confidential data and crucial service. This results in secure network connection and data communication. The components of security programs are authority, framework, assessment, planning and maintenance.

In a denial of service attack, when attacker's attack messages are initiated from multiple hosts which are distributed over the network, it is called as Distributed Denial of Service (DDOS) attack. In contrast, when offender's attack messages are originated from a single host called as Single-Source Denial of Service (SDOS) attack. A DOS attack is a depraved attempt by a single attacker or a group of attackers to cripple an online service. The cause and effects of denial-of-service attacks could even become life-threatening. A group of terrorist attacked 19,000 French websites hit by DDOS on January 7, 2015. This attacked low level government as well as business websites. Several websites of the Paris had been hacked and defaced by ISIS flag. The few symptoms of the attacks are abnormal slowdown of network performance, inadequacy of a particular site, inefficiency to access any site etc. Usually DOS attackers are inspired by different following reasons-financial/economical gain, invariably slow network performance, revenge, ideological belief, intellectual challenge, service unavailability, cyber warfare (Prasad, 2014).

This paper discusses the various DOS attacks involved in each layers of the OSI model and solutions are provided for those attacks. We have provided the best solution for these attacks and even more solution for these attacks may be invented in the future. The impacts of attacks may vary in different platform or environment such that solutions will too have certain restrictions with respect to the domains. And also, we discuss about the significant of DOS attacks that all affected some of the industries. A detailed survey of DOS attack that all experienced by many of the countries all over the world. There are many attacks emerging as technology developing in parallel. We can't able to judge the best solution for the attacks, but we can able to take preventive measures to solve the issues or problems which may occur.

DDOS FILTERING PROCESS

The Figure 1 presents the process of Distributed Denial of Service as follows:

- Initially, the hacker attempt to gather information about the targeted system;
- Next step, using any basic techniques exploits the weakness of the system;
- DDOS sensor (any related mechanisms) is used to detect and filter these attacks;
- DDOS filter (any related tools), removes the detected attacks;
- Finally, the distributed customers can utilize the network without any issues.

Figure 1. Distributed denial of service

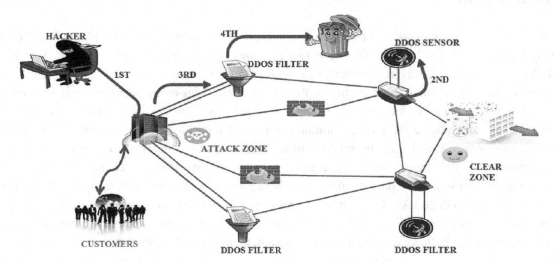

TAXONOMY OF DOS ATTACKS

The OSI model is a design of network system that allows communication among different systems. And it consists of seven layers, each layer possesses a different level view of the different requirements within network security. There are different types of DOS attacks. Sometimes may be on Client, Server or Network. These various attacks hack the genuine user's system using different techniques. Some attacks have permanent solutions while others may result on heavy loss of cost without any desire conclusion. The Figure 2 presents the various attacks mapping onto the Open System Interconnection (OSI) model.

ATTACKS AND SOLUTIONS IN OSI LAYERS

Application Layer

E-Mail Bombs

E-mail bomb is used to hang the program or ends the program prematurely. It is a dangerous code which consists of large number of mails that target on a particular system. This mail bombs is usually used to crash the email server or slow down the users system. When the user downloads these huge number of mails then the allocated space of the email sever is utilized. This leads to server crash. The main reason, the email bombers make their attacks to mess up the emails and harm the Internet Service Provider (ISP) that they target. It causes loss of connectivity, overload network connection, and consumes all system resources.

In order to prevent this attack use ISP to block email bombers, proxy servers is used to check the malware content and filter the messages from particular IP address and protocols before transmitting to the clients or users. Simple Mail Transfer Protocol (SMTP) is used to authenticate the messages before transferring to the destination system.

Figure 2. Taxonomy of DoS attacks

OSI LAYERS	ATTACKS	
APPLICATION LAYER	->E-Mail Bomb ->DNS ->HTTP ->Slow Read ->Tear Drop ->URL	->Buffer Overflow ->WSDL Probing ->Rudy ->XML Injection ->Malicious -> Resource Starvation
PRESENTATION LAYER	->TCP Handshake ->SSL Based DOS	
SESSION LAYER	->TELNET Brute Force ->TELNET DOS ->TELNET Communication Sniffing	
TRANSPORT LAYER	->Flooding ->UDP Flood ->ICMP Flood ->SYN Flood	->Infrastructure DDOS ->NTP Amplification ->Vampire ->DE-Synchronization Flood
NETWORK LAYER	->PING Flood ->Naphtha ->MITM ->Eavesdropping ->Node Impersonation ->Sybil ->Grey Hole ->Collision ->Wormhole	->Sleep Deprivation ->Rushing ->Smurf ->Selective Forwarding ->Sink Hole ->Hello Flood ->Reflection ->Exhaustion ->Land
DATALINK LAYER	->VLAN Hopping ->MAC Flooding ->Cache Poisoning	->ARP Spoofing ->DHCP Starvation
PHYSICAL LAYER	->Jamming ->Tampering ->Multipoint Crosstalk Crosstalk Jamming	->In-Band Jamming ->Mixed Security Domain ->Correlative Multipoint

DNS Flood

DNS flood is one of the DDOS attacks in which offender attempt to crash one or more Domain Name System (DNS) servers belonging to a particular zone. DNS server act as a "road map" to the internet, which helps the requestors to seek their server. This attack is another alternative of the UDP flood attack, since DNS servers rely on the UDP protocol for name resolution. The offender runs a script, generated from multiple servers. These scripts forward malformed packets from spoofed IP addresses. Randomized packet data helps offenders to prevent common DDOS protection mechanisms, like IP filtering.

First resolution, if you come to know the IP address of the offender then block traffic from those addresses using the firewall protection rules.

Second resolution, to reduce DNS flood use legitimate enterprise customers -Denial of Service-DDOS Protection.

HTTP Attack

Here the attacker main intention to attack a web server or application using HTTP GET or POST requests. HTTP flood attacks are volumetric attacks where a group of inter connected computers are exploited. This attack requires less bandwidth rather than the other attacks to hang up the targeted site or server.

Incapsula's Web Application Protection that analyzes and classifies all incoming site traffic. This is specifically designed to identify malicious bot traffic—stopping all HTTP floods and other Application Layer DDOS attacks.

Slow Read Attack

Slow read attack desires to cause an undetected denial of the service by exploding a TCP persist timer vulnerability. The attacker sends a legitimate HTTP request to server, but receives the response very slowly which forces the connection to stay open. The client forwards a zero window to the server that makes the server to assume that the client is now busy in reading the data.

NetScaler has intellectual to find such open connections and silently drop it as a part of attack protection. It is activated when large numbers of connections in small window size condition are accumulated.

Teardrop Attack

It forwards the fragmented packets to the targeted machine. The receiver machine is not able to reassemble the fragmented packets due to error in TCP/IP fragmentation reassembly. Thus, the packets overlap one another and crash the targeted network device.

The best way to fix this attack is by upgrading network hardware and software to secure from these attacks.

URL Attack

URL manipulation attack that make changes in the URL parameters and sends it back to the provider, insisting the web application to do various things like redirecting to third-party sites and access the sensitive files of the server.

To prohibit this attack, the web server should be configured as follows: Disable the display of files available in a directory that does not contain an index file; delete useless directories and files; delete unnecessary configuration options and delete unnecessary script interpreters.

Buffer Overflow Attack

When the buffer size exceeds, data start to overflow from one buffer to another buffer. Since the buffer can store some particular amount of data if it exceeds it flows somewhere else. This can corrupt the data contained in that buffer. The various prevention to this attack is indicated in Table 1.

Table 1. Preventions of buffer overflow

Preventions	Description
Stack Cookie	It is a piece of data which is used to predicate the buffer overflow and health of the system. If the stack cookie had been changed that indicates buffer overflow and the application is exited.
Data Execution Protection	It is available in some specific processor, which marks certain locations of the stack as non-executable locations. Hence these locations will not be executed.
Address Space Layout Randomization	It involves arranging the positions of key data locations like positions of libraries, heap, and stack in process address space. This randomization of virtual memory address makes exploitation of a buffer overflow more difficult, but in some cases, possible.
Deep Packet Inspection	It can detect buffer overflow using attack signatures. It blocks packets that have known attack signature or No-Operation instructions (NOP).

WSDL Probing

In this attack, hacker examine the Web Service Definition Language (WSDL) interface to expose sensitive information like invocation patterns, technology implementations, services ports, bindings available to customers and associated vulnerabilities. This form of probing may accomplish to perform serious attacks e.g. parameter tampering, malicious content injection, command injection, etc. Thus, hacker may submit some special characters or malicious code to the Web service and may cause a denial of service condition or unauthorized access to database.

It's necessary to protect WSDL file or provide limit access to it. Inspect the functions exposed by WSDL interface and ensure it's not vulnerable to injection. Check the function naming convention because it is easy to guess function name and may be an entry point for an attack.

RUDY Attack

RUDY attack is a low and slow attack tool that is used to crash a web server by accepting long form fields. It searches the targeted website and detects the web forms. After identifying the forms, it sends a HTTP POST request with long content length header field of one byte sized packet information at equal intervals of time. To prevent detection, this information is sent in the form of small chunks at slow rate which makes a backlog of application threads and hence it prevents the server from closing the connection.

This attack is difficult to detect due to the unexpected high fluctuations on the network. One of the ways to detect is by monitoring the server resources. For example, it can able to identify the server memory, connection tables, thread application and also includes long and idle open network connection. The misuse can be identified and traced based upon the behavior analysis of open server connection. Incapsula's security services are used to monitor the incoming requests to the server from the clients.

XML Injection Attack

In this, attacker tries to inject XML commands and aims to modify XML structure. Hence it may lead to violation of security objectives like Integrity, Access Control due to the modification of payment data and unauthorized admin login.

This XML injection attack can be prevented by properly managing and sanitizing any user's input before the execution. This attack can be avoided by monitoring all the input carefully. This can be done by removing all the single and double quotes from the user input. Thus, proper functions and syntax from the Extensible Markup Language (XML) library must use.

Malicious Attack

Malware or malicious software is a program or file which will harm a user computer. Thus, malware includes computer Viruses, Worms, Trojan Horses and also Spyware. These programs are used to gathers information about a user computer without any user permission.

Anti-malware software is used to clear up this malware attack. This is used to find the malware file in the user system and prevents from accessing the resources from the user's system.

Resource Starvation Attack

It is also called as disk space attack which is used to access the particular resources on the specific system until it uses the resources completely. For example, the attacker attacks particular web site by sending requests continuously to create baskets or users.

Radmin is used to detect this attack and can avoid it.

Presentation Layer

TCP Handshake Spoof Attack

This handshake spoof crucial reverses client and server machine functionality, with the compromised client's port reacting as a server receptor, and the server's port reacting as a client receptor. Initially client sends SYN packet to the server. The malicious server sends back a SYN packet rather than a SYN-ACK packet. But the client wrongly responds with a SYN-ACK packet to the server. Finally, the server completes the handshake by forwarding an ACK packet to the client's SYN-ACK (Aamir, 2013).

TCP Handshake Spoof attacks can be prevented by dropping out-of-turn SYN or SYN-ACK packets using Sophos Firewall (SF). Sophos Firewall control, terminate TCP connection when the packets are not found in the related state record. Hence, spoofed packets are dropped before it enters the network. SF finds this traffic as invalid traffic and administrators can recognize this type of traffic by using the Packet Capture tool.

SSL Based DDOS Attacks

The Hacker's Choice (THC) is a tool which works after establishing normal Secure Sockets Layer (SSL) handshake but then instantly requests a renegotiation of the encryption method. As soon as the renegotiation finished, it requests another renegotiation and so on. This makes the server sniffle and lead resources unavailable to legitimate users due to resource exhaustion.

Another SSL based DDOS attack tool is the Pushdo botnet is used to send garbage data to a target SSL server. This SSL protocol is computationally expensive and it consumes extra workload to process garbage data as a legitimate handshake on the server.

The prevention process includes the burden of implementing encryption and decryption mechanisms. As a result, these serious attacks require extremely sophisticated DDOS protection mechanisms.

Session Layer

TELNET Brute Force Attack

In brute force attack the attacker uses a program to guess the password using various combinations to crack the password.

To preclude the brute force attack issue, change the password frequently and use high strong password like using uppercase letters, lowercase letters, and numerals.

TELNET DOS Attack

This attack is used to disturb the communication between two network devices by consuming the entire bandwidth of the connection. Here the attacker sends unusual and unwanted data in order to stifle the connection. Hence the real communication will not be able to access the connection as well as it will not function.

To avoid the telnet DOS attack, update the hardware version in order to reduce these attacks.

TELNET Communication Sniffing

The main security issue of this attack is encryption. The communication happens between remote and network device where data are communicated in the form of plain text. Here the attacker can able to view the device configuration as well as the password used to connect to the device.

Use appropriate encryption mechanism.

Transport Layer

Flooding Attack

Flooding attack is used to make the network or service unavailable by submerging large amount of traffic in network. It fills the host buffer and checks whether there is no further connection made with that host. The different types of flooding attacks as follows.

UDP Flood Attack

User Datagram Protocol (UDP) attack is like DOS attack which is used to send large number of UDP packets to the random ports on the remote network. This result the distant network to check whether the application is listening to the ports or not, if not they reply by ICMP destination unreachable packet. Hence it forces the targeted system to send many ICMP packets leading to unreachable by other clients. The attacker can able to spoof the IP address of UDP packets, determine that more ICMP return packets do not reach to sender, and removes the identity of their network location.

To prohibit from this attack use firewall to block malicious UDP packets.

ICMP Flood Attack

Internet Control Message Protocol (ICMP) is used for error messaging and do not exchange data between systems. It follows with TCP packets when connecting to the server. It is used to overload the targeted networks bandwidth (Mirković, 2002).

To defend from this attack use 'Watch and Block Method'. This method is used to monitor the ICMP traffic to the targeted system and drops the packet if it exceeds the threshold for specific duration of time.

SYN Flood Attack

It is like DOS attack in which the attacker sends order of SYN requests to the targeted system to consume server resources to make the system not to respond to valid traffic (Chu, 2011).

To prevent from this attack use following techniques: firewalls, proxies, filtering, SYN cache, SYN cookies, micro blocks, RST cookies, stack tweaking.

Infrastructure DDOS Attack

It is used to overload the network infrastructure by using the large number of bandwidths. For example, by sending excessive connection request without responding to confirm the connection.

A proxy server is used to exclude this attack by using cryptographic hash tags and SYN cookies.

NTP Amplification Attack

Network Time Protocol (NTP) attack is a reflection attack in which the attacker attacks the NTP servers to submerge the targeted system with UDP traffic. In the NTP amplification attack, the attacker sends 'Get MonList' request to the NTP server to spoof the IP address. The NTP server responds with list of IP address. When the response is larger than the request, amplifies the amount of traffic in the server this leads to degradation of service.

Incapsula's protects from volumetric DOS attack and proxies used to filter amount of traffic which can harm the targeted system.

Vampire Attack

Vampire attack is an attack in which malicious node creates and send messages causes more energy consumption of network and that leads to reduction of batteries of the network. It consists of two type's attack they are: attack on stateless protocol-carousel and stretch attack; attack on state full attack.

To avoid this attack, they have proposed algorithm to modify the forwarding phase of PLGP.

De-Synchronization Attack

De-synchronization attack blocks the communication between parties or nodes. It is one of the RFID threat in which tag's key are stored in the back-end database and tag's memory would not be the same.

To avoid this attack, they have proposed hash-based RFID mutual authentication protocol for security.

Network Layer

Ping Flood

By using a ping command, offender tries to harm, disable or crash the targeted system by sending malicious or oversized packets. This attack is called Ping of Attack. Recently, a new form of POD attack – Ping Flood in which the targeted computer is attacked by sending ICMP packets simultaneously via ping without waiting for responses.

To defend this attack, disable the ICMP service.

NAPTHA Attack

Here malicious user attempts to maximize processes and minimize fake connections with the victim, leaving it alive until the TCP connection time out. Once the connection reached low rate, server will automatically drop any new incoming connection request. It is a complex process because offender must finish all bogus connections as planned by the offender. Server creates new thread for each request and rejects when a new request arises such that when the maximum thread limit is attained.

Early Client Authentication Method (ECAM) used to authenticate the client's login before assigning the connection. Fake requests are dropped and consequently processes and threads are active only for clients who had successful login.

Man in the Middle: MITM Attack

It is a form of cyber-attack, attacker inserts information into a conversation between two parties, portray both parties and access information that are transferred between parties. MITM attacks are correlated with 802.11 security, as well as with wired communication systems. For example, online banking and e-commerce sites are frequently abused by this attack. So, malicious actor can catch sensitive information like login credentials and account details.

For a secure connection is Virtual Private Network (VPN) can used because it extends a private network across a public network.

Use some privacy software like Hide My IP that provides reliable proxy servers and encryption between the parties.

To authenticate the user, Secure Shell (SSH) tunnel is used which consists of an encrypted tunnel created through SSH protocol connection (i.e.) SSH uses public-key cryptography.

Eavesdropping

Eavesdropping is an electronic attack where digital communications are intercepted by malicious users. It aims to capture packets from the network transmitted by other systems and scan the data. This is due to lack of encryption services. Generally black hat offender perform this attack. For example, they attempt to attack government agencies, such as National Security Agency (Sheikh, 2010).

The best security method is encryption process which defense against eavesdropping.

NODE Impersonation Attack

Here the node attempt to send an altered version of a message received from the genuine user, in order to show the misbehavior and pretend as if the message coming from the real user.

To inhibit this problem, a unique identity is given for each node so that can avoid misguide of an offender.

SYBIL Attack

It happens when an insecure system is hijacked to claim multiple identities. This makes the hacked system to think that the attacker has large influence. Hence, by having these identities an attacker attempt to steal information or disrupt communication.

By establishing trusted certification to identify and verify each system via certificate authority.

Resource testing is used to examine computing power, storage space, network bandwidth and other parameters to determine whether these collections are from a legitimate resource.

Greyhole Attack

An offender modifies the sequence number of the message and route to the source. Now the source routes the packet to its destination according to the attacker's route. Such that the intermediate attacker will stop all the data packet forwarding process (Fatema, 2014).

To avoid this problem, use Data Routing Information algorithm (DRI). It also takes more time for node decision routing process.

Collision Attack

Collision attack occurs between two nodes when messages are transmitted at same frequency simultaneously.

To exclude this attack, use error correcting codes.

Wormhole Attack

It gives shortest mock routing path than the genuine path within the network; this can daze the routing mechanisms this delays the data packet transmission.

To clear up this attack, use four-way handshaking messages exchange technique or can also use private channel.

Sleep Deprivation Attack

It is a dangerous attack where the intruder explodes to drain the battery power of the sensor node to the minimum level. So, it affects the life time of the node. The hacker sends request to the target in order to pretend as if a legal request and making the node to wait for a long period of time. Thus, it leads to the battery power consumption of the node (Das, 2014).

It is difficult to detect this attack. But the impact can be minimized by the below techniques; a) Random Vote Selection b) Round Robin Fashion and c) Hashing Method. This hashing is having high ranking compared with the others.

Rushing Attack

Rushing attack exploits the network by forwarding high speed packets and obtain access. In a group communication, offender receives packet and forward to other node at a high speed, so the node gets this error packet first because of high frequency speed and rejects other legitimate packets (Das, 2014).

To prevent this attack can use reliable neighbor detection and route discovery process.

The concept of threshold can be used by fixing a threshold range for a transmission. So, all the nodes must receive the packets at the fixed time period. If there is a rushing of a packet, then the neighbor node will intimate about the offender and identifies it.

Smurf Attack

It is a form of Disturbed Denial of Service attack which provides computer networks disabled. The perpetrator creates a network packet associated with a false IP address called as spoofing. The packet is available with an ICMP ping message which denotes that the packet received network must reply. These replies or echoes, are forwarded back to network IP addresses once again, to set an infinite loop. Finally causes the complete network slump.

To mitigate this attack, ensure to block directed broadcast traffic coming into the network. Determine whether the configure hosts and routers not responding to ICMP echo requests.

Selective Forwarding Attack

Selective forwarding attack is like DOS attack which attacks a certain node or a group of nodes. In this attack, the malicious node selectively drops the packets or modifies the packets of the node or a group of nodes.

To quick fix this attack, use multipath routing technique, monitor the nodes before forwarding the messages to other nodes and watchdog can be used to supervise the system.

Sinkhole Attack

It is a type of attack in which the malevolent node tries to draw all the possible traffic through the compromised node by communicating its fake routing update.

To defend this attack, use quintessential scheme to make awareness in the network from malicious node and use cryptographic methods for security.

Hello Flood Attack

It is not a valid node in the network and sends hello flood request to the genuine node and break the security of the network (Singh, 2010).

To prohibit this attack, we use "identity verification protocol" which is used to verify both direction links between nodes.

Reflection Attack

Reflection attack attacks the authentication system which uses same protocol in both directions. The main intention of the attacker is to trap the targeted system by providing the result of its own challenge.

To inhibit this attack, both sender and receiver must respond their messages after their identity, use different keys for both directions.

Exhaustion Attack

Exhaustion attack occurs when it undergoes continuous collision and retransmission of messages till the sensor node becomes dead.

To exclude this attack, use time division multiplexing technique or limit the rate transmission.

Land Attack

This attack forward a special poison called spoofed packet to a system, which lead to system lock up. But it is different from TCP SYN flooding because the attacker sends spoofed targeted IP address to both source and destination. So, this result, the system replies to itself.

Firewalls can be used to discard this type of poisonous packet. Additionally, routers must be configured with both ingression and egression filters to block all traffics which includes where the source and destination IP addresses are the same.

Datalink Layer

VLAN Hopping

A VLAN hopping attack allows packets from one VLAN to pass into another VLAN, without first pass through router. There are two ways to attack, switch spoofing and double tagging. Sniffing the traffic on all VLANs is possible. Thus, attacker can discover the sensitive information's like username and password from user's network.

Ensure that all user ports are assigned as access mode ports. Any unused ports must be disabled and set as access mode ports by default.

MAC Flooding Attack

This attack is also called Content Addressable Memory (CAM) flooding attack. A switch is flooded with packets, in which each packet contains different source Media Access Control (MAC) addresses. The purpose of this attack is to consume the limited memory space of switch to store the MAC address to physical port translation table. So, it causes the switch to enter a state called fail open mode, thus all incoming packets are broadcast out of all ports like hubs. A malicious user can use this packet sniffer running in a compromising mode to expose sensitive data.

Offer Port Security- advanced switch configurations can limit the number MAC addresses when connected with the port. MAC addresses also be authenticated against an Authentication, Authorization and Accounting (AAA) server.

CACHE Poisoning

In this attack depends on the presence of exploitable Domain Name System (DNS) software vulnerabilities. When the attacker has sent a malicious DNS response, then the corrupted data cached by the real DNS name server. So, DNS cache is poisoned. When the future users visit, the corrupted domain will be routed to the new IP address selected by the attacker. Until the poisoned cache is removed, users will be receiving unauthorized IP addresses from the DNS.

To prevent this attack, configure DNS name servers with the following:

- Restrict recursive queries;
- Store only related data to the desired domain;
- Ensure that DNS server clears any unrelated service responses.

ARP Spoofing

This attack is also called as ARP poison routing (APR) or ARP cache poisoning. To monitor the address of the network card, offender attacks Ethernet LAN by upgrading the targeted system's ARP cache with both a fake Address Resolution Protocol (ARP) request and reply packets such that to change the Ethernet MAC address. So, the packets are sent to offender's system first which in turn not visible to the user.

An open source solution for anti - ARP spoofing like ARP handler inspection (ARPON) can be used. This compact ARP handler finds sand blocks ARP spoofing. Thus, anti- ARP spoofing is possible through different vendors.

DHCP Starvation

The tools like Gobbler, Yersinia, and Metasploit are public hacking tool to perform Dynamic Host Configuration Protocol (DHCP) starvation. It broadcasts huge number of DHCP requests with spoofed MAC addresses continually. These addresses utilize large amount of space from the DHCP server. Hence legitimate user cannot make use of the resources from this server. So, it lead to DHCP resource starvation.

Attacks can be mitigated by Port Security. Limit the number of MAC addresses on the port. During the DHCP request, monitor default settings of the CHADDR field.

Physical Layer

Jamming Attack

A jamming attack is used to jam the radio frequencies used for communication between end nodes of the network. This prevents the communication between the nodes in the network.

Channel switching algorithm is used to save the network against the jamming attack. Channel switching anti-jamming can prevent maximum network from this attack.

Tampering Attack

The attacker attacks the nodes in the network based upon the nature of the wireless sensor network. The attacker accesses the resources from the nodes and prevents the end user or genuine user from accessing the resources.

To prevent this attack in sensor network, masking the packet, obscure the device, and implement Low-Probability of Intercept (LPI) radio techniques.

Multi-Point Crosstalk

Here the Wavelength Specific Switch (WSS) which specifically renege the routes. This nature of light leads to crosstalk within the switch grants for the injected signal interferes slightly upon the legitimate signal. Finally, compounding affect is created on multiple WSS (White, 2008).

To prevent this attack, secure switches are needed.

In-Band Jamming

This attack induces noise into the bandwidth of the network. The defender gathers tolerance of the system using fingerprints of the network. The main aim of this attack is interruption of the service (White, 2008).

It can be detected using the fingerprint left behind on the network and also can gather wavelength of the channel.

All Optical Network-Mixed Security Domains

Mixed security domain jamming happens if one or more wavelengths are added to insecure domain. This produces crosstalk within the secured domain (White, 2008):

- Eliminate the use of mixed security domain;
- Define separate wavelengths for the two security domains.

Correlative Multi-Pont Crosstalk Jamming

It is similar to multipoint crosstalk jamming, but a specific wavelength is implanted instead of random wavelength (White, 2008).

Secure the switch in order to avoid this attack.

CASE STUDY

Hackers have started to sale, shared malicious code ejected by booters involved in online game world. Last year, defender exploited network traffic about 10-20 gbps. But at present it increased to 100gbps. When we consider web app attacks like SQL injection, Local File Inclusion, Remote File Inclusion, PHP injection, Command injection, Java injection and Malicious File Upload. At present, it is accounted about 178.85 million web application attacks. In 2015 application attacks about 163.62 million represented

91.48% were sent over http. Local File Inclusion is at the top vector 71.54%, then SQLi at 24.20% and 15.23 million attacks over HTTPS. The bar chart in Figure 3 presents Industries Targeted By DDOS Attack On 2015.

Some of the top countries affected by web application attacks, U.S. was one of the top country getting affected IPs at 52.42%, as follows China (11.39%), Brazil (6.09%) and India (5.33%). The pie chart in Figure 4 presents Countries Affected By DDOS Attacks On 2015.

From the above attacks, we infer that hacking contributors are tremendously increasing attacks on mobile phones since 2011. In fact, there was a huge data loss on 2011, 855 incidents over 174 million compromised records. According to the security report from 2013 to 2014 new malwares are increased from 83 million to 142 million. Of the downloaded malware, 52 percent of malware was contained in PDF files and 3 percent in Office files. In 2015 network security, found more than 400 malware incidents on the client's android devices. The Figure 5 presents Mobile Hacking by DDOS Attacks performed by various defenders.

Figure 3. Industries targeted by DDOS attack on 2015

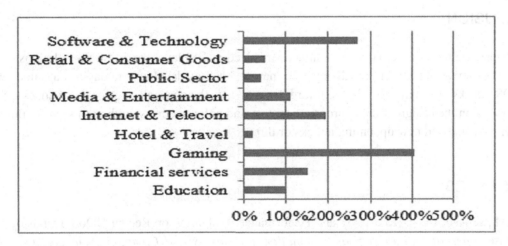

Figure 4. Countries affected by DDOS attacks on 2015

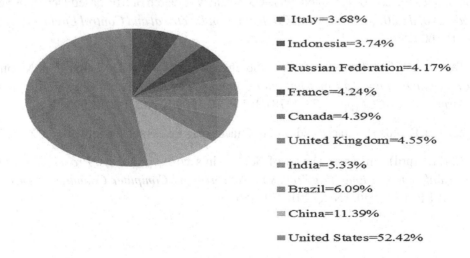

Figure 5. Mobile hacking by DDOS attacks

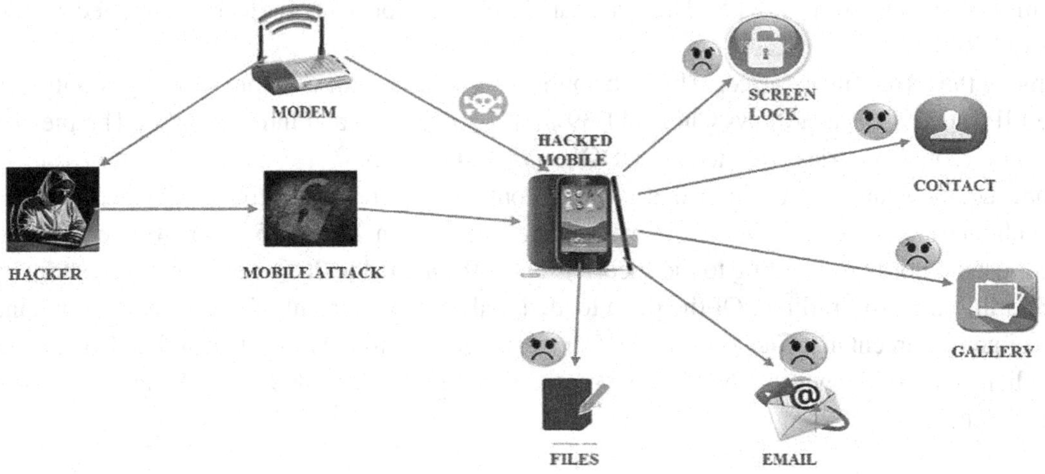

CONCLUSION

In this paper, we have discussed various attacks involved in OSI layers and also the solutions of those attacks. The increased internet growth organizes new technology development day-to-day, along with it new DOS attacks also may arise. In the future, we may face the consequences of those attacks. So, we have to focus on the design of the appropriate system and policies corresponding to security threat. By this way, we can avoid new upcoming attacks or threats.

REFERENCES

Aamir, M., & Arif, M. (2013). Study and Performance Evaluation on Recent DDoS Trends of Attack & Defense. *International Journal of Information Technology and Computer Science*, 5(8), 54–65. doi:10.5815/ijitcs.2013.08.06

Chu, L., Huo, Z., & Liu, L. (2011, September). The security research of SIP-based Denial of Service attack. *Proceedings of the 2011 International Conference on Electrical and Control Engineering*. 10.1109/ICECENG.2011.6057845

Das, K., & Taggu, A. (2014, September). A comprehensive analysis of DoS attacks in Mobile Adhoc Networks. *Proceedings of the 2014 International Conference on Advances in Computing, Communications and Informatics ICACCI* (pp. 2273-2278). IEEE. 10.1109/ICACCI.2014.6968561

Fatema, N., & Brad, R. (2014). Attacks and counterattacks on wireless sensor networks. arXiv:1401.4443

Jain, M. K. (2011, April). Impact of Denial-of-Service in security protocols. *Proceedings of the 2011 International Conference on Emerging Trends in Networks and Computer Communications (ETNCC)* (pp. 142-147). IEEE. 10.1109/ETNCC.2011.5958503

Kumar, G. (2004). Understanding Denial of Service (Dos) Attacks Using OSI Reference Model. *International Journal of Education and Science Research, 1*(5), 10–17.

Mirković, J., Prier, G., & Reiher, P. (2002, November). Attacking DDoS at the source. *Proceedings of the 10th IEEE International Conference on Network Protocols* (pp. 312-321). IEEE. 10.1109/ICNP.2002.1181418

Prasad, K. M., Reddy, A. R. M., & Rao, K. V. (2014). DoS and DDoS Attacks: Defense, Detection and Traceback Mechanisms-A Survey. *Global Journal of Computer Science and Technology, 14*(7).

Sheikh, R., Singh Chande, M., & Mishra, D. K. (2010, September). Security issues in MANET: A review. *Proceedings of the 2010 Seventh International Conference on Wireless And Optical Communications Networks (WOCN)* (pp. 1-4). IEEE.

Singh, V. P., Jain, S., & Singhai, J. (2010). Hello flood attack and its countermeasures in wireless sensor networks. *IJCSI International Journal of Computer Science Issues, 7*(3), 23–24.

White, J. S. (2008). The Missing Pieces: Physical Layer Optical Network Security. State University of New York Institute of Technology at Utica/Rome.

This research was previously published in the International Journal of Information Security and Privacy (IJISP), 11(4); edited by Michele Tomaiuolo and Monica Mordonini; pages 1-15, copyright year 2017 by IGI Publishing (an imprint of IGI Global).

Chapter 13
DDoS Attacks and Defense Mechanisms Using Machine Learning Techniques for SDN

Rochak Swami
National Institute of Technology, Kurukshetra, India

Mayank Dave
(iD) https://orcid.org/0000-0003-4748-0753
National Institute of Technology, Kurukshetra, India

Virender Ranga
(iD) https://orcid.org/0000-0002-2046-8642
National Institute of Technology, Kurukshetra, India

ABSTRACT

Distributed denial of service (DDoS) attack is one of the most disastrous attacks that compromises the resources and services of the server. DDoS attack makes the services unavailable for its legitimate users by flooding the network with illegitimate traffic. Most commonly, it targets the bandwidth and resources of the server. This chapter discusses various types of DDoS attacks with their behavior. It describes the state-of-the-art of DDoS attacks. An emerging technology named "Software-defined networking" (SDN) has been developed for new generation networks. It has become a trending way of networking. Due to the centralized networking technology, SDN suffers from DDoS attacks. SDN controller manages the functionality of the complete network. Therefore, it is the most vulnerable target of the attackers to be attacked. This work illustrates how DDoS attacks affect the whole working of SDN. The objective of this chapter is also to provide a better understanding of DDoS attacks and how machine learning approaches may be used for detecting DDoS attacks.

DOI: 10.4018/978-1-7998-5348-0.ch013

INTRODUCTION

Nowadays, the world has become digitally oriented and full of networking services. Networking is an essential part of our lives because of providing several flexible and easy way of communications. With the increasing growth in advanced network services, chances of cyber-attacks are also growing. There are various attacks that disturb the normal functioning of the networks. One of these attacks is Distributed denial of service (DDoS) attack (Mirkovic et al., 2004). DDoS has become the most frequently used attack for infecting the system's services. It tries to make the services unavailable for normal users by overwhelming it with a huge amount of traffic. DDoS attacks target the system's resources to disrupt the proper functioning of the system's services. Most commonly targeted resources by DDoS attacks are bandwidth, memory, and CPU. These attacks are rapidly growing year by year. As per Arbor's report (Novinson, 2018), DDoS attacks have increased from 1Gbps in 2000 to 100Gbps in 2010, and to more than 800Gbps in 2016 from the perspective of size. One of the biggest DDoS attacks targeted the GitHub in 2018 with a very high rate of traffic. One more such disastrous DDoS attack called "Dyn attack" happened in 2016. It affected the working of many sites such as PayPal, Amazon, GitHub, Netflix, and many more. This attack used a malware named "Mirai" to target these websites. To defend against these vulnerable attacks, more useful research work should be done and efficient intrusion detection system (IDS) should be designed. These IDS systems are very helpful in identifying the attacks in time. Many IDS systems have been developed by researchers and networking companies. A new networking technology "Software-defined networking" (SDN) has also become very famous due to its unique characteristics. Separation of control logic from its data forwarding devices and its centralized global visibility to the entire network topology are two main characteristics of SDN (Nunes et al., 2014). It can become very helpful in DDoS detection using these unique features. SDN can resolve various security issues of conventional as well as trending networking technologies. However, SDN also attracts DDoS attacks due to its centralized controller. DDoS attack targets the SDN controller by sending a large number of malicious packets. By targeting the SDN controller, the whole network can be compromised as a single point of failure. Therefore, efficient defense mechanisms are required to detect the attack in SDN. By overcoming these security issues, SDN serves as a security resolver in a more effective and better way. For these detection mechanisms, machine learning algorithms can be utilized (Michie et al., 1994). Machine learning is widely being used for cyber security. Various machine learning based IDS systems have been proposed by the researchers. They classify the traffic as malicious and normal traffic, which helps to identify the attack. Machine learning based IDS gives better classification results with high accuracy.

This chapter includes a brief literature review of DDoS attacks and its defense using machine learning based IDS. The chapter is organized as follows. Section 2 discusses various types of DDoS attacks and their behavior. A brief overview of working of SDN and the effect of DDoS is given in Section 3. Some major processing modules of an IDS are detailed in Section 4. Section 5 provides some machine learning based DDoS detection approaches. Section 6 provides research challenges in current machine learning solutions. Finally, Section 7 concludes the chapter.

DISTRIBUTED DENIAL OF SERVICE ATTACKS

DDoS is considered as one of the most serious attacks nowadays. A DDoS is a cyber-attack that attempts to block the online services by overwhelming requests for a time period (Gupta et al., 2009). The target system is forced to slow down, crash or shut down by the flooding of a large number of requests. DDoS attacker keeps the system busy for a certain period of time by forcing the system to serve illegitimate requests consequently denying the services to legitimate customers. One of the most important security principles of the CIA (Confidentiality, Integrity, and Availability) model is availability, which is compromised by DDoS attacks. According to a report (Goodin, 2018), a US based service provider was targeted by a 1.7Tbps attack on 5 March 2018. The attacker spoofed its victim's address and sent a number of packets with ping at a memcached server. The server responded by firing back as much as 50,000 times the data it received. This flooding of traffic was enough to exhaust the server and to deny the services for its legitimate users.

Resources constraints in most of the networking architectures are the main reasons behind the DDoS attacks. These types of attacks mainly consume the communication channel (bandwidth), storage capacity, and CPU processing power, etc.

There are various kinds of DDoS attacks. Different attackers of these attacks have different motives to target the victim. DDoS attacks are rapidly growing in the field of internet, which can be divided into categories as per their target of resource exhaustion.

DDoS attacks can be divided first into two categories as follows:

- **Connection-Based:** It is such type of attack where a connection must be established by the attacker for launching the attack via any standard protocol. These attacks usually affect the web server or applications. Some common examples are TCP and HTTP based attacks.
- **Connectionless:** An attack that does not require a connection/session to be established by the attacker with a victim. It can be launched very easily by transferring the packets to the victim. Some examples of this attack are UDP flooding, ICMP flooding, and many more.

Further, a DDoS attack can be put into the following three categories, which is illustrated in Figure 1.

Volume-Based Attacks

Volume based attacks are also called as flooding attacks. Flooding attacks are the most commonly used attacks to target a host. In general, 65% of the total reported DDoS attacks are flooding based as per the Arbor's networks (Calyptix, 2015). In this attack, a large volume of packets is forwarded to the target in order to exhaust its bandwidth. These attacks use multiple infected systems, i.e. botnet, zombienet allowing malicious traffic as legitimate. Common types of flooding-based attacks are:

- **UDP Flooding:** UDP is a connectionless protocol and UDP flooding is one of the most common attacks nowadays. The attacker here exhausts the target host with a huge number of UDP packets on the random ports. The target continually checks for application listening at that port. When the target host finds no application at that random port, it sends back an ICMP destination unreachable packet. This attack aims to exhaust the bandwidth and resources of the target host. UDP flooding attack is shown in Figure 2.

Figure 1. Taxonomy of DDoS attacks

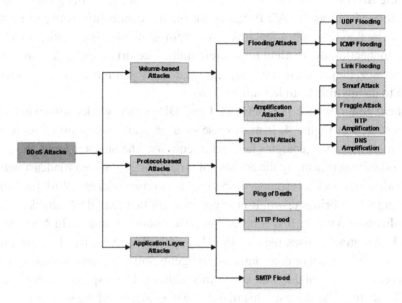

- **ICMP Flooding:** It is also known as Ping flooding attack. In ICMP flood, an attacker overwhelms the target host with a huge number of ICMP echo request (ping) packets. Consequently, the target host responds with the same number of echo reply packets that makes both the incoming and outgoing bandwidth of the network exhausted as shown in Figure 3. This attack can become the most successful in case of an attacker having more bandwidth than the victim.

Figure 2. UDP flooding

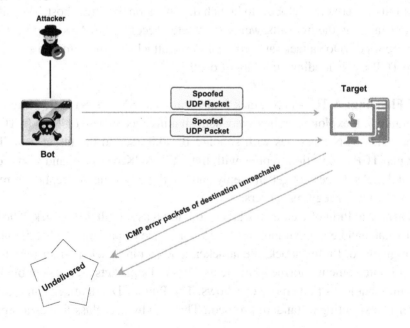

- **Link Flooding Attack:** It is a new type of DDoS attacks that is rapidly growing as a serious threat and can be abbreviated as "LFA". It can break off the connection between legitimate user and victim servers by flooding only a few links. An example of LFA is crossfire attack that can cut off the network connection by flooding only a few links. The origin of LFA is not detectable by any target host because they don't receive any message. They just receive low intensity flows that are not possible to distinguish from legitimate flows.

- **Smurf Attack:** Smurf attack is a network layer DDoS that works somewhat like ICMP flood attack as illustrated in Figure 4. It makes use of a program called smurf malware to enable its execution. Smurf malware generates fake echo requests. The attacker sends the echo request with spoofed IP source that is actually the address of target host, on an IP broadcast network. Each host on the network sends back a response to the spoofed source address. With this flooding of ICMP replies, the target host brings down. It is a type of amplification DDoS attack.

- **NTP Amplification Attack:** It is a reflection-based flooding attack. In Network Time Protocol (NTP) attack, the attacker uses the functionality of NTP servers for flooding on the target host with UDP traffic. The attacker constantly sends "get monlist" command (used for traffic count) to the NTP server with a spoofed IP that is victim's address. The response is sent to the victim server that will be larger than the request. This makes the degradation of the services for legitimate users.

- **DNS Amplification Attack:** It is also a reflection-based flooding attack. In DNS amplification attacks, the attacker exploits the functionality of a publicly accessible DNS server. They send fake DNS query requests with a spoofed IP that is the address of victim server to the DNS server. After receiving several DNS requests, DNS resolver replies back to the victim server with numerous DNS responses. This makes it slow down by overwhelming the victim server and degrades the service for the legitimate users.

Protocol-Based Attacks

These attacks exploit the network protocols to launch the attack on the target host. They attempt to target the connection state tables in the firewalls, web servers, etc. According to Arbor report (Calyptix, 2015), about 20% of the reported DDoS attacks are protocol-based attacks. Some common examples of protocol based attacks are TCP-SYN flooding and Ping of death.

- **TCP-SYN Flooding:** A TCP-SYN attack is also called as SYN or SYN flooding attack, which is shown in Figure 5. It exploits the three-way handshaking mechanism of TCP. In TCP-SYN attack, the attacker sends SYN messages with spoofed IP addresses to the target host. The target host makes an open TCP connection, replies with the SYN-ACK message, and waits for an acknowledgment (ACK). As it does not get any reply and continually waits for replies, it makes the target server unresponsive for legitimate users.

- **Ping of Death:** The Ping of Death attack is also known as long ICMP attack. The internet protocol generally can handle a maximum of 65,535 bytes size of packets. To handle larger packets, it has to be fragmented. In this attack, the attacker sends a ping packet larger than 65,535 bytes by fragmenting it into some malformed fragments. When the packets are reassembled, an over-sized packet is found that leads to memory overflows. The Ping of Death attack can crash or freeze the target server by exploiting a standard protocol. That is why it is classified as a protocol exploitation attack.

Figure 3. ICMP flooding

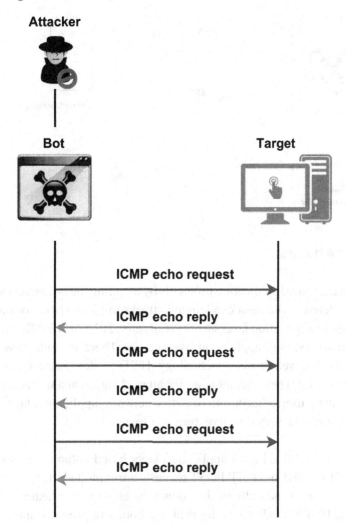

Figure 4. Smurf attack

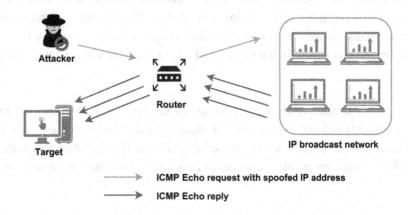

Figure 5. TCP-SYN attack

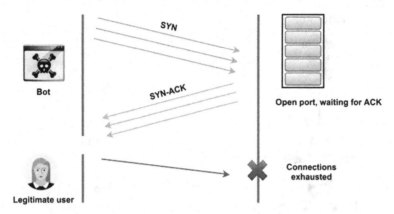

Application Layer Attacks

These attacks exploit the standard application protocols by targeting the online services, web servers, etc. These attacks are considered as the most challenging attacks to be identified or mitigated. As of 2013, 20% of attacks come under application layer attacks (Calyptix, 2015). HTTP flood, Slowloris, and DNS flood are the most common types of application layer attacks. There are some new forms of application layer attacks such as HTML, web browser technology, HTTPS, slow rate attacks, etc. An example of slow rate attack is slow HTTP. They attempt to attack an application in a way that they appear as actual requests from the legitimate users. According to Arbor network, application layer attacks are the most sophisticated attacks that can be very effective even at a low rate.

- **HTTP Flooding:** HTTP flood is an application layer based volumetric DDoS attack. In this attack, legitimate HTTP GET or HTTP POST requests are exploited to attack a web server or an application. It requires less bandwidth to slow down the target server instead of spoofed, reflection-based techniques. HTTP floods generally utilize a botnet (a group of interconnected computers that are malicious) with malware such as Trojan Horses.
- **SMTP Flooding:** SMTP flood is an application layer-based DDoS attack. In SMTP floods, an attacker exploits the SMTP server by sending a number of anonymous emails. The aim of SMTP attack is to overflow the inbox to slow down the server. The blocking of such emails is not the concern, these emails are automatically identified as spam. There is no way to prevent an email DDoS attack but the chances of being victimized can be reduced using some firewall and security systems.

Recently, a new DDoS attack known as Zero-day attack has appeared. The zero-day attack originates from a security vulnerability unknown to the software developers but known to the attackers. Any patches have not been released yet for this attack. It is named as Zero-day because it occurs before "Day 1", i.e. before the vulnerability becomes publicly known, and considered that the attack occurred on "Day 0".

SOFTWARE-DEFINED NETWORK

Software-defined network (SDN) has attained a great attention of the researchers in the last few years. The unique property of SDN is the decoupling of the control plane and the data plane (Kreutz et al., 2015; Hakiri et al., 2014). This separation provides agility and flexibility to the network. SDN makes it easy to update the changes required in the network policies as per the user's requirements. These changes have to be made in the control plane only, which reduces the cost of this process. Due to this significant property, SDN is tending to replace the conventional networks in which control and data plane are tightly integrated with each other. A centralized entity "controller" is placed in the control plane that manages and controls all the data plane devices. Therefore, decoupling of control and data plane, and centralized view are the two key characteristics of SDN (Goransson et al., 2016). The design architecture of SDN is described in Figure 6. The complete architecture of SDN is divided into three planes (layers) that are discussed as:

1.   **Data Plane:** It comprises of data forwarding devices, i.e. switches. These SDN switches are responsible for the forwarding of the incoming packets to the destined host. Switches are connected with each other. Each switch has a flow table that contains an entry for the packets. These entries have three fields: rule, action, and counter. On incoming of a packet at the switch, the rule is matched and if the rule doesn't match, the packet is transferred to the controller.

Figure 6. SDN architecture

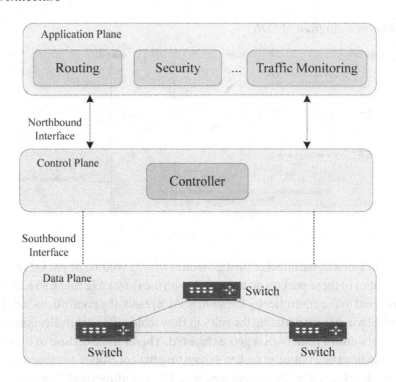

255

2. **Control Plane:** It contains a controller, which handles all the data plane devices. The control logic for the forwarding of packets is implemented in the SDN controller. Being a centralized entity, the controller has the capability of global visualization of the network. It decides whether a packet should be forwarded or dropped. The controller instructs the switch in the data plane to update the flow table rules timely. In the case of multi-controller scenario, the controllers communicate using east-west bound interfaces. The data plane devices communicate with the controller via a standard southbound protocol named "OpenFlow" (Tourrilhes et al., 2014).

3. **Application Plane:** This plane consists of various applications required as per the user's and network service's requirements. These applications are deployed over the controller. Some of these applications are network security, traffic monitoring, routing, load balancing, etc. Logics for the data plane devices are implemented in the controller by using these applications. The applications communicate to the controller via the northbound interface.

The packet forwarding between the SDN switches and controller is described in Figure 7. When a new packet come at the switch, it checks its flow table to find out an entry for the incoming packet. A *packet_in* message containing the header of the packet is sent to the controller if the rule doesn't match with the rule placed in the flow table. Then the controller sends back a message called *FlowMod* rule to the SDN switch S1 and S2. *FlowMod* rule instructs the switches to update the corresponding entry of the packet. Both the switches install new flow rules in their respective flow tables. Similarly, if the flow rule gets a match with flow table rule of the incoming packet, the switch takes an action, which is defined in the flow table and forwarded to the next destined switch.

Figure 7. Event-sequence diagram of SDN

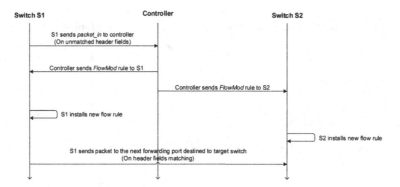

In the case of DDoS attack, the attacker host generates a huge volume of packets and sends to the targeted switch. Since rules of these packets do not match with the flow table rules, so a number of *packet_in* messages are transferred to the controller by the switch. As a result, the controller sends back a number of *FlowMod* rules to the switches for updating the rules in flow tables. The controller continuously sends the rule updating messages upto a limit until it gets exhausted. Therefore, flooding of these packets over the channel between switches and controller makes exhausting the controller's resources, switch-controller bandwidth, and switch's flow table. Due to controller and bandwidth exhaustion, legitimate users suffer from the unavailability of the controller's services. This results in dropping out the legitimate packets. It can be observed that DDoS attacks disrupt the functionality of the whole SDN network.

DDoS attacks most commonly target the bandwidth of the communication channel, other resources, i.e. memory, CPU, and power consumption of the system. Based on these targeted resources, the most affected parts of the SDN are listed:

- **Switch:** SDN switches have flow tables to store the packet forwarding rules and its header fields. But the storage capacity of these flow tables is very limited. Therefore, when a number of new packets are sent at a switch, all the storage of switch gets occupied. DDoS attack targets the switch's memory.
- **Switch-Controller Channel:** DDoS attacks send the flood of packets over the communication channel between switch and controller. This flooding of packets exhausts the bandwidth of the channel, which results in dropping the legitimate packets.
- **Controller:** A controller is the main functioning entity of SDN. SDN switches are not able to handle the DDoS attack packets, and then a message request is sent to the controller. Therefore, a large number of messages are transferred to the controller in the case of DDoS. It consumes the controller's resources, i.e. memory and processing that make it unable to serve the services to the legitimate users and the whole working of the network gets collapsed.

IDS FOR DDOS DETECTION

An intrusion detection system (IDS) is an essential entity for detection of the malicious activities in cyber security. It can be a software application or a hardware device that monitors and inspects the generated traffic in the network. An alert is issued automatically if IDS discovers any malicious activity. Nowadays machine leaning based IDS are being used due to its prediction capability. Machine learning techniques provide more accurate and predictive results. These IDS work better with the large datasets as compared to other IDS.

Figure 8. Modules of a machine learning based IDS (Moustafa et al., 2017)

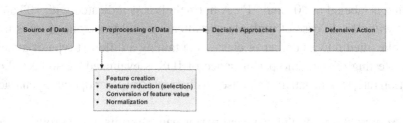

For attack detection, important working modules of a machine learning based IDS are discussed in this chapter as shown in Figure 8 (Moustafa et al., 2019). This IDS is based on machine learning approaches to identify an attack.

- **Sources of Data:** This module involves collecting the data (network traffic) containing normal and attack traffic. The sources of data can be either real-time data collection or available datasets. For collecting real-time data, the network is generated and captured with some packet analyzing tools. These captured packets are collected in a pcap file, which contains details of packets header, i.e. source IP address, destination IP address, source port, destination port, source/destination MAC address, protocol, timestamp, etc. To access the header fields, the pcap file is converted into a parsed file. Further, some useful features required for attack identification are computed using feature extraction techniques. For developing an effective IDS, there are various off-line datasets available. Most commonly used DDoS attacks datasets are KDD99, NSL-KDD, CAIDA 2017, UNSW-NB15, CICIDS2017, DARPA 2009, ISCX dataset.

- **Preprocessing of Data:** Preprocessing of datasets is an important step in machine learning because real-world data has generally missing values, duplicate values, errors, which may affect the performance of the IDS. Therefore, preprocessing improves the performance of the IDS by resolving these flaws. This step has some functions that are feature creation, feature reduction (feature selection is a special case of feature reduction), conversion of features and normalization. Feature creation is the creation of the features from the captured network packets using network sniffing tools such as Netmate, Scapy, tcpdump, Tcptrace, etc. Using the basic features (source and destination IP addresses), some significant features can also be derived that define network behavior. These derived features are helpful in identifying the attacker and source of the attack. Feature selection is a special case of feature reduction, which includes the selection of some features from an original set of features in the dataset. These features have relevant information only that can be important in the detection of malicious activities. Some most commonly used feature reduction techniques are Principle Analysis Component (PCA), Association Rule Mining (ARM), and Independent Component Analysis (ICA). Datasets have both numerical and text data values. It is required to convert the text data into numerical data. To perform an experiment on the dataset, feature conversion is an important step. Further, data is converted into a normalized form. Feature values are defined into an interval of [0, 1] using normalization function.

- **Decisive Approaches:** It comprises of various approaches to be performed on the preprocessed dataset. These approaches detect malicious activities by classifying them. Machine learning algorithms are used to classify the data into different classes. Different machine learning techniques are support vector machine (SVM), decision tree, artificial neural network (ANN), KNN, etc. It involves two parts in its processing: training and testing of the data. Mostly, binary classification is used which is labeled as "0" and "1". A normal class is indicated with "0" and attack class is represented with "1". In case of multiple classification problems, one class is normal and other classes are classified into a number of classes containing a different type of attack. Based on the training and testing of data, the performance of IDS is evaluated on some indicators i.e. accuracy, detection rate, true negative rate, false positive rate, receiver operating characteristics (ROC) curve, etc.

- **Defensive Action:** Based on the achieved performance results, an appropriate decision is taken and it is defined if the identified class of a packet is normal or attack. An alarm is generated if there is an attack and informed the administrator. Accordingly, the system administrator takes action to stop that malicious activity.

MACHINE LEARNING BASED DEFENSE SOLUTIONS

Machine learning (Adeli et al., 1994; Tsai et al., 2009) is widely being used in cyber security for the attack detection and classification of the normal and malicious data by the researchers. There is a large variety of machine learning based classification algorithms that are utilized for different purposes. All the algorithms have their own different pros and cons. Machine learning algorithms work on the training and testing of datasets. Most commonly used algorithms are support vector machine (SVM), random forest, decision tree, K-nearest neighbor (KNN) and so on. These machine learning methods work on two stages i.e. training and testing of the data. Performance of these methods is evaluated using some indicators that are accuracy, precision, true positive rate, f-measure, etc. In this section, some proposed solutions by the researchers for DDOS attack detection are discussed.

Kokila et al. (2014) proposed an intrusion detection system against DDoS attacks in SDN. The proposed system used SVM as a classifier to detect the attack. For evaluation, a dataset Darpa 2000 was used. SVM achieved more accurate results with a less false positive rate as compared to some existing methods.

Vetriselvi et al. (2018) proposed an IDS to detect the attacks in SDN based on machine learning and genetic algorithms. The proposed IDS is built up with two modules. One module is responsible for detecting the attack and another module is used for classifying them. The first module is deployed in the SDN switches and the second one is built in the controller. The proposed method of attack detection reduces the load on the controller and also decreases the dependent nature of switches on the controller.

Barki et al. (2016) proposed an approach to detect the DDoS attacks in the SDN environment. The proposed approach is based on two components. The first component is signature IDS and the second one is advanced IDS. Four machine learning algorithms are analyzed for classification of the traffic into normal and malicious traffic. These machine-learning-based algorithms are Naive Bayes, KNN, k-means, and k-medoids. The classification algorithm with higher accuracy is used for the signature IDS. It identifies the normal and malicious behavior of the hosts. A list of malicious hosts is sent to the advanced IDS. The advanced IDS works on the basis of TCP three-way handshaking. The designed IDS is implemented on Ryu controller. Mininet (Yan et al., 2015) is used as an SDN based emulator for the experiment. The results show that Naive Bayes provides a higher detection rate. One disadvantage of the algorithm is that it takes more processing time as compared to using other classification algorithms.

In a research work, Abubakar et al. (2017) presented a machine learning based IDS for securing SDN from attacks. For simulation, a virtual testbed is designed using a star topology with hosts and servers connected to OpenFlow switches. To perform the experiment, OpenDaylight controller (Khattak et al., 2014) and open virtual switches are used with an emulator – Mininet. In the presented work, a signature-based IDS – Snort is used for developing an IDS to detect the attacks. A signature-based IDS is not capable to detect all types of attacks. Therefore, authors also implemented a flow-based IDS using neural network, which has a feature of pattern recognition. It works as an anomaly-based detection. It is combined with signature-based IDS, which can detect attacks that are not detected by signature-based IDS. NSL-KDD dataset is used for the training of the proposed model. Used attack types in this work are DoS, R2L, probe, and U2R. Results show that the proposed model achieves accuracy up to 97%.

da Silva et al. (2016) proposed a framework "ATLANTIC" that uses entropy-based information theory to measure the deviations in the flow table. ATLANTIC utilizes machine learning classification technique to classify the traffic flows. It presents a combination of attack detection, classification, and mitigation tasks in one framework. It consists of two operational phases. The First phase is a lightweight phase, which includes traffic monitoring and attack detection. The second phase is the heavyweight phase, which is responsible for the classification of traffic and mitigation of the attack. In this framework, after capturing all the network traffic flows, features are extracted to perform the classification. Extracted features are *packet_count, byte count,* and *duration.* To classify the traffic flows, SVM is used in the proposed framework. For mitigation, all the malicious packets are blocked and new firewall rules are modified in the flow table. Experiments are performed on Mininet and Floodlight controller. To evaluate the performance of the framework, port scanning and TCP-SYN DDoS attacks are launched. As per the achieved results, all the modules perform well by minimizing the detection overhead.

Ye et al. (2018) designed a DDoS detection model using SVM classification algorithm. For simulation, Mininet and Floodlight controller are used. The proposed attack detection model involves functions performed as part of it: flow statistics collection, features extraction from these flow statistics, and classifying the traffic as malicious using classification algorithm. These flow statistics are extracted from entries in switch's flow table. Six features are used computed for the training of the classifier. In the proposed model, TCP, ICMP, and UDP traffic are used for the evaluation of the experiment. Results show a high detection accuracy.

Yu et al. (2018) designed a model for DDoS attack detection in vehicular networks. The proposed solution is based on SDN capabilities and machine learning. It works on a trigger method which depends on *packet_in* message for timely responding. In the proposed model, features are extracted based on the flow table entries and some useful entropy-based features are also computed. With the help of all these features, a classification model is trained and evaluated. Results show that detection model reduces the attack detection time and has a low false alarm rate.

Chen et al. (2018) proposed a DDoS attack detection system for SDN. In this system, XGBoost classifier is used as an attack detection method in the SDN controller. Attacks, i.e. switch-controller bandwidth congestion and controller's resource exhaustion are discussed in the proposed work. These works include attack traffic generation and packets capturing using simulation tools, and the performance of the detection system is tested. For training the model, an existing dataset is used. As per results, the proposed system achieves accuracy of 98.53%.

Most of the research works have discussed flooding DDoS attacks in SDN. In a research work, Ahmed et al. (2017) presented a DNS query-based DDoS mitigation model. The proposed model involves maintaining traffic statistics and filtering the malicious packets out. It uses a Dirichlet process mixture model to differentiate malicious traffic from normal traffic. Experiments are performed on the real-time data that was collected from network traffic trace files. For classification, features are extracted that are number of transmitted packets, source and destination bytes and duration. Results show that the proposed model performs well for the detection of the DDoS attack as well as for the HTTP and FTP traffic.

Some researchers proposed defense solutions against by developing some intelligence capabilities in the SDN switches. One of these works is presented by Han et al. (2018). Authors proposed a cross-plane DDoS attack defense framework named OverWatch. This framework works on the idea of collaborative intelligence between switches and controller. This framework consists of two modules that are attack detection and reaction. The detection module is responsible for flow monitoring on the SDN switches and an ML classification system on the controller.

These discussed attack detection mechanisms are summarized in Table 1.

Table 1. Machine learning based detection mechanisms against DDoS

Authors	Classification Algorithm	Type of Attacks	Simulation Tools
Kokila et al. (2014)	SVM	BreakIn, DDoS, IPSweep	-
Vetriselvi et al. (2018)	SVM	SYN Flood, port scan	Scapy, Floodlight, Mininet
Barki et al. (2016)	Naive Bayes, KNN, k-means, and k-medoids	TCP-SYN flood	Ryu, Mininet
da Silva (2016)	SVM	Port Scan, TCP-SYN flood	Floodlight, Mininet
Ahmed et al. (2017)	DPMM clustering approach	DNS query-based DDoS	-
Ye et al. (2018)	SVM	UDP, ICMP, TCP-SYN flood	Floodlight, Mininet
Yu et al. (2018)	SVM	UDP, ICMP, TCP-SYN flood	Floodlight, Mininet
Abubakar et al. (2017)	Neural network	DoS, Probe, U2R, and R2L attacks	OpenDaylight, Mininet
Chen et al. (2018)	XGBoost	UDP, ICMP, TCP-SYN flood	POX, Mininet
Han et al. (2018)	Autoencoder based classification	UDP, CIMP, TCP-SYN flood	Ryu, Real-time scenario

RESEARCH CHALLENGES

This chapter discussed an overview of many existing research works for DDoS detection in SDN, which are based on machine learning. Machine learning is a very effective and significant technique in cyber security for the classification of malicious and normal network traffic. Machine learning based IDS are commonly used in the solving some tasks including regression, prediction and classification But there are also some issues existed that are discussed as:

- Machine learning based IDS provide prediction results with more accuracy. However, in most of the work attack detection approaches are not evaluated for real traffic. All the proposed IDS systems and defense solutions have been measured using already provided datasets, which is not an efficient way. Therefore, there is a need to do more research work in the direction of machine learning based IDS system's development. Researchers should propose such detection and mitigation systems that can be effectively used for the real traffic environment, and that have been evaluated with generated attack traffic.
- There is one more challenge is that a proposed defense solution works for a particular type of DDoS attack. So efficient features should be extracted for the classification of the multiple types of attack and normal traffic. This can be helpful to develop a solution that can be applied for the various DDoS attacks.

CONCLUSION

DDoS attacks have become one of the most vulnerable attacks for the networks. They are becoming stronger with the advancement of the network technologies, which make suffered the legitimate users for the network services. Some efficient solutions should be developed for the detection and mitigation of these vulnerable attacks. In this chapter, an overview of various common types of DDoS attacks has been discussed. Different layers of the SDN architecture and impacts of DDoS attacks have also been presented in the chapter. This chapter also includes a discussion of required steps in an IDS that is based on machine learning classification. Finally, authors provided some machine learning based solutions for DDoS detection in SDN. Machine learning based IDS are more efficient in the case of large datasets and provide more accurate classification results. They have the better prediction capability because of having training of the data. There is a requirement of developing efficient machine learning based defense solutions for the real-time network traffic.

REFERENCES

Abubakar, A., & Pranggono, B. (2017, September). Machine learning based intrusion detection system for software defined networks. In *2017 Seventh International Conference on Emerging Security Technologies (EST)* (pp. 138-143). IEEE. 10.1109/EST.2017.8090413

Adeli, H., & Hung, S. L. (1994). *Machine learning: neural networks, genetic algorithms, and fuzzy systems*. Hoboken, NJ: John Wiley & Sons.

Ahmed, M. E., Kim, H., & Park, M. (2017, October). Mitigating DNS query-based DDoS attacks with machine learning on Software-defined networking. In 2017 IEEE Military Communications Conference (MILCOM) (pp. 11-16). IEEE. doi:10.1109/MILCOM.2017.8170802

Barki, L., Shidling, A., Meti, N., Narayan, D. G., & Mulla, M. M. (2016, September). Detection of distributed denial of service attacks in software defined networks. In *2016 International Conference on Advances in Computing, Communications and Informatics (ICACCI)* (pp. 2576-2581). IEEE. 10.1109/ICACCI.2016.7732445

Calyptix. (2015). DDoS Attacks 101: Types, targets, and motivations. Retrieved from https://www.calyptix.com/top-threats/ddos-attacks-101-types-targets-motivations/

Chen, Z., Jiang, F., Cheng, Y., Gu, X., Liu, W., & Peng, J. (2018, January). Xgboost Classifier for DDoS Attack Detection and Analysis in SDN-Based Cloud. In *2018 IEEE International Conference on Big Data and Smart Computing (BigComp)* (pp. 251-256). IEEE. 10.1109/BigComp.2018.00044

da Silva, A. S., Wickboldt, J. A., Granville, L. Z., & Schaeffer-Filho, A. (2016, April). ATLANTIC: A framework for anomaly traffic detection, classification, and mitigation in SDN. In *Proceedings 2016 IEEE/IFIP Network Operations and Management Symposium (NOMS)* (pp. 27-35). IEEE. 10.1109/NOMS.2016.7502793

Goodin, D. (2018). *US service provider survives the biggest recorded DDoS in history*. Retrieved from https://arstechnica.com/information-technology/2018/03/us-service-provider-survives-the-biggest-recorded-ddos-in-history/

Goransson, P., Black, C., & Culver, T. (2016). *Software defined networks: A comprehensive approach*. Burlington, MA: Morgan Kaufmann.

Gupta, B. B., Joshi, R. C., & Misra, M. (2009). Defending against distributed denial of service attacks: Issues and challenges. *Information Security Journal: A Global Perspective, 18*(5), 224-247.

Hakiri, A., Gokhale, A., Berthou, P., Schmidt, D. C., & Gayraud, T. (2014). Software-defined networking: Challenges and research opportunities for future internet. *Computer Networks, 75*, 453–471. doi:10.1016/j.comnet.2014.10.015

Han, B., Yang, X., Sun, Z., Huang, J., & Su, J. (2018). OverWatch: A cross-plane DDoS attack defense framework with collaborative intelligence in SDN. *Security and Communication Networks, 2018*, 1–15. doi:10.1155/2018/9649643

Khattak, Z. K., Awais, M., & Iqbal, A. (2014, December). Performance evaluation of OpenDaylight SDN controller. In *Proceedings 2014 20th IEEE International Conference on Parallel and Distributed Systems (ICPADS)* (pp. 671-676). IEEE. 10.1109/PADSW.2014.7097868

Kokila, R. T., Selvi, S. T., & Govindarajan, K. (2014, December). DDoS detection and analysis in SDN-based environment using support vector machine classifier. In *Proceedings 2014 Sixth International Conference on Advanced Computing (ICoAC)* (pp. 205-210). IEEE. 10.1109/ICoAC.2014.7229711

Krazit, T. (2018). *What are memcached servers, and why are they being used to launch record-setting DDoS attacks?* Retrieved from https://www.geekwire.com/2018/memcached-servers-used-launch-record-setting-ddos-attacks/

Kreutz, D., Ramos, F. M., Verissimo, P., Rothenberg, C. E., Azodolmolky, S., & Uhlig, S. (2015). Software-defined networking: A comprehensive survey. *Proceedings of the IEEE, 103*(1), 14–76. doi:10.1109/JPROC.2014.2371999

Michie, D., Spiegelhalter, D. J., & Taylor, C. C. (1994). Machine learning. *Neural and Statistical Classification, 13*.

Mirkovic, J., & Reiher, P. (2004). A taxonomy of DDoS attack and DDoS defense mechanisms. *Computer Communication Review, 34*(2), 39–53. doi:10.1145/997150.997156

Moustafa, N., Creech, G., & Slay, J. (2017). Big data analytics for intrusion detection system: Statistical decision-making using finite dirichlet mixture models. In *Data analytics and decision support for cybersecurity* (pp. 127–156). Cham, Switzerland: Springer. doi:10.1007/978-3-319-59439-2_5

Moustafa, N., Hu, J., & Slay, J. (2019). A holistic review of network anomaly detection systems: A comprehensive survey. *Journal of Network and Computer Applications, 128*, 33–55. doi:10.1016/j.jnca.2018.12.006

Novinson, M. (2018). *8 biggest DDoS attacks today and what you can learn from them.* Retrieved from https://www.crn.com/slide-shows/security/8-biggest-ddos-attacks-today-and-what-you-can-learn-from-them

Nunes, B. A. A., Mendonca, M., Nguyen, X. N., Obraczka, K., & Turletti, T. (2014). A survey of software-defined networking: Past, present, and future of programmable networks. *IEEE Communications Surveys and Tutorials, 16*(3), 1617–1634. doi:10.1109/SURV.2014.012214.00180

Tourrilhes, J., Sharma, P., Banerjee, S., & Pettit, J. (2014). SDN and OpenFlow Evolution: A standards perspective. *Computer*, *47*(11), 22–29. doi:10.1109/MC.2014.326

Tsai, C. F., Hsu, Y. F., Lin, C. Y., & Lin, W. Y. (2009). Intrusion detection by machine learning: A review. *Expert Systems with Applications*, *36*(10), 11994–12000. doi:10.1016/j.eswa.2009.05.029

Vetriselvi, V., Shruti, P. S., & Abraham, S. (2018, January). Two-level intrusion detection system in SDN using machine learning. In *Proceedings International Conference on Communications and Cyber Physical Engineering 2018* (pp. 449-461). Springer, Singapore.

Yan, J., & Jin, D. (2015, June). VT-Mininet: Virtual-time-enabled mininet for scalable and accurate software-defined network emulation. In *Proceedings of the 1st ACM SIGCOMM Symposium on Software Defined Networking Research* (p. 27). ACM.

Ye, J., Cheng, X., Zhu, J., Feng, L., & Song, L. (2018). A DDoS attack detection method based on SVM in software defined network. *Security and Communication Networks*.

Yu, Y., Guo, L., Liu, Y., Zheng, J., & Zong, Y. (2018). An efficient SDN-based DDoS attack detection and rapid response platform in vehicular networks. *IEEE Access: Practical Innovations, Open Solutions*, *6*, 44570–44579. doi:10.1109/ACCESS.2018.2854567

This research was previously published in Security and Privacy Issues in Sensor Networks and IoT edited by Priyanka Ahlawat and Mayank Dave; pages 193-214, copyright year 2020 by Information Science Reference (an imprint of IGI Global).

Chapter 14
Global Naming and Storage System Using Blockchain

Chanti S.
Pondicherry University, Pondicherry, India

Taushif Anwar
https://orcid.org/0000-0002-6937-7258
Pondicherry University, Pondicherry, India

Chithralekha T.
Pondicherry University, Pondicherry, India

V. Uma
https://orcid.org/0000-0002-7257-7920
Pondicherry University, Pondicherry, India

ABSTRACT

The global naming systems are used to resolve the DNS (domain name system) queries by providing the IP address of a particular domain. Humans are familiar in remembering the text rather than numbers. So the DNS servers help in resolving the human-readable domain names into system understandable IP address. In the current DNS architecture, there are several threats that cost a lot of damage to the organizations. At the earlier stage, DNS protocol lacks security assurance in place. To solve this issue, they introduced DNSSEC (subsequent DNS) as an additional layer of trust on top of DNS by providing authentication. Still, the current DNS servers couldn't address issues such as DoS/DDoS attacks. To address all these issues, blockchain technology offers an innovative method to handle those challenges. The existing naming systems are centralized, which is a major problem in achieving security.. The main aim of this chapter is to provide an overview of blockchain technology and a brief introduction to blockchain-based naming and storage systems.

DOI: 10.4018/978-1-7998-5348-0.ch014

INTRODUCTION

The Domain Name System (DNS) is introduced in the early days of the internet and mainly used for an academic and military purpose (Wei-hong, Meng, Lin, Jia-gui, & Yang, 2017). DNS is used to translate the human-readable names into the numerical address of the computer. At the early stage, a host file is maintained to store the human-readable name to represent the numerical address of a computer on ARPANET (Wikipedia, n.d.). Maintaining the host files in the long turn becomes much complex and to overcome this, Paul Mockapetris created the Domain Name System in early 1980s.

The DNS lacks in security features because they didn't think that the Internet will become popular and spread globally. Denial of Service Attack (DoS) becomes a major security threat to the DNS (Bisiaux, 2014). To overcome those security issues, DNSSEC is introduced to address the security problems created on DNS (Marrison, 2015). DNSSEC provides the authenticity and integrity of the information in DNS. But, the DNSSEC fails to address the confidentiality of the data because the data is not encrypted and so anyone can see the information and there is a possibility that the manipulation of information is also carried out.

Blockchain is a decentralized peer-to-peer network, in which all the nodes in the network share the same information (Wikipedia, 2019a). It is like a public ledger that is available with all the nodes in the network and so any type of insertion or updation of records can be ubiquitous. Bitcoin is the cryptocurrency used in blockchain for transferring digital money in a peer-to-peer network more securely (Crosby, Pattanayak, Verma, Kalyanaraman, 2016). The blockchain network is fully decentralized and there is no third party in between them (Iansiti & Lakhani, 2017; Pilkington, 2016). In the initial stages, the blockchain is used for the digital transaction using cryptocurrencies. In blockchain, the miner is a peer in the network who mines the set of transaction to create a new block and miners are rewarded for successful creation of a block. Later, the technology behind the blockchain is used for many purposes. Some real-time application of blockchain technologies are: voting system using blockchain, in food industry the blockchain helps end user to see all the stages from the former to the customer, blockchain based land registration process, blockain based DNS and so on (Foroglou & Tsilidou, 2015). Blockchain can be used for global naming and storage system that is fully decentralized and it also maintains the security level as higher (Wang, Wang, Guo, Du, Cheng, & Li, 2019). The blockchain based naming system can address the security issues in the traditional DNS.

A secured naming system is required to protect the privacy of the internet users. The structure of this book chapter is given as follows: Section-1 explains the basic concepts of DNS like how it works, what are the components and parties involved in creating a domain name and so on. Section-2 is about the potential threats systems. (For example, Denial of service attack, Zero-day attack, DNS cache poisoning, DNS hijacking) that current DNS couldn't failed to address. Section-3 provides the alternative solutions that are available to provide a secure internet i.e., blockchain based naming and storage system. Namecoin, Blockstack, Nebulis, Bitforest are the existing blockchain based naming systems. Finally section-4 provides the conclusion of the book chapter.

1. DOMAIN NAME SYSTEM (DNS)

Domain Name System (DNS) is a core part of the internet that translates the human-readable domain to the system understandable IP address (Wikipedia, n.d.; Brain, Chandler, & Crawford, 2002). Humans are familiar in remembering the text rather than numbers. So DNS servers are like internet phone that maintains the IP address of all domains. When the user search for any website (for example, www.google. com), the DNS server provides the IP address (216.58.195.238) of www.google.com and by using it the user connects to that server.

1.1. Components of DNS

The DNS servers have three main components Domain Name Space, Name Server, and Resolver. Each component is explained below in detail:

1.1.1. Domain Name Space

Domain Name Space is a hierarchical representation of domain names on the internet. In this hierarchy, one root server along with number of top-level domains are present. From the top-level domains, subdomains are registered. Likewise, it can go up to 127 levels. The top-level domains will have the information of their child nodes. Figure 1 shows the hierarchy of the Domain Name Space.

Figure 1. Hierarchy of the domain name space

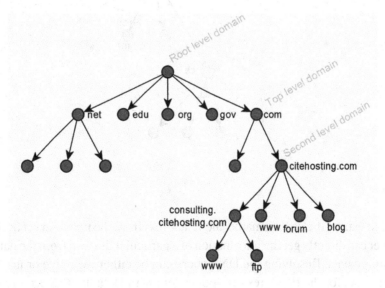

1.1.2. Name Server

Name servers store the information related to domain names and their corresponding IP addresses. It is very difficult to store all the DNS entries in a single server. Therefore, a delegation of the DNS server is required. The complete namespace is divided into zones. A DNS zone is any distinct, contiguous portion of the domain name space in the Domain Name System (DNS) for which administrative responsibility has been delegated to a single manager (Wikipedia). These zones are authoritative for the domain information they contain. Figure 2 explains the zones, where '.com' will be root, abc.com will be the primary domain and xyz.abc.com will be the secondary domain. The name servers are of two types- authoritative servers and caching server. The authoritative name server is again classified into primary name servers and secondary name servers.

Figure 2. DNS Hierarchy with Zone Files

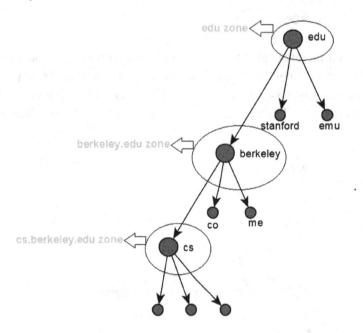

1.1.3. Resolver

Resolvers are used to extract the domain name and IP address from the name server according to the user request. The resolver can directly get the information of a particular domain from the name server without any additional requirements. Resolving the DNS query can be either recursive or iterative. In recursive processes, the client asks for the IP address of google.com with Default DNS server and it provides the IP address. If it is not available, the Default DNS server contacts the root server to resolve the query. In return, the root server provides the '.com' server information. Now the Default DNS requests the IP address with '.com' server and it provides the IP address of google.com server. But in case of an iterative process, if the IP address of google.com is not available, then it queries the other DNS server to get the IP address. Figure 3 shows the recursive process and figure 4 shows the iterative process.

Figure 3. Recursive DNS Query Process

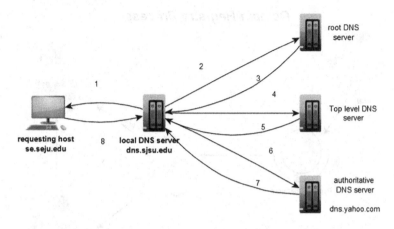

Figure 4. Iterative DNS Query Process

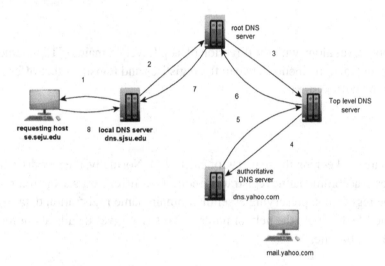

1.2. Domain Name Registration Processes

To register a domain, the registrant should register the domain with ICANN-accredited registrar (Parsons, Coffman, & Rechterman, 2011; Thoke, 2019; Network Solutions, n.d.). Later the registrar will check for the availability of the domain and the request will be considered only if it is available. For every domain, there will be an expiry date and it offers the renewal of ownership. The owner of a domain can also resell their domain(s) through the registrar. There are five parties that are involved in this process of registration of the domain as shown in figure 5.

1.2.1. ICANN

The institution, Internet Corporation for Assigned Names and Numbers (ICANN) is a non-profit organization that administrates the task assigned for both IP address and domain names. ICANN is responsible

Figure 5. Domain registration process and the parties involved in it

Domain Registry Process

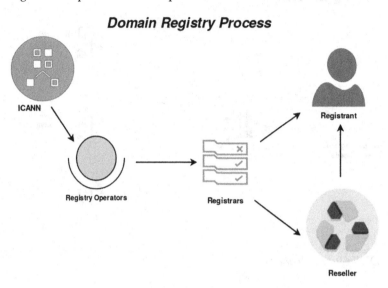

for handling the root server along with the direction of Top Level Domains (TLD) name scheme process. The system makes mutual agreements between the registries and registrars that offer the foundation for the creation of the WHOIS system.

1.2.2. Registry

Registries are incharge of keeping the registry for each TLD. Normally, the registries have some obligations that comprises of accommodating registration requests from registrars. It also communicates directly from domain name registrants, preserving essential domain name registration data in a database and it broadcasts the zone file data with the help of name servers (i.e. gives details about the site information of a domain name) via Internet.

1.2.3. *Registrar*

Registrars are an organization licensed by ICANN and authorized by the registries to deal with domain names. They are tied up by the Registrar Accreditation Agreement (RAA) with ICANN and they create their contracts with the registries. The registrar responsibilities are set out by RAA which includes WHOIS database maintenance, entry of data to registries, alleviate WHOIS queries by the public, safeguarding details of domain name registrants, and obeying RAA conditions regarding termination period of the domain name registration.

1.2.4. *Reseller*

Several domain name registrants choose to register the domains via **reseller** for the organization. These organizations made an agreement with registrars and offer services like email mailboxes, web hosting, etc. Resellers sell registrar(s) services through the mutual agreement between them; because of that, they are not licensed by ICANN. However, these types of domain registration still support the registration for whom they are reselling.

1.2.5. *Registrant*

The domain name has been registered by **domain name registrant.** The registrant may be a person or organization. Generally, domain name registrant registers their domain through online or through reseller who is available at that time. In addition to the domain name registering, the domain names itemized on name servers are required in order to customize the domain name to reach the internet as quickly as possible through domain name registrant. Sometimes, if the registrar cannot compromise this service on that time, domain name registrant is accountable for obtaining or presenting his or her own name server.

2. CHALLENGES IN USING THE CURRENT DNS SERVERS

ICANN is a non-profit organization that only maintains all the registries of DNS. The DNS servers are prone to several attacks, which can increase gradually. DNSSEC is an additional layer of protection that protects users from intruders. But still, several attacks are happening by spoofing the records, poisoning the DNS entries and so on. Some major DNS attacks have been discussed here.

2.1. DNS Spoofing/ Cache Poisoning

In DNS Spoofing (Wikipedia, 2019b), the attackers corrupt the DNS entries of a particular domain and it is cached by the resolver. When the user tries to access the site, the resolver provides the wrong IP address that redirects the user to attackers' server. This results in redirection of users to a spoofed site. Figure 6 describes the DNS spoofing process.

Figure 6. DNS spoofing attack

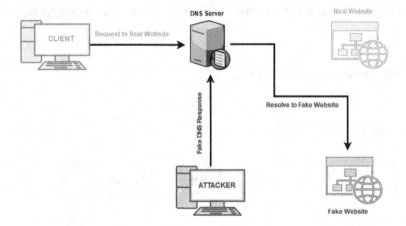

2.2. Denial of Service Attack (DoS)

The Denial of Service Attacks (Fulton, 2016; Rouse, n.d.) is done to prevent the legitimate internet user to access the website by flooding or crashing the server. Rarely the attacker crashes the server and most of the time they flood the server by sending multiple spoofed packets. This slows down the system for legitimate users. For example, if a user sends a request packet to the site, in response the server has to reply the client's request as shown in figure 7. In a DoS attack, the server receives hundreds and thousands of requests which delays the intended users' service.

Figure 7. Denial of service attack (DoS)

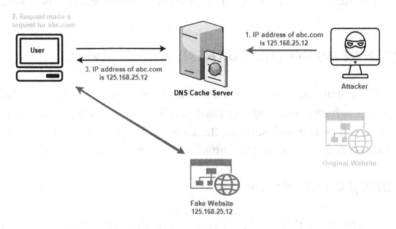

2.3. Distributed Denial of Service Attack (DDoS)

The Distributed Denial of Service Attack (DDoS) (Rouse, n.d.; Yusof, Udzir, & Selamat, 2019) is the advanced level of DoS attack, where the attacker targets the particular website or the server with multiple corrupted computers for flooding. The DoS attack uses a single computer to attack the target as shown in figure 8. But in DDoS, the attacker uses the multiple compromised computers together to shut down or crash the server.

Figure 8. Distributed denial of service (DDoS)

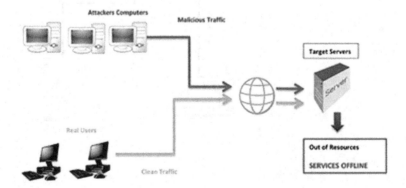

2.4. Zero Day Attack

Zero Data vulnerability (Rijnetu, 2017) is a fault within the software, hardware which is not known to the developers. The zero-day attack occurs only when the attacker finds the loophole in the system hardware or software and attacks the system before the developer comes to know about the flaw. The complete life cycle of Zero day vulnerability is shown in figure 9.

Figure 9. Zero day attack life cycle

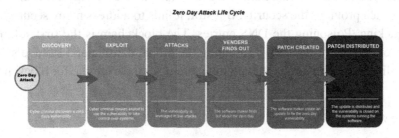

2.5. DNS Hijacking

DNS hijacking (Qadir, 2018) is one type of DNS attack, in which the user gets the wrong IP address for the requested domain. In this attack, the intruder modifies the DNS entries by installing the malicious code in the user system and modifies the host files. Otherwise, affects the DNS server by replacing IP address of a domain with the IP address of a server which is under the control of the attacker. In figure 10, it is clearly shown how the attacker changes the DNS entries.

Figure 10. DNS hijacking

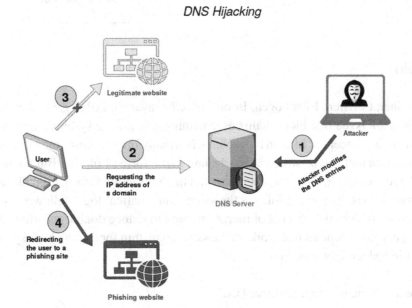

3. BLOCKCHAIN BASED NAMING AND STORAGE SYSTEM

The blockchain-based naming system provides the internet in a decentralized manner, where there is no centralized entity to provide the service. It also addresses the current security issues facing by the traditional DNS. In recent years, many blockchain based naming system had been developed and it provides the correct information to the users in a decentralized manner. According to Zooko Wilcox-O'Hearn (2001), any naming system should satisfy the three principles of Zooko's Triangle as shown in the figure 11. Human readable, secure and decentralized are the three principles and the traditional DNS provides only two principles (i.e. human readable and secure). DNSSEC is an additional layer of traditional DNS which provides the security. But still, it fails to address many security issues like DoS, DDoS, DNS Hijacking, Poisoning the DNS entries. The blockchain is the first solution that satisfies all the principles of Zooko's triangle in developing the global naming and storage system. Namecoin, Blockstack, Nebulis, and Ethereum based naming system are the example for blockchain DNS.

Figure 11. Zooko's triangle

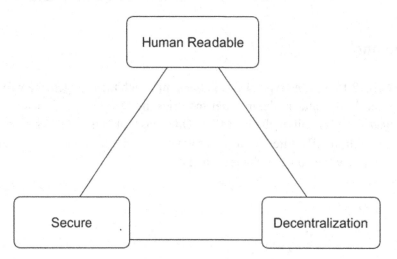

3.1. Namecoin

Namecoin (Kalodner, Carlsten, Ellenbogen, Bonneau, & Narayanan, 2015) is an alternative to the current DNS system and it is the first blockchain based naming and storage system. Namecoin is originally developed based on the concept of bitcoin blockchain. Normally bitcoin stores the information related to a particular transaction that can be stored in blockchain in the form of blocks. But namecoin is a modified version of bitcoin that stores the content other than the transaction information like registration and storing the domain names. Namecoin follows the same mathematical logic followed by bitcoin during mining and it also introduces the concept of merged mining to reduce double spending. Merged mining helps in allowing cryptocurrencies that work on the same algorithm for mining both symmetrically. The main purpose of introducing Namecoin is:

- To provide an alternative to traditional DNS.

- It won't depend on any third-party for Censorship- resistance (Only the owner have the right to make changes on the domain that they purchased).
- It provides security, privacy and very fast.
  - **Security**: Fingerprint of the certificate owned by an owner is stored in the blockchain, which is trusted because of its proof of work.
  - **Privacy**: There is no resolver to resolve the domain name in Namecoin (all the data is stored locally). So the user can get the IP address of the required domain locally without a resolver.
  - **Fast**: It takes less time for getting the IP address of a Domain because it doesn't depend on any resolver. DNS takes 100ms to resolve a domain whereas Namecoin takes only 3ms to resolve a domain.

Namecoin is the first Blockchain based naming system that satisfies all the three conditions of Zooko's triangle (Human-meaningful, Decentralized, and secure). Using namecoin, we can register a domain, resolve the domain names registered using blockchain, renew the domains, and transfer the ownership to other users. The Name server operator, registrars, registries are not required in Namecoin Blockchain. Unlike traditional DNS, the blockchain based naming system (namecoin) doesn't have too many top-level domains. All the domains registered using namecoin will have '.bit' as a top-level domain. Due to limited storage capacity in blocks, namecoin can only offer the domain names of 64 characters length. In Blockchain, every node in the network contains the complete information of all the transaction available locally. Namecoin provides two types of storage facilities i.e. locally stored Blockchain and remotely stored Blockchain. Namecoin can address the DNS attacks like *Packet interception, ID guessing and query prediction, Name chaining (similar to cache poisoning), Betrayal by trusted servers, authenticated denial of domain names, Denial of service attack, and wildcards*. The Namecoin addresses the following questions:

1. How does Namecoin work?
   – Using Blockchain technology.

2. What are the current shortcomings of the DNS system?
   – Centralized control and no encryption is offered.

3. Which of the shortcomings of the DNS does Namecoin address?
   – All the attacks listed above only when the data is stored locally.

4. Can Namecoin match the robustness of the DNS?
   – Yes. P2p systems that ensure all nodes with fewer resources.

5. What are the consequences for the different organizational roles like DNS operators, registrars, (root) registries, etc.?
   – Name server operators, registrars, and registries are not required in Namecoin.

6. How would a transition scenario from the DNS to Namecoin look like?
   – Using a client application and parallel resolving of queries.

3.2. Blockstack

Blockstack is a blockchain based naming system developed after the deployment of Namecoin. They found that one single miner is holding more than 51% of computational power on Namecoin blockchain (Ali, Nelson, shea, & Freedman, 2016). In Blockchain, the 51% attack is very dangerous and it impacts the security of blockchain. If the one miner or mining pool (set of miner formed as a group) contains more than 51% of computational power, they can deny the legitimate transaction and double spending is also possible. Namecoin uses merged mining, which is not practically feasible. This is the reason why they used bitcoin in their update blockchain based naming system called Blockstack and the complete architecture is shown in figure 12. The Blockstack addresses the following:

- Identified the 51% attack in Namecoin blockchain.
- The issues faced with merged mining.
- Successful migration from Namecoin to Blockstack.
- Introduced a new design for the blockchain based naming system.

In Blockstack, blockchain is at the bottom layer and on top of it, there is a logical layer for maintaining the naming system. It uses blockchain to achieve the consensus on the state of the naming system and bind these names to the data. Based on the consensus protocol of the blockchain, Blockstack can provide all operations like registering the names, updates, transferring the ownership of the domain name. This can be done by separating control pane from the data plane.

The control plane is for registering the human-readable domain names. The first layer of the control plane is blockchain and the second layer is a virtualchain (logical layer) on top of the blockchain. Once the domain name is registered, binding of domain names with the respective hash (name, hash) is done and binds with the owner's key pairs.

Figure 12. Blockstack architecture (Ali et al., 2016)

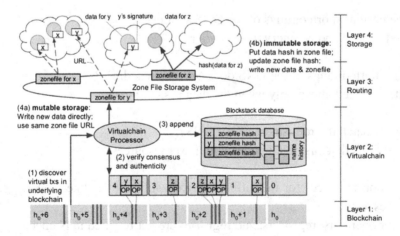

The data plane is to store the data and make it available for everyone. Since the blockchain has limited storage, the Blockstack uses a separate layer to store the data and access these data through zone file. It works similar to traditional DNS, but it identifies the data by hash value or URL. Storage systems like S3 and IPFS are used and the data values are signed with owners' public key before storing so that only the owner can modify the content with the help of a private key.

Blockstack contains four layers, in which two layers are in control plane and two layers are in the data plane. Each of these layers is explained below in detail.

3.2.1. *Layer 1: Blockchain*

The blockchain inhabits the lowermost tier and is utilized for two purposes: it stores the series of Blockstack operations and it offers agreement on the basis of the order were the operations are written. Blockstack operations are encrypted during transactions based on the principal of blockchain.

3.2.2. Layer 2: Virtualchain

Layer 2 is the virtualchain which is present over the blockchain. Virtualchain describes novel operations that don't require any changes to the blockchain principles. Most of the Blockstack operations are carried out in virtualchain layer in addition to that the data in metadata are encrypted during a legal blockchain transaction. The execution of Blockstack operations are carried out in virtualchain layer but only the raw data transactions are shown by the Blockchain nodes. The virtualchain also outlines the rules for accepting or rejecting Blockstack operations. If the blockstack operations are accepted then the virualchain stores the data universally along with the condition that state variations at any certain state. Different kinds of state machines are developed with the help of Virtualchain. Presently, Blockstack has a distinct state machine for universal naming and storage method.

3.2.3. *Layer 3: Routing*

The blockstack maintains the routing layer apart from the storage. The routing layer helps to discover the data. Blockstacks support multiple storage providers which solve the problem of data storage. Like traditional DNS, the blockstack uses zone files to store the Routing Information. The zone files are stored in the routing layer. If the user wants to verify the integrity of the zone files, it can be done by simply verifying the hash values. The zone files contain the hash values that bind the names with their respective data.

3.2.4. *Layer 4: Storage*

The storage layer is the top layer in the blockstack that maintains the actual data. Every information stored is signed digitally with the owners key. Blockstack provides two types of storage facilities.

1. **Mutable Storage**: Mutable storage is the default way of storage provided by blockstack. The zone file contains the URI that identifies the data and the data is stored only after signing it with the owners' private key. The zone file remains the same but the data can be altered according to the owner's concern. The user can check the integrity of the data through the name owner's public key.

2. **Immutable Storage**: The immutable storage is also same as mutable storage but it maintains an additional TXT file in a zone file that stores the hash values. In immutable storage, the data once entered cannot be altered. So, when there is any modification in the data it is updated accordingly. The users can check the integrity of the zone file and the data with the hash values and the public key of the owner. In order to maintain the most updated information in the zone files, the updates are considered as a transaction.

3.3. Nebulis

Nebulis is a decentralized and uncensorable internet that uses IPFS as storage, a transport layer and ethereum based blockchain for DNS activities (Mosakheil, 2018). Nebulis contains smart contracts with some set of rules that administrates the creation of new clusters. The root contract creates the clusters and these clusters are autonomous contracts that control the top-level domains. Within the clusters, they have their own indexes that help in mapping the owners' ethereum address to a UTF-8 encoded string URL and later maps resources with IPFS Hash. Like another mining process, if a new record is created in Nebulis blockchain, the system awards a token called Dust (DST). The entire nebulis system is divided into several core contracts of the system as shown in the figure 13.

- **Nebulis:** Responsible for the creation & administration of clusters, zones, and redirection of queries.
- **Whois:** Search for the existence of domains and clusters.
- **Resolver:** Resolves the URL and returns the IPFS resource.
- **Who:** Who is a contract that holds the domains, address and the link to the database node of a new user who creates a domain.
- **Zones:** Portion of users managed as a group.
- **Clusters:** A cluster is top-level-domains that can be created by anyone by generating the Dust. Within a cluster, we can create as many domains as possible.
- **Root/Branch/Node:** All the entries in a cluster are indexed alphabetically and it can go up to three levels.
- **Parser/Regex:** Only a valid character sets is activated during the cluster creation.
- **Ox:** Ox contracts pay the miners for the domains that are ejected.

3.4. Bitforest

Bitforest is a blockchain based naming system that combines the features of Blockstack and EthIKS (Dong, Kim, & Boutaba, 2018). In Bitforest they maintain a centralized lookup service for policy enforcement and uses blockchain data structure. This is to increase the efficiency of mapping the names with their hash values. Dues to centralized storage, it is very conformable for administrators. Based on the existing blockchain, Bitforest follows the following three principles:

1. **Blockchain Portability**: The bitforest blockchain won't rely on any particular blockchain. The blockchains with its security based on the concept of spending the unspent transaction output at once. Bitforest adopts all blockchain based on their application and compatibility.

Figure 13. The nebulis system with different contracts

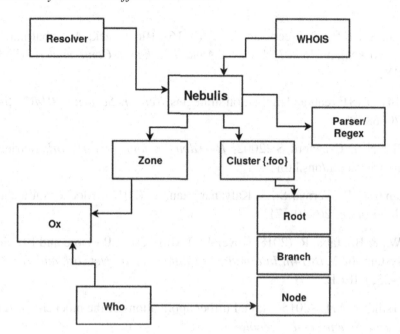

2. **Centralized Administration**: Managing the namespace is done centralized to provide better security and flexible administration. A centralized provider can increase performance by indexing the blockchain and maintaining blockchain data structures as existing "hybrid" blockchain naming systems.
3. **Decentralized Identity Retention**: The administration is centralized but no identity. There is a chance that an attacker can modify the name-value bindings without any authorization from the owner. In such cases, the identity retention is very much helpful.

CONCLUSION

In this chapter, we have explained about DNS (a naming system that resolves the human-readable domain names into the system understandable IP addresses), components of DNS, security threats and addressing mechanisms focused on current DNS. DNSSEC has been introduced to address the security issues in DNS, which is not a feasible solution. Then the blockchain is introduced as an alternative naming and storage system. Further we explained about blockchain, how it works, a complete blockchain based naming and storage system and some existing blockchain based DNS in detail. Namecoin is the first blockchain based naming system and later Blockstack, Nebulis and Bitforest are developed. Even blockchain has its own limitations like storage limit, requires more computation power, and 51% attack (a single miner holds more than 51% of computation power). Blockstack addressed the storage issue by storing the information in a separate layer. Since blockchain is an emerging technology, more research is required to address the issues.

REFERENCES

Ali, M., Nelson, J., Shea, R., & Freedman, M. J. (2016). Blockstack: A global naming and storage system secured by blockchains. In *2016 USENIX Annual Technical Conference (USENIX ATC 16)* (pp. 181-194). USENIX.

Bisiaux, J. Y. (2014). DNS threats and mitigation strategies. *Network Security, 2014*(7), 5–9. doi:10.1016/S1353-4858(14)70068-6

Brain, M., Chandler, N., & Crawford, S. (2002). *How domain name servers work.* Retrieved from https://computer.howstuffworks.com/dns.htm

Crosby, M., Pattanayak, P., Verma, S., & Kalyanaraman, V. (2016). Blockchain technology: Beyond bitcoin. *Applied Innovation, 2*(6-10), 71.

Dong, Y., Kim, W., & Boutaba, R. (2018, November). Bitforest: a Portable and Efficient Blockchain-Based Naming System. In *2018 14th International Conference on Network and Service Management (CNSM)* (pp. 226-232). IEEE.

Foroglou, G., & Tsilidou, A. L. (2015, May). Further applications of the blockchain. *12th Student Conference on Managerial Science and Technology.*

Fulton, S. (2015, February 20). *Top 10 DNS attacks likely to infiltrate your network.* Retrieved from https://www.networkworld.com/article/2886283/top-10-dns-attacks-likely-to-infiltrate-your-network.html#slide3

Iansiti, M., & Lakhani, K. R. (2017). The truth about blockchain. *Harvard Business Review, 95*(1), 118–127.

Kalodner, H. A., Carlsten, M., Ellenbogen, P., Bonneau, J., & Narayanan, A. (2015, June). *An Empirical Study of Namecoin and Lessons for Decentralized Namespace Design.* WEIS.

Marrison, C. (2015). Understanding the threats to DNS and how to secure it. *Network Security, 2015*(10), 8–10. doi:10.1016/S1353-4858(15)30090-8

Mosakheil, J. H. (2018). *Security Threats Classification in Blockchains.* Retrieved from https://repository.stcloudstate.edu/cgi/viewcontent.cgi?article=1093&context=msia_etds

Network Solutions. (n.d.). *6 Steps to Registering a Successful Domain Name.* Retrieved from http://www.networksolutions.com/education/registering-domain-names/

Parsons, R. R., Coffman, J. T., & Rechterman, B. J. (2011). *U.S. Patent No. 7,996,457.* Washington, DC: U.S. Patent and Trademark Office.

Pilkington, M. (2016). 11 Blockchain technology: principles and applications. *Research handbook on digital transformations, 225.*

Qadir, M. (2018, April 5). *What is DNS hijacking and How It Works?* Retrieved from https://www.purevpn.com/blog/dns-hijacking/

Rijnetu, I. (2017). *Security Alert: MS Office Zero Day and DNS Vulnerabilities Can Impact Users*. Retrieved from https://heimdalsecurity.com/blog/security-alert-microsoft-vulnerabilities-in-office-and-dns/

Rouse, M. (n.d.). *DNS Attack*. Retrieved from https://searchsecurity.techtarget.com/definition/DNS-attack

Thoke, O. (2019, June 24). *Understanding Domain Names and the Registration Process*. Retrieved from https://www.lifewire.com/domain-names-and-registration-process-3473709

Wang, J., Wang, S., Guo, J., Du, Y., Cheng, S., & Li, X. (2019). A Summary of Research on Blockchain in the Field of Intellectual Property. *Procedia Computer Science*, *147*, 191–197. doi:10.1016/j.procs.2019.01.220

Wei-hong, H. U., Meng, A. O., Lin, S. H. I., Jia-gui, X. I. E., & Yang, L. I. U. (2017). Review of blockchain-based DNS alternatives. *3*(3), 71-77.

Wikipedia. (2019a, June 26). *Blockchain*. Retrieved from https://en.wikipedia.org/wiki/Blockchain

Wikipedia. (2019b). *DNS spoofing*. Retrieved from https://en.wikipedia.org/w/index.php?title=DNS_spoofing&oldid=891592674

Wikipedia. (n.d.). *Special*. Retrieved from https://en.wikipedia.org/w/index.php?title=Special

Wilcox-O'Hearn, Z. (2001). *Names: Distributed, secure, human-readable: Choose two*. Retrieved from https://web.archive.org/web/ 20011020191610/http://zooko.com/distnames.html

Yusof, A. R. A., Udzir, N. I., & Selamat, A. (2019). Systematic literature review and taxonomy for DDoS attack detection and prediction. *International Journal of Digital Enterprise Technology*, *1*(3), 292–315. doi:10.1504/IJDET.2019.097849

This research was previously published in Transforming Businesses With Bitcoin Mining and Blockchain Applications edited by Chanti S., Taushif Anwar, Chithralekha T. and V. Uma; pages 146-165, copyright year 2020 by Business Science Reference (an imprint of IGI Global).

Chapter 15
Performance Evaluation of Web Server's Request Queue against AL–DDoS Attacks in NS–2

Manish Kumar

Punjabi University, Department of Computer Engineering, Patiala, India

Abhinav Bhandari

Punjabi University, Department of Computer Engineering, Patiala, India

ABSTRACT

As the world is getting increasingly dependent on the Internet, the availability of web services has been a key concern for various organizations. Application Layer DDoS (AL-DDoS) attacks may hamper the availability of web services to the legitimate users by flooding the request queue of the web server. Hence, it is pertinent to focus fundamentally on studying the queue scheduling policies of web server against the HTTP request flooding attack which has been the base of this research work. In this paper, the various types of AL-DDoS attacks launched by exploiting the HTTP protocol have been reviewed. The key aim is to compare the requests queue scheduling policies of web server against HTTP request flooding attack using NS2 simulator. Various simulation scenarios have been presented for comparison, and it has been established that queue scheduling policy can be a significant role player in tolerating the AL-DDoS attacks.

INTRODUCTION

In today's digital era, the Internet has become the most common and widely used means of communication. Online services such as banking, shopping, gaming, social media and cloud storage are growing rapidly. Thus, its usage has been increased exponentially (INTERNET USAGE STATISTICS, 2015). The users communicate with each other through digital devices that interact via various protocols like ICMP, TCP, UDP, FTP, HTTP, and SMTP. Vulnerabilities in the protocols help the attackers to launch the attacks that may lead to severe loss especially in the financial sector. Few examples of attack types

DOI: 10.4018/978-1-7998-5348-0.ch015

are wiretapping, port scanning, the man in the middle, Denial of Service (DoS), E-Mail spamming and phishing. Among these attacks, DoS attack is the most critical one as its strength has increased much in the last few years (Worldwide Infrastructure Security Report, Volume XI, 2016). DoS attacks deny the services provided by the network or the servers to the legitimate users by overwhelming the resources. The attackers overload the resources by employing thousands of compromised machines into the attacks from all over the world; therefore, called Distributed Denial of Service (DDoS) attacks (McDowell, 2009).

Over the years, DDoS attackers have developed more strategic techniques to achieve their targets. They are now becoming more sophisticated since they are perpetrating the DDoS attacks of furtive nature that may prove to be very harmful. The attackers are now moving towards the stealthier DDoS attacks i.e. Application Layer Distributed Denial of Service (AL-DDoS) attacks. These attacks without causing any harm at the network layer and the transport layer reach the application layer (Durcekova, Schwartz, & Shahmehri, 2012). Consequently, the attackers are now posing a huge threat to the Internet Community and a significant challenge for the defenders of DDoS attacks.

From the past DDoS attack incidents on prominent organizations like Yahoo, eBay, Facebook, Twitter, US Banks and many others (Sachdeva, Singh, Kumar, & Singh, 2010; Zeb, Baig, & Asif, 2015; Mosharraf, 2015), it is noticeable that even a little unavailability of the web services can cause huge damage. By mimicking the behavior of legitimate users, AL-DDoS attacks have made this problem even more severe. So, to maintain the high availability of web services to legitimate users, during AL-DDoS attacks, is a major challenge. In this paper, the authors have evaluated the performance of web server's request queue policies so that the availability of web services can be sustained by tolerating the AL-DDoS attacks. The key contributions of the paper are:

- To review various types of HTTP based AL-DDoS attacks with an aim to get insight into the problem of AL-DDoS attacks;
- To launch the HTTP request flooding AL-DDoS attack by modifying the WebTraf module available in NS-2 Simulator;
- To evaluate and compare the performance of web server's request queue scheduling policies during HTTP request flooding attacks using relevant performance metrics like successful transactions, failed transactions, response time and server throughput.

RELATED WORK

By defending against DDoS attacks only through detection and traceback techniques does not completely solve the ever-growing problem of these attacks. The reason behind is to discriminate the attack packets from that of legitimate clients has become even more challenging due to legitimate mimicking behavior of AL-DDoS attacks. Moreover, the mimicking behavior of AL-DDoS attacks also increases the false positive and negative rates. However, the tolerance and impact analysis of DDoS attacks are also crucial to counter against these dreadful attacks. In 2003, (Xu & Lee, 2003) proposed a defense system that can sustain high availability of web services during the DDoS attacks. For this, the authors have segregated the legitimate traffic from the DDoS attack traffic by using a HTTP redirect message. They had measured the performance of this system by game theoretical framework. In (Farhat, 2006), the author proposed an implicit token scheme (ITS) so that the TCP services can be protected from DoS attacks. The researchers in (Beitollahi & Deconinck, 2009) conducted an empirical study to tolerate

DoS attacks by using the Fosel architecture. Other tolerance mechanisms proposed in the literature are based on intrusion tolerance (Lin & Tseng, 2004; Ficco & Rak, 2011) and avoidance of DDoS attacks (Bellaïche & Grégoire, 2011; Kang, Park, Yoo, & Kim, 2013).

Furthermore, most of the studies have been carried out in measuring the impact of DDoS attacks on the network layer. A few attempts have been made to analyze the impact of DDoS attacks on web servers. Jelena et al. (Mirkovic, et al., 2006, 2007) measured the impact of DoS attacks and also proposed the several metrics by taking into consideration the QoS requirements. In (Wu & Yue, 2008), the performance of the web and FTP server under low rate DoS attacks is assessed. Sachdeva et al. (Sachdeva, Kumar, Singh, & Singh, 2009), analyzed the web server's performance during DDoS attacks by using various performance metrics such as throughput, response time, average serve rate, percentage link utilization and survival ratio. In (Aamir & Arif, 2013), authors evaluated the performance of FTP server under AL-DDoS attacks using OPNET simulator by CPU utilization and task processing time. To evaluate the impact of DDoS attacks, Bhandari et al (Bhandari, Sangal, & Kumar, 2014) have comprehensively described the various performance metrics which can be used to detect, mitigate, traceback and measure the impact of DDoS attacks launched on network, transport and application layer. In (Gonzalez, Gosselin-Lavigne, Stakhanova, & Ghorbani, 2014), authors studied the impact of slow rate and low rate AL-DDoS attacks on modern web servers by using only one metric i.e. loss.

After a comprehensive literature review, the authors found that there are no real AL-DDoS attack datasets available. Most of the researchers in the field of DDoS defense are validating their findings by either using the old benchmarked datasets like WorldCup98 (WorldCup98, 1998), CAIDA2007 (The CAIDA "DDoS Attack 2007" Dataset, 2007) or by simulated datasets. Lack of availability of real and public datasets of DDoS attacks has enforced many researchers to simulate the attacks. In the paper (Xie & Yu, 2009), the authors conducted the experiments using NS-2 Simulator to validate their proposed approach. Many researchers are simulating the attacks that are emulated with the real (non-attack) traffic traces. The authors in (Liao, Li, Kang, & Liu, 2015) used the Clarknet HTTP dataset and simulated the attack records for conducting the experiments. In (Yu, Fang, Lu, & Li, 2009; Ye & Zheng, 2011; Zhou, Jia, Wen, Xiang, & Zhou, 2014; Dantas, Nigam, & Fonseca, 2014; Park, Iwai, Tanaka, & Kurokawa, 2014; Singh, Kumar, & Bhandari, 2015), the researchers also used the simulated environment.

Due to non-availability of the real AL-DDoS attack dataset, the authors of this paper have also conducted the experiments using the simulated approach.

APPLICATION LAYER DDOS ATTACKS

Application Layer DDoS (AL-DDoS) attacks are the ones that target the web or database servers to overwhelm their resources. This attack can simply be carried out by requesting a large file from the server repeatedly such that the resources of the server like CPU, I/O bandwidth and memory gets consumed. If a single source sends the high number of requests, these can be controlled and rate limited by the server. However, the attackers manage to send an enormous number of requests with the widely-distributed bots having non-spoofed IP addresses. The application layer DDoS attacks target the services of the application layer of TCP/IP model such as web surfing, E-Mail, and other web services. Hence, these attacks are also known as Layer 7 attacks.

According to (Akamai, 2015), most of the application layer attacks are carried with the use of HTTP protocol. In fact, the attackers mostly employ HTTP GET requests to saturate the resources of the targeted server. Moreover, even the secured protocol HTTPS is not relinquished by the attackers. As a result, this can be concluded from here that HTTPS can automatically secure the connections for the data like user ids, passwords through their encryption mechanism but the connections through HTTPS cannot safeguard the availability of services of the application layer. For today, application layer attacks are the primary cause of concern because they are tough to detect due to their mimicking behavior with the flash event. A flash event is a sudden increase in legitimate access to a famous website beyond the tolerable limits of its server causing congestion, which results in non-availability of services.

Types of AL-DDoS Attacks

To launch the attacks, the attackers are exploiting various application layer protocols like HTTP, FTP, TELNET, SMTP, DNS, and SIP. In this paper, only attacks launched by exploiting the vulnerabilities of HTTP protocol are discussed.

Request Flooding Attacks

Request flooding attacks are those in which the server is flooded with the high number of HTTP GET/POST requests than it can handle normally (Ranjan, Swaminathan, Uysal, & Knightly, 2006; Zargar, Joshi, & Tipper, 2013). In a session, the number of requests sent is more than usual. Suppose a server can handle 5000 requests at any instant of time then the attackers would try to send more than 5000 requests at that instant of time so that the servers get busy in handling those illicit requests and deny the services intended for the legitimate users. The example of this kind of attack is excessive VERB single session.

In Excessive VERB Single Session (RioRey, 2014), the attackers send an excessive number of HTTP GET/POST requests in a single session using HTTP 1.1 (non-persistent) feature. By doing so, attackers create very less number of sessions to send a large number of requests to the targeted server. This attack can easily surpass the defense mechanisms based on session rate limit.

Asymmetric Attacks

Asymmetric attacks are different from request flooding attacks in that the request rate is not higher than the normal, but the HTTP GET/POST requests contain high workload requirements which are to be provided by the server (Ranjan, Swaminathan, Uysal, & Knightly, 2006; Zargar, Joshi, & Tipper, 2013). This type of attack causes more damage to the server because of heavy workload requirements. The example of asymmetric attack is multiple VERB single request attack.

In Multiple VERB Single Request (RioRey, 2014), a huge number of requests are not sent one after the other, rather multiple requests are embedded in a single HTTP GET /POST request packet. By this, the attackers manage to send very low packet rate, but each packet contains multiple requests. Hence, high load resources of the server are compromised by the attackers with a small number of packets. Therefore, these are very hard to detect due to the failure of packet inspection techniques.

Session Flooding Attacks

In contrast, to request flooding attacks, Session flooding attacks consists of a vast number of session establishment connection requests i.e. in this type of attack, a large number of session connections are set up by the attackers (Zargar, Joshi, & Tipper, 2013). The attackers flood the server by sending numerous HTTP GET/POST requests so that the legitimate users could not avail their services. Excessive VERB is the common example of this type of attack.

In Excessive VERB attack (RioRey, 2014), a large number of valid HTTP GET requests are sent by the attackers through the bots, towards the targeted server. The source addresses of the bots are non-spoofed which reflects the appropriate behavior of the normal user. The attackers try to consume all the server resources by requesting large sized files so that the server becomes busy and start denying the services to the legitimate users.

Repeated Single (One-Shot) Attacks

These types of attacks are stealthier as they are a combination of request flooding attacks and asymmetric attacks. The attacker sends the heavy requests repeatedly, and each heavy request is transmitted in a different session (Ranjan, Swaminathan, Uysal, & Knightly, 2006; Institute, 2013). The attacks comprising of these types are recursive GET and random recursive GET attacks.

In Recursive GET attacks (RioRey, 2014), the attackers send a large number of GET requests to several pages or images repeatedly. These attacks explicitly mimic the behavior of legitimate users and are difficult to detect.

In Random Recursive GET attacks (RioRey, 2014), numerous pages of websites like news sites and forum sites are requested randomly and repeatedly with valid page reference numbers so that every GET request seems different from the others. These kinds of attacks are the modification of repeated GET attacks.

Application Exploit Attacks

Instead of exploiting the protocol vulnerabilities, these types of attacks specifically target the applications which are not well developed; like an application has a poor design. The vulnerabilities in the applications are exploited by the attackers so that the server becomes unavailable to the legitimate users (Institute, 2013). Faulty application attack is an example of these attacks.

In Faulty Application attacks (RioRey, 2014), the applications having a faulty design or poor integration of databases are misused. It includes buffer overflows, SQL Injection, hidden field manipulation and cookie poisoning. Mostly attackers issue complex SQL database queries which consume high CPU cycles, memory or even can corrupt the database.

Slow Request/Response Attacks

Attacks of this kind can be launched from a very less number of bots that mimic the legitimate user behavior. Therefore, these types of attacks are hard to detect. In slow request/response attack, either the attacker sends the fractional part of the requests from various bots or keeps the receiving window very short (Cambiaso, Papaleo, & Aiello, 2012; Zargar, Joshi, & Tipper, 2013). Examples of this type of attack are Slowloris attack; HTTP fragmentation attack, Slowpost attack and Slow read attack.

In Slowloris Attack (Damon, et al., 2012), the attackers send incomplete HTTP GET requests headers to the targeted server that allocate its resources for each request after establishing each connection. In this way, attackers slowly and gradually increase the number of requests that saturate the web server up

Figure 1. Slowloris DDoS attack

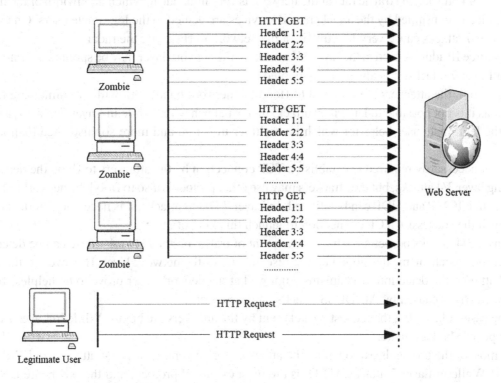

to its maximum connection holding capacity. This attack is also known as slow headers attack. Figure 1 shows the scenario of Slowloris attack.

In HTTP Fragmentation Attack (RioRey, 2014), valid HTTP packets are split up into very short fragments. These tiny fragments are sent at very slow pace before the server time out. A large number of similar requests hold all the connections that can be offered by the server. Hence, the legitimate user's requests are not entertained due to the scarcity of connections.

In Slowpost Attack (Damon, et al., 2012), this attack is popularly known as R-U-Dead-Yet (RUDY) attack. It is similar to Slowloris, but it uses HTTP POST requests to flood the server with gradually increasing incomplete requests. The body of the HTTP POST requests is sent in an intermissive way such that the server keeps waiting for other parts and slowly all the connections are held by the illicit requests resulting in denying of services to the legitimate clients.

In Slow Read DoS Attack (Park, Iwai, Tanaka, & Kurokawa, 2014), the response from the server is read very slowly as compared to the slowly sending of requests. The attackers send the valid HTTP GET/POST requests and read the response in a slow manner by keeping the receiving window size very short as compared to servers sending window. In this way, many requests are sent to keep the web server busy with too many open connections and finally the actual clients do not get their share.

Layer 3/4 Vs. Layer 7 DDoS Attacks

There are many differences observed between the Layer 3/4 attacks and AL-DDoS (Layer 7) attacks. For the better understanding of Layer 7 attacks and layer 3/4, differences between them are discussed below. Table 1 summarizes these differences.

In layer 3/4 attacks, the traffic rate at the network is very high due to which bandwidth of the network gets completely consumed by the attackers and services are denied to the legitimate users. On the other hand, Layer 7 attacks cause very low traffic at the network to fly under the radar.

The source IP address used in the layer 3/4 attacks at the network layer may be spoofed or non-spoofed while in Layer 7 attacks, it is always non-spoofed.

In layer 3/4, the attackers are required to flood the network bandwidth without mimicking the user behavior as it is not possible to launch an attack, in normal behavior. While in Layer 7 attacks, attackers mimic the legitimate user behavior which is stealthier in nature and more sophisticated than layer3/4 attacks.

It is not necessarily required to establish a TCP connection by the attackers to flood the network for launching layer 3/4 attacks, but the attackers may use other protocols also to flood the network. The other protocols like ICMP and UDP can be utilized. In Layer 7 DDoS attacks, it is necessary for the attackers to establish the successful TCP connection to launch this kind of attack.

As layer 3/4 attacks perpetrate a massive amount of traffic on the network, these can be detected by using various mechanisms developed by the researchers for the network layer. However, in the case of Layer 7 attacks, the detection mechanisms employed at the network layer prove to be helpless because very low traffic is caused by AL-DDoS attacks on the network.

In the case of layer 3/4, the request packets sent by the attackers are bogus. While in Layer 7 attacks, these appear to be legitimate.

The most of the protocols exploited by the attackers for launching layer 3/4 attacks are ICMP, UDP, and TCP. While in Layer 7 attacks, HTTP is the most exploited protocol and the others are DNS, SIP, and VoIP.

Table 1. Layer 3/4 v/s layer 7 DDoS attacks

Characteristics	Layer 3/4 DDoS Attack	Layer 7 DDoS Attack
Traffic Rate at the network	High	Low
Source IP Address	Spoofed or Non-Spoofed	Non-Spoofed
Mimicking Legitimate Behavior	No	Yes
TCP Connection	Not necessarily required	Necessarily required
Detection on the network	Possible	Not possible
Request Type	Bogus	Genuine
Packet Type	ICMP, UDP	HTTP,DNS, SIP, VoIP

METHODOLOGY AND SIMULATION SETUP

To analyze the impact of HTTP request flooding AL-DDoS attack on the request queue scheduling algorithms of the server, widely accepted open source simulator, The Network Simulator 2 (NS-2), has been used (The Network Simulator - ns-2). There are two scheduling algorithms, i.e. First Come First Serve (FCFS) and Shortest Task First (STF), available in WebTraf Module of NS-2 implemented on server's request queue. Their performance during the HTTP Request Flooding AL-DDoS attack has been compared by the authors. The methodology consists of three phases as shown in Figure 2.

Generation of Traffic (Phase I)

As discussed earlier, the HTTP request flooding attacks cause very low traffic on the network and overwhelm the resources of the server by sending large number of legitimate looking requests over a genuine TCP connection. Therefore, to launch this attack the authors generated the traffic in such a way that the bandwidth of the network is not fully consumed but the request queue of the server gets overloaded. To make the simulation more realistic, the authors have set the traffic parameters after carefully inspecting the two publicly available famous HTTP datasets. The examined datasets are Clarknet-HTTP (ClarkNet-HTTP, 1995) and CSIC HTTP (HTTP DATASET CSIC 2010, 2010).

Figure 2. Flow chart of methodology

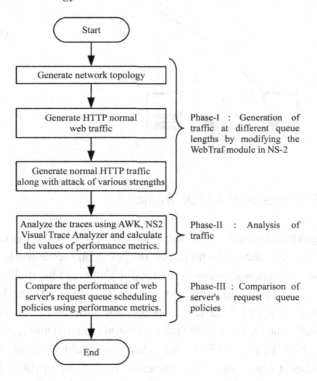

Generation of Network Topology

In (Rajab, Zarfoss, Monrose, & Terzis, 2007; Yu, Guo, & Stojmenovic, 2015), the study about botnets divulge that a botmaster can deploy a very few number of active bots into the attacks as compared to actual legitimate users. Accordingly, the authors of this paper have taken 10% of the clients as active attacking bots and rest 90% as legitimate. A topology of 100 nodes (90 legitimate clients and 10 attackers) and one web server has been used in the simulations. The bandwidth of the bottleneck link is set at 100 Mbps and of other links is 20 Mbps. The bandwidth is adjusted in such a way that no congestion occurs at the network to successfully simulate the application layer normal and attack traffic. Figure 3 shows the small representation of topology used.

Figure 3. Network topology

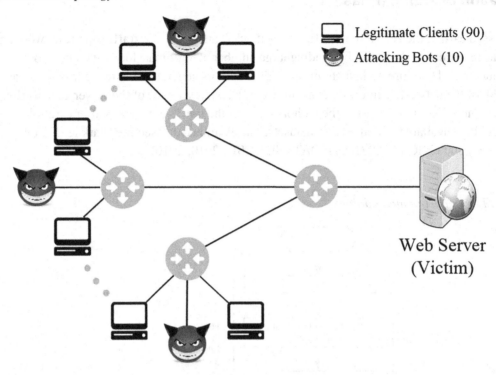

Generation of HTTP Normal and Attack Traffic

In the simulation, the aggregated bandwidth of the generated traffic by all the nodes did not exceed the bandwidth of the bottleneck. So, there was no packet dropping on the network. However, the dropping of requests by the web server's request queue confirmed the attack. This makes the detection of attack difficult in the lower layers and the mimicking of normal user behavior is exhibited.

The normal application layer HTTP traffic is generated for both the FCFS and STF queue policies in a separate manner. Secondly, the attack is launched to generate normal and attack traffic by varying the strength of the attack for both FCFS and STF. For exhaustive evaluation, the attack strength was first increased to 20% and further it was subsequently increased by 20% up to 100%. Furthermore, the queue length of the server was also varied from 250 to 500 and 500 to 1000. The simulation has been run for 3000 seconds and the other parameters are shown in Table 2.

Modification in NS-2

NS-2 is an open source simulator. Two languages namely OTcl and C++ are used in NS-2 to define the front end and the back end respectively. To generate the AL-DDoS attack the source code of internal mechanism at back end in NS-2 defined using C++ has been modified. For modification, two steps have been followed. Firstly, the code of WebTraf module of the NS-2 simulator has been comprehensively studied. The various C++ source files related to WebTraf module have been analyzed. Secondly, the part of the source code of webtraf.cc file has been modified to generate the attack. The modified code is shown below.

Table 2. Parameters of simulated traffic

Parameter	Legitimate Client	Attacker
Traffic Type	HTTP over TCP	HTTP over TCP
No. of Sessions	1000	2000
Session Rate	Exponential avg. 1	Exponential avg. 0.8/0.6/0.4/0.2/0
Number of pages per session	Constant 5	Constant 20
Launch Time	0.1 s	500 s
Page Size	Exponential avg. 1	Exponential avg. 5
InterPage Rate	Exponential avg. 0.01	Exponential avg. 0.01
Object Size	Exponential avg. 2 Shape 1.2	Exponential avg. 2 Shape 1.2

```
Node* WebTrafPool:: picksrc(){
int n = 0;
if (npg < 10){
n = int(floor(Random:: uniform(0, nClient_ -10)));
assert((n >= 0) && (n < nClient_));
return client_[n];
}
else{
n = int(floor(Random:: uniform(nClient_ -10, nClient_)));
assert((n >= 0) \&\& (n < nClient_));
return client_[n];
}
}
```

In WebTraf module, there was no facility to control the functioning of the different nodes in a particular way i.e. at any instant either all nodes can act as legitimate clients or attackers. To simulate the AL-DDoS attack in a realistic manner, we have modified the code that is shown above. On the basis of number of pages per session, the nodes are set up as legitimate clients as well as attackers. In this case, if the number of pages per session is less than 10 then node is setup as legitimate client otherwise it is an attacking bot. In this way, the normal and AL-DDoS attack traffic has been generated.

Analysis of Traces (Phase II)

In this phase, the analysis of the traffic is done by using AWK programming (Aho, Kernighan, & Weinberger, 1987) and NS2 visual trace analyzer (Rocha, 2012). Also, the values of the performance metrics have been calculated. The various performance metrics on the basis of which traffic has been analyzed and the performance of request server's queue policies has been compared are discussed below:

1. **Successful Transaction Rate:** It is the number of Web requests successfully completed in a period of time, divided by the length of time (in seconds) (Yeager & McGrath, 1996). It can be measured out in transactions/second (TPS):

$$Avg.\ TPS_{successful} = \frac{No.\ of\ successfully\ completed\ HTTP\ Web\ requests}{Total\ Time\ Taken} \tag{1}$$

2. **Failed Transaction Rate:** It represents the number of Web requests failed during a period of time (Yeager & McGrath, 1996; Bhandari, Sangal, & Kumar, 2014). It can also be measured out in transactions/second (TPS):

$$Avg.\ TPS_{failed} = \frac{No.\ of\ HTTP\ Web\ requests\ failed}{Total\ Time} \tag{2}$$

3. **Average Response Time:** It is the time from when a HTTP request is sent by the client until the first response is received by the client (Bhandari, Sangal, & Kumar, 2014). It is measured in seconds:

$$Avg.\ Response\ Time\left(in\ seconds\right) = \frac{\sum_{1}^{N}\left(T_{Resp} - T_{Req}\right)}{N} \tag{3}$$

where:
T_{Rep} = Time at which the request is sent by the client
T_{Req} = Time at which the first response is received by the client
N = Total number of requests

4. **Server Throughput:** It is the total number of bytes of data transferred by the server for the completed requests divided by the total time taken (Yeager & McGrath, 1996). It is measured in bytes per second:

$$Server\ Throughput\left(Bytes\ per\ second\right) = \frac{Total\ bytes\ served\ by\ server}{Total\ Time} \tag{4}$$

Comparison of Server's Request Queue Policies (Phase III)

For performance evaluation, three queue sizes are considered in this work for web servers. Generally, the sizes of the request queue vary from server to server according to the popularity of the website and the intrinsic resources (memory, CPU cycles, Database Bandwidth and I/O Bandwidth) of the web server. The default request queue limit of the Apache Web Server is 256 (Apache HTTP Server Version 2.4 Documentation) and in Microsoft IIS 6.0 is 1000 (Configuring a Request Queue Limit (IIS 6.0)). Hence, the authors of this paper have considered a queue size of 250 for a web server hosting website that may be of less popularity, queue size of 500 for moderate popularity and 1000 for highly populated websites.

The comparison of the web server's request queue policies using the performance metrics is done by two ways:

1. The performance of FCFS and STF is evaluated by taking the specific queue sizes i.e. the queue policies are compared using all performance metrics with 250, 500 and 1000 as queue sizes;
2. The performance of queue sizes for FCFS and STF is measured to ascertain the better request queue size for each scheduling policy.

RESULTS AND DISCUSSION

A scheduling policy of the request queue along with its size can substantially affect the performance of the web server during HTTP request flooding attacks. Thus, the authors have evaluated the performance of the queue policies and compared them to determine which queue policy performs better against these attacks.

Comparison of FCFS and STF on Specific Queue Sizes

The scheduling policies FCFS and STF are compared in this sub-section on the basis of individual queue sizes by using various performance metrics. Queue Size of 250, 500 and 1000 are taken separately to evaluate the performance of these scheduling policies.

Successful Transactions

Of all the total transactions initiated, the number of successful transactions should be more for indicating the better performance of the queue. This tells the number of requests that are successfully served by the server. The results calculated at different queue sizes of 250, 500 and 1000 are shown in Figure 4 (a), (b) and (c) respectively.

Figure 4. Successful transactions on specific queue sizes

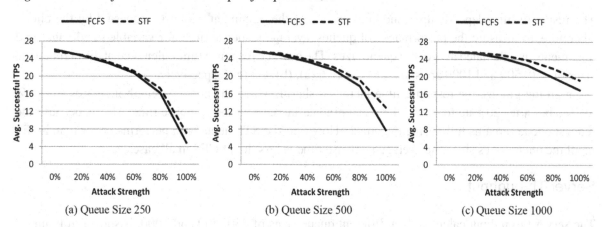

(a) Queue Size 250   (b) Queue Size 500   (c) Queue Size 1000

It can be observed that the number of successful transactions per second (TPS) decreases as the attack strength increases in all the queue sizes. But STF policy is better than FCFS here as successful transactions are always more in all queue sizes and at all attack strengths.

Failed Transactions

For higher performance of the web server's request queue, the number of the failed transactions should be less. For FCFS and STF queue scheduling policies, the number of failed transactions calculated at queue sizes of 250, 500 and 1000 are shown in Figure 5 (a), (b) and (c) respectively.

Figure 5. Failed transactions on specific queue sizes

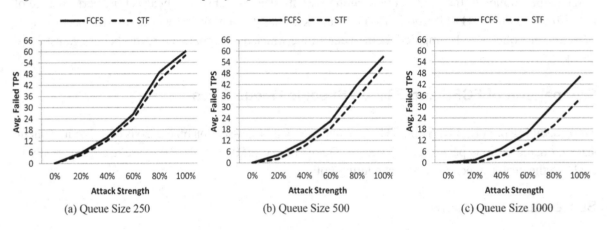

(a) Queue Size 250   (b) Queue Size 500   (c) Queue Size 1000

In all the queue sizes, with increase in attack strength the number of failed transactions increases. However, STF queue performs better than FCFS queue because in all queue sizes the number of failed transactions per second (TPS) are less with STF than FCFS at all the attack strengths.

Average Response Time

The response time depends upon the kind or size of the document which is requested by the client. Therefore, to measure the performance of queues, average response time, for variable sized pages and documents, is calculated at specific queue sizes. The average response time calculated at different queue sizes of 250, 500 and 1000 are shown in Figure 6 (a), (b) and (c) respectively.

In all the graphs, the response time increases sharply when the attack strength increases from 0% to 20% but after 20% up to 100%, there is a gradual increase in the response time. This is because the request queue remains full during the attack. However, the STF queue still performs better than FCFS in all the queue sizes since the average response time is less than FCFS in all cases.

Server Throughput

The server throughput calculated, at different queue sizes of 250, 500 and 1000, is shown in Figure 7 (a), (b) and (c) respectively.

Figure 6. Average response time on specific queue sizes

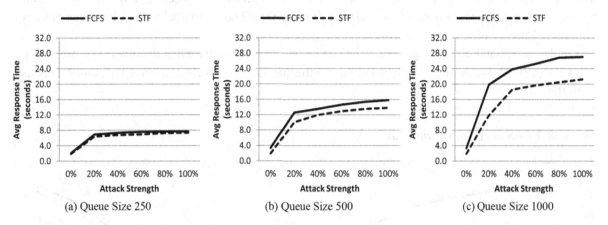

(a) Queue Size 250   (b) Queue Size 500   (c) Queue Size 1000

Figure 7. Server throughput on specific queue sizes

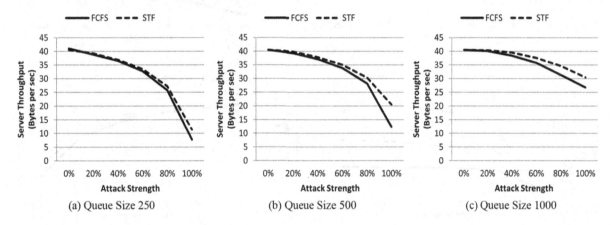

(a) Queue Size 250   (b) Queue Size 500   (c) Queue Size 1000

The server throughput decreases with increase in attack strength in all the queue sizes. Therefore, the resource utilization of server decreases. Among STF and FCFS, the server throughput is more in STF which can be examined easily from the graphs shown.

Performance of FCFS and STF with Varying Queue Sizes

As described earlier, the size of the request queue may vary from server to server. The performance of FCFS and STF has been measured on queue sizes of 250, 500 and 1000 during the attack. This measurement determines at what size the request queue performs better.

FCFS Queue

The average successful transactions, failed transactions, average response time and server throughput for FCFS queue at queue sizes of 250, 500 and 1000 are shown in Figure 8. The number of successful transactions and server throughput do not increase much by increasing the queue size from 250 to 500. Though, by increasing the queue size from 500 to 1000, there is large increase in the successful transactions and the server throughput. The number of failed transactions also decreased in the same manner by varying the queue sizes from 250 to 500 and 500 to 1000. The reason behind is, the queue now can hold more number of requests at a time to serve more transactions.

On the other hand, the average response time increased extensively when the queue size was varied from 250 to 1000. This indicates that by increasing the queue size, the clients receive the slower response from the server.

Figure 8. FCFS queue at varying queue sizes

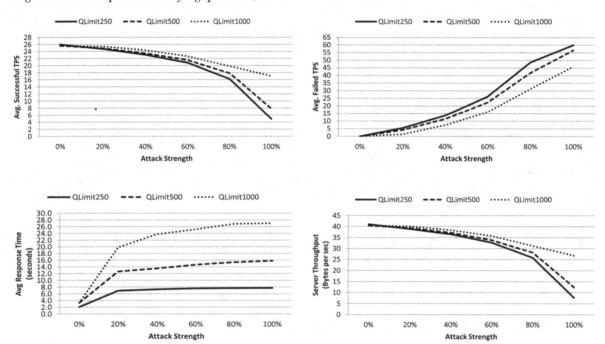

STF Queue

Figure 9 shows the performance of STF Queue on varying the queue sizes from 250 to 500 and 500 to 1000.

In case of STF Queue, the rate of successful transactions and server throughput also increased from queue size of 250 to 1000. But, it can be noted that these are more as compared to the FCFS Queue. Correspondingly, the rate of failed transactions and average response time is less in STF queue as compared to FCFS Queue.

During attack, the larger size of the request queue can increase the number of successful transactions and server throughput but it also increases the average response time. It can be noted that if a moderate queue size is chosen with a proficient queue policy like STF rather than FCFS, it can improve the performance of the web server during the HTTP request flooding attacks with more successful transactions and server throughput along with less average response time.

Figure 9. STF queue at varying queue sizes

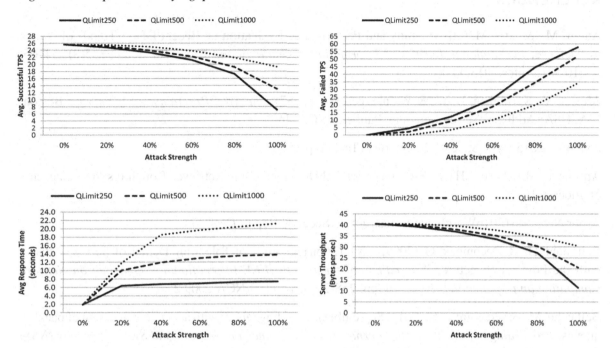

CONCLUSION AND FUTURE WORK

AL-DDoS attacks have grown up a serious threat to the web servers for maintaining the high availability of its services. As perspective to web server's point of view, there needs a strong mechanism that can easily tolerate against these sophisticated attacks without deploying the defense solution. In this paper, the authors have measured the performance of different request queues scheduling algorithms on the web server against the AL-DDoS attacks with an aim to provide a tolerating method. It has been concluded from the simulations performed that, STF queue outperforms FCFS queue at different queue sizes i.e. 250, 500 and 1000. It has also been found that with increasing the size of the request queue of the web server, the number of successful transactions and server throughput increased. However, there is also an increase in the average response time. Hence, there is a tradeoff between the rate of successful transactions, failed transactions, server throughput and average response time.

However, certain key issues could not be established to the desired due to certain limitations and can act as avenues for future research work. Some of the important issues are:

1. This study has a limited scope because of the non-availability of various other request queue scheduling algorithms in NS2. This study can be extended by exploring other queue scheduling algorithms by modifying the NS2 code;
2. Though the parameters of simulations have been set by taking into consideration of study of real datasets still, there is a question of acceptability for real world scenarios. In near future, we will validate these policies in a closed environment by the process of emulation.

REFERENCES

Aamir, M., & Arif, M. (2013). Study and Performance Evaluation on Recent DDoS Trends of Attack \& Defense. *International Journal of Information Technology and Computer Science*, 5(8), 54–65. doi:10.5815/ijitcs.2013.08.06

Aho, A. V., Kernighan, B. W., & Weinberger, P. J. (1987). *The AWK Programming Language*. Boston, MA, USA: Addison-Wesley Longman Publishing Co., Inc.

Akamai. (2015). The State of the Internet (Tech. rep.).

Apache. (n. d.). Apache HTTP Server Version 2.4 Documentation. Retrieved from https://httpd.apache.org/docs/2.4/

Arbor Networks(2016Worldwide Infrastructure Security Report (Vol. 11).

Beitollahi, H., & Deconinck, G. (2009, July). Empirical Study of Tolerating Denial-of-Service Attacks with the Fosel Architecture. *Proceedings of the Eighth IEEE International Symposium on Network Computing and Applications NCA '09* (pp. 258-261). 10.1109/NCA.2009.22

Bellaïche, M., & Grégoire, J. C. (2011, September). Avoiding DDoS with active management of backlog queues. *Proceedings of the 2011 5th International Conference on Network and System Security (NSS)* (pp. 310-315). 10.1109/ICNSS.2011.6060021

Bhandari, A., Sangal, A., & Kumar, K. (2014). Performance Metrics for Defense Framework against Distributed Denial of Service Attacks. *International Journal of Network Security*, 5(2), 38.

CAIDA. (2007). DDoS Attack 2007 Dataset. Retrieved from https://www.caida.org/data/passive/ddos-20070804_dataset.xml

Cambiaso, E., Papaleo, G., & Aiello, M. (2012). Taxonomy of Slow DoS Attacks to Web Applications. In S. Thampi, A. Zomaya, T. Strufe, J. Alcaraz Calero, & T. Thomas (Eds.), *Recent Trends in Computer Networks and Distributed Systems Security* (Vol. 335, pp. 195–204). Springer Berlin Heidelberg. Retrieved from; doi:10.1007/978-3-642-34135-9_20

The Internet Traffic Archive. (1995). ClarkNet-HTTP. Retrieved from http://ita.ee.lbl.gov/html/contrib/ClarkNet-HTTP.html

Damon, E., Dale, J., Laron, E., Mache, J., Land, N., & Weiss, R. (2012). *Hands-on Denial of Service Lab Exercises Using SlowLoris and RUDY. Proceedings of the 2012 Information Security Curriculum Development Conference* (pp. 21–29). New York, NY, USA: ACM; Retrieved from http://doi.acm.org/10.1145/2390317.2390321

Dantas, Y. G., Nigam, V., & Fonseca, I. E. (2014, Sept). A Selective Defense for Application Layer DDoS Attacks. *Proceedings of the 2014 IEEE Joint Intelligence and Security Informatics Conference (JISIC)* (pp. 75-82). IEEE. 10.1109/JISIC.2014.21

Durcekova, V., Schwartz, L., & Shahmehri, N. (2012, May). Sophisticated Denial of Service attacks aimed at application layer. Proceedings of *ELEKTRO '12* (pp. 55–60). doi:10.1109/ELEKTRO.2012.6225571

Farhat, H. (2006). *Protecting TCP Services from Denial of Service Attacks. Proceedings of the 2006 SIGCOMM Workshop on Large-scale Attack Defense* (pp. 155–160). New York, NY, USA: ACM; Retrieved from http://doi.acm.org/10.1145/1162666.1162674

Ficco, M., & Rak, M. (2011, June). Intrusion Tolerant Approach for Denial of Service Attacks to Web Services. *Proceedings of the 2011 First International Conference on Data Compression, Communications and Processing (CCP)* (pp. 285-292). 10.1109/CCP.2011.44

Gonzalez, H., Gosselin-Lavigne, M. A., Stakhanova, N., & Ghorbani, A. A. (2014). The Impact of Application-Layer Denial-of-Service Attacks. *Case Studies in Secure Computing: Achievements and Trends*, 261.

Infosec Institute. (2013, October 24). Layer Seven DDoS Attacks. Retrieved from http://resources.infosecinstitute.com/layer-seven-ddos-attacks/

Instituto de Tecnologías Físicas y de la Información. (2010). HTTP DATASET CSIC 2010. Retrieved from http://www.isi.csic.es/dataset/

Internet Usage Statistics. (2015, November 30). Stats. Retrieved from http://www.internetworldstats.com/stats.htm

Kang, S.-H., Park, K.-Y., Yoo, S.-G., & Kim, J. (2013). DDoS avoidance strategy for service availability. *Cluster Computing*, *16*(2), 241–248. doi:10.100710586-011-0185-4

Liao, Q., Li, H., Kang, S., & Liu, C. (2015). Application layer DDoS attack detection using cluster with label based on sparse vector decomposition and rhythm matching. Security and Communication Networks, 8(17), 3111-3120. Retrieved from doi:10.1002ec.1236

Lin, S.-C., & Tseng, S.-S. (2004). Constructing detection knowledge for DDoS intrusion tolerance. *Expert Systems with Applications*, *27*(3), 379–390. Retrieved from http://www.sciencedirect.com/science/article/pii/S0957417404000417 doi:10.1016/j.eswa.2004.05.016

McDowell, M. (2009, November 04). Understanding Denial-of-Service Attacks. *US-CERT*. Retrieved from https://www.us-cert.gov/ncas/tips/ST04-015

Microsoft Technet. (n. d.). Configuring a Request Queue Limit (IIS 6.0). Retrieved from https://www.microsoft.com/technet/prodtechnol/WindowsServer2003/Library/IIS/9701f9dd-d40b-4d24-a2df-1d1abc13f764.mspx?mfr=true

Mirkovic, J., Fahmy, S., Reiher, P., Thomas, R., Hussain, A., Schwab, S., & Ko, C. (2006). Measuring impact of dos attacks. *Proceedings of the DETER Community Workshop on Cyber Security Experimentation*.

Mirkovic, J., Hussain, A., Wilson, B., Fahmy, S., Reiher, P., Thomas, R., & Schwab, S. (2007). *Towards User-centric Metrics for Denial-of-service Measurement. Proceedings of the 2007 Workshop on Experimental Computer Science.* New York, NY, USA: ACM; Retrieved from http://doi.acm.org/10.1145/1281700.1281708

Mosharraf, N. a. (2015). Foundations and Practice of Security. In F. a.-A. Cuppens (Ed.), 7th International Symposium, FPS 2014, Montreal, QC, Canada (Revised Selected Papers). Cham: Springer International Publishing. doi:10.1007/978-3-319-17040-4_23

Park, J., Iwai, K., Tanaka, H., & Kurokawa, T. (2014, Oct). Analysis of Slow Read DoS attack. *Proceedings of the 2014 International Symposium on Information Theory and its Applications (ISITA)* (pp. 60-64). IEEE.

Rajab, M. A., Zarfoss, J., Monrose, F., & Terzis, A. (2007). *My Botnet is Bigger Than Yours (Maybe, Better Than Yours): Why Size Estimates Remain Challenging. Proceedings of the First Conference on First Workshop on Hot Topics in Understanding Botnets,* Berkeley, CA, USA (pp. 5–5). USENIX Association. Retrieved from http://dl.acm.org/citation.cfm?id=1323128.1323133

Ranjan, S., Swaminathan, R., Uysal, M., & Knightly, E. (2006, April). DDoS-Resilient Scheduling to Counter Application Layer Attacks Under Imperfect Detection. *Proceedings of the 25th IEEE International Conference on Computer Communications INFOCOM '06* (pp. 1-13). 10.1109/INFOCOM.2006.127

RioRey. (2014). Taxonomy of DDoS Attacks. Taxonomy of DDoS Attacks.

Rocha, F. (2012). *NS2 visual trace analyzer. NS2 visual trace analyzer.*

Sachdeva, M., Kumar, K., Singh, G., & Singh, K. (2009, March). Performance Analysis of Web Service under DDoS Attacks. *Proceedings of the IEEE International Advance Computing Conference IACC '09* (pp. 1002-1007). 10.1109/IADCC.2009.4809152

Sachdeva, M., Singh, G., Kumar, K., & Singh, K. (2010, January). DDoS Incidents and their Impact: A Review. *The International Arab Journal of Information Technology*, 7(1), 14–20.

Singh, B., Kumar, K., & Bhandari, A. (2015, October). Simulation study of application layer DDoS attack. *Proceedings of the 2015 International Conference on Green Computing and Internet of Things (ICGCIoT)* (pp. 893-898). 10.1109/ICGCIoT.2015.7380589

The Internet Traffic Archive. (1998). WorldCup98. Retrieved from http://ita.ee.lbl.gov/html/contrib/WorldCup.html

The Network Simulator - ns-2. (n. d.). Retrieved from http://www.isi.edu/nsnam/ns/

Wu, Z.-J., & Yue, M. (2008). Research on the performance of low-rate DoS attack. *Journal on Communications*, 6, 016.

Xie, Y., & Yu, S. Z. (2009, February). Monitoring the Application-Layer DDoS Attacks for Popular Websites. *IEEE/ACM Transactions on Networking*, 17(1), 15–25. doi:10.1109/TNET.2008.925628

Xu, J., & Lee, W. (2003, February). Sustaining availability of Web services under distributed denial of service attacks. Computers. *IEEE Transactions on*, 52(2), 195–208.

Ye, C., & Zheng, K. (2011, December). Detection of application layer distributed denial of service. Proceedings of the 2011 International Conference on Computer Science and Network Technology (ICCSNT) (Vol. 1, pp. 310-314). IEEE.

Yeager, N. J., & McGrath, R. E. (1996). *Web server technology: the advanced guide for World Wide Web information providers.* Morgan Kaufmann.

Yu, J., Fang, C., Lu, L., & Li, Z. (2009). A lightweight mechanism to mitigate application layer DDoS attacks. In *Scalable Information Systems* (pp. 175–191). Springer International Publishing. doi:10.1007/978-3-642-10485-5_13

Yu, S., Guo, S., & Stojmenovic, I. (2015, January). Fool Me If You Can: Mimicking Attacks and Anti-Attacks in Cyberspace. *IEEE Transactions on* Computers, *64*(1), 139–151.

Zargar, S., Joshi, J., & Tipper, D. (2013). Fourth). A Survey of Defense Mechanisms Against Distributed Denial of Service (DDoS) Flooding Attacks. *IEEE Communications Surveys and Tutorials*, *15*(4), 2046–2069. doi:10.1109/SURV.2013.031413.00127

Zeb, K., Baig, O., & Asif, M. K. (2015, March). DDoS attacks and countermeasures in cyberspace. *Proceedings of the 2015 2nd World Symposium on Web Applications and Networking (WSWAN)* (pp. 1-6). 10.1109/WSWAN.2015.7210322

Zhou, W., Jia, W., Wen, S., Xiang, Y., & Zhou, W. (2014). Detection and defense of application-layer DDoS attacks in backbone web traffic. *Future Generation Computer Systems*, *38*, 36–46. Retrieved from http://www.sciencedirect.com/science/article/pii/S0167739X13001672 doi:10.1016/j.future.2013.08.002

This research was previously published in the International Journal of Information Security and Privacy (IJISP), 11(4); edited by Michele Tomaiuolo and Monica Mordonini; pages 29-46, copyright year 2017 by IGI Publishing (an imprint of IGI Global).

Chapter 16
Evaluation of the Attack Effect Based on Improved Grey Clustering Model

Chen Yue

School of Information Technology and Network Security, People's Public Security University of China, Beijing, China

Lu Tianliang

Collaborative Innovation Center of Security and Law for Cyberspace, People's Public Security University of China, Beijing, China

Cai Manchun

Collaborative Innovation Center of Security and Law for Cyberspace, People's Public Security University of China, Beijing, China

Li Jingying

School of Information Technology and Network Security, People's Public Security University of China, Beijing, China

ABSTRACT

There are a lot of uncertainties and incomplete information problems on network attack. It is of great value to access the effect of the attack in the current network attack and defense. This paper examines the characteristics of network attacks, there are problems with traditional clustering that index attribution is not clear and the cross of clustering interval. A two-stage grey synthetic clustering evaluation model based on center-point triangular whitenization weight function was proposed for the attack effect. The authors studied the feasibility of applying this model to the evaluation of network attack effect. Finally, an example is given, which showed the model could evaluate the effect of the denial-of-service attack precisely. It is also shown that the model is viable to evaluate the attack effect.

DOI: 10.4018/978-1-7998-5348-0.ch016

1. INTRODUCTION

With the rapid development of modern computer technology, the dependence of people on the computer network is deepening. The network attack is the main way to tamper with people's networks, access to confidential information threatening the people's privacy and security. Because of the wide range of design and complex factors, the research of assessing the research of assessing the effect of network attack is a very important part of network attack and defense.

In 1982, Professor Deng had put forward the grey clustering method (Deng, 1982), which is widely used in many fields now, such as teaching evaluation, ecological evaluation and so on, which provides a great help for researchers. There are many uncertainties in the network attack bringing great difficulties to the evaluation work. The authors have improved the grey clustering method based on the selection of whitenization weight function and use it to evaluate the effect. At the same time, in order to solve the problem that traditional whitenization weight function has a certain overlapping in grey judgment that affects the result of evaluation, this paper proposed two-stage grey synthetic clustering evaluation model that based on center-point triangular whitenization weight function.

2. RELATED WORKS

2.1. Research on Network Attack Effect

The main research method of network attack effect evaluation is to evaluate the network attack effect through the designed model. Wang, Xian, and Wang (2005) presented a network effect evaluation model based on network entropy, which is based on the concept of entropy in information theory. In order to solve the problem of inaccurate data of some evaluation indexes, Cao, Zhang, and Wu (2009) proposed a network attack effect evaluation system based on fuzzy set, which makes the results more reasonable and effective. Wang, Jiang, and Xian (2009) proposed a method based on the attribute importance of rough set to reduce the subjectivity in the process of determining the weight of evaluation index. There is research work related to the effects of specific network attacks, such as denial of service attack and other evaluation methods (Wang, 2013) (Li, Zhang, & Zhu, 2015).

2.2. Research on Grey Theory

Grey theory is a kind of method to study the problem which has a little and uncertain information (Liu, 2014). Wang (2012) evaluated teachers' professional ability based on grey absolute degree to decide the rank of the teachers' professional training. Zhao, Zheng, and Zhao (2012) proposed an evaluation mode of the 3G network attack effectiveness based on AHP and grey relational analysis and use grey correlation analysis method to reduce the subjective effects brought by the AHP. Gao, Xu, and Wang (2011) used grey clustering to build a hierarchical network security evaluation system for power enterprises, and divided the network attacks into different levels through clustering. The evaluation system improved the display capabilities of the network security situation, and solved the human disturbance problem existed in the original system. Zhao (2013) presented a network protection capability evaluation model from information protection and defense to analyze the ability of target network protection. The application of grey theory provides an effective way to solve this kind of problem in view of the characteristic of the large amount of uncertainty in the network attack.

3. GREY CLUSTERING EVALUATION MODEL

3.1. Concept of Grey Clustering

Grey clustering refers to divide the index into some interval according to the whitenization weight function, and the researchers judge the index belonging to what kind of grey class by calculating the kinds of index data, and finally determine the definition of the classification.

3.2. Grey Clustering Evaluation Model

- **Definition 1:** Set the evaluation index j is divided into k grey class, each index weight is $\omega_j(j= 1,2, ..., s)$, $\sum_{j=1}^{m}\omega_j = 1$. Then $\sigma_i^k = \sum_{j=1}^{m} f_j^k(x_{ij})\omega_j$, the researchers call σ_i^k is the grey clustering factor.

- **Definition 2:** Then the researchers get clustering factor matrix as $\sum = \left(\sigma_i^k\right) = \begin{bmatrix} \sigma_1^1 & \sigma_1^2 & ... & \sigma_1^s \\ \sigma_2^1 & \sigma_2^2 & ... & \sigma_2^s \\ ... & ... & ... & ... \\ \sigma_n^1 & \sigma_n^2 & ... & \sigma_n^s \end{bmatrix}$.

  δ_i^k is the normalized clustering factor, and $\delta_i^k = \sigma_i^k / \sum_{k=1}^{s}\sigma_i^k$.

- **Definition 3:** Then the researchers call $\Pi = \left(\delta_i^k\right) = \begin{bmatrix} \delta_1^1 & \delta_1^2 & ... & \delta_1^s \\ \delta_2^1 & \delta_2^2 & ... & \delta_2^s \\ ... & ... & ... & ... \\ \delta_n^1 & \delta_n^2 & ... & \delta_n^s \end{bmatrix}$ is the normalized clustering

  factor matrix.
- **Definition 4:** When the clustering isn't obvious difference, if $\varphi_i \in \left[1+(k-1)(s-1)/s, 1+k(s-1)/s\right]$ then the researchers think the object i belonging to the kth class.

3.3 The Construction Process of Evaluation Model

Step 1: Determine the assessment index and the grey class

The index is divided into s grey class, and the evaluation index $j(j=1,2,...,m)$ is also divided into the corresponding s grey class. Set the range of values of $\lambda_k(k=1,2,...,s)$ for the k grey class to be determined as $\left[\lambda_{k-1}, \lambda_{k+1}\right], k = 1,2,...,s$.

Step 2: Constructing the whitenization weight function

The traditional endpoint triangle-based whitenization weight function has the problem of interval intersection, and the white weight function based on the center point does not exist this phenomenon. Connect the point(λ_k,1)and the center point(λ_{k-1},0)of the (k-1)th section and the center point(λ_{k+1},0) of the (k+1)th section, then the corresponding section of the triangle whitenization weight function is obtained. For $f_j^1(x)$ and $f_j^s(x)$, respectively, the lower measure of the weight function and the upper limit measure of the whitenization weight function, in order to avoid the problem of traditional center point whitenization weight function that the range of the value of the cluster index to the left and right extension. Shown as Figure 1:

Step 3: Determine the weight of the index: determine the weight of each assessment index as ω_j(j=1,2,...,s).

Step 4: Calculate the grey clustering factor: $\sigma_i^k = \sum_{j=1}^{m} f_j^k(x_{ij})\omega_j$. Among them, $f_j^k(x_{ij})$ is the whitenization weight function in the corresponding interval, and ω_j is the weight of each index in Step 3.

Step 5: Calculate the normalized clustering factor: $\delta_i^k = \sigma_i^k / \sum_{k=1}^{s}\sigma_i^k$. Because $\sum_{k=1}^{s}\sigma_i^k = 1$, $\delta_i^k = \sigma_i^k$.

Step 6: Evaluate the significant difference value θ: if the maximum value of θ(θ≥0.5) the researchers think it is easy to identify that means the difference between each value is obvious, so the maximum clustering factor is determined according to the principle of maximum degree of membership, then go to Step 7; Otherwise the researchers can determine the maximum clustering factor according to definition 4, then go to Step 8.

Step 7: Judge the grey class, and get the evaluation result: according to $\max_{1\leq k\leq s}\{\delta_i^k\} = \delta_i^{k*}$, the researchers conclude object i belong to the grey class k^*.

Step 8: Calculate the weighted decision vector: η=(1,2,...,s)^T.

Step 9: Calculate the synthetic evaluation clustering factor vector: $\varphi_i^k = \eta \cdot \delta_i^k, \varphi_i = (\varphi_1^1, \varphi_1^2, ..., \varphi_i^s), i = 1, 2, ..., n$.

Step 10: judge the grey class, and get the evaluation result: according to $\max_{1\leq k\leq s}\{\delta_i^k\} = \delta_i^{k*}$, the researchers conclude object belong to the grey class k^*.

Figure 1. The two-stage triangle whitenization weight function

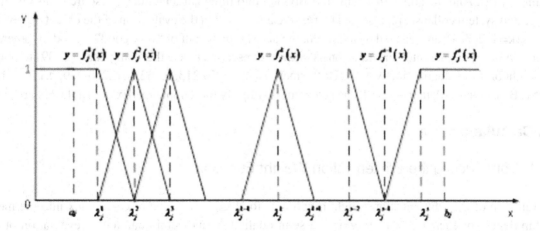

4. EXPERIMENT

4.1. Experimental Sample

In this validation experiment, the researchers use the denial of service attack as the target of the attack effect evaluation. Denial of service attack effects are not publicly disclosed data sources, and the purpose of this experiment is to compare and verify the feasibility of the proposed model. In order to ensure the accuracy of the experimental results, and compared with the existing algorithms, the researchers use the experimental data in the Peng (2011)'s paper to verify the accuracy of the results. The specific experimental data are shown in Table 1.

Table 1. Experiment sample

Attack	a	b	c	d	e	f	g
1	92%	78%	81%	34%	9.5s	2.5m	srvc
2	10%	61%	30%	14%	1.1s	7.5m	rc
3	28%	40%	30%	16%	4.5s	0.9m	rc
4	71%	81%	94%	35%	6.5s	9m	sysc
5	20%	10%	22%	1%	0.1s	0.15m	rc
6	94%	79%	68%	40%	3.2s	2.7m	sysc
7	74%	71%	58%	10%	1.8s	3.25m	srvc
8	13%	10%	20%	20%	7.0s	5.35m	rc
9	80%	40%	48%	11%	3.1s	4.25m	rc
10	20%	17%	20%	11%	4.4s	7m	rc

DoS attacks send a lot of information to make the network can't respond timely, and disabled the normal service. the researchers select index including: CPU variation, memory variation, bandwidth utilization, packet loss rate, response time, recovery time, attack mechanism, which are represented by column (a)-(g). And the attack mechanism is divided into three parts including resource consumption, service and system collapse, represented by rc, srvc and sysc. On the evaluation of the object 4 grey categories (k=1, 2, 3, 4), are selected by to present the classes, on behalf of "very good", "good", "general", "poor". In order to guarantee the data consistency, the researchers use the Wang et al. (2009) to obtain the weight of the evaluation index of the DoS attack effect ω= {0.213, 0.162, 0.122, 0.089, 0.113, 0.136, 0.165}. Based on the data in Table 1, the researchers simplify the sample matrix, so Table 2 is obtained.

4.2. Calculation

4.2.1. Constructing the Whitenization Weight Function

The function of the whitenization weight function is to change the value of each index into the membership degree of each grey category. It is a semi-qualitative and semi-quantitative evaluation of the evaluation indicators. The preference degree of the assessment can be determined by the whitenization

Table 2. Sample matrix

Attack	a	b	c	d	e	f	g
1	0.92	0.78	0.81	0.34	9.5	2.50	2
2	0.10	0.61	0.30	0.14	1.1	7.50	1
3	0.28	0.40	0.30	0.16	4.5	0.90	1
4	0.71	0.81	0.94	0.35	6.5	9.00	3
5	0.20	01.0	0.22	0.01	0.1	0.17	1
6	0.94	0.79	0.68	0.40	3.2	2.70	3
7	0.74	0.71	0.58	0.10	1.8	3.25	2
8	0.13	0.10	0.20	0.20	7.0	5.35	1
9	0.80	0.40	0.48	0.11	3.1	4.25	1
10	0.20	0.17	0.20	0.11	4.4	7.00	1

weight function. According to the principle of the maximum membership degree, the evaluation index is determined. According to the steps 1 and 2, the researchers get all the indicators about the whitenization weight function of the grey class, as shown in Table 3:

4.2.2. Calculate the Grey Clustering Factor and the Normalized Clustering Factor

Grey clustering factor is one of the most important steps to determine the evaluation index. According to the grey clustering factor of each index in each grey interval, the grey class of the index is judged. Because the grey clustering factor is usually not a unity vector, it is necessary to deal with the grey clustering factor vector.

Table 3. The whitenization weight function

Fisrt Grey Class	Second Grey Class	Third Gery Class	Fourth Grey Class
$f_1^1\left(c_1^1,\infty\right)=f_1^1(0.9,\infty)$	$f_1^2\left(-,c_1^2,+\right)=f_1^2(-,0.7,+)$	$f_1^3\left(-,c_1^3,+\right)=f_1^3(-,0.5,+)$	$f_1^4\left(0,c_1^4\right)=f_1^4(0,0.3)$
$f_2^1\left(c_2^1,\infty\right)=f_2^1(0.8,\infty)$	$f_2^2\left(-,c_2^2,+\right)=f_2^2(-,0.65,+)$	$f_2^3\left(-,c_2^3,+\right)=f_2^3(-,0.4,+)$	$f_2^4\left(0,c_2^4\right)=f_2^4(0,0.1)$
$f_3^1\left(c_3^1,\infty\right)=f_3^1(0.8,\infty)$	$f_3^2\left(-,c_3^2,+\right)=f_3^2(-,0.6,+)$	$f_3^3\left(-,c_3^3,+\right)=f_3^3(-,0.4,+)$	$f_3^4\left(0,c_3^4\right)=f_3^4(0,0.2)$
$f_4^1\left(c_4^1,\infty\right)=f_4^1(0.4,\infty)$	$f_4^2\left(-,c_4^2,+\right)=f_4^2(-,0.2,+)$	$f_4^3\left(-,c_4^3,+\right)=f_4^3(-,0.1,+)$	$f_4^4\left(0,c_4^4\right)=f_4^4(0,0.01)$
$f_5^1\left(c_5^1,\infty\right)=f_5^1(8,\infty)$	$f_5^2\left(-,c_5^2,+\right)=f_5^2(-,6,+)$	$f_5^3\left(-,c_5^3,+\right)=f_5^3(-,1,+)$	$f_5^4\left(0,c_5^4\right)=f_5^4(0,0.1)$
$f_6^1\left(c_6^1,\infty\right)=f_6^1(8,\infty)$	$f_6^2\left(-,c_6^2,+\right)=f_6^2(-,6,+)$	$f_6^3\left(-,c_6^3,+\right)=f_6^3(-,2,+)$	$f_6^4\left(0,c_6^4\right)=f_6^4(0,0.25)$
$f_7^1\left(c_7^1,\infty\right)=f_7^1(3,\infty)$	$f_7^2\left(-,c_7^2,+\right)=f_7^2(-,2,+)$	$f_7^3\left(-,c_7^3,+\right)=f_7^3(-,2,+)$	$f_7^4\left(0,c_7^4\right)=f_7^4(0,0.1)$

According to the steps 4 and 5, the grey clustering factor and the normalized grey clustering factor are obtained, and the clustering factor matrix is also obtained:

$$\Pi=\left(\delta_i^k\right)=\sigma=\sigma_i^k=\begin{vmatrix} 0.00 & 0.20 & 0.15 & 0.65 \\ 0.36 & 0.33 & 0.21 & 0.10 \\ 0.44 & 0.45 & 0.13 & 0.00 \\ 0.00 & 0.00 & 0.39 & 0.61 \\ 0.90 & 0.10 & 0.00 & 0.00 \\ 0.00 & 0.18 & 0.24 & 0.58 \\ 0.00 & 0.37 & 0.52 & 0.11 \\ 0.58 & 0.10 & 0.26 & 0.06 \\ 0.08 & 0.52 & 0.29 & 0.11 \\ 0.54 & 0.24 & 0.15 & 0.07 \end{vmatrix}$$

4.2.3. Calculate the Synthetic Evaluation Clustering Factor Vector

By the clustering factor matrix, it can be known that the grey clustering factor of Attack 2 in the fourth and third grey classes is only 0.03, which is not scientific according to the principle of the maximum membership degree to ensure the grey class. Therefore, it is needed to calculate the synthetic clustering factor of each attack.

According to step 9, the researchers get: $\varphi_1=1.5507$, $\varphi_2=2.9446$, $\varphi_3=3.3095$, $\varphi_4=1.3919$, $\varphi_5=3.9053$, $\varphi_6=1.5910$, $\varphi_7=2.2647$, $\varphi_8=3.2071$, $\varphi_9=2.5813$, $\varphi_{10}=3.2520$.

4.2.4. Get the Evaluation Result

According to the grey synthetic cluster evaluation method, the evaluation results are obtained:

$\varphi_1,\varphi_4,\varphi_6 \in [1, 1+3/4]$, it indicates the effect of Attack1,4,6 is very good ;
$\varphi_7 \in [1+3/4, 1+6/4]$, it indicates the effect of Attack 7 is good;
$\varphi_2,\varphi_9 \in [1+6/4, 1+9/4]$, it indicates the effect of Attack 2,9 is general;
$\varphi_3,\varphi_5,\varphi_6,\varphi_{10} \in [1+9/4, 4]$, it indicates the effect of Attack 3,5,6,10 is poor.

4.2.5 Compare with different models

According to the experiment, the experimental results obtained from different models are given, as shown in Table 4:

It is obvious in Table 4, when the significant difference value isn't significant, the maximum membership degree is simple in judging the grey class. But evaluation based on the synthetic clustering has a more detailed division and solves the problem that different clustering factor is close to the data making the result is difficult to classify; Peng (2011)'s model is given in the division of whitenization weight function, without considering the problem of whitenization function number interval overlap, resulting in the sum of clustering factor of the signal index is not 1, which caused the error.

Table 4. Compare with different models

Attack	General evaluation results of fixed weight based on improved triangular function	The synthetic evaluation results of clustering Peng (2011)'s paper	The Synthetic clustering evaluation results based on improved triangular function	Significant Difference Value θ	Significant test	consistency
1	First class	First class	First class	0.45	No	Yes
2	Fourth class	Third class	Third class	0.03	No	No
3	Third class	Third class	Fourth class	0.01	No	No
4	First class	First class	First class	0.22	No	Yes
5	Fourth class	Fourth class	Fourth class	0.80	Yes	Yes
6	First class	First class	First class	0.34	No	Yes
7	Second class	Second class	First class	0.15	No	Yes
8	Fourth class	Third class	Third class	0.32	No	No
9	Third class	Fourth class	Second class	0.41	No	No
10	Fourth class	Third class	Fourth class	0.30	No	No

In this paper, the grey clustering evaluation model based on improved trigonometric function is good to avoid this problem, and it can evaluate the effect of the denial of service attack more accurately. As in the evaluation of the Attack 2, 8, 9, the researchers get different results between the method of synthetic clustering and the way of the principle of maximum degree of membership, which shows the method of synthetic clustering more scientific. In the same way, according to the Attack 10, the results show that the interval overlap will have a certain impact on the experimental results.

5. CONCLUSION

Grey theory is of great practical value to evaluate the effect of network attack with the characteristics of "little data" and "poor information". This paper uses grey clustering model for network attack effect evaluation. In order to solve the problem that ownership is not clear by the general clustering evaluation method of maximum degree of membership, the researchers propose the method of the synthetic clustering. At the same time, the grey clustering evaluation model based on improved triangular whitenization weight function is used to solve the problem of the cross of clustering interval, which makes the result more accurate. The feasibility of the model is verified by experimental examples.

ACKNOWLEDGMENT

This work was supported by the National Nature Science Foundation of China (No.61602489) and NSFC-Zhejiang Joint Fund for the Integration of Industrialization and Informatization (No. U1509219).

REFERENCES

Cao, Y., Zhang, L., & Wu, H. (2009). An Evaluation System for Network Attack Effect Based on Fuzzy. In *Proceedings of International Conference on E-Business and Information System Security*, Changsha, China. 10.1109/EBISS.2009.5137923

Deng, J. L. (1982). Control problems of grey systems. *Systems & Control Letters*, *1*(5), 288–294. doi:10.1016/S0167-6911(82)80025-X

Gao, K. L., Xu, R. Z., & Wang, X. F. (2011). A Study of Hierarchical Network Security Situation Evaluation System for Electric Power Enterprise based on Grey Clustering Analysis. In *Proceedings of International Conference on Computer Science & Service System*, Nanjing, China.

Li, F. W., Zhang, X. Y., & Zhu, J. (2015). Network security situational awareness model based on information fusion. *Journal of Computer Applications (C)*, *35*(7), 1882–1887.

Liu, S. F. (2014). *Grey system theory and Application*. Beijing, BJ: Science Press.

Peng, Z. M. (2011). *The Research on Key Evaluation Technique of Network Attack Effectiveness* [Master's thesis]. National University of Defense Technology, Changsha, China.

Wang, F. (2013). *Research on Detection and Reaction of Distributed Denial of Service Attacks*. Unpublished doctoral dissertation, National University of Defense Technology, Changsha, China.

Wang, H. M., Jiang, L., & Xian, M. (2009). Grey evaluation model and algorithm of network attack effectiveness. *Journal of Communication*, *30*(11A), 17–22.

Wang, Y. J., Xian, M., & Wang, G. Y. (2005). Study on effectiveness evaluation of computer network attacks. *Computer Engineering and Design*, *26*(11), 2868–2901.

Wang, Z. (2012). Evaluation of the teachers' occupation ability based on grey system theory. In *Proceedings of International Conference on Fuzzy Systems and Knowledge Discovery*, Shenyang, China. 10.1109/FSKD.2012.6234038

Zhao, S., Zheng, K. F., & Zhao, J. P. (2012). Evaluation model of 3G network attack effectiveness based on AHP and GRA. In *Proceedings of Academic annual conference of* China Communication Association, Zhangjiajie, China.

Zhao, X. L. (2013). Research on the ability of network protection evaluation based on grey theory. *Electronic Design Engineering*, *21*(24), 26–28.

This research was previously published in the International Journal of Digital Crime and Forensics (IJDCF), 10(1); edited by Feng Liu; pages 92-100, copyright year 2018 by IGI Publishing (an imprint of IGI Global).

Section 3
Detection and Prevention: Internet of Things and Smart Devices

Chapter 17
Security in IoT Devices

N. Jeyanthi
https://orcid.org/0000-0002-6141-5467
VIT University, India

Shreyansh Banthia
VIT University, India

Akhil Sharma
VIT University, India

ABSTRACT

An attempt to do a comparison between the various DDoS attack types that exist by analysing them in various categories that can be formed, to provide a more comprehensive view of the problem that DDoS poses to the internet infrastructure today. Then DDoS and its relevance with respect to IoT (Internet of Things) devices are analysed where attack types have been explained and possible solutions available are analysed. This chapter does not propose any new solutions to mitigating the effects of DDoS attacks but just provides a general survey of the prevailing attack types along with analysis of the underlying structures that make these attacks possible, which would help researchers in understanding the DDoS problem better.

INTRODUCTION

Distributed Denial of Service attacks pose an imminent threat to the internet infrastructure, where the frequency of these attacks have increased in recent times many folds. Attackers constantly modify their attacking techniques to work around defence mechanisms in place, leaving the researchers to play catch-up with them. There is no silver bullet solution to this problem because each attack fundamentally differs from the other with respect to the part of the network system that it attacks, the way it attacks, the resources with which it attacks etc. With so many variables in place it's tough categorise solutions to these problems.

DOI: 10.4018/978-1-7998-5348-0.ch017

Now coming to DDoS attacks and their relation to IoT devices we have a scenario where according to IDC, the IoT market will hit evaluation of $7.1 trillion in revenue by 2020. Gartner predicts the IoT devices base to expand to 26 billion units by 2020. This gives us a perspective on the importance of IoT in our futures but at the same time this technology is susceptible to exploitation because of the security gaps that exist in the communication technologies that these devices employ.

We hope that this survey would go a long way in simplifying the myriad categories of attacks that are possible, thereby helping the research community to direct their research towards specific targets, enabling this focussed effort to make a bigger impact.

TAXONOMY OF THE DDOS ATTACK METHODS

Classifying by Degree of Automation

1. **Manual Attacks:** The offender physically try to find inaccessible machines for susceptibility, splits them, then proposes the attack code, and after charges the outset of the attack (Mirkovic & Reiher, 2002). After all the actions, it leads to progression of semi-automated attacks of DDoS.
2. **Semi-Automatic Attack:** The DDoS Network comprises of handler and specialist slave machines. The select, misuse and taint stages are automated. In the utilization stage, the offender species the attack sort, on-set, span and the casualty by means of the handler to specialists. Attacker tries to set up scripts for scanning and fitting of the attack code, then he uses those machines to define the type of attack and the address of the victim (Mirkovic & Reiher, 2002).
3. **Direct Communication:** Attack in type is done through strong-coding of IP address of handler machines in the attack code that is later introduced on the agent side (Houle & Weaver, 2001). The agent and handler mechanisms need to know each other's ID keeping in mind the end goal to impart. Every operator then reports its status to the handlers, who store its IP address in a record for later correspondence (Mirkovic & Reiher, 2002).
4. **Indirect Communication:** Through this attack a level of duplicity is expanded for the serviceability of a DDoS network. Late attacks give the case of utilizing IRC channels for specialist/handler correspondence. The utilization of IRC administrations replaces the capacity of a handler, since the IRC channel offers adequate namelessness to the offender.
5. **Attacks with Random Scanning:** Every composed host inquiry random addresses within the IP address area (Paxson & Weaver, 2003). This probably creates a high traffic volume since several machines research the same addresses. (CRv2) performed random scanning.
6. **Attacks with Hit-list Scanning:** A machine acting hit-list scanning finds all addresses from an outwardly provided list (Paxson & Weaver, 2003). When it finds the harmful machine, it will send one-half of the initial hit-list to the receiver and keeps the other half of the hit-list. This method grants for nice propagation speed (due to exponential spread) and no collisions throughout the scanning section.
7. **Attacks with Permutation Scanning:** In this scanning method, major composed machines share a typical pseudo-random permutation of the IP address area; every IP address is structured to the index during this permutation. A machine starts finding by using the index got from its IP address as a start line. Whenever it sees an already infected machine, it chooses a brand new random begin point (Mirkovic, Prier & Reiher, 2002).

Classifying by Exploited Vulnerability

There are two sub-categories under this section, protocol attacks and Brute-force attacks.

1. Protocol attacks abuse a particular element or execution bug of some convention introduced at the casualty so as to devour abundance measures of its assets (Mirkovic & Reiher, 2002). Illustrations incorporate the TCP SYN attack, the CGI request attack and the confirmation server attack (Seltzer, 2014) In the confirmation server attack, the attacker make use of the fact that the indication process of validation consumes notably more resources than fake signature generation.
2. Brute force attacks are performed by starting a boundless measure of apparently genuine transactions (Seltzer, 2014). Since an upstream system can typically convey higher traffic volume than the victim system can handle, this depletes the victim's assets.

Classifying by Attack Rate Dynamics

1. **Continuous Rate Attacks:** The majority of identified attacks deploy an eternal rate mechanism. Once the onset is commanded, agent machines generate the attack packets with full force. This quick packet flood disrupts the victim's services quickly, and then finally ends up in attack detection (Wang, 2006).
2. **Variable Rate Attacks:** These are more guarded in their engagement, which they vary the rate of attack to avoid detection and response. Based on the rate modification mechanism attacks with increasing rate and unsteady rate are differentiated below:
3. **Increasing Rate Attacks:** Attacks that have a bit by bit increasing rate result in a slow exhaustion of victim's resources. A phase transition of the victim may be therefore gradual that its services degrade slowly over an extended fundamental measure, so delaying detection of the attack (Wang, 2006).
4. **Fluctuating Rate Attacks:** Attacks that have a unsteady rate modify the attack rate supported the victim's behaviour, often relieving the result to avoid detection (Mirkovic & Reiher, 2002). At the acute finish, there's the instance of pulsing attacks. Throughout pulsing attacks, agent hosts sporadically abort the attack and resume it at a later time.

CLASSIFYING BY IMPACT

Classified by Activity Level: Preventive Mechanism

The goal of preventive mechanisms is either to eliminate the likelihood of DDoS attacks altogether or to alter potential victims to endure the attack while not denying services to legitimate clients.

Attack avoidance mechanisms modify the system configuration to eliminate the prospect of a DDoS attack. They secure based on the target.

System or framework security methods increment the general security of the framework, guarding against ill-conceived gets to the machine, expelling application bugs and updating protocol establishments to avert interruptions and abuse of the framework.

Protocol security address the issue of terrible design of protocol. Numerous protocols contain operations that are modest for the customer yet costly for the server. Such protocols can be abused to draining the assets of a server by starting huge quantities of concurrent transactions (Cisco, 2008)

1. **Reactive Mechanism:** Reactive mechanisms attempt to reduce the impact of associate degree attack on the victim. So as to achieve this goal they have to find what type of attack and reply to it.
2. **Mechanisms with Pattern Attack Detection:** The kind of methods that spread out the pattern detection store the signatures of known type attacks in a data storage system. Every communication will be monitored and compared with data storage entries to find the occurrences of DDoS attacks. Drawback of this method is that it can only predict known attacks and it cannot be used for new attacks (Mirkovic & Reiher, 2002).
3. **Mechanisms with Anomaly Attack Detection:** The kind of mechanism which spread out inconsistency detection have a normal system behaviour. Advantage is that it can used for unknown attacks.
4. **Mechanisms with Hybrid Attack Detection:** It combines the pattern and anomaly-based detection, by using the data about attacks found by anomaly detection and to discover unique attack signs and then updates the storage system (Incapsula, 2016).
5. **Mechanisms with Third-Party Attack Detection:** Methods that dispose an unbiased observer detection do not handle the detection process themselves, but depend on a message comes from outside that signals the occurrence of the attack and provides characterization of the attack (Incapsula, 2016).

Based on response strategy we define reactive methods as:

1. **Agent Identification Methods:** This methodology give the victim with data regarding the identity of the machines that are acting the attack (Incapsula, 2016). This information will then be combined with alternative response approaches to mitigate the impact of the attack.
2. **Rate-Limiting Mechanisms:** These methods enforce a rate limit on a stream that has been characterised as vicious by the detection mechanism. Rate limiting may be an easy response technique that's typically deployed once the detection method features a high level of false positives or cannot exactly characterize the attack stream. The disadvantage is that they permit some attack traffic through, therefore very high scale attacks would possibly still be effective even though all traffic streams are rate-limited (Meena & Jadon, 2014).
3. **Reconfiguration Mechanisms:** These strategies modify the structure the inter-mediate network to either add additional resources to the sufferer or to separate the attack machines. Examples: reconfigurable overlay networks asset replication kind of services, attack segregation methods (Meena & Jadon, 2014).

Table 1. Comparison table of various DDOS attacks

Type of attacks 1)Volumetric Attack	2)Reflected Attack	3) UDP Flood	4) Ping Of Death	5) TCP SYN Flood	6) Slowloris
How it is being done: Attacker sends large traffic to overwhelm the bandwidth of the site.	Sends a request to an IP that will yield a big response, spoof the source IP to that of the actual victim.	Attacker send's UDP datagrams to victim with spoofed source address.	The victim is attacked by sending corrupt packets that could fail the system.	Attacker creates many half-open connections to target - Send SYN packet -Ignore SYN+ACK response.	It accomplishes this by creating connections to the aimed server, but sending only a partial request to it.
Major Causes: Causes a large amount of traffic congestion.	Causes the site to be slow down with requests until the server resources are exhausted.	Disturbs random ports on the intended host with IP packets also contains UDP datagrams. Also, threats the firewalls.	Damage the local area networks. Server can freeze, reboot or crash.	Target is to exploit server CPU memory. To crash the system.	This ultimately excess the maximum connection pool, and leads to denial of additional connections from legitimate clients.
Possible way of doing: Usually botnets or traffic from spoofed IPs generating high bps/pps traffic volume.	Usage of a possibly legitimate third party component to send the attack traffic to a victim.	Attacked host will receive the junk-filled UDP packets to ports, get reply with ICMP destination unreachable packet.	Sends data packets above the max. Limit (65,536 bytes) that TCP/IP allows.	Attacker sends repeated SYN packets to every port on the targeted server, may be using a fake IP address.	Attack will hold as many connections to the target web server open for as long as possible.
Example: Phishing, click fraud through BOTNET.	Example: Reflective DNS response attack.	Example: UDP Unicorn	Example: C:\ windows>ping -l 65600. It might hang the victim's computer as it crosses max. limit.	Example: On SunOS this may be done by the command: netstat -a -f inet. Large number of connections in the state "SYN_RECEIVED" could indicate that the system is being attacked.	Example: Sending incomplete request by slowloris: "GET /$rand HTTP/1.1\r\n" "Host: $sendhost\ r\n" "Content-length: 32\r\n";

CLASSIFICATION OF DDOS ATTACKS BASED ON THE LAYER IN THE NETWORK THAT IS AFFECTED

This part of chapter exhaustively compares types of DDOS attacks on the basis of layers. It also tells there how attacker attacks, discusses the attack mechanism and the after effects of them. It also gives the examples of attack on each type of layers. Here we briefly discuss the attacks on the basis of level and then we will gradually talk about attacks in the layers (Li, Zhou, Li, Hai & Liu, 2011)

DDOS attack can attack on different levels namely:

1. Network device level
2. OS level
3. Application level
4. Protocol feature level

Network Device Level: It consists of data link layer and physical layer. In this level attacker uses the weak points of a router to attack and hence takes down the system (Xie & Yu, 2009)

OS level: In this level the attacker takes the advantage of the vulnerability of the OS features and hence they are more effective as they can attack any system having that (Xie & Yu, 2009).

Application Level: This level consists of session, presentation and application layers. In this level attacker scans the port and hence finds the unguarded part of application and use this mechanism to take down the mobile networks (Ahn, Blum & Langford, 2004).

The protocol level: the attacker takes great advantage of the feebleness of some of the features of protocol such as the acknowledgement from client by the server in TCP's three-way handshake (Li, Zhou, Li, Hai & Liu, 2011).

Now we classify the attacks based on the layers they affect:

1. **Physical Layer**
   a. **Node Tampering Attack:** Node of the network is damaged and tampered in this. Destroyed node because gaps among sensor hence communication is not effective.
   b. **Jamming Attack:** Jamming is interference with radio reception to deny the Authorized user of a communication channel. It renders the node which is jammed unable to communicate with others in the network (Khanna, Venkatesh, Fatemieh, Khan & Gunter, 2012).

2. **Link / MAC Layer**
   a. **Collision Attack:** In physical radio channel, an attacker can wilfully cause collisions or corruption at the link layer. Attacker can disrupt key elements of packets, such as fields that contribute to checksums or the checksums themselves (Dean, Franklin & Stubblefield, 2001).
   b. **Interrogation Attack:** Small messages (such as queries) may elicit larger responses. For example, an attacker may be able to replay a broadcast initialization command, causing nodes in network to time synchronization procedures. Such unauthenticated or stale messages provide an easy way for traffic amplification. It is known as solicitation of energy-draining responses interrogation (Dean, Franklin & Stubblefield, 2001).

3. **Network layer**
   a. **TCP Flooding:** Initializingcolossal number of TCP based connections (of spoofed IP address) with victim and not notifying the same that it has received the data by the server (known as TCP ACKNOWLEDGE attack). Many requests are left unanswered due to unavailability of connections for authorized clients (Because capacity is limited on a given server) (Dean, Franklin & Stubblefield, 2001).
   b. **ICMP Flooding:** Sending big amount of ICMP packets towards bandwidth of the victim. Network congestion is observed due to unavailability of bandwidth to true clients (Dean, Franklin & Stubblefield, 2001).
   c. **UDP Flood:** Sending large amount of UDP packets towards victim's bandwidth. Network is congested due to unavailability of bandwidth to true clients (Tian, Bi &Jiang, 2012).

4. **Transport layer**
   a. **Syn Flood:** Attacker sends many requests to a target's system to consume server resources to make the system unavailable to authorized traffic.

5. **Application layer**
   a. **HTTP Flooding:** Initiating colossal number of TCP connections with victim and sending heavy processing of requests through HTTP is also major problem. Unavailability of server's

processing cycles for legitimate users because there are many unanswered requests from clients (All servers remains busy for answering attacker's requests of heavy data requests)

b. **FTP Flooding:** Establishing heavily large number of TCP connections with victim and sending requests for bigger processing through FTP communication. Unanswered requests become pending because of unavailability of processing cycles of the server for true clients, server remains busy for answering attackers' requests of heavy processing (Li, Zhou, Li, Hai & Liu, 2011).

DDoS Attacks in Non-Wired Networks

Non-wired networks (Wireless networks) are vulnerable to many kinds of attacks which includes distributed denial of service attacks also. Their main vulnerability is shared medium because of which many attacks are possible to exploit wireless stations. It is possible in these ways: (Douceur, 1987)

1. Wireless sensor networks (WSN)
2. Mobile ad hoc networks (MANET)
3. Wireless local area networks (WLAN)

1. DDoS Attacks and IoT Devices

On 21st October 2016, Dyn, which is one company that controls much of internet's DNS infrastructure, was hit by the Mirai botnet in an attack which was considered as the biggest DDoS attack till date. The reason this attack was so effective was because this botnet consisted primarily of IoT devices that are categorically more vulnerable to getting infected by the "botnet" malware which transforms them into slave machines which then participate in the attack.

This incident has shifted the focus of the research community on securing the IoT devices to prevent such attacks in the future. This survey is a step towards that direction in which we aim to compare the various attack strategies that are used to exploit computers and IoT devices, compare them and also compare the underlying structures that leave these devices vulnerable to such attacks.

2. Wireless Sensor Networks: A Technology that Connecting IoT Devices

Wireless sensor networks are sensor networks that consist of low-power, low-cost, multifunctional sensor nodes that are small in size and communicate untethered across short distances.

In these, sensor nodes are densely deployed in large numbers either inside a phenomenon or close to it and are tasked with gathering and processing data before transmitting it (Weilian, Sankarasubramaniam & Cayirci, 2002).

Two interesting features of such networks are:

1. The position on these nodes can be random if the situation warrants, whereby they become versatile for deployment in areas where the terrain isn't easily accessible or during disaster relief efforts. This is made possible by the network protocols and algorithms used in these sensors that are self-organising in nature.

2. These nodes do not transmit raw data because of the presence on a processor on board which allows them to so simple processing and transmit only necessary partially processed data to the sink, hence reducing the computation effort for a single device.

These sensor nodes usually consist of the following hardware components:

1. Sensor module
2. Processing module
3. Memory chip
4. Transceiver module
5. Power unit

In WSNs, sensors are linked through a wireless medium like radio, infrared or optical media. Data is collected in the sensor fields through collaboration between various sensor nodes. Then the data is transmitted back to the sink using a multi-hop infrastructure less architecture after which the sink then communicates with the manager node using internet connectivity. The factors that affect these networks include but are not limited to, fault tolerance, scalability, production costs, operating environment, sensor network topology, hardware constraints, transmission media and power consumption (Weilian, Sankarasubramaniam & Cayirci, 2002)

3. Security Issues with WSNs

Wireless sensor networks provide us with a viable alternative to be used in situations where traditional network architectures can't be used and thus are used byte military, health care systems, disaster relief efforts etc. In such cases, it is critical for these sensors to be secure and resistant to exploitation, but the underlying communication technologies that these sensors apply are vulnerable to exploitation and in need of serious security protocols. Thus, exploitation of these networks can be categorised in three categories: (Shi & Perrig, 2004)

1. **Attacks on Service Integrity Constraints:** These include making the sensor pass false data values to the sink which are then sent to the user thereby compromising the data integrity of the system.
2. **Attacks on Privacy and Authentication:** These can be solved by using standard cryptographic techniques which prevent outsider attacks.
3. **Attacks on Network Availability:** These usually constitute of DoS attacks that prevent the user from accessing the collected data because the network resources are being consumed by an army of infected bots that attack different layers of the network. This area will be further expanded upon in the following paragraphs.

1. **DoS Attack on the Physical Layer in WSNs:** The physical layer in WSNs is responsible for representation bits, data rate synchronisation, providing an interface between the devices and the medium, line configuration and transmission modes. This layer is vulnerable to the following types of attacks: (Akyildiz, 2002)
   a. **Jamming:** In this type of attack, the nodes are prevented from communicating with each other because the medium is flooded with packets from the attacker. This is a problem here

because the nodes are randomly distributed and rely on each other for transfer of data to the sink, so even if a small portion of the network is affected, the entire network can be brought down. Typical defences against this include spread spectrum communications variations and code spreading.

b. **Node Tampering:** This can happen when the attacker has access to the nodes physically and can extract sensitive information from them by accessing them physically. One solution to this involves tamper-proofing the physical structure of the node and putting fail-safes in place in case the physical package is tampered with.

2. **DoS Attack on the Link Layer:** The link layer makes sure that there are reliable point-to-point and multi-point connections in the network by ensuring that multiplexing of data streams, medium access, data frame detection, and error control is taken care of. This layer is susceptible to the following attacks: (Akyildiz, 2002)

a. **Collisions:** Here an attacker can plan a collision in between packets leading to a change occurring in the data section of these packets which then causes a checksum mismatch at the receiving end leading to the packet being sent again. This consumes extra network recourse and can lead to costly exponential back-off in certain media access control protocols. Typical defence against this includes traditional error-correcting protocols like Hamming code being used.

b. **Exhaustion:** The attacker here can cause repeated collisions, which causes repeated attempts to retransmit the corrupted packets, which then lead to resource exhaustion of the network resources. A viable workaround to this is application of rate limits to the MAC admission control so that the network can ignore excessive requests, thus preventing resource exhaustion. Another technique that can be used is time-division multiplexing where each node is given a time slot in which they can transmit the data.

c. **Unfairness:** An attacker can cause unfair distribution of resources by using the above-mentioned attacking techniques. Here the attacker doesn't outright cut off access to the network resources but degrades them to an extent where the network becomes practically unusable for the other nodes. This can be prevented by using smaller frames which don't allow the attacker to occupy the communication channel effectively but at the same time this then affects the efficiency of the data delivery of the packets.

3. **DoS Attacks on Network layer:** This layer is primarily tasked with maintaining the power efficiency of the nodes while transmitting data, maintaining the data-centricity of the nodes, and ensure attribute based addressing and location awareness in the nodes. The technologies usually used in this layer are usually Bluetooth, IrDA, Wi-Fi, ZigBee, RFID, NUWB, NFC, Wireless Hart etc. The attacks this layer is vulnerable to are:

a. **Spoofed, Altered, or Replayed Routing Information:** This is achieved by altering or spoofing the routing information in order to disrupt the traffic by creation of routing loops, attracting or repelling network traffic from select nodes, extending and shortening source routes, generating fake error messages, partitioning the network, and increasing end-to-end latency. Possible solutions include appending a message authentication code in the end of the message or adding time stamps and counters in messages (Karlof & Wagner, 2003) (Perrig, 2002).

b. **Selective Forwarding:** This exploits the assumption that all nodes accurately forward the received messages because of which an attacker can create a malicious node that selectively forwards some messages while drops all others. This can be dealt with by using multiple paths to send the data or finding the malicious node and treating it as failed node until it can be recovered so that an alternative path can be formed (Karlof & Wagner, 2003).

   c.   **Sinkhole:** In here the attacker makes a compromised node more attractive to the surrounding nodes by manipulating the routing table values of that node because of which all the traffic is routed through that node and selective forwarding as an attack becomes more potent (Karlof & Wagner, 2003).

   d.   **Sybil:** Here the compromised node will represent more than one value to the other nodes which severely affects protocols and algorithms like fault-tolerant schemes, distributed storage, and network-topology maintenance (Karlof & Wagner, 2003) (Newsome, 2004).

   e.   **Wormholes:** Here data packets can be relocated from their original position in the network by tunnelling the bits of the data over a wormhole in the network. Packet leashes have proven to be an effective mechanism against this type of attack (Karlof & Wagner, 2003) (Hu, Perrig & Johnson, 2003).

   f.   **Acknowledgment Spoofing:** In this a compromised node can spoof the acknowledgments of the packets being routed through it to provide false information to the nearby nodes. (Karlof & Wagner, 2003)

   g.   **Homing:** Here the attacker will search for cluster heads and key managers that have capabilities to shut down the entire network.

   h.   **Hello Flood Attacks:** In many protocol if a node receives a hello packet then there is an assumption that the sender in within in range. This can be exploited by using a high-powered transmitter to trick a large number of nodes that they are neighbours with the sender node and if this is combined with broadcasting of a superior route to the base station, all these nodes will attempt transmission to these attacking nodes, despite it being actually out of their ranges (Karlof & Wagner, 2003).

   i.   **Protocol Exploitation Flooding Attacks:** Here the attacker exploits some specific features of the victim's protocols to deplete the resources of the networks.

4.   **DoS Attacks on the Transport Layer:** The transport layer in WSNs provides end to end reliability of data transmission and congestion control. The possible attacks in this layer are: (Akyildiz, 2002)

   a.   **Flooding:** This involves flooding of the communication channels using unnecessary messages and high traffic.

   b.   **De-Synchronisation:** Here fake messages will be created on one or both the endpoints requesting retransmissions for correction of an error that doesn't exists. This results in loss of network resources.

5.   **DoS Attack on the Application Layer:** The application layer in WSNs carries out traffic management in the network and also provides software for different applications to access the data in a particular form and execute queries. Here a DoS attack is carried by making the sensor nodes generate a lot of traffic towards the base station/sink (Alkhatib, & Baicher, 2012; Pathan, 2010). Some other DoS attacks are as follows: (Saxena, 2007) (Sen, 2009) (Padmavathi & Shanmugapriya, 2009)

   a.   Neglect and Greed Attack

   b.   Interrogation

   c.   Black Holes

   d.   Node Subversion

   e.   Node malfunction

    f.   Node Outage

    g.   Passive Information Gathering

    h.   False Node

    i.   Message Corruption

4. RFID Tags: The Technology that Connects IoT Devices

RFID, in the context of IoT, primarily consist of information tags which can interact with each other automatically. This technology allows a reader to activate a transponder on a radio frequency tag attached to, or embedded in, an item, allowing the reader to remotely read and/or write data on the RFID tag (Das, 2002; ITAA, 2004; Want, 2004). These tags use radio waves for cooperating and transferring information between each other without the need for the arrangement to be in the same observable pathway or in physical contact. It is uses Automatic Identification and Data Catch (AIDC) to do this.

Figure 1. RFID components

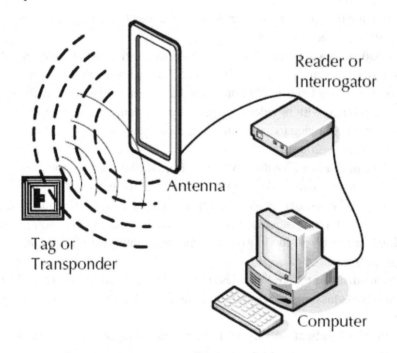

A RFID is made up of the following components:

1.   **RFID tags (Transponders):** In a tag, the microchip has a radio wire embedded inside it. A RFID tag consists of memory units which contains an identifier called Electronic Product Code (EPC). A RFID tag works along with a RFID reader, where the EPC of the former is used to identify it when the latter is scanning for tags. As per the classification provided in (Mirkovic & Reiher, 2002), the types of RFID tags are:

2. **Active Tag:** These contain their own transmitters and a power source to maintain data integrity and the capability to transmit data on their memory chips through a broadcast. These usually operate in the ultra-high frequency band (300 MHz – 3 GHz) because of which they can offer a data transmitting range of 100 meters. Two categories of Active tags are:

    a. **Transponders:** These are activated on receiving a radio signal from the reader, upon which the power up and respond with a signal. Since they don't actively transmit radio waves, they conserve battery life.

    b. **Beacons:** These are used in more real time scenarios, where data needs to be transmitted continuously or at continuous intervals. These, unlike transponders, emit signals at a pre-set interval.

3. **Semi-Passive Tag:** These are also called Battery-Assisted RFID tags which include a crucial feature of active tags. These use a power source to maintain data integrity while use the reader's signal to generate power to transmit the response and the data subsequently.

4. **Passive Tag:** These tags do not contain an internal battery but instead use the electromagnetic signal sent by the reader to generate power to respond and transfer data. These are also activated only on receiving a signal from the reader, upon which they perform data transfer of their EPC when in the range of the reader.

5. **RFID readers (Transceivers):** This works as a detector to identify a tag based on it's interaction with the EPC of the tag once it responds back.

5. Security Issues in RFID

RFID as a technology was developed with the intention of optimizing performance over resilience and security, because of which it suffers from various security vulnerabilities, and these gaps become an issue when RFID tags find their use in critical applications across various industries. In the subsequent paragraphs these vulnerabilities will be explained and various proposed security mechanisms will also be looked upon.

The four most common security vulnerabilities that are found in RFID chips are the following: (Burmester, Mike & Medeiros, 2007) (Xiao, Qinghan, Gibbons & Lebrun, 2009)

1. **Unauthorized Tag Disabling:** Here the attacker can cause the RFID tags to move into a state in which they are no longer functional which results in these tags become temporarily or permanently disabled or malfunction on being read by a reader by giving incorrect information. This problem is further aggravated by the fact that these tags are mobile in nature because of which they can manipulated by readers from a distance, thereby avoiding detection. A possible response to this problem could be each tag having a permanent private identifying key which will be shared with the backend servers, which then use this key to decode the response generated by the tag upon a scan, which again has been encoded with the same private key.

2. **Unauthorized Tag Cloning:** Here the tag's integrity is attacked upon by which the attacker can capture the tag identification information using a reader from a distance. Using this information, exact same tags can be created which can be easily passed under scanners, leaving the counterfeit security measures unusable. These can be prevented by making the identification data of a tag private.

3. **Unauthorized Tag Tracking:** Here the attack is on the privacy and security of the customer using the RFID tag where the tag can be tracked using a reader which can then be used to extract confi-

dential information of the customer. Thus, a user isn't guaranteed protection against attacks on his privacy and confidentiality while using these tags and hence it's a problem in this respect. This can be prevented by making sure that the values of a response appear to the attacker as randomly and uniformly distributed.

4. **Replay Attacks:** These attacks are on the integrity of the tags where the attacker uses the response generated by the tag against a rogue reader trying to get the identification information of that tag. The response here is intercepted, recorded and replayed when required against a scanner thereby the availability of the tag can be faked to gain access to sites where these tags are being used as access tokens. To deal with these the tag's responses to every server challenge must be unique, this can be achieved by making server challenges and tag responses should be unpredictable.

5. **Killing Tag Approach:** Here the attacker tries to permanently disable the tag. This can be done by using the kill command on the tag. To prevent against this, upon manufacturing, each tag is given a password but due to limited memory and processing capabilities, this password can be easily cracked using a brute force method.

6. **De-Synchronisation Approach:** Here the attacker uses a jamming technique to permanently destroy the authentication capability of a RFID tag by preventing synchronisation between the tag and the reader.

Other than these, some other security gaps in RFID tags are: (Saxena, 2007) (Sen, 2009) (Singla & Sachdeva, 2013)

- Reverse Engineering
- Power Analysis
- Eavesdropping
- Man-in-the-middle attack
- Spoofing
- Viruses
- Tracking

CONCLUSION

Preventive measures that are present to protect these structures against various attacks and their viability in various scenarios were analysed. The aim for this chapter was to provide a researcher interested in the field of DDoS attacks, a starting point from where they can delve into any specific field of this vast, complex problem that affects all of us today. Also focussed on the IoT device vulnerabilities that make them a ripe target for attackers to employ them as DDoS bots or attack them using a DDoS attacks, at the same time critically analysing the various methods in place to secure these devices against these very attacks. In conclusion, we would like to suggest that more effort should be diverted towards securing these security gaps in the network infrastructure that exist before going for further development of networking capabilities because the future devices can be proofed against exploitation but the old insecure devices and protocols in use pose the real threat.

REFERENCES

Ahmad, A. A. A., & Baicher, G. S. (2012). Wireless sensor network architecture. *IPCSIT, 35*, 11-15.

Ahn, L. V., Blum, M., & Langford, J. (2004). Telling humans and computers apart automatically. *Communications of the ACM, 47*(2), 56–60. doi:10.1145/966389.966390

Akyildiz, I. F., Weilian Su, Sankarasubramaniam, Y., & Cayirci, E. (2002, August). A Survey on Sensor Setworks. *IEEE Communications Magazine, 40*(8), 102–114. doi:10.1109/MCOM.2002.1024422

Burmester, M., & De Medeiros, B. (2007). RFID security: attacks, countermeasures and challenges. *The 5th RFID Academic Convocation, The RFID Journal Conference*.

Cisco. (2008). *Strategies to protect against Distributed Denial of Service Attacks*. Document ID:13634. Cisco.

Crosby & Wallach. (2003). Denial of service via algorithmic complexity attacks. *Proceedings of USENIX Security 2003*.

DDoS Attack Types and Mitigation. (n.d.). Retrieved from https://www.incapsula.com/ddos/ddos-attacks

Dean, D., Franklin, M., & Stubblefield, A. (2001). An algebraic approach to IP traceback. *Proceedings of Network and Distributed Systems Security Symposium (NDSS)*, 3–12.

Defending Against Denial of Web Services Using Sessions. (2006). NEC Europe Ltd.

Douceur. (2002). The sybil attack. *IPTPS*, 251–260.

Ganesan, Govindan, Shenker, & Estrin. (2001). Highly-resilient, energy-efficient multipath routing in wireless sensor networks. *Mobile Computing and Communications Review, 4*(5).

Gligor, Blaze, & Ioannidis. (2000). Denial of service - panel discussion. *Security Protocols Workshop*.

Houle, K.J., & Weaver, G.M. (2001). *Trends in Denial of Service Attack Technology*. CERT Coordination Center.

Hu, Y.-C., Perrig, A., & Johnson, D. B. (2003, April). Packet Leashes: A Defense Against Wormhole Attacks in Wireless Networks. *Proceedings - IEEE INFOCOM*.

Karlof, C., & Wagner, D. (2003). Secure Routing in Wireless Sensor Networks: Attacks and Countermeasures. *Proc. First IEEE Int'l. Wksp. Sensor Network Protocols and Applications*, 113–27. 10.1109/SNPA.2003.1203362

Khanna, S., Venkatesh, S. S., Fatemieh, O., Khan, F., & Gunter, C. A. (2012). Adaptive Selective Verification: An Efficient Adaptive Countermeasure to Thwart DoS Attacks. *IEEE/ACM Transactions on Networking, 20*(3), 715–728. doi:10.1109/TNET.2011.2171057

Li, K., Zhou, W., Li, P., Hai, J., & Liu, J. (2009). Distinguishing DDoS Attacks from Flash Crowds Using Probability Metrics. In *Proceedings of 3rd Intl Conference on Network and System Security* (NSS 09). IEEE.

Meena & Jadon. (2014). Distributed Denial of Service Attacks and Their Suggested Defense Remedial Approaches. *International Journal of Advance Research in Computer Science and Management Studies, 2*(4).

Mirkovic, J., Prier, G., & Reiher, P. (2002). Attacking DDoS at the Source. *Proceedings of the ICNP 2002*.

Mirkovic, J., & Reiher, P. (2002). A Taxonomy of DDoS Attack and DDoS Defense mechanisms. *Proceedings of the 2nd ACM SIGCOMM Internet Measurement Workshop*.

Newsome, J. (2004). The Sybil Attack in Sensor Networks: Analysis and Defenses. *Proc. IEEE Int'l. Conf. Info. Processing in Sensor Networks*. 10.1145/984622.984660

Padmavathi, G., & Shanmugapriya, D. (2009). *A survey of attacks, security mechanisms and challenges in wireless sensor networks*. arXiv preprint arXiv: 0909.0576

Pathan. (2010). Denial of Service in Wireless Sensor Networks: Issues and Challenges. In A. V. Stavros (Ed.), *Advances in Communications and Media Research* (Vol. 6). Nova Science Publishers, Inc.

Paxson, V., & Weaver, N. (2003). *DDoS protection strategies*. Stanford.

Perrig, A., Szewczyk, R., Tygar, J. D., Wen, V., & Culler, D. E. (2002, September). SPINS: Security Protocols for Sensor Networks. *Wireless Networks, 8*(5), 521–534. doi:10.1023/A:1016598314198

Saxena, M. (2007). *Security in Wireless Sensor Networks-A Layer based classification*. Technical Report. Centre for Education and Research in Information Assurance & Security-CERIAS, Purdue University. Retrieved from pages.cs.wisc.edu/~msaxena/papers/2007-04-cerias.pdf

Seltzer. (2014, June). Brute and protocol attacks. *Zero Day*.

Sen. (2009). A Survey on Wireless Sensor Network Security. *International Journal of Communications Network and Information Security, 1*(2), 59-82.

Shi, E., & Perrig, A. (2004, December). Designing Secure Sensor Networks. *Wireless Commun. Mag., 11*(6), 38–43. doi:10.1109/MWC.2004.1368895

Singla, A., & Sachdeva, R. (2013). Review on Security Issues and Attacks in Wireless Sensor Networks. *International Journal of Advanced Research in Computer Science and Software Engineering, 3*(4). Retrieved from www.ijarcsse.com

Thatte, G., Mitra, U., & Heidemann, J. (2011). Parametric Methods for Anomaly Detection in Aggregate Traffic. *IEEE/ACM Transactions on Networking, 19*(2), 512–525. doi:10.1109/TNET.2010.2070845

Tian, H., Bi, J., & Jiang, X. (2012). An adaptive probabilistic marking scheme for fast and secure trace-back. *Networking Science*. DOI: doi:10.100713119-012-0007-x

Xiao, Gibbons, & Lebrun. (2009). RFID Technology, Security Vulnerabilities, and Countermeasures. In *Supply Chain the Way to Flat Organization*. Intech.

Xie, Y., & Yu, S. Z. (2009). Monitoring the Application-Layer DDoS Attacks for Popular Websites. *IEEE/ACM Transactions on Networking*, *17*(1), 15–25. doi:10.1109/TNET.2008.925628

This research was previously published in Security Breaches and Threat Prevention in the Internet of Things edited by N. Jeyanthi and R. Thandeeswaran; pages 96-116, copyright year 2017 by Information Science Reference (an imprint of IGI Global).

Chapter 18
Cyber–Physical System and Internet of Things Security:
An Overview

Thomas Ulz
Graz University of Technology, Austria

Sarah Haas
Infineon Austria AG, Austria

Christian Steger
Graz University of Technology, Austria

ABSTRACT

An increase of distributed denial-of-service (DDoS) attacks launched by botnets such as Mirai has raised public awareness regarding potential security weaknesses in the Internet of Things (IoT). Devices are an attractive target for attackers because of their large number and due to most devices being online 24/7. In addition, many traditional security mechanisms are not applicable for resource constraint IoT devices. The importance of security for cyber-physical systems (CPS) is even higher, as most systems process confidential data or control a physical process that could be harmed by attackers. While industrial IoT is a hot topic in research, not much focus is put on ensuring information security. Therefore, this paper intends to give an overview of current research regarding the security of data in industrial CPS. In contrast to other surveys, this work will provide an overview of the big CPS security picture and not focus on special aspects.

INTRODUCTION

In recent years, customers' demands for personalized products increased rapidly (Adomavicius & Tuzhilin, 2005). To account for these customer requests, traditional mass production facilities need to be altered such that personalized products can be manufactured in a cost-effective way. One possible

DOI: 10.4018/978-1-7998-5348-0.ch018

way to achieve this goal is to make factories smart by enabling the interconnection of all devices involved in the manufacturing process. The term Smart Factory was introduced by Zuelke (2010) when he described his vision of a factory-of-things. According to Zuelke, in such a factory-of-things, smart objects could interact with each other using Internet of Things (IoT) and cyber-physical systems (CPSs) concepts (Weiser, 1991) (Mattern & Floerkemeier, 2010), (Lee, 2008). Recent high-tech initiatives such as Germany's Industry 4.0 further extend the vision of smart factories beyond providing cost effective personalized products. In these initiatives, smart factories utilize self-organizing multi-agent systems that operate without human assistance. In addition, also big data analysis will play a major role in future smart factories in order to optimize production processes.

To account for the envisioned functionalities of a smart factory, devices ranging from battery operated sensors up to big data servers need to be interconnected. Due to the diversity of devices which might be resource constraint, standard web protocols such as HTTP often cannot be applied, thus making Web of Things (WoT) concepts infeasible. Instead, lightweight protocols and concepts from the IoT can be applied. IoT concepts in industrial contexts offer advantages but also critical disadvantages. One advantage is the possibility to control and reconfigure machines such that personalized products can be manufactured (Gibson, Rosen, Stucker et al., 2010). However, connecting production machinery to the Internet also results in issues that do not arise in traditional production facilities. Machinery that is accessible through the Internet implicates security and safety issues; security breaches in industrial contexts may lead to the loss of highly confidential data or may even threaten employees' lives (Cheng, Zhang, & Chen, 2016).

Security, however, is often not considered in industrial IoT research as current main topics in research are enabling technologies and production strategies. Therefore, the intention of this work is to present an overview of current security related research on industrial IoT and CPSs. In contrast to other works, the authors intend to give a broad overview of security aspects, not focusing on single special topics. This broad overview, however, is given in a compact form to present the big picture of IoT and CPS security. An overview of all topics discussed in this work is presented in the big picture shown in Figure 1.

This work is structured as follows. As background information, attack taxonomies are given and different types of attacks are discerned in Section Attack Taxonomies. Also in this Section, challenges of CPS security and differences compared to traditional IT systems are discussed. This section also lists current research trends regarding CPS security. To highlight the importance of IoT and CPS security, recent attacks targeting IoT devices and CPSs are presented in Section Attacks. The subsequent sections discuss security enhancing technologies on different layers as shown in Figure 1. Section Network Security lists network related security problems and solutions. Issues and fixes related to device security are discussed in Section Device Security where hardware and software related topics are discussed. This work is then concluded with Section Conclusion where also current hot research topics are briefly discussed.

ATTACK TAXONOMIES

Attacks in information security often are associated with the resulting "CIA" (Confidentiality, Integrity, Availability) triad security attributes that are broken by the respective attack. The three security attributes, as defined in principle by Saltzer and Schroeder (1975), are:

- **Confidentiality:** The property of information that is protected from unauthorized persons, entities or processes.

- **Integrity:** The property of information that is protected from being modified in an authorized, undetected manner during its entire life-cycle.
- **Availability:** Describes the property of information being available when it is needed such that the information system can serve its purpose.

Besides these three most commonly referred to security attributes, there are also many other attributes such authenticity, possession, or non-repudiation.

Attacks on cyber-physical systems can be further divided into two categories (Ravi, Raghunathan, Kocher, & Hattangady, 2004). Attacks corresponding to the first category, logical attacks can be conducted using existing communication interfaces. Logical attacks typically target software weaknesses and can be done remotely. The second category of attacks, physical and side-channel attacks, usually requires an attacker to have physical access to the hardware. An attacker that is able to physically access the targeted hardware is then able to attack both, the software and hardware weaknesses of a system.

Figure 1. Big picture of IoT and CPS related security measures as discussed in this work
Source: Big Picture.

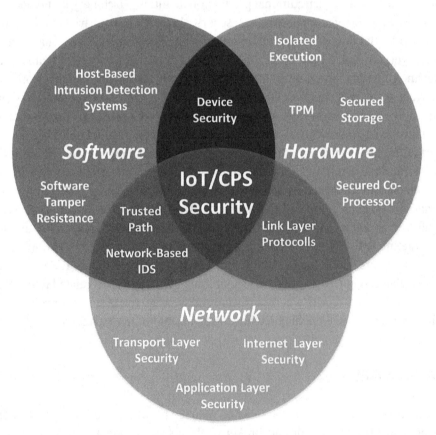

Logical Attacks

Logical attacks can target either a single device or a whole network. Hansman and Hunt (2005) give a categorization of possible attacks on network and computer systems. Most of these attacks can also occur in CPSs or IoT systems.

- **Viruses and Worms:** Malicious software components executed at the targeted system. The malicious code is often spread and even updated via a network. Viruses and worms might compromise data confidentiality and integrity as well as the availability of systems.
- **Exploits:** By using weaknesses in a software or hardware implementation, attackers are able to perform various operations such as injecting malicious code or revealing secret data. Exploits include, for example, buffer overflows or various code injections (e.g. SQL-injection, cross site scripting). These attacks also target the confidentiality, integrity and availability of a system.
- **Denial of Service (DoS):** In DoS attacks, the aim is to make the service provided by the targeted system unavailable. This can be achieved in various ways such as flooding a server with a high amount of requests. This kind of attack targets the availability of a system.
- **Network Attacks:** In this type of attack, network related vulnerabilities are used to attack a system. The goal is often to redirect traffic to a malicious system. Examples of attacks include man-in-the-middle attacks or DNS spoofing. The targeted CIA attributes are confidentiality, integrity and availability.
- **Password Attacks:** Attackers try to reveal users' password in order to gain unauthorized access to a system. THIS can be done, for example, via brute force attacks or dictionary attacks. All three CIA attributes might be compromised by such attacks.

The above listed attacks are general attacks on network and computer systems. Pasqualetti et al. (2013) discuss logical attacks that are mainly relevant for CPSs. In contrast to the previously mentioned attacks, these attacks often target information regarding the physical process attached to a CPS.

- **Deception Attacks:** In deception attacks, wrong data (such as sensor data or control data) is injected into the CPS. On the one hand, an attacker might inject data that is false and unrelated to the system; however, such attacks might easily be detected. On the other hand, an attacker might first try to learn a system's behavior and then inject data based on the learned standard behavior (stealthy deception attack) which is harder to detect. This type of attack targets the integrity and as a possible consequence also the availability of a CPS.
- **Replay Attacks:** In replay attacks, an attacker first captures data produced by a CPS which also can be encrypted. After capturing that data, the attacker then injects this data into the system at a later point in time. In contrast to deception attacks, an attacker does not necessarily need to have any knowledge about the sent data. This type of attack also targets the integrity and availability of a CPS.

Physical and Side-Channel Attacks

Physical and side-channel attacks always compromise the confidentiality, integrity, and availability of CPSs due to the information revealed by them. These attacks can be categorized by two criteria: an attacker's behavior and the attack's degree of invasiveness. First, an attacker's behavior can be used to distinguish attacks (Kocher, Lee, McGraw, Raghunathan, & Moderator-Ravi, 2004):

- **Active Attack:** An attacker actively tries to induce faults into the hardware, for example, by injecting power spikes. In unprotected devices, this may lead to failures in the executed software which then might reveal keys or weaknesses of the implementation.
- **Passive Attack:** An attacker passively observes physical properties of the hardware, for example, a CPU's power consumption. These physical properties might reveal details about the implementation or even confidential data such as keys.

The second type of categorization can be done depending on an attack's degree of invasiveness (Kocher, Lee, McGraw, Raghunathan, & Moderator-Ravi, 2004):

- **Invasive Attack:** In invasive attacks, there is no limit regarding the actions an attacker might take. Possible actions include removing the packaging, probing internal bus lines or even permanent changes to the circuits of a hardware element.
- **Semi-Invasive Attack:** In semi-invasive attacks the attacker does not change the attacked hardware. Although semi-invasive attacks often include the de-packaging of hardware, no physical contact with the internal components is made. Desired faults are injected by, for example, using radiation or light to attack the hardware.
- **Non-Invasive Attack:** In non-invasive attacks the attacker observes properties of the hardware without damaging or changing it. Such properties include side-channels (Le, Canovas, & Clédiere, 2008) such as the power consumption or the timing of a certain part of software.

An overview of potential attacks, categorized by these two criteria can be seen in Table 1. All of these attacks can be applied to CPSs.

Table 1. Physical attacks categorized according to Section Attack Taxonomies

	Active	**Passive**
Invasive	Circuit Changes, Forcing, …	Probing, …
Semi-Invasive	Light Attacks, Radiation Attacks, …	Inspecting the Hardware, EM Attacks, …
Non-Invasive	Spike Attacks, Low Voltages, …	Side-Channel Attacks (Power, Timing, …)

Attacks extracted from (Weingart, 2000) and (Anderson, Bond, Clulow, & Skorobogatov, 2006).

CPSs are, by definition, seen as an embedded system or controller that is attached to a physical process. The physical process can be monitored using sensors or actively influenced by a CPS using actuators. A wide range of systems can be classified as CPS, such as smart grids, process control systems, (autonomous) robotic systems, (autonomous) car systems, medical devices, and many more. Such systems provide various potential points of attack inside a CPS as depicted in Figure 2. There, y is seen as the output of a process, for example, sensor measurements and u are the control commands sent to the physical process. The potential attacks on such CPSs and their implications can be categorized into five

Figure 2. Potential points of attacks inside a CPS
Adapted from (Cardenas, Amin, & Sastry, Secure Control: Towards Survivable Cyber-Physical Systems, 2008). Source: Attack Points.

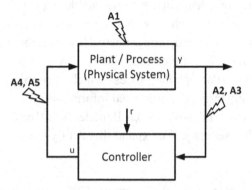

groups (adapted from Cardenas, Amin, & Sastry, Secure Control: Towards Survivable Cyber-Physical Systems, 2008). A1 are attacks targeted directly at the physical process itself. The aim of such attacks could be actuators or even a physical attack against the plant. A2 are so called deception attacks. In these kinds of attacks the adversary induces false information $\tilde{y} \neq y$ by attacking, for instance, a sensor. Possible information that can be forged includes measurements or the time associated to measurements. A3 represent DoS attacks where an attacker prevents the controller from receiving the physical process' output. A4 represent attacks where an adversary attacks the controller and induces false control commands $\tilde{u} \neq u$. These manipulated control commands could harm and destroy the physical process. A5 is similar to A3; an adversary attacks the data transportation from the controller to the physical process. Because of its nature, this attack is also a DoS attack.

Challenges and Research Trends

The challenges regarding IoT security are manifold (Jing, Vasilakos, Wan, Lu, & Qiu, 2014); therefore, the authors identify four major challenges. (i) A high number of insecure devices is supposed to be already connected to the Internet. Many devices were shown to be vulnerable to simple intrusion attacks by a large scale study (Cui & Stolfo, 2010). The study results show that about 13 percent of all discovered devices are configured with factory default passwords; the carna botnet revealed 1.2 million devices with weak passwords or no password set at all (Le Malécot & Inoue, 2014). (ii) There is believe that current security measures such as public-key infrastructures will not scale to the large number of IoT devices (Roman, Najera, & Lopez, 2011). (iii) As most IoT devices are highly constraint devices, finding a single weak link to attack could be an easy task for attackers. Therefore, efficient security algorithms need to be developed to mitigate attacks. (iv) Being in control of a single device could already lead to failures of many services. Thus, each involved component needs to be secured.

In the context of CPSs, even more security challenges arise compared to traditional ICT systems (Cardenas et al., 2009). For example, a challenge could arise through the necessity for security related software updates that often require reboots of the updated system or additional redundant systems to prevent reboots. Reboots are critical as the physical process also needs to be stopped in order to avoid potential problems. Restarting a physical process such as a power plant will take magnitudes longer than restarting, for example, a personal computer (PC). Regarding the CIA attributes a shift in priorities between CPSs and ICT systems can be found. Protecting data confidentiality is crucial for systems processing private data while for CPSs that interact with a physical process their availability is in most cases more important than data confidentiality. Another challenge is the need for real-time availability of CPSs. Many traditional IT systems such as web services only need to provide availability of their service with no requirements regarding real-time aspects. However, the major difference between CPSs and traditional IT systems is that CPSs are connected to a physical process. Attacks might target the physical process itself or intend to damage the process which even might threaten human lives. In traditional it systems, attacks mostly target the processed information.

Lun et al. (Lun, D'Innocenzo, Malavolta, & Di Benedetto, 2016) describe current trends and hot topics in research related to CPS security. We expand this list by current research trends regarding the challenges mentioned by us:

- Countermeasures against special attacks targeting CPSs (deception, false data injection, etc.) (Kim & Poor, 2011; Lo & Ansari, 2013)
- Prevention, detection and mitigation of attacks (Chaojun, Jirutitijaroen, & Motani, 2015), (Huang, Li, Campbell, & Han, 2011)
- Ensuring integrity of data in case of attacks (Kwon, Liu, & Hwang, 2014), (Vuković & Dán, 2014)
- Security measures for resource constraint devices such as sensors (Mishra, Shoukry, Karamchandani, Diggavi, & Tabuada, 2015; Mo, Weerakkody, & Sinopoli, 2015; Höller, Druml, Kreiner, Steger, & Felicijan, 2014)
- Security concepts for specific CPS application fields (e.g. Power Grid, Autonomous Vehicles, etc.) (Xue, Wang, & Roy, 2014; Zhu & Basar, 2015)
- Security measures for controllers (Dadras, Gerdes, & Sharma, 2015; Urbina et al., 2016)

Lun et al. also state that focus regarding CPS application is almost entirely on power grids. The research interest in the field of communication aspects is very low which is surprising as communication is an essential topic for all networks. This work shows that many topics are addressed currently but many more need to be approached to provide solutions for real world applications of CPSs.

ATTACKS

Cyber-attacks targeting CPSs became the focus of public attention in recent years. The probably best known cyber-attack that focused on physically destroying a target was Stuxnet. Stuxnet's only goal, contrary to traditional worms, was to harm a target instead of stealing, manipulating or erasing information. However, Stuxnet was not the first attack that harmed a physical process. Some other and earlier attacks are listed in Table 2 (collected and adapted from Miller & Rowe, 2012).

New Attack Dimension

All attacks listed in Table 2 reportedly successfully manipulated or destroyed a physical process. Recently, attacks have not tried to harm a physical process or device, but have tried to capture devices in order to use them in botnets (Dagon, Gu, Lee, & Lee, 2007). Because of their large number, IoT devices are a favored target to be used in botnets (Pa, et al., 2015). In addition, IoT devices are online 24/7,

Table 2. Attacks

Attack	Reported Description and Sources
Siberian Pipeline Explosion (1982)	The first known cyber-attack targeting critical infrastructure. A trojan planted in a control system caused the explosion of a Siberian pipeline (Daniela, 2011).
Chevron Emergency Alert System (1992)	Chevron's alert system was disabled by a fired employee. The undetected attack threatened people in 22 states in the USA and parts of Canada (Denning, Cyberterrorism: The Logic Bomb versus the Truck Bomb, 2000).
Worcester, MA Airport (1997)	An attacker successfully disabled a telephone computer that serviced Worcester Airport. The outage affected services such as the aviation control tower, the airport fire department or the airport security and thus threatened human lives (Denning, Cyberterrorism: The Logic Bomb versus the Truck Bomb, 2000).
Gazprom (1999)	Attackers supported by a disgruntled employee gained access to the central switchboard that controls the gas flow in pipelines. The attackers reportedly used a trojan horse to gain access (Denning, Cyberterrorism: Testimony Before the Special Oversight Panel on Terrorism Committee on Armed Services US House of Representatives, 2000).
Davis-Besse Nuclear Power Plant (2003)	The Davis-Besse nuclear power plant in Ohio, USA was infected by a worm that disabled the plant's safety parameter display system and the plant process computer for several hours (Beggs, 2006).
CSX Corporation (2003)	Train signaling systems in Florida, USA were shut down by a fast spreading worm. There are no major incidents caused by this attack; however still many lives were threatened by it (Nicholson, Webber, Dyer, Patel, & Janicke, 2012).
Stuxnet (2010)	Stuxnet attacked Iranian nuclear facilities exploiting zero-day vulnerabilities. The worm tried to destroy centrifuges by frequently switching between high and low speeds which ultimately led to the failure of these centrifuges (Langner, 2011).
Night Dragon (2011)	Five global energy and oil companies were attacked by a combination of social engineering, trojans and using Windows exploits. The attacks are said to have been ongoing for about two years. Although no damage has been detected, data such as operational blueprints were stolen (Nicholson, Webber, Dyer, Patel, & Janicke, 2012).
Flame (2012)	Flame, a piece of malware was found on computers operating in Iran, Lebanon, Syria, Sudan and other places in the Middle East and North Africa. The malware was used to extract documents but also opened a backdoor that allowed adding any new functionality that could be used to harm the systems under attack (Lee D., 2012).
HAVEX (2014)	The HAVEX malware primarily targeted the energy sector, collecting data from attacked systems and leaving backdoors to control systems. Through these backdoors, the connected physical process could be controlled in a malicious way and therefore could also be manipulated or destroyed by attackers (Hentunen & Tikkanen, 2014).
Black Energy (2015)	Initially known as a botnet (Lee, Jeong, Park, Kim, & Noh, 2008), Black Energy changed its purpose in 2015. Ukrainian power plants infected were infected with a trojan through a backdoor opened by Black Energy. The trojan then tries to destroy the system by deleting certain files relevant for booting the system (ICS-CERT, 2016).

Mainly collected and adapted from (Miller & Rowe, 2012).

which makes them even better suited to be used in botnets. In 2014 both, Sony's and Microsoft's gaming platforms were attacked by a large number of infected IoT devices (Somani, Gaur, & Sanghi, 2015). The number of infected devices is rising since, culminating in a recent attack that reached traffic peaks of 620 gigabits per second (Gallagher, 2016). In this attack, an IoT botnet called Mirai was involved in attacking DNS services. The Mirai botnet comprises of devices such as WiFi routers and IP cameras. According to a study, the number of DDoS attacks in 2016 increased by 71 percent when compared to 2015 (Daws, 2016). The attacks originated from countries shown in Figure 3. As the number of IoT devices will continue to grow, also the number of associated attacks will increase.

Figure 3. Top origins of DDoS attacks
(Daws, 2016). Source: DDoS Origins.

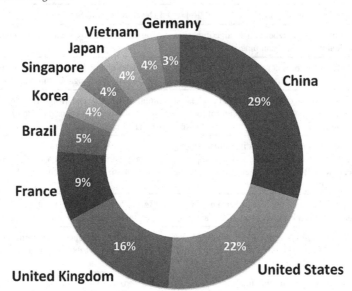

NETWORK SECURITY

In the context of initiatives such as Industry 4.0 (Referat, 2013), more CPSs are going to be connected to the Internet. These CPSs process confidential data and control production relevant processes. Therefore, securing the data transfer between these devices is of high importance. According to the Internet protocol suite, there are four layers: Link Layer, Internet Layer, Transport Layer and Application Layer (see Figure 4). All four of these layers are capable of providing different security measures that are going to be discussed in this section. In most cases, security measures on multiple levels are needed as sufficient security cannot be provided by one layer due to information not being available. For instance, information such as IP addresses that might be required to detect certain kinds of attacks are not available at the link layer.

Link Layer

On the link layer, there are a couple of protocols that are used in the IoT. The protocols that are of most interest when discussing security are wireless protocols, as this type of communication offers by far more weaknesses than wired communication. For example, eavesdropping in a wireless network can be as easy as positioning a malicious device in the communication range of the attacked devices. However, also wired communication technologies can be attacked if communication is not properly secured. The technologies that are seen as most promising (Zorzi, Gluhak, Lange, & Bassi, 2010) for the IoT are Wireless LAN, Near Field Communication and 802.15.4 based technologies such ZigBee. Therefore, these three technologies are analyzed regarding their security vulnerabilities in industrial usage (Plósz, et al., 2014).

Figure 4. TCP/IP protocol architecture layers with protocols discussed in this work
Source: TCP.

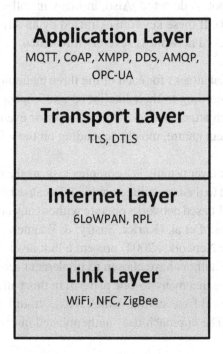

- **Wireless LAN (Wi-Fi):** Wi-Fi is a wireless communication technology that has its origin in personal computers. Wi-Fi operates in frequency bands of 2.4 GHz or 5 GHz with a communication range of approximately 100 meters. This rather high range allows adversaries to attack Wi-Fi networks without being, for instance, in the same building. Wi-Fi standards include authentication and encryption mechanisms such as WEP and WPA. The security of Wi-Fi communication therefore relies on the confidentiality of these keys. If, for instance, an adversary is in possession of a Wi-Fi network's WPA key, ongoing communication can be read by the adversary. Therefore, key cracking key cracking by eavesdropping Wi-Fi communication is one of the biggest threats against this technology.
- **Near Field Communication (NFC):** NFC is a wireless communication technology that is based on RFID standards. NFC has a typical communication range of 10 cm and operates at a radio frequency of 13.56 MHz. Because of NFC's limited communication range, attacks need to be conducted in close proximity to the NFC devices. Although communication is limited to a couple centimeters, eavesdropping might be possible in a range of up to 10 m (Haselsteiner & Breitfuß, 2006). Currently there is no dedicated NFC standard for authentication and access control. Therefore, unauthorized access to NFC devices is seen as the most critical issue with NFC. To mitigate the problem of unauthorized access, application layer security must be implemented.
- **802.15.4/ZigBee:** Zigbee is intended to be used in low power wireless networks. ZigBee operates in the ISM (industrial, scientific and medical) radio bands and allows for communication up to a range of approximately 20 m. The 802.15.4 standard allows higher layers to provide security; therefore, ZigBee implements security features such as authentication, encryption, and key establishment. ZigBee also defines a so-called Trust-Center that is a special node responsible for

storing network keys (Lennvall, Svensson, & Hekland, 2008). The biggest weakness of ZigBee is rogue nodes that might not be detected. Also, in many installations master keys are factory installed (Baronti et al., 2007). If these keys are extracted by an adversary with physical access to a device, security of the attacked network is severely threatened.

Plósz et al. (2014) list potential attacks for each of the three technologies, Wi-Fi, NFC, and ZigBee. All attacks are then assessed according to their likelihood and impact. This assessment yields a final rank highlighting the risk of each attack. Attacks with a major or even critical risk are listed in Table 3. The threats listed are of different nature, mostly depending on the wireless technology's architecture and communication range.

Improving security at the link layer usually is a complex task, as the overhead imposed by security at this layer is significant compared to the transmitted payload. Because most CPSs are resource constraint devices, a large number of 802.11 based networks operate without any cryptographic protection (Hurley, 2003). To mitigate this issue, Karlof et al. (Karlof, Sastry, & Wagner, TinySec: A Link Layer Security Architecture for Wireless Sensor Networks, 2004) present a link layer security architecture tailored for resource constraint devices. The authors have chosen to implement security measures at the link layer, because CPSs often communicate in a many-to-one pattern. In this pattern, many sensors and actuators communicate their data to a central base station, which makes traditional end-to-end security such as SSH, TLS or IPSec infeasible. The approach uses authenticated encryption to secure the transported payload at the link layer.

Table 3. Link Layer protocols and possible attacks with major or critical risks

	Threat	**Highest Risk**
Wi-Fi	WEP Shared Key Cracking	Confidentiality
	WPA-PSK Cracking	Confidentiality
	Application Login Theft	Confidentiality, Authenticity
	Intercepting TCP, SSH, SSL	Confidentiality, Integrity, Authenticity
	Evil Twin Access Point	Confidentiality, Availability, Integrity, Authenticity
	Device Cloning	Confidentiality, Integrity, Authenticity
NFC	Clone or Modify Portable Reader Device	Confidentiality, Authenticity
	Wormhole / Relay Attack	Authenticity
	Rogue Node	Confidentiality, Availability, Integrity, Authenticity
	Unauthorized Access to Node	Confidentiality, Authenticity
ZigBee	Rogue Node	Confidentiality, Integrity, Authenticity
	Device Cloning / Firmware Replacement	Confidentiality, Integrity, Authenticity
	Security Parameter Extraction by Physical Access	Confidentiality, Authenticity
	Plaintext Key Capture	Confidentiality, Integrity, Authenticity

Plósz et al., 2014.

Internet Layer

Security measures implemented at the Internet layer increased in popularity when the Internet Engineering Task Force (IETF) started the IP Security Working Group. The goal of this working group was to design cryptographic security for IPv6 that could also be ported to IPv4 (Oppliger, 1998). The result, IPSec, is widely known and supported nowadays as it is capable of providing data confidentiality and integrity by mitigating network attacks. IPSec is very popular and integrated in IPv6; therefore, the focus for the rest of this section will be on approaches that are capable to detect attacks at the Internet layer.

IETF introduced IPv6 for Low power Wireless Personal Area Networks (6LoWPAN) for resource constraint IoT devices. 6LoWPAN enables these devices to be connected to the Internet by compressing standard IPv6 headers. Kasinathan et al. (2013) present an approach that includes an Intrusion Detection System (IDS) and DoS detection into 6LoWPAN. A network based IDS analyzes the 6LoWPAN traffic to detect intrusion attempts and to raise alerts in case of detected attacks. The IDS approach helps to detect and mitigate network and DoS attacks and thus, increases confidentiality, integrity and availability of a CPS. The presented network based approach requires the inclusion of IDS Probe nodes that are allowed to analyze all packets, irrelevant of the actual recipient. In case of an attack, the IDS then alerts the DoS protection manager that then further collects data to verify the potentially ongoing DoS attack. The authors claim that their distributed hybrid approach is capable of detecting DoS attacks reliably.

The Routing Protocol for Low-Power and Lossy Networks (RPL) is a standardized routing protocol for IoT devices that use 6LoWPAN. Attacks against routing protocols were successfully applied against wireless sensor networks (WSNs) as well (Karlof & Wagner, 2003). Wallgren et al. (Wallgren, Raza, & Voigt, 2013) propose to place IoT IDSs at the root nodes of RPL routing trees, thus, giving the IDS a global view. This allows the routing protocol, for instance, to exclude malicious nodes from the routing tree in order to prevent network attacks. By excluding malicious nodes, confidentiality, integrity, and availability of a CPS can be increased. In their approach, ICMPv6 messages protected by IPSec with ESP are used to detect anomalies in the network. Wallgren et al. also show that the inclusion of an IDS introduces only a small overhead in power consumption of about 10 percent.

Transport Layer

Transport Layer Security (TLS) is considered to be of utmost importance in IoT applications (Garcia-Morchon, Kumar, Struik, Keoh, & Hummen, 2013). Although considered by some as an application layer protocol, the authors put TLS into the transport layer as its name suggests. Similar to the Internet layer, conventional protocols of the transport layer cannot directly be applied to IoT devices because of resource limitations. Especially in low-power lossy networks, protocols such as conventional TLS cannot be applied. TLS is a stream oriented protocol building on TCP that suffers from frequent packet loss in the form of delays. As an alternative to TLS, the Datagram Transport Layer Security (DTLS) protocol that is using UDP was introduced. DTLS provides the same protection mechanisms as TLS and does not influence the underlying packet transport. Thus, DTLS is able to provide confidentiality and integrity of transferred data by mitigating network attacks. A gateway from the Internet (TLS) to a lossy IoT network (DTLS) is proposed by Brachmann et al. (2012) in order to be able to provide end-to-end security between networks. The DTLS protocol is often used to implement IoT related security mechanisms such as a two-way authentication (Kothmayr, Schmitt, Hu, Brünig, & Carle, 2013) that uses X.509 certificates and an Elliptic Curve Diffie Hellman (EC-DH) key agreement process. By using this approach, both communication partners are authenticated and an encrypted communication is enabled. Kothmayr et al. (2013) show that securing a connection using DTLS imposes minimal overhead for the involved devices and also conclude that the usage of dedicated security hardware such as Trusted Platform Modules (TPM) will further decrease the overhead in power consumption and delay. TPMs and other security related hardware concepts will be discussed in Section Device Security.

Application Layer

Application layer protocols are an essential part when discussing communication in the context of IoT. There is a wide range of protocols that also might be suitable for an industrial context. IoT application layer protocols such as MQTT, CoAP, or DDS typically provide a very low protocol overhead that enables these protocols to efficiently transport the huge amount of data created by IoT devices. To meet the security requirements of industrial IoT applications, these existing protocols need to be adapted. Therefore, existing IoT application layer protocols will be evaluated regarding their built-in security features and the available security extensions for the protocols.

- **MQTT:** MQTT is based on the publish/subscribe principle and uses a client-server architecture (Standard, 2014). Clients publish messages to a specific topic or subscribe to a topic using a so-called broker. The broker is a server which manages the distribution of messages in the network. MQTT Messages are sent using TCP to enable reliable message delivery. Before clients can send and receive messages, they have to connect to the broker. The CONNECT message, sent by the client, contains optional fields for username and password that can be used for authentication. These fields are the only built-in security features MQTT provides. Due to these scarce security mechanisms, OASIS highly recommends the use of TLS (Dierks, 2008) to secure messages from attackers. Unfortunately, TLS suffers from attacks such as BEAST or CRIME (Sarkar & Fitzgerald, 2013). To overcome the issues with TLS and to provide reliable security for MQTT, Singh et al. (Singh, Rajan, Shivraj, & Balamuralidhar, 2015) propose the use of Key/Cipher text Policy-Attribute Based Encryption (KP/CP-ABE) that relies on lightweight Elliptic Curve Cryptography (ECC). ABE using lightweight ECC supports broadcast encryption. Encrypting a broadcast message enables many clients to decrypt a message. ABE are of the types Ciphertext Policy based ABE (CP-ABE) and Key Policy based ABE (KP-ABE). CP-ABE provides private key generation over a set of attributes and uses an access tree to encrypt the data. KP-ABE generates a user's private keys based on an access tree depending on the user's privileges. In KP-ABE the data is encrypted over a set of attributes. The combination of CP/KP-ABE provides data confidentiality and also provides access control. Another approach to secure MQTT was made by Niruntasukrat et al. (Niruntasukrat, et al., 2016) who proposed an authorization mechanism based on the OAuth 1.0 authentication algorithm. With this algorithm, a device can generate an access token to be allowed to subscribe to a specific resource. This authorization only approach is designed for highly constraint devices which cannot carry TLS or perform cryptographic functions.
- **CoAP:** CoAP relies on the request/response principle between endpoints using a client/server architecture (Shelby, Hartke, & Bormann, 2014). Clients can request specific resources using URIs with HTTP media types such as GET. Requests and responses are sent using UDP to keep the protocols footprint small. Although CoAP uses UDP for transport it also offers modes for guaranteed message delivery. CoAP itself does not provide any security features. To secure the sent messages

anyway, the RFC 7252 requires the implementation of DTLS (Modadugu & Rescorla, 2004) but allows the NoSec mode to be used where DTLS can be disabled. DTLS, similar to TLS, results in a huge overhead compared to CoAP's overhead. Therefore, Raza et al. (2013) propose Lithe, a lightweight DTLS integration for CoAP. The integration is, among others, done by using the principle of 6LoWPAN header compression mechanisms (Hui & Thubert, 2011). The header compression for DTLS reduces the overhead for the complete handshake headers by about 33%. There are also other approaches such as proposed by Capossele et al. (2015) or Ukil et al. (2014) that try to secure CoAP by manipulating DTLS to reduce the packet overhead and number of messages.

- **XMPP:** XMPP is based on a client/server architecture (Saint-Andre, Smith, Tronçon, & Troncon, 2009) and uses XML to structure the data sent between clients and servers. All clients in a specific domain are connected to one server. Servers can connect to other servers to enable inter domain communication. The communication between client and server can be secured using TLS; the communication between servers however does not necessarily need to be secured. Therefore, the RFC 6120 (Saint-Andre, 2011) recommends end-to-end encryption between clients in different networks to provide data security. One approach to secure XMPP was done by Celesti et al. (2013), who proposed SE Clever. SE Clever is the secure extension of an existing middleware for cloud computing. The security extensions enable XMPP to (i) sign the sent XML files with private key of the sender, (ii) attach content encrypted with receiver's public key to the message body, (iii) attach a session key for symmetric encryption, and (iv) attach signed timestamps. These extensions enable a secure XMPP middleware without establishing TLS connections.

- **DDS:** DDS is a protocol for real-time, high-performance data exchange between clients (Pardo-Castellote, 2003) that relies on the publish/subscribe principle but does not require a broker to distribute messages. DDS clients simply publish data to topics and other clients subscribe to the topics. DDS' architecture is similar to the one of bus systems where every client is connected to the bus. Data is transported using TCP, UDP or any other transport specification. DDS does not provide any security features; therefore, TLS or DTLS should be used to protect the data from manipulation or theft.

- **AMQP:** AMQP is a message-oriented protocol based on publish/subscribe and point-to-point communication (Vinoski, 2006). AMQP uses a broker to distribute messages. The broker provides an exchange service and a message queue service. The exchange service is used to send data to a specific receiver where the data is stored in a queue the receiver can read from. The exchange service uses point-to-point communication with the broker as a forwarding device. The message queue service copies the same message to each client that has subscribed to the message topic. The message queue service uses the publish/subscribe principle for data distribution; the messages are sent using TCP but AMQP can be extended to also use UDP. AMQP does not provide any security features; therefore, Vinoski (2006) recommends the use of TLS to provide data security. Besides TLS no other security extensions for AMQP were proposed yet.

- **OPC-UA:** OPC-UA is based on a client/server architecture using the request/response principle (Mahnke, Leitner, & Damm, 2009). Each client needs an OPC-UA client implementation that uses the OPC-UA communication stack to create request messages. The client's communication stack communicates with the server's communication stack by sending the request messages. The server's communication stack forwards the request to the server implementation. The server implementation provides the response which is sent to the client by using the server's and client's communication stacks. Furthermore, subscriptions and notifications can be sent between client and server using a publish/subscribe principle (Cavalieri, Cutuli, & Monteleone, 2010). OPC-UA provides two different communication modes for message exchange. The first mode, UA Web Services, uses web services secured with HTTPS to communicate. The second mode is named UA Native and sends data in plain text using TCP. Besides HTTPS, OPC-UA provides a huge amount of built-in security features. The security features include:

- **Session Encryption:** Transmitted messages are encrypted with 128 bit or 256 bit keys.
- **Message Signing:** Messages are signed to prevent data manipulation.
- **Sequenced Packets:** Sequencing eliminates the possibility of replay attacks.
- **Authentication:** OpenSSL certificates are used to authenticate systems or applications.
- **User Control:** Login credentials must be provided by users to access applications.

Because OPC-UA already provides extended security features, no proposed security extensions exist for this protocol. Due to these security features, OPC-UA generates a huge overhead compared to other protocols.

Table 4. Security analysis of existing IoT application protocols

	Built-In Security	Extended Security	Provides
MQTT	User/Password Authentication	TLS, KP/CP-ABE (Singh, Rajan, Shivraj, & Balamuralidhar, 2015), Authorization (Niruntasukrat, et al., 2016)	Confidentiality, Integrity
CoAP	None	DTLS, Lithe (Raza, Shafagh, Hewage, Hummen, & Voigt, 2013)	Confidentiality, Integrity
XMPP	None	TLS/SASL, SE Clever (Celesti, Fazio, & Villari, 2013)	Confidentiality, Integrity
DDS	None	TLS/DTLS	Confidentiality, Integrity
AMQP	None	TLS	Confidentiality, Integrity
OPC-UA	Sequencing, Encryption, Authentication, Signing, User Control	None	Confidentiality, Integrity

DEVICE SECURITY

When connecting CPSs to the Internet, securing the device itself is as important as securing the communication between devices. Communicating over an unsecured channel might threaten the confidentiality and integrity of transferred data. Leaving weaknesses at a device itself, however, might lead to bigger issues such as the device being overtaken. Such an overtaken device could then forward confidential data to adversaries' servers, use the device in botnet related attacks or even manipulate the device's intended behavior. The security of a whole network is threatened if an adversary possesses a single device belonging to it. The adversary might apply any type of physical attack to reveal confidential data or even keys stored on the device under attack. These keys could then be used to connect malicious devices to the network without anyone noticing. To counteract all kinds of attacks at the device level, so-called tamper resistance needs to be achieved in software as well as in hardware. A system's tamper resistance can be split into four different steps (Ravi, Raghunathan, & Chakradhar, 2004):

- **Attack Prevention:** Attack Prevention techniques should complicate attacks that target CPSs and thus make the attacks infeasible. Possible techniques include packaging, special hardware design, and software design.
- **Attack Detection:** Attack Detection should detect potential attacks as soon as possible to minimize the effect of them. Possible techniques include, for example, a run-time detection of malicious memory accesses.
- **Attack Recovery:** Attack Recovery is essential in the case of a detected attack to take appropriate countermeasures and to check that the system returns to a normal operation state. Possible techniques include, for example, locking the system or rebooting the system.
- **Tamper Evidence:** Tamper Evidence is responsible for keeping track of past attacks that can be used for inspection later. Tamper evidence be protected from being reversed. Thus, techniques such as seals or wires that have to be cut can be used.

Software

Tamper resistance is a security feature that often is associated with hardware components. However, also software measures can and need to be taken to provide tamper resistance of executed code (Lie, et al., 2000). Horne et al. (Horne, Matheson, Sheehan, & Tarjan, 2001) propose a self-checking code mechanism that can be integrated into existing code segments to provide tamper resistance. Aucsmith et al. (1996) present an approach for tamper resistant software that uses so-called Integrity Verification Kernels to check if software is operating as intended. Integrity verification kernels are self-modifying, self-decrypting, self-checking and installation unique code segments that communicate with other kernels to create an interlocking trust model. Software tamper resistance is able to mitigate physical and side-channel attacks that passively inspect a device and try to reveal data from information such as timings. Thus, these approaches are able to provide data confidentiality. The authors also list design principles for tamper resistant software (Aucsmith, 1996):

- **Secret Dispersion:** Secret Dispersion is used to evenly spread confidential information throughout the whole system. For instance, if a key is distributed in the whole memory instead of being stored in a single location, an attacker is hindered from revealing the whole secret by randomly guessing and observing the correct position in memory.
- **Obfuscating and Interleaving:** This principle converts a program into a state that is harder to understand for humans without changing the functionality of the obfuscated code. Obfuscated code is used to hide its logic and purpose to prevent tampering and reverse engineering.
- **Installation of Unique Code:** Installation of unique code is used to mitigate class attacks (Ouyang, Le, Liu, Ford, & Makedon, 2008) by checking that each code has a unique component. Uniqueness can be added to software by different unique code sequences or encryption keys.
- **Interlocking Trust:** This is the principle of code components relying on other code segments to effectively perform their tasks. Not only are code segments responsible for their own functionality, but also for maintaining and verifying the integrity of other components. Thus, each software

component is monitored by another component of the system which forms an interlocking trust relationship between components.

Although software tamper resistance can increase a system's security, it has two major drawbacks compared to tamper resistant hardware. First, most CPSs are constrained in their processing capabilities which limits the feasibility of adding security features in software. Second, software tamper resistance has been shown to be prone to many attacks (Oorschot, Somayaji, & Wurster, 2005), (Wurster, van Oorschot and Paul, & Somayaji, 2005). Therefore, software tamper resistance cannot be relied on to provide a device's security without other security measures.

IDSs are another measure to increase CPS security by potentially detecting viruses, worms, DoS attacks, network attacks, or password attacks. Thus, increasing the confidentiality, integrity, and availability of CPSs. Mitchell and Chen (2014) state the importance of IDSs for CPSs as an unnoticed adversary could set up an attack that is more harmful than attacks that are immediately recognized. The authors further categorize CPS IDSs by their detection technique and the used audit material. The detection technique defines how such IDSs need to be trained and how misbehaving code is detected.

- **Knowledge Based Approach:** These approaches identify runtime features based on specific patterns of misbehavior (Whitman & Mattord, 2011). Because knowledge based approaches only react to known bad code segments, the false positive rate of such approaches is usually low.
- **Behavior Based Approach:** These IDSs approaches identify runtime features that differ from the ordinary (Whitman & Mattord, 2011). Depending on what is defined as ordinary, these IDSs need to be trained live or on supervised data. The advantage of such approaches is that they do not need to previously see the exact code they need to detect. However, the machine learning aspect increases the false positive rate.

In the context of CPSs, there are two possible ways to collect data for analysis.

- **Host Based IDS:** Host based IDSs analyze logs recorded on a single node. The advantage of host based approaches is their independence of other nodes and the corresponding ease of detecting host-level misbehavior (Mitchell & Chen, 2014).
- **Network Based IDS:** These approaches analyze network activity to find compromised nodes (Kasinathan, Pastrone, Spirito, & Vinkovits, 2013). The advantage of this approach is that other, dedicated, and non-compromised nodes are used to identify misbehaving nodes in a network. Dedicated nodes could be equipped with external power sources and more computational power (Wallgren, Raza, & Voigt, 2013).

However, in the context of CPSs, also other indicators such as the physical process itself could be used for intrusion detection. Cardenas et al. (2009) state that traditional IDSs only analyze device or network logs while control systems could be used to monitor the physical process. Anomalies in the physical process could be an indicator for an ongoing attack that might not be detected by traditional IDSs.

Hardware

Secure hardware components need to provide a number of security properties in order to increase the overall security of a system (Vasudevan, Owusu, Zhou, Newsome, & McCune, 2012). The properties considered most important are the following three:

- **Isolated Execution:** A fundamental concept in hardware security is the so-called security by isolation concept (Vasudevan, Owusu, Zhou, Newsome, & McCune, 2012). In this concept, an execution environment is split into two worlds, the normal world and the secure world. The normal world is then used as general-purpose execution environments (GPEE) while the secure world servers as a secure execution environment (SEE). The security by isolation principle can be realized using different hardware elements (Anderson, Bond, Clulow, & Skorobogatov, 2006), on a single CPU (ARM TrustZone (Winter, 2008), Intel Trusted Execution Technology (TXT), AMD SVM), or in software (Madnick & Donovan, 1973). Isolated execution allows software developers to run certain parts of their software in complete isolation from other code that is executed at the same device. Current operating systems (OS) provide isolation at a process level. Security by isolation helps to mitigate the impact of viruses and worms as well as exploits. Also, passive physical and side-channel attacks can be mitigated and thus, confidentiality, and integrity of CPSs is increased. The drawback with this approach is that, if the OS itself is compromised, also the isolation mechanisms are circumvented. Also, Bond and Anderson (2001) highlight that secured execution environments can be targeted by so-called API attacks. The simplest form of such an attack is to issue valid API commands in an unexpected sequence. To account for this type of attack, measures such as security analysis (for example Common Criteria Certification (Mellado, Fernandez-Medina, & Piattini, 2007)) needs to be conducted.
- **Secured Storage:** The need to store confidential data such as key material on a CPS highlights the importance of secured storage. A secured storage therefore should be capable of guaranteeing data integrity and secrecy for any kind of data. Storage secured by software measures is considered to be insecure, as any physical attack can be applied to storage media that is extracted from its coating (Vasudevan, Owusu, Zhou, Newsome, & McCune, 2012). A (now already outdated but simple) possible approach to mitigate physical attacks is to seal the storage by embedding it inside a protective coating that makes the hardware resistant against invasive attacks (Tuyls, et al., 2006). Such protective coatings enable read-proof hardware by being sprayed on traditional hardware. The coating is doped with several random dielectric particles that help to (i) absorb light and UV-light, (ii) make the coating very hard, (iii) provide a certain capacitance of the coating that can be measured by sensors inside of it. These properties not only mitigate physical attacks but also help to identify an ongoing attack by sensing the coating's capacity.
- **Trusted Path:** To provide confidentiality, authenticity and availability for a connection between software and a peripheral such as a sensor, a trusted path needs to be used (Zhou, Gligor, Newsome, & McCune, 2012). Trusted Path are essential to mitigate the problem of malicious applications that try to manipulate data such that a CPS or the associated physical process could be damaged.

Besides these three mentioned properties, Vasudevan et al. (2012) list two additional important properties. Remote Attestation is used to verify the origin of messages from software modules, for example, a remote server could verify the correctness of a client's OS kernel and application. Remote attestation therefore provides data integrity. Secure Provisioning allows data to be sent to a specific software part running on a specific hardware module. For example, data could only be sent to services that were previously verified using remote attestation. Secure provisioning therefore also provides data integrity. Stankovic (2014) notes that in order to meet the security requirements defined for CPSs, hardware support is needed in addition to software mechanisms. He further states that so-called tamper resistant hardware modules will be essential in providing encryption, authentication, attestation, and secured storage.

- **Security Co-Processors:** These are one example of such tamper resistant hardware components (Smith & Weingart, 1999). The security principle used by security co-processors to increase security is isolated execution. Security co-processors are used as trusted devices that execute critical software parts in a tamper resistant environment. The software components that are most frequently executed on security co-processors are cryptographic algorithms such as encryption, decryption, signing and verification (Mclvor, McLoone, & McCanny, 2003). The execution of cryptographic algorithms is especially vulnerable to physical attacks as so-called side-channel attacks can be used to reveal key material or other confidential data (Standaert, Malkin, & Yung, 2009), (Mangard, Oswald, & Popp, 2008). Because side-channel weaknesses might make other security measures such as secured storage useless, the focus in cryptographic co-processor design is often in eliminating all side-channels (Tiri, et al., 2005). In addition to cryptographic operations, there are also other use-case scenarios for security co-processors such as intrusion detection. Zhang et al. (2002) propose to run IDS software on a tamper resistant co-processor instead of a host processor for increased security. This approach has four advantages according to the authors: (i) the intrusion detection is independent from other software components, (ii) the interface between the security- and host processor is very simple, so it is hard to exploit, (iii) the security co-processor can boot the device into a well-known state, (iv) statements made by the software running on a security co-processor can be fully trusted. Security co-processors will be especially useful in the context of cyber-physical systems (Feller, 2014) where, for instance, controller software could be executed in a secure manner. If CPSs are used in industrial processes, many new scenarios such as smart maintenance (Lesjak, et al., 2015) need to be considered for which security co-processors provide confidentiality, integrity, and availability.
- **Trusted Platform Modules (TPM):** TPM are standardized hardware components often associated with personal computers because of their size and power requirements. TPMs typically comprise of several components such as a cryptographic co-processor and secured storage. The CIA attributes provided by a TPM are therefore a combination of the attributes provided by these components. TPMs are capable of providing confidentiality, integrity, and availability for CPSs. Because of the size requirements, CPSs often emulate a TPM's functionality in software (Aaraj, Raghunathan, & Jha, 2008), (Strasser & Stamer, 2008), which poses security risks as well as problems regarding the power consumption of CPU-intensive cryptographic operations. TPMs are decreasing in size, so they nowadays are also included into CPSs (Kinney, 2006) and even smartcards (Akram, Markantonakis, & Mayes, 2014).
- TPM can be used to increase security in CPSs in various other ways too. Hutter and Toegl (2010) present a TPM that is extended by NFC functionality to provide a trusted channel between two devices. The TPM chip is further used for remote attestation that provides trust that the device is not modified in a malicious way. Kothmayr et al. introduce a two-way authentication (Kothmayr, Schmitt, Hu, Brünig, & Carle, 2013) and end-to-end encryption (Kothmayr, Schmitt, Hu, Brünig,

& Carle, 2012) that relies on TPMs in both devices to generate and store RSA keys, and to perform cryptographic operations. Because many IoT devices are resource constraint, the authors argue that TPMs not only need to be included for tamper resistance but also to handle the overhead imposed by using cryptographic security measures. According to Hu et al. (Hu, Tan, Corke, Shih, & Jha, 2010), including TPM into CPSs increases the system's overall price by an average of only 5 percent.

Another possible security feature when using TPM is the so-called authenticated boot as specified by the Trusted Computing Group (TCG). Authenticated boot is a passive method that stores integrity measures such as hashes of software components on the TPM. When booting a device, the integrity measure is applied again and compared against the stored value before loading and executing the software. This security mechanism, however, can only be used to protect a software's integrity at boot time; malicious code that is loaded at run time cannot be detected by such a TPM assisted system. A simple solution to that problem would be to reboot a potentially compromised system to restore a secured system state (Hendricks & Van Doorn, 2004). Raciti and Nadjm-Tehrani (2012) address the problem of many CPSs such as smart meters: the unsecured connection between sensor and controller. They argue that although TPM are included in many solutions nowadays, vulnerabilities persist that still allow CPSs to be attacked. To mitigate some problems, Raciti and Nadjm-Tehrani suggest to include an anomaly detection system in addition to a TPM chip in order to detect potential attacks targeting the communication between sensor and controller.

Tamper resistant hardware is shown to increase security by mitigating various types of physical and also logical attacks. However, as prices for such hardware devices are decreasing, also low cost attacks targeting tamper resistant hardware are possible (Anderson & Kuhn, 1997), (Bao et al., 1997). Anderson and Kuhn (Anderson & Kuhn, Tamper Resistance - a Cautionary Note, 1996) state that trusting a system because of its tamper resistant components is problematic as such systems are broken frequently.

CONCLUSION

The number of IoT devices is rapidly rising and forecasted to reach 50 billion devices by 2020 (Evans, 2011). Initiatives such as Industry 4.0 and Smart Manufacturing will further boost this trend, as they envision connecting production machinery to the Internet. These so-called cyber-physical production systems are attractive targets for adversaries for a number of reasons.

- The number of connected devices is still rapidly increasing while most devices are online 24/7.
- A large number of currently connected devices has no proper security mechanisms implemented or is using default credentials.
- Most of the CPSs are resource constraint which does not allow to implemented traditional security measures.
- Many CPSs process confidential data. Attacks can therefore be used for industrial espionage.
- Attacks might aim at damaging the physical process which could threaten human lives.

Trends in emerging CPS threats (Marinos, Belmonte, & Rekleitis, 2015) show that the number of all top 10 attacks such as DoS attacks, cyber espionage and physically damaging attacks are increasing compared to last year's report. This further highlights the importance of CPS security.

Due to these reasons, an overview of CPS security is given in this work. To be able to categorize attacks as well as the applied countermeasures, the authors have given attack taxonomies for logical as well as for physical attacks. The authors also have shown recent major attacks that increased the public attention regarding IoT security. After that, security measures are discussed for two major aspects of CPSs: on a network level and on the device level. On the network level, all TCP/IP layers and their protocols have been evaluated regarding potential security measures. On device level, software measures and potential security increasing hardware components have been presented. Simply combining some of the presented security measures however might harm a system more than it improves its security (Krawczyk, 2001). Also, a tradeoff between security and other parameters such as overhead needs to be made. Therefore, this publication tends to present an overview of current security related topics rather than suggest to apply certain solutions.

REFERENCES

Aaraj, N., Raghunathan, A., & Jha, N. K. (2008). Analysis and Design of a Hardware/Software Trusted Platform Module for Embedded Systems. *ACM Transactions on Embedded Computing Systems*, 8.

Adomavicius, G., & Tuzhilin, A. (2005). Personalization Technologies: A Process-Oriented Perspective. *Communications of the ACM*, *48*(10), 83–90. doi:10.1145/1089107.1089109

Akram, R. N., Markantonakis, K., & Mayes, K. (2014). Trusted Platform Module for Smart Cards. In *Proceedings of the 2014 6th International Conference on New Technologies, Mobility and Security (NTMS)* (pp. 1-5).

Anderson, R., Bond, M., Clulow, J., & Skorobogatov, S. (2006). Cryptographic Processors - A Survey. *Proceedings of the IEEE*, *94*(2), 357–369. doi:10.1109/JPROC.2005.862423

Anderson, R., & Kuhn, M. (1996). Tamper Resistance - a Cautionary Note. In *Proceedings of the second Usenix workshop on electronic commerce*, 2, pp. 1-11.

Anderson, R., & Kuhn, M. (1997). Low Cost Attacks on Tamper Resistant Devices. In *Proceedings of the International Workshop on Security Protocols* (pp. 125-136).

Aucsmith, D. (1996). Tamper Resistant Software: An Implementation. In *Proceedings of the International Workshop on Information Hiding*, (pp. 317-333).

Bao, F., Deng, R. H., Han, Y., Jeng, A., Narasimhalu, A. D., & Ngair, T. (1997). Breaking Public Key Cryptosystems on Tamper Resistant Devices in the Presence of Transient Faults. In *Proceedings of the International Workshop on Security Protocols* (pp. 115-124).

Baronti, P., Pillai, P., Chook, V. W., Chessa, S., Gotta, A., & Hu, Y. F. (2007). Wireless sensor networks: A survey on the state of the art and the 802.15. 4 and ZigBee standards. *Computer Communications*, *30*(7), 1655–1695. doi:10.1016/j.comcom.2006.12.020

Beggs, C. (2006). Proposed Risk Minimization Measures for Cyber-Terrorism and SCADA Networks in Australia. In *Proceedings of the 5th European conference on information warfare and security (ECIW 2006, Helsinki). Academic Publishing, Reading, UK*, (pp. 9-18).

Bond, M., & Anderson, R. (2001). API-Level Attacks on Embedded Systems. *Computer, 34*(10), 67–75. doi:10.1109/2.955101

Brachmann, M., Keoh, S. L., Morchon, O. G., & Kumar, S. S. (2012, July). End-to-End Transport Security in the IP-Based Internet of Things. In *Proceedings of the 2012 21st International Conference on Computer Communications and Networks (ICCCN)* (pp. 1-5). IEEE.

Capossele, A., Cervo, V., De Cicco, G., & Petrioli, C. (2015). Security as a CoAP resource: an optimized DTLS implementation for the IoT. In *Proceedings of the 2015 IEEE International Conference on Communications (ICC)* (pp. 549-554). 10.1109/ICC.2015.7248379

Cardenas, A. A., Amin, S., & Sastry, S. (2008). Secure Control: Towards Survivable Cyber-Physical Systems. In *Proceedings of the 28th International Conference on, Distributed Computing Systems Workshops ICDCS'08* (pp. 495-500).

Cardenas, A. A., Amin, S., Sinopoli, B., Giani, A., Perrig, A., & Sastry, S. (2009). Challenges for Securing Cyber Physical Systems. In *Proceedings of the Workshop on future directions in cyber-physical systems security*, (p. 5).

Cavalieri, S., Cutuli, G., & Monteleone, S. (2010, May). Evaluating Impact of Security on OPC UA Performance. In *Proceedings of the 3rd International Conference on Human System Interaction*, (pp. 687-694). 10.1109/HSI.2010.5514495

Celesti, A., Fazio, M., & Villari, M. (2013). SE CLEVER: A secure message oriented Middleware for Cloud federation. In *Proceedings of the 2013 IEEE Symposium on Computers and Communications (ISCC)*, (pp. 35-40). 10.1109/ISCC.2013.6754919

Chaojun, G., Jirutitijaroen, P., & Motani, M. (2015). Detecting False Data Injection Attacks in AC State Estimation. *IEEE Transactions on Smart Grid, 6*(5), 2476–2483. doi:10.1109/TSG.2015.2388545

Cheng, P., Zhang, H., & Chen, J. (2016). *Cyber Security for Industrial Control Systems: From the Viewpoint of Close-Loop*. CRC Press. doi:10.1201/b19629

Cui, A., & Stolfo, S. J. (2010). A Quantitative Analysis of the Insecurity of Embedded Network Devices: Results of a Wide-Area Scan. In *Proceedings of the 26th Annual Computer Security Applications Conference* (pp. 97-106). 10.1145/1920261.1920276

Dadras, S., Gerdes, R. M., & Sharma, R. (2015). Vehicular Platooning in an Adversarial Environment. In *Proceedings of the 10th ACM Symposium on Information, Computer and Communications Security* (pp. 167-178).

Dagon, D., Gu, G., Lee, C. P., & Lee, W. (2007). A Taxonomy of Botnet Structures. In *Proceedings of the Computer Security Applications Conference, 2007. ACSAC 2007. Twenty-Third Annual* (pp. 325-339).

Daniela, T. (2011). Communication Security in SCADA Pipeline Monitoring Systems. In *Proceedings of the 2011 RoEduNet International Conference 10th Edition: Networking in Education and Research* (pp. 1-5).

Daws, R. (2016, 11). Akamai: IoT botnet set a record in a year when DDoS attacks increased 71 percent. IoT Tech News.

Denning, D. E. (2000). Cyberterrorism: Testimony Before the Special Oversight Panel on Terrorism Committee on Armed Services US House of Representatives. *Focus on Terrorism, 9.*

Denning, D. E. (2000). Cyberterrorism: The Logic Bomb versus the Truck Bomb. *Global Dialogue, 2.*

Dierks, T. (2008). *The Transport Layer Security (TLS) Protocol Version 1.2.* IETF. doi:10.17487/rfc5246

Evans, D. (2011). The Internet of Things. *How the Next Evolution of the Internet is Changing Everything* (Whitepaper). *Cisco Internet Business Solutions Group, 1,* 1–12.

Feller, T. (2014). Towards Trustworthy Cyber-Physical Systems. In *Trustworthy Reconfigurable Systems* (pp. 85–136). Springer.

Gallagher, S. (2016, 10). Double-dip Internet-of-Things botnet attack felt across the Internet. *Ars Technica.*

Garcia-Morchon, O., Kumar, S., Struik, R., Keoh, S., & Hummen, R. (2013). *Security Considerations in the IP-based Internet of Things.* IETF.

Gibson, I., Rosen, D. W., Stucker, B., & ... (2010). *Additive Manufacturing Technologies* (Vol. 238). Springer. doi:10.1007/978-1-4419-1120-9

Hansman, S., & Hunt, R. (2005). A taxonomy of network and computer attacks. *Computers & Security, 24,* 31-43.

Haselsteiner, E., & Breitfuß, K. (2006). Security in Near Field Communication (NFC). In *Proceedings of the Workshop on RFID security.*

Hendricks, J., & Van Doorn, L. (2004). Secure Bootstrap Is Not Enough: Shoring up the Trusted Computing Base. In *Proceedings of the 11th workshop on ACM SIGOPS European workshop.* 10.1145/1133572.1133600

Hentunen, D., & Tikkanen, A. (2014). *Havex Hunts For ICS/SCADA Systems.* F-Secure.

Höller, A., Druml, N., Kreiner, C., Steger, C., & Felicijan, T. (2014). Hardware/Software Co-Design of Elliptic-Curve Cryptography for Resource-Constraint Applications. In *Proceedings of the 51st Annual Design Automation Conference.* ACM. 10.1145/2593069.2593148

Horne, B., Matheson, L., Sheehan, C., & Tarjan, R. E. (2001). Dynamic Self-Checking Techniques for Improved Tamper Resistance. In *Proceedings of the ACM Workshop on Digital Rights Management,* (pp. 141-159).

Hu, W., Tan, H., Corke, P., Shih, W. C., & Jha, S. (2010). Toward Trusted Wireless Sensor Networks. *ACM Transactions on Sensor Networks, 7*(1).

Huang, Y., Li, H., Campbell, K. A., & Han, Z. (2011). Defending False Data Injection Attack on Smart Grid Network Using Adaptive CUSUM Test. In *Proceedings of the 2011 45th Annual Conference on Information Sciences and Systems (CISS)* (pp. 1-6).

Hui, J., & Thubert, P. (2011). *Compression format for IPv6 datagrams over IEEE 802.15. 4-based networks*. IETF.

Hurley, C. (2003). *The worldwide wardrive: The myths, the misconceptions, the truth, the future*. Defcon.

Hutter, M., & Toegl, R. (2010). A Trusted Platform Module for Near Field Communication. In *Proceedings of the 2010 Fifth International Conference on Systems and Networks Communications* (pp. 136-141). 10.1109/ICSNC.2010.27

ICS-CERT. (2016). *Cyber-Attack Against Ukrainian Critical Infrastructure*.

Jing, Q., Vasilakos, A. V., Wan, J., Lu, J., & Qiu, D. (2014). Security of the Internet of Things: Perspectives and challenges. *Wireless Networks, 20*(8), 2481–2501. doi:10.100711276-014-0761-7

Karlof, C., Sastry, N., & Wagner, D. (2004). TinySec: A Link Layer Security Architecture for Wireless Sensor Networks. In *Proceedings of the 2nd international conference on Embedded networked sensor systems* (pp. 162-175). 10.1145/1031495.1031515

Karlof, C., & Wagner, D. (2003). Secure routing in wireless sensor networks: Attacks and countermeasures. *Ad Hoc Networks, 1*(2-3), 293–315. doi:10.1016/S1570-8705(03)00008-8

Kasinathan, P., Pastrone, C., Spirito, M. A., & Vinkovits, M. (2013). *Denial-of-Service detection in 6LoWPAN based Internet of Things. In WiMob* (pp. 600–607). doi:10.1109/WiMOB.2013.6673419

Kim, T. T., & Poor, H. V. (2011). Strategic Protection Against Data Injection Attacks on Power Grids. *IEEE Transactions on Smart Grid, 2*(2), 326–333. doi:10.1109/TSG.2011.2119336

Kinney, S. L. (2006). *Trusted Platform Module Basics: Using TPM in Embedded Systems*. Newnes.

Kocher, P., Lee, R., McGraw, G., Raghunathan, A., & Moderator-Ravi, S. (2004). Security as a New Dimension in Embedded System Design. In *Proceedings of the 41st annual Design Automation Conference,*(pp. 753-760).

Kothmayr, T., Schmitt, C., Hu, W., Brünig, M., & Carle, G. (2012). A DTLS Based End-To-End Security Architecture for the Internet of Things with Two-Way Authentication. In *Proceedings of the 2012 IEEE 37th Conference on, Local Computer Networks Workshops (LCN Workshops)* (pp. 956-963).

Kothmayr, T., Schmitt, C., Hu, W., Brünig, M., & Carle, G. (2013). DTLS based security and two-way authentication for the Internet of Things. *Ad Hoc Networks, 11*(8), 2710–2723. doi:10.1016/j.adhoc.2013.05.003

Krawczyk, H. (2001). The Order of Encryption and Authentication for Protecting Communications (or: How Secure Is SSL?). In *Proceedings of the Annual International Cryptology Conference* (pp. 310-331). 10.1007/3-540-44647-8_19

Kwon, C., Liu, W., & Hwang, I. (2014). Analysis and Design of Stealthy Cyber Attacks on Unmanned Aerial Systems. *Journal of Aerospace Information Systems, 11*(8), 525–539. doi:10.2514/1.I010201

Langner, R. (2011). Stuxnet: Dissecting a Cyberwarfare Weapon. *IEEE Security \& Privacy, 9*, 49-51.

Le, T.-H., Canovas, C., & Clédiere, J. (2008). An Overview of Side Channel Analysis Attacks. In *Proceedings of the 2008 ACM symposium on Information, computer and communications security* (pp. 33-43). 10.1145/1368310.1368319

Le Malécot, E., & Inoue, D. (2014). The Carna Botnet Through the Lens of a Network Telescope. In *Foundations and Practice of Security* (pp. 426–441). Springer. doi:10.1007/978-3-319-05302-8_26

Lee, D. (2012, May). Flame: Massive cyber-attack discovered, researchers say. *BBC News*.

Lee, E. A. (2008). Cyber Physical Systems: Design Challenges. In *Proceedings of the 2008 11th IEEE International Symposium on Object and Component-Oriented Real-Time Distributed Computing (ISORC)* (pp. 363-369).

Lee, J.-S., Jeong, H., Park, J.-H., Kim, M., & Noh, B.-N. (2008). The Activity Analysis of Malicious HTTP-Based Botnets Using Degree of Periodic Repeatability. In *Proceedings of the International Conference on Security Technology SECTECH'08* (pp. 83-86).

Lennvall, T., Svensson, S., & Hekland, F. (2008). A Comparison of WirelessHART and ZigBee for Industrial Applications. In *Proceedings of the IEEE International Workshop on Factory Communication Systems* (pp. 85-88). 10.1109/WFCS.2008.4638746

Lesjak, C., Hein, D., Hofmann, M., Maritsch, M., Aldrian, A., Priller, P., . . . Pregartner, G. (2015). Securing Smart Maintenance Services: Hardware-Security and TLS for MQTT. In *Proceedings of the 2015 IEEE 13th International Conference on Industrial Informatics (INDIN)* (pp. 1243-1250).

Lie, D., Thekkath, C., Mitchell, M., Lincoln, P., Boneh, D., Mitchell, J., & Horowitz, M. (2000). Architectural Support for Copy and Tamper Resistant Software. *ACM SIGPLAN Notices, 35*(11), 168–177. doi:10.1145/356989.357005

Lo, C.-H., & Ansari, N. (2013). CONSUMER: A Novel Hybrid Intrusion Detection System for Distribution Networks in Smart Grid. *IEEE Transactions on Emerging Topics in Computing, 1*(1), 33–44. doi:10.1109/TETC.2013.2274043

Lun, Y., D'Innocenzo, A., Malavolta, I., & Di Benedetto, M. (2016). Cyber-Physical Systems Security: a Systematic Mapping Study.

Madnick, S. E., & Donovan, J. J. (1973). Application and Analysis of the Virtual Machine Approach to Information System Security and Isolation. In *Proceedings of the workshop on virtual computer systems* (pp. 210-224). 10.1145/800122.803961

Mahnke, W., Leitner, S.-H., & Damm, M. (2009). *OPC Unified Architecture*. Springer Science & Business Media. doi:10.1007/978-3-540-68899-0

Mangard, S., Oswald, E., & Popp, T. (2008). *Power Analysis Attacks: Revealing the Secrets of Smart Cards* (Vol. 31). Springer Science & Business Media.

Marinos, L., Belmonte, A., & Rekleitis, E. (2015). *Enisa Threat Landscape (Technical report)*. ENISA.

Mattern, F., & Floerkemeier, C. (2010). From the Internet of Computers to the Internet of Things. In *From active data management to event-based systems and more* (pp. 242–259). Springer. doi:10.1007/978-3-642-17226-7_15

Mclvor, C., McLoone, M., & McCanny, J. V. (2003). Fast Montgomery Modular Multiplication and RSA Cryptographic Processor Architectures. In *Conference Record of the Thirty-Seventh Asilomar Conference on* Signals, Systems and Computers (Vol. 1, pp. 379-384).

Mellado, D., Fernandez-Medina, E., & Piattini, M. (2007). A common criteria based security requirements engineering process. *Computer Standards & Interfaces*, *29*(2), 244–253. doi:10.1016/j.csi.2006.04.002

Miller, B., & Rowe, D. (2012). A Survey of SCADA and Critical Infrastructure Incidents. In *Proceedings of the 1st Annual conference on Research in information technology* (pp. 51-56). 10.1145/2380790.2380805

Mishra, S., Shoukry, Y., Karamchandani, N., Diggavi, S., & Tabuada, P. (2015). Secure State Estimation: Optimal Guarantees Against Sensor Attacks in the Presence of Noise. In *Proceedings of the 2015 IEEE International Symposium on Information Theory (ISIT)* (pp. 2929-2933).

Mitchell, R., & Chen, I.-R. (2014). A Survey of Intrusion Detection Techniques for Cyber-Physical Systems. [CSUR]. *ACM Computing Surveys*, *46*(4), 55. doi:10.1145/2542049

Mo, Y., Weerakkody, S., & Sinopoli, B. (2015). Physical Authentication of Control Systems: Designing Watermarked Control Inputs to Detect Counterfeit Sensor Outputs. *IEEE Control Systems*, *35*(1), 93–109. doi:10.1109/MCS.2014.2364724

Modadugu, N., & Rescorla, E. (2004). *The Design and Implementation of Datagram TLS*. NDSS.

Nicholson, A., Webber, S., Dyer, S., Patel, T., & Janicke, H. (2012). SCADA security in the light of Cyber-Warfare. *Computers & Security, 31*, 418-436.

Niruntasukrat, A., Issariyapat, C., Pongpaibool, P., Meesublak, K., Aiumsupucgul, P., & Panya, A. (2016). Authorization Mechanism for MQTT-based Internet of Things. In *Proceedings of the 2016 IEEE International Conference on Communications Workshops (ICC)* (pp. 290-295).

Oorschot, V., Somayaji, A., & Wurster, G. (2005). Hardware-Assisted Circumvention of Self-Hashing Software Tamper Resistance. *IEEE Transactions on Dependable and Secure Computing*, *2*(2), 82–92. doi:10.1109/TDSC.2005.24

Oppliger, R. (1998). Security at the Internet Layer. *Computer*, *31*(9), 43–47. doi:10.1109/2.708449

Ouyang, Y., Le, Z., Liu, D., Ford, J., & Makedon, F. (2008). Source Location Privacy against Laptop-Class Attacks in Sensor Networks. In *Proceedings of the 4th international conference on Security and privacy in communication networks* (p. 5). 10.1145/1460877.1460884

Pa, Y. M., Suzuki, S., Yoshioka, K., Matsumoto, T., Kasama, T., & Rossow, C. (2015). IoTPOT: Analysing the Rise of IoT Compromises. In *Proceedings of the 9th USENIX Workshop on Offensive Technologies (WOOT 15)*.

Pardo-Castellote, G. (2003). OMG Data-Distribution Service: Architectural Overview. *Proceedings of the 23rd International Conference on Distributed Computing Systems Workshops* (pp. 200-206).

Pasqualetti, F., Dörfler, F., & Bullo, F. (2013). Attack Detection and Identification in Cyber-Physical Systems. *IEEE Transactions on Automatic Control*, *58*(11), 2715–2729. doi:10.1109/TAC.2013.2266831

Plósz, S., Farshad, A., Tauber, M., Lesjak, C., Ruprechter, T., & Pereira, N. (2014). Security Vulnerabilities and Risks in Industrial Usage of Wireless Communication. In *Proceedings of the 2014 IEEE Emerging Technology and Factory Automation (ETFA)*, (pp. 1-8). 10.1109/ETFA.2014.7005129

Raciti, M., & Nadjm-Tehrani, S. (2012). Embedded Cyber-Physical Anomaly Detection in Smart Meters. In *Proceedings of the International Workshop on Critical Information Infrastructures Security*, (pp. 34-45).

Ravi, S., Raghunathan, A., & Chakradhar, S. (2004). Tamper Resistance Mechanisms for Secure Embedded Systems. In *Proceedings of the 17th International Conference on VLSI Design* (pp. 605-611).

Ravi, S., Raghunathan, A., Kocher, P., & Hattangady, S. (2004). Security in Embedded Systems: Design Challenges. *ACM Transactions on Embedded Computing Systems*, *3*(3), 461–491. doi:10.1145/1015047.1015049

Raza, S., Shafagh, H., Hewage, K., Hummen, R., & Voigt, T. (2013). Lithe: Lightweight Secure CoAP for the Internet of Things. *IEEE Sensors Journal*, *13*(10), 3711–3720. doi:10.1109/JSEN.2013.2277656

Referat, B. f. (2013). *Zukunftsbild Industrie 4.0*. Bundesministerium fuer Bildung und Forschung Referat.

Roman, R., Najera, P., & Lopez, J. (2011). Securing the Internet of Things. *Computer*, *44*(9), 51–58. doi:10.1109/MC.2011.291

Saint-Andre, P. (2011). *Extensible Messaging and Presence Protocol (XMPP): Core*. IETF. doi:10.17487/rfc6122

Saint-Andre, P., Smith, K., Tronçon, R., & Troncon, R. (2009). *XMPP: The Definitive Guide*. O'Reilly Media, Inc.

Saltzer, J. H., & Schroeder, M. D. (1975). The Protection of Information in Computer Systems. *Proceedings of the IEEE*, *63*(9), 1278–1308. doi:10.1109/PROC.1975.9939

Sarkar, P. G., & Fitzgerald, S. (2013). Attacks on SSL: A Comprehensive Study of Beast, Crime, Time, Breach, Lucky 13 & RC4 Biases.

Shelby, Z., Hartke, K., & Bormann, C. (2014). *The Constrained Application Protocol (CoAP)*. Tech. rep. IETF.

Singh, M., Rajan, M. A., Shivraj, V. L., & Balamuralidhar, P. (2015). Secure MQTT for Internet of Things (IoT). In *Proceedings of the 2015 Fifth International Conference on Communication Systems and Network Technologies (CSNT)* (pp. 746-751).

Smith, S. W., & Weingart, S. (1999). Building a high-performance, programmable secure coprocessor. *Computer Networks*, *31*(8), 831–860. doi:10.1016/S1389-1286(98)00019-X

Somani, G., Gaur, M. S., & Sanghi, D. (2015). DDoS/EDoS attack in Cloud: Affecting everyone out there! In *Proceedings of the 8th International Conference on Security of Information and Networks* (pp. 169-176). 10.1145/2799979.2800005

Standaert, F.-X., Malkin, T. G., & Yung, M. (2009). A Unified Framework for the Analysis of Side-Channel Key Recovery Attacks. In *Proceedings of the Annual International Conference on the Theory and Applications of Cryptographic Techniques* (pp. 443-461). 10.1007/978-3-642-01001-9_26

Standard, O. A. (2014). *MQTT Version 3.1*. OASIS.

Stankovic, J. A. (2014). Research Directions for the Internet of Things. *IEEE Internet of Things Journal*, *1*(1), 3–9. doi:10.1109/JIOT.2014.2312291

Strasser, M., & Stamer, H. (2008). A Software-Based Trusted Platform Module Emulator. In *Proceedings of the International Conference on Trusted Computing* (pp. 33-47).

Tiri, K., Hwang, D., Hodjat, A., Lai, B., Yang, S., Schaumont, P., & Verbauwhede, I. (2005). A Side-Channel Leakage Free Coprocessor IC in 0.18 μm CMOS for Embedded AES-based Cryptographic and Biometric Processing. In *Proceedings of the 42nd Design Automation Conference* (pp. 222-227).

Tuyls, P., Schrijen, G.-J., Škorić, B., Van Geloven, J., Verhaegh, N., & Wolters, R. (2006). Read-Proof Hardware from Protective Coatings. In *Proceedings of the International Workshop on Cryptographic Hardware and Embedded Systems* (pp. 369-383).

Ukil, A., Bandyopadhyay, S., Bhattacharyya, A., Pal, A., & Bose, T. (2014). Lightweight security scheme for IoT applications using CoAP. *International Journal of Pervasive Computing and Communications*, *10*(4), 372–392. doi:10.1108/IJPCC-01-2014-0002

Urbina, D. I., Giraldo, J. A., Cardenas, A. A., Tippenhauer, N. O., Valente, J., Faisal, M., ... Sandberg, H. (2016). Limiting the Impact of Stealthy Attacks on Industrial Control Systems. In *Proceedings of the 2016 ACM SIGSAC Conference on Computer and Communications Security* (pp. 1092-1105). 10.1145/2976749.2978388

Vasudevan, A., Owusu, E., Zhou, Z., Newsome, J., & McCune, J. M. (2012). Trustworthy Execution on Mobile Devices: What Security Properties Can My Mobile Platform Give Me? In *Proceedings of the International Conference on Trust and Trustworthy Computing* (pp. 159-178). Springer Berlin Heidelberg. 10.1007/978-3-642-30921-2_10

Vinoski, S. (2006). Advanced Message Queuing Protocol. *IEEE Internet Computing*, 10(6).

Vuković, O., & Dán, G. (2014). Security of Fully Distributed Power System State Estimation: Detection and Mitigation of Data Integrity Attacks. *IEEE Journal on Selected Areas in Communications*, *32*(7), 1500–1508. doi:10.1109/JSAC.2014.2332106

Wallgren, L., Raza, S., & Voigt, T. (2013). Routing Attacks and Countermeasures in the RPL-based Internet of Things. *International Journal of Distributed Sensor Networks*, *9*(8), 794326. doi:10.1155/2013/794326

Weingart, S. H. (2000). Physical Security Devices for Computer Subsystems: A Survey of Attacks and Defenses. Advanced Message Queuing Protocol*International Workshop on Cryptographic Hardware and Embedded Systems* (pp. 302-317). 10.1007/3-540-44499-8_24

Weiser, M. (1991). The Computer for the 21st Century. *Scientific American*, *265*(3), 94–104. doi:10.1038cientificamerican0991-94

Whitman, M. E., & Mattord, H. J. (2011). *Principles of Information Security*. Cengage Learning.

Winter, J. (2008). Trusted Computing Building Blocks for Embedded Linux-based ARM TrustZone Platforms. In *Proceedings of the 3rd ACM workshop on Scalable trusted computing* (pp. 21-30). 10.1145/1456455.1456460

Wurster, G., van Oorschot and Paul, C., & Somayaji, A. (2005). A generic attack on checksumming-based software tamper resistance. In *Proceedings of the 2005 IEEE Symposium on Security and Privacy (S\&P'05)*, (pp. 127-138). 10.1109/SP.2005.2

Xue, M., Wang, W., & Roy, S. (2014). Security Concepts for the Dynamics of Autonomous Vehicle Networks. *Automatica*, *50*(3), 852–857. doi:10.1016/j.automatica.2013.12.001

Zhang, X., van Doorn, L., Jaeger, T., Perez, R., & Sailer, R. (2002). Secure Coprocessor-based Intrusion Detection. In *Proceedings of the 10th workshop on ACM SIGOPS European workshop* (pp. 239-242). 10.1145/1133373.1133423

Zhou, Z., Gligor, V. D., Newsome, J., & McCune, J. M. (2012). Building Verifiable Trusted Path on Commodity x86 Computers. In *Proceedings of the 2012 IEEE Symposium on Security and Privacy* (pp. 616-630). 10.1109/SP.2012.42

Zhu, Q., & Basar, T. (2015). Game-Theoretic Methods for Robustness, Security, and Resilience of Cyberphysical Control Systems: Games-in-Games Principle for Optimal Cross-Layer Resilient Control Systems. *IEEE Control Systems*, *35*(1), 46–65. doi:10.1109/MCS.2014.2364710

Zorzi, M., Gluhak, A., Lange, S., & Bassi, A. (2010). From Today's Internet of Things to a Future Internet of Things: A Wireless-and-Mobility-Related View. *IEEE Wireless Communications*, *17*(6), 44–51. doi:10.1109/MWC.2010.5675777

Zuehlke, D. (2010). SmartFactory - Towards a factory-of-things. *Annual Reviews in Control*, *34*(1), 129–138. doi:10.1016/j.arcontrol.2010.02.008

KEY TERMS AND DEFINITIONS

CIA: Security attributes confidentiality, integrity, and availability that need to be protected. Many attacks target one or multiple of these attributes.

Industrial IoT: Inspired by initiatives such as Industry 4.0 or Smart Manufacturing, IoT concepts are applied to industrial machinery. These machines are connected to the Internet, thus making them accessible from everywhere.

Intrusion Detection System: Used to monitor networks or devices to detect ongoing attacks. In combination with other measures, also successfully defeated attacks should be detected by IDSs.

Logical Attack: Logical attacks can be conducted using existing interfaces to a device, such as network interfaces or a debug interface. This type of attack can be done remotely without physical access to the device.

Network Security: Due to IoT devices and even CPS being connected with other devices and even the Internet, security at the network layer needs to be provided. Security measures can be applied at different network layers such as the transport layer.

Physical Attack: Physical attacks require physical access to the device under attack. This type of attack can be invasive, semi-invasive or non-invasive, which denotes the severity of modifications an attacker performs with the attacked device.

Tamper Resistance: Devices that should not reveal any confidential information need to be tamper resistant. Tamper resistance is achieved mostly through hardware measures but can also be realized in software only.

This research was previously published in Solutions for Cyber-Physical Systems Ubiquity edited by Norbert Druml, Andreas Genser, Armin Krieg, Manuel Menghin and Andrea Hoeller ; pages 248-277, copyright year 2018 by Engineering Science Reference (an imprint of IGI Global).

Chapter 19
Advanced Network Data Analytics for Large-Scale DDoS Attack Detection

Konstantinos F. Xylogiannopoulos
University of Calgary, Calgary, Canada

Panagiotis Karampelas
Hellenic Air Force Academy, Dekelia, Greece

Reda Alhajj
University of Calgary, Calgary, Canada

ABSTRACT

Internet-enabled devices or Internet of Things as it has been prevailed are increasing exponentially every day. The lack of security standards in the manufacturing of these devices along with the haste of the manufacturers to increase their market share in this area has created a very large network of vulnerable devices that can be easily recruited as bot members and used to initiate very large volumetric Distributed Denial of Service (DDoS) attacks. The significance of the problem can be easily acknowledged due to the large number of cases regarding attacks on institutions, enterprises and even countries which have been recently revealed. In the current paper a novel method is introduced, which is based on a data mining technique that can analyze incoming IP traffic details and early warn the network administrator about a potentially developing DDoS attack. The method can scale depending on the availability of the infrastructure from a conventional laptop computer to a complex cloud infrastructure. Based on the hardware configuration as it is proved with the experiments the method can easily monitor and detect abnormal network traffic of several Gbps in real time using the minimum hardware equipment.

DOI: 10.4018/978-1-7998-5348-0.ch019

INTRODUCTION

In recent years, the number of Internet enabled devices is increasing everyday exponentially. According to Ericsson Mobility Report (Ericsson, 2016) in the third quarter of 2016 there are more than 7.5 billion mobile subscriptions worldwide and most of the half of them are broadband. In most of the countries the penetration rate is over 100% which means that there are more mobile devices than the population. In UK in the first quarter of 2016 the percentage of mobile users between the adult population was 93% while more than 71% of the adult population use smart phones and 66% of the mobile users use their smart phone to access the Internet as reported by OfCom (OfCom, 2017). Apart from smart phones, other internet-enabled devices have appeared such as smart TVs, watches, security cameras, printers, washing machines, etc. which are connected to the Internet either directly or through pairing with a smart phone. All these devices are potential victims of the malevolent hackers who wish to exploit security weaknesses of the new devices and the privacy insensitivity or even ignorance of the users. As the number of the devices is increasing and as more and more types of devices are Internet-connected, the possibility of a device high jacking is also increasing. The most apparent reason for this is stealing private information such as financial information, personal emails and photos, etc. which can be used by the attacker for personal gain. However, someone would wonder why someone would like to take control of a smart washing machine apart from playing a trick on the device owner? A smart device, part of the Internet of Things (IoT), since it is connected to Internet is a valuable resource of the network and can be used in the service of, for example, a bot network to attack other legitimate users of the network. This type of attacks has already been reported (Kührer et al., 2014) especially using devices such as routers, VoIP gateways, network printers and surveillance cameras. Latest reports from various security firms have disclosed several serious attempts for distributed denial-of-service volumetric attacks attributed to IoT botnets. An example of such a DDoS attack was reported on September 2016 against the Brian Krebs's security blog. An attack that created traffic of over 600 Gbps and was attributed to an IoT botnet created by Mirai malware (Bertino & Islam, 2017). The same month another attack was reported against the OVH French webhost at 1.1 or more Tbps (US CERT, 2017). On October 21st, 2016, Dyn Service Provider in the US experienced the largest so far reported DDoS attack of more than 1 Tbps which again is attributed to the infected from Mirai malware IoT devices (Arbor Networks, 2016).

In addition to the proliferation of internet-enabled devices and the corresponding security issues that have raised, there is also a proliferation of electronic services that are available through the cloud infrastructure that have also become the main target of several DDoS attacks. The consequences of such attacks in the cloud infrastructure are not only catastrophic to the attacked services but they may also affect other services that are not in the spot due to the possible migrations of the virtual machines of these other services during the attack (Somani, Gaur & Sanghi, 2015). In other cases, some services may depend or may serve other websites and as a result when an attack disrupts the operation of the former, the latter also experience problems. As an example of how a DDoS attack in a Service Provider can affect other services is the aforementioned case of Dyn which is a dynamic DNS service provider offering services to several other companies such as Etsy, PayPal, Microsoft, GitHub, Reddit, Twitter, etc. As a result of the 21st of October attack to Dyn, several services of the other companies were not accessible at least to the East coast of United States (Arbor Networks, 2016). Other services, that are directly targeted, are usually those of commercial companies such as Yahoo, Dell, eBay, Amazon, ZDNet, British Telecom and in 2015 Blizzard WoW, GitHub, New York Magazine, Dreamhost and several other services which may experience downtime from few minutes to several hours due to DDoS attacks. Governmental services are also frequently targeted by DDoS attacks and several incidents have been reported in the past in several countries such as Georgia, Estonia, Ukraine, Syria, UK, USA, etc. (Loukas & Oke, 2010) and more recently on November 2016 in Liberia which suffered a large DDoS attack from a mirai enabled botnet (Kolkman, 2016).

The Internet traffic due to the increasing number of DDoS attacks has been increased correspondingly (Wang, Yufu & Jie, 2015) and as a result it becomes more difficult and sophisticated to monitor and detect this type of attacks since bot networks utilize different techniques to initiate an attack. For example, the attacks can target different protocols using different techniques such as TCP SYN, TCP RST, TCP NULL, UDP, ICMP, DNS, SSDP, NTP and other protocols while sometimes the attackers are launching more complicated attacks targeting all types of intrusion detection systems (Nexusguard, 2016) making the detection let alone the mitigation of a DDoS attack very difficult.

For that reason, security researchers and experts are trying to develop techniques to confront DDoS attacks and mitigate their consequences either these are technical or financial. In this context, several different techniques can be found in the literature; they attempt to either detect or to stop a DDoS attack something which is very difficult due to the diverse characteristics of each attack as mentioned before. J. Mikrovic (Mirkovic, 2002) reported that the main characteristics which make a DDoS practically undetected are the geo-dispersion of the botnets that are used, the sophisticated methods that the attackers are using to cover their traces e.g., by IP spoofing, the diverse attacks to different network protocols, the availability of different attack tools such as LOIC (Low Orbit Ion Canon), HULK (HTTP Unbearable Load King), Tor's Hammer, PyLoris, Trinoo, Stacheldraht, (Infosec Institute, 2013), or mirai and leet botnets (Zawoznik & Bekerman, 2016) etc. The most important reason though that allows the utilization of a great number of resources to initiate a DDoS attack is the security weaknesses that exist in the software systems, the illiteracy of users who fail to take the necessary precautions to secure their system, e.g., to update their operating system and install antivirus software in conjunction with the inherent characteristics of IoT devices. More specifically (Bertino and Islam, 2017) reported that the heterogeneity of protocols, devices and platforms used by the manufacturers as well as the mobility of this type of devices are the main weaknesses that make IoT devices vulnerable since there are no security standards yet and the environment they operate may not be always secure or monitored. If someone also accounts the very large number of such devices e.g. sensors it may be very difficult, costly or even impossible to configure and constantly monitoring them.

The solution to this problem can be the regulation of the manufacturing process of such devices e.g., coming with predefined security standards but also the creation of novel and advanced methods and tools for information assurance. These techniques should be able to early detect very large DDoS attacks from any source such as those recently reported by using advanced data analytics in real time as the method proposed in this paper.

The rest of the paper is organized as follows: Section 2 presents a review of the most important DDoS detection methods. Section 3 presents the proposed DDoS detection approach. Section 4 presents the experimental results by the application of the proposed methodology to an existing publicly available very large dataset with DDoS attack data; also, experimental results are reported and discussed. Finally, the conclusions and future work is presented.

RELATED WORK

The diversity of the DDoS attacks and their corresponding sources has led security researchers to attempt to apply a wide range of methods either to prevent DDoS attacks or to early detect the initiation of the attack and take the appropriate measures to defend their infrastructure. According to Mirkovic and Reiher (Mirkovic & Reiher, 2004) detection and prevent mechanisms are classified in two broad categories: the preventive and reactive methods. Preventive methods aim at deterring a DDoS attack by taking the appropriate measures to increase the hardware or software security of the infrastructure. This can be achieved in the software level, e.g., with the deployment of automatic updating schemes to minimize exposure to security holes or by monitoring user and access rights to detect potential risks that escaped the attention of the initial installation of the systems or regular auditing of the software systems for suspicious activities. At hardware level, the installation of firewalls, honeypots and intrusion detection systems can prevent attacks to the infrastructure. Another type of preventive methods aims to alleviate the consequences of a DDoS attack by balancing the payload of the attack intelligently to either more resources if they are available or to resources that are not actually used and thus limit the effects of the attack to the active infrastructure. In terms of cost, while the software hardening of the systems and the revision of security policies and processes may be affordable, the installation of sophisticated firewalls and intrusion detection systems is more expensive and difficult to maintain especially for small or medium companies. However, when it comes to the increase of the available resources then only very large Internet Service Provider may justify the cost and be able to absorb a large-scale DDoS attack coming from a very large botnet.

Reactive methods on the other hand aim to detect patterns or anomalies in the traffic of a network. Pattern detection methods utilize a database of known signatures of attacks and compare those signatures with the current traffic. If similarities are detected, then the network administrator is notified for further actions. Anomaly detection methods identify anomalies in the normal traffic of the network. Unexpected spikes are identified as DDoS attempts and are reported to the network administrators. In this case, it is very important to early identify the developing DDoS attack in order to have time to take the appropriate measures against the malevolent IPs and drop the corresponding network packets that will cause problem. Thus, a successful reactive method must early detect the emerging attack by identifying the anomalies in the traffic of the network or a specific pattern that escalates.

None of the above-mentioned methods can be considered as 100% successful since as it was mentioned in the Introduction, DDoS attacks are very sophisticated and perpetually new attack methods are introduced. In this context, security researchers are always testing novel concepts to promptly detect a DDoS attack. These methods are usually addressing three stages of the DDoS defence process: the detection phase, the classification phase and finally the response (Oke, Loukas & Gelenbe, 2007). However, there are methods that address only the two first stages, i.e., the detection and clarification stage and then notify the network administrator for final decision and response since the most essential effort is needed in the detection and decision-making stage while the response stage in most of the cases is trivial, e.g., by blocking the suspicious IPs, or IP ranges, limiting the available network bandwidth for a specific subnetwork, etc. Thus, focusing on the first two stages, we can found methods that have been proposed so far which range from pattern or signature detection using artificial neural networks, data mining, statistical analysis and hybrid techniques.

Artificial neural network methods apply machine learning techniques using patterns or signatures that have already been detected in order to predict whether the network traffic resembles those patterns and can be part of a DDoS attack. Usually such a methodology involves multiple stages, e.g., monitoring various features of the network traffic which then are fed to the artificial network in order to analyse them and based on previous data finally decide whether a DDoS attack is likely in progress or not (Öke & Loukas, 2007). The accuracy of such a methodology depends on various factors, e.g., the training dataset which may not contain patterns of a new type of DDoS attack, or the selected features identified in the first stages may not be similar to the DDoS attack in progress and thus the detection may not be possible.

As mentioned DDoS attacks overwhelm a legitimate service with tons of artificial traffic that cannot be served on a reasonable time frame by the service and thus the service stops responding to all requests. As the data flood the service, data mining techniques are employed to analyse the data stream and decide whether this flow of data is a DDoS attack or normal traffic. The most frequent data mining techniques employed for this purpose are feature selection and classification techniques (Kim et al., 2004) to select the attributes of the traffic data that need to be analysed and then a classification algorithm is utilized to decide whether the data stream belongs to a DDoS attack or not. Another data mining technique that can be used in DDoS attack detection is a combination of classification and association rule mining algorithms in which a classification technique, e.g., C4.5 can be applied to develop a learning model for known attack types while the association rule learning algorithm analyses the traffic and recognizes relationships between the classes identified in the learning model (Yu et al., 2013). Some newer methods in this category, in the effort to understand the behaviour and characteristics of a botnet which creates the DDoS attack traffic, use other classification techniques such as Boosted Decision Trees, Naïve Bayesian Classification, Support Vector Machine (Kirubavathi & Anitha, 2016), Expectation-Maximization Clustering (Garcia et al, 2014) and Hidden Markov model for pattern matching (Kim et al, 2012).

Statistical analysis techniques are also applied to identify anomalies in the normal network traffic (Thapngam et al., 2012). Usually this can be achieved by monitoring and modelling the normal network traffic and if the traffic deviates from a predetermined threshold this will be considered suspicious and potentially a DDoS attack. As it can be understood, the success of this type of detection methods is very sensitive to the selection of threshold since a small increase in the traffic due to an important announcement or a popular item posted in a website may be considered as a DDoS attack while it is simply increased temporary traffic. Another drawback of this type of methods is that low intensity attacks that take a long time to escalate may not be detected if the threshold is automatically refined based on the hourly or daily traffic.

Finally, several researchers have proposed hybrid detection methods that combine features of the other categories in order to improve the success rate of the detection. In (Wang et al., 2012) a hybrid method that uses multistage detection which comprise Markov's prediction and wavelet singularity detection is proposed to detect DDoS attacks. Another hybrid method (Hwang et al., 2007) combines anomaly detection with weighted association rules to produce attacks' signatures that could be used in a future DDoS attack. According to the reported results the hybrid methods outperform the corresponding constituent methods if used separately.

OUR APPROACH

The method proposed in this paper is able to monitor traffic in a medium to large networking environment and early warn the network administrators in case of a large-scale DDoS attack as it can detect the increase of network traffic by analyzing it in real-time. The main advantage of the method is that it can run in a conventional computer and scale up automatically to any available resources increasing significantly the volume of the traffic it can monitor. The method has been tested using a range of different hardware configurations such as an i7 processor on mobile computer, to a desktop i7 computer with 4 cores and a server with Intel Xeon dual processors with 12 cores demonstrating consistent and scaled up results according to the hardware configuration.

The method is based in the Reduced Suffix Array data structure presented by the authors in (Xylogiannopoulos, Karampelas, Alhajj, 2016) which allows ARPaD algorithm (Xylogiannopoulos, Karampelas, Alhajj, 2014) to detect all repeated patterns in a sequence. The data structure and the algorithm have been altered and optimized to accommodate the particularities of the network packets.

With the use of the actual suffix strings we can construct a similar to a suffix array data structure for fixed width substrings such as the IP strings of length 12. In order to perform this in we had to convert all IP strings to the same length, i.e., 12 by adding leading zeros in octets that do not have length three, i.e., for single digit octets adding two leading zeros while for double digit octets adding one zero. By doing this, ARPaD can then analyse the strings of the IPs and detect all repeated patterns, which in this case are domains, subdomains, subnets or actual hosts when the string is a full IP address of length 12.

However, in the current paper we will base our analysis on a new data structure introduced in (Xylogiannopoulos, Karampelas, Alhajj, 2016) which allows the classification of the suffix array to smaller classes. The major advantage of the newly introduced data structure is that it allows the parallel execution of the ARPaD over each class and, therefore, the significant acceleration of the analysis. The use of the new data structure requires though major transformations to the methodology originally presented in (Xylogiannopoulos, Karampelas, Alhajj, 2016). More specifically, the recording of IP addresses as exist in the IPv4 protocol does not allow to take full advantage of the LERP-RSA because only 3 classes can be created based on the decimal system for Classification Level 1, i.e., IP address strings starting with 0, 1 and 2. Actually the last class sample space is significantly smaller since it can take values up to 255 only and not up to 299 (Xylogiannopoulos, Karampelas, Alhajj, 2016). Even if we use Classification Level 2 (the two first digits) again we cannot have an almost uniformly distribution of the strings which will accelerate the analysis. Due to the small number of classes, the improvement is not significant. In order to take full advantage of the classification, whenever a new packet arrives, instead of using the decimal representation of IPv4 address, we convert each octet of the address to the hexadecimal equivalent, e.g., IP address 123.45.6.78 will be transformed to 7B.2D.6.4E and the corresponding string will be 7B2D064E. Doing this we have achieved two significant improvements: (1) the length of our IP address string is not anymore 12 but 8, which is by 1/3 smaller and will help for a faster analysis of the IP addresses list and (2) since the values of the octets have changed from 0-255 to 00-FF this means that we can classify our data structure using hexadecimal system and create 16 classes which can cover the whole sample space of possible octets. Another important aspect of this transformation is that allows us to execute our method over the new IPv6 protocol directly, with the new addressing scheme. The only change that has to take place is to transform every empty octet "::" to double zeros, i.e., ":00:"

After the creation of classes, the next step is to lexicographically sort each one based on the IP address string. For this purpose, the merge sort algorithm can be used which has complexity O(nlogn) and it is the slowest part of the process. The last step in our method is to execute in parallel the ARPaD over each one of the 16 classes, if we use Classification Level 1. If we use Classification Level 2, which means we have 256 classes, there is high possibility that the hardware cannot allow us the parallel execution over all classes simultaneously. In this case we can execute in semi-parallel mode depending on the maximum number of threads allowed by our hardware and OS.

This analysis can return every IP that occurs at least twice in the IP list. Yet, the Network Administrator can set different parameters and thresholds, which can be either static or dynamic, and raise a warning signal for a potential DDoS attack. The analysis can be performed following different schemes: (1) using a fixed time interval analysis at which the IP addresses are collected and analyzed every specific timespan, e.g., 1 minute, 5 minutes etc., (2) using fixed number of packets, e.g., 100,000 for which whenever the specific number of packets has been collected, can be analysed regardless of the timespan they occurred and (3) a combination of the above where the Network Administrator can set a criterion to execute the analysis based on which threshold is met first (time or packets). All these parameterizations depend on the hardware and bandwidth available to the infrastructure used and can be determined and adjusted dynamically by the Network Administrator.

The completion of the IP addresses analysis will initiate the detection phase which will identify potential threats based on a set of custom variables, set by the Administrator. In order to experimentally test and verify the methodology we have created a prototype application which: (1) implements the current methodology, (2) detects the geolocation of each IP prefix (domain, subdomain, subnet and host), (3) provides aggregate and grouped results information to the Network Administrator and (4) visualizes the comprehensive results. The Network Administrator can use the application to provide a number of variable thresholds to define custom warning signals of a potential DDoS attack. Some of the metrics available are (1) the percentage change of traffic per time interval, (2) the percentage change of traffic per country, (3) region or domain of the IP, (4) time zone of the IP geolocation, etc. All or combinations of the above can be used to characterize an IP as suspicious, e.g., a sudden increase of packets from a region where the time zone is in the middle of the night and cannot be justified. Even more, it is possible to directly identify to whom a domain or host IP belongs which can allow Network Administrator to decide if this can be a suspicious traffic that can lead to a DDoS attack. This information can be provided in real time to the Network Administrator who can decide to block the communication in the level of hosts, domains, countries or geographical regions from accessing the network resources and allow legitimate users to continue using the services without experiencing any degradation.

EXPERIMENTAL ANALYSIS

For the experiments, as mentioned above a range of different of-the-shelf hardware configurations were used to prove the high performance and scalability of the method. Table 1 summarizes the characteristics of the different hardware configurations.

Table 1. Hardware configuration for the experiments

	Configuration 1	Configuration 2	Configuration 3
Computer Type	Laptop	Desktop	Server
Processor	i7-6700HQ	i7-4790	Xeon E5-2620
Frequency	2.6	3.6	2.4
Cores	4	4	2x6
Logical processors	8	8	24
RAM	16	32	32

The dataset used in the experiments comprises the Booters – Analysis of DDoS-as-aService Attacks (Santanna et al. 2015). The dataset contains traffic generated by a round of 9 different files (Table 2) including IP addresses from botnets cleaned from normal traffic. This affects significantly the outcome of the analysis since no conclusion can be made from the perspective of distinguishing malicious traffic from legitimate, yet, the dataset is very helpful in determining the performance of the methodology using different, conventional hardware.

Table 2. Dataset information per file (Santanna et al. 2015)

File	Packets	Duration (sec)	Average Packet Rate/sec
1	12,947,222	295.06	2,633
2	9,054,436	280.66	1,936
3	13,239,142	289.28	2,746
4	31,643,406	490.96	3,867
5	2,167,847	378.54	344
6	9,795,411	138.75	4,236
7	16,746,986	538.02	1,868
8	5,758,016	169.32	2,040
9	13,281,044	155.04	5,140

Advanced ARPaD algorithm (Xylogiannopoulos, 2017) can detect all repeated patterns in a sequence and in our case every IP address which has accessed the server at least twice and every domain, subdomain or subnet by breaking down the IP address to octets (Table 3). Of course, during a potential DDoS attack low frequency IP addresses may not be of high priority since in their majority could be characterized as legitimate traffic. Individual IP address of low frequencies can be many, yet, they might be from the same subnet or domain and that is why this kind of analysis is of extreme importance. Our purpose is to try to identify IP addresses, domains and subnets with extremely high number of occurrences. Based on other qualitative characteristics and the thresholds a Network Administrator can set, these high frequent IPs can be characterized as possible threats and block them. We executed our experiment in 10 rounds using 256 classes for the IP addresses (Classification Level 2), one for each one of the 9 files of the dataset and one for all files combined in one large file in order to calculate an average execution time. Also, multiple of sixteen threads are used to analyze in parallel classes for each one of each IP prefix.

Depending on the available hardware and resources, all threads can be executed in parallel, something which although gives incredible fast processing time it also means that 256 threads should run in parallel. Unfortunately, with our available hardware at the time of the experiments something like this was not possible and, therefore, the process was executed in semi-parallel mode in steps of multiples of 16 threads. For example, while the laptop was able to run 64 threads before the CPU utilization gets almost to 100%, the Xeon with 24 logical cores was able to run 176 threads before the CPU reaches almost 100% utilization. As we can observe there is an important difference in the number of IP addresses analyzed per second by almost similar CPUs (i7 with 2.6GHz and 3.6GHz) with the second having 25% better performance for IPs per second. Yet, when a double Xeon CPU with multiple cores is used (even

Table 3. Top ten most occurring IPs per octet for combined dataset

xxx.xxx.xxx.xxx	Occur.	xxx.xxx.xxx.	Occur.	xxx.xxx.	Occur.	xxx.	Occur.
113.235.30.255	507,098	113.235.60.	1,657,627	113.235.	14,529,762	113.	19,454,081
113.235.60.173	504,402	113.235.54.	1,183,731	103.117.	2,456,209	103.	7,307,447
113.235.38.149	504,332	113.235.38.	1,074,255	103.115.	1,878,261	117.	6,468,359
113.235.62.251	501,772	103.117.75.	853,251	253.80.	1,271,667	253.	5,519,965
113.235.54.59	499,488	113.235.30.	774,193	105.239.	715,237	111.	4,969,406
113.235.78.121	496,548	103.115.71.	727,497	95.69.	694,534	109.	4,829,574
113.235.68.187	473,988	113.235.88.	725,827	111.203.	657,722	251.	4,476,491
113.235.88.57	472,316	113.235.44.	724,834	113.247.	635,000	107.	4,228,699
113.235.60.247	462,105	103.115.91.	682,890	107.111.	586,178	99.	3,319,476
113.235.52.91	458,820	113.235.12.	600,407	113.125.	569,903	247.	3,304,235

with lower frequency at 2.4GHz) the number of IP addresses analyzed is significantly increased. The ability of LERP-RSA to create the data structure in multiple small classes and ARPaD to analyze all these classes in full-parallel or semi-parallel mode is the catalytic factor for outstanding performance. As the number of cores is increased the ability to analyze significantly larger number of IP addresses per second is proportionally increased.

In Table 4 we can observe the average number of IP addresses analyzed by each hardware configuration per second. As we can see the laptop with the i7 CPU managed to analyze approximately 4 million IP addresses per second while the desktop with the i7 CPU but with higher frequency can analyze approximately 5 million IP addresses. However, the double Xeon CPU with 24 logical processors, three times more than the two others, can analyze approximately 12 million IP addresses per second (approximately 300% and 240% respectively) regardless that the CPU has lower frequency than both others. The significant larger number of cores allowed us to execute multiple parallel processes and, therefore, analyze more IP addresses per second. In case of significant large traffic of hundreds Gbps or even Tbps, a cluster of multicore CPUs such as Xeon could potentially easily perform the task of real time analysis of the traffic.

Table 4. Average execution performance per hardware configuration

	Configuration 1	Configuration 2	Configuration 3
Total combined IPs	114,633,510	114,633,510	114,633,510
Average IPs analyzed per second	4,000,000	5,000,000	12,000,000
Approximate total combined execution time	29 sec	23 sec	10 sec

In the four graphs of Figure 1 the occurrences per octets are demonstrated in each graph. As we can observe for each case there are few IPs in each category (domain, subnets, full addresses) which dominate the majority of the traffic. For example, in graph 1 in Figure 1, domain 113.xxx.xxx.xxx has almost 20 million packets out of the 114 in total, while 103.xxx.xxx.xxx which is the next one more frequent has only approximately 7.3 million. Domain 113.xxx.xxx.xxx can be analyzed further in order to extract valuable information about traffic because subnet 113.235.xxx.xxx has more than 14.5 million packets while all other 62 subnets of 113.xxx.xxx.xxx have approximately 5 million packets, which implies that the 113.235.xxx.xxx is the major consumer of the network resources. Thus, the network administrator in a real-life situation can fast detect and block the appropriate domains or subnets in order to avoid network resources exhaustion without blocking legitimate users.

Figure 1. Occurrences per octets and IPs

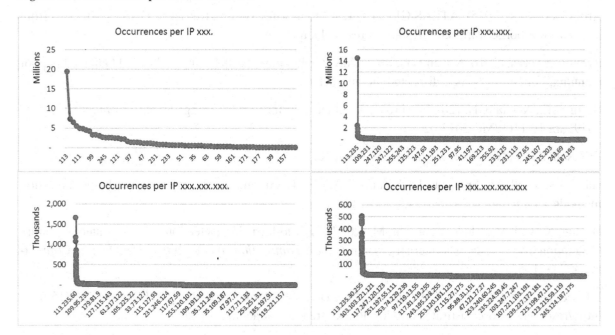

CONCLUSION

In this paper, we have proposed an innovative method that automatically and efficiently detects a very-large DDoS attack. The algorithm as it was proved in the experimental analysis can run in a conventional of-the-shelf computer system monitoring the network traffic. The method based on the experiments can scale up to consume more resources according to the available bandwidth of the network and the corresponding available resources.

Based on an advanced data mining technique, our method takes advantage of the very fast ARPaD algorithm and the newly introduced, high efficient, LERP-RSA data structure. The algorithm analyses IP prefixes and the results can be grouped based on different characteristics like the number of occurrences or geolocation information. Such analyses can be used as an early warning system for a DDoS attack and help the network administrator to prevent a potential attack while is developing and block possibly suspicious IPs. The efficiency of the method has been tested in a dataset of 114 million packets over a 2 to 8 minutes traffic from the Booters dataset (Santana, 2015). Although files cover different time spans for the total 114 million packets, ARPaD algorithm managed to perform the analysis in less than half a minute in worst case comparing to the 2 minutes that the fastest attack took place for just 13 million packets.

In the future, the method can be further developed to monitor additional properties of the network traffic such as specific protocols, packet sizes, etc. something that could improve the time required to detect an attack but could also improve the overall accuracy of the method.

REFERENCES

Arbor Networks. (2015). ATLAS Global Threat Monitoring System. Retrieved October 10, 2015 from http://www.arbornetworks.com/resources/research/attack-map

Arbor Networks. (2016, November). IoT DDoS attacks show the stakes have changed Quick take: poor planning, not an IoT Botnet, disrupted the internet.

Bertino, E., & Islam, N. (2017, February). Botnets and Internet of Things Security. *Computer*, *50*(2), 7679. doi:10.1109/MC.2017.62

Ericsson. (2016, November). Ericsson Mobility Report.

Garcia, S., Grill, M., Stiborek, J., & Zunino, A. (2014). An empirical comparison of botnet detection methods. *Computers & Security*, *45*, 100-123.

Hwang, K., Cai, M., Chen, Y., & Qin, M. (2007). Hybrid Intrusion Detection with Weighted Signature Generation over Anomalous Internet Episodes. *IEEE Transactions on* Dependable and Secure Computing, *4*(1), 41–55.

Infosec Institute. (2013). DOS Attacks and Free DOS Attacking Tools. Retrieved October 2, 2015 from http://resources.infosecinstitute.com/dos-attacks-free-dos-attacking-tools/

Kim, D. H., Lee, T., Kang, J., Jeong, H., & In, H. P. (2012). Adaptive pattern mining model for early detection of botnet-propagation scale. *Security and Communication Networks*, *5*(8), 917–927. doi:10.1002ec.366

Kim, M., Na, H., Chae, K., Bang, H., & Na, J. (2004). A combined data mining approach for DDoS attack detection. In Information Networking. Networking Technologies for Broadband and Mobile Networks (pp. 943-950). Springer Berlin Heidelberg. doi:10.1007/978-3-540-25978-7_95

Kirubavathi, G., & Anitha, R. (2016). Botnet detection via mining of traffic flow characteristics. *Computers & Electrical Engineering*, *50*, 91–101. doi:10.1016/j.compeleceng.2016.01.012

Kolkman, O. (2016, November 4). The DDoS Attack Against Liberia - we must take collective action for the future of the Open Internet. *Internet Society*. Retrieved March 1, 2017 from https://www.internetsociety.org/blog/tech-matters/2016/11/ddos-attackagainst-liberia-we-must-take-collective-action-future-open

Kührer, M., Hupperich, T., Rossow, C., & Holz, T. (2014). Hell of a handshake: Abusing TCP for reflective amplification DDoS attacks. In *Proceedings of the USENIX Workshop on Offensive Technologies (WOOT)*.

Loukas, G., & Oke, G. (2010). Protection against denial of service attacks: A survey. *Computer J. British Computer Society*, *53(7)*, 1020–1037.

Mirkovic, J. (2002, January 23). *D-WARD: DDoS network attack recognition and defense* [PhD dissertation prospectus]. UCLA.

Mirkovic, J., & Reiher, P. (2004). A taxonomy of DDoS attack and DDoS defense mechanisms. *SIG-COMM Computer Communication Review*, *34(2)*, 39–53. doi:10.1145/997150.997156

NexuGuard. (2016). Distributed Denial of Service (DDoS) Threat Report Q4 2016.

OfCom. (2017). OfCom Independent regulator and competition authority for the UK communications industries. 2017. Facts & Figures. Retrieved March 1, 2017 from http://media.ofcom.org.uk/facts/

Öke, G., & Loukas, G. (2007). A Denial of Service Detector based on Maximum Likelihood Detection and the Random Neural Network. *The Computer Journal*, *50(6)*, 717–727. doi:10.1093/comjnl/bxm066

Oke, G., Loukas, G., & Gelenbe, E. (2007) Detecting denial of service attacks with bayesian classifiers and the random neural network. *In Proceedings of the IEEE International Fuzzy Systems Conference FUZZ-IEEE '07* (pp. 1-6). 10.1109/FUZZY.2007.4295666

Santanna, J. J., van Rijswijk-Deij, R., Hofstede, R., Sperotto, A., Wierbosch, M., Granville, L. Z., & Pras, A. (2015, May). Booters-An analysis of DDoS-as-a-service attacks. In *Proceedings of the 2015 IFIP/IEEE International Symposium on Integrated Network Management* (pp. 243-251). IEEE. 10.1109/INM.2015.7140298

Somani, G., Gaur, M. S., & Sanghi, D. (2015). DDoS/EDoS attack in cloud: affecting everyone out there! In *Proceedings of the 8th International Conference on Security of Information and Networks (SIN '15)* (pp. 169-176). New York, NY: ACM. 10.1145/2799979.2800005

Thapngam, T., Yu, S., Zhou, W., and Makki, S. K. (2012). Distributed Denial of Service (DDoS) detection by traffic pattern analysis. In *Peer-to-Peer Networking and Applications*.

US-CERT. (2017). Heightened DDoS Threat Posed by Mirai and Other Botnets. Retrieved March 1, 2017 from http://www.us-cert.gov/ncas/alerts/TA16-288A

Wang, D., Yufu, Z., & Jie, J. (2010). A multi-core based DDoS detection method. In *Proceedings of the 2010 3rd IEEE International Conference Computer Science and Information Technology (ICCSIT)* (Vol. 4, pp.115-118).

Wang, F., Wang, H., Wang, X., & Su, J. (2012). A new multistage approach to detect subtle DDoS attacks. *Mathematical and Computer Modelling*, *55(1)*, 198–213. doi:10.1016/j.mcm.2011.02.025

Xylogiannopoulos, K. F. (2017) Data Structures, Algorithms and Applications for Big Data Analytics: Single, Multiple and All Repeated Patterns Detection in Discrete Sequences. Unpublished doctoral thesis

Xylogiannopoulos, K. F., Karampelas, P., & Alhajj, R. (2014). Analyzing very large time series using suffix arrays. *Applied Intelligence*, *41(3)*, 941–955. doi:10.100710489-014-0553-x

Xylogiannopoulos, K. F., Karampelas, P., & Alhajj, R. (2016, January). Real Time Early Warning DDoS Attack Detection. In *Proceedings of the 11th International Conference on Cyber Warfare and Security* (pp. 344-351)

Xylogiannopoulos, K. F., Karampelas, P., & Alhajj, R. (2016). Repeated Patterns Detection in Big Data Using Classification and Parallelism on LERP Reduced Suffix Arrays. *Applied Intelligence*, *45*(3), 567–597.

Yu, J., Kang, H., Park, D., Bang, H.-C., and Kang., D. W. (2013). An in-depth analysis on traffic flooding attacks detection and system using data mining techniques. *Journal of Systems Architecture*, *59*(10), 1005-1012.

Zawoznik, A., & Bekerman, D. (2016). 650Gbps DDoS Attack from the Leet Botnet. *Incapsula*. Retrieved March 1, 2017 from https://www.incapsula.com/blog/650gbpsddos-attack-leet-botnet.html

This research was previously published in the International Journal of Cyber Warfare and Terrorism (IJCWT), 7(3); edited by Graeme Pye and Brett van Niekerk; pages 44-54, copyright year 2017 by IGI Publishing (an imprint of IGI Global).

Chapter 20
Malware Threat in Internet of Things and Its Mitigation Analysis

Shingo Yamaguchi
Yamaguchi University, Japan

Brij Gupta
National Institute of Technology, Kurukshetra, India

ABSTRACT

This chapter introduces malware's threat in the internet of things (IoT) and then analyzes the mitigation methods against the threat. In September 2016, Brian Krebs' web site "Krebs on Security" came under a massive distributed denial of service (DDoS) attack. It reached twice the size of the largest attack in history. This attack was caused by a new type of malware called Mirai. Mirai primarily targets IoT devices such as security cameras and wireless routers. IoT devices have some properties which make them malware attack's targets such as large volume, pervasiveness, and high vulnerability. As a result, a DDoS attack launched by infected IoT devices tends to become massive and disruptive. Thus, the threat of Mirai is an extremely important issue. Mirai has been attracting a great deal of attention since its birth. This resulted in a lot of information related to IoT malware. Most of them came from not academia but industry represented by antivirus software makers. This chapter summarizes such information.

INTRODUCTION

In September 2016, Brian Krebs' web site "Krebs on Security" came under a massive DDoS attack (Krebs, 2016). This attack was caused by a new type of malware called Mirai. Mirai primarily targets IoT devices such as security cameras and wireless routers. This is because IoT devices feature large volume, pervasiveness, and high vulnerability (Kolias, Kambourakis, Stavrou, &Voas, 2017). As a result, a DDoS attack raised from infected IoT devices tends to become massive and disruptive. Thus, the threat of Mirai is an extremely important issue.

DOI: 10.4018/978-1-7998-5348-0.ch020

This chapter introduces malware's threat in IoT and then analyzes the mitigation methods against the threat. It consists of two parts. In the former part, we describe Mirai's threat, attack, mechanism, and mitigation methods. In the beginning, we trace the history from Mirai's birth. Next, we illustrate the mechanism of Mirai's infection and attack. Against the threat, there are some mitigation methods such as rebooting infected devices and using an IoT worm called as Hajime which blocks Mirai. In the latter part, we present a mathematical model of the infection phenomenon of Mirai. We regard the infection phenomenon as a multi-agent system and express it with agent-oriented Petri net called as Petri nets in a Petri net (PN^2 for short). Intuitively, a PN^2 is a Petri net in which each token is a Petri net again. PN^2 is not only as a graphical and mathematical modeling tool but also useful as a simulation tool. We reflect the mitigation methods into the PN^2 model and evaluate the methods of the model. We illustrate the dynamic behavior of the mitigation methods with the simulation of the model. We finally conclude this chapter by summarizing our key points and give future research directions.

MALWARE IN INTERNET OF THINGS: MIRAI

Threat and Attack

Mirai (means "future" in Japanese) is a malware which changes IoT devices into malicious bots and creates the network of bots called botnet. The botnets can be used to perform large-scale network attacks typified by DDoS attacks. We shall trace Mirai's history to show its threat and attack.

- **Discovery (August 31, 2016):** A malware research group MalwareMustDie reported the discovery of Mirai. See [MalwareMustDie. (2016)].
- **Early Major Attacks (September 2016):** The first attack came on September 18, 2016. It targeted a French cloud hosting company OVH [Bonderud, D. (2016)]. At about the same time as the first attack, another attack fell on Brian Krebs' website "Krebs on Security" [Krebs, B. (2016)]. It reached 620 Gbps that means twice the size of the largest attack in history. In addition, a United States Domain Name System provider Dyn was exposed to attacks on October 21, 2016 [York, K. (2016)]. Major internet services such as Amazon and Twitter were made unavailable. These massive and disruptive attacks and threats made Mirai well-known.
- **Source Code Released (September 30, 2016):** The author of Mirai "Anna-senpai" posted the source code of Mirai on Hack Forums as open source [Statt, N. (2016)]. Later, it was removed by the administrator of Hack Forums. For the academic purpose, it has also been archived to Github: https://github.com/jgamblin/Mirai-Source-Code.
- **Variant (December 2017):** The released source code enabled anyone not only to implement Mirai but also to evolve Mirai into new variants. In December 2017 researchers discovered a variant of Mirai called "Satori" [360 netlab. (2017)]. Satori has higher infectivity than Mirai by using vulnerabilities in IoT devices. In the following month, a variant of Satori called "Okiru" was found. Okiru becomes able to target more architectures like ARC [Arzamendi, P., Bing, M. & Soluk, K. (2018)]. Following Satori and Okiru, more than ten variants of Mirai have been discovered. That number of variants will continue to increase.

Figure 1. Countries possessing the infected IoT devices before and after the outbreak of Mirai (Nakao, 2018)

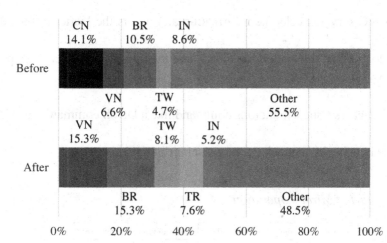

Mirai infected over 300,000 IoT devices in 164 countries (Devry, 2016). Figure 1 illustrates the difference in countries possessing the infected IoT devices before and after the outbreak of Mirai (Nakao, 2018). Before the outbreak, the top 5 countries were China (14.1%), Brazil (10.5%), India (8.6%), Vietnam (6.6%), and Taiwan (4.7%). After the outbreak, the top 5 countries were changed to Vietnam (15.3%), Brazil (15.3%), Taiwan (8.1%), Turkey (7.6%), and India (8.6%). This means that malware activity was moving to emerging markets and developing countries.

Mechanism

A Mirai botnet is composed of three major components: bots, command and control (C&C) server, and loader. In Sinaović and Mrdovic (2017), the authors analyzed the source code for Mirai.

- **Bot:** Runs on an infected device. It consists of three modules: scanner, killer, and attack. Scanner module uses telnet and looks for other vulnerable IoT devices. Killer module kills the processes that use ports 22, 23 and 80 and reserves those ports. Attack module executes the command issued by attackers.
- **C&C Server:** Used by attackers to maintain a botnet and to send malicious commands to the botnet.
- **Loader:** Turns a discovered vulnerable IoT device into a new bot. After logging in, the loader downloads and executes an architecture-dependent malicious binary code.

Mirai takes the following operational steps (See Figure 2):

- **Infection Phase**
  Step 1: An IoT device infected by Mirai, i.e. bot, searches for another IoT device which uses port 23 or 2323. If discovering such a device, the bot attempts to log-in with the list of easy-to-guess username and password pairs.

Step 2: If logging in successfully, the bot sends the discovered device's information to the C&C server.

Step 3: The C&C server checks the information and orders the loader to turn the device into a new bot.

Step 4: After logging in, the loader downloads and executes an architecture-dependent malicious binary code.

- **Attack Phase**

Step 5: Once attackers issue a malicious command like a DDoS command, the C&C server relays it to the bots.

Step 6: All the bots begin to attack the target server in unison.

Figure 2. Sequence chart of Mirai's operation

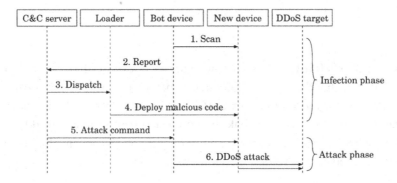

Mitigation

The US Computer Emergency Readiness Team (US-CERT) gave the following steps to remove Mirai from an infected IoT device in US-CERT. (2016)., Bertino and Islam (2017):

Step 1: Disconnect the device from the network.
Step 2: Perform a reboot. It clears Mirai from the device.
Step 3: If the password is easy-to-guess, change it to a strong password.
Step 4: Should reconnect to the network only after rebooting and changing the password. If the device is reconnected before changing the password, it could be shortly reinfected by Mirai.

In addition, in order to prevent Mirai's infection, the US-CERT recommends the users and administrators to take the following precautions:

- Ensure that all default passwords are changed to strong passwords
- Update IoT devices with the latest security patches
- Disable Universal Plug and Play (UPnP) on routers unless it is absolutely necessary
- Purchase IoT devices from secure companies
- Allow devices to operate only on a home network with a secured Wi-Fi router.

- Monitor ports 23 and 2323. Mirai attempts illegal login by using telnet.
- Look for suspicious traffic on port 48101. Infected devices often attempt to spread Mirai by using this port.

In Nakao (2018), the author has proposed to make use of darknet, honeypot, and sandbox for the proactive response of cyber security. Darknet monitoring is simple and useful for monitoring wider networks. Honeypot and sandbox can be used to emulate vulnerable IoT devices to capture malware and analyze them in detail. He has pointed out that IoT malware problem is already too big to be solved with only manufacturers' effort.

In October 2016, a new type of worm called *Hajime* (means "beginning" in Japanese) was reported by the Security Research Group at Rapidity Networks, Inc. (Edwards & Profetis, 2016) Just like Mirai, Hajime infects IoT devices. The crucial difference from Mirai is that Hajime has neither DDoS capabilities nor attacking code except for the propagation module. Instead, it displays a message which warns the user of the risk of malware (Grange, 2017). In addition, Hajime blocks ports which Mirai uses to infect a device. Hajime is an unethical way but has practically mitigated the threat of Mirai. Thus we can consider Hajime as one of the mitigation methods against the threat of Mirai.

MITIGATION ANALYSIS

Modeling of Mirai's Infection Phenomenon

In Tanaka and Yamaguchi (2017), the authors regarded Mirai's infection phenomenon as a multi-agent system and expressed it with PN^2. The mapping among Mirai's infection phenomenon, multi-agent system, and PN^2 is shown in Table 1. Since Mirai and IoT devices respectively have objectives and behave autonomously to achieve the objectives, they are regarded as autonomous agents. An IoT network enables them to interact with each other, thus it is considered as an environment.

Table 1. Mapping among Mirai's infection phenomenon, multi-agent system, and PN^2

Mirai's Infection Phenomenon	Multi-Agent System	PN^2
Mirai, IoT device	Autonomous agent	Agent net
IoT network	Environment	Environment net

PN^2 is a Petri net-based mathematical tool for modeling and analysis of multi-agent systems. This chapter assumes that the readers have some knowledge about Petri net and preferably even know PN^2. For the formal definitions and analysis techniques, the readers are referred to Yamaguchi, Bin Ahmadon, and Ge, (2016) and Hiraishi (2001). A PN^2, as its name suggests, is a Petri net (called an *environment net*) in which each token is a Petri net (called an *agent net*) again. Each agent net represents an autonomous agent. It has a state which can be changed by the fire of its transition. The environment net represents an environment in which agents interact and move. Each transition in the environment net is synchronized with the transitions in one or more agent nets. The synchronization is decided through dynamic binding by label. In Nakahori and Yamaguchi (2017), the authors have developed a software tool called *PN2Simulator* for editing and simulating PN². Figure 3 shows a screenshot of PN2Simulator. The left-side of PN2Simulator shows an environment net, while the right-side shows agent nets. A user can edit those nets through direct manipulation and can execute them by playing a token game interactively. PN2Simulator can highlight which transitions are enabled.

Figure 3. Screenshot of PN2Simulator

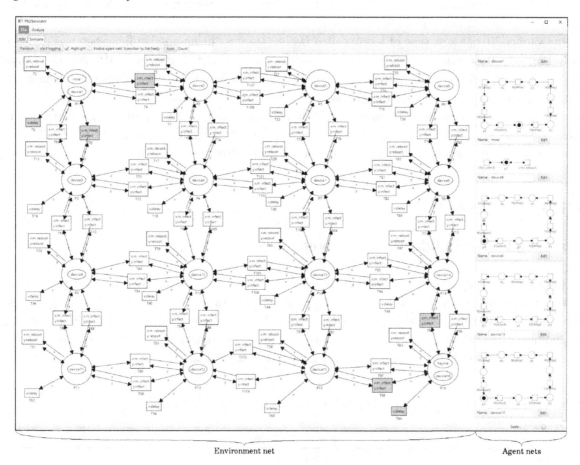

Environment net   Agent nets

Mirai repeatedly infects IoT devices. This behavior can be modeled as the agent net N_{mirai} shown in Figure 4. Transition t1 represents an infection action by Mirai. An IoT device is initially normal. Once a device is infected by Mirai, it becomes a bot. This behavior can be modeled as the agent net N_{device} shown in Figure 5. Transition t1 represents an infection action by the infected device. An IoT network consists of nodes. A node may or may not connect to another node directly. Figure 6 shows an environment net N_{net} which represents a line topology network consisting of three nodes. Each transition of the environment net represents that Mirai infects a device. For example, transition T1 represents that Mirai of place P1 infects the device of place P2.

Figure 4. Agent net N$_{mirai}$ which represents Mirai

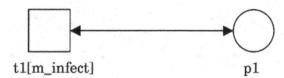

t1[m_infect]   p1

Figure 5. Agent net N$_{device}$ which represents an IoT device

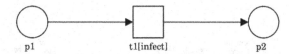

p1   t1[infect]   p2

Tokens are used to represent a state. An agent net N have zero or more tokens at each place. The state with one token only at place p is denoted by [p]. (N, [p]) denotes N with [p]. For agent nets N_{mirai} and N_{device}, the initial state is [p1]. Environment N_{net} has zero or more (N_{mirai}, [p1]) and/or (N_{device}, [p1]) in each place as tokens. A token game on N_{net} enables us to simulate Mirai's infection phenomenon. Figure 7 shows a state transition of N_{net} with the following initial state:

Node 1: The device device1 has already been infected by Mirai and is a bot, which is represented as ($N_{device1}$, [p2]) and (N_{mirai}, [p1]) at place P1;

Node 2: The device device2 is normal, which is represented as ($N_{device2}$, [p1]) at place P2; and

Node 3: The device device3 is normal, which is represented as ($N_{device3}$, [p1]) at place P3.

This initial state s_0 is illustrated in Figure 7 (a). In s_0, transition T1 is enabled. This means that Mirai attempts to infect device2. The occurrence of T1 in s_0 results in a new state s_1 shown in Figure 7 (b). Mirai is characterized by self-reproduction. Mirai at place P1 produces a copy of itself at place P2, and the copy infects device2. In s_1, transition T3 is enabled. This means that Mirai attempts to infect device3. The occurrence of T2 in s_1 results in a new state s_2 shown in Figure 7 (c). In s_2, all the devices have been infected by Mirai. In this state, there is no longer a transition that can occur.

Figure 6. Environment net N$_{net}$ which represents a line topology network consisting of three nodes

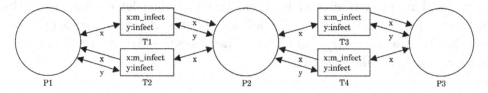

Figure 7. A state transition of N$_{net}$ from the initial state with one Mirai

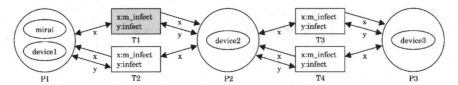

(a) *The initial state s$_0$. Mirai has already infected `device1` and attempts to infect `device2`.*

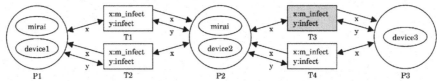

(b) *The state s$_1$ just after Mirai infected `device2`. Mirai attempts to infect `device3`.*

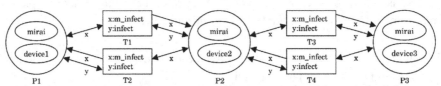

(c) *The state s$_2$ just after Mirai infected `device3`. There is no longer device which Mirai can infect.*

Modeling of Mitigation Methods

In Yamaguchi and Tanaka (2018), to evaluate mitigation methods against Mirai, the authors reflected them into the PN² model. The analysis was focused on two methods: rebooting and the use of Hajime.

One method is to reboot infected devices. Mirai stays only on the dynamic memory of an infected device, so it could be removed if the device is rebooted. Figure 8 shows an agent net N_{mirai}' of Mirai that is removed by rebooting. This is an extension of N_{mirai} of Figure 4. Transition t2 represents a reboot action by Mirai. This method is simple but carries the risk of reinfection if the device is not updated. Even though an IoT device became a bot, it can be returned to normal by rebooting. However, the device is not always rebooted immediately after the infection. Therefore some delay would be introduced until the reboot. Figure 9 shows an agent net N_{device}' of IoT device that is returned to normal by rebooting after some delay. This is an extension of N_{device} of Figure 5. Transitions t2 and t3 respectively represent a delay action and a reboot action by the infected device.

Figure 8. Agent net N$_{mirai}$' of Mirai that is removed by rebooting. This also means agent net N$_{hajime}$'

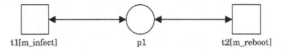

Figure 9. Agent net N_{device}' of IoT device is returned to normal by rebooting after some delay

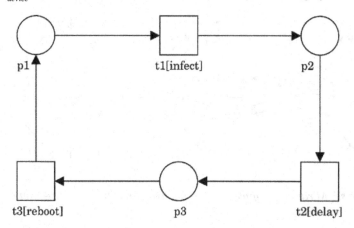

The other method is to use Hajime. Hajime has the same infection capability as Mirai. Once Hajime infects a device, it protects the device against Mirai. Unfortunately, if the infected device was rebooted, Hajime and its effect would be lost. This behavior is considered to be the same as that of Mirai. Therefore, Hajime was modeled as an agent net N_{hajime}' which has the same structure as N_{mirai}'.

Figure 10 shows an environment net N_{net}' which includes rebooting devices after some delay. This is an extension of N_{net} of Figure 6. As an example, for agents at place P1, transitions t5 and t6 respectively represent a reboot action and a delay action.

Figure 11 shows a state transition of N_{net}' with the following initial state.

Node 1: Device1 has already been infected by Mirai, which is represented as ($N_{device1}$', [p2]) and (N_{mirai}', [p1]) at place P1;

Node 2: Device2 is normal, which is represented as ($N_{device2}$', [p1]) at place P2; and

Node 3: Device3 has already been infected by Hajime, which is represented as ($N_{device3}$', [p2]) and (N_{hajime}', [p1]) at place P3.

Figure 10. Environment net N_{net}' which includes rebooting devices after some delay

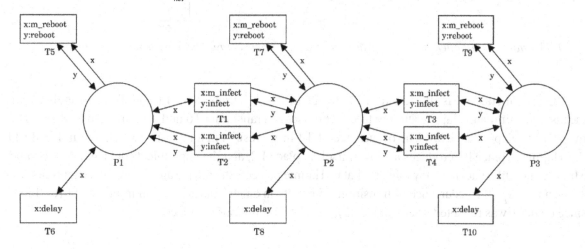

Figure 11. A state transition of N_{net}' *from the initial state with one Mirai and one Hajime*

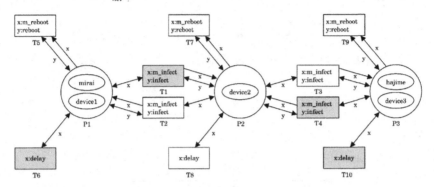

(a) *The initial state* s_0'. *Mirai and Hajime have respectively infected* `device1` *and* `device3`, *and they attempt to infect* `device2`.

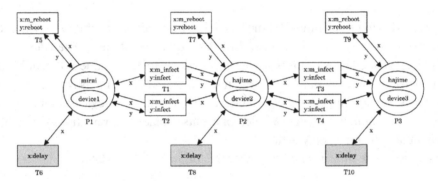

(b) *The state* s_1' *just after Hajime infected* `device2`. *At this time, Mirai cannot infect it any longer.*

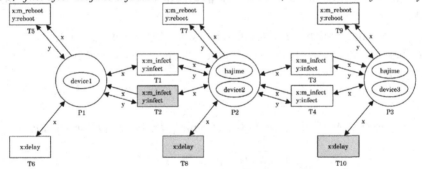

(c) *The state* s_2' *just after* `device1` *was rebooted after some delay. Mirai exists no more in place* `P1`.

This initial state s_0' is illustrated in Figure 11 (a). In s_0', transitions T1 and T4 are enabled. This means that Mirai and Hajime attempt to infect device2. Transitions T6 and T10 are also enabled. This means time elapses as delay. The occurrence of T4 in s_0' results in a new state s_1' shown in Figure 11 (b). Hajime at place P3 produces a copy of itself at place P2, and the copy infects device2. At this time, Mirai cannot infect device2 any longer. That is, Hajime protects the device against Mirai. After transition T6 occurs in s_1', the occurrence of transition T5 results in a new state s_2' shown in Figure 11 (c). In s_2', since device1 was rebooted after some delay, Mirai exists no more in place P1.

Figure 12. The grid network used in the first experiment

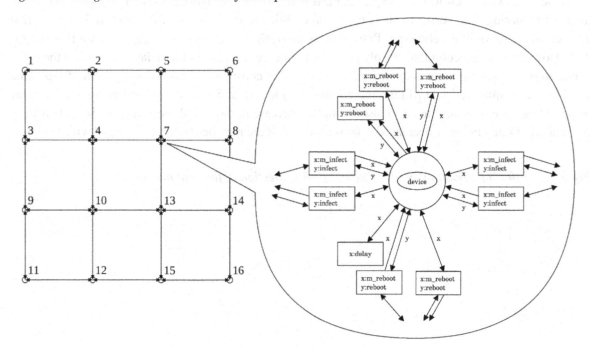

Evaluation of Mitigation Methods

In Yamaguchi, Tanaka, and Bin Ahmadon (in press), the authors evaluated the effect of the mitigation methods against Mirai through two simulation experiments of the PN^2 model.

In the first experiment, they used a grid network composed of 16 nodes. It is illustrated in Figure 12. They measured the infection rate of Mirai (= the number of devices infected by Mirai / the total number of devices) after 1,000 steps under the following condition:

- The delay of rebooting is 0, 1, 2, 3, 4, or 5 steps;
- The initial number n of Hajime is 0, 1, 2, or 3; and
- In the initial state, one Mirai is put at node 1 and n Hajime are put as follows: The first, the second, and the third are respectively at nodes 6, 11, and 16.

Table 2. Result of the experiment for the grid network

Initial Number of Hajime	Delay of Rebooting [Steps]					
	0	1	2	3	4	5
0	23.4%	70.3%	83.5%	89.0%	92.0%	93.5%
1	17.7%	40.5%	44.7%	44.5%	45.2%	46.2%
2	13.8%	26.6%	29.8%	30.7%	33.9%	33.1%
3	13.1%	20.7%	22.1%	24.0%	24.2%	24.8%

Table 2 shows the result of the experiment. It is illustrated in Figure 13. The horizontal axis is the delay of rebooting. The vertical axis is the mean of Mirai's infection rate for 1,000 trials. Let us first consider the case of only rebooting. Rebooting reduced the infection rate to 23.4% when the delay is zero. However, the infection rate steeply increased with the increase in the delay. Even when the delay is one step, the infection rate became 70.3%. Next, let us consider the case of using both of rebooting and Hajime. Hajime reduced Mirai's infection rate to less than 50% without depending on the delay of rebooting. The infection rate decreased with the increase in the initial number of Hajime. However, the reduction rate gradually decreased. The reason is that the network became saturated with Hajime.

Figure 13. Effect of rebooting and Hajime to Mirai's infection in the grid network

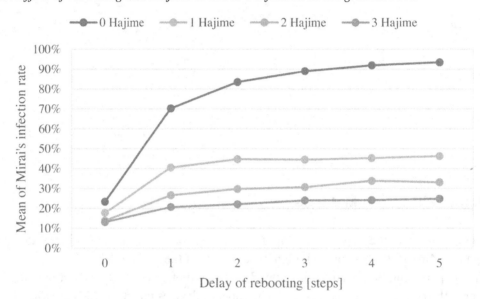

Figure 14. The hierarchy network used in the second experiment

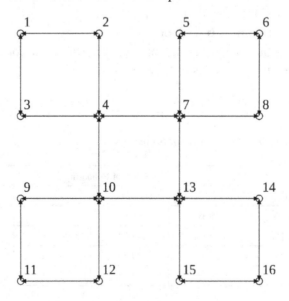

In the second experiment, they used a hierarchy network composed of 16 nodes, which is a ring network of ring networks. It is illustrated in Figure 14. They measured the infection rate of Mirai under the same condition as the first experiment.

Table 3 shows the result of the experiment for the hierarchy network. It is illustrated in Figure 15. The horizontal and vertical axes respectively have the same meaning as those of Figure 13. Let us first consider the case of only rebooting. Rebooting reduced Mirai's infection rate to 4.9% when the delay is zero. The hierarchy network could reduce more the infection rate than the grid network because of the restriction of network structure. However, the infection rate steeply increased with the increase in the delay. Even when the delay is one step, the infection rate became 61.4%. Next, let us consider the case of using both of rebooting and Hajime. Hajime showed higher effect than the case of the grid network because of the same reason as the case of only rebooting.

Table 3. Result of the experiment for the hierarchy network

Initial Number of Hajime	Delay of Rebooting [Steps]					
	0	1	2	3	4	5
0	4.9%	61.4%	79.3%	86.2%	90.7%	92.0%
1	4.9%	38.8%	42.9%	45.0%	47.4%	47.1%
2	3.3%	25.2%	28.7%	29.0%	33.1%	31.2%
3	3.3%	19.1%	18.9%	21.3%	21.9%	22.1%

In addition, the authors of this chapter conducted a simulation experiment to investigate the relationship between the size (the number of nodes) of grid network and the effect of the mitigation methods. They measured the infection rate of Mirai after 1,000 steps under the following condition:

- The size (the number of nodes) of grid network is 9 (=3×. 3), 16 (=4×. 4), or 25 (=5×5);
- The delay of rebooting is 3 steps;
- The initial number n of Hajime is 0, 1, 2, or 3; and
- In the initial state, one Mirai is put at node 1 and n Hajime are put as follows: The first, the second, and the third are respectively at the lower-right, the lower-left, and the upper-right corner nodes.

Table 4 shows the result of the experiment. It is illustrated in Figure 16. The horizontal axis is the size of grid network. The vertical axis is the mean of Mirai's infection rate for 1,000 trials. Even though the size of grid network varied, Mirai's infection rate did not almost change. The influence of network size is smaller than that of network topology. This suggests that the network topology should be emphasized rather than size.

Figure 15. Effect of rebooting and Hajime to Mirai's infection in the hierarchy network

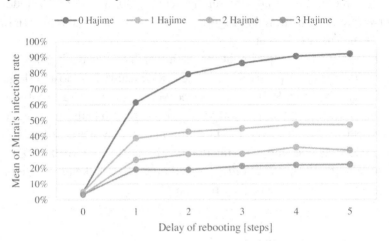

Figure 16. Relationship between the size of grid network and the effect of the mitigation methods

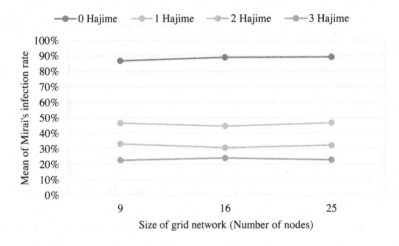

CONCLUSION

This chapter presented IoT malware Mirai's threat and then analyzed the mitigation methods against the threat. They were written in two parts. At the former part, we first traced Mirai's history to show its threat and attack. Next, we revealed Mirai's mechanism from both the static structure and dynamic behavior. Then, we described mitigation methods against the threat. At the latter part, we first explained a PN^2 model of Mirai's infection phenomenon. Next, we reflected the mitigation methods into the PN^2 model. Then, we evaluated the methods through the simulation of the model. The evaluation result shows:

- **Rebooting:** Drastically reduces Mirai's infection rate when the delay is zero. The effect, however, is rapidly lost with the increase in the delay
- **Hajime:** Reduces Mirai's infection rate to less than half without depending on the delay of rebooting. The reduction rate, however, gradually decreases with the increase in the initial number of Hajime.

Table 4. Result of the experiment in the case of varying the size of grid network

Size of Grid Network	Initial Number of Hajime			
	0	1	2	3
9	86.8%	46.6%	33.2%	22.7%
16	89.0%	44.5%	30.7%	24.0%
25	89.2%	46.7%	32.2%	22.9%

Is Hajime a "white worm"? Hajime continues to stay at the infected device even though completing the protection against Mirai. Since Hajime still has a remote control mechanism, it should not stay at the devices once the protection completed. It is an interesting future work to turn Hajime into "white worm". In Yamaguchi and Leelaprute (2019), the authors have proposed to extend Hajime to turn it into "white worm" by introducing lifespan to Hajime. In addition, in Yamaguchi (2019), the author has proposed to further extend the time-limited Hajime by introducing the secondary infectivity (the ability to infect a device infected by Mirai). In Molesky, M.J., & Cameron, E.A. (2019), the authors have proposed a perspective of how to utilize white worm technology while overcoming some of its many challenges by balancing individual, business, and government objectives.

Another future work is to develop how to dynamically put Hajime in response to the infection status of Mirai. In Tanaka, Yamaguchi, and Arata (2019), the authors have analyzed the effect of network structure on Mirai's infection. This chapter should become a trigger to interest researchers and engineers in this domain.

REFERENCES

Arzamendi, P., Bing, M., & Soluk, K. (2018). *The ARC of Satori*. Retrieved from https://www.netscout.com/blog/asert/arc-satori

Bertino, E., & Islam, N. (2017). Botnets and Internet of Things Security. *IEEE Computer*, *50*(2), 76–79. doi:10.1109/MC.2017.62

Bonderud, D. (2016). *Leaked Mirai Malware Boosts IoT Insecurity Threat Level*. Retrieved from https://securityintelligence.com/news/leaked-mirai-malware-boosts-iot-insecurity-threat-level/

Devry, J. (2016). Mirai Botnet Infects Devices in 164 Countries. Retrieved from https://www.cybersecurity-insiders.com/mirai-botnet-infects-devices-in-164-countries/

Edwards, S., & Profetis, I. (2016). *Hajime: Analysis of a decentralized internet worm for IoT devices*. Retrieved from https://security.rapiditynetworks.com/publications/2016-10-16/hajime.pdf

Grange, W. (2017). *Hajime battles Mirai for control of the Internet of Things*. Retrieved from https://www.symantec.com/connect/blogs/hajime-worm-battles-mirai-control-internet-things

Grange, W. (2017). *Hajime battles Mirai for control of the Internet of Things*. Retrieved from https://www.symantec.com/connect/blogs/hajime-worm-battles-mirai-control-internet-things

Hiraishi, K. (2001). A Petri-net-based model for the mathematical analysis of multi-agent systems. *IEICE Trans. on Fundamentals*, *E84-A*(11), 2829–2837.

Kolias, C., Kambourakis, G., Stavrou, A., & Voas, J. (2017). DDoS in the IoT: Mirai and other botnets. *IEEE Computer*, *50*(7), 80–84. doi:10.1109/MC.2017.201

Krebs, B. (2016). *KrebsOnSecurity Hit With Record DDoS*. Retrieved from https://krebsonsecurity.com/2016/09/krebsonsecurity-hit-with-record-ddos/

MalwareMustDie. (2016). *MMD-0056-2016 - Linux/Mirai, how an old ELF malcode is recycled*. Retrieved from http://blog.malwaremustdie.org/2016/08/mmd-0056-2016-linuxmirai-just.html

Molesky, M. J., & Cameron, E. A. (2019). Internet of Things: An Analysis and Proposal of White Worm Technology. *Proc. of IEEE ICCE 2019*, 4. 10.1109/ICCE.2019.8662111

Nakahori, K., & Yamaguchi, S. (2017). A support tool to design IoT services with NuSMV. *Proc. of IEEE ICCE 2017*, 84–87. 10.1109/ICCE.2017.7889238

Nakao, K. (2018). Proactive cyber security response by utilizing passive monitoring technologies. *Proc. of IEEE ICCE 2018*. 10.1109/ICCE.2018.8326061

360. netlab. (2017). *Warning: Satori, a Mirai Branch Is Spreading in Worm Style on Port 37215 and 52869*. Retrieved from https://blog.netlab.360.com/warning-satori-a-new-mirai-variant-is-spreading-in-worm-style-on-port-37215-and-52869-en/

Sinaović, H., & Mrdovic, S. (2017), Analysis of Mirai malicious software. Prof. of SoftCOM 2017, 1-5.

Statt, N. (2016). *How an army of vulnerable gadgets took down the web today*. Retrieved from https://www.theverge.com/2016/10/21/13362354/dyn-dns-ddos-attack-cause-outage-status-explained

Tanaka, H., & Yamaguchi, S. (2017). On modeling and simulation of the behavior of IoT devices malwares Mirai and Hajime. *Proc. of IEEE ISCE 2017*, 56–60.

Tanaka, H., Yamaguchi, S., & Arata, T. (2019). Consideration of IoT structure in mitigation against Mirai malware. *Proc. of IEEE ICCE-Berlin 2018*.

US-CERT. (2016). *Heightened DDoS threat posed by Mirai and other botnets*. Retrieved from https://www.us-cert.gov/ncas/alerts/TA16-288A

Yamaguchi, S., Bin Ahmadon, M. A., & Ge, Q. W. (2016). Introduction of Petri Nets: Its Applications and Security Challenges. In B. Gupta, D. P. Agrawal, & S. Yamaguchi (Eds.), *Handbook of Research on Modern Cryptographic Solutions for Computer and Cyber Security* (pp. 145–179). Hershey, PA: IGI Publishing. doi:10.4018/978-1-5225-0105-3.ch007

Yamaguchi, S., & Leelaprute, P. (2019). Hajime worm with lifespan and its mitigation evaluation against Mirai malware based on agent-oriented Petri net PN2. *Proc. of IEEE ICCE 2019*, 4. 10.1109/ICCE.2019.8662079

Yamaguchi, S., & Tanaka, H. (2018), Modeling of infection phenomenon and evaluation of mitigation methods for IoT malware Mirai by agent-oriented Petri net PN2. *Proc. of IEEE ICCE-TW 2018*, 271-272.

Yamaguchi, S., Tanaka, H., & Bin Ahmadon, M. A. (in press). Modeling and Evaluation of Mitigation Methods against IoT Malware Mirai with Agent-Oriented Petri Net PN^2. *International Journal of Internet of Things and Cyber-Assurance*. doi: 10.1504/IJITCA.2019.10021463

York, K. (2016). *Read Dyn's Statement on the 10/21/2016 DNS DDoS Attack*. Retrieved from https://dyn.com/blog/dyn-statement-on-10212016-ddos-attack/

This research was previously published in Security, Privacy, and Forensics Issues in Big Data edited by Ramesh C. Joshi and Brij B. Gupta; pages 363-379, copyright year 2020 by Information Science Reference (an imprint of IGI Global).

Chapter 21

Zero–Crossing Analysis of Lévy Walks and a DDoS Dataset for Real–Time Feature Extraction:
Composite and Applied Signal Analysis for Strengthening the Internet–of–Things Against DDoS Attacks

Jesus David Terrazas Gonzalez

Department of Electrical and Computer Engineering, University of Manitoba, Winnipeg, Canada

Witold Kinsner

Cognitive Systems Laboratory, Department of Electrical and Computer Engineering, University of Manitoba, Winnipeg, Canada & Telecommunications Research Laboratories (TRLabs), Winnipeg, Canada

ABSTRACT

A comparison between the probability similarities of a Distributed Denial-of-Service (DDoS) dataset and Lévy walks is presented. This effort validates Lévy walks as a model resembling DDoS probability features. In addition, a method, based on the Smirnov transform, for generating synthetic data with the statistical properties of Lévy-walks is demonstrated. The Smirnov transform is used to address a cyber-security problem associated with the Internet-of-things (IoT). The synthetic Lévy-walk is merged with sections of distinct signals (uniform noise, Gaussian noise, and an ordinary sinusoid). Zero-crossing rate (ZCR) within a varying-size window is utilized to analyze both the composite signal and the DDoS dataset. ZCR identifies all the distinct sections in the composite signal and successfully detects the occurrence of the cyberattack. The ZCR value increases as the signal under analysis becomes more complex and produces steadier values as the varying window size increases. The ZCR computation directly in the time-domain is its most notorious advantage for real-time implementations.

DOI: 10.4018/978-1-7998-5348-0.ch021

1. INTRODUCTION

The Internet has become an important part of our society in numerous ways, such as in economics, government, business, and daily personal life. An increasing amount of critical infrastructures (e.g., power grid and air traffic control) are managed and controlled via the Internet (Knowles, Prince, Hutchison, Disso, & Jones, 2015; Kriaa, Pietre-Cambacedes, Bouissou, & Halgand, 2015; Özçelik & Brooks, 2015), in addition to traditional infrastructure for communication. Today's cyberspace is full of attacks, such as Distributed Denial of Service (DDoS), information phishing, financial fraud, email spamming, and so on (Karim, Salleh, Shiraz, Shah, Awan, & Anuar, 2014; Yu, 2004).

Among various Internet based attacks, denial-of-service (DoS) attack is a critical and continuous threat in cybersecurity (Kinsner, 2012). DoS attacks are implemented by either forcing a victim computer to reset or consume its resources (e.g., access to application programming interfaces (APIs) (Balkanli, Alves, & Zincir-Heywood, 2014), CPU cycles, memory or network bandwidth (Beitollahi & Deconinck, 2014; Bhuyan, Kashyap, Bhattacharyya, & Kalita, 2014). Hence, the targeted computer no longer provides its intended services to legitimate users. When the DoS attacks are organized by multiple distributed computers, it is called distributed denial-of- service (DDoS) attack, which is a popular attack method in the cyberspace (Kaspersky Lab., 2014). Network security branches into three categories: confidentiality, availability and integrity. DDoS attacks belong to the availability category (Yu, 2004).

Despite all the efforts from industry participants and academia, DDoS attack is still an open problem. Some of the essential reasons for this passive situation are: (1) the no security design of the ARPANET network. The Internet came from this private network, ARPANET. As a private network, there were very limited security concerns in the original design (Peng, Leckie, & Ramamohanarao, 2007). This private network became a public network in the 1990s, and now many killer applications are running on the Internet, such as e-business. Security patches have been developed and installed to circumvent the inherent vulnerabilities, however, the effectiveness of these efforts are sometimes limited. For example, the Internet was designed stateless, therefore, a receiver has no information about which routers a received packet went through. Hence, it is easy to perform source IP spoofing; (2) Internet is the largest man-made system in human history. Cyberspace is huge and complex, and stays in an anarchy status; (3) Cyber attackers are enjoying one incredible advantage of the cyberspace: it is hard for defenders to technically identify attackers. Moreover, there lacks international laws or agreements among nations to bring cyber criminals to justice who commit crimes in one country but are living in other countries; (4) Hacking tools and software are easy to obtain. An attacker may not need profound knowledge of networking or operating systems to initiate a cyber attack (Yu, 2004). This paper proposes the study of Lévy walks and explores their connection to real DDoS datasets considering the similarities in their probability distribution functions (pdf).

Biologists have found that mobility patterns of foraging animals (e.g., spider monkey, albatrosses (seabirds), jackals, and marine predators) resemble what physicists have long called Lévy-walks (Atkinson, Rhodes, Macdonald, & Anderson, 2002; Ramos-Fernandez, Morales, Miramontes, Cocho, Larralde, & Ayala-Orozco, 2004; Viswanathan, Afanasyev, Buldyrev, Murphy, Prince, & Stanley, 1996). The term "Lévy-walk" was coined by (Shlesinger, Klafter, & Wong, 1982) to explain atypical particle diffusion not governed by Brownian motion (BM) (Rhee, Shin, Hong, Lee, Kim, & Chong, 2011; Rhee, Shin, Hong, Lee, & Chong, 2008).

Patterns of human mobility have features resembling Lévy walks (e.g., heavy-tail flight and pause-time distributions and the superdiffusive nature of mobility (Rhee et al., 2011)). Some deviations from pure Lévy walks, in human mobility, occur due to various factors specific to humans (e.g., geographical constraints such as roads, buildings, obstacles and traffic) (Rhee et al., 2008). General examples of Lévy-processes are: Poisson processes, compound Poisson processes, BM, Gamma processes, inverse Gaussian processes, and those with stable distributions (Kyprianou, 2014).

Biological systems exhibiting Lévy-walks have been of inspiration for designing adaptive behaviour in robotic applications and artificial agents. The behaviour imitation of biological creatures has contributed to the advancement of adaptive searching (Nurzaman, Matsumoto, Nakamura, Koizumi, & Ishiguro, 2009). Motion of bacteria responding to the presence of chemical concentration gradients, aka bacterial chemotaxis, has been adopted and implemented to realize simple yet effective searching behaviour for gradient-inducing targets in robots or artificial agents (Rhee et al., 2011). Lévy-walks are also applied in complex mobile sensing scenarios related to the Internet-of-Things (IoT), where smartphones are taking a central role. Smartphones allow crowd-sourced sensing in the IoT because of their embedded different types of sensors (e.g., camera, microphone, GPS, thermometer, accelerometer, and communications like Wi-Fi, Bluetooth, and near field communications (NFC)) (Thejaswini, Rajalakshmi, & Desai, 2014). Due to the nature of human mobility, smartphones are immersed in scenarios subjected to Lévy-walks when monitoring environmental factors like temperature, humidity, urban noise pollution, carbon footprint, air pollution, and urban traffic (Thejaswini et al., 2014).

The search problem distinguishes between two kinds of interacting organisms: either a "searcher" (e.g., forager, predator, parasite, pollinator, the active gender in the mating process) or else a "target" (e.g., prey, food, the passive gender for mating) (Viswanathan et al., 1996). When compared to BM, it is known that the probability for returning to previously visited site of a particle making a Lévy-flight is smaller, and therefore advantageous when target sites are sparsely and randomly distributed (Rhee et al., 2011).

The nature of the searching drive can be guided almost entirely by external cues, either by the cognitive (memory) or detective (e.g., olfaction and vision) skills of the searcher. Nevertheless, in certain situations the movement is non-oriented, thus becoming a stochastic process (Stark & Woods, 2002) in essence. Therefore, in such cases (and even when a small deterministic component in the locomotion exists) it is a random search that defines the outcomes of biological activities (e.g., a predator cannot search for so long without finding food, or it will perish). It is known that Lévy-walks search patterns lead to optimal outcomes in computing (e.g., computer data bases and networks). These outcomes are possible because Lévy-walks can be applied not only to continuous spaces, but also to discrete ones (e.g., inherent discrete nature of searches in Internet or memory search in neural-networks) (Viswanathan, Raposo, & da Luz, 2008).

Since Lévy-walks reflect the nature of Internet traffic and relate to cybersecurity dynamics, using a time-domain feature extraction amenable for real-time computation is proposed. An example of such a technique is the zero-crossing rate (ZCR), evaluated over a moving window of either a fixed size or a variable size, whose parameters are selected formally. In the simplest form, the ZCR is a monoscale measure. The ZCR can be extended to multiscale and polyscale measures (Kinsner, 2014; Kinsner, 2011; Kinsner, 2007a; Kinsner, 2007b). Notice that there is no evidence in the literature that previous research in this niche has been conducted.

The well-known ZCR is a measure that estimates the complexity of a waveform directly in the time domain. It provides the general trends in the level of their overall frequency contents, thus conveying useful information about the signal (Rangayyan, 2002). This estimation of frequency in a signal is a companion to spectral transforms such as the monoscale short-time Fourier transform or the multiscale wavelet transform. The classical usage of ZCR in the analysis of biomedical signals is now expanded to the cybersecurity realm through this research.

Implementations of ZCR to operate in the frequency domain for signal analysis are available in the literature (Shenoy & Seelamantula, 2015). This is termed as the spectral zero-crossing rate (SZCR), where either the real or the imaginary parts of the frequency spectrum are considered. Signal analysis through SZCR provides information related to the transient locations within a temporal observation window. Signal analysis based on ZCR finds applications in spectral estimation, seismology, and speech processing (Kay & Sudhaker, 1986; Kedem, 1986; Rangayyan, 2002; Uppu & Mujumdar, 2012). Particularly in speech processing, ZCR has been utilized for voice activity detection (Benyassine, Shlomot, Su, Massaloux, Lamblin, & Petit, 1997), fundamental frequency estimation, formant extraction (Sreenivas & Niederjohn, 1992), and features formulation for speech recognition (Shenoy & Seelamantula, 2015). Signal analysis via ZCR has also been applied in practical applications such as speech signal analysis to perform speech versus silence decision and to discriminate between voiced and unvoiced sounds (Rangayyan, 2002). The problem of blind symbol estimation in carrier systems in which the modulation is unknown has been resolved applying analysis by ZCR. This research example affirms that ZCR as a signal processing technique possesses strong merits for both feature formulation and extraction even without knowledge about the system under analysis and its parameters (Elgenedy, & Elezabi, 2013).

Many signals are quasistationary, as is the case of speech, and their properties (e.g., level-crossings, zero-crossings, energy, and information theoretic related features) are often studied by segmenting them in windows that are stationary within that specific window (Shenoy & Seelamantula, 2012). Even though speech is a non-stationary signal, it remains nearly unvaried for small segments (i.e., for 10 to 50 ms) (Jalil, Butt, & Malik, 2013).

Stationarity ranges from wide sense stationarity (WSS) to strong sense stationarity (SSS). New and versatile approaches that stay away from extremes have been proposed in the literature, as is the case of finite sense stationarity (FSS) (Terrazas Gonzalez & Kinsner, 2013).

The rest of this paper is organized by providing the necessary background about DDoS attacks, the need of cognitive computing for detecting and mitigating attacks in cyberspace, Lévy-flights, ZCR, followed by the design of experiments and testing, experimental results and discussion of their relevance.

2. BACKGROUND

2.1. Overview of DDoS Attacks Types

Launching an effective DDoS attack requires cyber attackers to firstly establish a network of computers, which is known as a botnet or army. The individual controlling a botnet is called botmaster or botnet owner. Attackers take advantage of various techniques (referred to as scanning techniques) to find vulnerable hosts on the Internet to gain access to them (Peng et al., 2007; Stone-Gross, Cova, Gilbert, Kemmerer, Kruegel, & Vigna, 2011; Cho, Caballero, Grier, Paxson, & Song, 2010). The next step for the attacker is to install programs (known as attack tools) on the compromised hosts. The headquarters of a botnet is called command-and-control (C&C) server. The C&C server communicates with its bots for updating the attack tools, and issuing an attack orders (Yu, 2004).

Sustaining C&C servers from detection may require botnet programmers: (1) setting up intermediate nodes as stepping-stones between the C&C server and bots, and (2) encrypting the messages of their communication with cryptographic techniques (Stinson, 2006). Avoiding evictions may require botnet programmers using techniques like IP flux or domain flux, to conceal their C&C servers (Yu, 2004).

Two different DDoS attack classes: typical DDoS attack and distributed reflection denial-of-service (DRDoS) attack. Unlike a typical DDoS attacks, a DRDoS attack network consists of C&C servers and reflectors. In a DRDoS attack, the bots, led by C&C servers, send a stream of packets with the victim's IP address as the source IP address to uninfected machines (reflectors). A variation of a DDoS attack in cloud computing is the economic denial-of-sustainability (EDoS) attack (Sqalli, Al-Haidari, & Salah, 2011) or the fraudulent resource consumption (FRC) attack (Idziorek, Tannian, & Jacobson, 2013). DDoS defense can be classified into three categories: detection, mitigation and traceback (Yu, 2004).

Methods documented in the literature for DDoS attacks detection include: activity profiling (Feinstein, Schnackenberg, Balupari, & Kindred, 2003; Moore, Shannon, Brown, Voelker, & Savage, 2006), packet filtering (El-Atawy, Al-Shaer, Tran, & Boutaba, 2009; Soldo, Markopoulou, & Argyraki, 2009), sequential change-point detection (Chen & Hwang, 2006; Wang, Jin, & Shin, 2007), wavelet analysis (Barford, Kline, Plonka, & Ron, 2002; Tang & Cheng, 2011), among others. The methods mentioned beforehand are based on specific features or fingerprints of DDoS attacks (Ayres, Sun, Chao, & Lau, 2006; Kim, Lau, Chuah, & Chao, 2006; Kompella, Singh, & Varghese, 2007; Wang et al., 2007). Hence, these detection methods are passive and incapable of detecting new forms of DDoS attacks (Yu, 2004).

DDoS hit and run attacks consist of short packet bursts at regular or random intervals over a long period of time usually. What makes these threats different from other DDoS attacks is that they can last for days or even weeks. In addition, unlike other attacks, they are not continuous and are designed to specifically exploit slow-reacting anti-DDoS solutions. Despite the sophistication of other kinds of DDoS threats, hit and run attacks are of interest to attackers because of their low cost and ease of deployment (Imperva, 2015).

DDoS hit and run attacks wreak havoc with "on-demand" DDoS mitigation solutions that need to be manually engaged/disengaged with every burst. Such attacks are presently changing the face of the anti-DDoS industry, pushing it toward "always on" integrated solutions. Any mitigation that takes more than a few seconds is simply unacceptable (Imperva, 2015).

DDoS hit and run attacks last from 20 to 60 minutes in duration typically. After causing some collateral damage to a target, hit and run attacks occur again usually after another 12 to 48 hours. Common DDoS prevention solutions, such as generic routing encapsulation (GRE) tunneling and domain name system (DNS) rerouting, have become ineffective in dealing with hit and run attacks (Imperva, 2015).

In fact, hit and run attacks are becoming the most prominent threat in cyberspace in and on itself. On September 20, 2016, the website of a renowned security journalist Brian Krebs was hit with one of the largest distributed denial of service attacks (DDoS) to date, 620-665 Gbps (Krebs, 2016). It is almost twice the previous DDoS attack record holder of 363 Gbps seen previously this year, which was in the form of a reflection attack. Ten days later, the source code for Mirai, the botnet malware behind the attacks, was leaked. It was found that the Mirai botnet was responsible for a slew of GRE floods using a hit-and-run tactic (peaking at 130 Gbps and 280 Mpps) that were mitigated on August 17, 2016, by Incapsula. This DDoS attack uncovered 49,657 unique IPs hosting Mirai-infected devices distributed in 164 countries (mostly CCTV cameras, but also DVRs and routers). Mirai's C&C is coded in Go (a recent language developed by Google), while its bots are coded in C. Mirai is built for two core purposes: (1) locate and compromise IoT devices (via wide-ranging scans of IP addresses to locate under-secured IoT devices accessible with weak login credentials breakable through dictionaries) to further grow the botnet, and (2) launch DDoS attacks based on instructions received from the C&C. Some interesting features that Mirai has are: (1) capabilities to circumvent security solutions, (2) a hardcoded list of IP addresses for the bots to avoid (e.g., department of defense) when scanning so that ironically attention is not drawn to their activities (suggesting that the attack may have not been launched by professional cybercriminals, but yet highly skilled coders), and (3) a "territorial" nature by holding killers scripts to eradicate other worms and Trojans (e.g., killing processes using SSH, Telnet, and HTTP; and locating and eliminating competing botnet processes from memory) and preventing remote connection of the hijacked devices (Zeifman, Bekerman, & Herzberg, 2016).

Certainly, the Dyn DDoS attack on October 21, 2016, targeting its domain name servers (DNS), impacted various multinational Internet companies (e.g., Amazon, Twitter, GitHub, the New York Times, Pandora, Reddit, Pinterest, Shopify, Okta, Netflix, among others big-name outages) with the Mirai botnet. This novel DDoS attack has raised serious concerns about the security of the IoT where Botnets of things (BoT) are starting to appear (Imperva, 2016). Dyn claims that the sophisticated DDoS attack targeting its infrastructure involved 10s of millions of IP addresses (York, 2016).

Information security has three core elements: confidentiality, integrity, and availability. Availability is just as important as the other two elements. Data might be just fine, but no one can access it. DDoS attacks are no longer minor inconveniences, nor are they solely used by unsophisticated adversaries. As attackers harness botnets made of IoT devices or launch amplification attacks using network time protocol (NTP) and other network protocols, these attacks will get bigger and more damaging (Rashid, 2016).

The prime targets in the IoT for malicious parties wanting to add them to their botnets include and are not limited to smart appliances like smart televisions, refrigerators, laundry machines, dishwashers, toasters, home security systems, and automated thermostats (Pierson, 2016). Technically any computing system with networking capabilities is a potential in the new form of botnets that are IoT based. It can be impossible to tell whether or not a device has been compromised as it works exactly as they normally would. The IoT is not only expanding rapidly in the commercial realm, but also in specialized industrial networks where it is known as the Industrial Internet-of-Things (IIoT). The rapid growth of the many flavours of the IoT is a serious cybersecurity concern. Many IoT devices are capable of being compromised with malware. This puts a compromised system on the same network with home personal computers, corporate servers, and even sensitive government data (Pierson, 2016).

The IoT is the wave of the future, a world of autonomous cars and intelligent sidewalks and a scheme of a reality where needs are met before existing. The IoT allows everyone to have access to information whenever needed. During this journey to the future, it is important that to balance the growth of technology with security. After all, if millions of homes in the United States alone are going to be filled with smart devices in the next years, security should not be an afterthought (Pierson, 2016).

The research presented here aims for the completion of two goals. Firstly, comparing the pdfs of a real DDoS attack and the mathematical model of Lévy walks, and secondly analyzing the DDoS dataset via ZCR. Both of these research goals represent part of the ground-braking efforts found in the literature for matching the DDoS attack pdf to a mathematical model and analyzing a DDoS dataset with ZCR. Hence, these parts are relevant angles in this research, which highlight their potential applications for detection of DDoS attacks.

2.2. The Need of Cognitive Computing Based Cybersecurity Detection and Mitigation

The solutions to the new forms of cyberthreats are not based on static countermeasures, but highly self-aware computing systems. Such design approach is offered by the area of cognitive computing. This new area envisions new applications like cognitive machines, which are expected to act not only autonomously and be aware of their environment (including other machines and also human beings), but also in an increasingly intelligent and cognitive manner (Kinsner, 2006). Cognitive machines should have a high quality perception layer so that they would translate the perceived signals into information, also understanding its meaning, in a more human-like way (Kinsner, 2006). The development path for creating cognitive machines is based on human perception, attention, concept creation, cognition, consciousness, executive processes guided by emotions and value, and symbiotic conversational human-machine interactions (Kinsner, 2006). The motivation for developing such cognitive machines additionally allows gaining a better understanding of the cognitive capabilities of the human brain. Examples of cognitive machines research include cognitive radio, cognitive radar, and cognitive monitors (Kinsner, 2006). The IoT demands cognitive networking engines for making cyberspace a better place. However, in order to fulfill that goal there is a need for developing strong features helpful in classification.

Some developments related to cognitive informatics are: (1) designing highly secure cryptosystems (Terrazas Gonzalez & Kinsner, 2011), (2) assessment of the security degree of cryptosystems (Terrazas Gonzalez & Kinsner, 2012a; Terrazas Gonzalez & Kinsner, 2012b), (3) creating new paths in cognitive informatics bridging the gap from information to intelligence (Patel, Patel, Shell, Wang, Rolls, Howard, Raskin, Kinsner, Murtagh, & Bhavsar, 2015), (4) envisioning cognitive machines (Kinsner, 2006) or (5) designing high quality features for enhancing machine learning applications (e.g., Harada, Iwasaki, Mori, Yoshizawa, & Mizoguchi, 2014), among others. This research follows a new multiscale approach for designing high quality features that could be potentially helpful in cyberthreats detection and mitigation.

2.3. Lévy-Flight Foraging Hypothesis

A single and instantaneous displacement, in the Lévy-walks context, is known as Lévy-flight because its expression does not consider a time cost dependent on the distance. Lévy-walks take time into consideration (Rhee et al., 2011). According to the Lévy-flight foraging hypothesis (Viswanathan, Buldyrev, Havlin, da Luz, Raposo, & Stanley, 1999), since Lévy-flights optimize random searches biological organisms must exploit Lévy-flights (Viswanathan et al., 2008).

A Lévy-walk is a process where at each time step j the random walker makes an instantaneous jump ℓ_j chosen from a probability distribution function (pdf) $P(\ell)$ that has a power law tail in the long-distance regime (Viswanathan et al., 2008):

$$P(\ell) \sim \ell^{\mu} \tag{1}$$

with $1 < \mu \leq 3$. For $\mu < 3$ the second moment of $P(\ell)$ diverges and for $\mu < 2$ the first moment also diverges (Viswanathan et al., 2008). When $\mu \geq 3$, a special case, the Gaussian distribution emerges, while $\mu \leq 1$ corresponds to pdfs that cannot be normalized (Viswanathan et al., 1999).

Lévy-walks and -flights lead to super diffusion, which implies that the mean squared displacement of the position of the walker scales super linearly with time t. This concept is expressed as:

$$\left\langle x^2 \right\rangle \sim t^{2H} \tag{2}$$

where H represents the Hurst exponent (Viswanathan et al., 2008).

Lévy walks posses scale invariant and fractal properties (Kinsner, 2016). Zooming into a true Lévy-walk trajectory reveals a substructure with statistically identical properties to the original structure.

The Lévy probability distribution function, named after the French mathematician Paul Lévy, is formally defined as (Kinsner, 2016):

$$f_X(x) = \frac{\sqrt{\sigma}}{\sqrt{2\pi}\left(x-\mu\right)^{3/2}} e^{-\frac{\sigma}{2(x-\mu)}} \tag{3}$$

where σ and μ are the scale and location parameters respectively. Some important features of the Lévy distribution are: (1) it is defined for a non-negative random variable X, (2) its support takes higher values than its location parameter ($x \geq \mu$), and (3) its support is semi open extending to positive infinity $[\mu, \infty)$.

2.4. Zero-Crossing Rate Analysis

An intuitive indication of how "busy" a signal becomes can be estimated by the number of times it crosses either the zero-activity line for alternating signals, or some other reference level for oscillating signals. The ZCR is defined as the number of times the signal crosses the reference within a specified interval.

In its simplest form, the frequency of a sinusoid is estimated as half the number of zero-crossing counts per second (Shenoy & Seelamantula, 2015). More formally, ZCR is a measure of "frequency composition" of a signal, which is more valid for narrowband signals such as sinusoids (Jalil, Butt, & Malik, 2013). A sinusoid of frequency F_0 sampled with a frequency F_s produces F_s/F_0 samples per cycle, which posses two zero crossings per cycle. This results in the ZCR defined as (Jalil et al., 2013):

$$Z = \frac{2F_0}{F_s} \tag{4}$$

The interpretation of the average ZCR for broadband signals is less precise. However, the use of short-time average ZCR could provide good estimates of the signal properties (Jalil et al., 2013).

The definitions of ZCR for discrete computation is defined as (Jalil et al., 2013):

$$Z_n = \sum_{m=-\infty}^{\infty} \left|\left| \text{sgn}\left(x[n]\right) - \text{sgn}\left(x[m-1]\right) \right|\right| w[n-m] \tag{5}$$

where $\text{sgn}(\bullet)$ is defined as the sign function and $w[\bullet]$ represents the window containing a stationary segment of the signal under analysis.

The sign function is represented as (Jalil et al., 2013):

$$\text{sgn}(x[n]) = \begin{cases} 1, & x[n] \geq 0 \\ -1, & x[n] < 0 \end{cases} \qquad (6)$$

and the stationary window is (Jalil et al., 2013):

$$w[n] = \begin{cases} \dfrac{1}{2N}, & 0 \leq n \leq N-1 \\ 0, & \text{otherwise.} \end{cases} \qquad (7)$$

where N represents the total number of samples contained in the window. An estimation of the frequency content of a signal is provided by the ZCR by the occurrences, in a given time interval/frame, of a sign change in a given signal. The rate at which zero crossings occur is a simple measure of the frequency content of a signal.

Zero-crossing rate is very useful for discriminating a broadband signal from noise. Furthermore, ZCR helps in determining the beginning and the end of segments of interest in a signal (Jalil et al., 2013).

3. DESIGN OF EXPERIMENTS AND VERIFICATION

3.1. DDoS Dataset Access: Packets Count and Packets Length Analysis

Access to a DDoS dataset was granted through the United States Department of Homeland's PREDICT Project. This DDoS dataset contains an attack between two sites: (1) The Information Sciences Institute at the University of Southern California (ISI/USC) located in Marina del Rey California, California and (2) The Colorado State University (CSU) located in Fort Collins, Colorado. The ISI/USC hosted one attacker system (IP address: 145.233.157.236) and six recursive DNS servers (IP addresses: 145.233.157.224, 145.233.157.228, 145.233.157.232, 145.233.157.233, 145.233.157.234, and 145.233.157.235), while the CSU provided a single system as an intended target (IP address: 144.154.222.228). All data files containing the DDoS attack recording are in extensible record format (ERF), compressed with bzip2 (Department of Homeland Security (DHS) of the United States of America: PREDICT Project, 2013).

In this DDoS attack, all non-attack traffic has been anonymized and scrubbed. Since the attack traffic has been generated as part of an experiment (completely under control), it is known to not have any privacy concerns, and the payloads of traffic specific to the attack have been preserved (Department of Homeland Security (DHS) of the United States of America: PREDICT Project, 2013).

Attack queries are replayed at 400 packets per second, each packet containing a UDP DNS query, which is directed to one of the six ISI/USC servers in a round-robin fashion. Each IP packet is 64 bytes long, thus the bit rate of the attack before amplification/reflection is 64*400*8=205 Kbps. The data collection starts at 21:52:45 and ends at 22:25:32 on 17 June 2013. Within this window of time, the DDoS attack starts at 22:00:12 and concludes at 22:15:34. This dataset contains 59,928,921 packets from which the following relevant information is available: time stamp, source, destination, length, and protocol (Department of Homeland Security (DHS) of the United States of America: PREDICT Project, 2013). Within this Internet traffic segment, the DDoS attack packets count and packets length are shown in Figures 1 and 2 respectively. It is from these time series that the pdfs are further derived

Figure 1. Packets counts of Internet traffic in 100ms time intervals. The packets count averages are shown as a cyan coloured waveform. In the abscissa's axis, the numbers 4,469 and 13,393 denote the beginning and end of the DDoS attack.

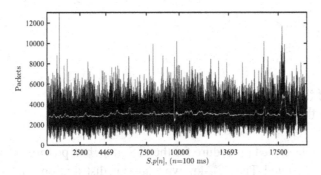

Figure 2. Internet traffic data rate in time intervals of 1s. The traffic data rate averages are shown as a cyan coloured waveform. In the abscissa's axis, the numbers 4,469 and 13,393 denote the beginning and end of the DDoS attack.

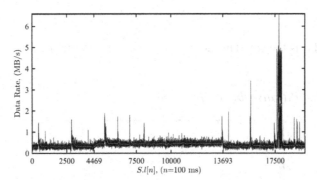

to observe their shapes. The Internet traffic features shown in Figures 1 and 2 are further investigated for resemblance of Lévy like distributions. Next, a method for prescribing arbitrary pdfs is introduced.

3.2. Generation of Prescribed Probability Distribution Functions (pdfs)

Synthetic generation of a process with the characteristics of a Lévy distribution is fundamental in this research. In order to achieve this objective, pseudo-random samples from a prescribed pdf are generated. This is a central procedure in the preparation of experiments in applied probability, statistics, computing, and physics (Olver & Townsend, 2013).

3.2.1. Inverse Transform Sampling

A classical approach is the inverse transform sampling (ITS), Smirnov transform, in which pseudo-random samples $U_{1,...,}U_N$ are generated from a uniform distribution U on the interval [0,1] and then transformed by $F_X^{-1}(U_1)$, ..., $F_X^{-1}(U_N)$, where F_X is the cumulative distribution function (CDF) of the prescribed pdf (Olver & Townsend, 2013). The uniform distribution is used in communication theory, in queuing models, and in situations where no a priori knowledge favouring the distribution of outcomes except for the end-points exists. The uniform distribution is formally defined as (Stark & Woods, 2002):

$$U = f_X(x) = \begin{cases} \dfrac{1}{b-a}, & a < x[n] < b \\ 0 & \text{otherwise.} \end{cases} \tag{8}$$

3.2.2. Verification of the Generation of the Gaussian Distribution through the Smirnov Transform

Following the previously described procedure for the ITS, it is then possible to verify that a prescribed Gaussian distribution is generated. The well-known Gaussian distribution, shown in Figure 3, is defined as (Stark & Woods, 2002):

$$f_X(x) = \frac{1}{\sqrt{2\pi\sigma^2}} e^{-\frac{1}{2}\left[\frac{x-\mu}{\sigma}\right]^2} \tag{9}$$

where μ is the mean and σ is the standard deviation (σ^2 is the variance).

Figure 3. Gaussian probability distribution function

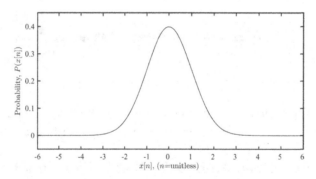

Through the ITS, the Gaussian CDF defined as:

$$F_X(x) = \frac{1}{2}\left[1 + \text{erf}\left(\frac{x-\mu}{\sigma\sqrt{2}}\right)\right] \tag{10}$$

and displayed in Figure 4, allows the remapping of the supports and probability weights from the uniform pdf to the Gaussian pdf.

A realization of random noise featuring a uniform distribution is shown in Figure 5, which only shows the first 1,000 samples. The length of this series is 200,000 samples long for the purposes of the experiments run in this research.

Figure 4. Cumulative distribution function of the Gaussian distribution

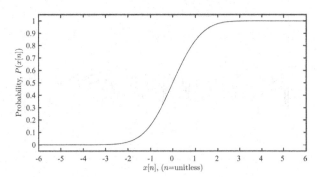

By making the uniform random noise shown in Figure 3 undergo through the ITS, with the prescribed Gaussian CDF shown in Figure 4, a series with the properties of a Gaussian distribution is obtained. This transformation is demonstrated in Figures 4 and 5, which denote the Gaussian random noise and its probability mass function (pmf) respectively.

Figures 6 and 7 serve as verification of the correct implementation of the ITS. Obtaining a pmf with a Gaussian like shape in Figure 7 is a clear indication of the supports and probability weights remapping through ITS.

Figure 5. A realization of uniform random noise with a length of 1000 samples

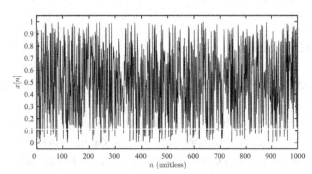

3.3. Zero-Crossing Rate Analysis of a Known Signal

This subsection explores the detection of the ZCR of an ordinary sinusoid with $F_0 = 1,000$ Hz and a $F_s = 10,000$ Hz over a time period of 100s. This experiment is intended to detect the sinusoid frequency and serves as implementation verification of the ZCR technique depicted previously by (5). Figure 8 shows the results of applying ZCR to the sinusoid described above. It is seen that a value of ZCR= 2,000 is obtained for each time window lasting one second (w= 10,000 samples). The value for this particular case being ZCR= $2F_0$ follows the fact that a sinusoid crosses zero twice.

In this section, the verification of the implementations of the Smirnov transform and ZCR has been presented. The next section elaborates on the experiments that are the core of this research.

Figure 6. Gaussian random noise

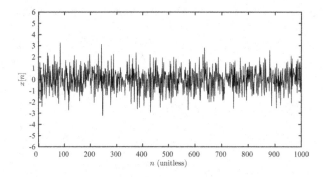

Figure 7. Gaussian probability mass function

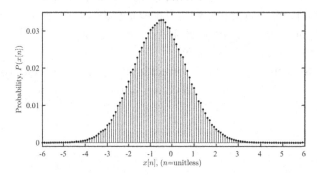

4. EXPERIMENTAL RESULTS

4.1. DDoS Attack: pmfs of Packets Count and Packets Length

From the DDoS dataset, packets count and packets length time series depicted in Figures 1 and 2, the frequency of occurrence of the events corresponding to both categories has been obtained. This is then used to visualize the pmfs of the packets count and packets length in the DDoS attack as shown in Figures 9 and 10.

Figure 8. Zero-crossing rate of a sinusoid with $F_0 = 1,000$ Hz

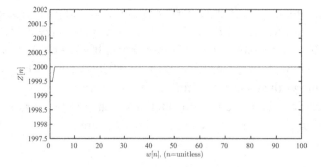

Figure 9. Packets count pmf in DDoS attack

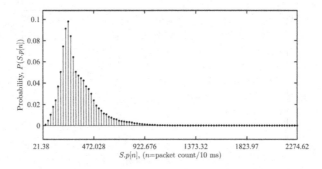

Figure 10. Packets length pmf in DDoS attack

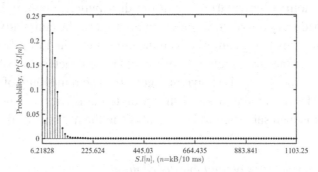

4.2. Generation of Synthetic Lévy-Walks Through a Prescribed Probability Distribution Function

Since the core of this research is Lévy-walks, the generation of a synthetic process with the characteristics of the Lévy distribution is posed, realized, and further investigated through ZCR. The Lévy distribution previously defined in (3) is shown in Figure 11. The location and scale parameters are set to $\mu=0$ and $\sigma=1/2$. The CDF of the Lévy distribution is shown in Figure 12. These parameters are chosen with these values to create a smooth long tailed pdf as demonstrated by Figure 11.

Figure 11. Lévy probability distribution function

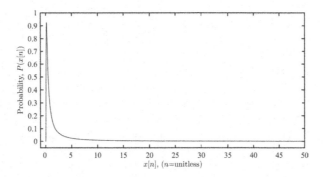

Figure 12. Cumulative distribution function of the Lévy distribution

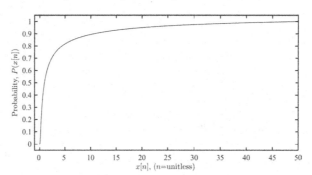

The realization of random noise featuring a uniform distribution shown in Figure 5 is fed through the ITS with the prescribed Lévy distribution shown in Figure 11. The cumulative distribution function depicted in Figure 12 allows mapping samples from the uniform to the Lévy distributions.

Figures 13 and 14 denote the generation of a series with the characteristics of the Lévy distribution. The pmf with Lévy like characteristics is shown in Figure 14. The remapping of the supports and probability weights through ITS from the uniform distribution to the Lévy distribution has been achieved. The synthetic Lévy-walk is then subjected to ZCR analysis in the next subsection.

Figure 13. Series with the properties of the Lévy distribution

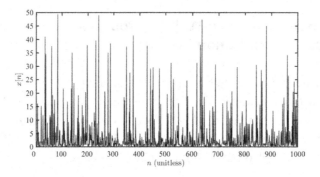

Figure 14. Lévy probability mass function

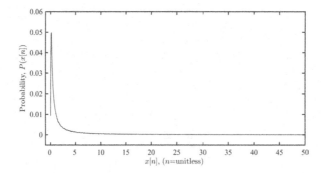

4.3. Zero-Crossing Rate Analysis of the Composite Signal

This section analyzes a composite digital signal (800,000 samples long). This signal has four distinct sections (200,000 samples long each): (1) Uniform noise, (2) a sinusoid with F_0= 1,000 Hz, (3) Gaussian noise, and (4) the synthetically Lévy-walk generated in the previous section. It is possible to identify these four different segments in Figures 15 to 18, whose features are further examined in the next section. The composite signal, in these four figures, is analyzed varying through four different window sizes. These different windows are 128 samples (Figure 15), 256 samples (Figure 16), 512 samples (Figure 17), and 10,000 samples (Figure 18), which correspond to 1562, 781, 390, and 20 windows per section under analysis respectively.

Figure 15. Zero-crossing rate analysis for a window size of 128 samples

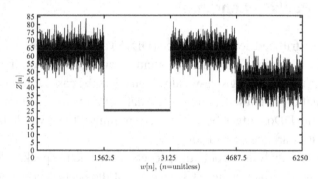

Figure 16. Zero-crossing rate analysis for a window size of 256 samples

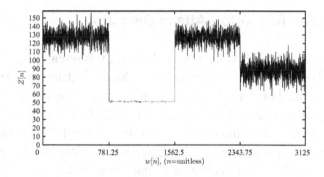

Figure 17. Zero-crossing rate analysis for a window size of 512 samples

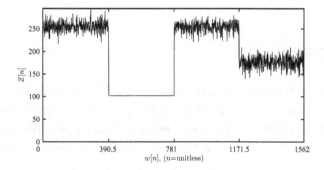

Figure 18. Zero-crossing rate analysis for a window size of 10,000 samples

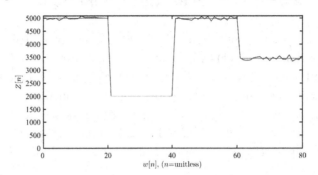

4.4. Zero-Crossing Rate Analysis of the DDoS Dataset Packets Count and Packets Length

The dataset describing a distributed denial of service (DDoS) attack is inspected in this subsection. This dataset is analyzed via ZCR within a varying-size window and focusing on the packets count and the packets length (bandwidth). The varying size-window considers the cases studies previously of 128, 256, and 512 samples. The dual focus in the features of the dataset aims to determine which of them would match the occurrence of the DDoS attack best. This determining if there would be clear resemblance of the attack occurrence in its start and conclusion.

The ZCR windows for the analysis for both the packets count and the packets length are 128 samples, 256 samples, and 512 samples. The graphic ZCR analysis of the packets count and length are shown in the sets of Figures 19 to 21 and Figures 22 to 24, respectively.

4.5. Embedded Hit and Run DDoS Attack Detection

During the close inspection of the DDoS dataset available for this research, an embedded DDoS attack with the properties and fingerprint of a hit and run attack has been detected. This embedded DDoS attack is shown in Figure 25 and lasts for approximately 40 seconds. Twelve bar markings are seen in this figure, which denote typical activity of a hit and run DDoS attack. Two of these bars, second and fifth, are not very high in bandwidth. It is important to mention that this DDoS dataset has been inspected actively in the literature and finding the resemblance to what seems to be a hit and run DDoS attack is reported by the first time via the efforts made through this research. It is also important to point out that the presence of this hit and run attack is not documented in the description provided by the facilitators of this dataset.

5. DISCUSSION OF RESULTS

Two prescribed probability distribution functions (pdfs), the Gaussian and the Lévy, are considered in this paper. The former is used for implementation validation of the Smirnov transform and the latter is the focus of this research. The Smirnov transform can be utilized for prescribing an arbitrary pdf, which in this paper has been demonstrated by synthetically generating two distinct probability distributions in

Figure 19. Zero-crossing rate analysis of the DDoS dataset packets count for a window size of 128 samples

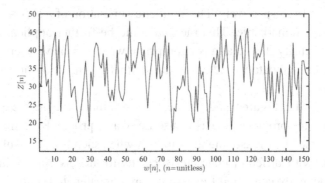

Figure 20. Zero-crossing rate analysis of the DDoS dataset packets count for a window size of 256 samples

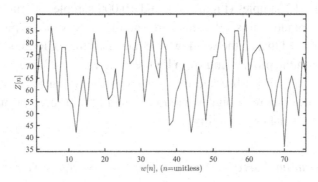

Figure 21. Zero-crossing rate analysis of the DDoS dataset packets count for a window size of 512 samples

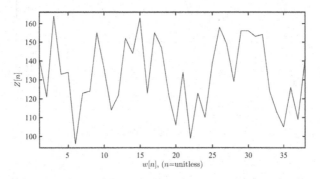

Figure 22. Zero-crossing rate analysis of the DDoS dataset packets length for a window size of 128 samples

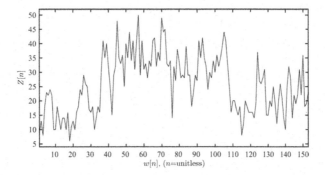

their discrete form (pmfs). The characteristic shapes of both the Gaussian and the Lévy pdfs have been obtained in Figures 7 and 14, respectively. The synthetic generation of a series with the characteristics of the Lévy distribution is remarkable. This method could be further applicable to modeling of processes relevant in cybersecurity. This claim is appropriate when pdfs have been derived from real data. Hence, a pdf derived from real data would allow the synthetic generation of series with the statistical characteristics of real data.

From the results obtained in Figure 9 and 10, it can be seen that these pmfs clearly resemble the Lévy probability distribution. This provides a basis to use Lévy as a probabilistic model that resembles the properties of Internet traffic. This reasoning also applies when such traffic is subject of a DDoS attack.

Four distinct signals with different characteristics (uniform noise, an ordinary sinusoid, Gaussian noise, and the synthetically generated Lévy-walk) are concatenated, into a composite signal. This composite signal is analyzed with ZCR utilizing four different window sizes, 128 samples (Figure 15), 256 samples (Figure 16), 512 samples (Figure 17), and 10,000 samples (Figure 18). The ZCR average values of the two types of random noise, the sinusoid, and the Lévy walk are plotted in blue, green, and red respectively. It is observed that as the window size increases the ZCR value becomes steadier. This phenomenon can be seen in the progression from Figure 15 to Figure 18 and it is directly related to the sensitivity of the window size. It is observed that a bigger window causes a smaller variability in the ZCR values obtained. Furthermore, a bigger window would have a more prominent filtering impact, which in turn is a cause for smaller variability.

Figure 23. Zero-crossing rate analysis of the DDoS dataset packets length for a window size of 256 samples

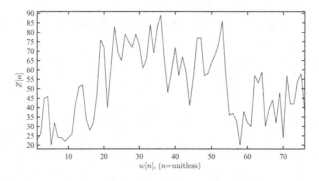

Figure 24. Zero-crossing rate analysis of the DDoS dataset packets length for a window size of 512 samples

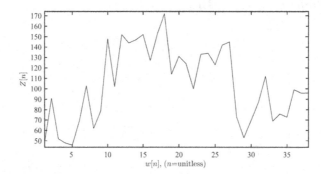

Figure 25. Embedded negligible DDoS attack with the properties of what is considered a hit and run attack

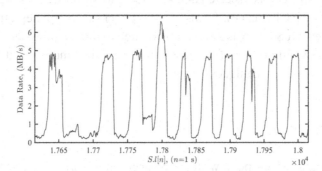

The two random types of noise included in the signal, uniform and Gaussian in the first and third sections respectively, posses the highest ZCR values. These values are averaging 63.5 (Figure 15), 127.5 (Figure 16), 255 (Figure 17), and 5,000 (Figure 18) as denoted by the blue lines. The reason for the ZCR value to be increasing is that a bigger window size, with potentially more zero-crossings, is considered subsequently. It should be stated here that the ZCR values for random noise are not representative of its frequency contents, as both the estimation of high frequency broadband signals through ZCR is not precise.

The value of the ZCR of the ordinary sinusoid depicted in the second section of the four figures appears to be very steady. The reason for this ZCR value being so constant is that the number of zero-crossings of a sinusoid follows a known and predictable pattern. The sinusoid ZCR average value (denoted in green) is of 25.4, 51.1, 102.7, and 2000, for the 128, 256, 512, and 10,000 window sizes respectively. The reason for the big jump for a window size of 10,000 samples is to verify that the double (2,000 Hz) of the fundamental frequency (1,000 Hz) of the sinusoid is obtained. This follows from the verification of the implementation of ZCR that was previously described in section three.

For the synthetically generated Lévy-walk signal case, it can be seen that it is located between the ZCR values for the ordinary sinusoid and the two forms of random noise. The average value (denoted in red) of ZCR for the synthetic Lévy-walk rank in 43.8, 88, 176.8, and 3,447 for the 128, 256, 512, and 10,000 window sizes, respectively.

From the extracted ZCR values shown in Figures 15 to 18, a reliable method has been presented. The four experiments validate the differentiation of the synthetic Lévy-walk. These findings provide a strong justification for potentially using these features in signal classification. These features, which are based in ZCR, can clearly fingerprint the four different sections present in the composite signal used for experimentation in the previous section.

The overall structure of behaviour change through the different sections in the composite signal is maintained in the analysis through different window sizes. This structure becomes better defined as the window size increases as shown in Figures 17 and 18.

The analysis of the DDoS dataset by ZCR visually demonstrates that the packets count shows no correlation to the attack occurrence. Nevertheless, all window sizes selected (128, 256, and 512 samples) for the ZCR analysis of the packets length visually point to the identification of both the start and conclusion of the DDoS attack. Figures 22 to 24 show a high correlation with the bandwidth shown in Figure 2. This similarity particularly resembles the DDoS attack occurrence. However, the three window sizes show no indication of having detected the DDoS hit and run attack. This fact verifies why such attacks are trending now in cyberspace. It is expected that the DDoS form of hit and run attack and its variations would become more pervasive in the new forms of cyberattacks. Nevertheless, the non-detection of the hit and run version of the DDoS attack is more likely related to the window sizes used so far. The detection of hit and run DDoS would require finer resolution analysis windows and possibly some support from alternate signal processing techniques.

6. CONCLUSION

A method for prescribing arbitrary pdfs, with the Smirnov transform as its base, has been evaluated. This method was used to generate a reliable synthetic process with the characteristics of Lévy-walks, which reflect the dynamics of Internet traffic and has potential for being relevant in cybersecurity. A Lévy-walk pdf has been obtained after the transformation method has been applied to uniform noise. The method for prescribing arbitrary pdfs works effectively for any distribution as long as this would have a continuous CDF. This has advantages like: (1) overcoming the difficulty of accessing real data that featuring a given pdf, or (2) synthetically generating a series with a desired pdf as presented in the implementation verification and experimentation in this research.

It has been demonstrated that the Lévy probability distribution is a suitable mathematical model for resembling Internet traffic. This even in the presence of a cyberattack as is the case of a DDoS. This finding is of relevance for the cybersecurity research that is looking constantly for strengthening the cyberspace, particularly IoT, against cyberattacks.

The direct computation in the time-domain for obtaining the ZCR is advantageous for real-time implementations of feature extraction of signals. This feature extraction has been applied successfully to a composite signal embedding characteristics like uniform noise, a sinusoid, Gaussian noise, and the synthetically generated Lévy-walk. The analysis of this composite signal through windows of different sizes has consistently shown that the ZCR values obtained have a degree of locality, which becomes more defined as the window size value increases the number of samples considered in it. Similarly, three of the sections (i.e., uniform noise, Gaussian noise, and Lévy-walk) embedded in the composite signal appear to reflect some complex dynamics in the evolution of the ZCR value.

Additionally, this study provides an insight about the ability of ZCR to identify sections in a composite signal having different properties embedded, as demonstrated through four different experiments. The main finding in this work has been that the different signals have been identified consistently. For Lévy walks, it has been shown that the ZCR value is between an ordinary sinusoid and a random noise. Together with other features, the ZCR can be used for identification of significant transitions in a complex signal.

Furthermore, the practical application of ZCR in cybersecurity has been shown by inspecting a dataset containing a documented DDoS attack. This inspection unveiled clearly the beginning and the end of the DDoS attack when inspecting its bandwidth (packets length) within the selected varying-size window (128, 256, and 512 samples). This is a remarkable and critical part in this study because ZCR can assist in real-time identification of DDoS attacks.

REFERENCES

Atkinson, R. P. D., Rhodes, C. J., Macdonald, D. W., & Anderson, R. M. (2002). Scale-free dynamics in the movement patterns of jackals. *Oikos*, *98*(1), 134–140. doi:10.1034/j.1600-0706.2002.980114.x

Ayres, P. E., Sun, H., Chao, H. J., & Lau, W. C. (2006). ALPi: A DDoS defense system for high-speed networks. *IEEE Journal on Selected Areas in Communications*, *24*(10), 1864–1876. doi:10.1109/JSAC.2006.877136

Balkanli, E., Alves, J., & Zincir-Heywood, A. N. (2014). Supervised learning to detect DDoS attacks. *Proceedings of the 2014 IEEE Symposium on Computational Intelligence in Cyber Security, 2014 CICS* (pp. 1–8), Orlando, FL, USA. http://doi.org/10.1109/CICYBS.2014.7013367

Barford, P., Kline, J., Plonka, D., & Ron, A. (2002). A signal analysis of network traffic anomalies. *Proceedings of the 2nd ACM SIGCOMM Workshop on Internet Measurement* (pp. 71–82). inproceedings, New York, NY, USA: ACM. http://doi.org/10.1145/637201.637210

Beitollahi, H., & Deconinck, G. (2014). ConnectionScore: A statistical technique to resist application-layer DDoS attacks. *Journal of Ambient Intelligence and Humanized Computing*, *5*(3), 425–442. doi:10.100712652-013-0196-5

Benyassine, A., Shlomot, E., Su, H., Massaloux, D., Lamblin, C., & Petit, J.-P. (1997, September). ITU-T recommendation G.729 annex B: A silence compression scheme for use with G.729 optimized for V.70 digital simultaneous voice and data applications. *IEEE Communications Magazine*, *35*(9), 64–73. doi:10.1109/35.620527

Bhuyan, M. H., Kashyap, H. J., Bhattacharyya, D. K., & Kalita, J. K. (2014). Detecting distributed denial of service attacks: Methods, tools and future directions. *The Computer Journal*, *57*(4), 537–556. doi:10.1093/comjnl/bxt031

Chen, Y., & Hwang, K. (2006). Collaborative detection and filtering of shrew DDoS attacks using spectral analysis. *Journal of Parallel and Distributed Computing*, *66*(9), 1137–1151. doi:10.1016/j.jpdc.2006.04.007

Cho, C. Y., Caballero, J., Grier, C., Paxson, V., & Song, D. (2010). Insights from the inside: A view of botnet management from infiltration. *Proceedings of the 3rd Conference on Largescale Exploits and Emergent Threats, Botnets, Spyware, Worms, and More, USENIX*.

Department of Homeland Security (DHS) of the United States of America. (2013). PREDICT Project. Scrambled Internet trace measurement dataset. Retrieved from http://www.isi.edu/ant/lander

El-Atawy, A., Al-Shaer, E., Tran, T., & Boutaba, R. (2009). *Adaptive early packet filtering for defending firewalls against DoS attacks. In 2009* (pp. 2437–2445). IEEE INFOCOM; doi:10.1109/INFCOM.2009.5062171

Elgenedy, M. A., & Elezabi, A. (2013). Blind symbol rate estimation using autocorrelation and zero crossing detection. *Proceedings of the 2013 IEEE International Conference on Communications ICC '13*, Budapest, Hungary (pp. 4750–4755). http://doi.org/10.1109/ICC.2013.6655324

Feinstein, L., Schnackenberg, D., Balupari, R., & Kindred, D. (2003). Statistical approaches to DDoS attack detection and response. *Proceedings of the 2003 DARPA Information Survivability Conference and Exposition* (Vol. 1, pp. 303–314). http://doi.org/10.1109/DISCEX.2003.1194894

Harada, T., Iwasaki, H., Mori, K., Yoshizawa, A., & Mizoguchi, F. (2014). Evaluation model of cognitive distraction state based on eye tracking data using neural networks. *Int. J. Softw. Sci. Comput. Intell.*, *6*(1), 1–16. Doi:10.4018/ijssci.2014010101

Idziorek, J., Tannian, M. F., & Jacobson, D. (2013). The insecurity of Cloud utility models. *IT Professional. IT Professional*, *15*(2), 22–27. doi:10.1109/MITP.2012.43

Imperva. (2015). *The top 10 DDoS attack trends*. Imperva.

Imperva. (2016). The DDoS attack on Dyn: A recap from Imperva. Retrieved from http://www.informationsecuritybuzz.com/articles/ddos-attack-dyn-recap-imperva/

Jalil, M., Butt, F. A., & Malik, A. (2013). Short-time energy, magnitude, zero crossing rate and autocorrelation measurement for discriminating voiced and unvoiced segments of speech signals. *Proceedings of the 2013 International Conference on Technological Advances in Electrical, Electronics and Computer Engineering, 2013 TAEECE*, Konya, Turkey (pp. 208–212). http://doi.org/10.1109/TAEECE.2013.6557272

Karim, A., Salleh, R., Shiraz, M., Shah, S., Awan, I., & Anuar, N. (2014). Botnet detection techniques: Review, future trends, and issues. *Computers & Electronics*, *15*(11), 943–983. doi:10.1631/jzus.C1300242

Kaspersky Lab. (2014). *Global IT Security Risks Survey 2014 – Distributed Denial of Service (DDoS) Attacks*. Moscow, Russia: Kaspersky Lab.

Kay, S. M., & Sudhaker, R. (1986). A zero crossing-based spectrum analyzer. *IEEE Transactions on Acoustics, Speech, and Signal Processing*, *34*(1), 96–104. doi:10.1109/TASSP.1986.1164784

Kedem, B. (1986). Spectral analysis and discrimination by zero-crossings. *Proceedings of the IEEE*, *74*(11), 1477–1493. doi:10.1109/PROC.1986.13663

Kim, Y., Lau, W. C., Chuah, M. C., & Chao, H. J. (2006). PacketScore: A statistics-based packet filtering scheme against distributed denial-of-service attacks. *IEEE Transactions on Dependable and Secure Computing*, *3*(2), 141–155. doi:10.1109/TDSC.2006.25

Kinsner, W. (2006). Towards cognitive machines: Multiscale measures and analysis. *Proceedings of the 5th IEEE International Conference on Cognitive Informatics ICCI '06*, Beijing, China (Vol. 1, pp. 8–14). Doi:10.1109/COGINF.2006.365667

Kinsner, W. (2007a). A unified approach to fractal dimensions. *International Journal of Cognitive Informatics and Natural Intelligence*, *1*(4), 26–46. doi:10.4018/jcini.2007100103

Kinsner, W. (2007b). Is entropy suitable to characterize data and signals for cognitive informatics? *International Journal of Cognitive Informatics and Natural Intelligence*, *1*(4), 34–57. doi:10.4018/jcini.2007040103

Kinsner, W. (2011). It's time for multiscale analysis and synthesis in cognitive systems (Keynote speech). *Proceedings of the 2011 10th IEEE International Conference on Cognitive Informatics & Cognitive Computing ICCI*CC '11* (pp. 7–10). 10.1109/COGINF.2011.6016116

Kinsner, W. (2012). Towards cognitive security systems. *Proceedings of the 2012 IEEE 11th International Conference on Cognitive Informatics & Cognitive Computing ICCI*CC '12,* Kyoto, Japan (p. 539). 10.1109/ICCI-CC.2012.6311207

Kinsner, W. (2014). Polyscale analysis and fractional operators for cognitive systems. *Proceedings of the 2014 IEEE 13th International Conference on Cognitive Informatics & Cognitive Computing, 2014 ICCI*CC* (pp. 6–7), London, UK. http://doi.org/10.1109/ICCI-CC.2014.6921433

Kinsner, W. (2016). *Fractal and Chaos Engineering: Lecture Notes*. Winnipeg, MB, Canada: University of Manitoba.

Knowles, W., Prince, D., Hutchison, D., Disso, J. F. P., & Jones, K. (2015). A survey of cyber security management in industrial control systems. *International Journal of Critical Infrastructure Protection, 9*, 52–80. doi:10.1016/j.ijcip.2015.02.002

Kompella, R. R., Singh, S., & Varghese, G. (2007). On scalable attack detection in the network. *IEEE/ACM Transactions on Networking, 15*(1), 14–25. doi:10.1109/TNET.2006.890115

Krebs, B. (2016). KrebsOnSecurity hit with record DDoS. Retrieved from https://krebsonsecurity.com/2016/09/krebsonsecurity-hit-with-record-ddos/

Kriaa, S., Pietre-Cambacedes, L., Bouissou, M., & Halgand, Y. (2015). A survey of approaches combining safety and security for industrial control systems. *Reliability Engineering & System Safety, 139*, 156–178. doi:10.1016/j.ress.2015.02.008

Kyprianou, A. E. (2014). *Fluctuations of Lévy Processes with Applications: Introductory Lectures* (2nd ed.). Heidelberg, Germany: Springer. doi:10.1007/978-3-642-37632-0

Moore, D., Shannon, C., Brown, D. J., Voelker, G. M., & Savage, S. (2006). Inferring Internet denial-of-service activity. *ACM Trans. Comput. Syst., 24*(2), 115–139. Doi:10.1145/1132026.1132027

Nurzaman, S. G., Matsumoto, Y., Nakamura, Y., Koizumi, S., & Ishiguro, H. (2009). Yuragi-based adaptive searching behavior in mobile robot: From bacterial chemotaxis to Lévy walk. *Proceedings of the 2008 IEEE International Conference on Robotics and Biomimetics, 2008 ROBIO,* Bangkok, Thailand (pp. 806–811). http://doi.org/10.1109/ROBIO.2009.4913103

Olver, S., & Townsend, A. (2013). Fast inverse transform sampling in one and two dimensions. *Mathematics: Numerical Analysis, 29*.

Özçelik, İ., & Brooks, R. R. (2015). Deceiving entropy based DoS detection. *Computers & Security, 48*, 234–245. doi:10.1016/j.cose.2014.10.013

Patel, S., Patel, D., Shell, D. F., Wang, Y., Rolls, E. T., Howard, N., ... Bhavsar, V. C. (2015). Cognitive informatics and computational intelligence: From information revolution to intelligence revolution. *Int. J. Softw. Sci. Comput. Intell. IJSSCI, 7*(2), 50–69. doi:10.4018/IJSSCI.2015040103

Peng, T., Leckie, C., & Ramamohanarao, K. (2007). Survey of network-based defense mechanisms countering the DoS and DDoS problems. *ACM Comput. Surv., 39*(1). Doi:10.1145/1216370.1216373

Pierson, R. M. (2016). DDoS attack sheds new light on the growing IoT problem. Retrieved from http://readwrite.com/2016/10/24/dyn-ddos-attack-sheds-new-light-on-the-growing-iot-problem-dl4/

Ramos-Fernandez, G., Morales, J. L., Miramontes, O., Cocho, G., Larralde, H., & Ayala-Orozco, B. (2004). Lévy walk patterns in the foraging movements of spider monkeys. *Behavioral Ecology and Sociobiology, 55*, 223–230. doi:10.100700265-003-0700-6

Rangayyan, R. M. (2002). *Biomedical Signal Analysis: A Case-Study Approach*. Piscataway, NJ, USA: IEEE Press.

Rashid, F. Y. (2016). Dyn DDoS attack exposes soft underbelly of the cloud. Retrieved from http://www.infoworld.com/article/3134023/security/dyn-ddos-attack-exposes-soft-underbelly-of-the-cloud.html

Rhee, I., Shin, M., Hong, S., Lee, K., & Chong, S. (2008). On the Levy-walk nature of human mobility. *Proceedings of the 27th IEEE Conference on Computer Communications, 2008 INFOCOM,* Phoenix, AZ, USA (pp. 924–932). 10.1109/INFOCOM.2008.145

Rhee, I., Shin, M., Hong, S., Lee, K., Kim, S. J., & Chong, S. (2011). On the Levy-walk nature of human mobility. *IEEE/ACM Transactions on Networking, 19*(3), 630–643. doi:10.1109/TNET.2011.2120618

Shenoy, R. R., & Seelamantula, C. S. (2012). Spectral zero-crossings: Localization properties and application to epoch extraction in speech signals. Proceedings of the 2012 International Conference on Signal Processing and Communications, 2012 SPCOM, Bangalore, India (pp. 1–5). http://doi.org/10.1109/SPCOM.2012.6290218

Shenoy, R. R., & Seelamantula, C. S. (2015). Spectral zero-crossings: Localization properties and applications. *IEEE Transactions on Signal Processing, 63*(12), 3177–3190. doi:10.1109/TSP.2015.2420538

Shlesinger, M. F., Klafter, J., & Wong, Y. M. (1982). Random walks with infinite spatial and temporal moments. *Journal of Statistical Physics, 27*(3), 499–512. doi:10.1007/BF01011089

Soldo, F., Markopoulou, A., & Argyraki, K. (2009). *Optimal filtering of source address prefixes: Models and algorithms. Proceedings of* INFOCOM '09 (pp. 2446–2454). IEEE. Doi:10.1109/INFCOM.2009.5062172

Sqalli, M. H., Al-Haidari, F., & Salah, K. (2011). EDoS-shield - A two-steps mitigation technique against EDoS attacks in Cloud computing. *Proceedings of the 2011 4th IEEE International Conference on Utility and Cloud Computing UCC '11* (pp. 49–56). Doi:10.1109/UCC.2011.17

Sreenivas, T. V., & Niederjohn, R. J. (1992). Zero-crossing based spectral analysis and SVD spectral analysis for formant frequency estimation in noise. *IEEE Transactions on Signal Processing, 40*(2), 282–293. doi:10.1109/78.124939

Stark, H., & Woods, J. W. (2002). *Probability and Random Processes with Applications to Signal Processing. Prentice Hall* (3rd ed.). Upper Saddle River, NJ, USA: Pearson-Prentice Hall.

Stinson, D. R. (2006). *Cryptography: Theory and Practice* (3rd ed.). Boca Raton, FL, USA: CRC Press Inc.

Stone-Gross, B., Cova, M., Gilbert, B., Kemmerer, R., Kruegel, C., & Vigna, G. (2011). Analysis of a botnet takeover. *IEEE Security & Privacy Magazine*, *9*(1), 64–72. doi:10.1109/MSP.2010.144

Tang, J., & Cheng, Y. (2011). Quick detection of stealthy SIP flooding attacks in VoIP networks. *Proceedings of the 2011 IEEE International Conference on Communications ICC '11* (pp. 1–5). 10.1109/icc.2011.5963248

Terrazas Gonzalez, J. D., & Kinsner, W. (2011). A modular dynamical cryptosystem based on continuous-interval cellular automata. *International Journal of Cognitive Informatics and Natural Intelligence. International Journal of Cognitive Informatics and Natural Intelligence*, *5*(4), 27. doi:10.4018/jcini.2011100106

Terrazas Gonzalez, J. D., & Kinsner, W. (2012a). A modular dynamical cryptosystem based on continuous-interval cellular automata. In Y. Wang (Ed.), *Cognitive Informatics for Revealing Human Cognition: Knowledge Manipulations in Natural Intelligence* (pp. 261–286). Hershey, PA, USA: IGI Global. Doi:10.4018/978-1-4666-2476-4

Terrazas Gonzalez, J. D., & Kinsner, W. (2012b). Evaluating the security level of a cryptosystem based on chaos. *International Journal of Software Science and Computational Intelligence*, *4*(3), 80–120. doi:10.4018/jssci.2012070105

Terrazas Gonzalez, J. D., & Kinsner, W. (2013). Comparison of selected cryptosystems using single-scale and poly-scaly measures. *Proceedings of the 2013 12th IEEE Intern. Conf. on Cognitive Informatics & Cognitive Computing ICCI*CC '13*, New York, NY, USA. Doi:10.1109/ICCI-CC.2013.6622230

Thejaswini, M., Rajalakshmi, P., & Desai, U. B. (2014). Novel sampling algorithm for Levy-walk based mobile phone sensing. *Proceedings of the 2014 IEEE World Forum on Internet of Things WF-IoT '14*, Seoul, South Korea (Vol. 2, pp. 496–501). 10.1109/WF-IoT.2014.6803217

Uppu, R., & Mujumdar, S. (2012). Lévy exponents at critical excitation of nanostructured random amplifying media. *Proceedings of the 2012 International Conference on Fiber Optics and Photonics PHOTONICS '12*, Chennai, India (pp. 1–3) . 10.1364/PHOTONICS.2012.M3A.3

Viswanathan, G. M., Afanasyev, V., Buldyrev, S. V., Murphy, E. J., Prince, P. A., & Stanley, H. E. (1996). Levy flight search patterns of wandering albatrosses. *Nature*, *381*(6581), 413–415. doi:10.1038/381413a0

Viswanathan, G. M., Buldyrev, S. V., Havlin, S., da Luz, M. G. E., Raposo, E. P., & Stanley, H. E. (1999). Optimizing the success of random searches. *Nature*, *401*(6756), 911–914. doi:10.1038/44831 PMID:10553906

Viswanathan, G. M., Raposo, E. P., & da Luz, M. G. E. (2008). Lévy flights and superdiffusion in the context of biological encounters and random searches. *Physics of Life Reviews*, *5*(3), 133–150. doi:10.1016/j.plrev.2008.03.002

Wang, H., Jin, C., & Shin, K. G. (2007). Defense against spoofed IP traffic using hop-count filtering. *IEEE/ACM Trans. Netw.*, *15*(1), 40–53. Doi:10.1109/TNET.2006.890133

York, K. (2016). Dyn statement on 10/21/2016 DDoS attack. Retrieved from http://dyn.com/blog/dyn-statement-on-10212016-ddos-attack/

Yu, S. (2014). *Distributed Denial of Service Attack and Defense*. New York, NY, USA: Springer; doi:10.1007/978-1-4614-9491-1

Zeifman, I., Bekerman, D., & Herzberg, B. (2016). Breaking down Mirai: An IoT DDoS botnet analysis. Retrieved from https://www.incapsula.com/blog/malware-analysis-mirai-ddos-botnet.html

This research was previously published in the International Journal of Software Science and Computational Intelligence (IJSSCI), 8(4); edited by Brij Gupta and Andrew W.H. Ip; pages 1-28, copyright year 2016 by IGI Publishing (an imprint of IGI Global).

Chapter 22

Taxonomy of Distributed Denial of Service (DDoS) Attacks and Defense Mechanisms in Present Era of Smartphone Devices

Kavita Sharma

National Institute of Technology Kurukshetra, India

B. B. Gupta

National Institute of Technology, Kurukshetra, India

ABSTRACT

This article describes how in the summer of 1999, the Computer Incident Advisory Capability first reported about Distributed Denial of Service (DDoS) attack incidents and the nature of Denial of Service (DoS) attacks in a distributed environment that eliminates the availability of resources or data on a computer network. DDoS attack exhausts the network resources and disturbs the legitimate user. This article provides an explanation on DDoS attacks and nature of these attacks against Smartphones and Wi-Fi Technology and presents a taxonomy of various defense mechanisms. The smartphone is chosen for this study, as they have now become a necessity rather than a luxury item for the common people.

1. INTRODUCTION

Communication is the basic requirement of human beings after air, water, food, clothes, and shelter. As human beings are social animals, they need to communicate. If the history of communication is looked upon, there was only one medium of communication; direct communication where a person communicated with another person present in front of him/her through direct talking. This was followed by exchanging written notes initially in near-by places followed by far-off places through birds like pigeons. They continued up to our recent past, but their mode upgraded by continuously removing associated limitations. Graham Bell changed the field of communication by introducing telephone to the world that

DOI: 10.4018/978-1-7998-5348-0.ch022

revolutionized the communication sector. The telephone was further modified into cellular or mobile phones. Initially, these were only used for communicating voice. However, modern mobile phones are too much different from initial mobile phones. At the same time, computer and laptop industries have grown largely. People started to perceive the need for the computer and mobile phones in daily life. Laptops were developed so that they could be carried from one place to another, but they were still bulky (Zargar, Joshi, & Tipper, 2013).

Therefore, a need was felt to propose several computing features in mobile phones as they can be carried in the pocket easily. Mobiles slowly turned to be a media with much more facilities than simple voice communication devices and were further developed as Smartphone. The smartphone is a huge success to the communication sector, and its variety, sale, and facilities are increasing day-by-day. With an increasing utilization of Smartphone in the public domain, they have become vulnerable to security attacks. There are many types of security attacks, but we emphasize here on DoS to current two Smartphone operating system iOS and Android (Zargar & Joshi, 2010).

DDoS attack targets that Smartphone a linked to the Internet. This attack generally performed in a group form to a Smartphone and attempt is made to disrupt each other's operations in the network. These have some common reasons to attack, but the organizations realize its impact only after the attack has occurred. Oftentimes, attacks form a part of cyber crimes where the main aim is to bring down the competitor's operating system. These attacks can be repelled by analyzing attacker's nature and the path used by him/her for sending DDoS messages. To combat this problem, many organizations are providing DDoS mitigation & DDoS protection services (Al Quhtani, 2017; Yao, Ruohomaa & Xu, 2012). The target and the solution of DoS attacks are shown in Figure 1.

Figure 1. Target and solution of DoS attacks (source: authors' work)

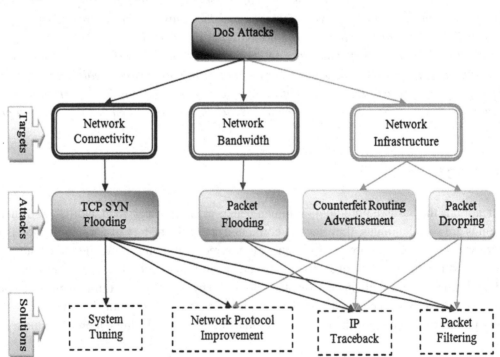

DDoS is used to interrupt a legitimate user by overwhelming all the resources and bandwidth of the mobile. This is achieved by performing simultaneous attacks from multiple sources.

To launch DDoS attacks (Alomari, Manickam, Gupta, Karuppayah & Alfaris, 2012; Gupta, Misra & Joshi, 2008; Chhabra, Gupta & Almomani, 2013), following two techniques are generally used:

1. **Malford Packets:** In this technique, the attacker sends some malformed packets in the network to perplex the victim.
2. **Interruption:** In this technique, attacker attacks in either of two ways:
   ○ Exhausting the resources of legitimate users
   ○ Exhausting the server resources of legitimate users

DDoS attacks are initiated remotely by creating botnet in the network; which further hires zombie (Trojan horse / Worm) to attack the network. Our Contribution to this paper is several. Initially, our main aims to review the recent research work of the DDoS attacks and its defense mechanisms in Smartphone as per today scenario. As cited, there are numerous studies on the DoS attack over mobile and computer technology. Still, only a few researchers explained the DDoS attack in the Smartphone devices. Authors mainly explored the DDoS attack and their defense mechanisms for computer technology. For example, Zaroo (2002) investigated the different facet of DDoS attacks and their defence techniques. Arora, Kumar and Sachdeva (2011) explored that Internet is rising at a fast pace; which has escorts to raise the vulnerability of the network. The biggest threat is the DDoS attack. An overview of the DDoS problem and major factors causing DDoS attacks has been also expressed. Therefore, another contribution of this paper is the taxonomy of DoS attacks in Smartphone. In addition, by analysing specific research work in DDoS attack, we also discuss some issues and challenges in defending the Smartphone beside DDoS attack. This gives enhanced information to recognizing of the DDoS attack problem in Smartphone, present solution for the research gap. The smartphone, being an increasingly popular device is vulnerable to DDoS Attack. There is much security flows in almost all Smartphone operating system, which makes them vulnerable to DDoS Attack. We will cover the main popular operating system like Android and iOS. "Permanent Denial of Service" (PDoS) is also recognized as Phlasing. Where in the damage is to an extent that even hardware needs to be reinstalled or completely replaced. This attack may be much faster than DDoS and necessitates few more resources than DDoS attack and pure targeted to hardware (Mirkovic & Reiher, 2004).

This paper is structured as follows: Section 2, presents related work of DDoS attack in the Smartphone. Section 3 discusses the overview of Smartphone and its operating system. Section 4 discusses the DDoS attack architecture in detail. Taxonomy of DoS attacks on Smartphone is presented in section 5. Taxonomy of defense mechanisms against DDoS attacks is discussed in section 6. Finally, Section 7 concludes the paper and discusses the scope for future work.

2. RELATED WORK

The Smartphone is a hardware device that includes both characteristics of the mobile device as well as the computer with some advanced features. In simple words, it can be defined as the hybrid of mobile and computer technology. It can be used from simple communication to software designing, running and installing different software, which was not earlier possible in mobile phones. Today, Smartphone contains several new facilities like accelerometer, map guide, etc. They have so much of facilities that they have to begin to challenge personal computers. The modern generation of mobile device and the operating systems like iOS, Android, Windows, and RIM are a great success. They are an easy target for security breaches and attacks (Dondyk, Rivera & Zou, 2013).

Jailbreaking and rooting are two terms used for gaining root access in iPhone and Android respectively (Miller, Honoroff & Mason, 2007). Users can add a capability to remotely access their device by the installation of SSH server. This requires jailbreaking on an iOS device. The simple reason behind jailbreaking requirement is that the user can install those applications, which didn't get approval from Apple's certificate authority. Vulnerabilities present with source can be explained for jailbreaking current generation iPhones. On the other hand, Hardware revision generally requires patching.

SSH server can itself be vulnerable for iOS security. If anybody gets default passwords and/or superuser value, he/she can change it and can remotely access the device. An attacker could steal information and even execute the system call.

Installing and using the server for an Android-based device does not require root access. However, unlike devices, those which are run in the root of Android and have SSH server installed, are less valuable. There is no such concept of superusers and passwords. So, there is no default value for an attack to the user. Many efforts have been made in Android to save the root. Manufacturers have released hardware with security features that can cause devices to fail when the root is attacked. Historical highlights of DDoS attacks is shown in Table 1 and Defense mechanisms against DDoS attacks are shown in Table 2.

Table 1. Historical Highlights of DDoS Attacks; Source: Authors' work

S. No.	Year	Attack
1.	1999	Testimony of first DDoS attack was provided by Computer Incident Advisory Capability.
2.	2000	Yahoo website was infected for 2 hours.
3.	2002	Domain Name Server services were infected for few hours.
4.	2004	SCO group website was infected. No legitimate user was able to access it. The same website was attacked using the mydroom virus.
5.	2009	In South Korea, Mydroom virus code was reused for DDoS attacks on many government, media, and financial websites.
6.	2010	Mastercard, Paypal, Visacom, Postfinance, and Visa website faced DDoS attacks.
7.	2012	Serial DDoS attacks were performed on websites of 9 major U.S. Banks. These attacks were named as "Izz ad-din Qassam".
8.	2013	The DDoS attack on e-banking using Smartphone Trojans was reported in the 17th semi-annual report published by the Reporting and Analysis Centre for Information Assurance (MELANI).
9.	2014	Akamai, the company known for its cloud services, detected 17 DDoS attacks which had generated traffic of more than 100 Gbps.

Table 2. Defense Mechanisms against DDoS Attacks; Source: Authors' work

S. No.	Year	Author	Research Article	Explanation
1.	2002	Zaroo, 2002	"A Survey of DDoS attack and some DDoS defense mechanism"	Different facets of DDoS attacks and defense techniques covered.
2.	2004	Mirkovic & Reiher, 2004	"A taxonomy of DDoS attack and DDoS defense mechanisms"	Common and significant features of attack approach, defense tools and the specific approaches of these tools against DDoS attacks are discussed. These approaches have created a better solution.
3.	2004	Specht & Lee, 2004	"Distributed Denial of Service: Taxonomy of Attacks, Tools, and Countermeasures"	Similarity and pattern of different DDoS attacks are explained. They have also included the software used to perform the attack that helped in generalizing solution for fighting against DDoS attacks.
4.	2004	Chen, Longstaff & Carley, 2004	"Characterization of defense mechanisms against distributed denial of service attack"	Describes the congestion based, anomaly based & source based techniques of DDoS attack. Defense is classified based on both destination network & source work filtering.
5.	2011	Mishra, Gupta & Joshi, 2011	"A Comparative study of Distributed Denial of Service Attacks, Intrusion Tolerance and Mitigation Techniques"	Classifications & defense mechanism used to detect prevent and tolerate the DDoS attacks are given.
6.	2012	Beitollahi & Deconinck, 2012	"Tackling Application-layer DDoS Attacks"	A method Connection Scores against application-layer, which resists the DDoS attack (DDoS attack exploits network and destroys the victim server with the help of zombie).
7.	2012	Devi & Yogesh, 2012	"An Effective Approach to Counter Application Layer DDoS Attacks"	Detection of DDoS attacks during normal flows as well as flows from the Flash Crowd.
8.	2013	Bhuyan, Kashyap, Bhattacharyya et al., 2013	"Detecting Distributed Denial of Service Attacks: Methods, Tools, and Future Directions"	A comprehensive study of DDoS attacks, detection methods, & tools used in wired networks.
9.	2013	Sivabalan & Radcliffe, 2013	"A Novel Framework to detect and block DDoS attack at the Application layer"	An algorithm for detecting and blocking DDoS attacks in Network layer in case of failure of Application Layer methodology.
10.	2013	Sanmorino & Yazid, 2013	"DDoS Attack Detection Method and Mitigation Using Pattern of the Flow"	By using pattern flow entries, they handled a DDoS attack on the firewall. Tests were carried out using three scenarios: normal network environment, unsecured network, and secure network.
11.	2013	Zargar, Joshi & Tipper, 2013	"A Survey of Defense Mechanisms Against Distributed Denial of Service (DDoS) Flooding Attack"	DDoS attack problem is explained and categorized. Existing countermeasures are classified based on where and while, can prevent, detect, & respond to the DDoS flooding attacks.
12.	2014	Liao, Li, Kang et al., 2014	"Feature extraction and construction of application layer DDoS attack based on user behaviour"	DDoS is a big black hole in the network security and web service is a mainly susceptible application. Authors have analyzed the user behaviour as per the web log.
13.	2014	Arora, Kumar & Sachdeva, 2011	"Impact Analysis of Recent DDoS Attacks"	The Internet is growing at a fast pace; which has led to increase in the vulnerability of the network. The biggest threat is the DDoS attack. An overview of the DDoS problem and major factors causing DDoS attacks has been expressed.

3. OVERVIEW OF SMARTPHONE

Smartphone devices on which Android OS runs allows only manufacturers and cellular carriers to modify its operating system. It is a closed access system and is referred to as a new cellular tradition. However, making its source code available represents a general computing tradition (Singh & Sharma, 2016). Smartphone platform consists of two elements: General purpose computing environment, and Cellular environment.

The general-purpose computing environment helps the owner to interact with Smartphone including user interface GUI, mathematical computation, and graphics, while cellular environment contains baseband chip that interacts with the mobile network (Figure 2). While doing a call, operating system hands voice stream to baseband chip for transmission (Sharma & Gupta, 2016). These interactions protect and secure device owner's communication and protect cellular carrier network (Traynor, Enck, McDaniel & Porta, 2009).

Figure 2. Smartphone Platform; Source: Authors' work

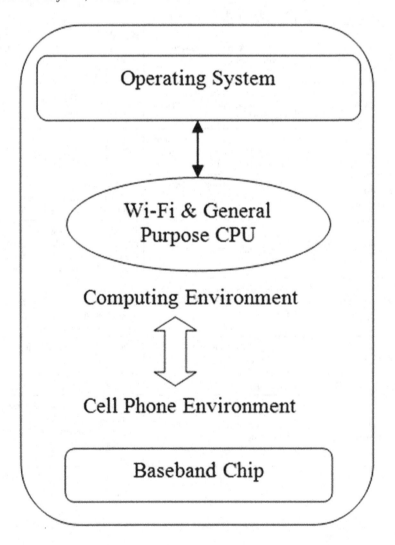

3.1. iPhone Operating System (iOS)

Apple's iPhone is one of publicize and most popular product. Apple released its first iPhone on June 29, 2007. It proved to be of great success, outpacing traditional mobile companies like Nokia, Motorola, & LG. It is a mobile phone included with the music player, video player, digital camera, images, data library and many things. It has very useful widgets for road maps, weather conditions, location with email & many other internet capabilities. Features of iPhone include a soft and user-friendly keypad and a capability to amalgamate calls easily as well as obtain voicemail information visually. It contains some of its prior released iPods facility. It has a fully advanced web browser with zoom-in and zoom-out feature; automatically switch onto the best Wi-Fi network that makes internet surfing easy, convenient and better than ever. Multi-touch display allows gliding, scrolling along with zooming (Apple iOS Software, 2017; Pandya, 2008).

3.2. Android

Google defined Android as "The First truly, open and compression platform for the mobile device, all of the software to run a mobile phone but without the proprietary obstacles that have hindered mobile innovation." Android is an arrangement of the following three major components: "A free, open-source operating system (OS) for mobile devices, an open-source development platform" for developing the application, and the device that runs Android OS.

The Android architecture comprises five layers (Enck, Octeau, McDaniel & Chaudhuri, 2011):

1. **Linux Kernel:** Android is developed as on Linux Kernel version 2.5 for core system services, which include process management and APC. It also provides a link between the hardware and the android layer (Kim, Smith & Shin, 2008);
2. **Libraries Layer:** It is just above the Kernel Layer and contains various C and C++ core libraries such as SSL. It provides the useful tool to upper layers used by application framework services;
3. **Android Runtime Layer:** Similar to Java & .Net, Android also has its own runtime & virtual machine; to deal with the application memory. Android runtime also manages the process lifetime. The virtual machine is Dalvik process virtual machine. It executes application files index format (Wyatt, 2018);
4. **Application Framework Layer:** It is used to create Android applications as this layer provides system server, which contains various modules for managing the device and interaction with them using Linux;
5. **Application Layer:** This is the layer on which all the application (from native applications to third-party applications) are built using apl libraries. It is the topmost layer in the software attack and compromises of both user and system applications, which have been installed and executed on the device.

Android is said to be open source, while it is open only to some extent. It is open at the user level and the system level but closed at the chip level. Individuals are not allowed to access source code file, which interfaces with baseband, camera, and other many devices of the system. While a developer can change elements at the user application level, he/she is not permitted and can't change elements at another level of the OS (Reisinger, 2013).

Threats of malware have also been observed in Android. For example, DroidDream & DroidDream Light; which materialized in Android market in mid-2011, challenged Android security implications. These applications steal confidential data and are similar to Trojan (Shrivastava & Kumar, 2017).

Malware that achieves root access can pose the serious challenge of security in Android. Root access permits malware to access low-level functionality of Operating System and can bypass most of the operating system protection. The malware can also flash device ROM and modify the operating system with a harmful mimic. It could lead to denial of service attacks (Sadeghi, Bagheri, Garcia & Malek, 2017).

3.3. Windows

Windows is developed by Microsoft for Smartphone. Windows mobile phones are not well-suited by dwarf platform but it has the good number of users. Windows Phone, Microsoft formed an innovative user interface, emphasizing a designed language called "Modern" (which was earlier acknowledged as "Metro"). Unlike its predecessor, it is originally aimed at the consumers rather than the enterprise market. It was initially originated in October 2010 with Windows Phone 7 and 8.1, which were released in concluding form by developers on April 14, 2014 (Zhang, Liang, Li, Liu, Zhao & Chen, 2018).

3.4. Attacks on Current Generation Smartphone

Jailbreaking and rooting are two respectively terms used for gaining root access in iPhone and Android. Users can add a capability to remotely access their device by installation SSH server. This requires jailbreaking of the iOS device. A simple reason behind jailbreaking requirement is that the user can now install the applications, which have not get approval from Apple's certificate authority. Vulnerabilities present with the source are feasible by jailbreaking current generation iPhones. Any patching requires hardware revision (Bose, 2008).

SSH server can itself be vulnerable for iOS security. As anyone gaining default passwords and super-user value, it can remotely access device unless the user has changed. An attacker could steal information and even issue system calls (Becher, 2009).

In an android based device, installing or using server does not require root access. However, unlike devices, those are having Android, i.e., rooted and have SSH server installed, are less valuable. There is no concept of superusers and passwords, and there is no default act of values for an attack on the user. Many efforts have been made in android to prevent rooting and manufacture have released hardware with security features that can cause devices to full, fail as attempted to root (Beitollahi & Deconinck, 2012).

4. DDOS ATTACK ARCHITECTURE

DoS refer to denial of service and major security attacks, which are faced in the digital world. It is simply denied use to a service or application, which a legitimate user is authorized to use. It is an attempt, to build machine or network resources occupied by the intended user. Motives for DoS attack is varied but usually consist of an effort to provisionally or permanently interrupt or suspended service. The denial of service attack is a violation of acceptable-polices and laws of the individual nation (Ranjan, Swaminathan, Uysal & Knightly, 2006).

There is two most common type of DoS attack: Crash services and Flood service. The DDoS attack does not attack a particular protocol/system. It can prove to be fatal for a huge network. The attacker analyzes weakness of the network, discovers the victim; and infects it by a malicious code (Peng, Leckie & Ramamohanarao, 2007). The infected machine further discovers victim machines and infects them. This process keeps on continuing with the connected machines; till a botnet is created. The system that is compromised and creates infection is called Master/handler or Zombie. Master gives the instruction to zombies and accordingly zombies perform the designated operation in the network. DDoS attack consumes resources of the victim system like bandwidth, memory CPU cycles, and allocated buffer (Carl, Kesidis, Brooks & Rai, 2006).

There are two most common forms of DoS attack: Direct DDoS Attack, and Reflective DDoS Attack.

DDoS flooding attacks are classified differently based on two major criteria as (Douligeris & Mitrokotsa, 2004): Protocol-Based, and Botnet Based. Additionally, IRC based and Web based occurs.

Protocol-Based Attacks

Protocol-Based attacks are presented in figure 3, where two types of DDoS Attacks are presented: (1) Network/Transport level DDoS flooding attack, and (2) Application level DDoS flooding attack.

Network/Transport level DDoS flooding attack can be done on packets follow TCP, UDP, ICMP and DNS Protocols. This is further categorized into four attacks: (1) Flooding attack: In this, attacker interrupts legitimate user connectivity by using resources of victim network's bandwidth, like UDP flood, ICMP flood, etc., (2) Protocol exploitation flooding attack: In this, the attacker exploits the malicious program of victim's protocol and consumes victim resources; (3) Reflection based flooding attack: In this, an attacker sends a forgery message in the network and the victim gets the response to messages back and exhausts victim's resources; and (4) Amplification-based flooding attacks: In this, the attacker sends a large size of the message or multiple messages to the victim; so that the traffic is increased and the bandwidth is exhausted (Wang, Jin & Shin, 2007).

Application level DDoS flooding attack presumes that the attacker disturbs the legitimate user and accesses their services like CPU, memory, bandwidth. DNS amplification flooding attack and SIP flooding attack are two well-known flooding attacks in application level (Abliz, 2011).

4.1. Botnet Based Attacks

It is used to launch DDoS attacks on the network. Where in a large, a number of zombies are used in the distributed network and zombie's IP address is spoofed by an attacker. It makes the process of tracing back the traffic and zombies very difficult. In the botnet, an attacker controls all zombies. In this, a set of the installed program in the system is used for communication with another system. This system is infected by the zombie and the victim system is attacked (Liu, Xiao, Ghaboosi, Deng & Zhang, 2009). An attacker sends the command to the handler and handler executes this command and sends it to the bots; that forces bots to attacks the victim system. It can be classified into three parts while only two are used to launch DDoS flooding attacks as per figure 4.

Figure 3. Protocol-Based DDoS Flooding Attack Classification; Source: Authors' work

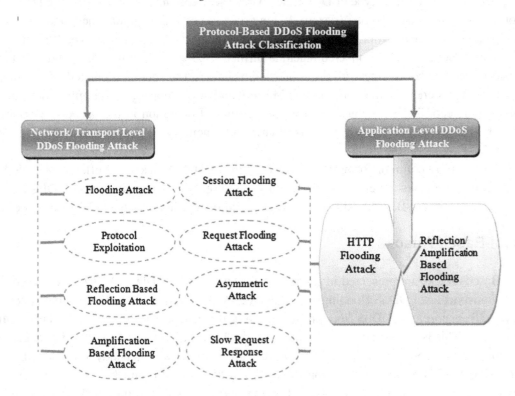

Figure 4. Botnet Based DDoS Flooding Attack Classification; Source: Authors' work

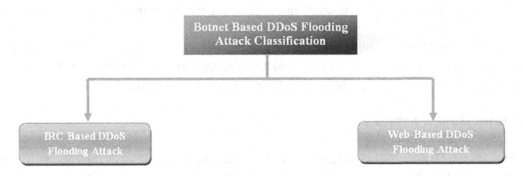

4.1.1. IRC based

The client-server architecture is used to attack online instant messaging. The attacker uses IRC port as the handler and sends the command to bots to share malicious code with the network. It can be executed with botnet tool, which has been developed for DDoS attacks such as TRINTY V3.

4.1.2. Web based

In this, HTTP is used to send the command to bots. It becomes difficult to trace and detect DDOS command and structure, as the attacker hides everything within valid HTTP traffic. Bots are configured & managed via PHP script and encrypted communication is used over HTTP/HTTPS. Three types of botnet tools used are: Black energy, Orbit –ION cannon, and ALDI.

5. TAXONOMY OF DOS ATTACKS ON SMARTPHONE

DoS attack is different from those attack that steals personal information as in DoS attack is made to prevent using services. Even after much hardware and software advancement, one of the major problems with android service is power consumption. An attacker can drain the battery life of device if the network is attacked (Li & Im, 2011; Devi & Yogesh, 2012):

1. **SYN Attack:** When time frame is too short then attackers use this technique to generate heavy network traffic. In this attack, an attacker repeatedly changes the level of TCP connection through on /off to the aimed device and performed very rapidly as possible. Generated Network traffic can drain off the battery. However, such attacks can also be simply carried out on other devices (Wyatt, 2018).
2. **Ping Flooding Attack:** It is based on the firmware feature of the ping command on most of the operating system. This can be utilized to generate the huge amount of network traffic to the targeted device. It does not require any open TCP parts, so it is better than SYN attack for the attacker, as SYN attack have this drawback (Nakashima & Oshima, 2006).

SYN attack and Pink flooding attack are active in draining the battery of a Smartphone while ping attacks are especially, effective and are attractive because of lack of any firewalls on Smartphone. However, it necessitates several circumstances to be fulfilled for its successful operation which make it inferable. But, it is a striking option for attacking (Apple, 2018).

Depleting Smartphone power makes the user unable to use, thus making the situation worse. This type of attack is called *Denial of Sleep*. These are flooding attack, which generates a large amount of network traffic for drainage the power (Mulliner, 2009).

5.1. Denial of Convenience Attack to Smartphone

Most popular Smartphone and iPhone are susceptible to Denial-of-Convenience (DoC) attack. It is one of the specific types of DoS attack. In this scheme, Smartphones are reprised of using internet services. Android and iPhone have a unique feature to automatically switch on the Wi-Fi access and doesn't utilize the limited broadband data plan for the users. But, these devices don't check whether the Wi-Fi access point (AP) has an internet connection or not. An attacker can use this flaw to reject appropriate service to the legitimate user on these Smartphone (Swami & Tschofenig, 2006).

DoC attacks are easy to launch, as it only requires a Wi-Fi AP that does not have the Internet connection. This can be done simply through a computer equipped with probable Wi-Fi adapter. When

Smartphone come into range of this AP, it does not have any interest in connection. Thus, the user will not be allowed to use Internet services.

5.2. iMessage DDoS Attack on iPhone

It is a recent quite new DDoS attack, and damaging. Several iOS developed became victims of an iMessage DDoS attack that crashed their app, inhibited the matching devices, and make them unable to use. These attacks used simple Apple scripts and when the attackers executed to send unlimited, fast pace- the number of messages, may be a number of large messages, the app would either crash or would shell our notification at an annoyingly, frustratingly, and alarming rate (Dixon & Mishra, 2010).

However, till now these types of attacks have been seen to be limited to a small group of people. It has been observed only for devices that have been jailbroken. However, the vulnerability of iPhone that has not jailed broken, are expected to be included in the future. They are also prone to such attacks and anybody can be a victim. In addition, they have a potential of becoming widespread, can easily communicate attacker for this DDoS attack, as it requires e-mail address of the person to be attacked. Once the e-mail address is obtained DDoS attack can be easily performed (Chen, Hwang & Ku, 2007). These types of DDoS attack are able to install these devices, as iMessage queue need to be cleared in order to perform any other actions. This attack can also be performed by mass sending of Unicode character for large messages, which ends up crashing of iMessage app and preventing the user from reopening it. As per (Robinson, G., & Weir, G. R., 2015, September), there are no real and effective solutions to this problem besides disability iMessage app (Russello, Conti, Crispo & Fernandes, 2012).

6. DEFENSE AGAINST SMARTPHONE DDOS ATTACKS

This attacker-victim relationship follows the principle of a funnel; in which attacker is placed at the top-end and victim at the narrow bottom end obtains all the attack flows produced by the attacker (Geva, Herzberg & Gev, 2014; Daswani, Mysen, Rao, Weis, Gharachorloo & Ghosemajumder, 2008; Tariq, Hong & Lhee, 2006).

6.1. Defense Against Smartphone Attacks (Mirkovic & Reiher, 2004)

Defense against static identified validation attack is using the similar approach to NSCI feature used by the Microsoft Windows. This can be called as authentication verified whether the currently connected AP has a running Internet connection or not without requiring user's authentication (Miller, Pearce, Grier, Kreibich & Paxson, 2011).

The process consists of two phases:

1. The smartphone comes in the vicinity of Wi-Fi AP and a Wi-Fi connection is established (Xie, Song, Jaeger & Zhu, 2008). Wi-Fi authentication sends a validation process to validation server and waits for the response. If the response doesn't come within specified time, AP is considered invalid. However, if the response is received, it performs second step (Habib, Jacob & Olovsson, 2008).

2. It composed of validation key, which is stored in Smartphone to retrieves validation key received from validation server.

If the both AP matches the same then only AP is considered to valid else it is considered invalid.

Defense against Dual channel validation attack is defined as follows. An attacker with a good technical knowledge can defeat the security of static validation, as validation key is static. In order to prevent fake validation response, dynamic validation key can be utilized. It is done by relying on the distinctive broadband data channel of Smartphone that cannot be simply attacked or blocked by an attack (Bickford, O'Hare, Baliga, Ganapathy & Iftode, 2010; Huegen, 2000).

The process consists of five phases: "(1) Smartphone's encounters with accessible Wi-Fi AP; it generates an indiscriminate key & sends it along with a MAC address to validate a server via the cellular network. This data, however, can be sent as an SMS/TCP packet (Miller, Pearce, Grier, Kreibich & Paxson, 2011, July); (2) Validation server stores a random key in a table that is used as the MAC address of the Smartphone as the index (Shrivastava, Sharma & Rai, 2010, December); (3) The smartphone is transmitted from mobile broadband to Wi-Fi connection; Smartphone sends a challenge to validation server with its MAC address (Daswani, Mysen, Rao, Weis, Gharachorloo & Ghosemajumder, 2008); (4) The validation server or AP will send the response to the corresponding Smartphone's MAC address; and (5) Validation response is compared against that generated earlier by the Smartphone. The Wi-Fi connection is considered valid if these two keys match; otherwise invalid" (Reisinger, 2013).

Defense against Network Performance Monitoring Attack is defined as follows. Dual channel validation can be compromised by selective internet traffic throttling if the attacker has Internet access. The dual channel validation is because they are not a priori in the validation list (Wong, 2005).

If an attacker has the Internet connection, he/she can execute DoS attack by permitting validation process to achieve validation server while blocking the entire traffic (Gupta & Badve, 2017).

This problem can be resolved through talking defense into consideration for the network identification. If the traffic is blocked in such a case, the network awareness protocol would identify the network performance and identify that traffic. If it is lesser than its lower bound called threshold limit, then it would resume data services. From mobile broadband, the common approach is to do packet drops, instant throughput, and average through the output (Shrivastava & Kumar, 2017).

In SYN flooding attacks, attacker drains the memory assigned for TCP connection by releasing many uncompleted connections. This is a kind of DoS or DDoS attack for flooding victim. The mainly trendy approach of initiating the DoS or DDoS attack is flooding's victim network. However, it can be prevented by using a firewall that filters out spontaneous traffic before it can accomplish victim's node. SYN flooding can be prevented by blocking SYN from fake source IP address (Kim, Smith & Shin, 2008).

6.2. Defense Mechanisms of Application-Level DDoS Flooding Attacks

These mechanisms observe the server and client behaviour, and then detect unwanted packet/traffic in the network and drop the malicious request (Wei, Mao, Jeng, Lee, Wang & Wu, 2012). The major methods besides application level DDoS flooding attacks are as follows (Sivabalan & Radcliffe, 2013): Destination based (server-side) methods & DDoS Defence Categorization. The Destination based (server-side) methods are as follows: (1) Defense against Reflection/Amplification Attacks: Machine learning techniques are used to identify malicious traffic from different protocols like SIP and DNS, and (2) DDoS-Shield: Statistical approaches are used to identify HTTP session.

DDoS attacks do not have any common characteristics. So, it is difficult to solve this problem and DDoS is difficult to trace back. It is classified into four parts: "Submissive Defense Mechanism, Categorization by Counter Defense Mechanism, Categorization by Action, and Classification by Defense Deployment Position".

6.2.1. Submissive Defense Mechanism

It is performed when the DDoS attack is detected. Submissive defense mechanism performs traffic restrictive, blocking & filtering through examining inbound network traffic. It is categorized into two different parts: Identifying Mechanism & Counter mechanism (Keshariya & Foukia, 2010).

Identifying Mechanism is based on the following categories: "(1) Traffic Degree Monitoring: It is easy and fast approach to identify traffic monitoring, although it cannot distinguish between actual attack & flash attack; (2) Source IP Address Monitoring: According to packet analysis, it can be identified and differentiated between real attack and crowd flash attack; and (3) Packet Attribute Analysis: It analyzes features of the packet and then identifies the attack."

Counter Mechanism: When attack signs are detected, defense mechanism should execute several counters measures. Following measures includes: (1) Filtering: Filter is spoofed with IP packet. It is efficient when it is installed on a universal scale; (2) Congestion Control: The packet flow is analyzed and attack is detected in the network. It is unsuccessful if low bandwidth is detected; (3) Submission Trace-Back: It identifies DDoS attack root source & starts functionality subsequent to the attack starts and is easy to install. The drawback is that it takes time to set up the path; which is inappropriate for a quick defense scheme; (4) Reproduction: This procedure necessitates no additional overhead. If the attacking environment is distributed, the recourses can still be shattered by the attack.

6.2.2. Categorization by Counter Defense Mechanism

It endeavours to manage the attack as early as possible; so that damages can be reduced. It consists of four parts: (1) Base end defense: It faces high false alarm and is less responsive to come across attack signs, (2) Mapping trackback: It observes malicious packet path and reconstructs the attack path; (3) Packet marking traceback: It is not effective when the number of attack nodes increases. It takes figure print of the router IP address and no extra packet is stored and (4) Protocol-based defense: It is not extensively installed as it is a barrier to manage the DDoS attack.

6.2.3. Categorization by Action

It is categories into three parts: (1) Invasion Prevention: It is a good way to remove DDoS attack. It has universally synchronized filters, and traffic can be attacked and blocked before damage resources; (2) Invasion detection: the Previous signature is identified and data mining, techniques are applied, and (3) Invasion response: When the attack is detected; root node is identified and the attacked traffic is blocked. Traffic pattern analysis, ICMP traceback, etc., techniques are in use.

6.2.4. Categorization by Defense Deployment Position

It is categories into three parts: (1) Basic Network Mechanism: Attack is detected before entering into the network layer. Egress filter abolishes the spoofed packets approaching from the closest source; (2) Transitional Network Mechanism: Transitional network can follow the traffic and traceback; (3) Destination Network Mechanism: Uses the high computational algorithm to combat from attack.

6.3. DDOS Defence Performance Measurement Metrics

These measurements are classified into two categories (Choi, Oh, Jang & Ryou, 2010, August): Defence Strength (Accuracy, Sensitivity, Specificity, Precision, Reliability, & False Negative Rate) and Compromise-ability (Delay in recognition/reaction, System performance deprivation, Passive, Active or Proactive, Holistic defense, Operational complication, Usability, Deployment location, & Scalability)

6.4. Cyber–Insurance and DDoS Flooding Attack

The current scenario of cyber related attacks is increasing day by day. The cyber defense strategy is based on the cyber risk management that identifies & handles the data & network security risks. The cyber insurance provides the authenticity of the product when any organization needs to purchase. It protects from risk and financial transfers that cannot be reduced to cyber insurance. Cyber insurance companies still do not have the solutions to these risks (Khari, Shrivastava, Gupta & Gupta, 2017).

7. CONCLUSION

In this paper, we have discussed the Smartphone security problems and allied challenges. Denial of service is an endangered security attack for new generation Smartphone and Jailbreaking and unblocking are the most prominent attacks. These are primarily categorized into three classes based on the operating system of Smartphone viz. iOS, Android, and Windows. In this paper, we have discussed attacks related to Smartphone related computer technology in much detail. Moreover, we have explored the importance of DoS and DDoS and prospective defensive solutions in the Smartphone. We have also explored different parameters to compute the accuracy & performance of the defense systems. Flooding attacks are initiated through bulk SMS and MMS in phones. Wi-Fi too has a major role in these attacks. This can be used to evaluate various mechanisms and get the finest solution in a specified environment. Finally, we have discussed different challenges that are accommodate by self-protective systems alongside DDoS attacks in the Smartphone while detecting, filtering & identifying such attack traffic and future research scope to cope with such attacks in a well-organized and competent way. Moreover, as per the practical implications of the presented research is concern, we have discussed, most of the security issues and challenges against Smartphone and Wi-Fi technology. Especially, we have discussed impact and countermeasures against DoS and DDoS attacks. In future, we will design and develop some efficient solutions to protect Smartphone and Wi-Fi technology against various DoS and DDoS attacks. Moreover, we will also explore various tools and dataset to evaluate the performance of the proposed solutions.

REFERENCES

Abliz, M. (2011). Internet denial of service attacks and defense mechanisms (technical report). *University of Pittsburgh, Department of Computer Science.*

Al Quhtani, M. (2017). Data Mining Usage in Corporate Information Security: Intrusion Detection Applications. *Business systems research journal, 8*(1), 51-59.

Alomari, E., Manickam, S., Gupta, B. B., Karuppayah, S., & Alfaris, R. (2012). Botnet-based distributed denial of service (DDoS) attacks on web servers: classification and art. arXiv:1208.0403

Apple. (2018). Apple iOS Software. Retrieved from http://www.apple.com/ios/

Arora, K., Kumar, K., & Sachdeva, M. (2011). Impact analysis of recent DDoS attacks. *International Journal on Computer Science and Engineering, 3*(2), 877–883.

Becher, M. (2009). Security of smartphones at the dawn of their ubiquitousness [Doctoral dissertation]. Universität Mannheim.

Beitollahi, H., & Deconinck, G. (2012). Tackling application-layer DDoS attacks. *Procedia Computer Science, 10*, 432–441. doi:10.1016/j.procs.2012.06.056

Bhuyan, M. H., Kashyap, H. J., Bhattacharyya, D. K., & Kalita, J. K. (2013). Detecting distributed denial of service attacks: Methods, tools and future directions. *The Computer Journal, 57*(4), 537–556. doi:10.1093/comjnl/bxt031

Bickford, J., O'Hare, R., Baliga, A., Ganapathy, V., & Iftode, L. (2010, February). Rootkits on smart phones: attacks, implications and opportunities. In *Proceedings of the eleventh workshop on mobile computing systems & applications* (pp. 49-54). ACM. 10.1145/1734583.1734596

Bose, A. (2008). Propagation, detection and containment of mobile malware [Doctoral dissertation]. University of Michigan.

Carl, G., Kesidis, G., Brooks, R. R., & Rai, S. (2006). Denial-of-service attack-detection techniques. *IEEE Internet Computing, 10*(1), 82–89. doi:10.1109/MIC.2006.5

Chen, L. C., Longstaff, T. A., & Carley, K. M. (2004). Characterization of defense mechanisms against distributed denial of service attacks. *Computers & Security, 23*(8), 665–678. doi:10.1016/j.cose.2004.06.008

Chen, Y., Hwang, K., & Ku, W. S. (2007). Collaborative detection of DDoS attacks over multiple network domains. *IEEE Transactions on Parallel and Distributed Systems, 18*(12), 1649–1662. doi:10.1109/TPDS.2007.1111

Chhabra, M., Gupta, B., & Almomani, A. (2013). A novel solution to handle DDOS attack in MANET. *Journal of Information Security, 4*(03), 165–179. doi:10.4236/jis.2013.43019

Choi, Y. S., Oh, J. T., Jang, J. S., & Ryou, J. C. (2010, August). Integrated DDoS attack defense infrastructure for effective attack prevention. In *Proceedings of the 2010 2nd International Conference on Information Technology Convergence and Services (ITCS)*. IEEE. 10.1109/ITCS.2010.5581263

Daswani, N., Mysen, C., Rao, V., Weis, S., Gharachorloo, K., & Ghosemajumder, S. (2008). Online advertising fraud. *Crimeware: understanding new attacks and defenses, 40*(2).

Devi, S. R., & Yogesh, P. (2012, July). An effective approach to counter application layer DDoS attacks. In *Proceedings of the 2012 Third International Conference on Computing Communication & Networking Technologies (ICCCNT)*. IEEE. 10.1109/ICCCNT.2012.6395941

Dixon, B., & Mishra, S. (2010, June). On rootkit and malware detection in smartphones. In *Proceedings of the 2010 International Conference on Dependable Systems and Networks Workshops (DSN-W)* (pp. 162-163). IEEE. 10.1109/DSNW.2010.5542600

Dondyk, E., Rivera, L., & Zou, C. C. (2013). Wi–Fi access denial of service attack to smartphones. *International Journal of Security and Networks, 8*(3), 117–129. doi:10.1504/IJSN.2013.057698

Douligeris, C., & Mitrokotsa, A. (2004). DDoS attacks and defense mechanisms: Classification and state-of-the-art. *Computer Networks, 44*(5), 643–666. doi:10.1016/j.comnet.2003.10.003

Enck, W., Octeau, D., McDaniel, P., & Chaudhuri, S. (2011, August). A study of android application security. In *Proceedings of the 20th USENIX conference on Security* (pp. 21-21). USENIX Association.

Geva, M., Herzberg, A., & Gev, Y. (2014). Bandwidth distributed denial of service: Attacks and defenses. *IEEE Security and Privacy, 12*(1), 54–61. doi:10.1109/MSP.2013.55

Gupta, B. B., & Badve, O. P. (2017). Taxonomy of DoS and DDoS attacks and desirable defense mechanism in a cloud computing environment. *Neural Computing & Applications, 28*(12), 3655–3682. doi:10.100700521-016-2317-5

Gupta, B. B., Misra, M., & Joshi, R. C. (2008). FVBA: A combined statistical approach for low rate degrading and high bandwidth disruptive DDoS attacks detection in ISP domain. In *Proceedings of the 16th IEEE International Conference on Networks ICON '08*. IEEE. 10.1109/ICON.2008.4772654

Habib, S. M., Jacob, C., & Olovsson, T. (2008, December). A practical analysis of the robustness and stability of the network stack in smartphones. In *Proceedings of the 11th International Conference on Computer and Information Technology ICCIT '08* (pp. 393-398). IEEE. 10.1109/ICCITECHN.2008.4803083

Huegen, C. A. (2000). Network-Based Denial of Service attacks (CISCO systems). Retrieved from. http://www.pentics.net/denial-of-service/presentations/msppt/19980513_dos.ppt

Keshariya, A., & Foukia, N. (2010). DDoS defense mechanisms: a new taxonomy. In *Data privacy management and autonomous spontaneous security* (pp. 222–236). Berlin, Heidelberg: Springer. doi:10.1007/978-3-642-11207-2_17

Khari, M., Shrivastava, G., Gupta, S., & Gupta, R. (2017). Role of Cyber Security in Today's Scenario. In Detecting and Mitigating Robotic Cyber Security Risks (pp. 177–191). Hershey, PA: IGI Global. doi:10.4018/978-1-5225-2154-9.ch013

Kim, H., Smith, J., & Shin, K. G. (2008, June). Detecting energy-greedy anomalies and mobile malware variants. In *Proceedings of the 6th international conference on Mobile systems, applications, and services* (pp. 239-252). ACM. 10.1145/1378600.1378627

Li, B., & Im, E. G. (2011). Smartphone, promising battlefield for hackers. *Journal of Security Engineering*, *8*(1), 89–110.

Liao, Q., Li, H., Kang, S., & Liu, C. (2014, July). Feature extraction and construction of application layer DDoS attack based on user behavior. In *Proceedings of the 2014 33rd Chinese Control Conference (CCC)*, (pp. 5492-5497). IEEE. 10.1109/ChiCC.2014.6895878

Liu, J., Xiao, Y., Ghaboosi, K., Deng, H., & Zhang, J. (2009, December). Botnet: Classification, attacks, detection, tracing, and preventive measures. *EURASIP Journal on Wireless Communications and Networking*, (1), 1184–1187. doi:10.1155/2009/692654

Miller, B., Pearce, P., Grier, C., Kreibich, C., & Paxson, V. (2011, July). What's Clicking What? Techniques and Innovations of Today's Clickbots. In DIMVA (pp. 164-183). doi:10.1007/978-3-642-22424-9_10

Miller, C., Honoroff, J., & Mason, J. (2007). Security evaluation of Apple's iPhone. *Independent Security Evaluators*, 19.

Mirkovic, J., & Reiher, P. (2004). A taxonomy of DDoS attack and DDoS defense mechanisms. *Computer Communication Review*, *34*(2), 39–53. doi:10.1145/997150.997156

Mishra, A., Gupta, B. B., & Joshi, R. C. (2011, September). A comparative study of distributed denial of service attacks, intrusion tolerance and mitigation techniques. In *Proceedings of the 2011 European Intelligence and Security Informatics Conference (EISIC)* (pp. 286-289). IEEE. 10.1109/EISIC.2011.15

Mulliner, C. (2009, March). Vulnerability analysis and attacks on NFC-enabled mobile phones. In *Proceedings of the International Conference on Availability, Reliability and Security ARES'09* (pp. 695-700). IEEE. 10.1109/ARES.2009.46

Nakashima, T., & Oshima, S. (2006, August). A detective method for SYN flood attacks. In *Proceedings of the First International Conference on Innovative Computing, Information and Control ICICIC '06* (Vol. 1, pp. 48-51). IEEE. 10.1109/ICICIC.2006.3

Pandya, V. R. (2008). iPhone security analysis [Doctoral dissertation]. San Jose State University.

Peng, T., Leckie, C., & Ramamohanarao, K. (2007). Survey of network-based defense mechanisms countering the DoS and DDoS problems. *ACM Computing Surveys*, *39*(1), 3, es. doi:10.1145/1216370.1216373

Ranjan, S., Swaminathan, R., Uysal, M., & Knightly, E. (2006, April). DDoS-Resilient Scheduling to Counter Application Layer Attacks Under Imperfect Detection. In *INFOCOM 2006. 25th IEEE International Conference on Computer Communications. Proceedings*. IEEE. 10.1109/INFOCOM.2006.127

Reisinger, D. (2013). Android, iOS growing 10 times faster than PCs did in the 1980s. *CNET News*.

Robinson, G., & Weir, G. R. (2015, September). Understanding android security. In *Proceedings of theInternational Conference on Global Security, Safety, and Sustainability* (pp. 189-199). Springer, Cham.

Russello, G., Conti, M., Crispo, B., & Fernandes, E. (2012, June). MOSES: supporting operation modes on smartphones. In *Proceedings of the 17th ACM symposium on Access Control Models and Technologies* (pp. 3-12). ACM.

Sadeghi, A., Bagheri, H., Garcia, J., & Malek, S. (2017). A taxonomy and qualitative comparison of program analysis techniques for security assessment of android software. *IEEE Transactions on Software Engineering*, *43*(6), 492–530. doi:10.1109/TSE.2016.2615307

Sanmorino, A., & Yazid, S. (2013, March). DDoS attack detection method and mitigation using pattern of the flow. In *Proceedings of the 2013 International Conference of Information and Communication Technology (ICoICT)* (pp. 12-16). IEEE. 10.1109/ICoICT.2013.6574541

Sharma, K., & Gupta, B. B. (2016). Multi-layer defense against malware attacks on smartphone wi-fi access channel. *Procedia Computer Science*, *78*, 19–25. doi:10.1016/j.procs.2016.02.005

Shrivastava, G., & Kumar, P. (2017). Privacy Analysis of Android Applications: State-of-art and Literary Assessment. *Scalable Computing: Practice and Experience*, *18*(3), 243–252.

Shrivastava, G., Sharma, K., & Rai, S. (2010, December). The Detection & Defense of DoS & DDoS Attack: A Technical Overview. In *Proceeding of ICC* (Vol. 27, p. 28).

Singh, V., & Sharma, K. (2016, March). Smartphone Security: Review of Challenges and Solution. In *Proceedings of the Second International Conference on Information and Communication Technology for Competitive Strategies* (p. 8). ACM.

Sivabalan, S., & Radcliffe, P. J. (2013, April). A novel framework to detect and block DDoS attack at the application layer. In *TENCON Spring Conference* (pp. 578-582). IEEE. 10.1109/TENCON-Spring.2013.6584511

Specht, S. M., & Lee, R. B. (2004, September). Distributed Denial of Service: Taxonomies of Attacks, Tools, and Countermeasures. In ISCA PDCS (pp. 543-550).

Swami, Y. P., & Tschofenig, H. (2006, December). Protecting mobile devices from TCP flooding attacks. In Proceedings of first ACM/IEEE international workshop on Mobility in the evolving internet architecture (pp. 63-68). ACM. doi:10.1145/1186699.1186717

Tariq, U., Hong, M., & Lhee, K. S. (2006). A comprehensive categorization of DDoS attack and DDoS defense techniques. In *Advanced Data Mining and Applications* (pp. 1025-1036).

Traynor, P., Enck, W., McDaniel, P., & Porta, T. L. (2009). Mitigating attacks on open functionality in SMS-capable cellular networks. *IEEE/ACM Transactions on Networking*, *17*(1), 40–53. doi:10.1109/TNET.2008.925939

Wang, H., Jin, C., & Shin, K. G. (2007). Defense against spoofed IP traffic using hop-count filtering. *IEEE/ACM Transactions on Networking*, *15*(1), 40–53. doi:10.1109/TNET.2006.890133

Wei, T. E., Mao, C. H., Jeng, A. B., Lee, H. M., Wang, H. T., & Wu, D. J. (2012, June). Android malware detection via a latent network behavior analysis. In *Proceedings of the 2012 IEEE 11th International Conference on Trust, Security and Privacy in Computing and Communications (TrustCom)* (pp. 1251-1258). IEEE. 10.1109/TrustCom.2012.91

Wong, L. W. (2005). *Potential Bluetooth Vulnerabilities in Smartphones*. AISM.

Wyatt, T. (2018) Security alert: Android trojan ggtracker charges premium rate sms messages. Retrieved from http://blog.mylookout.com/2011/06/security-alertandroid-trojan-ggtracker-charges-victims-premiumrate-sms-messages

Xie, L., Song, H., Jaeger, T., & Zhu, S. (2008, April). A systematic approach for cell-phone worm containment. In *Proceedings of the 17th international conference on World Wide Web* (pp. 1083-1084). ACM. 10.1145/1367497.1367667

Yao, Y., Ruohomaa, S., & Xu, F. (2012). Addressing common vulnerabilities of reputation systems for electronic commerce. *Journal of Theoretical and Applied Electronic Commerce Research*, 7(1). doi:10.4067/S0718-18762012000100002

Zargar, S. T., Joshi, J., & Tipper, D. (2013). A survey of defense mechanisms against distributed denial of service (DDoS) flooding attacks. *IEEE Communications Surveys and Tutorials*, 15(4), 2046–2069. doi:10.1109/SURV.2013.031413.00127

Zargar, S. T., & Joshi, J. B. (2010, October). A collaborative approach to facilitate intrusion detection and response against DDoS attacks. In *2010 6th International Conference on Collaborative Computing: Networking, Applications and Worksharing (CollaborateCom)*. IEEE. 10.4108/icst.collaboratecom.2010.46

Zaroo, P. (2002). A survey of DDoS attacks and some DDoS defense mechanisms. In *Advanced Information Assurance (CS 626)*.

Zhang, L. L., Liang, C. J. M., Li, Z. L., Liu, Y., Zhao, F., & Chen, E. (2018). Characterizing privacy risks of mobile apps with sensitivity analysis. *IEEE Transactions on Mobile Computing*, 17(2), 279–292. doi:10.1109/TMC.2017.2708716

This research was previously published in the International Journal of E-Services and Mobile Applications (IJESMA), 10(2); edited by Mirjana Pejic-Bach; pages 58-74, copyright year 2018 by IGI Publishing (an imprint of IGI Global).

Section 4
Detection and Prevention: Social Media and the Cloud

Chapter 23
The Improved LSTM and CNN Models for DDoS Attacks Prediction in Social Media

Rasim M. Alguliyev

Institute of Information Technology, Azerbaijan National Academy of Sciences, Baku, Azerbaijan

Ramiz M. Aliguliyev

 https://orcid.org/0000-0001-9795-1694

Institute of Information Technology, Azerbaijan National Academy of Sciences, Baku, Azerbaijan

Fargana J Abdullayeva

 https://orcid.org/0000-0003-2288-6255

Institute of Information Technology, Azerbaijan National Academy of Sciences, Baku, Azerbaijan

ABSTRACT

Automatic identification of conversations related to DDoS events in social networking logs helps the organizations act proactively through early detection of negative and positive sentiments in cyberspace. In this article, the authors describe the novel application of a deep learning method to the automatic identification of negative and positive sentiments in large volumes of social networking texts. The authors present classifiers based on Convolutional Neural Network (CNN) and Long Short-Term Memory (LSTM) to address this problem domain. The improved CNN and LSTM architecture outperform the classification techniques that are common in this domain including classic CNN and classic LSTM in terms of classification performance, which is measured by recall, precision, f-measure, train loss, train accuracy, test loss, and test accuracy. In order to predict the occurrence probability of the DDoS events the next day, the negative and positive sentiments in social networking texts are used. To verify the efficacy of the proposed method experiments is conducted on Twitter data.

DOI: 10.4018/978-1-7998-5348-0.ch023

1. INTRODUCTION

Recently, cyber-attacks have become widespread, targeting giant corporations such as Sony, Verizon, Yahoo, Target, JP Morgan, Ashley Madison, and government agencies. Cyber-attacks are cause of leakage of sensitive information of users, loss of lives, the destruction of critical infrastructures.

The most common cyber-attacks are DDoS (Distributed Denial of Service) attacks (Kaur et al., 2017), uses multiple compressed systems to cut or stop the services of hosts connected to the Internet (Carl et al., 2006). Usually, web servers of the bank or credit card payment networks are the target of such attacks. Therefore, a single attack may cause considerable loss (Matthews, 2014). Detecting and predicting DDoS attacks is a challenging task (Bleakley & Vert, 2014; Imamverdiyev & Abdullayeva, 2018). The purpose of the traditional DDoS detection system is to distinguish malicious packet traffic from normal traffic (Mirkovic & Reiher, 2004). The malicious traffic in the network occurs after the DDoS attack takes place. In the detection of DDoS attacks prior to occurring the data of the social network have a great importance. On the basis of social media data, it is possible to track the traces of subjects targeted by the object.

Most information security experts believe that hacking attacks on businesses will be carried out through social media channels. Facebook, LinkedIn, Twitter are the most widely used networks. Social networks, besides allowing people to connect with each other, but also become a powerful political tool (Hua et al., 2013). Social media is regarded as the next big cybercrime vector (George, 2014).

At usual social media is considered as a sensor that collects information about various social events such as, disease epidemics, protests, elections and so on. The exponential growth of data containing the society opinion in the Web environment led researchers to focus on opinion mining and sentiment analysis of social media data (Ebrahimi et al., 2016). Among social media websites, the Twitter is a site that publishes more information on social issues, natural disasters, incidents and DDoS attacks planning. By analyzing Twitter, it is possible to identify the discussed events that will be occurred and analyze the trajectories (sources) of these events. Additionally, when analyzing the sentiments of the peoples related to the events which will be occurring, it is possible to get a lot of information about a certain event. Analysis of the sentimental traces allows to conduct the sentiment analysis by space and time, and predict the sentiments of the users in advance.

In (Liu & Zhang, 2012), the review of the various approaches related to opinion mining and sentiment analysis is provided. In (Jiang et al., 2011), the method for the providing classification of the sentiments in social media discussions into positive, negative, and neutral classes is proposed. This is a targeted sentiment analysis.

Another application area of the targeted sentiment analysis is to determine what do think people of one country about people of another country. In (Chambers et al., 2015), in order to model the relations between states, the "country-to-country sentiment data" are used. The data classification here is provided based on Bootstrapped classifiers.

The subject of the sentiment analysis is a text. There are two methods of sentiment analysis:

1. **Dictionary-based methods:** In (Taboada et al., 2011), sentiment analysis method, named as SO-CAL (Semantic Orientation CALculator) is proposed. Here in order to classify positive and negative sentiment, the dictionary is used. In this approach, each word is assigned a numerical value;

2. **Machine learning methods:** In the machine learning based sentiment analysis method, by using the statistical method called word embedding, each word is assigned values as a vector form and

the model trains these digitized sentences using machine learning or deep learning methods. SVM, Random Forest, and Naïve-Bayes are traditional machine learning methods, but CNN (Convolutional Neural Network), RNN (Recurrent Neural Network), LSTM (Long Short-Term Memory), GRU (Gated Recurrent Unit) are deep learning methods. In (Yoo et al., 2018), a system that analyzes and predicts the sentimental trajectory of the users, based on the events, recorded in real time discussions is proposed. Here the trajectory analysis and the sentiment analysis are both practically tested. To analyze and predict the sentiment, a deep learning method is applied and high results are obtained. To detect the events, the words such as crime, disaster, accident are used.

To predict cyber-attacks based on social media data, the extensive research is conducted. In (Khandpur et al., 2017), for the detection of the large-scale cyber-attacks such as DDoS, data breaches, and account hijacking, the supervised detection method based on social media data on Twitter is proposed. In this work, for the feature extraction and semantic structure modeling, the convolution kernels and dependency parses approaches are used. In (Ritter et al., 2015), the detection issue of DoS, data breaches and account hijacking attacks in Twitter discussions is considered. For this purpose, in the proposed approach, the label regularization, constrained semi-supervised EM and one-class SVM are used. The main objective of study (Suarez et al., 2018) is the monthly forecasting of the Twitter discussions about security attacks. For the detection of the incidents, l_1 regularization is used. To create security alarms based on users' sentiment data, the analysis of the Twitter discussions is conducted. This analysis is carried out on the basis of comparison of three supervised training algorithms which are Bayesian classification, Support Vector Machines and maximum entropy for text classification and the classifier with the best classification result is selected as the main classification model. After the implementation of the classification by applying the l_1 regularized regression, the forecasting is conducted. Regression is the best tool for predicting events given as linearly independent observations. In (Lippmann et al., 2017), for the detection of the cyber-attacks discussions provided on the Stack Exchange, Reddit and Twitter page the classifier based on hybridization of the TF–IDF, logistic regression, and linear SVM methods is proposed. In this work, to identify cyber-attack discussions, the keyword-based approach is used. The proposed approach searches on the basis of 200 keywords and phrases and calculates the frequency of these words in the document. A document containing more frequency number of keywords is assumed that document is more relevant to cyber attack topic. To implement the classification, the keywords such as "kit", "infected", "checksum", and the phrases such as "buffer overflow", "privilege escalation", "Distributed Denial of Service" are used. Here, the classifier generates a probability value that determines whether the document is related to the cyber attack topic discussion. This probability value allows assigning the document into the cyber or non-cyber classes.

Existing studies are based on the idea of training the system on classified samples and a fixed number of features. Such approaches cannot detect the cyber-attacks in dynamic nature.

The purpose of this paper is by means of self-learning methods to predict the likelihood of cyber-attack related words, interpreted in text type social media discussions. Attackers create unpleasant or negative sentiments in the social network texts against target object. The purpose of this paper is to predict the next day occurrence probability of the DDoS event, based on the social media discussions. Here as the time interval, a daily forecast is taken, however, the proposed method can make predictions for different time periods too. The input data of the model is text streams. For the converting words into vector form, embedding method is used.

The difference between this work from the existing ones is that there is no need to know the class of samples in advance.

The main contributions of this paper are:

- To predict the DDoS attack occurrence probability based on social media data, CNN model with 13 layers and improved LSTM model is proposed;
- In the classification of the data, the class labels are not used;
- In the detection of positive and negative sentiments, feature extraction and selection are not performed.

This paper consists of the following sections: In section 2, Backgraund study presented. Section 3 describes the problem statement formulation. Section 4 summarizes some of the methods used in the DDoS prediction based on social media data. In section 5, an improved CNN model is provided. In section 6, an improved LSTM model is provided. In section 7, the results of the comparative analysis of the proposed method with existing methods are described. Section 8 presents the conclusion of this work.

2. BACKGROUND STUDY

2.1. Information Security Events

2.1.1. Denial of Service Attacks (DoS)

The DoS is designed to deny the liveness properties (e.g. uptime) of a web service to other users. These attacks are most often accomplished by an agent who amplifies requests for a network service with no other intention but to saturate the service beyond some capacity of the resources behind that device (e.g. bandwidth, processing or memory).

2.1.2. Data Breach

Data breach is an attack which implements sophisticated techniques to pilfer a collection of personal or digital credentials. The effects of a data breach if unmitigated may result in the fraudulent use of personal information. However, early detection may alert affected users to monitor for fraud and initialize preventative measures such as updating credentials. Data breach attacks my elicit signals from social media such as early discovery and warnings generated by affected users who discover fraud, further this may be useful to other users whose stolen personal information (e.g. credit card) has not yet been exploited.

2.1.3. Account Hijacking

Account hijacking may involve an intruder guessing, cracking, or using default passwords to gain unauthorized access to user accounts or system privileges. Account hijacking usually focuses on the problem of determining an unknown user password by using techniques including brute force attacks, dictionary attacks (using frequently used passwords).

2.2. Cybersecurity Data

Sources of cybersecurity data in the field of information security are divided into two classes:

1. **Formal sources:** For example, the NIST National Vulnerability Database (NVD), United States Computer Emergency Readiness Team (US-CERT) and so on;
2. **Non-formal sources:** For example, developer forums, chat rooms and social media platforms like Twitter, Reddit, and Stack Overflow.

These sources publish information about security vulnerabilities, threats, and attacks. Automatic retrieval appropriate information relevant to the field from OSINT (Open-source intelligence) data is one of the key issues that attract the attention of researchers. OSINT covers data collected from open sources, such as newspapers, magazines, social networking sites, video sharing sites, wiki pages, blogs, and so on.

DDoS Cyber-attacks Data. Statistical information on DDoS type cyber attacks is available at www. digitalattackmap.com. The purpose of this website is to visualize global DDoS attacks and is created with a collaborative effort of the Arbor Networks and Google Ideas organizations.

In this paper, to analyse DDoS events the Twitter data is used.

2.3. Cyber Attacks and Forensic

For disclosure of the cyber-attack crimes, the cyber forensics are used. The forensic of the cyber attacks is the complicated issue (Shackelford, 2009).

Cyber forensic is used for collecting, evaluating and storing evidence from computer-related crimes (Jr & Menendez, 2002). Although the forensic investigation is useful, the ability of this approach to identify the motives behind cyber-attacks is limited.

2.4. Motivations Behind the Cyber-Attacks

Cyber-attacks are viewed as technical and social events (Sakaki et al., 2010). The socio-technical progress of the IT infrastructure of the country and its economy can seriously affect the likelihood of the country being attacked (Mezzour, 2015). Cyber-attacks are closely related to social, political, economic, and cultural (SPEC) motivations (Ghandi et al., 2011). For the prevention of the cyber-attacks effectively, the social and technical progress and the motivation of the cyber-attacks should be taken into account.

3. PROBLEM STATEMENT

The main research question to investigate is whether tweet streams contain useful information for DDoS defense. Our task is to predict the likelihood that a DDoS event will occur to a certain target in the day d given the tweet stream over a history period X related to the monitored target. X is a sequence of N^p days $\left(X = \left\{ d^{N^p}, ..., d^2, d^1 \right\} \right)$ immediately before d, where d^1 is the day before d and $d^i > d^{i+1}$. N^p can be arbitrarily large. The set of tweets posted on d^i is denoted as $d^i = \left\{ t^1, t^2, ..., t^{N_i^d} \right\}$ denotes the number of tweets of the day d^i. Each tweet consists of a sequence of words $t^j = \left\{ w^1, w^2, ..., w^{N_j^t} \right\}$.

In this work, to transform words into numbers, word embedding method is used. In the input level, we represent each word w^k with a K dimensional embedding, thus mapping a tweet t^j into a matrix:

$$t^j = \left\{ e\left(w^1\right), e\left(w^2\right), ..., e\left(w^{N_j^t}\right) \right\} \tag{1}$$

3.1. Primary Goal of Proposal

The primary goal of sentiment prediction in this work we can describe as follows. Assume $D \subset X \times Y$ be the dataset that contains the sentiments, where $X = \{x_1, x_2, ..., x_n\}$ is the set of sentiments so that $x_i(x_1, x_2, ..., x_m)^T$ is an m dimension feature vector for i^{th} sentiment. Also, let $Y = \{p, n\}$ be the set of class labels in binary classification problem in which positive and negative sentiments are denoted by p and n, respectively. The goal is to assign the right label from Y to each sentiment.

4. RELATED WORKS

For the predicting DDOS attacks based on social media data, by applying the above-mentioned dictionary-based and machine learning methods, various approaches are proposed.

In (Jiang et al., 2011), social media is used as a crowdsourcing sensor for the getting up insight about cyber-attacks, which willing to occur in the feature. In this work, to detect cyber-attacks such as DDoS, data breaches, and account hijacking, by using seed event triggers, an unsupervised approach is proposed.

In (Chambers et al., 2015), to modeling relationships between states, the Twitter data is used. Here, the experiments are conducted on the state by state sentiment data, and these data is placed on the web page http://www.usna.edu/Users/cs/nchamber/nations/index.html. This dataset consists of information about positive and negative discussions.

In (Sapienza et al., 2018), based on Twitter and Darknet data, a Mirai DDoS attack forecasting method is suggested. To detect attacks, a dictionary with listed attack terms is used. This dictionary contains the names of some malicious ransomware programs, such as wannacry, wannacrypt, petya, wcry, petrwrap and the proposed method can detect those words accurately. Here at first, cyber-security related headers are scanned, then by using the text mining methods, relevant terms are identified and non-relevant terms are removed. The drawback of this approach is that the model is unable to detect new types of attacks when new attack names are not included in the dictionary.

To test the impact of an attack, send attacks and received attacks are taken as dependent variables, and the parameters such as Network Bandwidth, GDP and Internet Users per 100 populations, ICT, CPIA and country-to-country average sentiment score are taken as independent variables, and the correlation between variables is evaluated (Kumar & Carley, 2016a). To perform correlation evaluation, the Pearson correlation method is used. To find the source and target countries of the cyber-attacks the network visualization is used. In this work, by using quadratic assignment procedure (QAP) the correlation between cyber-attack networks was found. From the correlation, it was revealed that countries with high bandwidth and corruption are the best source for DDoS attacks. Because countries with high bandwidth can provide hosting services to any number of computers to implement broadband DDoS attacks. In addition, it is determined that the countries with high Per-capita-GDP indicator and better Information and Communication Technologies (ICT) infrastructure become as targeted countries. In this work along with the attack data, the data showing the country's level taken from the World Bank website, such as the Information and Communication Technologies (ICT) infrastructure, Per-capita-GDP, Country Policy and Institutional Assessment (CPIA) corruption and Internet Users per 100 population data are also used. Here information about international Internet network bandwidth is taken from www. econstats.com, for the creating of the alliance-and hostility network an information from Correlates of War (www.coorelatesofwar.org) web-page is used. For the tracking relation trend of countries toward each other, the USNA (http://www.usna.edu/Users/cs/nchamber/nations/index.html) data is used.

In (Kumar & Carley, 2016b), a cyber-attack detection method based on decision tree algorithm is proposed. Here the attack probability is calculated on the basis of the Bayesian theorem. To track the relationships of the countries toward each other, based on Twitter sentiments (http://www.usna.edu/Users/cs/nchamber/nations/index.html) the sentiment trends are constructed and the comparison of this trend with the trend constructed on the basis of DDoS data, derived from the Arbor Networks (http://www.digitalattackmap.com), is conducted. The experiments suggest that the negative discussions within the discussions conducted against the certain country increase the occurrence probability of the cyber-attacks to that country, and the presence of positive sentiments to the country reduces it. In the paper, the analysis of this landscape in specific countries is described in detail.

In (Mittal et al., 2016), conceptual approach called CyberTwitter is proposed, which analysis cybersecurity-related discussions and generates timely alarms for security analysts. To conduct the experiments, the OSINT dataset is used.

The fact that the data on Twitter has real-time nature, it is enabled researchers to make important decisions from highly influential events. This type of information is used in the analysis of emergency events, such as earthquakes (Sakaki et al., 2010), forest fires (Longueville et al., 2009), terrorist attacks (Oh et al., 2011), natural disasters (Vieweg et al., 2010) and so on. These applications of Twitter have turned it into the most reliable source of OSINT data.

In the Twitter, many companies, such as Adobe (@AdobeSecurity), Github (@githubstatus), WhatsApp (@wa status) publish information about security incidents, related to their products. Here individual users also publish information about encountered new gaps.

The comparative description of the different approaches by various metrics is given in Table 1.

In the methods mentioned in Table 1, attack detection is provided based on the training of the system on classified samples. This approach is not suitable for attack detection in dynamic environments.

To predict the likelihood of cyber-attack related words, interpreted in text type social media discussions self-learning methods are needed.

5. AN IMPROVED CNN MODEL

An improved Convolutional Neural Network (CNN) is employed in this research. CNN is a subset of deep learning which has attracted a lot of attention in recent year. The CNN architecture consists of three different types of the layer: convolutional layer, pooling layer, and a fully connected layer (Goodfellow & Bengio, 2016).

Table 1. Comparative description of existing approaches by various metrics

	Reference	Dataset	Aim	Method	Classes
1.	(Chambers et al., 2015)	Country-to-country sentiment data http://www.usna.edu/Users/cs/nchamber/nations/index.html	Detection of international relations based on social media	Bootstrapped classifiers	Positive tweets, Negative tweets
2.	(Kumar & Carley, 2016b)	DDoS Cyber-attacks Data collected from the website www.digitalattackmap.com; country-to-country sentiment data http://www.usna.edu/Users/cs/nchamber/nations/index.html	Cyber-attack detection	Decision tree algorithm, Bayesian theorem	Cyber-attack (Yes, No)
3	(Mittal et al., 2016)	OSINT (Open–source intelligence) dataset	Analysis of cyber security related discussions		Cyber-attack (Yes, No)
4.	(Khandpur et al., 2017)	Users' status updates and blog posts-based text streams	Extract and encode cyberattacks reported and discussed in social media	Structured query expansion-based retrieval algorithm	Cyber-attack (Yes, No)
5.	(Kumar & Carley, 2016a)	World Bank data www.econstats.com, "Correlates of War" www.coorelatesofwar.org, USNA (http://www.usna.edu/Users/cs/nchamber/nations/index.html)	Analysis of cyber security related discussions	Pearson correlation, Quadratic assignment procedure (QAP)	Cyber-attack (Yes, No)

5.1. Convolutional Layer

It consists of filters (kernels) which slide across the input data. A kernel is a matrix to be convolved with the input data and stride controls how much the filter convolves across the input data. This layer performs the convolution on the input data with the kernel using Equation (2). The output of the convolution is also known as the feature map.

The convolution operation is as follows:

$$y_k = \sum_{n=0}^{N-1} x_n h_{k-n} \tag{2}$$

where x is input data, h is the filter, and N is the number of elements in x. The output vector is y. The subscripts denote the n-th element of the vector.

5.2. Pooling Layer

This layer is also known as the down-sampling layer. The pooling operation reduces the dimension of output neurons from the convolutional layer to reduce the computational intensity and prevent the overfitting. The max-pooling operation is used in this work. Max-pooling operation selects only the maximum value in each feature map and consequently reducing the number of output neurons.

5.3. Fully Connected Layer

This layer has full connection to all the activations in the previous layer. The rectifier linear unit (ReLu) is used in this work as an activation function for the convolutional layers (1, 3, 5, 7, 9, 11, and 12). The activation function is an operation which maps an output to a set of inputs. ReLu function is defined by the Equation (3):

$$\Phi(x) = \max(0, x) \tag{3}$$

The final output decision of the CNN model is based on the weights and biases of the previous layers in the network structure. Hence, the weights and biases of the model are updated with Equation (4) and Equation (5) respectively for each layer:

$$\Delta W_l(t+1) = -\frac{x\lambda}{r}W_l - \frac{x}{n}\frac{\partial C}{\partial W_l} + m\Delta W_l(t) \tag{4}$$

$$\Delta B_l(t+1) = -\frac{x}{n}\frac{\partial C}{\partial B_l} + m\Delta B_l(t) \tag{5}$$

where $W, B, l, \lambda, x, n, m, t, C$ represents the weight, bias, layer number, regularization parameter, learning rate, the total number of training samples, momentum, updating step, and cost function respectively.

The parameters used to train the CNN model are lambda regularization, learning rate, and momentum. These parameters can be tuned according to the dataset in order to achieve optimum performance. The lambda is to prevent overfitting of the data. The learning rate is to control how fast the network learns during training and momentum helps to convergence the data. The parameters lambda, learning rate, momentum is set to 0.04, 0.001, and 0.99, respectively in this work.

5.4. Architecture of The Improved CNN

Figure 1 shows the architecture of the CNN structure with 20808 input sample lengths where the green, blue, and red color signify the kernel size, max-pooling, and fully connected layer respectively. This proposed deep CNN architecture constructed on thirteen layers and includes five convolutional, five max-pooling, and three fully connected layers.

Step 1: The input layer (Layer 0) is convolved using Equation (2) with a kernel of size 6 to produce Layer 1.
Step 2: Then, a max-pooling of size 2 is applied to every feature map (Layer 2).
Step 3: After the max-pooling operation, the number of neurons is reduced.
Step 4: Again, the feature map in Layer 2 is convolved with a kernel of size 5 to produce Layer 3.
Step 5: A max-pooling operation of size 2 is applied to every feature map (Layer 4), reducing the number of neurons.
Step 6: Then, feature map from Layer 4 is convolved with a kernel of size 4 to produce Layer 5.

Step 7: Again, a max-pooling of size 2 is applied to reduce the number of neurons in the output layer (Layer 6).

Step 8: The feature map in Layer 6 is again convolved with a kernel size of 4 to produce the next layer (Layer 7).

Step 9: A max-pooling of size 2 is applied to the feature map (Layer 8).

Step 10: The feature map in Layer 8 is convolved with a kernel of size 4 to produce Layer 9.

Step 11: Max-pooling of size 2 is applied to every feature map in Layer 10.

Step 12: In Layer 10, the neurons are fully connected to neurons in Layer 11.

Step 13: Layer 11 is fully connected to neurons in Layer 12.

Step 14: Finally, Layer 12 is connected to the last layer (Layer 13) with 2 output neurons. (representing the positive and negative classes).

Figure 1. An Improved CNN

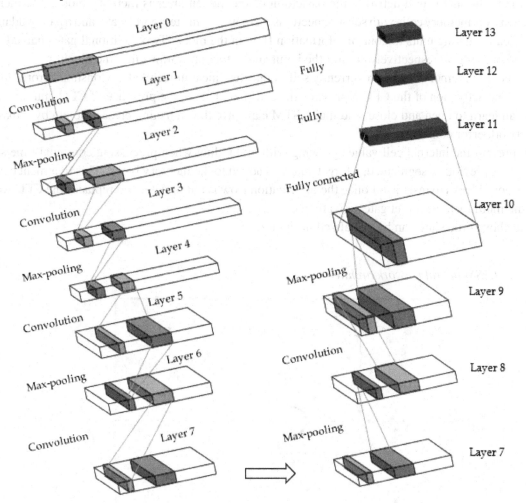

A conventional 1D with a batch size of 10 is employed in this work to train CNN. A batch size is the number of samples used for each training update. The batch size of 10 is chosen in this work.

A total of 140 epochs of training were run in this work. An epoch refers to one iteration of the full training set.

6. AN IMPROVED LSTM MODEL

LSTM (Long Short-Term Memory neural network) is proposed in this study to predict the occurrence probability of the DDoS events based on social media sensor data. LSTM neural network was initially introduced by Hochreiter and Schmidhuber in 1997 (Hochreiter & Schmidhuber, 1997), and the primary objectives of LSTM are to model long-term dependencies and determine the optimal time lag for time series problems. These features are especially desirable for DDoS event prediction in the network domain.

An LSTM is composed of one input layer, one recurrent hidden layer, and one output layer. Different from the traditional neural network, the basic unit of the hidden layer is memory block. The memory block contains memory cells with self-connections memorizing the temporal state, and a pair of adaptive, multiplicative gating units to control information flow in the block. Two additional gates named input gate and output gate respectively control the input and output activations into the block.

The core of memory cell is a recurrently self-connected linear unit called as Constant Error Carousel (CEC). The activation of the CEC represents the cell state. Due to the presence of CEC, multiplicative gates can learn to open and close, and thus LSTM can solve the vanishing error problem by remaining the network error constant.

To prevent the internal cell values growing without binding when processing continual time series that are not previously segmented, a forget gate was added to the memory block. This treatment enables the memory blocks to reset itself once the information flow is out of date, and replaces the CEC weight with the multiplicative forget gate activation.

The above procedure can be visualized in Figure 2.

Figure 2. LTSM neural network architecture

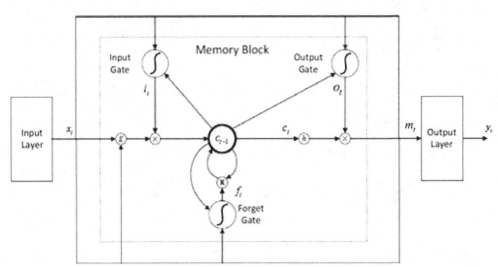

The model input is denoted as $x = (x_1, x_2, \ldots, x_t)$, and the output sequence is denoted as $y = (y_1, y_2, \ldots, y_t)$, where t is the prediction period. In the context of DDoS events prediction, x can be considered as historical input data (e.g. DDoS incidents), and y is the estimated incident. The objective of LSTM is to predict DDoS event incident in the next time step based on prior information without specifying how many steps should be traced back. To implement this goal, the predicted DDoS event incident time will be iteratively calculated by following Equations (6)-(11):

$$i_t = \delta\left(W_{ix}x_t + W_{im}m_{t-1} + W_{ic}c_{t-1} + b_i\right) \tag{6}$$

$$f_t = \delta\left(W_{f_x}x_t + W_{fm}m_{t-1} + W_{fc}c_{t-1} + b_f\right) \tag{7}$$

$$c_t = f_t \otimes c_{t-1} + i_t \otimes g\left(W_{cx}x_t + W_{cm}m_{t-1} + b_c\right) \tag{8}$$

$$o_t = \delta\left(W_{ox}x_t + W_{om}m_{t-1} + W_{oc}c_t + b_0\right) \tag{9}$$

$$m_t = o_t \otimes h\left(c_t\right) \tag{10}$$

$$y_t = W_{ym}m_t + b_y \tag{11}$$

where $\otimes$ represents the scalar product of two vectors, and $\sigma(\bullet)$ denotes the standard logistics sigmoid function defined in Equation (12):

$$\sigma\left(x\right) = \frac{1}{1 + e^{-x}} \tag{12}$$

The memory block is outlined in a box, and consists with an input gate, an output gate and a forget gate, where the outputs of three gates are respectively represented as i_t, o_t, f_t. The activation vectors for each cell and memory block are denoted as c_t and m_t, respectively. The weight matrices W and bias vectors b are utilized to build connections between the input layer, output layer and memory block.

Training LSTM is based on Back-Propagation using the stochastic gradient descent (sgd) method. The common objective function is to minimize the RMSLE (Root Mean Squared Logarithmic Error).

RMSLE is to compare the predictive value with the true value, and is calculated as the square root of the squared bias plus squared standard error:

$$RMSLE = \sqrt{\frac{1}{n}\sum_{i=1}^{n}\left(\log\left(a_i + 1\right) - \log\left(b_i + 1\right)\right)^2} \tag{13}$$

where n is the total number of observations in the testing dataset, a_i is predicted value, and b_i is the actual value. RMSLE is a method to measure the error rate, so smaller RMSLE value indicates more accurate model.

7. EXPERIMENTS

We propose a method for the detection of the DDoS attacks in social media. For this purpose, the proposed method first analyzes and then predicts the sentimental traces in the content, related to DDoS events.

7.1. Experiment Environment

The test process of the model that detects DDoS attacks on social media is provided on the Data Center of Institute of Information Technology of Azerbaijan National Academy of Sciences (AzScienceNet), in the following environment: Ubuntu 16.04.3 LTS amd64 system, 331.2 GB memory, 2933.437 CPU MHz.

The implementation of the method is conducted on the Python and Tensorflow. In this study, for implementation and experiments, Twitter data is used. Twitter, which can be said to be a representative social media site. Here US tweet data is used which is collected by work (Wang & Zhang, 2017).

Various experiments are performed to verify the accuracy of the proposed method. In the used dataset 3048 row of the dataset is positive, and the 17761 row is negative. The prediction of the DDoS attack is proved by using a dictionary with listed attack terms. This dictionary contains the names of some DDoS attacks programs, such as UFONet, Low Orbit Ion Cannon (LOIC), also malicious ransomware programs such as wannacry, wannacrypt, petya, wcry, petrwrap and ather security related words such as hackers, ddos, dos, denial distributed, wikileaks dos, lulzsec, and so on. The proposed method detects these words accurately. In order to find optimal parameters in the proposed model, the neural network is tested at different values of parameters.

The sentimental analysis model is constructed based on improved CNN and LSTM algorithms. The detection accuracy and test results for various metrics of the improved CNN and LSTM models are shown in Table 2.

Table 2. Comparison of the improved CNN and LSTM Models with traditional CNN and LSTM models

	Recall	Precision	F-Measure	Train Loss	Train Accuracy	Test Loss	Test Accuracy
CNN (proposed)	**0.8455**	0.8923	**0.8683**	0.0919	0.7761	**0.1272**	**0.7744**
CNN (Wang & Zhang, 2017)	0.3469	**0.9297**	0.5053	**0.0126**	**0.9925**	0.8932	0.4026
LSTM (Wang & Zhang, 2017)	0.5364	**0.9154**	0.6764	**0.0025**	**0.9925**	0.2030	0.5487
LSTM (proposed)	**0.7522**	0.8865	**0.8138**	0.1098	0.7090	**0.1354**	**0.6974**

As shown from the results of experiments in Table 2, the improved CNN and LSTM models have produced better results compared to traditional CNN and LSTM models. The experiments are conducted by changing the parameters and the optimal results in LSTM network are obtained in BATCH_SIZE

= 10, EPOCHS = 140, lr = 0.001, momentum = 0.99, decay = 1e-6, nesterov = True values, but in CNN network at BATCH_SIZE = 10, EPOCHS = 500 values and are added to the Table 2. In addition, to improve the results, the kernel regularizer (l2=0.2), BatchNormalization, Weight regularizer (l2 = 0.03) layers are added to the LSTM network, and kernel regularizer (l2 = 0.04) and Dropout = 0.25 layers are added to the CNN network. In each model the optimization function is sgd (stochastic gradient descent), the activation function is relu (rectified linear unit) and the loss function is RMSLE (Root Mean Squared Logarithmic Error).

As shown from the Table 2, it is seen that the traditional CNN algorithm has been trained the neural network with little loss and high accuracy (Train Loss = 0.0126, Train acc = 0.9925), but these parameters have been significantly worsened during the testing process. Here the Test loss = 0.8932 and Test acc = 0.4026 show that the neural network has caused a great deal of loss during prediction and almost could not carry out the prediction (Test acc = 0.4026) well. In addition, traditional CNN model has a higher value for precision (0.9297) and low value for recall (0.3469). Better models have to higher values for precision and recall. Weaker models might have high precision (for example, 95%) but low recall (for example, 50%) when it identifies samples of one class largely correct, but it mislabels samples of another class. This landscape can be easily seen from Figure 3.

Figure 3. CNN (Ref. (Wang & Zhang, 2017))

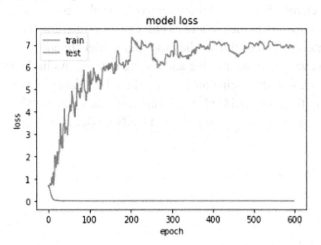

In good prediction models, the dynamics of the test line must be in the direction of the train line and should be as close to it as possible. But here, the opposite landscape is observed. The same landscape can be seen in the traditional LSTM model. Thus, despite the fact that in LSTM model the training loss and training accuracy are Train Loss = 0.0025, Train acc = 0.9925 respectively, but testing loss and testing accuracy of this model were Test loss = 0.2030, Test acc = 0.5487. In addition, traditional LSTM model is also has a higher value for precision (0.9154) and low value for recall (0.5364). This condition is also cannot be considered as a good result. Because here the traditional LSTM model can recognize the 54 percent of points in the dataset, while other points it can't recognize and allows a lot of losses. It can be visualized as follows (Figure 4).

Figure 4. LSTM (Ref. (Wang & Zhang, 2017))

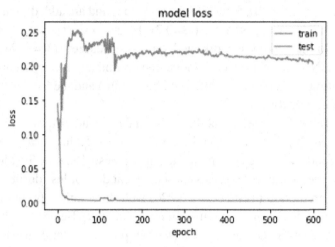

In this work, as mentioned above, by adding various layers to the proposed CNN and LSTM models very high results are obtained in the model. So, the training of the improved CNN model is conducted with low loss and high accuracy, and the loss and accuracy parameters of the model have obtained 0.0919 and 0.7761 values respectively. In this model during testing is also good results are achieved. Thus, the Test loss and Test acc parameters of the model has obtained the 0.1272 and 0.7744 values, respectively. It seems here, that the training and testing of the proposed model are conducted very well. There is not big jumping between the values of the training and testing metrics. As in the training phase, the model is trained with high accuracy, in the testing phase, it predicted the data points very properly. In addition, the precision and recall of the improved CNN model are also has a higher value, e.g. 0.8923 and 0.8455, respectively. The prediction accuracy of the proposed CNN model is visualized in Figure 5.

Figure 5. An improved CNN

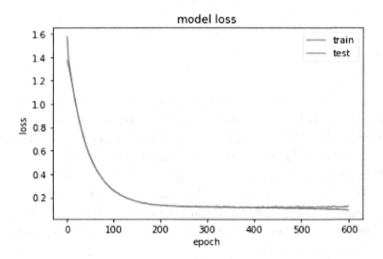

Here the training curve is the almost complete overlap of the test curve. In the proposed LSTM model the good results are also achieved. So, by allowing the low loss in the training of the model, the loss and accuracy parameters of the model have obtained 0.1098 and 0.7090 values, respectively. During the testing, with a slight difference compared to the training phase, also good results are obtained and test loss and test accuracy parameters have obtained the values as Test loss = 0.1354, Test acc = 0.6974. In addition, the precision and recall of the improved LSTM model are also has a higher value, e.g. 0.8865 and 0.7522 respectively.

The predictive accuracy of the improved LSTM model is visualized in Figure 6.

From the visual representation of the LSTM model, it seens that the test curve with the training curve conducted prediction accurately, with very little loss.

Figure 6. An improved LSTM

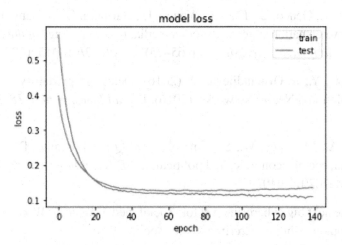

8. CONCLUSION AND FUTURE WORK

In this study, for the detection of DDoS attacks from the social media text data a deep learning method is employed to automatically identify the two classes of sentiments, positive and negative. To categorize the positive and negative class a 13-layer deep CNN and improved LSTM model is developed. We have performed a comprehensive evaluation of our approach and achieved recall, precision, f-measure, train loss, train accuracy, test loss, and test accuracy of 0.85, 0.89, 0.87, 0.09, 0.78, 0.13 and 0.77, respectively, in detecting DDoS attack related content from social media streams.

Future work is aimed at extending the attack class, as well as modeling the successive dependencies of cyber attacks (from the emergence to reporting). This will help to capture features such as the prevalence of attacks against specific institutions or countries in specific time periods.

ACKNOWLEDGMENT

This work was supported by the Science Development Foundation under the President of the Republic of Azerbaijan – Grant N° EIF-KETPL-2-2015-1(25)-56/05/1.

REFERENCES

Bleakley, K., & Vert, J. P. (2011). The group fused Lasso for multiple change-point detection. arXiv:1106.4199.

Carl, G., Kesidis, G., Brooks, R. R., & Rai, S. (2006). Denial-of-service attack detection techniques. *IEEE Internet Computing*, *10*(1), 82–89. doi:10.1109/MIC.2006.5

Chambers, N., Bowen, V., Genco, E., Tian, X., Young, E., Harihara, G., & Yang, E. (2015). Identifying political sentiment between nation states with social media. In *Proceedings of the conference on empirical methods in natural language processing*, (pp.65–75). 10.18653/v1/D15-1007

Ebrahimi, M., Suen, C. Y., & Ormandjieva, O. (2016). Detecting predatory conversations in social media by deep Convolutional Neural Networks. (2016). *Digital Investigation*, *18*, 33–49. doi:10.1016/j.diin.2016.07.001

Gandhi, R., Sharma, A., Mahoney, W., Sousan, W., Zhu, Q., & Laplante, P. (2011). Dimensions of cyber-attacks: Cultural, social, economic, and political. *IEEE Technology and Society Magazine*, *30*(1), 28–38. doi:10.1109/MTS.2011.940293

George, T. (2014). The next big cybercrime vector: Social media. *Security Week*. Retrieved from https://www.securityweek.com/next-big-cybercrime-vector-social-media

Goodfellow, I., Bengio, Y., & Courville, A. (2016). *Deep Learning*. MIT press.

Hochreiter, S., & Schmidhuber, J. (1997). Long short-term memory. *Neural Computation*, *9*(8), 1735–1780. doi:10.1162/neco.1997.9.8.1735 PMID:9377276

Hua, T., Lu, C. T., Ramakrishnan, N., Chen, F., Arredondo, J., Mares, D., & Summers, K. (2013). Analyzing Civil Unrest through Social Media. *Computer*, *46*(12), 80–84. doi:10.1109/MC.2013.442

Imamverdiyev, Y. N., & Abdullayeva, F. J. (2018). Deep learning method for denial of service attack detection based on restricted Boltzmann machine. *Big Data*, *6*(2), 159–169. doi:10.1089/big.2018.0023 PMID:29924649

Jiang, L., Yu, M., Zhou, M., Liu, X., & Zhao, T. (2011). Target-dependent twitter sentiment classification. In *Proceedings of the 49th annual meeting of the association for computational linguistics: Human language technologies* (Vol. 1, pp. 151–160).

Jr, A. M., & Menendez, D. (2002). *Cyber forensics: a field manual for collecting, examining, and preserving evidence of computer crimes* (2nd ed.). CRC Press.

Kaur, P., Kumar, M., & Bhandari, A. (2017). A review of detection approaches for distributed denial of service attacks. *Systems Science & Control Engineering, 5*(1), 301–320. doi:10.1080/21642583.2017.1331768

Khandpur, R. P., Ji, T., Jan, S., Wang, G., Lu, C. T., & Ramakrishnan, N. (2017). Crowdsourcing cybersecurity: Cyber attack detection using social media. In *Proceedings of the 2017 ACM on Conference on Information and Knowledge Management* (pp. 1049–1057). New York, NY: ACM. 10.1145/3132847.3132866

Kumar, S., & Carley, K. M. (2016a). Approaches to understanding the motivations behind cyber attacks. In *Proceedings of the IEEE Conference on Intelligence and Security Informatics* (pp. 307-309). 10.1109/ISI.2016.7745496

Kumar, S., & Carley, K. M. (2016b). Understanding DDoS cyber-attacks using social media analytics. In *Proceedings of the IEEE Conference on Intelligence and Security Informatics* (pp. 231-236). 10.1109/ISI.2016.7745480

Lippmann, R. P., Weller-Fahy, D. J., Mensch, A. C., Campbell, W. M., Campbell, J. P., Streilein, W. W., & Carter, K. M. (2017). Toward finding malicious cyber discussions in social media. In The AAAI-17 workshop on artificial intelligence for cyber security (pp. 203-209).

Liu, B., & Zhang, L. (2012). *A survey of opinion mining and sentiment analysis. In Mining text data* (pp. 415–463). Springer.

Longueville, B. D., Smith, R. S., & Luraschi, G. (2009). Omg, from here, I can see the flames!: A use case of mining location based social networks to acquire spatio-temporal data on forest fires. In *Proceedings of the International Workshop on Location based Social Networks* (pp. 73-80). 10.1145/1629890.1629907

Matthews, T. (2014). *Incapsula survey: What DDoS attacks really cost businesses.* Incapsula Inc.

Mezzour, G. (2015). Assessing the global cyber and biological threat [Ph.D. dissertation].

Mirkovic, J., & Reiher, P. (2004). A taxonomy of DDoS attack and DDoS defense mechanisms. *Computer Communication Review, 34*(2), 39–53. doi:10.1145/997150.997156

Mittal, S., Das, P. K., Mulwad, V., Joshi, A., & Finin, T. (2016). CyberTwitter: Using Twitter to generate alerts for cybersecurity threats and vulnerabilities. In *Proceedings of the IEEE/ACM international conference on advances in social networks analysis and mining* (pp. 860-867).

Oh, O., Agrawal, M., & Rao, H. R. (2011). Information control and terrorism: Tracking the mumbai terrorist attack through Twitter. *Information Systems Frontiers, 13*(1), 33–43. doi:10.100710796-010-9275-8

Ritter, A., Wright, E., Casey, W., & Mitchell, T. (2015). Weakly supervised extraction of computer security events from Twitter. In *Proceedings of the 24th international conference on World Wide Web* (pp. 896-905). 10.1145/2736277.2741083

Sakaki, T., Okazaki, M., & Matsuo, Y. (2010). Earthquake shakes twitter users: real-time event detection by social sensors. In *Proceedings of the 19th international conference on World Wide Web* (pp. 851-860). 10.1145/1772690.1772777

Sapienza, A., Bessi, A., Damodaran, S., Shakarian, P., Lerman, K., & Ferrara, E. (2017). Early warnings of cyber threats in online discussions. In *Proceedings of the IEEE international Conference on Data Mining Workshops* (pp. 667-674). 10.1109/ICDMW.2017.94

Shackelford, S. (2009). From nuclear war to net war: Analogizing cyber attacks in international law. *Berkeley Journal of International Law*, *25*(3), 191–251.

Suarez, A. H., Perez, G. S., Medina, K. T., Hernandez, V. M., Meana, H. P., Mercado, J. O., & Sanchez, V. (2018). Social sentiment sensor in Twitter for predicting cyber-attacks using ℓ1 regularization. *Sensors (Basel)*, *18*(5), 1–17.

Taboada, M., Brooke, J., Tofiloski, M., Voll, K., & Stede, M. (2011). Lexicon-Based Methods for Sentiment Analysis. *Computational Linguistics*, *37*(2), 267–307. doi:10.1162/COLI_a_00049

Vieweg, S., Hughes, A. L., Starbird, K., & Palen, L. (2010). Microblogging during two natural hazards events: What Twitter may contribute to situational awareness. In *Proceedings of the SIGCHI Conference on Human Factors in Computing Systems* (pp. 1079-1088). 10.1145/1753326.1753486

Wang, Z., & Zhang, Y. (2017). DDoS event forecasting using Twitter data. In *Proceedings of the 26th international joint conference on artificial intelligence* (pp. 4151-4157).

Yoo, S. Y., Song, J., & Jeong, O. (2018). Social media contents based sentiment analysis and prediction system. *Expert Systems with Applications*, *105*, 102–111. doi:10.1016/j.eswa.2018.03.055

This research was previously published in the International Journal of Cyber Warfare and Terrorism (IJCWT), 9(1); edited by Graeme Pye and Brett van Niekerk; pages 1-18, copyright year 2019 by IGI Publishing (an imprint of IGI Global).

Chapter 24
The HTTP Flooding Attack Detection to Secure and Safeguard Online Applications in the Cloud

Dhanapal A
VIT University, Chennai, India

Nithyanandam P
VIT University, Chennai, India

ABSTRACT

Cloud computing is the cutting edge and has become inevitable in all forms of computing. This is due to its nature of elasticity, cost-effectiveness, availability, etc. The online applications like e-commerce, and e-healthcare applications are moving to the cloud to reduce their operational cost. These applications have the vulnerability of a HTTP flooding Distributed Denial of Service attack in the cloud. This flooding attack aims to overload the application, making it unable to process genuine requests and bring it down. So, these applications need to be secured and safeguarded against such attacks. This HTTP flooding attack is one of the key challenging issues as it shows normal behaviour with regard to all lower networking layers like TCP 3-way handshaking by mimicking genuine requests and it is even harder in the cloud due to the cloud properties. This article offers a solution for detecting a HTTP flooding attack in the cloud by using the novel TriZonal Linear Prediction (TLP) model. The solution was implemented using OpenStack and the FIFA Worldcup '98 data set for experimentation.

INTRODUCTION

Cloud computing aids start-ups, small and medium level organization to reduce their capital investment (Salesforce, 2015) on the infrastructure front and use those investments towards their core business accomplishments. National Institute of Standards and Technology (NIST) defines the cloud computing

DOI: 10.4018/978-1-7998-5348-0.ch024

(NIST, 2017) is a model for enabling convenient on-demand network access to a shared pool of configurable computing resources such as networks, servers, storage, applications and services that can be rapidly provisioned and released with minimal management effort or service provider interaction. This cloud model promotes the availability and it exhibits the following five characteristics: on-demand self-service, broad network access, resource pooling, rapid elasticity and measured service.

Cloud Computing Classifications, Threats and Types

The cloud computing is classified based on the cloud services offered and cloud deployment scenario as follows:

- The cloud service delivery-based classifications are (WhatIsCloud, 2016a) Software as a Service (SaaS), Platform as a Service (PaaS) and Infrastructure as a Service (IaaS);
- The cloud deployment service models categories are (WhatIsCloud, 2016b) Private cloud, Public cloud, Hybrid cloud and Community Cloud.

Cloud Computing Threats

The cloud computing itself is evolving day by day. So, all the potential threats that are faced by computing technologies such as data breach, distributed denial of service, insider threat, malware injection, data loss, etc., are also applicable to the cloud computing (Ma, 2015) as well. It has become a question of how secure and safe the cloud computing for the business or business critical applications such as E-commerce, E-healthcare, financial services, online services like reservation system etc. Due to these security concerns, cloud computing adoption for business is very slow. The Distributed Denial of Service (DDoS) is one of the major threat to the cloud computing environment. There are multiple types of DDoS exists and they are explained in the next section.

Types of DDoS Attacks

The DDoS attacks are generally classified (Arbor Networks, 2019) (Radware, 2016) (Wikipedia, n.d.) into the following types:

- **Volumetric Attacks:** The attack is targeted to the network bandwidth. Examples are ICMP flooding, UDP flooding, etc.;
- **Protocol Attacks:** The server resources targeted in this type attack. Example is Ping of death;
- **Application Layer Attacks:** This aims to bring down the application services. The example is HTTP flooding attack.

The motivation behind DDoS attacks may be anything like bring down the competition, revenge, political reasons, etc. (Spacey, 2011) (Penta Security, 2016).

The Significance of Detecting HTTP Flooding DDoS Attack in the Cloud

The HTTP flooding attack detection in the cloud is very challenging. This has gained greater attention with the research community. There are few companies such as Arbor Networks, Radware, Incapsula, etc., are working actively on the DDoS solution:

- One of the recent surveys from Arbor Networks states that HTTP flooding is the topmost attack realized in the industry as shown in Figure 1;
- The CNN report (O'Brien, 2016), says that the number of websites such as Twitter, Netflix, Github, etc., are affected by flooding attacks;
- The CNN report (O'Brien, 2016) also adds that one of the leading public cloud service Amazon Web Services (AWS) too experienced the issue;
- The website tripwire (Bisson, 2016) captures the top 5 most significant application level DDoS attacks and those attacks are:
  - Attacks on services provided by Dyn, Inc.;
  - Attacks on blogs of American journalist and investigative reporter Brain Krebs;
  - Attacks on Hillary Clinton and Donald Trump campaign sites;
  - Attacks on Rio Olympics Websites;
  - An Attack on Russian Banks such as Sberbank and Alfabank;
- The article "Application attacks against clouds up 45%" (Korolov, 2015) states that 45% increase in application layer attacks in the cloud as per the report from Houston-based cloud security firm Alert Logic, Inc. This report prepared based on the security incidents over 3000 enterprise customers;
- The article "Denial-of-Service Attacks Meet the Cloud" (Robert Lemos 2010) covers the experts view on the DDoS attack over the cloud. It's emphasis on detection of HTTP flooding attacks over the cloud environment.

THE SPECIAL NEEDS AND COMPLEXITIES ASSOCIATED WITH THE CLOUD ENVIRONMENT

The following characteristics create the special needs and complexities associated with the HTTP flooding detection in the cloud environment:

- **Multi-tenancy model:** Multiple customers can be co-located in the same cloud environment. If anyone of the customer affected by the HTTP flooding attack causes a greater impact on the rest of clients as well as the cloud environment itself. Identifying the customer under attack in the multitenant environment is challenging and require special approach than the traditional model;
- **Virtualization and Elasticity:** Virtualization is the core concept of cloud computing. This helps cloud computing to achieve on-demand services, multi-tenancy, etc., with the help of virtualization. There shall be multiple virtual instances of the same customer is running across the different geographical locations of the cloud service provider (CSP). This requires special kind of HTTP flooding DDoS detection solution integrated with CSP environment even at the virtual routers and virtual instance level rather than typical intrusion detection system lies at the gateway;

Figure 1. Arbor network survey report

Percentage

	Count	Percentage
TCP/80	255057	12.91
UDP/53	148153	7.50
UDP/80	81526	4.13
UDP/4444	74402	3.77
TCP/443	66161	3.35

>   **TCP/80 (HTTP) is top target with UDP/53 (DNS) in second place.**

>   **UDP/80, in third place, is likely reflection activity targeting HTTP**

ARBOR

- **Computing Node:** The computing node (CN) is one more level of abstraction over virtualization and responsible for running virtual machine (VM) of the customer. Each CN may run VM's of the same or different customers. The CN also spread across various locations of the CSP. The HTTP flooding DDoS attack must be detected at each CN level. This mandate special kind of DDoS detection approach in the cloud environment.

The above points discussed underscores need for the special approach to detect the HTTP flooding attacks in the cloud environment.

THE CONTRIBUTION OF THE PROPOSED SOLUTION

The High Notes on the Contribution

- The proposed solution has introduced the concept of Tri-Zonal Linear Prediction (TLP) classification model in the cloud environment. This helps to classify and identify the attacks in a better manner rather than the traditional method. The details are discussed in upcoming section;
- The cloud has multiple possible HTTP flooding attack paths. All the paths need to be safeguarded from the attack and the same has been addressed in this work. The more details are covered in various possibilities of the HTTP flooding attack in cloud section;
- The TLP classification model is integrated into the cloud platform itself to inspect the HTTP request coming into the cloud so that it will detect any HTTP flooding attacks. The zone classification has the capability to detect the HTTP flooding attack within the same tenant, attacks from different tenants of the cloud and attack from the outside world to cloud;

- The solution helps the cloud provider to safeguard their internal cloud resources from such attacks in addition to the victim customer;
- The HTTP flooding attack is generated using the FIFA World Cup'98 real-time DDoS attack dataset.

The rest of the paper is organized as follows. The immediate next section explained the related works and critical reviews. Consecutively section captures details of the proposed solution architecture in details, followed by covers the Tri-Zonal classification model, the details on experimentation carried out, performance analysis and results are discussed. Finally, the conclusion and future direction of research are covered.

RELATED WORKS AND CRITICAL REVIEW

Authors have reviewed various works related to DDoS detection and mitigation. This section restricts the discussion to the most relevant papers and their critical reviews.

Karanpreet Singh et al. (2017) covered the detailed analysis of the Application layer HTTP flooding DDoS attack. It gives an excellent insight into HTTP flooding attack. Also, discussed the current research challenges and limitations in detecting the HTTP flooding DDoS attack. It formulates four research questions like what the strategies are used to launch an attack, what are the attributes involved in detection, what is the basic modelling used in detection and what are the software tools and data sets available for evaluation. It also discussed generalized protection mechanism, which involves multiple steps of processing and monitoring attributes such as traffic level, user level, detection attributes like management of active queue, scoring, etc. Also, filtering at different levels such as the packet, session, user, etc., are discussed. In real time, adoption and implementation of the generic solution do not meet the cloud requirement. It also involves the complexity of the practical implementation and costly from a perspective of resource, administration, etc.

Konstantin Borisenko et al. (2016) proposed a solution for detecting the DDoS attack in the cloud computing using data mining technique. The cloud environment used in this experiment is the OpenStack. This paper provided the solution for detecting HTTP flooding, TCP flooding, UDP flooding and ICMP flooding. The HTTP flooding carried out with the help of the tool known as Siege-3.1.0. This tool used to measure the performance of an application under heavy load condition (Jdfulmer, 2012). In the real-time, the characteristics of HTTP flooding vary drastically when compared to HTTP flooding generated using tools. The tool always exhibits the same kind of characteristics for all the HTTP requests generated, for example using the same set of source IP for generating the attack, HTTP URL in a request, kind of data being accessed, etc. So, the result of this solution may not yield the same result in the real-time. This paper has the gap in validating the solution against such real-time data set.

Ryotaro Kobayashi et al. (2016) classified the DoS attack into multiple types such as the impact on the service quality, method of attack, method of controlling the attack, layer of the protocol targets and scenario of the attack. It focused on providing the solution to HTTP flooding attacks. The notion of the paper is to have some intermediate server act in between the internet and the actual server known as control machine. Actual servers which serve the legitimate users and decoy machines used to fool the attackers as if the server is getting down. This paper discussed that control machine detects the attack and redirect it to decoy machines and continue to serve the legitimate users with the normal machine.

The problem with the proposed solution is the whole intelligence lies with control machine, if something goes wrong with control machine then the user cannot access anything, which is prone to single point failure. The reservation of the machine as decoy machine is the costly of the solution.

Shahanaz Begum et al. (2016) talked about DDoS detection and prevention in the private cloud. The proposed solution lacks in defining the architecture details on the detection and mitigation mechanism. The experimental setup has 3 virtual machines involved, and one has the web server running, and other two serve as bots. The attack generated with the proprietary tool. In the real-time environment, the number of parties involved is more and providing the solution with 3 virtual machines do not scale well in the real-time. The result exhibited may not be the same as the real-time scenario.

Tarun Karnwal et al. (2012) discussed vulnerabilities in each service models and proposed the architecture against XML and the HTTP flooding attacks. This paper failed to explain the deployment of the protection mechanism. It did not cover where the protection mechanism is implemented. It detected the flooding attack, based on the number of requests. In real-time, during flash web events the actual legitimate request may also be high. So, it lacks in giving clarity on how to suspect the incoming HTTP requests.

Ashaq Hussain Dar et al. (2016) discussed the various DDoS attack in the cloud and detection techniques with help of Eucalyptus private cloud setup. It used tools like hping3, slowhttptest. For the HTTP flooding and detection, the work used only two virtual machines as bots. The attack generated using the slowhttptest tool. The solution evaluated might not be sufficient to detect the real-time attacks and it may not work in the scaled environment where attack carried out with the huge number of bots.

Opeyemi Osanaiye et al. (2016) offered the DDoS detection solution in the cloud environment using packet inter-arrival time. This paper focused on determining the behavioral change of the user using the packet arrival time between consecutive packets. It used cumulative sum algorithm to calculate the change point. This solution might not work well when the user changes the attacking interval by means of adjusting the HTTP requests. This packet interval time can be used as one of the parameters to detect the DDoS attacks but considering it as the one and only parameter may not give expected results for the real-time applications.

Mohammed SALIM et al. (2018) recommended anomaly-based detection of the HTTP flooding attack. This paper identifies the attack using the behavioral changes with respect to URI in request. The solution did not consider the cloud environment. It has a gap in addressing cloud-specific requirements.

Mohamed Idhammad et al. (2018) proposed solution detects the HTTP flooding attack in the cloud environment. The network header entropy value used for classification and identification of the HTTP flooding attack. The Theoretic Entropy and Random Forest ensemble algorithms are used for the classifications. Though this paper discussed the solution for a cloud environment, the fundamental cloud characteristics are missed out. This limitation has a bigger impact on providing the appropriate solution for the cloud.

Hossein Abbasi et al. (2019) defined a machine-learning based approach to detect E-DoS attack in the cloud. The solution detects the attack based on the classification of client behavior as normal and abnormal. The proposed solution considers only virtualization aspect of the cloud and rest of the characteristic are missed. The various possible attack paths are not discussed in the cloud.

Trung V. Phan et al. (2019) offered a DDoS attack defense solution for SDN-Based cloud environment. This work proposed hybrid machine learning based approach to improve the traffic classification. This solution is focused on general DDoS attack in the SDN based cloud environment. The HTTP flooding is not discussed as part of the work. This has gaps in addressing various cloud characteristics.

Seth Djane Kotey et al. (2019) reviewed the existing defense mechanism against DDoS attacks and captured the strengths and their weakness of the solutions.

From the discussion and critical review of the various work done so far, still have the gaps in defining the solution for the HTTP flooding attack detection. The following section covers the proposed solution in detail and the experiment/results obtained.

PROPOSED SOLUTION ARCHITECTURE

In the proposed solution, the authors considered various points discussed in the special needs of cloud computing section. Figure 2 captures the proposed solution architecture model. This model covers the various aspects of the cloud environment:

- **Multi-tenancy:** The different colors of virtual machine (VM) shown in the architecture model indicates the different customers to realize multitenancy. The VMs with the same color belongs to a customer;
- **Compute Node:** The compute node (CN) given in the architecture consists of the virtual instance of multiple customers. Each CN has the capability to route the traffics with-in the clients, across the clients and to the outside world such as the internet;
- **Virtualization and Elasticity:** The CSP can add or remove the number of compute nodes as well as the number of VMs within the compute nodes dynamically. This covers the aspect of virtualization and elasticity of the cloud environment.

Figure 2. Proposed solution architecture

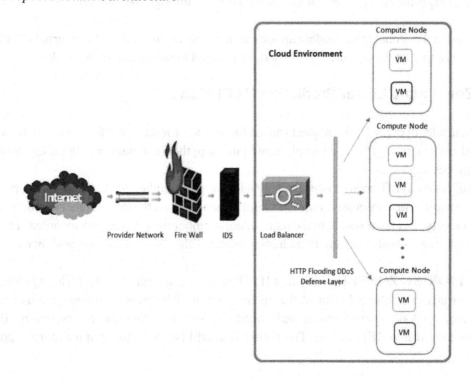

The HTTP flooding DDoS defense layer integrated into the cloud environment to protect each tenant as well as the CSP from the HTTP flooding DDoS attacks. This layer implements Tri-Zonal state technique to detect such HTTP flooding attacks. The details on Tri-Zonal state technique is discussed in the next section.

THE TRIZONAL STATE LINEAR PREDICTION (TLP) MODEL

The proposed novelty lies with implementation of Tri-Zonal State technique in the cloud environment. This involves multiple processing like sniffing, analyzing and classifying the incoming packets into the Tri-Zonal state. The HTTP flooding attack is notified to the cloud administrator for further action. Before getting into the details of Tri-Zonal state technique, the potential attacking scenarios explored in the subsection.

The Various Possibilities of the HTTP Flooding Attack in the Cloud

The possibilities of the HTTP flooding in the cloud environment (Dhanapal et al., 2019) are:

- The HTTP flooding attack can be carried out from multiple VMs of the same tenant. For example, different departments of the same organization can access the web services hosted by the organization;
- The HTTP attack shall be done by one or more VMs from other tenants hosted on the same cloud environment. The one of the details compromised tenant in the cloud shall generate attack to another tenant in the same cloud;
- The users from internet shall attack the web server running in the cloud environment. For example, compromised end users attack the web service through the internet.

The proposed Tri-Zonal state model captures all the internal as well as the external HTTP attacks. This makes sure that all the scenarios discussed are covered to detect any such attacks.

The Tri-Zonal State Linear Prediction (TLP) Model

Initially, the header of every HTTP request sniffed for the classification and forwarded to the web server in the cloud environment. This layer implemented using python language and the scapy module used for packet processing.

The details of the HTTP request like source IP address, port number, packet arrival time, packet inter-arrival time between two consecutive requests from the same source, the total number of requests received from the source, type of the resource in the request, port number pattern, etc., are recorded. These details used to classify the request from any IP address into one of the Tri-Zonal states as shown in Figure 3:

- **MONITORING ZONE:** The very first HTTP request from unknown IP address placed into this zone for analyzing the behavior of the client. If the user behaves in any suspicious manner like continuously flooding the request, malformed requests, etc., then the corresponding IP address will be moved into RED ZONE. The notification will be given to administrator for appropriate action;

Figure 3. The Tri-Zonal State Linear Prediction (TLP) model zone transitions

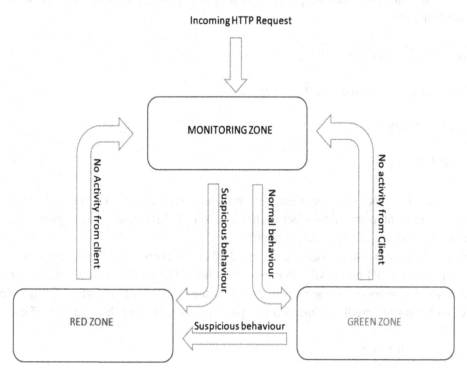

- **GREEN ZONE:** The HTTP requests from any known IP address in the MONITORING ZONE behaves in a legitimate manner like very reasonable number of requests to the web server, accessing the valid resource, reasonable bandwidth utilization, etc., then IP address is put into the GREEN ZONE. If the user behavior toggles after getting into the GREEN ZONE like the sudden spike in the request, etc., then the IP address put into RED ZONE and notified to the administrator for further action;
- **RED ZONE:** Any IP address in the MONITORING or GREEN zone behaves in a suspicious way like the continuous flooding of requests, malformed requests, invalid access to the resources, etc., are put into this zone. In case, there is no activity from IP address for the longer period after entering GREEN ZONE or RED ZONE, then the corresponding IP address will be moved into MONITORING ZONE and notification will be given to the administrator.

Mathematical Model

Every HTTP request from the clients recorded with following:

- The packet arrival timestamp from specific source IP address (PATS);
- Inter-arrival time between packets from specific source IP address in millisecond (IAT);
- The cumulative inter-arrival time between packets from specific source IP address (CIAT);
- The average inter-arrival time between packets for specific source IP address (AIAPT);
- The average number of requests from specific source IP address per millisecond (ANR);
- The total number of packets received from the specific source IP address (TNPR);

- The time difference between last packet and very first packet received from the same source IP address (TDLFP):

IAT = Current PATS - Previous PATS (1)

CIAT = $\sum$ Individual IAT of the specific source IP address (2)

AIAPT = (CIAT / TNPR) (3)

ANR = (TNPR / TDLFP) (4)

The Round-Trip Time (RTT) is considered as 1milliseccond (van der Mei et al., 2001) for the legitimate user. The average inter-arrival time between the packet (AIAPT) and the average number of request (ANR) used for classifying the behavior of the client.

The multiple linear regression models used to calculate the correlation between the HTTP flooding attack with respect to AIAPT and ANR behavior of the client. The predictor/independent parameters are AIAPT and ANR. The response is the determination of the HTTP flooding attack from the client. The linear model with multiple predictor/independent parameter denoted by the Equation (5):

$$Y = \beta_0 + \beta_1 x_1 + \dots + \beta_k x_k + \varepsilon$$ (5)

where:

- Y: Response to determine the HTTP flooding attack for the given predictor/independent parameter values;
- β_k: K^{th} population of the regression co-efficient;
- ε: Error term that follows a normal distribution with mean of zero;
- x_k: K^{th} term of predictor/independent parameter value.

The corresponding fitted equation is:

$$\acute{Y} = b_0 + b_1 x_1 + \dots + b_k x_k$$ (6)

where:

- x_k: K^{th} term of predictor/independent parameter value;
- b_k: Estimate of Kth population regression coefficient;
- $\acute{Y}$: Fitted response value to determine the HTTP flooding attack.

The coefficients of determination calculated using the R-square method and the Equation (7) represents the same:

Table 1. Classification based on the AIAPT and ANR Range of values

S. No	AIAPT Value Range	ANR Value Range	Classification
1	<= 0.5 RTT	<= 1RTT	The HTTP flooding attack - Very High-Risk Client
2	<= 1RTT	<= 5RTT	The potential attack - High Risk Client
3	<= 2RTT	<= 20RTT	Susceptible to attack - Medium Risk Client
4	<= 3RTT	<= 40RTT	Monitor the activity - Low Risk Client
5	>3RTT	>40RTT	Legitimate - Very Low Risk Client

$$R^2 = 1 - \frac{\sum \left(y_i - \hat{y} \right)^2}{\sum \left(y_i - \bar{y} \right)^2} \tag{7}$$

where:

- R^2: Co-efficient of determination;
- y_i: ith Observed response value;
- $\bar{y}$: Mean Response value;
- $\hat{y}$: ith Fitted response value.

Based on the experiment conducted the client's behavior classified into five different categories with respect to AIAPT & ANR values. Table 1 captured the details.

Figure 4. The OpenStack network instances with their IP address details

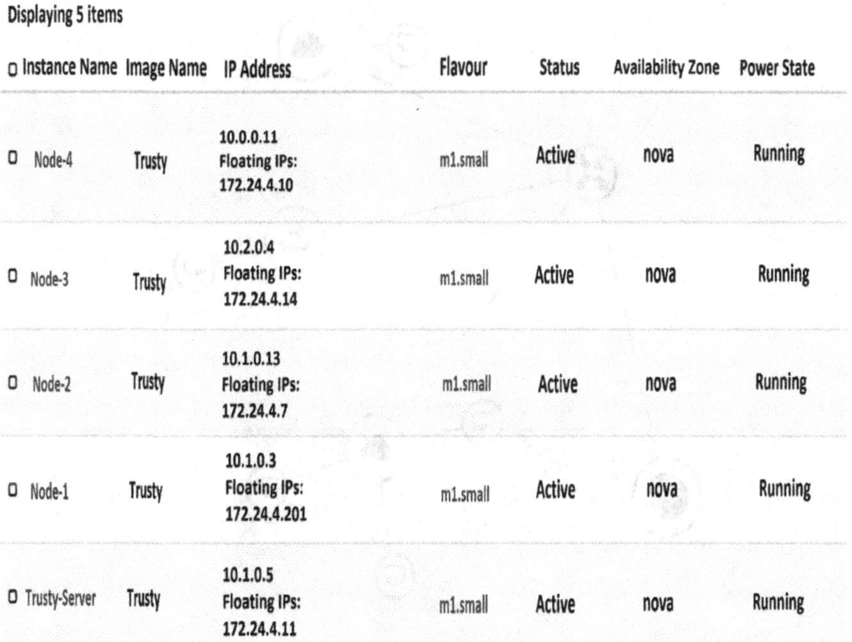

Displaying 5 items

☐ Instance Name	Image Name	IP Address	Flavour	Status	Availability Zone	Power State
☐ Node-4	Trusty	10.0.0.11 Floating IPs: 172.24.4.10	m1.small	Active	nova	Running
☐ Node-3	Trusty	10.2.0.4 Floating IPs: 172.24.4.14	m1.small	Active	nova	Running
☐ Node-2	Trusty	10.1.0.13 Floating IPs: 172.24.4.7	m1.small	Active	nova	Running
☐ Node-1	Trusty	10.1.0.3 Floating IPs: 172.24.4.201	m1.small	Active	nova	Running
☐ Trusty-Server	Trusty	10.1.0.5 Floating IPs: 172.24.4.11	m1.small	Active	nova	Running

EXPERIMENTATION, PERFORMANCE ANALYSIS AND RESULTS

The experimental environment has been created using OpenStack cloud. The OpenStack is an open source software freely available on the internet and it provides Infrastructure as a Service (IaaS) to the user.

OpenStack Testbed and Dataset Details

The proposed solution implemented in the OpenStack cloud environment. The Figure 4 shows the list of instances running on the OpenStack, their internal IP address as well as floating IP address.

The instance named as trusty-server, hosts the web application and its internal IP address is 10.1.0.5 and floating or external IP address is 172.24.4.11. The users from the internet can access the web application using IP address 172.24.4.11. The internal department of the same organization can access the web application using IP address 10.1.0.5. The instances Node-1, Node-2 and trusty-server belongs to the tenant- 1 and placed in the internal network address 10.1.0.X. The internal IP address of the Node-1 and Node-2 are 10.1.0.3 and 10.1.0.13 respectively. The external or floating IP address 172.24.4.201 allocated to Node-1 and 172.24.4.7 allocated to Node-2. The Node-3 is an instance of the tenant-2 and network allotted for tenant-2 is 10.2.0.X. The internal IP address of the Node-3 is 10.2.0.4, and corresponding external IP address is 172.24.4.14. Similarly, node-4 is a virtual instance of tenant-3 and placed in the network. The internal IP address of Node-4 is 10.0.0.11, and the floating IP address is 172.24.4.10. The corresponding OpenStack network topology details captured in Figure 5. The Tenant-1 is shown with three nodes, tenant-2 & tenant-3 represented with one node each. All three tenants connected to the router which acts as a gateway to the outside world.

Figure 5. The OpenStack network topology

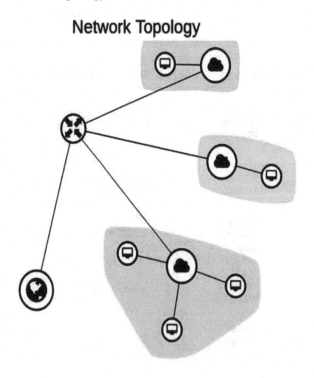

Network Topology

The authors used the IP Aliasing mechanism to assign multiple IP addresses to the single interface to mimic the multiple numbers of the bots in the cloud server. In each virtual instance running on the OpenStack are having internal as well as external IP addresses. Both IP addresses of the virtual instances also used as source IP addresses of the bots.

The FIFA World CUP 1998 real-time dataset (Arlitt et al., 2000) is a huge collection of 1.3 billion HTTP request to 33 servers across the different geographical regions. The dataset stored in the processed log format to hide the confidential information. This dataset is used in this research work to regenerate (Dhanapal et al., 2017) HTTP flooding DDoS attacks. The Wireshark tool used to capture the HTTP request coming to the web server.

Performance Analysis and Results

The HTTP flooding attack has been carried out on the web server running in the OpenStack cloud environment. The analysis is carried out based on the experimentation conducted. To represent the relationship between the HTTP flooding attack and predictor variables, the client's behavior is mapped as mentioned in Table 2.

Table 2. The client behavior – representation mapping

S. No	Clients Behavior Classification	Representation Value
1	The HTTP flooding attack - Very High-Risk Client	4
2	The potential attack - High Risk Client	3
3	Susceptible to attack - Medium Risk Client	2
4	Monitor the activity - Low Risk Client	1
5	Legitimate - Very Low Risk Client	0

The relationship between the average packet inter-arrival time from the specific source and the HTTP flooding attack is shown in Figure 6. The X-axis represents the client behavior based on Table 2. The Y-axis shows HTTP flooding attack detection. From the Figure 6, it is evident that the client behavior moving towards value 4 in the X-axis are generating attack to the web server in the cloud and these clients are plotted close to value 1 in Y-axis.

Similarly, the relationship between the average number of requests from a specific source and the HTTP flooding attack is shown in Figure 7. The X-axis indicates the client behavior based on the average number of requests from the specific source. The Y-axis shows HTTP flooding attack detection. It is clearly seen that the client behavior moving towards value 4 in the X-axis are generating attack to the web server in the cloud and the client plotted close to value 1 in Y-axis.

The ANOVA table of the multiple linear regression analysis for the experiment captured in Table 3. Table 4 captures the information like intercept and the coefficient for the predictor/independent parameters of the multilinear equation.

Figure 6. Average packet interval-arrival time in msec from specific source vs. The http flooding attack

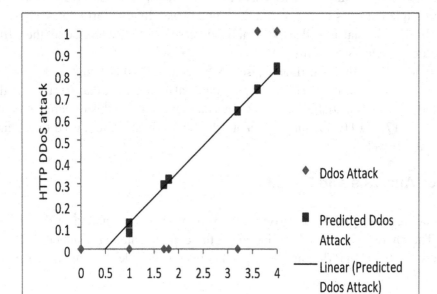

Figure 7. Average number of requests per millisecond from specific source vs. http flooding attack

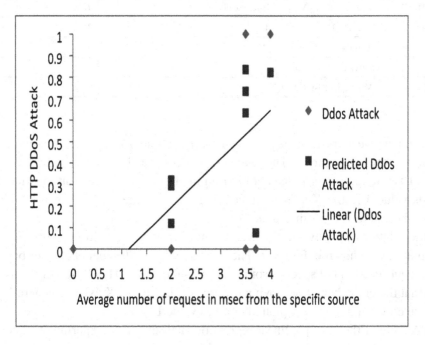

The formulation of the mathematical model for the proposed solution is:

$$Y = 0.25144\, x_1 - 0.02559\, x_2 - 0.08193 \tag{8}$$

where:

- x_1: The average inter-arrival time between packets for specific source IP address (AIAPT);
- x_2: The average number of requests from specific source IP address per second (ANR);
- Y: The HTTP flooding attack detection factor.

Table 3. The ANOVA table

ANOVA	df	SS	MS	F	Significance F
Regression	2	1.980242096	0.990121	12.420256	0.001508696
Residual	11	0.876900761	0.079718		
Total	13	2.857142857			

Table 4. Predictor variable co-efficient of the analysis

	Coefficients	Standard Error	t Stat	P-Value	Lower 95%	Upper 95%
Intercept	-0.08193378	0.172961591	-0.473711	0.6449688	-0.46261968	0.298752112
Average packet inter-arrival time in millisecond from specific source	0.251436782	0.075676191	3.3225349	0.0068007	0.084874609	0.417998954
Average number of request per millisecond from specific source	-0.02558653	0.097071113	-0.263585	0.7969718	-0.23923861	0.188065548

The snapshot of the normal and the HTTP flooding attack scenarios in the experiment are captured. Figure 8 shows the legitimate HTTP requests to the web server under the normal scenario. The X-axis represents the times, and Y-axis represents the number of packets per second. The same Figure 8 has a flash crowd observed around the time-period of 50sec.

The HTTP flooding attack scenario is shown in Figure 9. The X-axis represents time in seconds, and Y-axis represents the number of packets per second. It is evident that the number of requests is very high continuously as compared with normal scenario shown in Figure 8.

The web server has been continuously experiencing the HTTP request flooding from the various clients. This scenario is different from the scenario where momentary flash crowd depicted in Figure 6. In case of the flash crowd, the HTTP request is very high with the short span of time, whereas in the HTTP flooding attack the HTTP request rates remain high throughout the attacking interval. In this experiment, multiple clients shown in Figure 4 are sending out the HTTP flooding attack to the web server running on the trusty instance of the OpenStack. The snapshot of the HTTP flooding attack detection from the one of the clients 172.24.4.201 to the web server and the corresponding notification to the cloud administrator shown in Figure 10. The Wireshark packet capture of the HTTP flooding attack from the client 174.24.4.201 to the web server 172.24.4.11 depicted in Figure 11.

Figure 8. Workload capture during normal scenario with flash crowd

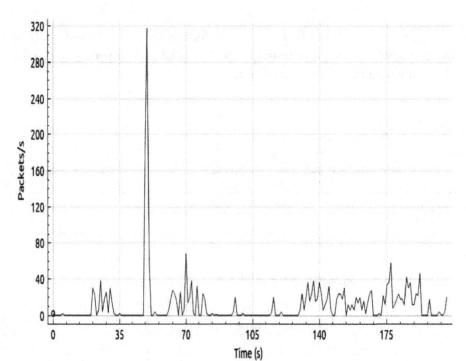

Figure 9. Workload capture during HTTP flooding attack

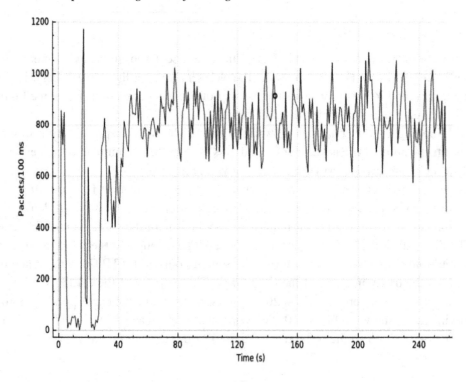

Figure 10. The HTTP flooding attack detection from 172.24.4.201 and notification to the administrator

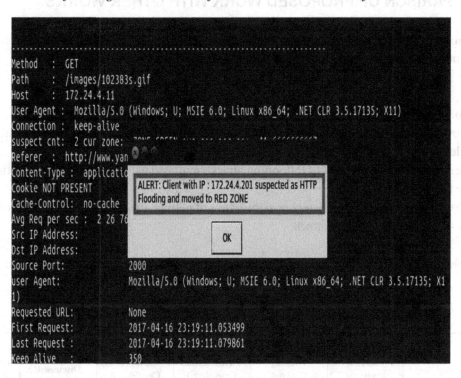

Figure 11. Wireshark packet capture during HTTP flooding attack

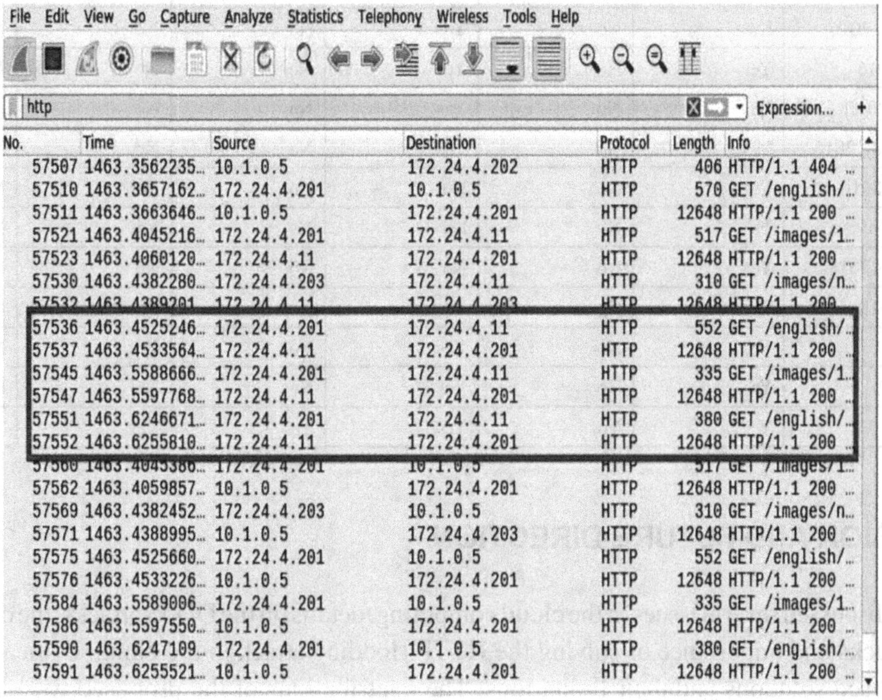

THE COMPARISON OF PROPOSED WORK WITH OTHER WORKS

This section compares the various existing works discussed with the proposed work. The comparison covers the multiple aspects that the proposed solution addressed when compared to existing works. The comparison study involves the perspective such as:

- The solution addressed the cloud specific issue;
- The coverage of core cloud characteristics such as multi-tenancy, elasticity, compute model is considered in the solution;
- The perspective of real-time HTTP flooding attack simulated using any available real-time dataset for the better results;
- The cloud environment has different possible ways of getting attacked. The proposed solution covers all such potential ways of attack.

The Table 5 depicts the comparison summary for easy understanding and interpretation.

Table 5. Comparison summary of the proposed work with other works

The Proposed Work by Authors	Cloud Specific Solution Proposed	Multi-Tenancy Covered	Elasticity/ Virtualization Considered	Compute Model Considered	Real Time DDoS Dataset Discussed/ Used	Multiple Cloud Attack Path Covered
Singh et al., 2017	No	No	No	No	Yes	No
Borisenko et al., 2016	Yes	No	Yes	Yes	No	No
Kobayashi et al., 2016	No	No	Yes	No	No	No
Begum et al., 2016	Yes	No	Yes	No	No	No
Karnwal et al., 2012	Yes	No	Yes	No	No	No
Hussain Dar et al., 2016	Yes	No	Yes	No	No	No
Osanaiye et al., 2016	Yes	No	No	No	Yes	No
Salim et al., 2018	Yes	No	No	No	Yes	No
Idhammad et al., 2018	Yes	No	No	No	No	No
Abbasi et al., 2019	Yes	No	Yes	No	No	No
Phan et al., 2019	Yes	No	Yes	No	Yes	No
John et al., 2019	Yes	No	Yes	No	No	No
Proposed Work	Yes	Yes	Yes	Yes	Yes	Yes

CONCLUSION AND FUTURE DIRECTION

The authors discussed several issues in the cloud computing, details on the DDoS attacks, the classification of DDoS attacks and importance of solving the HTTP flooding attack in the cloud. Critically reviewed several proposed solutions and their limitations. The contributions of the proposed work are covered. The proposed architecture model and the Tri-Zonal State Linear Prediction (TLP) Model is discussed in detail. Finally covered the experimentation of the implemented solution using the OpenStack cloud environment and thoroughly studied the results obtained and the corresponding snapshots are captured.

The future work is to provide more fine-grained control to the cloud administrator like defining the configuration of well-known GREEN ZONE clients, RED ZONE client's details and study the experimentation results and performance.

REFERENCES

Abbasi, H., Ezzati-Jivan, N., Bellaiche, M., Talhi, C., & Dagenais, M. R. (2019). Machine Learning-Based EDoS Attack Detection Technique Using Execution Trace Analysis. *Journal of Hardware and Systems Security*, 3(2), 164–176. doi:10.100741635-018-0061-2

Arlitt, M., & Jin, T. (2000). 1998 World Cup Web Site Access Logs. *IEEE Network*, 14(3), 30–37. doi:10.1109/65.844498

Bisson, D. (2016). *The 5 Most Significant DDoS Attacks of 2016*. Tripwire. Retrieved from https://www.tripwire.com/state-of-security/security-data-protection/cyber-security/5-significant-ddos-attacks-2016/

Borisenko, K., Smirnov, A., Novikova, E., & Shorov, A. (2016, July). DDoS attacks detection in cloud computing using data mining techniques. In *Industrial Conference on Data Mining* (pp. 197-211). Cham: Springer. doi:10.1007/978-3-319-41561-1_15

Dar, A. H., Habib, B., Khurshid, F., & Tariq Banday, M. (2016). Experimental analysis of DDoS attack and its detection in Eucalyptus private cloud platform. In *Proceedings of the Intl. Conference on Advances in Computing, Communications and Informatics (ICACCI)* (pp. 1718-1724). Academic Press. 10.1109/ICACCI.2016.7732295

Dhanapal, A., & Nithyanandam, P. (2018). A Review of Cloud Computing Adoption Issues and Challenges. *Recent Patents on Computer Science*, *11*, 1. doi:10.2174/2213275911666181114142428

Dhanapal, A., & Nithyanandam, P. (2017). An Effective Mechanism to Regenerate HTTP Flooding DDoS Attack using Real Time Data Set. In *Proceedings of the 2017 International Conference on Intelligent Computing, Instrumentation and Control Technologies (ICICICT)* (pp. 570-575). Academic Press. 10.1109/ICICICT1.2017.8342626

Dhanapal, A., & Nithyanandam, P. (2019). An OpenStack based cloud testbed framework for evaluating HTTP flooding attacks. *Wireless Networks*. doi:10.100711276-019-01937-4

Idhammad, M., Afdel, K., & Belouch, M. (2018). Detection system of HTTP DDoS attacks in a cloud environment based on information theoretic entropy and random forest. *Security and Communication Networks*. doi:10.1155/2018/1263123

Jdfulmer. (2012). *Joe Dog Software*. Retrieved from https://www.joedog.org/siege-home/

John, J., & Norman, J. (2019). Major Vulnerabilities and Their Prevention Methods in Cloud Computing. In Advances in Big Data and Cloud Computing (pp. 11-26). Springer. doi:10.1007/978-981-13-1882-5_2

Karnwal, T., Sivakumar, T., & Aghila, G. (2012). A Comber Approach to Protect Cloud Computing against XML DDoS and HTTP DDoS attack. In *Proceedings of the IEEE Students' Conference on Electrical, Electronics and Computer Science (SCEECS)* (pp. 1-5). doi:10.1109/SCEECS.2012.6184829

Kobayashi, R., Otani, G., Yoshida, T., & Kato, M. (2016). Defense Method of HTTP GET Flood Attack by Adaptively Controlling Server Resources Depending on Different Attack Intensity. *Journal of Information Processing*, 24(5), 802–815. doi:10.2197/ipsjjip.24.802

Korolov, M. (2015). *Application attacks against clouds up 45%.* CSO Online. Retrieved from http://www.csoonline.com/article/2991409/cloud-security/application-attacks-against-clouds-up-45.html

Kotey, S. D., Tchao, E. T., & Gadze, J. D. (2019). On Distributed Denial of Service Current Defense Schemes. *Technologies*, 7(1), 19. doi:10.3390/technologies7010019

Lemos, R. (2010). Denial of service attacks meet the cloud: 4 lessons. CIO. Retrieved from https://www.cio.com/article/2413818/denial-of-service-attacks-meet-the-cloud--4-lessons.html

Ma, J. (2015). *Top 10 Security Concerns for Cloud-Based Services.* Incapsula. Retrieved from https://www.incapsula.com/blog/top-10-cloud-security-concerns.html

Arbor Networks. (2019). *What is DDoS?* Retrieved from https://www.arbornetworks.com/research/ddos-resources

NIST. (2017). *NIST Cloud Computing Program – NCCP.* Retrieved from https://www.nist.gov/programs-projects/nist-cloud-computing-program-nccp

O'Brien, S.A. (2016). *Widespread cyberattack takes down sites worldwide.* CNN. Retrieved from http://money.cnn.com/2016/10/21/technology/ddos-attack-popular-sites/

Osanaiye, O., Choo, K.-K. R., & Dlodlo, M. (2016). Change-Point Cloud DDoS Detection using Packet Inter-Arrival Time. In *Proceedings of the 8th Computer Science and Electronic Engineering Conference (CEEC)* (pp. 204-209). Academic Press. 10.1109/CEEC.2016.7835914

Phan, T. V., & Park, M. (2019). Efficient Distributed Denial-of-Service Attack Defense in SDN-Based Cloud. *IEEE Access : Practical Innovations, Open Solutions*, 7, 18701–18714. doi:10.1109/ACCESS.2019.2896783

Radware. (2016). *DDoS Attack Definitions-DdoSPedia.* Retrieved from https://security.radware.com/ddos-knowledge-center/ddospedia/dos-attack/

Salesforce. (2015). *Why Move To The Cloud? 10 Benefits Of Cloud Computing.* Retrieved from https://www.salesforce.com/uk/blog/2015/11/why-move-to-the-cloud-10-benefits-of-cloud-computing.html

Salim, M., & Seçkin ARI (2018). Anomaly-Based Detection of Non-Recursive HTTP GET Flood DDoS Attack. In *Proceedings of the International Conference on Cyber Security and Computer Science (ICONCS'18)*, Safranbolu, Turkey. Academic Press.

Penta Security. (2016). *DDoS Top 6: Why Hackers Attack.* Retrieved from https://www.pentasecurity.com/blog/ddos-top-6-hackers-attack/

Shahanaz Begum, I., & Geetharamani, G. (2016). DDoS Attack detection and Prevention in Private Cloud Environment. *International Journal of Innovations in Engineering and Technology, 7*(3), 527–531.

Singh, K., Singh, P., & Kumar, K. (2017). Application layer HTTP-GET flood DDoS attacks: Research landscape and challenges. *Computers & Security, 65,* 344–372. doi:10.1016/j.cose.2016.10.005

Spacey, J. (2011). *The 5 Motives for DDoS Attack.* Simplicable. Retrieved from https://arch.simplicable.com/arch/new/the-5-motives-for-DDoS-attack

van der Mei, R. D., Hariharan, R., & Reeser, P. K. (2001). Web Server Performance Modeling. *Telecommunication Systems, 16*(3-4), 361–378. doi:10.1023/A:1016667027983

WhatIsCloud.com. (2016a). *Cloud Delivery Models.* Retrieved from http://whatiscloud.com/cloud_delivery_models/index

WhatIsCloud.com. (2016b). *Cloud Deployment Models.* Retrieved from http://whatiscloud.com/cloud_deployment_models/index

Wikipedia. (n.d.). *Denial-of-service attack.* Retrieved from https://en.wikipedia.org/wiki/Denial-of-service_attack

This research was previously published in the International Journal of Information System Modeling and Design (IJISMD), 10(3); edited by Remigijus Gustas; pages 41-58, copyright year 2019 by IGI Publishing (an imprint of IGI Global).

Chapter 25
DOS Attacks on Cloud Platform:
Their Solutions and Implications

Rohit Kumar

Chandigarh University, India

ABSTRACT

IaaS, PaaS, and SaaS models collectively form the Cloud Computing Infrastructure. The complexity of interrelationship of service models is very high and so security issue becomes essentials and must be developed with utmost care. Distributed DOS attacks are a major concern for different organization engaged in using cloud based services. The denial of service attack and distributed denial of service attacks in particular in cloud paradigms are big threat on a cloud network or platform. These attacks operate by rendering the server and network useless by sending unnecessary service and resource requests. The victims host or network isn't aware of such attacks and keeps providing recourses until they get exhausted. Due to resource exhaustions, the resources requests of genuine users doesn't get fulfilled. Severity of these attacks can lead to huge financial losses if, they are able to bring down servers executing financial services. This chapter presents DOS threats and methods to mitigate them in varied dimensions.

INTRODUCTION

Cloud computing has gained significant importance and has become obvious part of our day to day computation and communication needs. The cloud provides a platform for computation in terms of both hardware and software. The IaaS, PaaS and SaaS are cloud based services and provide online storage spaces, computational platform, customized software's etc. With more and more dependence on cloud computing, the issue of security becomes very important and is critical to the success of cloud based services. Many type of threats exists in cloud domain but, in this chapter we particularly focuses on Denial of Service attacks and methods to control them.

Denial of service attacks (DoS) are well known attacks and poses a serious problem in internet and other types of networks. The goal of DoS is to disturb the services and making them inaccessible to the user. In this kind of attack the network is rendered useless by attacking vehemently on the bandwidth and

DOI: 10.4018/978-1-7998-5348-0.ch025

connectivity. In these attacks the attacker sends a large stream of packets which causes huge congestion on the victims network. Due to this high congestion, the network cease to works and even a single request doesn't get served. In past there have been numerous attacks of these kind which targeted many famous internet sites and exposed their vulnerabilities. The distributed DOS called DDOS has been a complex and powerful technique to attack internet and its resources. As multiple machine or attackers can target a single machine; to identifying the real attackers for such attacks and to mitigate their effect is very difficult to achieve. The internet protocols like TCP/IP are well studied and some of them provides open resources access model which makes them easily targetable by the attackers. The attackers targets the some key loopholes in the internet system architecture to carry out such attacks. The DDOS attacks are called many to one attack as multiple sources attacks a single machine in well planned and synchronized way. These multiple attacker machines strangulates the target machine by huge data i.e. large volume of data or packet steams are sent to target machine to swamp it and efforts are made to make these packets genuine, this process renders the target useless. The traffic or data from multiple machines is transferred in aggregated and intelligent manner so that the target cannot distinguish among them and treat them as genuine and valid packets. The attacker usually knows the traffic handling capacity of the target and generates far more data than its capacity. The DDOS attack can damage the target form moderate to critical level. These attacks can lead the system to get shutdown, to corrupt files and usually results in total or partial loss of services.

The difficult thing about DDOS is that there is no clearly apparent feature which can lead to detection of these attacks. So, clear and direct methods to deal which such attacks aren't easy to devise and implement. The attackers now a days has access to user friendly and easy to use software's which assists in carrying out these attacks and averagely secured machine cannot handle such attacks.

The DoS attacking programs are devised with simple logic and occupy small memory making their handing easier. The attackers are vigilant and keep on devising new methods to carry out such attacks and its reverse is reciprocated by the defenders. The defenders must be pro-actively vigilant to secure their system. The DDOS handling technique are growing at a rapid rate but, a real panacea for such attacks is difficult to achieve. In practice multiple flavours of these attacks exists and providing a safe solution for all of them is very difficult to achieve. The mitigating techniques employed for such attacks tries to stop the attacker by making such attack difficult to carry out and making the attacker accountable for these attacks.

CLASSIFICATION OF DOS ATTACKS:

The DoS attacks can be carried out in different ways. The major distinguishing features has been mentioned here. Figure 1 presents the classification of DoS attacks. Below is a brief introduction to these attacks:

- **Network Device Level Attack:** DoS attacks in network device level can be caused by exhausting hardware resources of network devices (Douligeris, 2004) and by exploiting bugs in software also. One of the most common examples of such attack is buffer overrun attack. Some password checking routines are not well coded and can easily become target of buffer overrun attack by entering long passwords.

- **The OS Level Attacks:** These attacks are carried out by targeting the vulnerabilities in the underlying OS. One such attack Is Ping of death attack (S.F Rouger, 2012). In Ping death attacks large number of ICMP messages with data length larger than the capacity of standard IP packet are sent to target machine. This usually crashes the victims' machine and can incur unrecoverable losses.
- **Application-Based Attacks:** These attacks are carried out by finding the specific bugs in the application itself. The attacker tries to set the machine and application out of order and or makes it too slow to respond. Finger bomb (W. Paper, 2002) is one such application based attack.
- **Flooding Attacks:** Are very common and tries to choke the network and machine by sending it large voluminous data. Flood pinging is a commonly used attack using flooding method. The flooding attacks usually target the bandwidth of the victim's network by sending more data (meaning less data) than the network capacity. In some instances a server providing some services is overwhelmed with large service requests causing denial of service. The attacker uses a spoofed address to carry out such attacks to avoid detection.
- **Protocol Based Attacks:** The protocol feature based attacks tries to figure out possible loopholes in the protocols used for communication. One such attack is IP spoofing which can be done with moderate efforts. Many other kind of attacks targets DNS cache on name servers changing their configuration and changing the registration details of the web sites and other services. This usually results in wrong routing by the victim and ultimately he lends up at a wrong place.

Figure 1. Classification of DOS attacks

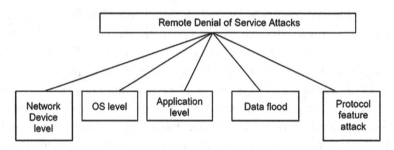

A Typical DDOS Policy

Figure 2 (a) and 2(b) presents a typical policy for carrying out DDOS attacks. Figure 2(b) is same as Figure 2(a) represents the actual attack environment for better understanding. This strategy consists of following four components:

1. The attacker
2. The compromised masters or handlers which can control other machines/agents
3. Compromised hosts which acts as zombie nodes and generates large volume of data.
4. The victim.

Figure 2. DDOS attack process

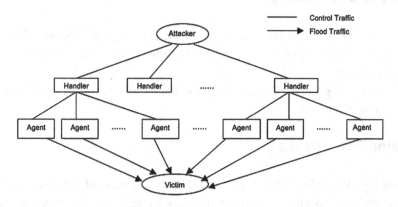

The real attacker doesn't carry out attacks directly but, uses handles and agents to carry out the desired attack. The handler nodes are compromised host and execute a specialized code on them. This code or program is capable of governing number of agents. The agents are the nodes which actually generate false requests and are called zombie hosts. These hosts also run a special program to generate large number of false requests.

Figure 3. DDOS architecture

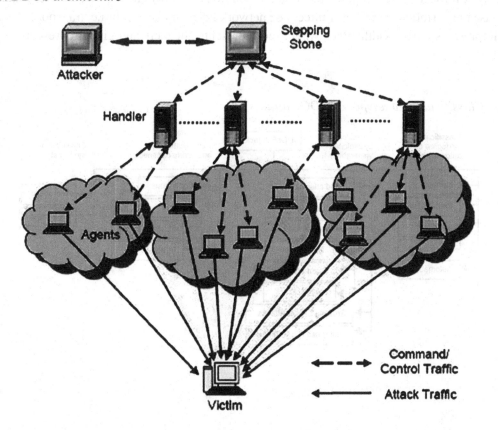

Different Types of DoS Attacks

Dos attacks can be carried out in number of ways and are evolving continuously. Figure 3 presents all kinds of DDOS attacks which depends upon degree of automation, by exploited vulnerability, attack are dynamics and by impact.

Some of these attacks are general DoS attacks and will not be discussed in detail But, attacks relevant to cloud domain will be discussed.

Cloud and Major DoS Attacks

The cloud provides a platform for computing through the utilization of software and hardware which empowers the users and organizations to perform their tasks efficiently. So, provision of robust security is pivotal to the success of cloud as it's a network based platform. The cloud providing virtualisation introduces vulnerabilities which includes DDOS, spoofing, sniffing and lot more which are obstruction in cloud growth. The main goal of this chapter is to provide comprehensible discussion of DoS attacks in context of cloud and to provide overview of techniques which provides mitigation from DoS attacks. Figure 3 provides a comprehensive list of all types of DoS attacks but, the present chapter focuses on key cloud based DoS attacks and their repercussions.

- **DDOS Attacks Impact on Layer 3 and 4 OSI:** Attack on these two layers are based on jeopardizing the network capacity. In these DDOS attack voluminous data is generated which targets the network infrastructure. High floods of data is sent to slow down the web server and gradually decrease the performance of Layer three, i.e., network layer and layer four i.e. transport layer. Figure 4 Represents a bandwidth attack where red represents attackers and green represents legitimate users.

Figure 4. Classification and types of DDOS attacks

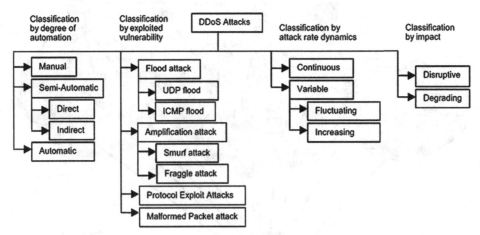

- **Flooding Attack:** SYN food attacks are common, simple but yet, powerful kind of DDOS attacks. The SYN attacks are performed by sending stream of packets with spoofed IP address. The recipient treats them as genuine and reserves resources for them. As the requests are so large in number that a given server runs out of its resources. The key to this attack is spoofed IP address for which a client actually doesn't exists. This fictitious client creates number of half connections to rob a server of its resources and renders it useless. Figure 5(a) presents the TCP connection setup process and Figure 5(b) shows how SYN floods affects the receiver and causes half closed connections.

Figure 5. Bandwidth attack

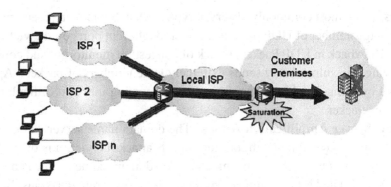

SYN flooding attacks are illustrated with following example:

- **TCP Connection Management:** The sender first establishes connection before actual transfer of data

Setup Process

- First set and initialize TCP variables, i.e., sequence number, buffers, flow control information, receiver window, etc.
- Then client initiates a connection
- Server responds to the client

Process of Three-Way Handshake

Step 1: Client sends TCP SYN seg. to server (seg. Stands for segment)
  ◦ It mention sequence number
  ◦ It contains no data
Step 2: Server gets SYN segment, which replies with SYNACK seg.
  ◦ Server reserves buffers
  ◦ Mentions server first sequence number
Step 3: The client node gets SYNACK, responds with ACK which may or may not contain data

Process of SYN Flooding and Its Steps

- Attacking computer uses spoofed address and sends multiple (flood) of request
- Victim machine reserves resources for every request
  - The connection state remain maintained until timeout
  - Half connections remains for fixed bound time
- Upon resource exhaustion legitimate requests from genuine users are declined

These steps just listed are classical example of DoS attack. These attacks don't harm the TCP connection initiating node, but forces the respondent to spawn a new thread for each service request.

- **UDP Attacks:** It is a most commonly observed type of DDOS attack in recent past. In UDP flood attack, a very large number of UDP packets are sent to different ports on the victim host by the attacker. Major Drawback in UDP Packets is lack of congestion monitoring and control system. The attacker knowing this vulnerability sends extremely large numbers of packets. Again this attacks are carried out by using IP address spoofing. The IP spoofing makes it difficult to control attack and to track the attacker.
- **Domain Name Server Amplification Attack:** The domain name server can be made to participate in DDOS attacks by wrong configuration. In this attack the victim is overwhelmed by large number of DNS replies which he never initiated. The domain name server is a publically accessible and open system and if programmed wrong can have sever repercussions. In DNS amplification attacks the response to the DNS request is quite large than the request itself. To perform this attack the attacker first creates a reliable domain name server and attaches a large garbage file with it. After this the attacker programs and commands zombies. These zombies have spoofed IP address of a victim machine and starts sending queries to the server. In response to the query the victim machine starts getting large replies ensuring resource exhaustion.
- **Internet Control Message Protocol (ICMP) Flooding Attacks:** This is a simple DDOS attack in which an attacker sends voluminous ICMP echo requests i.e. ping masseuses to slow done the receiver network and its associated services.
- **Smurf Attacks:** It is a ICMP kind of attack and operates by utilising broadcast IP address of a network. Here again the attacker utilizes the spoofed IP address to make the attack work. Using this spoofed IP it sends volumes of ICMP messages on the network and the victim in turn starts sending the replies. Figure 6 shows how an attacker sends a broadcast message with IP address of the victim host and then all devices are forced to reply to the victim host shown by red lines between the devices and victim.

Method

The attacker, i.e., DoS source sends ICMP message with wrong source address and wrong destination address. In ICMP message source address contains the address of the victim and destination address used is broadcast address. When this request reaches to the gateway (broadcast network) the gateway is not able to comprehend it and sends three ICMP replies to victim. Here three replies are created because gateway consists of three hosts and each host replies to the ICMP request from the attacker. In

Figure 6. TCP connection process

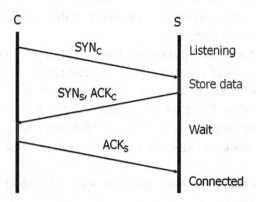

this process, the victim keep getting unnecessary replies and wastes its resources. In order to carry out these attacks the attacker must know the network topology very well.

- **Application Layer Attacks:** Application layer threats and attacks are hard to perceive in cloud based services, as they are difficult to be differentiated from authentic traffic, which intends makes the system vulnerable. Figure 7 Depicts Application Layer DDOS attacks which hampers the services of the application zone i.e. Web Server and Database Server.

Figure 7. SYN floods and half-closed connections

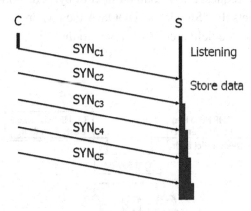

Application Layer DDOS Attacks

- **Request-Flooding Attacks:** All the major application layer protocols like HHTP GETs, DNS requests, and SIP Invites can participates in DDOS attacks though unwilling fully. All these attacks tries to overwhelm the server with genuine looking large number of requests (Shamsolmoali, 2014).

- **Application Layer Asymmetric Attacks:** Asymmetric Attacks send "high-workload" requests to the server. In these types of attacks the CPU, memory or disk space are completely brought down and their services are severely degraded.
- **Repeated One-Shot Attacks on Application Layer:** Attackers send one heavy request per session and in other words you can say attack load is spread around multiple sessions.
- **Application-Exploit Attacks:** These attacks finds out loopholes in the applications and makes these applications vulnerable. These types of attacks deliberately targets the application software to make them work in inappropriate manner and to take the control over application system. One of its common type of attacks is Structured Query Language (SQL) injection attack (Khajuria, 2013).
- **DDOS Attacks in Web Services:** Web applications available in cloud servers are hampered by these attacks they include:
- **Attack Using HTTP:** Non-specific request are targeted on the host, i.e., request of ambiguous nature are presented to the system. The web services are outperformed by extensively large process requests. Due to heavy use of resources (consumed/reserved by false requests), denial of services attacks are easily carried out and can result in huge losses in terms of data and functionality.
- **Malfunctioned HTTP:** Invalid packets are sent to the web servers which in-turn consumes server resources. The ZAFI.B is worm attack which best suites as an example for malfunctioned HTTP attack.
- **HTTP Request Attacks:** This type of attacks flood web servers with number of legitimate HTTP requests seeking to consume server resources to carry out DDOS attack.
- **HTTP Idle Attacks:** An attack that opens HTTP connections but then goes idle without actually sending a complete HTTP request but a small number of bytes dribbles out which never completes the request. Figure 8 depicts the "Slowloris" DDOS Attack where a prolonged and low bandwidth incomplete HTTP requests are delivered from a host to the server.

Figure 8. Smurf attack

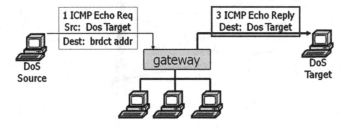

- **XML XXEA Attacks:** XML attacks target web application, which communicate through XML documents. Attackers construct a message which is malformed send it to the web applications. As shown in Figure 9 a message is sent from the client to the Web Application on the Cloud and which in turn gives response with a locally stored file address as ["/etc/hostname"]. If these requests, are made in abundance, can result in different losses.

Figure 9. Access zone and application zone

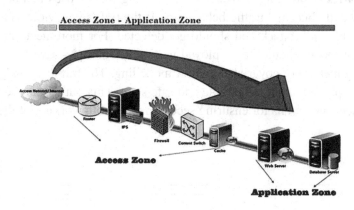

Detection and Mitigation Techniques Against DDOS Attacks

Numerous methods have been invented to tackle DDOS attack. Each of these mechanism tackles different variation of DDOS and cloud based attacks. Figure 10 presents all such possible methods. Among all of them few have been discussed here which are specific about cloud platform.

Figure 10. Idle attacks

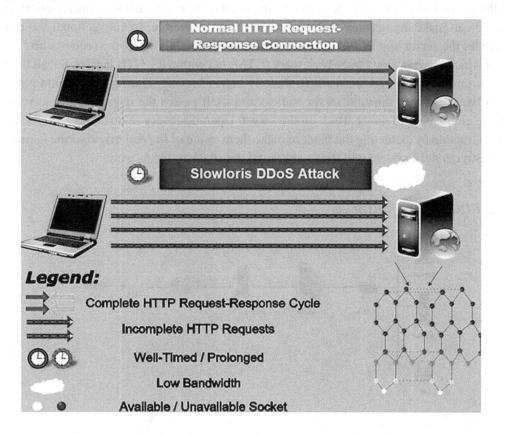

- **Covariance Matrix Modelling:** Covariance modelling theory tries to find out the differences between normal and abnormal traffic behaviours. If the traffic behaviour is quite abnormal then it can be a possible DoS attack and should get detected. For more accurate predication Multivariable variance model should be employed to capture multiple adverse factors. Figure 11 illustrates working method of covariance matrix modelling. The traffic is analysed and covariance matrix is used to predict about vulnerable and safe state. This output can be used to initiate and control the subsequent actions for ensuring secure, and smooth working of the system.

Figure 11. XML attacks

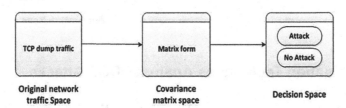

- **Cloud Trace Back Method (CTB):** Here major objective is to find out the real source of the attack and to protect a server form directly being attacked. CTB can be thought of as an extra layer of protection to safeguard the cloud network. The CTB is usually deployed at the edge routers of the network to close all source ends of the cloud network. If such systems are not put in place than it can make the network and server extremely vulnerable. In conventional setup the CTB precedes the server and all the server requests passes through it. All the requests first comes the CTB which places a cloud trace back mark (CTM) tag within the CTB header. So, all the requests passes through CTB and are marked properly before leaving. During this marking process the CTB removes the destination server address and itself passes the request to the server and thus ensure elimination of direct attack on the server. Upon discovery of an attack the victim asks for reconstruction by extracting the mark to make them aware of the real origin of the message. After reconstruction the system will start to filter out the attack traffic as well.

Figure 12. DDOS defence mechanism

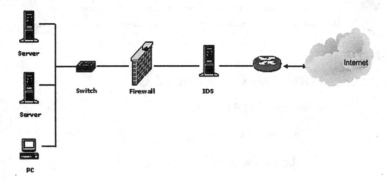

Intrusion Detection System (IDS) and Intrusion Prevention System

IDS is very important and essential security solution to safeguard a cloud network. If configured properly it can safeguards us from numerous vulnerabilities and attacks. In easier terms IDS is a systems to detect threats which originates in the network form any malicious computer or network. The IDS is a real time systems and it raises an alarm to alert network administrator in the event of possible threat. The IDS is intelligent enough to catch any unusual activity in the network. Upon receipt of alarm by the IDS the administrator takes the call and figures out the methods to safeguard the system. Depending upon the severity of the threat the administrator may take different actions like closing the connection etc. The IDS system must be updated regularly as newer threats keeps evolving regularly. The possible problem with IDS system is that they can safeguard us only from threats which they already know about. In case a new threat comes the IDS may fail completely. Figure 12 (a),12(b) presents a typical IDS system. If an intrusion is detected a message is delivered to notify the cloud servers.

Figure 13. Covariance matrix view

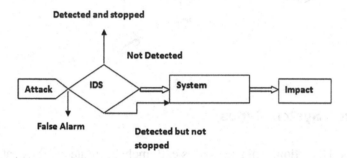

Figure 12(a) presents the placement of IDS system with respect to network and other componets. Figure 13 shows the actual filtering process. The IDS systesm raises an alarm on detection of attack. But, sometimes the IDS system raises false alarm but there is no occurrence of attack.

- **Intrusion Prevention System:** Intrusion prevention system (IPS) is an active system involved in preventing DoS attacks. This system can work without manual administration and can respond to newer threats easily and can adapt itself as per newer threats. IPS systems requires stricter configuration for effective working.
- **Differences Between IDS and IPS Systems:** IPS is bit different in functioning than the IDS system. There are few major difference between them. Table 1 presents the key differences between IDS and IPS Systems.

For optimal and best security both the IDS and IPS must be integrated together. With this integration the systems becomes bit complex but intelligent and secure. This setup is more powerful and can tackle newer kind of threats easily. Figure 14 shows a typical integration of IDS and IPS systems.

Table 1. Differences between IDS and IPS

IDS	IPS
• Detection Mode Only • Traffic replication required • Decoupling detection and reaction functionalities • IDS as good assistant for network administration • Usually used for testing rules	• Active Traffic Control • Original traffic required • Detection and reaction support • No administration assistance needed • Requires strict configuration • Two network cards bridging required

Figure 14. Placement of IDS

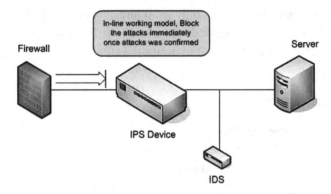

Intrusion Detection System Types

- **Signature-Based Detection:** This method is extremely accurate for those attacks which are well known attacks. Using this method, we can handle a broader range of known attacks and capability to figure out attacks remains considerably good. Disadvantage of this type of method is its efficiency which degrades when number of new attacks increases. This happens because it is based on signature and for every new attack it has to create a new signature and store it in its database to thwart future attacks. The big drawback of this approach is that the system is able to detect only those types of intrusion which matches a know predefined pattern. The method of signature based detection will not work properly when the attacker uses advanced technologies like Payload Encoders, NOP Generators and encrypted data channels (Ashwini Khadke, 2016). Other major problem with signature based attacks is that they suffers from the problem of false alarm i.e. the system may show the system in unsafe state though the system is in safe state.
- **Anomaly-Based Detection:** This approach generates a pattern of normal activity and if something deviates from the normal activity or processing patterns to certain different type of data processing/activity then anomaly based detection raises an alarm. The anomaly based system finds out the anomaly in the executing pattern (i.e., current processing) by checking the list of the normal activity processing types. Based on this if, something wrong is observed then the system automatically raises an alarm. Advantage of using this approach we can add new rules without tempering and modifying the existing ones. It is capable to find the new attacks easily. Disadvantage to use this approach is it goes off falsely sometimes which consumes time and processing speed (Shuyuan Jin, 2004).

- **Entropy-Based Method:** It is method to find the advent of DDOS attacks. This method clearly shows the fall in packet traffic or a sharp decrease from regular "fingerprint" profiles immediately after the start of DDOS attack. Severe DDOS attacks will mark a significant and immediate change in the entropy of the packet traffic monitored. These changes are even marked on small number of routers regardless of their position and kind of routing policy or algorithm they use to route the traffic (Raghav, 2013).

Stealthy DDOS Attacks in Cloud

A newer kind of DDOS attack called stealthy DDOS attacks have made their presence known in the security arena. These attacks are different from regular DDOS attacks in the way that their detection is difficult with the regular detection methods. In some of these attacks genuine users participates and try to gain information of the victim's computer and hosts. This involvement of real users makes their detection difficult. To detect these attacks extensive time series analysis needs to performed. In addition multi variance models can be used to detect these attacks (Zargar, 2013).

CONCLUSION

Cloud computing has lots of significance in today's competitive computing world. With the rise of cloud computing and its associated platforms security for these platforms has become vital and essential. In the present chapter denial of service attacks in context of cloud computing has been discussed. Different types of DOS attacks and working methods has been briefly discussed and presented. Different methods to control and mitigate the DOS and DDOS attacks have also been mentioned.

It can be concluded from the chapter that, to control such attacks multiple dimensions needs to be investigated and viable working methods needs to be envisaged. These attacks cannot be controlled by fixed kind of methods and algorithms. Instead some dynamic methods and policy must be implemented to detect and control these attacks like integration of IDS and IPS system.

xREFERENCES

Ashwini Khadke, C. (2016). *Review on Mitigation of Distributed Denial of Service (DDOS)*. Attacks in Cloud Computing. doi:10.1109/ISCO.2016.7726917

Douligeris, C., & Mitrokotsa, A. (2004). DDoS attacks and defense mechanisms: Classification. *Computer Networks*, *44*(5), 643–666. doi:10.1016/j.comnet.2003.10.003

Khajuria & Srivastava. (2013). Analysis Of The DDOS Defence Strategies In Cloud Computing. *International Journal Of Enhanced Research In Management & Computer Applications*, (2), 1-5.

Raghav, C. I. (2013). Intrusion Detection and Prevention in Cloud Environment. *Systematic Reviews*, (24), 21–30.

RougerS. F. (2012). Retrieved from http://www.akamai.com/dl/akamai/akamai-ebook-guide-to-multi-layered-web-security.pdf

Shamsolmoali. (2014). CDF: High rate DDOS filtering method in Cloud Computing. *Computer Network and Information Security*, 43-50.

Shuyuan Jin, C. (2004). A Covariance Analysis Model for DDOS Attack Detection. IEEE.

Zargar, S. T., Joshi, J., & Tipper, D. (2013). A Survey of Defense Mechanisms Against Distributed Denial of Service (DDOS)Flooding. *IEEE Communications Surveys and Tutorials*, 1–24.

This research was previously published in the International Journal of Information System Modeling and Design (IJISMD), 10(3); edited by Remigijus Gustas; pages 41-58, copyright year 2019 by IGI Publishing (an imprint of IGI Global).

Chapter 26
Denial of Service (DoS) Attacks Over Cloud Environment:
A Literature Survey

Thangavel M.

(iD) https://orcid.org/0000-0002-2510-8857
Thiagarajar College of Engineering, India

Nithya S
Thiagarajar College of Engineering, India

Sindhuja R
Thiagarajar College of Engineering, India

ABSTRACT

Cloud computing is the fastest growing technology in today's world. Cloud services provide pay as go models on capacity or usage. For providing better cloud services, capacity planning is very important. Proper capacity planning will maximize efficiency and on the other side proper control over the resources will help to overcome from attacks. As the technology develops in one side, threats and vulnerabilities to security also increases on the other side. A complete analysis of Denial of Service (DOS) attacks in cloud computing and how are they done in the cloud environment and the impact of reduced capacity in cloud causes greater significance. Among all the cloud computing attacks, DOS is a major threat to the cloud environment. In this book chapter, we are going to discuss DOS attack in the cloud and its types, what are the tools used to perform DOS attack and how they are detected and prevented. Finally it deals with the measures to protect the cloud services from DOS attack and also penetration testing for DOS attack.

DOI: 10.4018/978-1-7998-5348-0.ch026

INTRODUCTION

Cloud computing is an emerging trend in the field of Information Technology. Cloud computing provides scalable and flexible resources for the end users on demand. The cloud offers three levels of services. They are Infrastructure as a service (Iaas), Platform as a service (Paas), and Software as a service (Saas). In Infrastructure as a service, the consumer (customer) have the capability of processing, storage and other computing resources. The consumer can deploy and run the software, like operating systems and applications (E.g. Host firewall). In platform as a service, the consumer can create the applications using libraries, tools and programming languages offered by cloud service providers (cloud middleware's –E.g. Open nebula). The consumer cannot control the cloud infrastructure like operating systems, networks, and servers. In Software as a service, the consumer can make use of the applications that were created by the cloud service provider (E.g. Web based applications). Cloud characteristics include multi tenancy, device independence, resource pooling, measured services, resource allocation, scalability, use of third party services and energy efficiency.

Cloud computing provides the capabilities to store and process the data of the users and organizations in a third party (Cloud Service Provider) storage center. Cloud computing is one of the most innovative technologies in the present decade. In cloud computing, there are three types of cloud, namely, public cloud, private cloud and hybrid cloud. The advantages of cloud computing are cost saving, manageability and reliability. On the other side, there is a controversy in security and vendor lock in issue. In cloud computing, still some organizations cannot switch from one services to other services and it has not been completely evolved. This is called as vendor lock in. One of the major advantage of cloud computing is elasticity of the resources. The proper capacity planning is very necessary to manage the resources. Capacity planning means to plan the resources needed for the application in future. Pay as you go services is good as it needs to be paid only for the utilized resources. Capacity planning of resources will make us to handle multiple resources simultaneously.

In security aspect, there are so many attacks happening everyday like data theft, DOS attack and side channel attack, etc. Even though the cloud service providers provide the security standards, providing security in all aspects is quite difficult. In public cloud the vulnerable server or system and exploitation could happen easily. Other disadvantages are limited controls, technical difficulties, and downtime. Downtime is one of the disadvantages of the cloud service that affects the services when the internet connection goes down. In future, the security exploitation in cloud computing has to be managed effectively from the perspective of both providers and users.

COMMON ATTACKS ON CLOUD

Authentication Attack

Authentication is one of the vulnerable points in the cloud services. Generally authentication is provided for the users using username and password. Some of the developed organizations used site keys, virtual keyboards, and biometrics and shared secret questions. Most possible authentication attacks are i) brute force attack ii) shoulder surfing iii) Replay attack iv) Dictionary attack v) key loggers. We see in detail about all the above attacks. In a brute force attack, in order to break the username or password, we have to try all the possibilities (all possible combinations). In cloud, brute force attack is used to break the password which is in the encrypted form (encrypted text). In shoulder surfing, an attacker watches the employee or customer movements and tries to see the password when he/she types the password. This attack is also called spying. In Replay attack, an attacker intercept between the two valid users, capture the data and then retransmits the data frequently or in a delayed manner. This attack is also called Playback attack or reflection attack. Dictionary attack is to try out all the possible combinations of meaningful words in the dictionary to break the password (Ajey singh 2012). Key loggers is a software program and records the key pressed by the user. Key loggers monitor the user activities.

Denial of Service Attack

In DOS attacks, an attacker overloads the server by sending large number of requests and makes the server to un-respond to the valid users, at that time resource is not available to the user (Ramya 2015). DDOS attack which means many node systems attacking the one node systems at the same time by flooding the message.

Data Stealing Attack

Data stealing attack is similar to the authentication attack *(Kumar 2014)*. In this attack, an attacker tries to break the username and passwords and steal the confidential information of the user.

Flooding Attack

An attacker can create an unwanted data, when the server is overloaded with the most number of requests and at that time attacker sends this unwanted request also. At that time the server will process both the legitimate requests and invalid requests (Kumar 2014). This leads to the more CPU utilization causing flooding attack or flooding of the systems.

Malware Injection Attack

An attacker injects the virtual machine or malicious services (like Saas or Paas) in the cloud. The attacker has to make believe the service as valid service among the valid instances in the cloud system. If an attacker is successful in that, the cloud automatically redirects the valid user to the malicious implementation services (Shikha Singh 2014). If the attacker takes control of the service, he/she can gain access to the victim's (user) data in the cloud.

Man in The Middle Attack

In man in the middle attack, the attacker tries to intercept between the two users. An attacker tries to make a communication path and modify the communications. There are several types of man in the middle attacks, important MITM is i) DNS spoofing ii) session hijacking. In DNS spoofing, for example, an attacker can create a fake website for a bank, a user visiting the his/her bank website for internet banking at that time user was redirected to the attacker's website, after that attacker will gain all the credentials of the user (Chouhan 2016). DNS spoofing is done to get the credentials of the user by creating fake information's or fake website.

Side Channel Attack

In Side channel attack, an attacker tries to compromise the cloud by placing the malicious virtual machine in the target server (cloud server) and doing a side channel attack. Side channel attack is one of the security threats in cloud. Side channel attacks can be done in two ways: VM CO-RESIDENCE AND PLACEMENT, VM EXTRACTION. VM CO-RESIDENCE AND PLACEMENT- an attacker is fixing his/her malicious instance on the same physical machine as a target *(Shikha Singh 2014)*. VM EXTRACTION- the ability of malicious instance to utilize all the side channels and thus they are gaining information about the CO-RESIDENCE instances.

Wrapping Attack

In wrapping attack, attackers interrupt the process of the cloud server. This is done by a malicious SOAP (simple object access protocol) code element inserted in the TLS (Transport layer service) (Kumar 2014). After the code is inserted, the content is copied to the server; during the execution it interrupts the cloud server.

Attack on Hypervisor

Attacks in the hypervisor which lead to the compromise of security make whole cloud environment down. Hypervisor is the abstraction layer software between the virtual machine and hardware that comprise the cloud. If the attacker gains the control of operating systems, he/she can able to manipulate the data and even shut down or compromise the whole cloud services (Alani 2014). This attack on hypervisor is very low.

Resource Freeing Attack

Generally there are so many virtual machines are running on the same physical node in the cloud. The overall performance of the virtual machine will get down if another virtual machine over using the resources *(Alani 2014)*. So attack may done by the user to free up resources which are used in excess by the other user.

Attack on Confidentiality

In a cloud environment, security is the important aspect. Security is providing confidentiality (protect) the data from the unauthorized users. While we are concentrating on securing the data at the same time we have to think about providing security to the infrastructure as well. Attacks on confidentiality take place by social engineering, which an attacker eavesdrop or try to collect the encrypted passwords, keys, and identity of the cloud user *(Alani 2014)*. Most of the time an attacker will impersonate the identity of the user and gain the access of the user to get the confidential data.

Denial of Service Attack

A cloud environment is vulnerable to denial of service attack because of the network resources are completely shared between the client and cloud service providers(CSP). In a distributed denial of service attack, requests are sent to the victim from different sources by an attacker. An attacker tries to prevent the usage of required computer resources by the legitimate user. For which an attacker will flood the packets and disrupt the service and thereby increasing the bandwidth usage, preventing the authorized user to access it. This is generally called as a DOS / DDOS attack in a cloud environment (Gunasekhar 2014). The denial of service attack in cloud is shown in Figure 1, involving the request and responses.

Figure 1. DOS attack in cloud

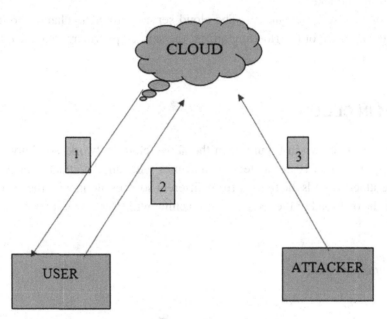

It is done as follows:

1. User's request to the cloud.
2. Cloud's response from the cloud.
3. The attacker tries to access the data from the cloud.

This DOS attack may cause to stop the service or shut down the service. It causes two kinds of impact in the cloud such as:

1. Direct denial of service, and
2. Indirect denial of service.

Direct Denial of Service

In the cloud environment, if the operating system faces large amount of workload in a particular service, at that time it provides more computational resource for that service like providing virtual machines in order to cope up with the assigned workload. Additional workload is given by the attacker to that particular service to stop or slow down the service.

Indirect Denial of Service

The indirect flooding attack causes the services provided on the same hardware servers to suffer severely from the workload. This is called as indirect denial of service. It depends upon the computational power under the control of the attacker.

Another important cause is accounting. The cloud service providers charge the user according to their resource usage. Because of the flooding attack, the service providers may raise the charge drastically for the cloud usage.

DDOS ATTACK IN CLOUD

DDOS attack in cloud in shown in Figure 2. In the above cloud network, so many servers are active and in each serving more than 10 computers or machines will run. An attacker targets any one of the machines, then the attacker sends the request from different sources along with the normal user (Somani 2015). Because of the overload of the request, the machine will slow down its performance.

Figure 2. DDOS attack in cloud

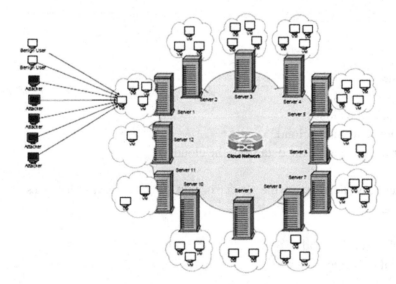

SYMPTOMS OF DOS/DDOS ATTACK

1.   Very slow network performance,
2.   Inability to access the service, website, or network,
3.   Unavailability of the website, and
4.   Increase in a large number of spam mails.

The above factors contribute much towards denial of service attacks.

TERMINOLOGY IN DDOS ATTACK

*   **Attacker:** An attacker is the root cause of the real attack in the cloud. To perform DOS attack, an attacker has to study the network topology clearly.
*   **Agent/ Handler:** The agent program coordinates the attack through the Zombies. This is also called as Master program. The agent will carry out the attack to the target victim.
*   **Zombies:** The agent carries out the attack to the victim. An attacker will gain access and the Zombies in the network will affect both the target as well as the host computer. This is also called as attack daemon agents.
*   **Victim:** The victim or target receives the attack. It is shown in Figure 3.

Figure 3. Elements of DOS attack in the cloud environment

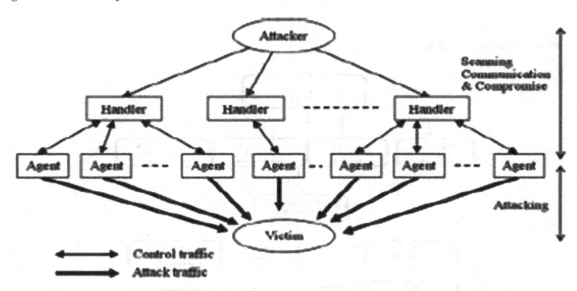

The attacker will send the command to the Handler. The handler will receive the execute command and this command will propagate to the attack daemon agent or Zombie. Then the attack daemon agent will start attacking the victim and results in the slowdown of the service or unavailability of the service.

DDOS ATTACKS CLASSIFICATION

Volume based Attack

In this attack, an attacker sends more chunks of data to overload the victim machine. This is also called as Bandwidth based attack (Vidhya 2014). Eg. ICMP floods, UDP floods.

Protocol Attack

In this attack, an attacker use protocols to overload the resources of the victim. Eg. SYN floods, Smurf attack and Ping of Death.

Application based Attack

In this attack, an attacker will send a large amount request to the target. This can be done through web based applications. Eg. HTTP DOS and XML DDOS attack.

METHODOLODY IN DDOS ATTACK

There are several methodologies used in the DDOS or DOS attack (Nagaraju 2014), it is shown in Figure 4. Other than this methodology, there are so many different types of attacks possible.

Figure 4. Taxonomy of DDOS attack

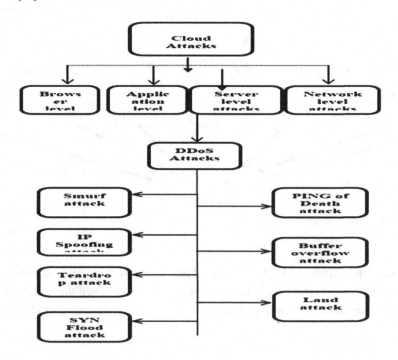

Smurf Attack

Smurf attack is the kind of distributed denial of service attack. In this, IP (Internet Protocol) and ICMP (Internet Control Message Protocol) protocols are used. ICMP packet is used to send the ECHO message and IP protocol is used to broadcast the messages. The Smurf attack is that the attacker sends large number ICMP packets as intended spoofed IP address (IP of victim's address is spoofed by the attacker), then these packets will broadcast in the cloud network by IP broadcast address. Normally the computer or machines in the network will reply to the source IP address, this will lead to the target machine flooded with traffic.

This will slow down the performance of the target machine and even it may stop the target from providing its services. This is generally called as Smurf attack. It is shown in Figure 5.

Figure 5. Smurf attack

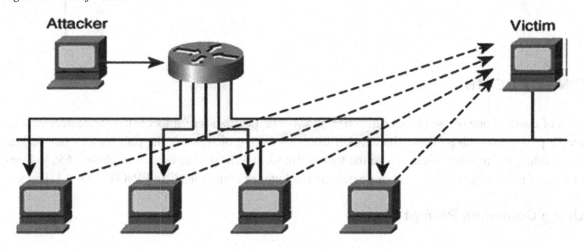

TOOL: HYENAE

Hyenae is a tool which we can use for Smurf attack. By using this tool we can perform man-in-the-middle attack, denial of service, distributed denial of service attack.

Features of Hyenae

1. UDP flooding,
2. TCP SYN flooding,
3. LAND attack,
4. DNS Query flooding,
5. ICMP Smurf attack, and
6. ICMP ECHO flooding.

The tool Hyenae screenshot is shown in Figure 6.

Figure 6. Screenshot for Hyena tool

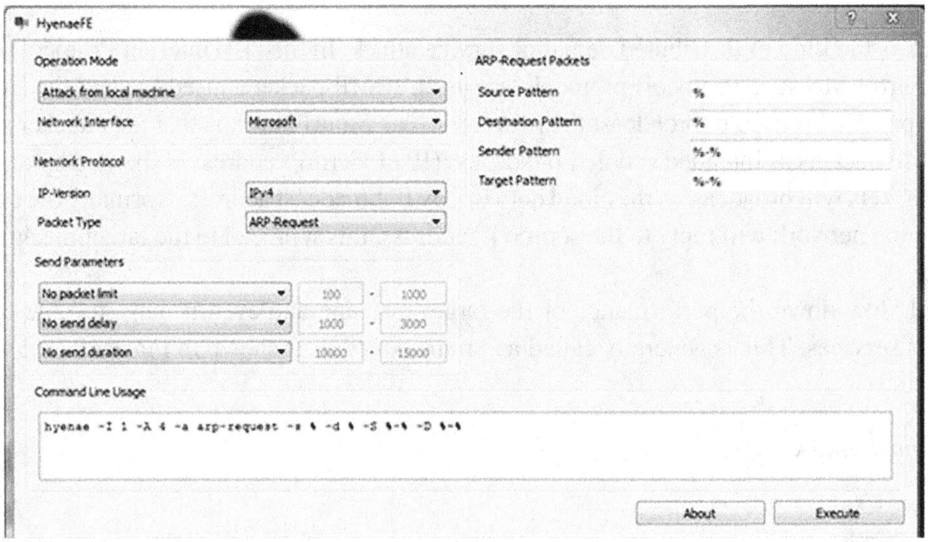

PING OF DEATH

Ping of death is one of the Denial of service attack. The IP (Internet Protocol) has the feature to send the IP packet into sub-packets. The attacker uses this feature of splitting the packets into sub-packets and sending the number of packets to the target. But In TCP/IP packet we can send only 65536 bytes of data. If an attacker tries to send more than 65536 bytes of data, it leads to PING OF DEATH attack.

Using Command Prompt

To perform ping of death attack, we can use command prompt of any operating system. In command prompt of windows OS, the attacker gives the command as ping –n 1000000 –l 65500, 216.58.220.361, where it is the IP address of www.google.com.

- **n:** Number of packets.
- **l:** Limitation of the packets.

When an attacker tries to send 1000000 numbers of packets which is more than the allowed bytes of data i.e 65536 at that time ping will not work and will not be able to give a reply from the IP address. This is called ping of death. It is shown in Figure 7. Ping of death is done by using the tool called CPU PING DEATH TOOL.

Figure 7. Ping of Death using Command Prompt

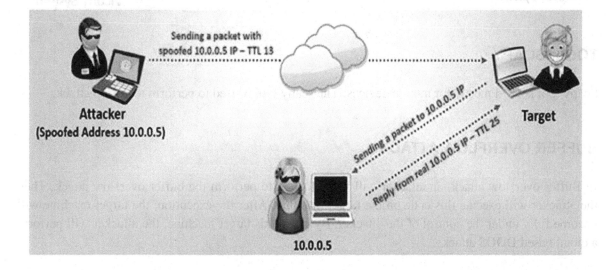

IP SPOOFING ATTACK

IP spoofing is generally used for Denial of service attack. Attacker changes the source IP (Internet Protocol) header field with the legitimate user IP address or an unreachable IP address. This causes the server in the cloud to wrongly lead to the legitimate user and server may unable to complete the task and affects the system performance. It is shown in Figure 8.

Figure 8. IP spoofing

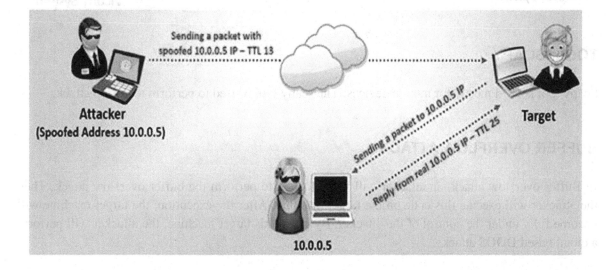

TOOL: NETWORK SPOOFER

This network spoofer is used in Android phone to spoof the network. It is used to break the Wi-Fi network. This tool shows that how the network is vulnerable to attacks like DOS attack etc.

TEAR DROP ATTACK

In teardrop packet, the Internet protocol packets are divided into small chunks and sent as fragments along with the source IP address. The reason for sending the fragments along with source IP address, is that it is easy to reassemble at the destination side.

When TCP/IP stack is overlapped with fragments, it is difficult to reassemble and it easily fails. This is known as Teardrop attack. Because of this attack, the system may even crash. The attacker sends the invalid overlapping values along with the fragments in the offset field. This leads to the crash of the system, when the victim is trying to re-assemble the packet. It is shown in Figure 9.

Figure 9. Tear Drop attack

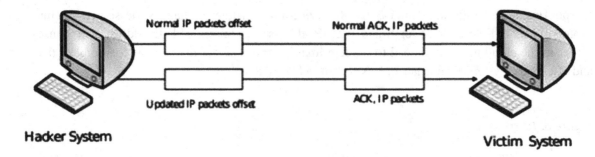

TOOL: SCAPY

Scapy tool is used mostly for mobile devices. The scapy tool is used to perform tear drop attack.

BUFFER OVERFLOW ATTACK

In Buffer overflow attack, an attacker will write a code to perform the buffer overflow attack. Then the attacker will execute this code on the target machine. After the execution, the target machine will become fully under the control of the attacker. By using this target machine, the attacker will perform a cloud based DDOS attack.

LAND ATTACK

In Land attack, an attacker will write a program called land.c, to modify the TCP SYN packets with the target IP address for both the source as well as the destination IP address. This causes the target itself to give the request and it gets crashed. This is one of the severe DOS attack similar to the ping attack.

Tool: Hyenae

Hyenae tool is used to perform land attack. Hyenae is also powerful tool and we can perform so many attacks like the man-in-the-middle attack, Denial of service attack, TCP Land attack.

SYN Flood Attack

In SYN FLOOD attack, the attacker will flood the TCP/IP packet to the target machine from the fake IP address. In the TCP handshake process, the packets are considered as a request and this TCP will respond by giving TCP /SYN_ACK message.

The target machine will wait for the ACK, but it is never received because the request is coming from the fake IP address. This leads to a half open connection. Then the target machine will be no more able to accept any requests, even if it comes from the legitimate user.

By using Hyena tool we can perform TCP/SYN flood attack. Already we discussed about this tool in the previous attacks.

SYN flood attack can be classified into three types:

1. Direct attack,
2. Distributed attack, and
3. Spoof based attack.

Direct Attacks

The attacker will send the large amount of SYN REQ to the server without spoofing their IP address. Then the attacker prevents the operating system to reply to the SYN ACK. This task is done by using the firewall rules either we can allow only the outgoing packets which allow only SYN out or allow the incoming packets, such that any SYN ACK is denied before reaching the local TCP.

Distributed Attack

The attacker will use the many compromised machines and botnets through internet to do the Distributed SYN flood attack. Then the attacker will use each changeable machine for a spoofed attack and multiple spoofed addresses. This kind of attack is difficult to be blocked or stopped.

Spoof Based Attack

In this spoof based attacks, the attacker uses the spoofed IP address. In this attack, the client will not respond to the SYN ACKs send to them or at present there is no client system available for that spoofed IP address, this is happening because of the assumption of the spoofed address that does not respond.

OTHER POSSIBLE DOS/DDOS ATTACK IN CLOUD ENVIRONMENT

- UDP FLOOD,
- ICMP FLOOD,
- HTTP DOS ATTACK,
- XML DDOS ATTACK, and
- DNS REFLECTION ATTACK OR AMPLIFICATION ATTACK.

APPLICATION DOS ATTACK

Possible attacks in cloud (Wong 2014) are as follows,

UDP Flood

In UDP (User Datagram Protocol) flood, an attacker sends large number of UDP packets to the ports on the target machine using an attack Daemon agent (Zombie). As soon as the target identifies this request is coming from the unwanted source, the target will reply with the destination unreachable ICMP packet.

Because of the unwanted reply, the network bandwidth is used more and this bandwidth is not available for the legitimate users. The above is the overall scenario of UDP flood. Let's see, in detail, about the UDP flood attack.

UDP flood attack is also a kind of bandwidth attack. This uses the user datagram protocol, which is a stateless protocol, that means there is no need of an established session between the server and the client. The UDP flood attack starts by sending the largest amount of UDP packets to the target machine. As soon as the target machine determines that there is no application waiting on the port, it will send the ICMP unreachable message for each UDP to the forged source IP address. So the attacker uses the spoofed IP address to send UDP packets to the target, thus the target is overloaded with large UDP traffic responders. This UDP flood attack will create a weakness of CHARGEN and ECHO services (Exploit the services). The purpose of the CHARGEN is to continue generating some random characters and sent them to the correct source, this ECHO service continuously responds to the services by echoing the random characters back to the CHARGEN services. The attacker can pipe out the CHARGEN to ECHO. This situation creates an infinite loop between two UDP services. For example HOST B echoes a packet to HOST A, then HOST A responds to the echo packet of HOST B until the exhaustion of some shared resources.

Most of the UDP floods happens for larger bandwidth DDOS attack greater than 1Gbps(gigabytes per second) because we can easily generate UDP packets from various different languages.

ICMP Flood

In ICMP FLOOD, the target will be loaded with ICMP ECHO request packets by the attacker. When the target machine tries to reply to the attacker, because of the maximum bandwidth utilization, target couldn't reply, this leads to inaccessibility to the legitimate users. Let's see, in detail, about the ICMP flood attack. ICMP flood attack is often called as Ping attack or Smurf attack. This is often used for Ping based DDOS attack. The attacker will send a large number of ICMP packets to the server and try to crash the TCP/IP stack and stops response to the incoming TCP/IP requests to the server. Some times Hping and custom perl scripts are installed on the Zombie machine to do the ICMP flood. Sometimes the SYN flood attack is launched together with the ICMP flood.

HTTP (HYPER TEXT TRANSFER PROTOCOL) DOS ATTACK

HTTP DOS attack is a type of attack will occur in the application level. For this attack, the attacker will use HTTP GET and HTTP POST messages to the victim. An attacker will send the more number of HTTP GET request to get some information and the server will load with get requests. This leads to the CPU and memory utilization and the victim will be unable to respond to other legitimate requests. The HTTP POST request is used to give input data (E.g. Forms). For this we require more computation from the server side. So, the HTTP POST DOS attack is complex than HTTP GET DOS attack.

There are three types of HTTP DOS attack:

- HTTP Malformed attack,
- HTTP Idle attack, and
- HTTP Request attack.

HTTP Malformed Attack

The attack happens when the Invalid HTTP packets are sent to the server and this results in the complete usage of the server resources. Eg. Zafi.B worm use malformed HTTP GET requests.

HTTP Idle Attack

HTTP connections are opened and left idle without sending the full request by the attacker. Eg. Slowloris. Slowloris means dribbling the small number of bytes or packets to keep the connection from timeout but it never completes the request.

HTTP Request Attack

HTTP request attack occur when a large number of legitimate requests are sent to the web server, which results in the consumption of server resources.

XML (EXTENSIBLE MARKUP LANGUAGE) DOS ATTACK

In X-DOS attack, the network is flooded with XML messages instead of packets inorder to prevent the legitimate users to access the network. The steps involved in X-DOS are,

- Exploit a known vulnerability.
- Flood the system with useless messages to exhaust.
- Attacker will try to hide their identities.
- Attacker will bypass a known defence that is in place to prevent it. This is also called as a REST based attack.

DNS (DOMAIN NAME SERVER) REFLECTION ATTACK

DNS reflection attack is also called as an amplification attack. It is a kind of distributed denial of service attack. An attacker sends a DNS name lookup request to the open DNS resolver from the spoofed source address (spoof the target address). The DNS server will send the DNS response to the spoofed source address. This response is larger than the DNS request. The attacker can amplify the traffic volume at the target. The attacker can use botnets to perform additional DNS queries, this results in overload of traffic. This type of attack is very difficult to block, because it is coming from the legitimate user from the authorized name servers.

The DNS reflection attack is possible by using the following:

- **Botnets:** In this DNS reflection attack, the attacker will compromise more numbers of online computers called as Botnets to send the DNS queries.
- **Source Address Spoofing:** When the attacker sends the DNS queries to open resolver, the source address of the DNS query is spoofed with target address rather than showing the real sender address. This is called as source address spoofing.
- **Malware:** This attack is triggered by botnets computer infected with malware EDNS0 (extension mechanism Domain name server). A 64 byte query is results in an 8x amplified 512 bytes UDP reply, if it's without EDNS0. EDNS0 will make the DNS requests to advertise their packet size and transfer the pack size larger than 512 bytes.
- **Open Recursion:** Open DNS resolvers which are generally called as servers on the internet, enables open recursion and provides the recursive DNS to response to anyone.

APPLICATION DOS ATTACK (ADOS)

Application DOS attack will use the vulnerability of the design, implementation and exploits it. Above all the attacks, the most recent and efficient attack is ADOS attack in recent times (Siva 2013). This prevents the access of the legitimate users to the services provided by CSP (Cloud Service Providers). This ADOS attack will disrupt the service rather than taking control of the service. This will happen mostly in the application layer.

The ADOS attack are broadly classified into four types:

1. Request Flooding Attack,
2. Repeated One shot Attack,
3. Application Exploit Attack, and
4. Asymmetric Attack,

Request Flooding Attack

The attacker tries to send heavy legitimate request to the server, the server will overload the session resources. Examples are HTTP, SIP INVITE'S, GET'S and DNS queries.

Repeated One Shot Attack

Repeated one shot attack occurs when high workload is sent to the server across many TCP sessions. This will slow down the service and shuts down the service on the server. This attack is similar to the asymmetric attack and request flooding attack.

Application Exploit Attack

Application exploit attack mainly focuses on the vulnerabilities of the application. It will exploit the application or server operating system by using the vulnerabilities of the application. Then it will allow the attacker to gain the control of the application in the cloud environment. Buffer overflow, SQL injection, Cookie poisoning, Hidden field manipulation and Scripting vulnerabilities are possible through this attack.

Asymmetric Attack

Asymmetric attack occurs when normal requests are in the need of large amount of computer resources, memory and disk space this leads to the degradation of the service.

THREATS OF DOS ATTACK IN CLOUD

X-DOS attack and H-DOS attack is one of the major threats of DOS in the cloud environment (Alotaibi 2015). There are three models in the cloud computing, they are Iaas, Paas, Saas. Cloud utilizes service oriented architecture (SOA) and web services to introduce the services.Web services and SOA are supported by Saas for many applications. When cloud users uses the web services in Saas, which leads to some vulnerabilities, by using this weakness an attacker tries to launch X-DOS and H-DOS attack in the cloud.

X-DOS attack uses the XML message to send to the web services or web server in the cloud. The message has the malicious content to exhaust all the resources and also exploits all the web service requests. When the attacker launches the X-DOS attack, this will flood the network with XML messages rather than packets, because of this the legitimate users are unable to use the network communication.

In H-DOS attack, the attacker uses HTTP Flooder to attack. The HTTP flooder starts up with 1500 threads. It has the capacity to send large number of HTTP requests to the web server to use all the communication channels. Till now there is no defined method to differentiate the legitimate and illegitimate packets.

SOLUTION TO THE X-DOS AND H-DOS ATTACK IN CLOUD

There are many approaches to mitigate X-DOS and H-DOS attack in the cloud environment. Using Cloud trace back method and Cloud protector (X-protector), can be implemented as discussed earlier in countermeasures of DOS. Another solution is a cloud defender system called cloud service queuing defender, that detects the X-DOS and H-DOS attack in an effective manner. Apart from X-DOS and H-DOS attack, there are so many types of DOS attack explained in the previous sections, which is also a severe threats to the cloud. To overcome the DOS attack, the detection and preventive methods are explained in the upcoming sections.

DETECTION OF DDOS ATTACK

In today's cloud environment all the DDOS/DOS attacks take place by using attack tool, malicious programs and botnets. There are so many detection techniques used to detect the DDOS attack. The detection techniques are used to identify and then discriminate the Unauthorized or Illegitimate packets.

The important detection techniques are:

1. Signature based detection,
2. Behaviour based detection,
3. Active profiling,
4. Wavelength based analysis, and
5. Sequential change point.

Signature Based Detection

Signature based detection technique is useful only if the communication is not encrypted.This technique capture the traffic packets and compare with the existing attack patterns (Sendi 2015). It is useful to get the information,i.e how the communication takes place between the attacker and Zombie computer.

Behaviour Based Detection

Behaviour based detection technique concept is normal behaviour of the traffic is designed based on the traffic patterns. If there is any deviation from the normal traffic then it is consider as abnormal traffic (Sendi 2015). Generally the threshold value is set in order to differentiate the normal traffic(traffic is low than the threshold value) or abnormal traffic traffic is higher than the threshold value).

Active Profiling

Active profiling defines the average rate of the packet flow and it will monitor the header information of the packet. Average rating of the packet flow is calculated by the elapsed time between the consecutive packets. The sum of all inbound and outbound of the average packet rates gives the activity of the network.

Network activity is determined by an average rate of the packet flow. If we want to analyze one individual packet, we have to follow the order of 264 flows including the protocols such as TCP, IP, ICMP and SNMP. This leads to the high dimensionality problem. So we are clustering by exhibiting the similar characteristics.

By the above concept, attack is detected by an increase in the number of distinct clusters and an increase in the activity levels of the clusters.

Wavelet Signal based Analysis

The wavelet signal based analysis provides the description about a global frequency, but it will not provide any details about time localization. The wavelet signal based analysis gives the frequency detail and concurrent time. The input signal will be in the form of spectral components. The input signals have the time localization anomalous signals and background noise. It will detect the traffic by separating the time localized signals and noise. By analyzing each spectral windows, it is used to determine the presence of anomalies. The anomalies may represent a network failure or an attack such as DOS etc.

Sequential Change Point Detection

Sequential change point detection will separate, if there is an abnormal change in the traffic statistics. This technique will filter the target traffic such as port, address, flow of a time series and protocol. The time series states that, when there is a statistical change in the time the DOS attack starts. CUSUM is an algorithm used in the sequential change point detection. It is a change point detection algorithm. CUSUM will operate on continuous slamped data and it needs only a minimum computational resource and low memory.

It will identify the DOS attack by analyzing the deviations from the actual expected average in the time series. If the deviation is below the bound (normal flow condition), the cusum statistics will decrease. If the deviation is above the bound (abnormal traffic change), the cusum statistics will increase. This algorithm helps us to identify the appropriate DOS attack.

TOOLS

- Tools to perform the DOS / DDOS attack
- Tools to protect a DOS / DDOS attack

Tools to Perform the DOS / DDOS Attack

The following tools are available to perform denial of service or distributed denial of service attack.

LOIC (Low Orbit Ion Canon)

Low Orbit Ion Canon is the most famous tool. It is very easy to use for the beginners those who have basic knowledge about DOS attack. This tool will perform an attack by sending HTTP, TCP and UDP requests to the target.

XOIC (High Orbit Ion Canon)

The high orbit ion cannon is the most powerful tool. It is used to perform a DOS attack on target websites and servers.

HULK (HTTP Unbearable Load King)

HULK tool is also used to perform DOS attack by sending a distinct request and creating a complicate traffic on the server.

DDOSIM Layer-7 DOS Simulator

DDOSIM layer-7 DOS tool is used to perform DDOS attacks by generating Zombie hosts which are used to create TCP connection in the target. There are so many features available to perform in this tool, such as, HTTP DDOS, SMTP DDOS, Application layer DDOS attack.

R U Dead Yet

R U Dead Yet tool is also called as RUDY. RUDY is used for HTTP POST attack. This tool is used in long form submission field by using the POST method.

Tor's Hammer

Tor's hammer tool will perform slow post written in a language called python. During the attack, to act as anonymous, it can run in a TOR network. It can kill the IIS and Apache server in a few minutes.

OWASP DDOS HTTP POST

OWASP DDOS HTTP POST is a DOS checking tool. This will check your server, whether it can able to defend against DDOS attack or not.

PHP DOS

PHP DOS tool is used to perform the denial of service attack against the website or IP address. The script is written in PHP.

Sprut

Sprut is also used for DDOS/DOS attack. It will perform multisystem TCP denial of service attacks.

DOS HTTP

This tool is used to perform effective HTTP flood. It is also used as HTTP flood testing tool for windows operating system. Features of this tool are HTTP redirection, URL verification and monitoring the tracks.

Tools to Protect a DOS / DDOS Attack

The following tools are available to protect from denial of service or distributed denial of service attack.

D-Guard Anti DDOS Firewall Tool

D-Guard anti DDOS firewall will protect the cloud network system from DDOS attack. It protects against super DDOS, SYN flood, ICMP flood and UDP flood.

Forti DDOS Tool

Forti DDOS is a protection tool against Denial of service attack. After deploying the Forti DDOS we can analyze the network traffic behaviour.

DDOS Defend Tool

DDOS defend will protect against web exploits like real time DOS, SQL Injection and cross site scripting attacks. It also provides network level DDOS protection as it undergoes intense scrubbing, HTTP, ICMP, UDP and TCP defense.

DOS Arrest

DOS arrest's security service (DSS) provides the customized view for the client's website from both inside and outside. It is an online reporting tool with most important features like load balancing where real time traffic could be shown. It is a single point of access through which we can login, modify, view or add.

Defencepro

Defencepro is the famous DDOS protection service providing security for DDOS attack, login page attack, SSL based flood attacks.

METHODS TO PROTECT DDOS ATTACK

The various methods to protect DDOS attacks are as follows,

Cloud Trace Back Model and Cloud Protector

Cloud trace back model is based on the algorithm called Distributed Packet Marking (DPM) whereas the cloud protector is based on back propagation neural network. Cloud trace back is used to identify the DDOS attack source and cloud protector is used to separate or differentiate the illegal message patterns. To avoid direct DDOS attack, cloud trace back is placed before webserver.

CLASSIE Packet Marking Approach

CLASSIE Packet is an intrusion detection system and this uses a decision tree classification algorithm. CLASSIE is placed at one hop distance from the host and finds the malicious packets by defining its own rules (Vidhya 2014).

Thus, CLASSIE Packet is used to prevent the HDOS and XDOS attack in the cloud network. The malicious packet is marked and carried all the way through a router and switches. IN RAD (reconstruction and Drop) placed at one hop distance from the target makes the decision whether to allow the packet or deny the packet. This method will reduce the DDOS attack rates. The malicious packets will be marked at the attacker's side and dropped at the target's side.

Cooperative Intrusion Detection System

An Intrusion Detection System (IDS) is deployed in every cloud computing environment. The IDS maintains a Block table for monitoring and log activities. When the packets are received, a comparison is made for a match in the block table, if match is found it will immediately allow the packet and if there is no match found and detects it as a malicious packet, then it will send an alert to the other IDS in the network. The majority votes of the IDS decides whether it's a true or a false alert. If it is a true alert, then the block table is updated with the new rule for future reference and if it is a false alert, it will not update in the block table.

For this method IDS needs four elements namely,

1. Intrusion detection,
2. Alert clustering,
3. Intrusion response and block, and
4. Cooperative operation.

These kinds of IDS are used to detect the early DDOS attack.

Filtering Tree Approach

Filtering tree approach is generally used in the application level layers. The user (client) request is converted to XML format and this XML format is converted to SOAP (simple object access protocol) with user IP address, user puzzle and user solution which are twice signed. The SOAP message is forwarded to the IP trace back where the incoming packets are compared with the table maintained in the IP trace back. If match is found, the packet is denied, otherwise it is forwarded to the Cloud Defender. Cloud defender has five filters namely, sensor filter, Double signature filter, Hop count filter, Puzzle resolver and divergence filter. After passing this entire filter it allows the packet. This filtering tree approach prevents the HDOS and X-DOS attack, but fails to prevent network and transport layer DOS attack.

Confidence based Filtering Approach

In Confidence based filtering approach, there are two time periods, one is Attack period and another one is Normal period. In normal period, it finds the correlation pattern for legitimate packets by extracting the attribute pair in the TCP/IP header. This correlation between the attribute pair is used to calculate the Confidence values. The confidence value is calculated to identify the trust between the attribute pair. If the frequency of the attribute pair is high, the confidence level also goes high. This is stored in the log file and considered as a normal profile.

During the attack period, every packet is calculated by the weighted average of confidence values of the attribute pair and it is called as CBF (confidence based filtering) score. In CBF, all the packets are compared to the threshold value inorder to allow or deny the packet. If the CBF score is lower than the threshold, the packet will be considered as a malicious packet and so it would be discarded. If the CBF score is higher than the threshold, the packet will be allowed.

Information Theory based Metric Method

In Information theory based metric method there are two phases such as, behaviour monitoring and behaviour detection. In behaviour monitoring phase, it will monitor the web user behaviour and entropy value is calculated for requests and the trust score is given to each user. This is generally called as a Non-attack period.

In behaviour detection phase, the entropy value is compared with the threshold value and if it exceeds the value, it is considered as a malicious packet and the packet is denied. If the entropy value is lesser than the threshold value, based on the trusted score restricted access is provided to the user.

COUNTERMEASURES FOR DDOS ATTACK

The countermeasures for the distributed denial of service attack in the cloud are as follows,

1. Secondary victims should be protected,
2. Neutralize the handlers,
3. Prevent the potential attacks,
4. Deflect the attacks,
5. Mitigate the attacks, and
6. Forensic the post attacks.

The various countermeasures above are explained in detail (Countermeasure 2015).

Secondary Victims should be Protected (in the Cloud Network Systems)

The secondary victims should always be protected from security issues by prevention techniques. This can avoid secondary victims to become Zombies. The system should check their own security, and by checking it should ensure that there is no agent program installed. The system should also check their DDOS agent traffic. The following measures should be taken to check and monitor the secondary victims,

- Awareness should be increased among the internet users about the security issues and its prevention techniques.
- Licensed Antivirus and Anti Trojan virus should be installed and updated often.
- Regular updates and configuration of the core hardware and software should be done.
- Uninstall unnecessary as well as unused application and disable unwanted services.
- Scan all the files from the external source, outside the network.

Another important thing in the cloud environment is price. In cloud, pricing should be fixed according to the usage of the services provided by the CSP (cloud service providers). This will allow only the legitimate users to access and avoids the DDOS attack in the cloud.

Neutralize the Handlers

One of the ways to stop the DDOS attack is to neutralize the handlers. This can be done in the following ways,

- Analyze the communication protocols and traffic patterns in the network.
- The DDOS attack deployed are compared to the number of agents. When we neutralize the handlers, it possibly renders many numbers of agents useless.
- The attack can come from a spoofed source address, thus we can prevent by neutralizing the handlers.

Prevent the Potential Attacks

We can prevent the DDOS attack by:

- Ingress Filtering,
- Egress Filtering, and
- TCP Intercept.

Ingress Filtering

In ingress filtering it will prohibit the attack, where the attacker trying to launch an attack from the spoofed IP address that does not obey ingress filtering rules. Ingress filtering will not protect against flooding attacks on the network.

It will have the strict traffic rules and it will not allow the packets if it has not come from the legitimate users. Another major advantage of ingress filtering is, it will trace the originator and its true source address.

Egress Filtering

In this method of traffic filtering, the IP header is initially scanned and checked whether it meets the criteria. If it meets the criteria, it is allowed into the network, otherwise it gets rejected. Egress filtering assures that unauthorized or malicious traffic will never initiate from the internal network.

TCP Intercept

To avoid the SYN flood attack, TCP intercept is introduced. In TCP intercept mode, it will intercept the SYN packets which are sent by the client to the server and find matches with an extended access list. If match is found, the TCP intercept establishes the connection to the server on behalf of the client and also establishes the connection to the client on behalf of the server. After the two half connections are made, the TCP intercept combines the connections transparently. This TCP intercept act as mediator between the client and the server. This TCP intercept mode prevents fake connections trying to reach the server. If a match is found, it will deny the request.

Deflect the Attack

One of the ways to deflect the attack is by using honey pots. The system which acts as a lure(tempt an attaccker) for the attacker and provides partial security is called honey pots. Honey pots not only protect the systems in the cloud network, but also track the activities of the attacker what they are trying to accomplish. Honey pots were specially designed to attract the DDOS attackers. The installation of the agent code within the honeypot avoids the legitimate system being compromised.

There are two types of honey pots namely, High interaction honeypot and Low interaction honeypot.

High Interaction Honeypot

It will simulate the complete layout of the entire network of the computers and its main aim is to capture the attacks. This will track and control all the activities in the network. Example for high interaction honeypot is a Honeynet.

Low Interaction Honeypot

It will simulate only the services often requested by the attacker. Here, multiple virtual machines run on one physical system consuming only few resources. It reduces the complexity of the virtual machine security. Example for low interaction honeypot is Honeyd.

Mitigate the Attacks

In two ways we can stop the DOS/DDOS attack:

1.   Load Balancing, and
2.   Throttling.

Load Balancing

Cloud service providers can increase their bandwidth, which prevents the servers going down. The above scenario is done to prevent the DOS / DDOS attack from happening. Another important thing is the replication server model, if there is a replication server, we can provide better load management and minimize the risk. This will mitigate the effect of Denial of service attack.

Throttling

Throttling helps to avoid DDOS attack in the cloud. This method enable the routers to handle more number of traffic in the network. It can also be used to filter the legitimate user traffic from fake DDOS attack traffic.

This throttling method is in the experimental stage. The major disadvantage is that throttling may trigger false alarms. Sometimes it will allow the malicious traffic and deny the authorized traffic.

Forensic the Post Attack

Among all the countermeasures, one of the important factor that investigate is the post attacks. This can be done in two ways:

1.   Traffic pattern analysis, and
2.   Run Zombie Zapper tool.

Traffic Pattern Analysis

During the DDOS attack, traffic pattern analysis helps to store the post attack data to analyze the traffic. The post attack data is helpful in changing load balancing and enhancing the anti attack measures.

This traffic pattern analysis is helpful for the admin to create a new filtering technique to prevent DDOS attack, this will avoid the traffic entering into the network. By analyzing the IDS (Intrusion Detection System) logs, firewall helps to identify the source of the DOS traffic.

Run Zombie Zapper Tool

When the providers are unable to ensure the security for the server and when DDOS attack begins, the IDS realizes large amount of traffic. At that time, the target victim starts running the Zombie Zapper tool acts as defence against TRINOO, TFN, Shaft and Stacheldraht. TRINOO is a set of computer programs that conducts DDOS attack. The tribe flood network is also the computer programs used to conduct DDOS attack. Shaft and Stacheldraht belong to the family of train and tfn, which is used to perform DDOS attack. The various Defence mechanisms and the model in which it can be applied for different attacks are shown in Table 1.

Table 1. DDOS attack Defence mechanisms

ATTACK	DEFENCE MECHANISM	APPLIED MODEL
Smurf attack	i) Routers should configure to disable the IP broadcast address. ii) Operating system should be configured properly.	IAAS
Ping of Death	Ping of death can be avoided by using most recent operating systems and network devices	IAAS and PAAS
IP spoofing attack	To avoid IP spoofing attack, we have to implement Hop count filtering technique as well as the IP to Hop count filtering technique.	PAAS
Tear Drop attack	Tear Drop attack can be avoided by using most recent network devices and operating systems	IAAS and PAAS
Buffer overflow attack	To write the code to avoid overflow and to check for the array boundaries and time limit consumption	SAAS
Land attack	i) Use most recent network device and OS (updated versions). ii) Drop the packets which have same IP address for both source and destination.	IAAS and PAAS
SYN flood attack	i) Firewall monitoring ii) Filtering techniques iii) SYN cache/SYN cookies approach	PAAS and IAAS
UDP flood	i) Rate limits on UDP traffic ii) Configure the router to disable the IP Broadcast transmission	IAAS and PAAS
ICMP flood	Configuring the routers to response only to legitimate ICMP packets	PAAS
HTTP DOS	i) We can provide defence by using IPS (Intrusion Prevention System). ii) We can use WAF (Web Application Firewall).	SAAS
XML DOS	Firewall monitoring and Intrusion Prevention System.	SAAS
DNS Reflection attack	i) Use Ingress filtering technique. ii) Limiting the DNS recursion by configuring the server to allow recursion for the list of authorized DNS servers.	SAAS and PAAS
A-DOS	To defence against DDOS attack we can use WAF (Web Application Firewall).	SAAS

PENETRATION TESTING

The penetration testing is done to identify the weakness and security loopholes in the cloud network. As a pen tester, we have to check the system have the ability to sustain for DOS attack or it gets crashed. To do a penetration testing, we have to do the following steps in the cloud network. It is shown in Figure 10 (Penetration 2015).

Define the Objective

As a penetration tester we have to define the objective. This helps the analyst to accomplish the goal of the test in the cloud.

Testing Heavy Loads on the Server

The Penetration tester, tests the server or the target by loading artificially to test the stability and performance of the cloud network. There are many tools available to test the heavy loads on the server.

Figure 10. Penetration testing

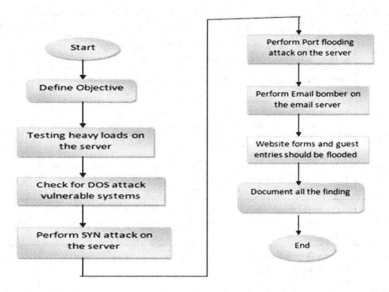

Web Server Test Tool

The web server test tool helps to perform a load test. It is a software tool to check the performance and stability of the web servers and web infrastructures.

Web Stress Tester Tool

This tool helps to check the stability of the proxy servers with SSL(secure socket layer)/TLS (transport layer security)enabled in the web servers.

Check for DOS Attack Vulnerable Systems

The penetration tester should check for the DOS attack vulnerable systems in the network by scanning the cloud network. To check the DOS attack vulnerable systems, several tools are available.

N-map Tool

N-map is the famous tool for port scanning. It is used to check the state of ports, services running on the port, operating system versions, firewall and filters.

Nessus Tool

Nessus is a vulnerability assessment tool. It is used for audit profiling, data discovery and vulnerability analysis.

Perform a SYN Attack on the Server

The penetration tester will try to do a SYN attack on the server. This can be done by bombarding the target by sending the request packets.

DOS HTTP tool

The DOS HTTP tool is used to perform SYN attacks on the server.

Sprut Tool

Sprut tool is also used perform Denial of service attack, especially SYN attack.

Perform Port Flooding Attack on the Server

The penetration tester should perform port flooding attack by sending large number of UDP or TCP packets to the target. The main aim of this attack is to make the port unusable and increase CPU utilization. To perform port flooding we can use the following tools.

Mutilate Tool

Mutilate is a tool which is used to see the open ports on the target. By using the open ports we can do the attack. This tool mainly concentrates on TCP/IP networks.

Pepsi5 Tool

Pepsi5 is a tool mainly focusing on UDP packets and it will show the size of the datagrams whereas it runs in the background.

Perform Email Bomber on the Email Server

The penetration tester will do an Email Bomber by sending a large number emails or bulk emails to the target server. If the target is withstanding enough, it will not crash. Otherwise the target would certainly crash. We can use the following tools to perform email bomber.

Mail Bomber

Mail Bomber is a tool to send a bulk amount of emails to the target server. These tools have the capability to hold separate mailing list. But it is not a free, open source tool requiring the payment of amount in dollars to use this tool.

Advanced Email Bomber

Advanced email bomber is able to send a personalized message (large amount of emails) to the subscriber using different predefined templates. This tool will deliver the message very fast and also tracks the feedback of the user.

Website Forms and Guest Entries should be Flooded

The penetration tester tests the online application forms by entering the lengthy entries to check causing it to crash. Generally DDOS attacker, try to enter the bogus entries to crash the website. To avoid this we are doing a penetration testing in the website forms.

Document all the Findings

The penetration tester should document the entire findings to report for future references.

CONCLUSION

In this chapter, we have analyzed that one of the major threat to the cloud environment is the denial of service attack. Most of the DOS attacks are performed to deprive resource utilization as the server would not be able to respond to the request. On preventing DOS attack, proper capacity planning will be achieved. When there is a proper capacity planning, we can easily manage the resources even though if there are massive amount of resources to be handled. To overcome the DOS attack, we need to follow some security techniques, mitigation strategies to overcome the attack. Thus, a detailed ananlysis of the impact, mitigation strategies, tools and the penetration testing is done for Denial of Service attack. Thus, the Denial of Service attack can be detected and prevented through the adherence of the DOS countermeasures.

REFERENCES

Alani. (2014). Securing the Cloud: Threats, Attacks, and Mitigation Techniques. *Journal of Advanced Computer Science and Technology*, 202-213.

Alotaibi. (2015). Threat in Cloud- Denial of Service (DoS) and Distributed Denial of Service (DDoS) Attack, and Security Measures. *Journal of Emerging Trends in Computing and Information Sciences, 6*(5).

Chouhan & Singh. (2016). Security Attacks on Cloud Computing with Possible Solution. *International Journal of Advanced Research in Computer Science and Software Engineering, 6*(1).

Gunasekhar, T., Thirupathi Rao, K., Saikiran, P., & Lakshmi, P. V. S. (2014). A Survey on Denial of Service Attacks. *International Journal of Computer Science and Information Technologies, 5*(2), 2373–2376.

Kilari & Sridaran. (n.d.). An Overview of DDoS Attacks in Cloud Environment. *International Journal of Advanced Networking Applications*.

Ramya, R., & Kesavaraj, G. (2015). A Survey on Denial of Service Attack in Cloud Computing Environment. *International Journal of Advanced Research in Education & Technology, 2*(3).

Shameli-Sendi, Pourzandi, Fekih-Ahmed, & Cheriet. (2015). Taxonomy of Distributed Denial of Service Mitigation Approaches for Cloud Computing. *Journal of Network and Computer Applications*, (October), 28.

Singh & Shrivastava. (2012). Overview of Attacks on Cloud Computing. *International Journal of Engineering and Innovative Technology, 1*(4).

Singh, S., Pandey, B. K., & Srivastava, R. (2014). Cloud Computing Attacks: A Discussion with Solutions. Open Journal of Mobile Computing and Cloud Computing, 1(1).

Siva, T., & Phalguna Krishna, E. S. (2013). Controlling various network based ADoS Attacks in cloud computing environment: By Using Port Hopping Technique. *International Journal of Engineering Trends and Technology, 4*(5).

Somani, G., Gaur, M. S., Sanghi, D., Conti, M., & Buyya, R. (2015). DDoS Attacks in Cloud Computing: Issues, Taxonomy, and Future Directions. ACM Comput. Surv., 1(1).

Venkatesa Kumar & Nithya. (2014). Improving security issues and security attacks in cloud computing. *International Journal of Advanced Research in Computer and Communication Engineering, 3*(10).

Vidhya, V. (2014). A Review of DOS Attacks in Cloud Computing. *IOSR Journal of Computer Engineering, 16*(5), 32-35.

Wong & Tan. (2014). A Survey of Trends in Massive DDOS Attacks and Cloud-based Mitigations. *International Journal of Network Security & Its Applications, 6*(3).

This research was previously published in Advancing Cloud Database Systems and Capacity Planning With Dynamic Applications edited by Narendra Kumar Kamila; pages 289-319, copyright year 2017 by Information Science Reference (an imprint of IGI Global).

Chapter 27
Distributed Denial of Service Attacks and Defense in Cloud Computing

Gopal Singh Kushwah
National Institute of Technology Kurukshetra, India

Virender Ranga
iD https://orcid.org/0000-0002-2046-8642
National Institute of Technology Kurukshetra, India

ABSTRACT

Cloud computing has now become a part of many businesses. It provides on-demand resources to its users based on pay-as-you-use policy, across the globe. The high availability feature of this technology is affected by distributed denial of service (DDoS) attack, which is a major security issue. In this attack, cloud or network resources are exhausted, resulting in a denial of service for legitimate users. In this chapter, a classification of various types of DDoS attacks has been presented, and techniques for defending these attacks in cloud computing have been discussed. A discussion on challenges and open issues in this area is also given. Finally, a conceptual model based on extreme learning machine has been proposed to defend these attacks.

INTRODUCTION

Cloud computing is one of the most promising technologies today. The services provided by cloud computing are grouped into three types, Software-as-a-Service (SaaS), Platform-as-a-Service (PaaS) and Infrastructure-as-a-Service (IaaS). SaaS provides various application programs. PaaS provides application development environments. IaaS provides processing power, memory etc. Security is a major concern in this area. The issues related to security in clouds are confidentiality, privacy, access control, integrity, and availability. Confidentiality means only authorized entities should have access to the data stored in the cloud. In the cloud, the data of users are stored away from their site and users do not have direct

DOI: 10.4018/978-1-7998-5348-0.ch027

control over data. Strong data confidentiality techniques are thus needed. The controlled disclosure of personal information of users comes under privacy. Only authorized entities should be provided information about cloud users. Access control ensures that a user should be able to access only those services to which he/she is authorized, not more. Access control should be provided fine-grained. Integrity means only authorized entities should be able to make changes in the data. If there is any change in the stored data, the owner of data should be able to identify the change. Also, if there is any loss or corruption of stored data, there should be a way to retrieve it. Availability means the services should be available all the time to legitimate users. There should be no denial of provided services to its users.

High availability is one of the most important features of cloud computing, it is affected by Distributed denial of service (DDoS) attacks. These attacks have made a huge loss to cloud computing as well as traditional IT infrastructure. In this attack, the attacker uses many compromised hosts to launch the attack. All these hosts work on the instructions provided by the attacker and send traffic to the target, to disrupt the services provided by it. Cloud computing has now become the new target for DDoS attackers as predicted in (Patrick, 2015). This was evidenced by (Seals, 2015) that most of the attacks in the first quarter of 2015 were on cloud-based systems. According to (Global IT security risks survey, 2015), 50% of the surveyed businesses experienced DDoS attacks in the year of 2014. The business' public website is the most affected service. In most of the cases, the website is not accessible. In some cases, a particular area of the website is affected, like login area. The most commonly reported effect of DDoS attack was increased page load time. The loss due to DDoS attacks to small and medium organizations is $52,000 per attack, while for large organizations this loss is $444,000 as depicted in (Global IT security risks survey 2014-Distributed denial of service (DDoS) attacks, 2014). The gaming industry has been the highest target for DDoS attacks in 2017 as shown by (McKeay & Fakhreddine, 2017a; McKeay & Fakhreddine, 2017b; McKeay & Fakhreddine, 2017c; McKeay & Fakhreddine, 2017d). Organization wise DDoS attack target information for the year 2017 is shown in figure 1. Average numbers of attacks per target have been 25, 32, 36 and 29 for Q1 2017, Q2 2017, Q3 2017 and Q4 2017, respectively. In view of these facts, there is a strong need of developing solutions for DDoS attack defense in cloud computing. The solutions for DDoS attacks can be developed using two approaches, proactive and reactive. The first approach is based on avoidance of attack and, the second approach is based on detection and mitigation of attack. In this chapter, some recent works done in DDoS attack defense in cloud computing have been discussed. A prediction based model for attack detection has also been proposed. Specifically, our contributions in this chapter are summarized as follows.

- To give a taxonomy of DDoS attacks.
- To present a literature survey on recent DDoS attack defense solutions in Cloud Computing.
- To discuss challenges and open issues in DDoS attack defense in cloud computing.
- To propose an extreme learning machine based model for defending DDoS attacks.

DDoS ATTACKS AND ITS TYPES

In DDoS attack, the attacker uses many machines to launch the attack. To perform the attack, a botnet of compromised machines is created. These machines are scattered through the Internet and follow instructions of the attacker during the attack. Some other machines called handlers are also used, which are more powerful than the bots. These handlers are directly connected to the attacker and relay the

Figure 1. Organization wise DDoS attack target (%) for 2017

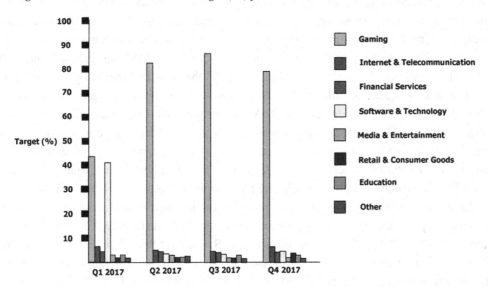

instructions of the attacker to the bots (as shown in Figure 2). DDoS attacks in cloud computing can be classified into four categories, Protocol-based, Network layer, Application layer and, Economical denial of sustainability (EDoS).

Protocol-Based Attacks

The attackers exploit the vulnerability of protocols to launch the attack. These attacks consume the processing power, memory capacity etc. of the victim machine. These attacks include ping of death (POD), Land, ARP poisoning, Teardrop, and SYN flood.

Ping of Death (POD)

In this attack, a ping request with a size larger than maximum allowable IP packet size is sent. It results in buffer overflow at the victim machine and its operating system can be crashed. Nowadays, the operating systems are made secured against these attacks.

Land

In this attack, spoofed IP address of the victim's machine is used for both source and destination addresses. The request with these addresses is sent to the victim, which results in heavy processing at the victim. Because it replies continuously to itself. This type of attack is no longer in use because networks are secured against these attacks.

Figure 2. DDoS attack

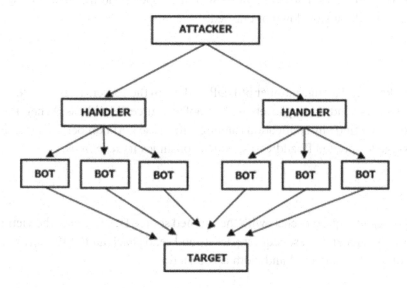

ARP Poisoning

In this attack, the cache used by the destination machine to store the MAC and IP addresses of the sender machine is changed. So, the sender machine cannot receive the reply from other machines.

Teardrop

In this type of attack, the fragment offset field of IP protocol is used. If there is any mismatch in this field then the reassembly process may be crashed. The attackers make some change in this field of the packets deliberately to crash the reassembly process at routers.

SYN Flood

In this attack, TCP connection procedure is exploited. An attacker sends many SYN packet to the server. In response to this, the server sends ACK and SYN to the attacker and waits for ACK from the attacker. The server stores the information about these connection states in a buffer. The attacker never sends ACK to the server. So, this buffer becomes full. Now, the server can not accept requests from legitimate clients for new connections.

Network Layer Attacks

ICMP Flood

In this type of attack, attackers send a huge amount of echo request messages to the victim. In response to these messages, the victim sends echo reply messages. It consumes both incoming and outgoing bandwidth of the victim. If an attacker sends requests with high speed and the victim is slow in processing these requests, then it will be slowdown or crashed.

UDP Flood

In this attack, attackers send a huge number of UDP packets to the server. These packets contain random port numbers. Attackers send these packets with spoofed source IP address. When the server process these packets, it does not find any application running with these port numbers. Thus it sends destination unreachable message to spoofed IP addresses, which consumes its resources.

Smurf Attack

In this attack, ICMP echo request packets with the spoofed source IP address of the victim are broadcast. A large number of hosts receive these request packets and sends back an ICMP reply to the victim. This results in exhaustion of the network bandwidth at the victim.

Application Layer Attacks

HTTP Flood

In this type of attack, malformed HTTP requests are used to exhaust web server resources. It creates HTTP POST or HTTP GET messages in such a way that seems legitimate. It uses Botnets for sending these messages to the server.

XML Flood

In this type of attack, malformed XML messages are used. This type of attack is performed when SOAP messages are used for communication in web services. SOAP messages are written in XML and sent through HTTP.

Slowris Attack

In this type of attack, attackers send multiple partial connection requests to the server. The server uses a separate thread for each such request. If the connection requests are not completed within a specific period then server terminates the connection. To avoid this, attackers send partial information again before the timeout. In that way, the server is not able to terminate the partial open connections and when the limit of simultaneously opened connection is reached, the server cannot accept new requests.

Back Attack

This type of attack is used against Apache web servers. In this attack, requests containing URL with a large number of forward slashes are sent. When the server receives such a request, it becomes down.

Rudy Attack (R U Dead Yet)

In this type of attack, the attacker sends an HTTP POST request to the server, intimating that a large amount of data will be submitted. Now, the attacker sends a small amount of data in next requests. The server thinks, the data is coming from slow connections and keeps the connection open. Attacker continues to send requests with small data, so the server keeps the connection open. When the limit of the connections, which can be handled by the server is reached, the server becomes down.

Economic Denial of Sustainability (EDoS)

This attack is different from others; it is not used to make cloud services un-available to legitimate users. It affects the billing amount of the service providers. Service providers use rented resources from the cloud providers and pay for these resources based on the service level agreements. The attackers send requests to the service provider's website so that it consumes more resources from the cloud provider and billing would be increased.

SOLUTIONS TO DDOS ATTACKS IN CLOUD COMPUTING

The literature related to DDoS attack defense has been focused on three types of techniques, attack detection and mitigation, attack prevention and, attack source traceback. In the first type of techniques, the attack is detected and then mitigated. In the second type of techniques, the attack is avoided from happening. The third type of techniques focus on finding the source of the attack.

Attack Detection and Mitigation

Soft Computing Techniques

In the work of (Vidal, Orozco, & Villalba, 2018), an artificial immune system based DoS attack mitigation system has been proposed. It detects and responds to attacks in the same way as the human immune system responds to protect the human body. It uses two types of detectors, spread across the network. First types of detectors are used to detect and block new types of attacks. The second types of detectors are used to detect and block only those attacks which have been previously identified by the first type of detectors. The authors in (Singh & De, 2017) proposed a method to detect application layer DDoS attacks. It uses a combination of multilayer perceptron and genetic algorithm to detect the attacks. The features used for classification are number of HTTP count, number of IP addresses, constant mapping function and fixed frame length. In the work of (Saied, Overill, & Radzik, 2016), the authors proposed a model to detect DDoS attacks based on ANN. It uses three ANNs for detection. First ANN is used with only TCP features. Second ANN is used with ICMP features, and third ANN is used with UDP features. The final output is based on the combination of the outputs received from these three ANNs. Based on the final output, attacks are determined. This model detects known as well as unknown attacks. In the work of (Sahi, Lai, Li, & Diykh, 2017), a machine learning based system for detecting and preventing TCP flood attacks has been proposed. First, source addresses of all incoming packets are compared against a blacklist table. Each entry in the table represents a malicious client, who has been identified in past.

All requests which have a match in the table, are terminated. The requests with the unmatched source address are forwarded to a classifier, which is based on least square support vector machine (LS-SVM). The packets identified as normal are forwarded to the cloud server, and those classified as malicious are terminated. The blacklist table is updated by adding the source addresses of malicious packets. In the work of (Pandeeswari & Kumar, 2016), the authors proposed a hypervisor level anomaly detection system. It is based on Fuzzy C means clustering and ANN. First, fuzzy c means clustering algorithm is used to divide a large training dataset into small clusters such that data within the same cluster are homogenous and data in different clusters are heterogeneous. This division of dataset improves the accuracy of training and reduces complexity. After that, each data cluster is used to train a separate ANN. The outputs of each ANN are aggregated using fuzzy aggregation to reduce the errors in detection. In the work of (Chonka, Xiang, Zhou, & Bonti, 2011), authors proposed a system for HTTP DoS and XML DoS attacks protection. It has two components, a cloud-based traceback, and cloud protector. Cloud traceback finds the source of the attack, it is based on service-oriented architecture. Cloud protector is used to filter attack packets, it is based on ANN. In the work of (Xiao, Qu, Qi, & Li, 2015), a method for DDoS attack detection in data centers has been proposed. It uses a K-nearest neighbor-based classifier and network flow data for attack detection. Correlation information of training data is used to improve the classification accuracy. To reduce the computation cost, a grid-based method has been proposed which reduces training data. In the work of (Iyengar, Banerjee, & Ganapathy, 2014), the authors proposed a fuzzy logic-based system to detect DDoS attacks. First, the model is trained i.e. fuzzy inference rules are constructed. To determine the logic, these rules are defined in the conditional form. These rules are based on those packet characteristics which show a significant change in their values during the attack. During detection, the system generates alert if the attack is found. For prevention, border router discards the packets from malicious sources. In the work of (Kushwah & Ali, 2017) authors proposed a solution for detecting DDoS attacks based on ANN and black hole optimization. In this solution, the black hole optimization algorithm has been used to train the ANN. The authors in (Kushwah & Ali, n.d.) proposed a model for detecting DDoS attacks, which is based on extreme learning machine. This model takes a very short time for training.

Statistical Techniques

In the work of (Wang, Miu, Luo, & Wang, 2018), a method for detecting and mitigating application-layer DDoS attacks based on sketch data structure has been proposed. To detect the attack, the divergence of the sketches between two consecutive cycles has been used. To measure the divergence, a variant of Hellinger distance has been used. To identify the malicious hosts directly, the detected abnormal sketches are used. The solution proposed by (Bharot, Verma, Sharma, & Suraparaju, 2018) uses Hellinger distance to measure the deviation of the current network traffic from the baseline traffic. If no significant deviation is found then traffic is forwarded to the legitimate request processing unit. In case of deviation, the traffic is forwarded for classification. After classification, normal requests are forwarded to the legitimate request processing unit. Malicious requests are forwarded to the intensive care response processing unit. In that unit, the attackers are trapped in a series of questions and meanwhile, sources of attack are determined and further traffic is blocked from those sources. In the work of (Behal & Kumar, 2017), the authors proposed the use of information theory metrics phi-entropy and phi-divergence for detecting DDoS attacks and flash events. These metrics are highly sensitive to any change in network traffic properties, so the attacks can be detected early. In the work of (Tan, Jamdagni, He, Nanda, & Liu,

2014), the authors proposed a multivariate correlation analysis based DoS attack detection system. In this model, first, a triangular area map generation technique is used to calculate the correlation between two distinct features of the same traffic record. After that, based on these correlation characteristics, a normal profile is created. During testing, correlation characteristics for current traffic are used to create a test profile. This test profile is compared with a normal profile to detect attacks. In the work of (Aborujilah & Musa, 2017), a covariance matrix based approach has been used to detect HTTP flood attacks. In the training phase, a normal profile is created. For creating a normal profile, the expected matrix and threshold matrix are calculated from covariance matrices of normal traffic. In the detection phase, the covariance matrix of real-time traffic is compared with the expected matrix. The deviation of the covariance matrix from the expected matrix more than the value of the threshold matrix represents an attack. In the work of (Dou, W. Chen, & J. Chen, 2013), the authors proposed a method to filter DDoS attacks based on correlation characteristics. First, a nominal profile is created. This is based on simultaneously appeared attribute pair's value called confidence. After that, for each attribute, a confidence score (CBF) is calculated and discarding threshold is determined. During attack detection, CBF score for all attributes is again calculated and compared with the nominal profile. Packets with a confidence score above discarding threshold are determined as legitimate. In the work of (Negi, Mishra, & Gupta, 2013), the authors proposed an enhanced confidence based filtering method for clouds. It addresses the problems of speed and database of the original method. To solve database problem, option field of IP header has been used for storage. The authors in (Vissers, Somasundaram, Pieters, Govindarajan, & Hellinckx, 2014), proposed a model for application layer HTTP and XML attacks. This model uses a normal profile based on the Gaussian distribution of various features. It has two phases, HTTP header inspection, and XML content inspection. In the first phase, requests are limited to avoid HTTP flood. After that, the SOAP action field is checked and size outliers are detected. In the second phase, first, spoofed SOAP action and WS-addressing are checked. After that, SOAP features are evaluated against the Gaussian model to detect outliers. In the work of (Koduru, Neelakantam, & Bhanu, 2013), a method for detecting EDoS attacks based on time spent on a web page (TSP) has been proposed. The authors observed that bots used in attack spend nearly zero time on a web page, this observation is used for attack detection. First, the mean of TSP during no attack period is calculated. During the attack period, deviation from mean represents an attack. In the work of (Idziorek, Tannian, & Jacobson, 2011), a detection approach for a new type of attack called the fraudulent resource consumption attack, has been proposed. Three metrics have been used in combination to detect this attack. According to the first metric, the popularity of web page and its frequency follows Zipf's law, if it does not follow then it may be an attack. The second measure is Spearman's footrule distance and the third measure is the overlap value.

SDN Based Techniques

The authors in (Hong, Kim, Choi, & Park, 2018) proposed a method for detecting and mitigating slow rate HTTP DDoS attacks based on SDN has been proposed. It uses an application which is installed on SDN controller. The application uses timeout based attack detection. When the attack is detected by the application, it requests the SDN controller to update its flow rules for blocking the traffic from the attacker. In the work of (Wang, Zheng, Lou, & Hou, 2015), a software-defined networking based solution for mitigating DDoS attacks has been proposed. It has two parts, attack detection module, and attack mitigation module. For detection, it uses a probabilistic inference graphical model. It has two properties, it can perform automatic feature selection and, it can overcome the data-shift problem by efficient update. The mitigation module uses predefined countermeasures to deal with attacks.

Other Techniques

In the work of (Baig, Sait, & Binbeshr, 2016), a solution based on controlled resource access for EDoS detection and mitigation has been proposed. It has two components, vFirewall, and VMInvestigator. A table of blacklisted IP addresses is maintained by vFirewall. The requests from sources with no matching IP in the table are forwarded to the cloud. The requests are forwarded to the VMInvestigator in two cases, either there is a match of IP address in table or auto-scaling threshold is exceeded. At first level, VMInvestigator uses some measures like user trust value and the number of concurrent requests from a user, to limit access to the cloud. At second level, a Turing test is performed. Based on the result of the test, access to the cloud is granted and corresponding user trust value is updated. In the work of (Tan et al., 2015), authors used computer vision technique for DDoS attack detection. The traffic records in this model are treated as images. To extract the correlation between traffic features and converting traffic records into images, a multivariate correlation analysis method has been used. For detection of attacks, Earth mover's distance dissimilarity measure has been used. In the work of (Somani, Gaur, Sanghi, Conti, & Buyya, 2017), A framework based on service resizing has been proposed to assist the mitigation of DDoS attacks. In the case of attack, the resources of victim service are shrunk to a minimum number. The resources taken from the victim are given to mitigation service for expanding its computation power. The resources for the victim service are expanded to its original number after the attack is mitigated. For minimizing the attack downtime, TCP tuning has been used. In the work of (Somani et al., 2015), a DDoS mitigation strategy has been proposed, which is based on accurate auto-scaling decisions. The attack is detected based on human behavior analysis and an IP blacklist table. The measure used for human behavior is the number of unique page requests from a single user in a specific time duration. If the number of requests for a web page from a single user is more than a specific number then it represents an attack. To provide quality of service to the legitimate users, it takes intelligent decisions for auto-scaling. In the work of (Wahab, Bentahar, Otrok, & Mourad, 2017), the authors proposed a model for optimally distributing the detection load to virtual machines. It results in maximizing attack detection under a limited amount of resources. It uses a trust model between the hypervisor and virtual machines based on objective and subjective sources. For aggregating these trust, the Bayesian inference has been used. A maximin game between hypervisor and attacker has been introduced on top of this trust model. The hypervisor tries to maximize the attack detection using limited resources and the attacker tries to minimize this. The result of the game provides an optimal distribution of detection load among various virtual machines to the hypervisor. In the work of (Bakshi & Dujodwala, 2010), the authors proposed a system for defending cloud based on intrusion detection system. An IDS is installed on the virtual switch which observes all incoming and outgoing traffic. If unexpected behavior is found then it checks acknowledgments from the senders. In case of not receiving acknowledgments, IDS requests honeypot to ping the source address. No reply from the source confirms the DDOS attack. To mitigate this attack, such types of sources are blocked and the server is moved to another virtual server.

Attack Prevention

In the work of (Luo, Chen, Li, & Vasilakos, 2017), the authors proposed a dynamic path identifier (D-PID) based approach to prevent DDoS flood attacks. In this approach, PIDs are used for inter-domain routing. These PIDs are dynamically changed. If an attacker succeeds to get PIDs, these can be used for a certain time only. Because, after that time these PIDs become invalid and the network discards the attack packets sent through these identifiers. If the attacker tries to get new PIDs for the attack, he has to increase attacking cost and it also makes the attack to be detected easily. In the work of (Wu, Zhao, Bao, & Deng, 2015), the authors proposed a new type of puzzle called software puzzle for resource inflated DoS attacks. The puzzle generation algorithm for these types of puzzles is not published in advance, but it is generated randomly when the server receives a request from the client. This approach has two advantages. First, the attacker can not prepare the solution for the puzzles in advance. Second, the attacker can not utilize the GPU system for puzzle software because it is not possible to convert the CPU based software system to its equivalent GPU version in real time. In the work of (Wang et al., 2014), the authors proposed a moving target based approach to defend DDoS attacks. It uses proxies between legitimate clients and the web server. In case of attack, the attack proxies are replaced with backup proxies. The attack clients are shuffled to new proxies. In this way, the attack traffic and legitimate traffic is segregated. This process of shuffling and assigning is continued until segregation is completed. For optimizing the segregation process, a greedy algorithm has been proposed. In the work of (Sqalli, Al-Haidari, & Salah, 2011), a model called EDoS Shield for mitigating EDoS attacks has been proposed. It has two components, a virtual firewall, and the verifier node. All incoming requests are applied to the virtual firewall. It uses a blacklist and a whitelist. Requests with a source address in blacklist are dropped, and in white list are forwarded to cloud. If the source address does not match with both lists then the packet is forwarded to the verifier node. This node performs a Turing test and based on the result of the test, permission to access the cloud is granted and lists at virtual firewall are also updated. In the work of (Al-Haidari, Sqalli, & Salah, 2012), the authors proposed a solution to mitigate EDoS attacks for spoofed source IP addresses, which is an extension to the original EDoS Shield. It uses the TTL value for detecting spoofed IP addresses. Blacklist and whitelist are also modified to store TTL values. In the work of (Kumar et al., 2012), the authors proposed an in-cloud scrubber service for EDoS attacks. The advantage of this type of service is, it can be used on –demand when required. The service provider is free from the burden of the defense process and they only need to pay for it. The service provider starts running in normal mode, when it observes attack symptoms then it calls the service and switches to suspended mode. The service produces two types of puzzles, one type for low rate attack and other for high rate attacks. In the work of (V. S. M. Huang, R. Huang, & Chiang, 2013), a multistage DDoS defense model has been proposed. First, it uses a source checking module to find the type of source based on the various lists maintained by this module. If the source is from blacklist then request is dropped and, if the source is from whitelist then it is forwarded to services. If the source is from block list then it is forwarded to Turing test module. Here, a puzzle is generated and supplied to the user. Based on the answer to the puzzle, the user is treated further. In the work of (Masood, Anwar, Raza, & Hur, 2013), the authors proposed a defense system based on access control and user behaviors. First, a challenge server is used, only those clients who pass the test of this server are allowed to go for next phase. In the next phase, called admission control, users are assigned hidden ports to access the server. This limits the number of users simultaneously accessing the server. For providing quality of service to different clients, their past behavior is used. Good clients are provided with more resources and bad clients are provided with fewer resources.

Attack Source Traceback

In the work of (Nur & Tozal, 2018), a technique for finding the source of attack has been proposed. It is based on probabilistic packet marking. It uses a modified record route option field of the IP protocol to make a path. In this technique, the IP addresses of visiting routers are stored until there is room. When there is no room then it stores the address with probability p and with probability 1-p it does not store. After finding the path, the DDoS defense is delegated to the upstream Internet service providers. In the work of (Foroushani & Zincir-Heywood, 2014), a model to defend DDoS attacks based on IP traceback has been proposed. It has three components, detection, traceback and traffic control. The detection module detects the attacks based on an unusual change in attack traffic. Traceback module finds the source of the attack based on deterministic flow marking. Traffic control module minimizes the attack traffic. The authors in (Katz-Bassett et al., 2010) developed a tool for creating the reverse path from destination to sources. In the work of (Xiang, Li, & Zhou, 2011), the authors proposed a system for detecting the DDoS attack and finding the source of that attack. For detection, it uses generalized entropy and information distance metrics. For finding the source of the attack, it uses information distance metric. In the work of (Yu, Zhou, Doss, & Jia, 2011), the authors proposed a traceback technique, which is not based on packet marking. It uses flow entropy variation for traceback. It has many advantages, it does not require memory intensive operations. It is efficiently scalable and robust against the population of packets. It is also independent of patterns of attack traffic.

ISSUES AND CHALLENGES IN DDOS DEFENSE IN CLOUD COMPUTING

- In detection schemes, the value of false alarms should be zero in the ideal case. But it is not always possible to reduce this value to zero, instead, it should be minimized. Designing schemes with a value of false alarms near to zero is still a challenging task.
- The detection accuracy of schemes should be very high, then only all attacks data is detected.
- Most of the detection schemes detect only those attacks which are available in the training dataset. They cannot detect new types of attacks. Schemes should be designed to detect known as well as unknown attacks.
- Training time for detection algorithms is also an issue. Schemes should be designed with minimal training time. When the classifier needs to be retrained with the new dataset, it should be done quickly.
- To select the right features for attack detection is also a challenge, as the accuracy of detection also depends on the number and type of selected features.
- The attack should be detected in the early stage, so it cannot create huge losses. Such early detection is also a challenge.
- The detection scheme should be fast enough to handle heavy traffic. It should be able to process and detect attacks in real time.
- Application layer attacks mimic the legitimate traffic, detecting these attacks is still challenging.
- In DDoS attack prevention, efficient generation and storage of puzzles, CAPTCHA etc. is difficult.

- It is difficult to trace back to the source of attack when IP spoofing is used.
- Majority of proposed schemes defend attacks at a particular single layer, designing a single scheme for defending attacks at multiple layers is still an open issue.

PREDICTION BASED DDOS ATTACK DETECTION

In this section, we propose a prediction based system to detect DDoS attacks. The proposed system is shown in Figure 3. All incoming requests from clients are accepted by the resource manager, which provides resources to these clients as needed. The request database stores information about the number of requests per time instance received by the resource manager. The predictor predicts the number of requests based on the information stored in the database. The attack detector compares the number of requests predicted by the predictor and actual requests received by the resource manager for a time instance. If the difference between these two values is greater than the threshold, an attack is detected. For prediction, extreme learning machine (ELM) has been used. It is a type of artificial neural network (ANN) which can be trained very quickly. ANN is a network of processing elements called neurons, which is based on the human neural system. These neurons are grouped into layers and, neurons in different layers are connected through weights. There are one input layer, one or more hidden layers, and one output layer. The input to this network is given by the input layer, the hidden layer performs the computations on these inputs and, output layer is used to generate the output of the system. The different types of computations in neurons are performed based on various activation functions, which may be a linear activation function, sigmoid activation functions etc.

First, ELM is trained and after training, it is used to predict the number of requests. During the training of the network, the weights between the input layer and the hidden layer are initialized randomly. The weights between the hidden layer and output layer are calculated based on the generalized inverse of the matrix, It means the network can be trained in a single step, it does not require iterations.

Figure 3. Proposed system

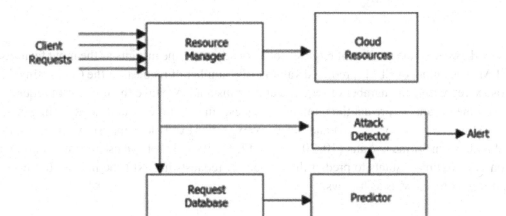

The ELM used in our system is shown in Figure 4. It has three layers, input, hidden and output. These layers have n, l, and 1 neuron, respectively. The weights between input and hidden layers are represented by matrix U and weights between hidden and output layers are represented by matrix V. Hidden layer biases are represented by b_j, for j=1 to l. The activation function is represented by f, which is defined by the following equation,

$$f(n) = \begin{cases} n, & For\ input\ layer \\ \dfrac{1}{1+e^{-n}}, & For\ other\ layes \end{cases} \tag{1}$$

Figure 4. Extreme learning machine

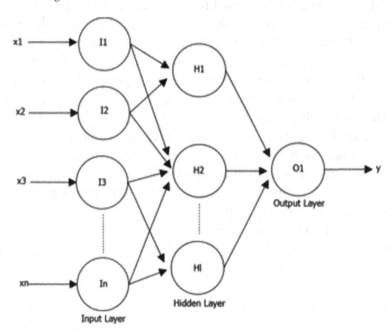

In this work, we used the number of requests for n consecutive time instants as the input features to be used in ELM. The output of ELM (predicted value) is the number of requests at the $(n+1)^{th}$ time instant.

Suppose x_i represents the number of requests at time instant i. We take the number of requests for n consecutive time instants to predict the number of requests in next time instant i.e. x_{n+1}. In general, the input of ELM is, $X=[x_1, x_2, x_3, ..., x_n]$ and output, $y=x_{n+1}$. For example, suppose we have a set of the number of requests in 8-time instants {10, 20, 15, 20, 17, 18, 19, 16}. Let, we use the number of requests at four consecutive time instants to predict the number of requests in next time instant. It means input and output matrix for ELM is as follows.

$$X=\begin{bmatrix} 10 & 20 & 15 & 20 \\ 20 & 15 & 20 & 17 \\ 15 & 20 & 17 & 18 \\ 20 & 17 & 18 & 19 \end{bmatrix} and \ Y=\begin{bmatrix} 17 \\ 18 \\ 19 \\ 16 \end{bmatrix}$$

Let N be the number of training samples used to train the ELM. These are of the form (X_i, t_i), where X_i represents the number of requests in *n* consecutive time instants and t_i represents the number of requests in $(n+1)^{th}$ time instant. The output can be modeled as

$$y_i=\sum_{j=1}^{l} v_j f(\boldsymbol{u}_j, b_j, Xi), \text{ for } i=1 \text{ to } N \tag{2}$$

Here, $\boldsymbol{u}_j \in R^n$ and $b_j \in R$, are parameters of the hidden layer and, $v_j \in R$ is the weight which connects j^{th} hidden neuron to the output neuron. Equation (2) can be written for all N samples as follows

$$Y=HV \tag{3}$$

where,

$$H=\begin{bmatrix} f(u_1,b_1,X_1) & \cdots & f(u_l,b_l,X_1) \\ \vdots & \ddots & \vdots \\ f(u_1,b_1,X_N) & \cdots & f(u_l,b_l,x_N) \end{bmatrix}, V=\begin{bmatrix} v_1^T \\ \vdots \\ v_l^T \end{bmatrix} \text{ and } Y=\begin{bmatrix} y_1^T \\ \vdots \\ y_N^T \end{bmatrix}$$

To minimize error $\|Y-T\|$, where $T = [t_1,t_2,\ldots, t_N]$ represents target value for all N samples, $\boldsymbol{u}_j$ and b_j can be randomly initialized. The output weights can be found by finding a least square solution of

$$V=H^\dagger T \tag{4}$$

here, † represents Moore-Penrose generalized inverse of a matrix. When the value of V is calculated, the ELM is trained. Now it can be used to predict the number of requests. It means that, to predict the number of requests at $(n+1)^{th}$ time instant, output $y= \sum_{j=1}^{l} v_j f(\boldsymbol{u}_j, b_j, X')$ is calculated. where, $X'=[x'_1,x'_2,$ $\ldots, x'_n]$ is a test sample which represents the number of requests received at previous *n* time instances.

Now, the value of *y* is compared with the actual number of requests received at $(n+1)^{th}$ time instant. If the difference between the number of requests actually received and number of requests predicted is more than the threshold then it determines attack. The value of the threshold is determined by using training dataset for attack and normal periods. The working of the proposed system is represented by the pseudo code in Figure 5.

Figure 5. Pseudocode for proposed system

```
Algorithm: Training
Input: Number of neurons (l), N training samples
Output: Trained ELM
    1.  Randomly initialize input-hidden weight matrix U
    2.  Randomly initialize hidden biases
    3.  for i=1 to N do
    4.      for j=1 to l do
    5.          calculate H_ij=f(u_j, b_j, Xi)
    6.      end for
    7.  end for
    8.  Calculate V=H†T

Algorithm: Attack Detection
Input: Test sample X', Trained ELM, Actual requests received y', threshold H
Output: Attack sample / Normal sample
    1.  Calculate y= ∑_{j=1}^{l} v_j f(u_j, b_j, X')
    2.  if |y'-y|>H
    3.      attack sample
    4.  else
    5.      normal sample
```

CONCLUSION

Distributed denial of service attack has been a big security issue for cloud computing. It prevents legitimate users from accessing cloud services. Developing defensive solutions against these attacks is a major research area. In this chapter, the solutions proposed by the researchers in recent years to defend DDoS attacks have been presented. Different types of DDoS attacks have also been discussed. A prediction based DDoS attack detection system has also been proposed. It is based on ELM. It predicts the number of requests at a particular time instance and compares this value with the number of requests actually arrived in that time instant. If the difference between these values is above the threshold then it represents an attack.

REFERENCES

Aborujilah, A., & Musa, S. (2017). Cloud-Based DDoS HTTP Attack Detection Using Covariance Matrix Approach. *Journal of Computer Networks and Communications*.

Al-Haidari, F., Sqalli, M. H., & Salah, K. (2012, June). Enhanced EDoS-shield for mitigating EDoS attacks originating from spoofed IP addresses. In *Trust, Security and Privacy in Computing and Communications (TrustCom), 2012 IEEE 11th International Conference on* (pp. 1167-1174). IEEE.

Baig, Z. A., Sait, S. M., & Binbeshr, F. (2016). Controlled access to cloud resources for mitigating Economic Denial of Sustainability (EDoS) attacks. *Computer Networks*, *97*, 31–47. doi:10.1016/j.comnet.2016.01.002

Bakshi, A., & Dujodwala, Y. B. (2010, February). Securing cloud from ddos attacks using intrusion detection system in virtual machine. In *Communication Software and Networks, 2010. ICCSN'10. Second International Conference on* (pp. 260-264). IEEE.

Behal, S., & Kumar, K. (2017). Detection of DDoS attacks and flash events using novel information theory metrics. *Computer Networks, 116*, 96–110. doi:10.1016/j.comnet.2017.02.015

Bharot, N., Verma, P., Sharma, S., & Suraparaju, V. (2018). Distributed Denial-of-Service Attack Detection and Mitigation Using Feature Selection and Intensive Care Request Processing Unit. *Arabian Journal for Science and Engineering, 43*(2), 959–967. doi:10.100713369-017-2844-0

Chonka, A., Xiang, Y., Zhou, W., & Bonti, A. (2011). Cloud security defence to protect cloud computing against HTTP-DoS and XML-DoS attacks. *Journal of Network and Computer Applications, 34*(4), 1097–1107. doi:10.1016/j.jnca.2010.06.004

Dou, W., Chen, Q., & Chen, J. (2013). A confidence-based filtering method for DDoS attack defense in cloud environment. *Future Generation Computer Systems, 29*(7), 1838–1850. doi:10.1016/j.future.2012.12.011

Foroushani, V. A., & Zincir-Heywood, A. N. (2014, May). TDFA: traceback-based defense against DDoS flooding attacks. In *Advanced Information Networking and Applications (AINA), 2014 IEEE 28th International Conference on* (pp. 597-604). IEEE.

Global IT security risks survey. (2014). *Distributed denial of service (DDoS) attacks.* Technical report, Kaspersky. Retrieved from https://media.kaspersky.com/en/B2B-International-2014-Survey-DDoS-Summary-Report.pdf

Global IT security risks survey. (2015). Technical Report, Kaspersky. Retrieved from https://media.kaspersky.com/pdf/global-it-security-risks-survey-2015.pdf

Hong, K., Kim, Y., Choi, H., & Park, J. (2018). SDN-Assisted Slow HTTP DDoS Attack Defense Method. *IEEE Communications Letters, 22*(4), 688–691. doi:10.1109/LCOMM.2017.2766636

Huang, V. S. M., Huang, R., & Chiang, M. (2013, March). A DDoS mitigation system with multi-stage detection and text-based turing testing in cloud computing. In *Advanced Information Networking and Applications Workshops (WAINA), 2013 27th International Conference on* (pp. 655-662). IEEE.

Idziorek, J., Tannian, M., & Jacobson, D. (2011, October). Detecting fraudulent use of cloud resources. In *Proceedings of the 3rd ACM workshop on Cloud computing security workshop* (pp. 61-72). ACM.

Iyengar, N. C. S., Banerjee, A., & Ganapathy, G. (2014). A fuzzy logic based defense mechanism against distributed denial of service attack in cloud computing environment. *International Journal of Communication Networks and Information Security, 6*(3), 233.

Katz-Bassett, E., Madhyastha, H. V., Adhikari, V. K., Scott, C., Sherry, J., Van Wesep, P., & Krishnamurthy, A. (2010, April). *Reverse traceroute* (Vol. 10). NSDI.

Koduru, A., Neelakantam, T., & Bhanu, S. M. S. (2013, October). Detection of economic denial of sustainability using time spent on a web page in cloud. In *Cloud Computing in Emerging Markets (CCEM), 2013 IEEE International Conference on* (pp. 1-4). IEEE.

Kumar, M. N., Sujatha, P., Kalva, V., Nagori, R., Katukojwala, A. K., & Kumar, M. (2012, November). Mitigating economic denial of sustainability (edos) in cloud computing using in-cloud scrubber service. In *Computational Intelligence and Communication Networks (CICN), 2012 Fourth International Conference on* (pp. 535-539). IEEE.

Kushwah, G. S., & Ali, S. T. (2017, August). Detecting DDoS attacks in cloud computing using ANN and black hole optimization. In *2017 2nd International Conference on Telecommunication and Networks (TEL-NET)* (pp. 1-5). IEEE.

Kushwah, G. S., & Ali, S. T. (in press). Distributed denial of service attacks detection in cloud computing using extreme learning machine. *International Journal of Communication Networks and Distributed Systems*.

Luo, H., Chen, Z., Li, J., & Vasilakos, A. V. (2017). Preventing distributed denial-of-service flooding attacks with dynamic path identifiers. *IEEE Transactions on Information Forensics and Security*, *12*(8), 1801–1815. doi:10.1109/TIFS.2017.2688414

Masood, M., Anwar, Z., Raza, S. A., & Hur, M. A. (2013, December). Edos armor: a cost effective economic denial of sustainability attack mitigation framework for e-commerce applications in cloud environments. In *Multi Topic Conference (INMIC), 2013 16th International* (pp. 37-42). IEEE. 10.1109/INMIC.2013.6731321

McKeay, M., & Fakhreddine, A. (2017a). *Akamai's state of Internet/Security Q1 2017 report*. Retrieved from https://www.akamai.com/us/en/multimedia/documents/ state-of-the-internet/q1-2017-state-of-the-internet-security-report.pdf

McKeay, M., & Fakhreddine, A. (2017b). *Akamai's state of Internet/Security Q2 2017 report*. Retrieved from https://www.akamai.com/de/de/multimedia /documents /state-of-the-internet/q2-2017-state-of-the-internet-security-report.pdf

McKeay, M., & Fakhreddine, A. (2017c). *Akamai's state of Internet/Security Q3 2017 report*. Retrieved from https://www.akamai.com/de/de/multimedia/documents/ state-of-the-internet/q3-2017-state-of-the-internet-security-report.pdf

McKeay, M., & Fakhreddine, A. (2017d). *Akamai's state of Internet/Security Q4 2017 report*. Retrieved from https://www.akamai.com/us/en/multimedia/documents/ state-of-the-internet/q4-2017-state-of-the-internet-security-report.pdf

Negi, P., Mishra, A., & Gupta, B. B. (2013). *Enhanced CBF packet filtering method to detect DDoS attack in cloud computing environment*. arXiv preprint arXiv:1304.7073

Nur, A. Y., & Tozal, M. E. (2018). Record route IP traceback: Combating DoS attacks and the variants. *Computers & Security*, *72*, 13–25. doi:10.1016/j.cose.2017.08.012

Pandeeswari, N., & Kumar, G. (2016). Anomaly detection system in cloud environment using fuzzy clustering based ANN. *Mobile Networks and Applications*, *21*(3), 494–505. doi:10.100711036-015-0644-x

Patrick, N. (2015). *Cybercriminals moving into cloud big time, report says*. Retrieved fromhttp://www. networkworld.com/article/2900125/malwarecybercrime/criminalsmoving-into-cloud-big-time-says-report.html

Sahi, A., Lai, D., Li, Y., & Diykh, M. (2017). An efficient DDoS TCP flood attack detection and prevention system in a cloud environment. *IEEE Access: Practical Innovations, Open Solutions, 5*, 6036–6048.

Saied, A., Overill, R. E., & Radzik, T. (2016). Detection of known and unknown DDoS attacks using Artificial Neural Networks. *Neurocomputing, 172*, 385–393. doi:10.1016/j.neucom.2015.04.101

Seals, T. (2015). *2015 DDoS Attacks Spike, Targeting Cloud*. Retrieved from http://www. infosecurity-magazine.com/news/q1-2015-ddos-attacks-spike/

Singh, K. J., & De, T. (2017). MLP-GA based algorithm to detect application layer DDoS attack. *Journal of Information Security and Applications, 36*, 145–153. doi:10.1016/j.jisa.2017.09.004

Somani, G., Gaur, M. S., Sanghi, D., Conti, M., & Buyya, R. (2017). Service resizing for quick DDoS mitigation in cloud computing environment. *Annales des Télécommunications, 72*(5-6), 237–252. doi:10.100712243-016-0552-5

Somani, G., Johri, A., Taneja, M., Pyne, U., Gaur, M. S., & Sanghi, D. (2015, December). DARAC: DDoS mitigation using DDoS aware resource allocation in cloud. In *International Conference on Information Systems Security* (pp. 263-282). Springer. 10.1007/978-3-319-26961-0_16

Sqalli, M. H., Al-Haidari, F., & Salah, K. (2011, December). Edos-shield-a two-steps mitigation technique against edos attacks in cloud computing. In *Utility and Cloud Computing (UCC), 2011 Fourth IEEE International Conference on* (pp. 49-56). IEEE.

Tan, Z., Jamdagni, A., He, X., Nanda, P., & Liu, R. P. (2014). A system for denial-of-service attack detection based on multivariate correlation analysis. *IEEE Transactions on Parallel and Distributed Systems, 25*(2), 447–456. doi:10.1109/TPDS.2013.146

Tan, Z., Jamdagni, A., He, X., Nanda, P., Liu, R. P., & Hu, J. (2015). Detection of denial-of-service attacks based on computer vision techniques. *IEEE Transactions on Computers, 64*(9), 2519–2533. doi:10.1109/TC.2014.2375218

Vidal, J. M., Orozco, A. L. S., & Villalba, L. J. G. (2018). Adaptive artificial immune networks for mitigating DoS flooding attacks. *Swarm and Evolutionary Computation, 38*, 94–108. doi:10.1016/j. swevo.2017.07.002

Vissers, T., Somasundaram, T. S., Pieters, L., Govindarajan, K., & Hellinckx, P. (2014). DDoS defense system for web services in a cloud environment. *Future Generation Computer Systems, 37*, 37–45. doi:10.1016/j.future.2014.03.003

Wahab, O. A., Bentahar, J., Otrok, H., & Mourad, A. (2017). Optimal load distribution for the detection of VM-based DDoS attacks in the cloud. *IEEE Transactions on Services Computing*.

Wang, B., Zheng, Y., Lou, W., & Hou, Y. T. (2015). DDoS attack protection in the era of cloud computing and software-defined networking. *Computer Networks, 81*, 308–319. doi:10.1016/j.comnet.2015.02.026

Wang, C., Miu, T. T., Luo, X., & Wang, J. (2018). SkyShield: A Sketch-Based Defense System Against Application Layer DDoS Attacks. *IEEE Transactions on Information Forensics and Security*, *13*(3), 559–573. doi:10.1109/TIFS.2017.2758754

Wang, H., Jia, Q., Fleck, D., Powell, W., Li, F., & Stavrou, A. (2014). A moving target DDoS defense mechanism. *Computer Communications*, *46*, 10–21. doi:10.1016/j.comcom.2014.03.009

Wu, Y., Zhao, Z., Bao, F., & Deng, R. H. (2015). Software puzzle: A countermeasure to resource-inflated denial-of-service attacks. *IEEE Transactions on Information Forensics and Security*, *10*(1), 168–177. doi:10.1109/TIFS.2014.2366293

Xiang, Y., Li, K., & Zhou, W. (2011). Low-rate DDoS attacks detection and traceback by using new information metrics. *IEEE Transactions on Information Forensics and Security*, *6*(2), 426–437. doi:10.1109/TIFS.2011.2107320

Xiao, P., Qu, W., Qi, H., & Li, Z. (2015). Detecting DDoS attacks against data center with correlation analysis. *Computer Communications*, *67*, 66–74. doi:10.1016/j.comcom.2015.06.012

Yu, S., Zhou, W., Doss, R., & Jia, W. (2011). Traceback of DDoS attacks using entropy variations. *IEEE Transactions on Parallel and Distributed Systems*, *22*(3), 412–425. doi:10.1109/TPDS.2010.97

KEY TERMS AND DEFINITIONS

Artificial Neural Network: A machine learning technique based on the working of the human brain.

Attack Detection: Detecting the attack while it is happening.

Attack Prevention: Preventing attack before it happens.

Cloud Computing: A technology that provides various types of resources on demand, on a pay-as-you-use basis.

Denial of Service Attack: An attack which makes a service un-available to its users. This attack is performed by single machine.

Distributed Denial of Service Attack: An attack that makes a service un-available to its users. This attack is performed by several machines.

Extreme Learning Machine: It is a special type of artificial neural network, which can be trained in a single step.

Source Trace Back: Finding the source of the attack.

This research was previously published in the Handbook of Research on the IoT, Cloud Computing, and Wireless Network Optimization edited by Surjit Singh and Rajeev Mohan Sharma; pages 41-59, copyright year 2019 by Engineering Science Reference (an imprint of IGI Global).

Chapter 28
Comparing Single Tier and Three Tier Infrastructure Designs against DDoS Attacks

Akashdeep Bhardwaj

University of Petroleum & Energy Studies, Dehradun, India

Sam Goundar

CENTRUM, Graduate Business School, Lima, Peru

ABSTRACT

With the rise in cyber-attacks on cloud environments like Brute Force, Malware or Distributed Denial of Service attacks, information security officers and data center administrators have a monumental task on hand. Organizations design data center and service delivery with the aim of catering to maximize device provisioning & availability, improve application performance, ensure better server virtualization and end up securing data centers using security solutions at internet edge protection level. These security solutions prove to be largely inadequate in times of a DDoS cyber-attack. In this paper, traditional data center design is reviewed and compared to the proposed three tier data center. The resilience to withstand against DDoS attacks is measured for Real User Monitoring parameters, compared for the two infrastructure designs and the data is validated using T-Test.

INTRODUCTION

Modern day cybercrime attacks are specific, targeted and designed to compromise high-value customer data, including personal, financial and corporate intellectual property. Distributed denial of service attacks are not just aimed to bring down network infrastructure, hog bandwidths or compromise applications, there is a bigger danger lurking behind these attacks targeting data security. Modern day Data center designs have evolved in recent times, migrating from in house, private hosting centers with physical servers to hybrid clouds, spread across multiple locations with Software Designed Networks (or SDNs), virtualized hosts, Application Centric Infrastructure (or ACIs) running automation for IT recovery, de-

DOI: 10.4018/978-1-7998-5348-0.ch028

tection tasks, accelerating application deployments in dynamic manner with DevOps policy model for network, storage, servers and services. Designing secure data centers has now becoming mandatory as well as challenging.

The motivation to perform this research firstly aims at designing a secure data center architecture, secondly with security implementations being highly complex, one off customized implementations as per client requirements, network architects and cloud providers tend to lean towards accelerating application and service delivery, dynamic scalability, resource availability, reduced operating costs and increasing business agility. The cloud providers tend to keep security on low priority which results in security gaps that impacts security and performance. As per the research performed, real time protection, Internet peering or use of dedicated protection technology right at the Data Center edge routers checking the inbound traffic seems to be the best way for proactively mitigating DDoS attacks targeting business which is proposed in this research paper.

LITERATURE SURVEY

Lonea at al. (2013) deployed a virtual machine based intrusion detection with graphical interface to monitor cloud fusion alerts by using Eucalyptus cloud architecture for front end and MySQL database for backend. Attacks are captured by Barnyard tool while using SNORT for signature based DDoS rules. Stacheldraht tool is utilized for generating the resource depletion data packets. These packets consist of UDP, TCP SYN and ICMP floods. These attack packets are captured during the attack and stored in the central MySQL database. However, a limitation in this signature based approach is that unknown or zero day attacks could not be detected.

Bakshi et al. (2010) proposed an Intrusion Detection based on Signature detection for DDoS by using virtual machines running SNORT to analyze both the real time in-bound and out-bound traffic. The defense framework identifies the attacker's IP Address and auto scripts an Access Control List configuration for dropping the entire packets from that IP Address and blacklisting it immediately.

Gul et al. (2011) have cited that to handle a large packet flow, an intrusion detection model that analyzes and reports on the attack packets is utilized. These reports should be shared with the cloud actors involved. To improve the performance of the Intrusion Detection System multi-threading techniques are used. The final evaluation concluded that the use of multi thread deployment as compared to a single threaded deployment is more efficient.

Zarepoor at al. (2014) proposed the use of a statistical filtering system with two levels of filtering. The first level of filtering involves removing the header fields of incoming data packets, then comparing the time to live (TTL) value with a predetermined hop count value. If the values are not similar, the packet is termed to be spoofed and immediately dropped. The second level of filtering involves comparing the incoming packet header with a stored normal profile header.

Zakarya (2013) proposes an entropy based detection technique that identifies attack flow based on distribution ratio using the attack packet dropping algorithm. The entropy rate identifies the attack flow, dropping the packets if the DDoS is confirmed. Cloudsim simulation shows an accuracy of almost 90%.

Vissers et al. (2014) utilize Gaussian Model to preform defense against application layer attacks on cloud services using the parametric technique. The use of malicious XML content in use requests inside SOAP resulted in the DDoS attacks. Initially the detection involves HTTP header inspection to detect any HTTP floods and SOAP action inspection. Then XML content processing action is checked for any spoofing by comparing previous data. While this works very well for existing DDoS attacks, the disadvantage is the inability to detect the new age threat vectors arising from new request schematics.

Girma et al. (2015) propose a Hybrid statistical model to classify the DDoS attack pattern using entropy based system and covariance matrix measuring the heightened data dependency. Similarly, Ismail et al. (2013) proposed a dual phase mathematical model with covariance matrix for detecting DoS attacks on cloud application services. The first phase involves baselining the normal traffic pattern by mapping into a covariance matrix. The next phase compares the current traffic with the baseline traffic pattern.

Bedi and Shiva (2012) propose securing cloud infrastructure from DDoS attacks using game theory. Both the legitimate and malicious virtual machine behaviors are modeled with a game inspired firewall defense.

Huang et al. (2013) propose a Multi-stage detection and text-based system with a Turing test to mitigate HTTP request flooding attacks. The system works in a modular fashion, with Source checking and counting modules intercepts in coming packets, the DDoS attack detection module checks for the DDoS attack, with the Turing test challenging the packets by using text based questions and answers to determine if the packet is suspicious. The attack detection module retrieves and records the traffic behavior of each virtual cluster for any suspicious traffic behavior by the inbound data packets. Turing testing module which is text-based receives the redirected blocked packets and presents a randomly selected question to the requester. Access is granted only if the question gets answered correctly. The question pool is updated regularly and the system is Linux kernel. Performance test suggested a low reflection ratio and high efficiency.

Chen et al. (2009) propose a three-layer DDoS defense mechanism based on web services. Combining web server characteristics using statistical filtering using Simplified Hop Count filtering algorithm (SHCF) and SYN Proxy Firewall at network, transport and application layer to filter malicious traffic and secure access for legitimate traffic. Limiting traffic at application layer is also applied inside a Linux kernel. These collaborative defense mechanisms provide sustained availability of the web services and can defend DDoS attacks effectively.

Xiao et al. (2009) propose putting forward an effective approach against DDoS attacks based on three-way handshake process. The proposal is based on discarding the first inbound handshake requests, these requests consume the computing resources. This ensures the new normal network requests can live easy, allowing new client requests even in DDoS attack duration, thereby raising the environment's overall security capability and the system protected against DDoS Attacks.

Durcekova et al. (2012) focuses on DDoS application layer attack detection, and these attacks have more impact than the traditional network layer denial of service attacks. The focus is on the DoS/DDoS attack description and consequently aimed at detecting application layer Denial of Service attacks and then proposed few methodologies to use for the application layer attack detection. While most current effort focuses on detection of network and transport layer attacks, two detection architectures for Web Application traffic monitoring are proposed, these help discover any dynamic changes in the normal traffic trends.

Akbar et al. (2015) propose a novel scheme based on Hellinger distance (HD) to detect low-rate and multi-attribute DDoS attacks. Leveraging the SIP load balancer for detecting and mitigating DDoS attacks is proposed. Usually DDoS detection and mitigations schemes are implemented in SIP proxy, however leveraging the SIP load balancer to fight against DDoS by using existing load balancing features is done with the proposed scheme implemented by modifying leading open source Kamailio SIP proxy server.

The scheme is evaluated by experimental test setup and found results are outperforming the existing prevention schemes in use against DDoS for system overhead, detection rate and false-positive alarms.

Selvakumar et al. (2015) propose application layer DDoS attack detection by logistic regression using modeling user behavior. Current solutions are able to detect only limited application layer DDoS attacks while the solutions can detect all types of application layer DDoS attacks tend to have huge complexities. To find an effective solution for the detection of application layer DDoS attack the normal user browsing behavior needs to be re-modeled so that a normal user and attacker can be differentiated. This method uses feature construction along with logistic regression for modeling the normal web user behavior in order to detect application layer DDoS attacks. The performance of the proposed method is evaluated in terms of the metrics such as total accuracy, false positive rate and detection rates. Comparing the logistic regression solution with existing methods, revealed results better than any of the current models in place.

Simulation study of application layer DDoS attack is performed by Bhandari et al. (2015). The impact of Web Service Application layer DDoS attacks is determined by using NS2 Simulator for a web cache model. These web attacks are launched on the server capacity to handle requests and to determine if any legitimate users would get impacted in receiving the required web application services. Transaction throughput, successful HTTP transactions, server queue utilization by legitimate users, transactions drops and Transaction survival ratio metrics are calculated to measure the impact of the attack.

DDOS ATTACK IMPLEMENTATION

Architecture Design and Implementation

The author implemented two infrastructure architectures for cloud based hoisting SaaS environments for testing the proposed theory against DDoS Attacks done by Nagar et al. (2016). The infrastructure designs are attacked at network and application layer with increasing ICMP size (3700 → 3805 bytes) and measured Real User Monitoring parameters as the criteria to determine performance and response of the two architectures during a DDoS attack. Application layer attack is performed with HTTP Flood GET attacks as described by Ghosh et al. (2016) The thread count is increased for reach request with slow socket HTTP attack. The logs are gathered using Wireshark as the sniffer in the network infrastructure.

The first infrastructure is implemented as having the same inbound and outbound exit gateway, which implies synchronous routing. This is implemented as a standard single tier data center design hosting a front-end web application portal and a backend SQL Database as a private cloud data center designed on single tier network infrastructure as shown in the Figure 1 below as reference from Data Center Site Infrastructure Tier Standard: Topology.

The second infrastructure implemented is the proposed secure three tier data center design, this design comprises of three tiers with different locations and IP Addressing scheme connected to each other with secure internal VPN links. This simulated Hybrid cloud architecture inform of two public clouds and one private cloud data center as shown in the Figure 2 below.

The first tier (Data Center # 1) is configured for network layer 3 & 4 defense with only simple Load Balancer features. The first tier is a private data center which has Network defenses in order to mitigate flood and volumetric attacks that could otherwise lead to network saturation issues as described by Jouini et al. (2016). The network level attacks are ICMP (Ping), UDP or SYN floods.

Figure 1. Single tier data center design

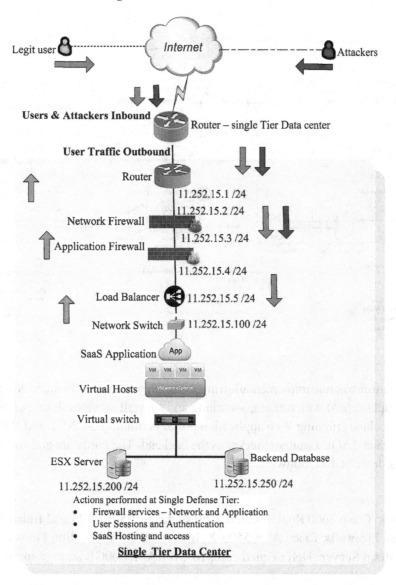

The second tier (Data Center #2) is configured for application layer 7 defense using Web Application Firewall and Load Balancing rules to maintain in bound user sessions as presented by Divakarla et al. (2016). SSL termination and defenses for DNS poisoning ARP spoofing, POST Flood and Malware detection is performed here.

After network and application attack cleanup in tier # 1 and tier #2, legitimate users remain in remaining traffic, now the users are directed to a hardened web server hosting only terminal services. Only by using this jump box are the users allowed to access the web application with a two-factor authentication. This third tier (Data Center #3) has the data center hosting web portal and database simulating the SaaS application for the users as shown by Asija et al. (2016). Portal access is allowed only on the jump box and outbound traffic routing is configured to exit from the second tier instead of returning via the original route of going back the same route.

Figure 2. Three tier network architecture

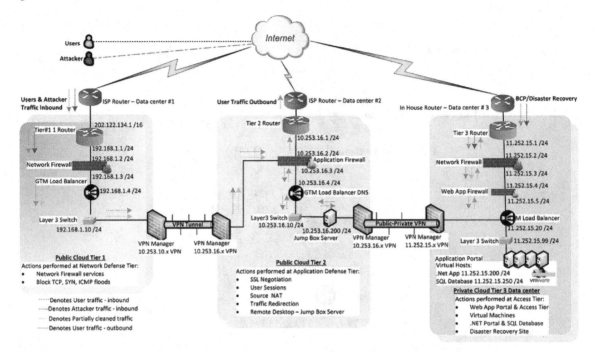

The data center infrastructure implementation involved hardware and software as described below. The two designs are implemented with routing, switching and firewall services. Imperva WAF is used with VMware virtual machines running Web application portal is running on .NET and IIS using Microsoft Windows Server OS and SQL Database Server as the backend. The hardware and software used for the implementation is described as follows.

- Hardware:
  - **Network**: Cisco 3600 Router, Cisco 3550 switches, F5 Big IP Load Balancer 4200v LTM
  - **Defense Firewalls**: Cisco ASA 5506-X, Imperva Web Application Firewall
  - **Bare Metal Server**: Dell i5 quad core, 16 GB RAM, 500GB storage space
- Software:
  - **Virtualization**: VMware Workstation ver10
  - **Application Servers**: Windows Server 2008 OS 64-bit with .NET, IIS & SQL 2008 Database
- DDoS Attack Tools:
  - **Low Orbit Ion Canon (LOIC):** UDP, TCP, HTTP GET Requests attacks
  - **R.U.D.Y**: Slow layer 7 attacks HTTP POST request with abnormally long content length headers
  - **Slowloris:** Opens multiple connections as long as possible, sends partial HTTP requests which never actually get completed which ends up consuming the target server's maximum of concurrent pool and sockets slowly and this is not detected.

PERFORMANCE ANALYSIS

DDoS attacks were performed on single tier and the proposed three tier infrastructure architecture and results gathered for real user monitoring parameters during the network attacks and validated using T Test hypothesis.

Single Tier Logs and Data Analysis

The below data and graphs illustrate the Network Firewall and Application layer logs and graphs for the DDoS attack performed on single tier data center architecture in order to determine the resilience for handling DDoS attacks.

In Figure 3 below Network firewall defense is implemented after attack#2 with ICMP, Page Load, Browser Throughput and Application Response as the key values.

Figure 3. Single tier network attack parameters

Attack#	Time (pm)	Buffer Size (bytes)	Echo Requests	Target Server IP	Real User Monitoring				Status code	Attack Vector Details
					Average ICMP (ms)	Page Load Response (ms)	Browser Throughput (rpm)	App server response (ms)		
Attack#1	13:00	3700	1000	11.252.15.100	6545	45	1800	1636	200	No standard network layer defense in place - single tier architecture Ping AppServer -n 1000 -l 3xxx Size: 3xxx, Echo request count: 1000
	13:30	3750	1000	11.252.15.100	6670	54	1856	1496	429	
	14:00	3760	1000	11.252.15.100	6575	55	1727	1624	200	
	14:30	3780	1000	11.252.15.100	6791	46	1627	1784	200	
	15:00	3790	1000	11.252.15.100	6583	41	1606	1713	429	
	15:30	3795	1000	11.252.15.100	6745	55	1806	1686	204	
	16:00	3800	1000	11.252.15.100	6790	50	1651	1488	429	
	16:30	3820	1000	11.252.15.100	6794	54	1761	1795	204	
	17:00	3810	1000	11.252.15.100	6690	47	1800	1833	503	
	17:30	3805	1000	11.252.15.100	6512	42	1849	1565	503	
	18:00	3820	1000	11.252.15.100	6692	48	1835	1726	503	
	18:30	3810	1000	11.252.15.100	6589	50	1635	1570	503	
	19:00	3805	1000	11.252.15.100	6995	50	1839	1663	503	
Attack#2	13:00	3750	1000	11.252.15.100	2795	30	1325	1297	200	Network Firewall Defense implemented: Attack vector categories of attack as ICMP/UDP/SYN floods
	13:30	3745	1000	11.252.15.100	2911	32	1327	1243	200	
	14:00	3760	1000	11.252.15.100	2805	29	1208	1298	200	
	14:30	3780	1000	11.252.15.100	2963	30	1306	1043	200	
	15:00	3770	1000	11.252.15.100	2746	29	1235	1097	200	
	15:30	3783	1000	11.252.15.100	2933	32	1245	1213	200	
	16:00	3780	1000	11.252.15.100	2988	28	1219	1228	200	

Figure 4 illustrates Real User Monitoring values obtained during an application layer attack on Single Tier network infrastructure in which Application firewall defense is implemented after attack#2 with ICMP, Page Load, Browser Throughput and Application Response key values.

Results of Single Tier Architecture attacks obtained before and during the DDoS attack is presented in Figure 5. The average ICMP, Browser Throughput, Page Load Response and Application server response is presented below.

Three Tier Logs and Data Analysis

DDoS attacks are performed on the designed network architectures and Network and Application attack results obtained for before and after attack scenarios. Network attacks like ICMP flood is done with 1000 ICMP echo requests with each increasing the attack buffer size from 3700 bytes to 3805 bytes. Application attack like HTTP Flood attack is done by increasing the thread count by "*GET /app/?id =*

437793 msg = BOOM%2520HEADSHOT! HTTP/1.1 Host: IP" and Slow socket buildup simulating slow web attacks by use of Perl. Logs and Data gathered is gathered from the network firewall, for each attack are displayed in Figure 6.

Results of Three Tier Architecture attacks obtained before and during the DDoS attack is presented in Figure 7. The average ICMP, Browser Throughput, Page Load Response and Application server response is presented below.

The below graph in Figure 8 presents the results of Three Tier Architecture attacks obtained before and during DDoS attack for ICMP Response.

Results of Three Tier Architecture attacks obtained before and during DDoS attack for Page Load Response is presented in Figure 9.

Results of Three Tier Architecture attacks obtained before and during DDoS attack for Browser Throughput is presented in Figure 10.

Results of Three Tier Architecture attacks obtained before and during DDoS attack for Application Server Response is presented in Figure 11.

Figure 4. Single tier architecture: Application attack logs

Date	Time (pm)	Threads Count	Average ICMP (ms)	Page Load Response (ms)	Browser Throughput (rpm)	App server response (ms)	Attack detected	ICMP Food Attack
					Real User Monitoring			
Attack#1	16:00	40	6544	40	1651	1728	GET /HTTP/1.1 404 204	layer defense in place - single tier architecture
	16:30	45	6511	51	1501	1566	GET /HTTP/1.1 404 204	
	17:00	50	6576	37	1555	1728	GET /HTTP/1.1 404 204	
	17:30	55	6525	45	1604	1598	GET /HTTP/1.1 404 204	
	18:00	60	6577	35	1669	1696	GET /HTTP/1.1 404 204	
	18:30	65	6567	38	1594	1575	GET /HTTP/1.1 404 204	
	19:00	70	6402	36	1674	1529	GET /HTTP/1.1 404 204	
	13:00	10	4239	24	1132	1053	GET /HTTP/1.1 404 204	
	13:30	15	4113	29	1182	1066	GET /HTTP/1.1 404 204	
	14:00	20	4184	30	1140	1200	GET /HTTP/1.1 404 204	
	14:30	25	4112	20	1219	1000	GET /HTTP/1.1 404 204	
	15:00	30	4233	22	1221	1184	GET /HTTP/1.1 404 204	WAF Defense implemented: Application layer attack vectors as HTTP attack, Slowloris attack performed
	15:30	35	3938	27	1106	1127	GET /HTTP/1.1 404 204	
Attack#2	16:00	40	4274	25	1258	1012	GET /HTTP/1.1 404 204	
	16:30	45	4269	25	1208	1000	GET /HTTP/1.1 404 204	
	17:00	50	4198	20	1256	1170	GET /HTTP/1.1 404 204	
	17:30	55	4167	26	1204	1176	GET /HTTP/1.1 404 204	
	18:00	60	4318	29	1244	1096	GET /HTTP/1.1 404 204	
	18:30	65	3951	29	1131	1002	GET /HTTP/1.1 404 204	
	19:00	70	3947	27	1203	1022	GET /HTTP/1.1 404 204	
	13:00	10	4059	28	1260	1038	GET /HTTP/1.1 404 204	
	13:30	15	4169	30	1187	1047	GET /HTTP/1.1 404 204	

Figure 5. Single tier network attack results

Raw Logs: Attack 1
Jan 27 2016 13:00:07 Warning [DDOS]:791366: UDP packet rate exceeded. Flow 192.168.0.100:2435 -> 11.252.15.100:2000. Limit 30. Current 3.
Jun 27 2016 13:30:15 Warning [DDOS]:810166: UDP packet rate exceeded. Flow 192.168.0.100:2435 -> 11.252.15.100:2000. Limit 30. Current 3.
Jan 27 2016 14:00:29 Warning [DDOS]:708372: DDoS packet L4 payload size is too big. Flow 226.61.80.115:53 -> 11.252.15.100:4696. Maximum 1280. Current 690.
Jan 27 2016 14:30:49 Warning [DDOS]:358374: DDoS packet L4 payload size is too big. Flow 158.91.47.243:53 -> 11.252.15.100:2001. Maximum 1280. Current 1.
Jan 27 2016 15:00:29 Warning [DDOS]:698373: DDoS packet from well-known UDP source port on 11.252.15.100 port 4619 has been detected. Current 9514
Jan 27 2016 15:30:11 Warning [DDOS]:687298: DDoS HTTP destination request rate exceeded. Flow 192.168.0.100:42091 -> 11.252.15.100:80. Limit 33. Current 870.
Jan 27 2016 16:00:15 Warning [DDOS]:635606: UDP packet rate exceeded. Flow 192.168.0.100:2435 -> 11.252.15.100:2000. Limit 30. Current 3.
Jan 27 2016 16:30:29 Warning [DDOS]:708372: DDoS packet L4 payload size is too big. Flow 226.61.80.115:53 -> 11.252.15.100:4696. Maximum 1280. Current 861.
Jan 27 2016 17:00:44 Warning [DDOS]:358374: DDoS packet L4 payload size is too big. Flow 158.91.47.243:53 -> 11.252.15.100:2001. Maximum 1280. Current 1.
Jan 27 2016 17:30:19 Warning [DDOS]:698373: DDoS packet from well-known UDP source port on 11.252.15.100 port 4619 has been detected. Current 9514
Jan 27 2016 18:00:17 Warning [DDOS]:628372: DDoS HTTP destination request rate exceeded. Flow 192.168.0.100:42091 -> 11.252.15.100:80. Limit 30. Current 693.
Jan 27 2016 18:30:17 Warning [DDOS]:638492: DDoS HTTP destination request rate exceeded. Flow 192.168.0.100:49031 -> 11.252.15.100:80. Limit 35. Current 547.
Jan 27 2016 19:00:09 Warning [DDOS]:793699: UDP packet rate exceeded. Flow 192.168.0.100:2435 -> 11.252.15.100:2000. Limit 30. Current 3.

Figure 6. Three tier architecture attack logs

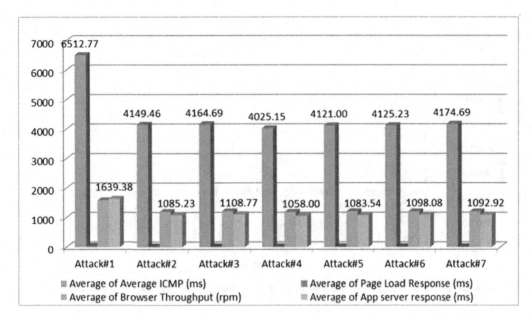

Figure 7. Three tier network architecture attack results

Attack#	Time (pm)	Buffer Size (bytes)	Echo Requests	Threads Count	Real User Monitoring				Status code	Attack Vector Details
					Average ICMP (ms)	Page Load Response (ms)	Browser Throughput (rpm)	App server response		
Attack#1	13:00	3700	1000	10	7655	50	1775	1528	200	
	13:30	3750	1000	15	7967	61	1826	1645	429	
	14:00	3760	1000	20	7202	70	1887	1517	200	
	14:30	3780	1000	25	7677	58	1773	1683	200	No standard network or application layer defense in place three tier architecture Ping AppServer -n 1000 -l 3xxx Size: 3xxx, Echo request count: 1000
	15:00	3790	1000	30	7993	65	1775	1692	429	
	15:30	3795	1000	35	6779	61	1850	1682	204	
	16:00	3800	1000	40	6016	63	1704	1534	429	
	16:30	3820	1000	45	7114	55	1804	1606	204	
	17:00	3810	1000	50	6242	50	1743	1547	503	
	17:30	3805	1000	55	7903	52	1751	1651	503	
	18:00	3820	1000	60	7766	72	1722	1685	503	
	18:30	3810	1000	65	6015	67	1860	1569	503	
	19:00	3805	1000	70	6042	64	1772	1674	503	
Attack#2	13:00	3700	1000	10	1746	11	1033	776	200	
	13:30	3750	1000	15	1574	15	947	859	200	
	14:00	3760	1000	20	1548	11	935	850	200	
	14:30	3780	1000	25	1798	18	871	715	200	
	15:00	3790	1000	30	1795	18	1000	739	200	Network & Web ApplicationFirewall Defense implemented: Attack vector categories of attack as ICMP/UDP/SYN floods performed.
	15:30	3795	1000	35	1549	15	888	736	200	
	16:00	3800	1000	40	1525	10	917	791	200	
	16:30	3820	1000	45	1827	12	878	807	200	
	17:00	3810	1000	50	1753	18	1029	768	200	
	17:30	3805	1000	55	1661	17	908	789	200	
	18:00	3820	1000	60	1733	11	1065	892	200	
	18:30	3810	1000	65	1685	17	1020	899	200	
	19:00	3805	1000	70	1536	11	1093	771	200	
	13:00	3700	1000	10	1697	16	906	701	200	
	13:30	3750	1000	15	1867	12	1028	823	200	
	14:00	3760	1000	20	1894	16	1016	857	200	
	14:30	3780	1000	25	1825	11	1093	710	200	

Below graphs displayed in Figure 12 and Figure 13 illustrate the availability trend metrics obtained after performing the DoS attacks on the single and three tier architectures for network and application layer design.

Figure 8. Real user monitoring: Average ICMP for single and three tier architectures

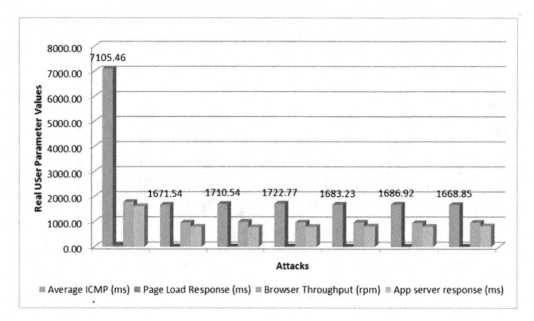

Figure 9. Real user monitoring: Page load response for single and three tier designs

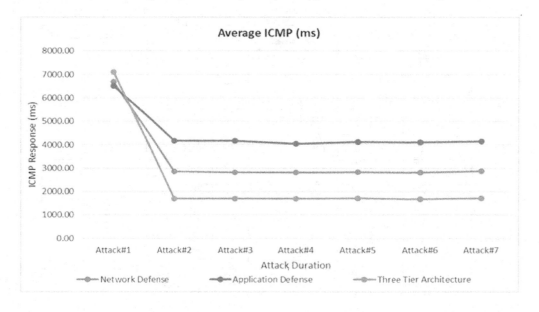

PERFORMANCE DATA VALIDATION

The author also performed Parametric Statistic T-test to validate the Real User Monitoring data obtained from Single and Three Tier architectures attack. The primary reason is to ensure there is no violations for the data that has been represented in a random sample from the test population, the distribution of the sample mean is normal and the variances of different real user parameter very similar.

Figure 10. Real user monitoring: Browser throughput for single and three tier designs

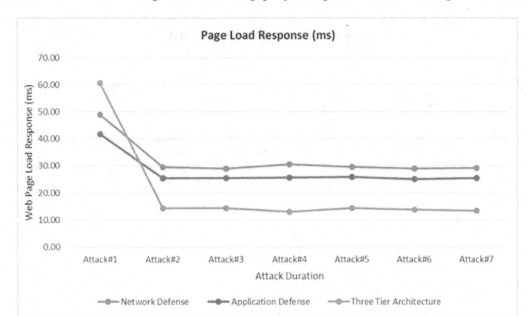

Figure 11. Real user monitoring: Application server response

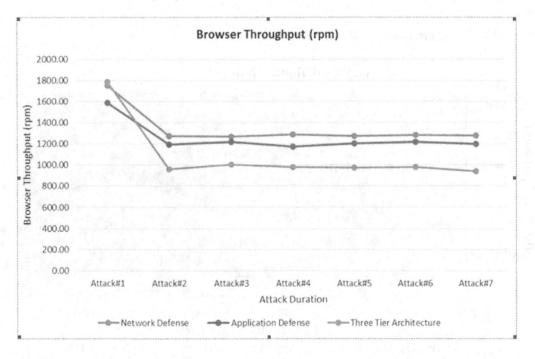

The null hypothesis assumed is that if the data violates these assumptions, then it is assumed the authors committed a Type I error which is more or less often than the alpha probability.

Interpreting the T-Test results (see Tables 1 to 13).

Figure 12. Real user monitoring: Application server response

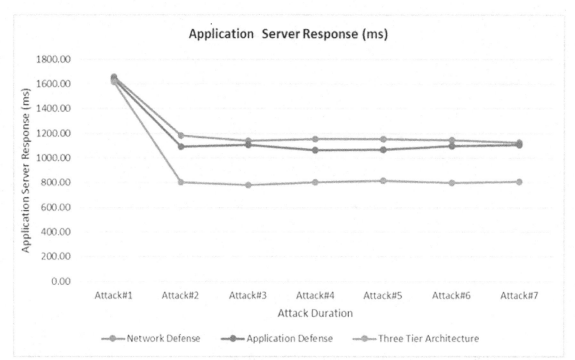

Figure 13. Single and three tier application response

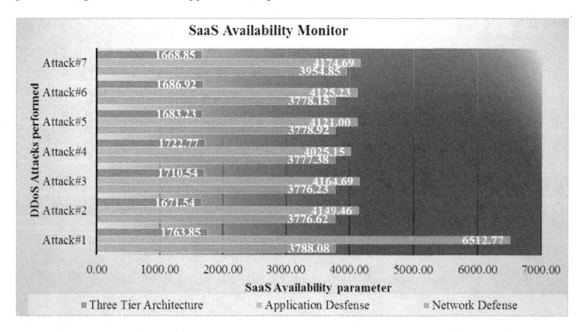

Table 1. T-test validation parameters

T	denotes the T-Test
DF(x)	denotes the degree of freedom for # of test performed
x.xx	denotes the 'T-Static' value of the calculations
p ≤ 0.05	Not likely to be a result of chance and A ≠ B, so the difference is significant, the Null hypothesis is incorrect – hence Null is rejected, relationship between A and B
p ≥ 0.05	Likely chance and A = B, so no significant difference, the Null hypothesis is correct – hence fail to reject the Null, no relationship between A and B

Table 2. Average ICMP for single tiers and three tiers

Attack#	Average ICMP (ms)		
	Network Defense	**Application Defense**	**Three Tier Architecture**
Attack#1	6690.08	6512.77	7105.46
Attack#2	2852.75	4166.33	1682.83
Attack#3	2823.75	4165.92	1691.67
Attack#4	2813.58	4031.92	1703.00
Attack#5	2839.67	4125.50	1713.25
Attack#6	2817.33	4101.67	1681.92
Attack#7	2874.67	4141.58	1705.25

Table 3. T-test summary for average ICMP

Variable	Observations	With Missing Data	Without Missing Data	Minimum	Maximum	Mean	Standard Deviation
6545	90	0	90	2618.000	6995.000	3342.400	1330.157
7655	90	0	90	1523.000	7993.000	2406.511	1860.344

Test Interpretation

H0: difference between two means $= 0$
Ha: difference between two means $\neq 0$

P-value is lower than the significance-level-alpha (0.05) – which infers that H0 – the null hypothesis can be rejected, the alternative hypothesis (Ha) is accepted.

Table 4. T-test for two paired sample data (single tier and three tiers)

95% Confidence Interval (CI) on Difference between the Two Means	
] 806.553,	1065.225 [
Difference	935.889
Observed value (t)	14.378
Critical value (ltl)	1.987
Degree of Freedom (DF)	89
Two-tailed P-value	< 0.0001
The ALPHA	0.05

Table 5. Page load response for single tiers and three tiers

Attack#	Page Load Response (ms)		
	Network Defense	Application Defense	Three Tier Architecture
Attack#1	49.00	41.77	60.62
Attack#2	29.58	25.50	14.42
Attack#3	28.92	25.58	14.33
Attack#4	30.58	25.67	13.00
Attack#5	29.50	25.92	14.42
Attack#6	29.08	25.08	13.83
Attack#7	29.17	25.42	13.33

Table 6. T-test summary for page load response

Variable	Observations	With Missing Data	Without Missing Data	Minimum	Maximum	Mean	Standard Deviation
45	90	0	90	27.000	55.000	32.000	7.213
50	90	0	90	10.000	72.000	20.311	16.593

Table 7. T-test for two paired sample data (single tier and three tiers)

95% Confidence Interval (CI) on Difference between the Two Means	
] 9.551,	13.827 [
Difference	11.689
t (Observed value)	10.865
ltl (Critical value)	1.987
DF	89
P-Value (Two-tailed)	< 0.0001
ALPHA	0.05

Table 8. Browser throughput for single tiers and three tiers

Attack#	Browser Throughput (rpm)		
	Network Defense	Application Defense	Three Tier Architecture
Attack#1	1753.23	1586.08	1787.85
Attack#2	1272.42	1191.75	957.58
Attack#3	1269.67	1216.67	1001.83
Attack#4	1285.75	1175.00	978.92
Attack#5	1273.75	1201.50	974.17
Attack#6	1283.58	1216.42	980.25
Attack#7	1278.58	1199.33	940.67

Table 9. T-test summary for browser throughput

Variable	Observations	With Missing Data	Without Missing Data	Minimum	Maximum	Mean	Standard Deviation
1800	90	0	90	1203.000	1856.000	1339.233	169.120
1775	90	0	90	850.000	1887.000	1080.478	287.208

Table 10. T-test for two paired sample data (single tier and three tiers)

95% Confidence Interval (CI) on Difference between the Two Means	
] 228.425,	289.086 [
Difference	258.756
Observed value (t)	16.951
Critical value (|t|)	1.987
DF	89
Two-tailed P-value	< 0.0001
The ALPHA	0.05

Table 11. Application server response for single tiers and three tiers

Attack#	Application Server Response (ms)		
	Network Defense	Application Defense	Three Tier Architecture
Attack#1	1659.92	1639.38	1616.38
Attack#2	1180.67	1090.50	801.75
Attack#3	1139.92	1108.25	780.83
Attack#4	1151.33	1065.83	805.83
Attack#5	1155.08	1066.67	819.75
Attack#6	1145.83	1097.17	797.83
Attack#7	1127.00	1108.00	810.17

Table 12. T-test summary for application server response

Variable	Observations	With Missing Data	Without Missing Data	Minimum	Maximum	Mean	Standard Deviation
1636	90	0	90	1001.000	1833.000	1221.733	196.171
1528	90	0	90	701.000	1692.000	913.744	286.449

Table 13. T-test for two paired sample data (single tier and three tiers)

95% Confidence Interval on the Difference between the Means	
] 276.857,	399.120 [
Difference	307.989
Observed value (t)	19.657
Critical value (|t|)	1.987
DF	89
Two-tailed P-value	< 0.0001
The ALPHA	0.05

CONCLUSION

As Cloud Computing technology adopts and advances towards embracing Cloud services, DDoS attacks have only increased in the past few years and show no signs of abating in volume, complexity or magnitude. The traditional IT defense systems on premise DDoS solutions or taken from ISPs can hardly be expected to take on the wide range of new types of dynamic attacks. DDOS attacks are becoming large enough to overwhelm Cloud provider's ability to absorb Server based attacks harness data center computational and networking resources to stage DDOS attacks of unprecedented volumes.

With Network firewall configured on the first tier and the Web Application Firewall (WAF) configured on the second tier, the author presented that network and application attack trend and real user monitoring graphs display a positive response for three tier design as compared to the single tier design when comparing ICMP TTL, Browser throughput, Page load response and the Application response. This lead to the confirmation that as compared to single tier architecture, the proposed three tier design architecture has a lot more resilience against DDoS attacks.

REFERENCES

Akbar, A., Zeeshan, T., & Muddassar, F. (2008). A Comparative Study of Anomaly Detection Algorithms for Detection of SIP Flooding in IMS. *Proceedings of the 2nd International Conference on Internet Multimedia Services Architecture and Applications (IMSAA)*. 10.1109/IMSAA.2008.4753934

Anteneh, G., Moses, G., Jiang, L., & Chunmei, L. (2015). Analysis of DDoS Attacks and an Introduction of a Hybrid Statistical Model to Detect DDoS Attacks on Cloud Computing Environment. *Proceedings of the 12th International Conference on Information Technology - New Generations (ITNG),* (pp. 212-217). doi:10.1109/ITNG.2015.40

Asija, R., & Nallusamy, R. (2016). Healthcare SaaS Based on a Data Model with Built-In Security and Privacy. *International Journal of Cloud Applications and Computing, 6*(3), 1–14. doi:10.4018/IJCAC.2016070101

Bakshi, A., & Yogesh, B. (2010). Securing Cloud from DDoS Attacks using Intrusion Detection System in Virtual Machines. *Proceedings of the 2nd International Conference on Communication Software and Networks (ICCSN'10)* (pp. 260–264). 10.1109/ICCSN.2010.56

Bedi, S., & Shiva, S. (2012). Securing Cloud Infrastructure against co-resident DoS attacks using Game Theoretic Defense Mechanisms. *Proceedings of the International Conference on Advances in Computing, Communications and Informatics (ICACCI)* (pp. 463-469). 10.1145/2345396.2345473

Bhandari, A., Sehgal, A., & Kumar, K. (2015). Destination Address Entropy-based Detection and Trace back approach against Distributed Denial of Service Attacks. *International Journal of Computer Network and Information Security, 8*, 9-20. doi:10.5815/ijcnis.2015.08.02

Birke, R., Qiu, Z., Pérez, J. F., & Chen, L. Y. (2016). Defeating variability in cloud applications by multi-tier workload redundancy. *Proceedings of the Conference on Computer Communications Workshops (INFOCOM WKSHPS).* 10.1109/INFCOMW.2016.7562127

Divakarla, U., & Chandrasekaran, K. (2016). Enhanced Trust Path between Two Entities in Cloud Computing Environment. *International Journal of Cloud Applications and Computing, 6*(3), 15–31. doi:10.4018/IJCAC.2016070102

Ghosh, P., Shakti, S., & Phadikar, S. (2016). A Cloud Intrusion Detection System Using Novel PRFCM Clustering and KNN Based Dempster-Shafer Rule. *International Journal of Cloud Applications and Computing, 6*(4), 18–35. doi:10.4018/IJCAC.2016100102

Gul, I., & Hussain, M. (2011). Distributed Cloud Intrusion Detection Model. *International Journal of Advanced Science and Technology, 6*(34), 71–82.

Huang, V., Huang, R., & Chiang, M. (2013). A DDoS Mitigation System with Multi-stage Detection and Text-Based Turing Testing in Cloud Computing. *Proceedings of the IEEE 27th International Conference on Advanced Information Networking and Applications Workshops (WAINA).* doi:10.1109/WAINA.2013.94

Jouini, M., & Rabai, L. B. (2016). A Security Framework for Secure Cloud Computing Environments. *International Journal of Cloud Applications and Computing, 6*(3), 32–44. doi:10.4018/IJCAC.2016070103

Lonea, M., Popescu, D., Prostean, Q., & Tianfield, H. (2013). Soft Computing Applications Evaluation of Experiments on Detecting DDoS attacks in Eucalyptus Private Cloud. *Proceedings of the 5th International Workshop Soft Computing Applications (SOFA)* (pp. 367–379). 10.1007/978-3-642-33941-7_34

Nagar, N., & Suman, U. (2016). Analyzing Virtualization Vulnerabilities and Design a Secure Cloud Environment to Prevent from XSS Attack. *International Journal of Cloud Applications and Computing*, *6*(1), 1–14. doi:10.4018/IJCAC.2016010101

Selvakumar, K., & Shafiq, R. (2015). Rule-based Mechanism to Detect Denial of Service (DoS) attacks on Duplicate Address Detection Process in IPv6 Link Local Communication. *Proceedings of the International Journal Conference on Reliability, Infocom Technologies and Optimization (ICRITO)*. doi:10.1109/ICRITO.2015.7359243

Shamsolmoali, P., & Zareapoor, M. (2014). Statistical-based Filtering System against DDOS attacks in Cloud Computing. *Proceedings of the International Conference on Advances in Computing, Communications and Informatics* (pp. 1234–1239). 10.1109/ICACCI.2014.6968282

Uptime Institute Professional Services. (2016) Data Center Site Infrastructure Tier Standard: Topology. Retrieved from http://www.gpxglobal.net/wp-content/uploads/2012/08/tierstandardtopology.pdf

Veronika, D., Žilina, S., Ladislav, S., & Shahmehri, N. (2012). Sophisticated Denial of Service attacks aimed at Application Layer. *Proceedings of the 9th International Conference (ELEKTRO)*. doi:10.1109/ELEKTRO.2012.6225571

Vissers, T., Somasundaram, S., Pieters, L., Govindarajan, K., & Hellinckx, P. (2014). DDoS Defense System for Web Services in a Cloud Environment. *Future Generation Computer Systems*, *37*, 37–45. doi:10.1016/j.future.2014.03.003

Zakarya, M. (2013). DDoS Verification and Attack Packet Dropping Algorithm in Cloud Computing. *World Applied Science Journal*, *23*(11), 1418–1424. doi:10.5829/idosi.wasj.2013.23.11.950

Zeng, X., Peng, X., Li, M., Xu, H., & Jin, S. (2009). Research on an Effective Approach against DDoS Attacks. *Proceedings of the International Conference on Research Challenges in Computer Science (ICRCCS)*. 10.1109/ICRCCS.2009.15

This research was previously published in the International Journal of Cloud Applications and Computing (IJCAC), 7(3); edited by B. B. Gupta and Dharma P. Agrawal; pages 59-75, copyright year 2017 by IGI Publishing (an imprint of IGI Global).

Section 5
Detection and Prevention: Smart Grid, Vehicular Ad–Hoc Networks, and Wireless Sensor Networks

Chapter 29
Denial of Service Attack on Protocols for Smart Grid Communications

Swapnoneel Roy
University of North Florida, USA

ABSTRACT

In this work, a denial of service (DoS) attack known as the clogging attack has been performed on three different modern protocols for smart grid (SG) communications. The first protocol provides authentication between smart meters (SM) and a security and authentication server (SAS). The second protocol facilitates secure and private communications between electric vehicles (EV) and the smart grid. The third protocol is a secure and efficient key distribution protocol for the smart grid. The protocols differ in either their applications (authentication, key distribution), or their ways of communications (usage of encryption, hashes, timestamps etc.). But they are similar in their purpose of design (for the smart grid) and their usage of computationally intensive mathematical operations (modular exponentiation, ECC) to implement security. Solutions to protect these protocols against this attack are then illustrated along with identifying the causes behind the occurrence of this vulnerability in SG communication protocols in general.

INTRODUCTION

The collective nature of a smart grid (SG) with many subsystems and networks, working together as a system of systems makes its components vulnerable to various kinds of attacks most of which can be performed remotely. Therefore, security has become a first class parameter in the development of SG, and many authentication and key management protocols have been designed and are continually being designed. Security protocols for the smart grid can be broadly classified into two major classes according to their functions:

DOI: 10.4018/978-1-7998-5348-0.ch029

1. Authentication, and
2. Key Management.

User authentication can enable a perimeter device (e.g., a firewall, proxy server, VPN server, or remote access server) to decide whether or not to approve a specific access request to gain entry to a computer network. It is necessary to be able to identify and authenticate any user with a high level of certainty, so that the user may be held accountable should his/her actions threaten the security and productivity of the network. The more confidence a network administrator has regarding the user's identity, the more confidence the administrator will have in allowing that user specific privileges, and the more faith the administrator will have in the internal records regarding that user.

Multi-factor authentication is an approach to cyber-security in which the user is required to provide more than one form of verification in order to prove his/her identity and gain access to the system. It takes advantage of a combination of several authentication factors. Commonly used factors include verification by:

1. Something a user knows (such as a password),
2. Something the user has (such as a smart card or a security token), and
3. Something the user is (such as the use of biometrics) (Stallings & Brown, 2008).

Due to their increased complexity, multi-factor authentication systems are harder to breach than those using any single factor.

Multiple factor authentication is needed to provide high-level security. But with the introduction of more factors, there are possibilities to introduce more vulnerability in the protocols that an attacker can exploit to launch an attack on them. Vulnerabilities are detected by static analysis before they are exploited. The root causes of CPU, stack, and other resource-exhaustion vulnerabilities (DoS) are often design flaws rather than programming errors. Several multi-factor authentication protocols in the literature involving smart cards, RFIDs, wireless networks, or digital signatures, rely on the usage of complex mathematical operations (e.g. ECC) for their security. Hence some level of protection should be added to them to guarantee total security against various kinds of attacks.

Key management is the management of cryptographic keys in a cryptosystem. This includes dealing with the generation, exchange, storage, use, and replacement of keys. It includes cryptographic protocol design, key servers, user procedures, and other relevant protocols. Key management concerns keys at the user level, either between users or systems. This is in contrast to key scheduling; key scheduling typically refers to the internal handling of key material within the operation of a cipher. Successful key management is critical to the security of a cryptosystem. In practice it is arguably the most difficult aspect of cryptography because it involves system policy, user training, organizational and departmental interactions, and coordination between all of these elements.

The nodes are all non-interactive in distributed key management protocols that are conventional. Every node is assumed to be able to independently learn about the keys shared with other nodes, without the assistance or intervention of any trusted third parties. The memory cost of each node in a non-interactive network has been proved to be N-1, where N is the total number of nodes in the network. This number does not depend on the kind of algorithms used to determine the pairwise keys. The pairwise key model, the Blom model and the Blundo model are optimum as non-interactive schemes in terms of their memory cost. However, as N grows, the memory requirement of non-interactive schemes grows exponentially.

This high memory requirement restricts their applications in many large-scale networks, such as ad hoc networks or sensor networks, which may involve hundreds to thousands of individual nodes.

To fix the problem of large memory requirements, and increase scalability of networks, interactions between nodes are implemented. Models like the Key Distributing Center (KDC) or the Key Trustee Center (KTC) have been developed to keep only a shared key with a trusted server that takes care of the key exchanging and agreement between nodes. However, KDC and KTC models have worse security issues than the non-interactive scheme, since they are single-point failure models. New key management protocols are developed that achieves a trade-off between the two extremes (fully-interactive (KDC/KTC), and the non-interactive) approaches. This way a balance between the memory cost, and security is made.

The way research works in the field in security especially while designing cryptographic protocols (for authentication and key management) is the security vulnerability analysis of one or more protocols leads to the design of new protocols. However, in most of these works, the authors present attacks on a previous protocol and propose a new protocol with assertions of the superior aspects of their protocol, while ignoring benefits that their new protocol does not attempt (or fails) to provide, and thus overlooking dimensions on which it performs poorly. Despite the lack of evaluation criteria, another common feature of these studies is that, there is no proper security justification (or even an explicit security model) presented, which explains why these protocols previously claimed to be secure turn out to be vulnerable.

One such vulnerability found in protocols is the denial of service (DoS). In a DoS attack, the adversary attempts to bring down a service thus preventing legitimate users access it. There are several ways to perform a DoS. DoS attacks when performed on a larger scale are called distributed denial of service (DDoS).

In this chapter, three recent communication protocols for the SG are analyzed for vulnerability to the *clogging attack*, which is a form of DoS. The first one by Nicanfar *et al.* (2014) is a protocol that provides authentication between smart meters (SM) and a security and authentication server (SAS). This protocol does not use timestamps. The second protocol we consider for analysis is by Tseng (2012). This protocol facilitates secure and private communications between electric vehicles (EV) and the smart grid, and uses timestamps. The third protocol by Xia *et al.* (2012) is a secure and efficient key distribution protocol for the smart grid.

Objectives of this Chapter

In order to demonstrate the vulnerabilities of the three modern protocols for smart grid communication considered a generalized cryptanalysis algorithm is applied to perform clogging attacks on these SG protocols that use computationally intensive operations like modular exponentiation and elliptic curve cryptography to guarantee security in the communication process. The attack results in the server side of the SG being forced to perform useless computationally intensive operations. This results in wastage of time and resources on the part of the server, and thus denial of service for legitimate users.

The first one by Nicanfar *et al.* (2014) is a protocol that provides authentication between smart meters (SM) and a security and authentication server (SAS). This protocol does not use timestamps. This protocol is shown to be vulnerable to the clogging attack. The vulnerability lies in the use of computationally intensive modular exponentiation by the server in the authentication process. In this analysis it is observed that using a timestamp would prevent clogging attack vulnerability in this protocol.

The second protocol we consider for analysis is by Tseng (2012). This protocol facilitates secure and private communications between electric vehicles (EV) and the smart grid, and uses timestamps. The vulnerability to clogging attack arises from the fact that no verification for the validity of the timestamps is performed in this protocol. A validity checking on timestamp added to the protocol makes it secure against the clogging attack.

The third protocol by Xia *et al.* (2012) is a secure and efficient key distribution protocol for the smart grid. It involves a trusted third party called the Trust Anchor (TA) that facilitates communication (in form of efficient key distribution) between the smart meters and service providers. The TA involves computationally intensive modular exponentiation that makes it vulnerable to clogging attack. Again, it is observed that the usage of timestamps with verification can make this protocol secure against clogging attack.

The three protocols differ in either their applications (authentication, key distribution), or their ways of communications (usage of encryption, hashes, timestamps etc.). But they are similar in their purpose of design (for the smart grid) and their usage of computationally intensive mathematical operations (modular exponentiation, ECC) to implement security.

It is observed that the usage of modular exponentiation or elliptic curve cryptography in protocols guarantees a higher level of security against much vulnerability, but it might also create vulnerability if it is used without an additional level of protection. The communication protocols analyzed in this chapter rely on either modular exponentiation or elliptic curve cryptography for their security. Hence some level of protection should be added to them to guarantee increased security against the clogging attack.

We conclude that additional techniques like usage of timestamps, usage of nonce, and encryption can be applied on these protocols to make them secure against the clogging attack.

Organization of this Chapter

The rest of this book chapter is organized as follows. The next section (Background) gives a brief overview of the research done in this area prior to this work and discusses the techniques employed in this work. The subsequent section (DoS attack on SG communication protocols) first describes the generic algorithm developed to launch the clogging attack on the various protocols analyzed in this chapter. Next the section describes each SG communication protocol in detail, performs clogging attack on them, and provides solutions for preventing the attack. Finally, the next sections summarize the work, discuss its significance, and propose possible future research directions.

BACKGROUND

This section summarizes the research done in the field of multi-factor authentication and key exchanging protocols in general, and also specifically for the smart grid (SG). The various kinds of attacks that are generally performed against these protocols are discussed, followed by two approaches to dealing with these attacks. Finally the approach taken in this chapter is briefly described.

A Research Snapshot of Security Protocols

The design and security analysis of authentication and key exchanging protocols has been an active area of research in recent years. Generally the security vulnerability analysis of one or more protocols leads to the design of new protocols. However, inmost of these studies, the authors present attacks on previous schemes and propose new protocols with assertions of the superior aspects of their schemes, while ignoring benefits that their schemes don't attempt (or fail) to provide, thus overlooking dimensions on which they perform poorly.

In addition to the lack of evaluation criteria, another common feature of these studies is that there is no proper security justification (or even an explicit security model) presented, which explains why these protocols previously claimed to be secure turn out to be vulnerable. Such an approach has generated a lot of literature, yet as far as we know, little attention has been paid to systematic design and analysis. The research history of this area can be summarized in Figure 1.

Figure 1. The design of security protocols

$$\text{New Protocol} \rightarrow \text{Broken} \rightarrow \text{Improved Protocol} \rightarrow \text{Broken Again}$$

$$\rightarrow \text{Further Improved Protocol} \rightarrow \cdots$$

In particular, the design of security protocols for the smart grid (SG) has picked momentum as a topic of research recently. Several protocols designed can be broadly classified as Authentication and Key Management according to their functions. Authentication protocols for the SG that mostly use more than one factor (are multi-factor) have been recently designed by (Lee *et al.* 2014; Nicanfar *et al.*, 2014; Saxena & Choi, 2015; Tseng, 2012). Some recent key management protocols for the SG have been designed by (Badra & Zeadally, 2013;, Benmalek & Challal, 2015; Demertzis *et al.*, 2015; Xia & Wang, 2012).

Most of these protocols have been designed on top of other protocols in the process making the previous protocols secure against various kinds of attacks (vulnerabilities). Figure 2 provides a chronological snapshot of security protocols. In this figure, protocols appearing below have evolved from making ones on top more secure, by finding out vulnerabilities in them. As an example, the evolution and subsequent enhancement of one of the protocol analyzed and enhanced in this chapter (Xia *et al.*, 2012) has been shown in Figure 2.

Various Kinds of Attacks on Protocols

Some common attacks that are generally considered during security analysis are man-in-the-middle, dictionary, password guessing, brute force, replay, denial of service, etc.

1. **Brute-Force Attack:** In this kind of attack, the adversary simply tries out all possible combinations of alphabets to obtain the correct password. Alternatively, the adversary could be a bit more intelligent to try to guess the password by obtaining some information about the user. Usually, users choose passwords, which are easy for them to remember. Hence passwords contain things like the year of birth, or a part of the user name or user ID. The adversary could gather such information to simplify his efforts to break the password (Apostol, 2012).
2. **Impersonation Attack:** In this kind of attack, the adversary pretends to be a legitimate user and gains access to the services meant for the legitimate user. The adversary might spoof the IP address of the legitimate user, or could intercept the messages sent by the user and use them to gain access to the server (Wei-Chi & Chang, 2005).

Figure 2. A snapshot of the evolution of security protocols

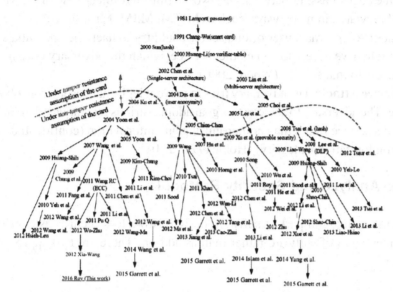

3. **Replay Attack:** In this kind of attack, the adversary intercepts a message with the identity and the password of the legitimate user. The adversary then waits till the legitimate user logs out of the service. Then he replays the message with the identity and the password to the server and gains access. Replay attacks are possible even when the user identity and password are encrypted (Syverson, 1994).

4. **Stolen Smart Card Attack:** In a password authentication scheme employing smart cards, the smart card contains the identity and password of the legitimate user. The stealing of the smart card by an adversary is equivalent to the stealing of a credit card. The adversary could enjoy service until all the servers to which the legitimate user has access are notified about the stolen smart card (Chen *et al.*, 2014).

5. **Stolen Server Database Attack:** In this kind of attack, the adversary steals the database maintained by the server that contains the user identities and passwords of the legitimate clients. Databases are not secured properly in most of the organizations. Database configurations are weak and insecure and easy to exploit. Database attacks go unnoticed as it takes less than 10 seconds to hack in and out of a database that is a major threat to organizations. Attackers use simple methods to break into databases, such as exploiting weak authentication, using default passwords and capitalizing on known vulnerabilities. The front-end client-server authentication store their passwords in their back-end databases and this connection are usually not secure. If the password is compromised, then the schema becomes vulnerable to attack which makes the protocol insecure. The adversary now has enormous power to do anything at his will (Wei-Chi *et al.*, 2004).

6. **Man-in-the-Middle Attack:** A man-in-the-middle attack is a similar strategy and can be used against many cryptographic protocols. One example of man-in-the-middle attacks is active eavesdropping, in which the attacker makes independent connections with the victims and relays messages between them to make them believe they are talking directly to each other over a private connection, when in fact the entire conversation is controlled by the attacker. The attacker must be able to intercept

all relevant messages passing between the two victims and inject new ones. Man-in-the-middle attacks are abbreviated in many ways, such as MITM, MitM, MiM or MIM.

7. **Insider Attack:** A legitimate user of one server could try to hack the credentials of another user. The victim might have access to some other service, which the adversary does not. The adversary thus gains access to that service (Wood, 2000).

8. **Denial of Service Attack:** The adversary tries to prevent legitimate users from obtaining the designated service. The adversary to achieve this goal adopts various techniques. This attack prevents the availability of a service rather than compromising any information (confidentiality), or modifying unauthorized information (integrity) (Houle *et al.*, 2001).

Approaches to Analyze and Security Protocols

Security has become an integral part of software design. Nowadays security is considered during the design and implementation of software rather than as add-on. There are two approaches to analyzing software for security:

1. **Static Analysis:** In this approach, the algorithm and the code after implementation are analyzed to find security vulnerabilities (Chess and McGraw, 2004; Garrett *et al.*, 2015; Harish and Roy, 2014; Roy *et al.*, 2011; Talluri and Roy, 2014). The advantage of static analysis is that it can find potential security violations without executing the application or, in the case of an algorithm analysis, even before the implementation is done.

2. **Dynamic Analysis:** In this approach, the software is executed and tested for potential vulnerabilities (Rahimi *et al.*, 1993; Russo & Sabelfeld, 2010; Sobajic & Pao, 1989; Yasinsac, 2001). One well-known technique is penetration testing in which the tester tries to be a hacker to break into a system (Petukhov & Kozlov, 2008).

Methodology Adopted in this Chapter

In this chapter, static vulnerability analysis is employed on three communication protocols for the SG. Specifically, static vulnerability analysis is performed to conclude if these protocols are vulnerable to clogging attack, a form of denial of service.

Static Analysis Technique

In this section, static analysis technique is illustrated in details, and how static analysis can be applied to detect security vulnerabilities is explained. Gary A. Kildall in (Kildall, 1973) introduced Data flow analysis. The general idea is to compute for each elementary program statement a set of information, which may reach it. The information could be variable names, arithmetic expressions, or values of variables. This depends on the objective of the specific analysis. A static program analysis, evaluates software, without executing it. This stands in contrast to a dynamic analysis that executes the code and observes its runtime behavior. Common techniques used in static analysis include model checking and data flow analysis. Model checking decides if a model of a system satisfies a given property. A data flow analysis computes information that reaches the program points of a program. As mentioned earlier, this work performs Static Vulnerability Analysis of various security protocols for the SG.

Static Analysis approach involves primarily three steps:

1. A Threat Model will be first formulated where the assumptions will be mentioned, and the common threats investigated for in the protocols would be identified.
2. The actual threat (vulnerability) analysis would be then performed on the protocols to find whether they are indeed vulnerable to the threats, and
3. Solutions to make the protocols secure against the threats will be then identified, and the application of the same on the protocols will be proved to make them secure against the identified threats.

The first step in the analysis of the protocols would be to design a threat model. Threat modeling is an approach for analyzing the security of an application. It looks at a system from a potential attacker's perspective. In the threat model, the assumptions under which the protocols would be analyzed statically to identify threats (vulnerabilities) in them are specified. The threat model would also consist of the various threats the protocols would be analyzed for.

Conventional multi-factor authentication and key exchanging protocols assume the attacker to have complete control over the communication channel between the parties in communication. In other words, the communication channel is considered insecure, and that the attacker can perform activities like eavesdropping, intercepting, inserting, deleting, and modifying any information (transmitted messages) over the communication channel.

The next step would be to choose authentication protocols to perform static cryptanalysis. As mentioned before, this work will only focus on protocols designed for the SG. Some of the other factors that will be considered to select protocols are:

1. How recent they are?
2. Different factors they use (e.g. Smart Cards, RFIDs, Memory drives, etc.).
3. What other means do they use to implement additional security (e.g. timestamps, nonce, encryption, hashes)?

The threat vulnerability analysis will be performed on these protocols to find whether they are indeed vulnerable to the threats. The last step would be to suggest solutions to prevent the identified attack in order to make the protocols more secure.

DoS ATTACK ON SG COMMUNICATION PROTOCOLS

The way most SG communication protocols (either authentication or key exchanging) work is that the client (usually a smart meter, or an electric vehicle, etc.) sends its credentials to the server (an authentication server, or a key distributing server, etc.) which then applies some mathematical operations (functions) to verify those credentials. These protocols usually work in different phases. The DoS attack illustrated in this chapter is applicable to various phases of the protocols cryptanalyzed.

The Denial of Service Attack

The main idea of the attack is the interception of the messages from the client to server containing the login credentials by the attacker. These messages are unencrypted in some protocols, while encrypted in others. They might (or might not) contain timestamps. The attacker then replays this intercepted messages several times to force the server perform computationally intensive mathematical operations (like modular exponentiation, elliptic curve cryptography, etc.) forcing the server to waste computational time and resources. Legitimate users are denied of any services that way. Algorithm 1 depicts the DoS attack, which is also known as the clogging attack (Garrett *et al.*, 2015).

Algorithm 1. The general algorithm for clogging attack

```
Intercept login message from client to server
if Timestamp is present then
    Modify timestamp to match requirements
else
    Keep message as is
end if
while The server is not completely clogged! do
    Replay the message to the server
end while
```

Conditions for the Attack

The clogging attack can be successfully performed on a protocol that uses computational resource intensive operations to perform authentication. Two such operations used by the protocol that are cryptanalyzed in this work are modular exponentiation and elliptic curve cryptography (ECC) operations. In the following section their computational resource intensiveness is illustrated.

Modular Exponentiation

Modular exponentiation ($y \equiv g^x \pmod{n}$) is an operation widely used in authentication protocols to guarantee security. In practice, the modulus n is a very large prime, and the exponent x, which is often a chosen random secret value, should be very large as well. Harish and Roy (2014) computed the energy consumed in computing the modular exponentiation y for fixed values of the parameters g, x, and n. They then compared it with common operations like addition, exclusive-OR, and multiplication. Figure 3 shows their result.

As seen in Figure 3, modular exponentiation consumer over a hundred times more (computational) energy over the other common operations. This proves the computational intensiveness of modular exponentiation. Therefore any protocol that uses modular exponentiation is vulnerable to the DoS attack in which, the attacker can exploit the computational resource intensiveness of modular exponentiation to launch the attack.

Figure 3. Comparison of normalized energy consumption of different operations (on log scale)
Source: Harish and Roy, 2014

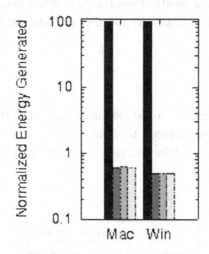

Elliptic Curve Cryptography

The ECC based operations are an alternative to modular exponentiation to perform authentication. The most commonly used ECC operations in authentication protocols are:

1. Bilinear pairing.
2. Scalar multiplication in group G.
3. Map-to-point conversion.

Let Tp, Ts, and $Tmap$ respectively be the time taken to perform a single bilinear pairing, scalar multiplication, and map-to-point conversation. The following have been proved in (Xu & Wu, 2015):

1. $Tp > Ts > Tmap$
2. $Tp \approx 3 \times Ts$
3. $Tp \approx 4 \times Tmap$

Further let $Tmodex$ be the time taken by one modulo exponentiation operation. It has been shown in (Farash and Ahmadian-Attari, 2014) that $Tp \approx 2 \times Tmodex$ to guarantee same level of security.

Elliptic Curve Cryptography (ECC) is a very widely used technique in multi factor authentication. ECC had been developed and used to reduce computational costs, but to provide the same level of security as other similar operations (e.g. modular exponentiation) provides. ECC thus finds its applications in various authentication protocols involving smart cards, RFIDs, wireless networks, digital signatures, and other factors. However, as the authors observe in (Farash and Ahmadian-Attari, 2014), the cost of one bilinear pairing that is an important operation of ECC is about two times higher than that of one modular exponentiation operation at the same security level. Therefore, the computationally intensive nature of ECC leaves a security loophole in the protocols by its usage. An attacker can force the server or the client to perform ECC operations repeatedly to clog them. This again results in one or all of them to waste resources by performing unnecessary computations.

It can be therefore concluded that all the ECC based operations bilinear pairing; scalar multiplication, and map- to-point conversation are quite computationally intensive. Therefore, a protocol that uses ECC operation has a potential vulnerability to DoS in which the attacker exploits the computational intensive nature of ECC operations.

Protocols Cryptanalyzed

Table 1 lists the protocols that have been shown to be vulnerable to the DoS attack by performing cryptanalysis on them. All the protocols considered are modern protocols designed for the smart grid. They differ in the usage of the type of mathematical operations, and the functionalities they provide.

Table 1. Protocols cryptanalyzed to perform DoS attack

Protocol	Tool(s) used for Authorization	Purpose of Protocol
Nicanfar *et al.* (2014)	Modular Exponentiation	Authentication for Smart Grid Communications.
Tseng (2012)	ECC (Bilinear pairing)	Authentication for Vehicle to Grid Network Communications.
Xia *et al.* (2012)	Modular Exponentiation	Key Exchanging for Smart Grids.

In the next sections, each of the protocols is illustrated, cryptanalyzed (attacked), and then a solution with its security analysis is provided to make the protocol secure against the DoS attack.

Nicanfar *et al.* (2014)

The protocol by Nicanfar *et al.* (2014) is a secure and efficient smart grid mutual authentication (SGMA) protocol. This protocol provides authentication between smart meters (SM) and a security and authentication server (SAS). In their paper, they propose a secure and efficient SG mutual authentication (SGMA) scheme and an SG key management (SGKM) protocol. SGMA claims to provide efficient mutual authentication between SMs and the security and authentication server (SAS) in the SG using passwords.

For a detailed description of the protocol the reader is referred to (Nicanfar *et al.*, 2014). Figure 4 briefly describes the protocol.

Attack on the Protocol

It is assumed that the attacker A has unlimited access to message sent back and forth the (insecure) channel. A performs the following steps:

1. Intercept the message $\{SN_{sm}, ID_{sm}, G_{sm}\}$ from SM to SAS.
2. Replay $\{SN_{sm}, ID_{sm}, G_{sm}\}$ to SAS.
3. SAS is forced to calculate G_{sas} each time it receives that message.

Figure 4. The SGMA protocol
Source: Nicanfar et al., 2014

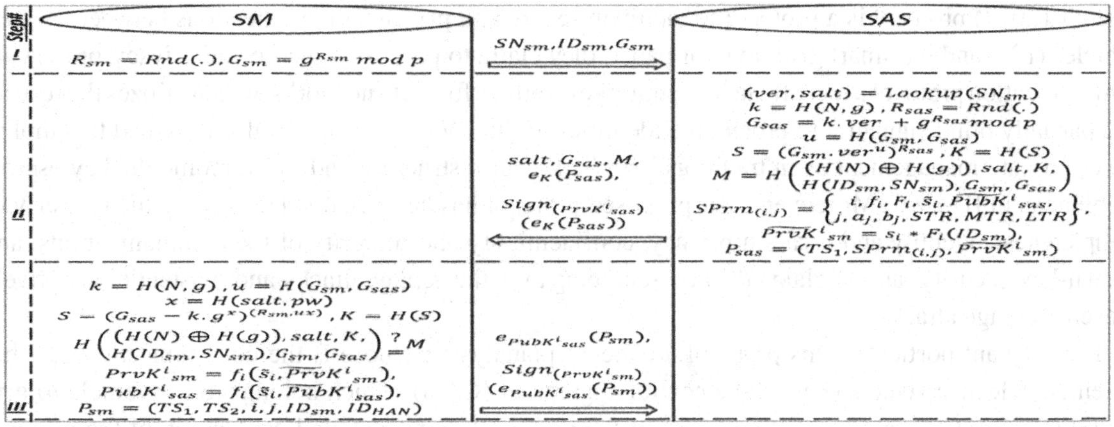

Since calculation of G_{sas} involves modular exponentiation computation, SAS will be clogged after some time only computing useless modular exponentiations, hence legitimate SMs would be denied of service.

It should be noted that even DoS-resilient mechanisms (e.g. timeout or locking an SM's account for a period of time after a predefined number of login failures) are introduced on the SAS's side (as mentioned in (Nicanfar *et al.*, 2014)), it may be not a real obstacle for attacker A as it can initialize new sessions with different intercepted identities in an interleaving manner. Hence, A can potentially perform the above attack procedure continuously, which will make the victimized SAS keep computing useless expensive modular exponentiation operations rather than any real work. Thus A clogs SAS with useless work and therefore A denies any legitimate SM service. If distributed DoS attacks are launched based on this strategy, the consequences will be more serious.

Proposed Countermeasures from the Attack

1. **Usage of Time Stamps:** One countermeasure from this attack for the SGMA protocol will be the addition of timestamp with the message $\{SN_{sm}, ID_{sm}, G_{sm}\}$. Let T_{sm} be the current system time of the SM while it sends the message to SAS. A hash of T_{sm} ($h(T_{sm})$) has to be added with the message. Therefore the SM sends the message $\{SN_{sm}, ID_{sm}, G_{sm}, T_{sm}, h(T_{sm})\}$. Upon receipt, SAS first recalculates $h(T_{sm})$ and compares it with the received hash value to ensure the timestamp has not been modified. SAS next checks whether $T_{sas} - T_{sm} \leq \Delta T$, where T_{sas} is the current system time of the SAS. This rules out the chances of DoS resulting from replays.

2. **Usage of Encryption:** Though this is not a good solution in terms of overhead, it will still prevent the DoS attack, if the message $\{SN_{sm}, ID_{sm}, G_{sm}\}$ is encrypted using either symmetric key, or public key encryption. This will however add overhead of key exchanging, and the encryption/decryption processes.

Tseng (2012)

Tseng's (2012) protocol is a protocol to facilitate secure and private communications between electric vehicles (EV) and the smart grid. In their paper, they claim to propose a secure and privacy-preserving communication protocol in certificateless public key settings for V2G networks, which utilizes the restrictive partially blind signature to protect the identities of the EV owners and is also designed to simplify the certificate management as in traditional public key infrastructure and to overcome the key escrow problem as in ID-PKC. Moreover, their proposed protocol has been claimed to achieve the property of completeness, identity and location privacy, confidentiality and integrity of the communications, and known-key security, and is claimed to be secure against the replay attacks and existential adaptively chosen message attacks.

The relevant portion of this protocol for the cryptanalysis purpose is the communication part between any electric vehicle (EV) and a central aggregator (CAG), which belongs to the vehicle to grid (V2G) network (the pass generation phase of the protocol). For a detailed description of the protocol the reader is referred to (Tseng, 2012). Figure 5 briefly describes the relevant portion of the protocol for our attack purpose.

Figure 5. The pass generation phase of Tseng's protocol
Source: Tseng, 2012

EV_i		CAG
1. Send $\{ID_i, M, t_1, Sig_i(H_1(ID_i \| M \| t_1))\}$ to the CAG	$\rightarrow$	**2.** Receive $\{ID_i, M, t_1, Sig_i(H_1(ID_i \| M \| t_1))\}$ Check the validity of the signature Compute $U = rP$, $a = e(P, Q)$, $b = e(M, Q)$ Compute $z = e(M, SK_j)$ Compute $k_1 = e(D_j, Q_i)$
3. Receive $\{U, a, b, z, t_2, HMAC_{k_1}(U \| a \| b \| t_2)\}$ Compute $k_1 = e(D_i, Q_j)$ Check the message integrity Compute $M' = \alpha M + \beta P$, $A = e(M', Q_j)$, $z' = z^{\alpha} y^{\beta}$ Compute $a' = a^u g^v$, $b' = a^{u\beta} g^{u\alpha} A^v$ Compute $U' = \lambda Q_j + U + \mu P$ Compute $c = H_2(M', U', A, z', a', b') + \lambda H_1(\Delta)$ Compute $c' = cu$	$\leftarrow$	Send $\{U, a, b, z, t_2, HMAC_{k_1}(U \| a \| b \| t_2)\}$ to EV_i
Send $\{c, t_3, HMAC_{k_1}(c \| t_3)\}$ to the CAG	$\rightarrow$	**4.** Receive $\{c, t_3, HMAC_{k_1}(c \| t_3)\}$ Check the message integrity Compute $S_1 = Q + cSK_j$ and $S_2 = cD_j + rH_1(\Delta)P_{pub}$
5. Receive $\{S_1, S_2, t_4, HMAC_{k_1}(S_1 \| S_2 \| t_4)\}$ Check the message integrity Check whether the following equations hold $e(P, S_1) = ay^c$ and $e(M, S_1) = bz^c$ If so, compute $S_1' = uS_1 + vQ_j$ and $S_2' = S_2 + \mu H_1(\Delta)P_{pub}$ The restrictive partially blind signature on (Δ, M') is $\{U', z', c', S_1', S_2'\}$ $Pass_i$ is $\{(\Delta, M'), (U', z', c', S_1', S_2')\}$	$\leftarrow$	Send $\{S_1, S_2, t_4, HMAC_{k_1}(S_1 \| S_2 \| t_4)\}$ to EV_i

Attack on the Protocol

It is again assumed that the attacker A has unlimited access to message sent back and forth along the (insecure) channel. A performs the following steps:

1. Intercept the message $\{ID_i, M, t_1, Sig_i(H_1(ID_i \| M \| t_1))\}$ from EV_i to CAG.
2. Replay $\{ID_i, M, t_1, Sig_i(H_1(ID_i \| M \| t_1))\}$ to CAG.
3. CAG is forced to calculate U, a, b, z, k_1 each time it receives that message.

Since calculation of the above parameters involve bilinear pairing (ECC) computation, the CAG will be clogged after some time only computing useless bilinear pairings, hence legitimate EVs would be denied of service.

Again, A can potentially perform the above attack procedure continuously by replaying messages it intercepted from every single EV. This will make the victimized CAG keep computing the useless expensive ECC operations rather than any real work. Thus A clogs the CAG with useless work and therefore A denies any legitimate EV service. Again, if distributed DoS attacks are launched based on this strategy, the consequences will be more serious.

Proposed Countermeasures from the Attack

1. **Usage of Time Stamps Checking:** It is quite surprising to note that this protocol includes time-stamps and their hashes in the messages from the EVs, but verifications of the timestamps are not done by the CAG, which makes this protocol vulnerable to this DoS attack. One countermeasure from this attack for the protocol will be the verification of timestamp t_1 by the CAG upon receipt of the message $\{ID_i, M, t_1, Sig_i(H_1(ID_i \| M \| t_1))\}$ from EV_i. CAG first recalculates $H_1(ID_i \| M \| t_1)$ and compares it with the received hash value to ensure the timestamp t_1 has not been modified. CAG next checks whether $t_2 - t_1 \leq \Delta T$, where t_2 is the current system time of the CAG. This rules out the chances of DoS resulting from replays.
2. **Usage of Encryption:** Though this is not a good solution in terms of overhead, it will still prevent the DoS attack, if the message $\{ID_i, M, t_1, Sig_i(H_1(ID_i \| M \| t_1))\}$ is encrypted using either symmetric key, or public key encryption. This will however add overhead of key exchanging, and the encryption/decryption processes.

Xia *et al.* (2012)

The protocol by Xia *et al.* (2012) is a secure and efficient key distribution protocol for the smart grid. They motivate the design of their scheme by mentioning that most of the proposed key management methods for the SG that uses either using public key or symmetric key have a lot of drawbacks. As mentioned earlier the Public Key Infrastructure (PKI) scheme, which is essentially a non-interactive scheme, has the memory usage issue that they term the manageably sized certificate revocation list (CRL) problem. The third-party setting schemes (e.g., Kerberos) may have a disconnection problem if the third-party server is out of power - the single point failure problem that was mentioned earlier. To avoid these concerns, they consider a third-party setting for key distribution for the SG letting the server work as a lightweight directory access protocol (LDAP) server without losing security, in an attempt to balance between the two extreme schemes.

Since the cost of a LDAP server is not too high, it is affordable that the server could be duplicated a few times in case one server loses the communication. Their proposed system is claimed to be able to provide secure communication between the smart meter and the service provider.

The relevant portion of their protocol for the cryptanalysis purpose is the message exchange between the smart meter (SM) and the trust anchor (TA). The TA is a trusted third party that manages the key distribution between the SMs and the service providers. For a detailed description of the protocol the reader is referred to (Xia *et al.*, 2012). Figure 6 briefly describes the protocol.

Figure 6. The key distribution protocol by Xia et al
Source: Xia et al., 2012

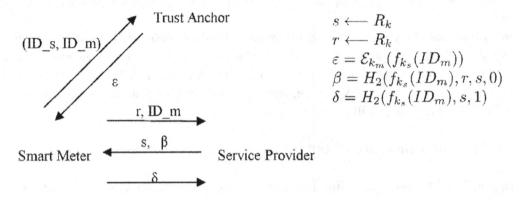

Attack on the Protocol

It is again assumed that the attacker A has unlimited access to message sent back and forth the (insecure) channel. A performs the following steps:

1. Intercept the message $\{ID_m, ID_s\}$ from SM to TA.
2. Replay $\{ID_m, ID_s\}$ to TA.
3. TA is forced to compute $k_s = H_1(ID_s{}^x \bmod p)$ each time it receives that message.

Since calculation of k_s involves modular exponentiation computation, the TA will be clogged after some time only computing useless modular exponentiations, hence legitimate SMs would be denied of service.

A can easily launch this attack on TA in a distributive manner (since the identities of the smart meters and the service providers are assumed to be public anyway).

Proposed Countermeasures from the Attack

1. **Usage of Time Stamps:** One countermeasure will be the addition of timestamp with the message $\{ID_m, ID_s\}$. Let T_m be the current system time of the SM while it sends the message to TA. A hash of T_m ($H(T_m)$) has to be added with the message. Therefore the SM sends the message $\{ID_m, ID_s, H(T_m)\}$. Upon receipt, the TA first recalculates $H(T_m)$ and compares it with the received hash value to ensure the timestamp has not been modified. TA next checks whether $T_{ta} - T_m \leq \Delta T$, where T_{ta} is the current system time of the TA This rules out the chances of DoS resulting from replays.
2. **Usage of Encryption:** Again, it will prevent the DoS attack, if the message $\{ID_m, ID_s\}$ is encrypted using either symmetric key, or public key encryption. This will however add overhead of key exchanging, and the encryption/decryption processes.

SOLUTIONS AND RECOMMENDATIONS

Table 2 summarizes the results obtained in this work. All the protocols have been found vulnerable against the clogging attack, a form of DoS. How the usage of timestamps can make them secure against this attack has been further illustrated.

Table 2. Summary of the results and solutions

Protocol	Vulnerability	Countermeasure
Nicanfar *et al.* (2014)	Denial of Service (Clogging attack)	• Usage of Timestamps • Usage of Encryption
Tseng (2012)	Denial of Service (Clogging attack)	• Implementing timestamps verification (checks) • Usage of Encryption
Xia *et al.* (2012)	Denial of Service (Clogging attack)	• Usage of Timestamps • Usage of Encryption

The usage of encryption has been noted to be another solution against the DoS attack. However, it must be emphasized that as everything has costs involved, the level of security needed will determine the nature of the countermeasure.

FUTURE RESEARCH DIRECTIONS

Research in security is continuous. Authentication protocols for various applications are designed, vulnerabilities are discovered in them, and new protocols secure against the vulnerabilities are designed as a result. The vulnerability of modern authentication and key exchanging protocols for smart grids illustrated in this work will lead to future protocols designs secure against this attack.

Of particular interests would be to design better solutions against the vulnerability than the ones designed in this work. For example, with the usage of timestamps, there is the problem of clock synchronization between various entities in the smart grid. With the usage of encryption comes a lot of overhead that increases costs.

Another solution might be to use nonce in place of timestamp in the protocols. But it remains to be seen how effective will that be. Also a dynamic analysis of the solutions (implementations) and their comparison is an interesting future research direction to pursue.

CONCLUSION

In this research, three advanced protocols for smart grids have been shown to be vulnerable to the clogging attack, which is a form of denial of service. The goal of this work has been to uncover the subtleties and challenges in designing this type of protocols. While mathematical operations like modular exponentiation and elliptical curve cryptography guarantee a certain level of security, this work shows that their usage might lead to an easily-exploitable vulnerability just in case they are used without an additional level of protection. Several other such protocols in the literature rely on the usage of such mathematical operations for their security. Therefore some level of protection should be added to them to guarantee total security against clogging attack.

REFERENCES

Apostol, K. (2012). *Brute-force attack*. Salu Publishing.

Badra, M., & Zeadally, S. (2013, April). Key management solutions in the smart grid environment. In *Wireless and Mobile Networking Conference (WMNC), 2013 6th Joint IFIP* (pp. 1-7). IEEE. 10.1109/WMNC.2013.6549050

Benmalek, M., & Challal, Y. (2015, August). eSKAMI: Efficient and Scalable multi-group Key management for Advanced Metering Infrastructure in Smart Grid. In Trustcom/BigDataSE/ISPA, 2015 IEEE (Vol. 1, pp. 782-789). IEEE.

Chen, B.-L., Kuo, W.-C., & Wuu, L.-C. (2014). Robust smart-card-based remote user password authentication scheme. *International Journal of Communication Systems*, 27(2), 377–389. doi:10.1002/dac.2368

Chess, B., & McGraw, G. (2004). Static analysis for security. *IEEE Security and Privacy*, 2(6), 76–79. doi:10.1109/MSP.2004.111

Demertzis, F. F., Karopoulos, G., Xenakis, C., & Colarieti, A. (2015). Self-organised Key Management for the Smart Grid. In Ad-hoc, Mobile, and Wireless Networks (pp. 303-316). Springer International Publishing. doi:10.1007/978-3-319-19662-6_21

Farash, M. S., & Ahmadian-Attari, M. (2014). A Pairing-free ID-based Key Agreement Protocol with Different PKGs. *International Journal of Network Security*, 16(2), 143–148.

Garrett, K., Talluri, S. R., & Roy, S. (2015). On vulnerability analysis of several password authentication protocols. *Innovations in Systems and Software Engineering*, 11(3), 167–176. doi:10.100711334-015-0250-x

Harish, P. D., & Roy, S. (2014, May). Energy oriented vulnerability analysis on authentication protocols for cps. In *Distributed Computing in Sensor Systems (DCOSS), 2014 IEEE International Conference on* (pp. 367-371). IEEE. 10.1109/DCOSS.2014.52

Houle, K. J., Weaver, G. M., Long, N., & Thomas, R. (2001). *Trends in denial of service attack technology*. Retrieved from: https://resources.sei.cmu.edu/asset_files/WhitePaper/2001_019_001_52491.pdf

Kildall, G. A. (1973, October). A unified approach to global program optimization. In *Proceedings of the 1st annual ACM SIGACT-SIGPLAN symposium on Principles of programming languages* (pp. 194-206). ACM. 10.1145/512927.512945

Lee, W. B., Chen, T. H., Sun, W. R., & Ho, K. I. J. (2014, May). An S/Key-like one-time password authentication scheme using smart cards for smart meter. In *Advanced Information Networking and Applications Workshops (WAINA), 2014 28th International Conference on* (pp. 281-286). IEEE.

Nicanfar, H., Jokar, P., Beznosov, K., & Leung, V. (2014). Efficient authentication and key management mechanisms for smart grid communications. *Systems Journal, IEEE, 8*(2), 629–640. doi:10.1109/JSYST.2013.2260942

Petukhov, A., & Kozlov, D. (2008). *Detecting security vulnerabilities in web applications using dynamic analysis with penetration testing. Computing Systems Lab.* Department of Computer Science,Moscow State University.

Rahimi, F. A., Lauby, M. O., Wrubel, J. N., & Lee, K. L. (1993). Evaluation of the transient energy function method for on-line dynamic security analysis. *Power Systems. IEEE Transactions on, 8*(2), 497–507.

Roy, S., Das, A. K., & Li, Y. (2011). Cryptanalysis and security enhancement of an advanced authentication scheme using smart cards, and a key agreement scheme for two-party communication. In *Performance Computing and Communications Conference (IPCCC), 2011 IEEE 30th International*. IEEE. 10.1109/PCCC.2011.6108113

Russo, A., & Sabelfeld, A. (2010). Dynamic vs. static flow-sensitive security analysis. In *Computer Security Foundations Symposium (CSF), 2010 23rd IEEE*, (pp. 186–199). IEEE.

Saxena, N., & Choi, B. J. (2015). State of the Art Authentication, Access Control, and Secure Integration in Smart Grid. *Energies, 8*(10), 11883–11915. doi:10.3390/en81011883

Sobajic, D. J., & Pao, Y.-H. (1989). Artificial neural-net based dynamic security assessment for electric power systems. *Power Engineering Review, IEEE, 9*(2), 55–55. doi:10.1109/MPER.1989.4310480

Syverson, P. (1994). A taxonomy of replay attacks [cryptographic protocols]. In *Computer Security Foundations Workshop VII, 1994. CSFW7. Proceedings*, (pp. 187–191). IEEE.

Talluri, S. R., & Roy, S. (2014). Cryptanalysis and security enhancement of two advanced authentication protocols. In Advanced Computing, Networking and Informatics (vol. 2, pp. 307–316). Springer. doi:10.1007/978-3-319-07350-7_34

Tseng, H. R. (2012, April). A secure and privacy-preserving communication protocol for V2G networks. In *Wireless Communications and Networking Conference (WCNC)* (pp. 2706-2711). IEEE. 10.1109/WCNC.2012.6214259

Wei-Chi, K., & Chang, S.-T. (2005). Impersonation attack on a dynamic id-based remote user authentication scheme using smart cards. *IEICE Transactions on Communications, 88*(5), 2165–2167.

Wei-Chi, K., Hao-Chuan, T., & Tsaur, M.-J. (2004). Stolen-verifier attack on an efficient smart card-based one-time password authentication scheme. *IEICE Transactions on Communications, 87*(8), 2374–2376.

Wood, B. (2000). An insider threat model for adversary simulation. SRI International. *Research on Mitigating the Insider Threat to Information Systems, 2*, 1–3.

Xia, J., & Wang, Y. (2012). Secure key distribution for the smart grid. Smart Grid. *IEEE Transactions on, 3*(3), 1437–1443.

Xu, L., & Wu, F. (2015). An improved and provable remote user authentication scheme based on elliptic curve cryptosystem with user anonymity. *Security and Communication Networks*, 8(2), 245–260. doi:10.1002ec.977

Yasinsac, A. (2001). Dynamic analysis of security protocols. In *Proceedings of the 2000 workshop on New security paradigms*, (pp. 77–87). ACM.

This research was previously published in Security Solutions and Applied Cryptography in Smart Grid Communications edited by Mohamed Amine Ferrag and Ahmed Ahmim; pages 50-67, copyright year 2017 by Information Science Reference (an imprint of IGI Global).

Chapter 30

IP–CHOCK Reference Detection and Prevention of Denial of Service (DoS) Attacks in Vehicular Ad–Hoc Network:
Detection and Prevention of Denial of Service (DoS) Attacks in Vehicular Ad–Hoc Network

Karan Verma
Central University of Rajasthan, India

ABSTRACT

Vehicular Ad-Hoc Network (VANET) is a subset of Mobile Ad-Hoc Network (MANET) and it is considered as a substantial component of Intelligent Transportation System (ITS). DoS attacks on VANET are varying and may be overwhelmed by VANET protocols, such as TCP or UDP flooding attacks. Different secure communications models can be used to detect and prevent IP spoofing DoS attacks, by which the attacks are committed by fraudulent and malicious nodes. In this chapter, an efficient detection method has been proposed to detect UDP flooding attacks, called Bloom-Filter-Based IP-CHOCK (BFICK). A prevention method using IP-CHOCK has also been proposed to prevent DoS, called Reference Broadcast Synchronization (RBS). In principle, the combined method is based on the IP-CHOCK filter concept of packets during an attack incident and with busy traffic condition. Fake identities from malicious vehicles can be analyzed with help of the existing reliable IP addresses. Beacon packets were exchanged periodically by all the vehicles to announce their presence and to forward it to the next node.

DOI: 10.4018/978-1-7998-5348-0.ch030

INTRODUCTION

Population growth has led to an increase in transportation needs, while advances in technology has motivated for the development of an Intelligent Transportation System (ITS). For ITS to work, each vehicle on road is equipped with communication devices, and they are communicating wirelessly with each other over a wireless network known as Vehicular Ad-hoc Network (VANET). In general, wireless network that supports user mobility is known as Mobile Ad-hoc Network (MANET). Hence, VANET is a sub-set of MANET, which today ITS is relying on VANET to powerfully implement it (Isaac, Zeadally, & Cámara, 2010; Wu, Chen, Wu, & Cardei, 2007). VANET can be expected to provide efficient transportation and management services.

In a VANET, vehicle nodes are mobile and interconnected through a wireless interface (Antolino Rivas, Barceló-Ordinas, Guerrero Zapata, & Morillo-Pozo, 2011; Sichitiu & Kihl, 2008). In the United States, the Federal Communication Commission (FCC) allocated a 75 MHz spectrum at 5.9 GHz for vehicular communications, which are of types of so-called Vehicle-to-Vehicle (V2V) and Vehicle-to-Infrastructure (V2I). Similar bands have been allocated in other countries (Aslam, Park, Zou, & Turgut, 2010; Lo & Tsai, 2007). As for protocols supporting VANET, Dedicated Short Range Communication (DRSC) is the underlying transport protocol, with its specification stated as IEEE 802.11p. It supports both public safety and licensed private operatives over V2V and V2I communications, in addition to upper-layer protocols for wireless access in a vehicular environment. Wireless Access for Vehicular Environment (WAVE)-IEEE 1609 protocols are also under development (Isaac et al., 2010; Raya & Hubaux, 2007) to support mobile communications.

As VANET is closely related to human daily life activities, it is expected that it shall provide reliable and secure communications, as nodes join or leave the network arbitrarily without human intervention. It is noted that data traffic in VANET will travel through multiple hops, and routed through vulnerable wireless media, thus exposing to security risks. Inter-vehicular communications (V2V) and Vehicle-to- Infrastructure communications (V2I) require applications that serve users and that secure their transportation goals (see: Figure 1). VANET has two main application categories: safety and non-safety (Wu et al., 2007). Safety applications are the focus of most research in the area of VANET systems. Although drivers have no ability to predict road conditions (Amadeo, Campolo, & Molinaro, 2013), with the aid of sensors, computer equipment, wireless communication devices and a combination of similar technologically equipped devices, it is possible to provide methods by which drivers can foresee the speed of other vehicles and assess possible risks. Through such systems, warnings are periodically sent to predict vehicular speeding to reduce the incidence of collisions (Zeadally, Hunt, Chen, Irwin, & Hassan, 2012). What is needed is to improve the application efficiency, which may effect in reducing number of fatalities and provide safer, cleaner and more comfortable road travel. Non-safety applications provide additional information for pleasant, convenient, and entertaining journey to users, while they are moving on roads. This class of application is categorized as infotainment.

Unfortunately, VANET comes with a set of challenges to both classes, especially safety. Due to its wireless communication capability in V2V and V2I modes, VANET is subjected to numerous threats that can lead to increase malicious attacks and service abuses (see: Figure 1) (Antolino Rivas et al., 2011; Y.-S. Chen, Hsu, & Yi, 2012; Y. Zhang & Cao, 2011).

Figure 1. Communications scenario in VANET

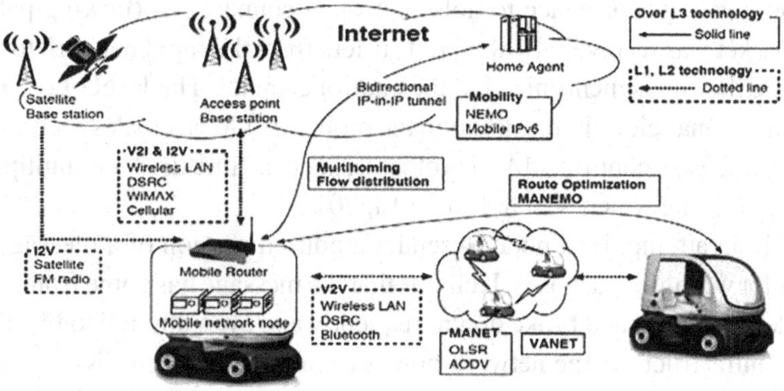

The unique characteristics of VANET are higher mobility and rapidly changing network topology caused by the high travel speed of nodes. Also, VANET is accompanied by some constraints due to:

1. Restricted roads;
2. Limited bandwidth due to absence of a central coordinator that controls and manages communications between nodes;
3. Disconnect problems due to frequent network fragmentation; and \
4. Fading signals caused by objects that form obstacles between communicating nodes (Ma, Wilson, Yin, & Trivedi, 2013; Mishra, Garg, & Gore, 2011; H. Wang, Zhang, & Shin, 2004).

Nevertheless, on the other side, the massive proliferation of Internet Service Provider (ISP) has also enabled personal mobile phones to have unprecedented Internet access for nearly everyone. This access is also available through VANET infrastructure. This has opened more opportunities for criminal innovations of unlawful and unethical activities, including attacks on vehicular and personal mobile applications (Jingle & Rajsingh, 2014). Furthermore, drivers have no ability to predict road conditions ahead, such as traffic speed and congestion or other risks. Vehicles often crash on roads due to congestion and other possibilities (J. K. Liu, Yuen, Au, & Susilo, 2014; Raya & Hubaux, 2007), but such risks can be reduced with the aid of sensors, computer equipment, wireless communication devices and other VANET devices. By using such equipment and devices, drivers are better informed to foresee road risks ahead. Hence, researchers working on VANET systems do so to achieve safe, clean (attack free traffic), and comfortable travelling conditions with secure communication between fast moving vehicles. The ultimate goal is to reduce the number of injuries and fatalities due to non-safe and not-informed driving environment (Muraleedharan & Osadciw, 2009; Park & Zou, 2008).

The expansion in transportation with respect to its technology and facilities requires a secure VANET infrastructure for proper communications and data transmissions. Appropriate management of VANET is a challenging task, which inputs to corresponding locations for counting nodes by changing bits of the bit levels. Devices involved are also work in open channel that make security a far more challenging task (Cheng, Yin, Wu, Zhang, & Liu, 2009). Due to vehicular mobility in an open channel area, it requests other vehicles to give way it or nearby OBUs for changing traffic lights. Various attackers use different approaches via illegal tasks that can interrupt VANET services (Karagiannis et al., 2011; Lin,

Sun, Ho, & Shen, 2007; Xiong, Chen, & Li, 2012). Attackers focus on attacking machines to the victim may also suffer from lower performance to hold half-open connections (tacking path of source node) until the last ACK packet was received. However, it suffers from the rapid network topology, their safety status messages while they are synchronized to the control channel. The level of security is achieved by changing pseudonyms as malicious jam. Although the problem of local clock synchronization is suffered in the context of media access control (MAC) protocols, such as time division multiple access (TDMA) overcome with activity (Tang, Chen, Chen, Liu, & Li, 2014).

'Impersonation' is an attempt by a node to send a modified version of a message received from an authentic originator for wrongful purposes. It claims that the message has come from the same originator. Hence, wireless links initialized and broke down frequently and even unpredictably. Due to node mobility and the dynamic infrastructure, the network now is even more insecure (Karagiannis et al., 2011).

After analyzing the discovered finding (Y.-S. Chen et al., 2012), DoS attacks are considered serious in any VANET environment. Various methods and applications have therefore, been used to detect and/ or prevent them. Even so, such methods and processes thus far utilized, did not meet the level of the challenges (Y. Chen & Hwang, 2006; Rahim et al., 2009; Zhao, Zhang, & Cao, 2007).

The recent growth and popularity of VANET and its use in various settings has prompted new scenarios, where secure operations are highly important. This is mainly due to VANET importance roles in many infrastructure-less environments and applications, especially in critical settings, such as vehicular and emergency rescue, as well as military and law enforcement usage. So to motivate the manufacturer to deploy VANET will get little incentive. VANET devices incorporating IP spoofing in the DoS attacks makes it even more difficult to defend against attacks. An efficient method is adapted to detect and defend against UDP flooding attacks under different IP spoofing types. The method makes use of a storage-efficient data structure and a Bloom-filter based IP-CHOCK detection method. This lightweight approach makes it relatively easy to deploy as its resource requirement is reasonably low. To solve the hidden terminal problem: virtual carrier sensing using network time synchronization is acquired. Since the synchronized collision phenomenon concerns with channel switching that is relatively easy to avoid. Moreover, for time slotted MACs are the best approaches. VANET also prone to interference and propagation issues, as well as different types of attacks and intrusions, that can harm ITS. A natural step was to adapt location-based operations to VANET. Specifically, the method outperformed others in achieving a higher detection rate yet with lower storage and computational costs. Until recently, these security and privacy issues for VANET have received little attention.

Nevertheless, various methodologies and frameworks have been proposed to detect and defend against DoS attacks. However, these solutions have significant drawbacks, including high computational overhead on intermediate routers, large memory space requirements, and high rates of false positives. Hence, the challenge is to lessen these impacts and to solve these problems in a comprehensive and integrated solution.

Hence, from the reviewed literature and the identified problem, there is an opportunity to improve the DoS attacks detection method, while at the same time providing extended defense mechanism against the attacks in VANET environment. Possibly, there are two ways to detect and defend against DoS attacks: one is to identify attack packets and filter those packets using BF, and the other is to locate the attack source and take defensive action through synchronization approach. It is expected that if these two approaches are combined together, then a more comprehensive and integrated solution to DoS attack can be realized.

BACKGROUND

VANET has been suffering from serious attacks and threats that cause the network service to breakdown. Attempts to render a mobile resource or service unavailable to intended users are called Denial of Service (DoS) attacks (Li, Hwang, & Chu, 2008; Muraleedharan & Osadciw, 2009). Due to a VANET's mobility and motion, it is easy for an attacker to initiate a threat, for example, flooding or spoofing (sybil, fabrication, alteration or reply) and disrupt the service. In addition to 'outsiders', such attackers even include network insiders (Y.-S. Chen et al., 2012; J. Wang & Yan, 2009; Zeadally et al., 2012). Initially, an attacker controls a large number of vulnerable hosts on the Internet by compromising them as shown in Figure 2. The attacker uses vulnerable mobile hosts to simultaneously send a huge number of packets to targeted vehicle nodes. Targets are either a specific network service or marked vehicles. Such victimized services are then disrupted due to an enormous quantity of data (Y.-Y. Chen, Wang, & Jan, 2013; Park & Zou, 2008).

Figure 2. A DoS attack scenario in a VANET environment

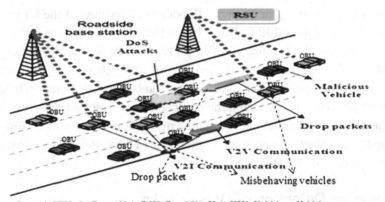

Legend: OBU- On-Board Unit, RSU- Road Side Unit, V2V- Vehicle-to-Vehicle,
V2I- Vehicle-to-Infrastructure

DoS attacks create such serious problems that a means for detecting and preventing them has become a priority because they are even more difficult to counter than IP spoofing. IP spoofing refers to a technique of misrepresenting a return address (i.e., through vehicle request) in a message. With IP spoofing, attackers gain unauthorized access to a vehicle or network by making it appear that a message has come from a certain trusted vehicle by spoofing the vehicle's IP address (Hamieh, Ben-Othman, & Mokdad, 2009; Mohandas & Liscano, 2008). Figure 2 shows that the technique that has been used for years and is commonly used in DoS attacks against commercial servers. Since attackers are mainly concerned with consuming network bandwidth and resources, they do not usually complete communications and transactions properly as they simply want to flood the victimized vehicle with as many messages as possible within a short period of time. In order to prolong the effects of attack, they spoof the requested IP addresses to make tracing and stopping the DoS as difficult as possible (Biswas, Miˇsic, & Miˇsic, 2012; G. Zhang et al., 2012).

IP-CHOCK

IP-CHOCK is a monitoring, filtering, speedy detection, and defense against flooding and spoofing attacks. It is standard for network management activities and is commonly used to filter and monitor network equipment (such as mobile vehicles, servers and routers (Kaur & Verma, 2012; Spaho et al., 2013)). The most external router in a series of routers and/or firewalls is the initial entry point of the boundary into network. It handles the initial rough filtering/inspection of externally-originating traffic for the next stage of filter/inspection routing. Congestion generally occurs at IP-CHOCK points in the network, where the total incoming traffic to a node exceeds the outgoing bandwidth. Proactively router sends a packet to the source to inform about congestion, which results in minimizing computation and fast detection and prevention of the malicious alarm. Connection points between a local area network and a wide area network are the most likely IP-CHOCK points. Offered IP-CHOCK is located at layer 3-network. Where mainly it is designed to limit fault currents to an acceptable level with this it also provides sufficient load sharing at the same time. Hence, IP-CHOCK can be used to detect and prevent any changes in the traffic with the matching of attack patterns.

The onset of a DoS attack is typically accompanied by an increased number of unsolicited packets originating from previous unseen or new source IP addresses arriving at the target vehicle. The DoS attack form the basis of the proposed IP-CHOCK based DoS attack detection and prevention approach to filterer, analyze, and track the incoming traffic (in term of the source IP addresses of the packets received). The IP-CHOCK is periodically invoked, at time intervals (e.g. 1 to 10 seconds), to analyze recent changes in the arrival of packet from new source IP addresses calculated. Whenever, an incoming packet is received, an IP-CHOCK calculated the number of new source IP addresses observed during a measurement interval. Its deployment at the source network can stop attack flow before they enter the Internet core and before they aggregate with other attack flows. Being close to the source, they can facilitate easier investigation of the attack.

Filtration Scheme for Detection of DoS Attacks

The Bloom-filter (BF) was first introduced in 1970 by Burton Bloom (Bloom, 1970). It is a probabilistic space-efficient data structure used to verify whether or not an element is a member of a set (Geravand & Ahmadi, 2013). Its structure offers a way to perform member queries that may result in false positives but never false negatives. The basic operations of a BF include membership testing and adding elements to the set. Presently, it is widely used in many applications such as databases, peer-to-peer networks, resource allocation and packet routing. For database application, it is used to reduce disk access to differential files (Geravand & Ahmadi, 2013; Sarela et al., 2011). As for routing, when a packet is received, the destination address in the packet is compared to each BF on the router and forwarded to matching interfaces. This mechanism does not store any individual addresses in the router. However, when addition and removal of multicast addresses is required, BF variant capable of doing these operations must be developed (Tarkoma, Rothenberg, & Lagerspetz, 2012).

Bloom-filter $B = \left(b_0, \ldots, b_{m-1}\right)$ is an array of m bits that represent an n element set $s = \left(x_0, x_1, \ldots, x_{n-1}\right)$. The element can be mapped to the BF by utilizing $k \geq 1$ hash functions, each of which maps the element to an integer range of [0, m–1]. An element is added to the BF by applying hashes to an element individually and by setting the bits at resulting positions in the BF to 1 (Tarkoma et al., 2012). Similarly, membership testing can be carried out by calculating the hashes of an element and checking whether all resulting bit positions in the BF are set to 1. BF is probability in the sense that membership testing may return false positive results, and this probability grows with the number of vehicles v_i added to the set because of the percentage of 1-bits in the bit array (El Defrawy & Tsudik, 2008).

The fundamental aim of this scheme is to detect against DoS attacks with features of detection and filtering mechanisms combined in a single scheme. Compared with the previously reported BF-based packet filtration protocols for security, the proposed protocol not only retains security properties, but also bears a smaller packet loss ratio and less transmission overhead, especially when the traffic is heavy. Thus, a new efficient and cooperative message filter protocol called 'BF with IP-CHOCK' has been proposed. BF with IP-CHOCK detection technique first extracts the IP addresses of the incoming network traffic. It then determines whether the source IP address has been seen previously or is a new IP address. The resulting time series of the rate of previously unseen or new IP addresses is then analyzed by the IP-CHOCK to identify whether the system (e.g., vehicle) is under attack. The system being protected against DoS attacks is represented in terms of two independent states: not under attack, which is the system state when receiving non-attack normal traffic, and under attack, the system state when receiving DoS attack traffic. Low-rate attacks can be as harmful as the high-rate ones, yet even more dangerous due to the fact that they are difficult for routers and counter-DoS mechanisms to detect. For each vehicle, this protocol probabilistically filters a certain percentage of the received messages based on its computing capacity, and then reports all the invalid messages detected (see: Table 1).

Clock Synchronization Scheme for Prevention of DoS Attacks

Clock Synchronization in wireless networks is extremely important for basic communication as it provides an ability to detect movement, location and proximity. Clock synchronization can be either proactive or reactive. Proactive time synchronization is performed continuously in order to support a synchronized network state for which it necessarily stands ready for future activity. For example, a single reference node can periodically disseminate its incidental time to other nodes that allow estimates of clock offsets (stored in the BF) with respect to the referenced time (Xiong et al., 2012). On the contrary, reactive synchronization is initiated only when synchronization is required. For example, unsynchronized mobility nodes may record the time of a certain event and send time stamps to a vehicle node. After data collection, the node can perform a synchronization procedure that transforms time-stamps from mobility nodes to its time (Bregni, 1997; Gillani, Shahzad, Qayyum, & Mehmood, 2013). VANET nodes can be synchronized either to an external time reference or by means of intra-network synchronization procedures. A Global Positioning System (GPS) receiver can serve as an external source of time for a wireless network, where time values are disseminated by a special node attached to the GPS receiver. In this event, network nodes are able to transform respective time values to the referenced time values, and vice versa, thus achieving time synchronization. Alternatively, the network can be synchronized internally by using the clock of some other nodes as the reference clock (store in the BF). VANET nodes can be synchronized to a certain guaranteed accuracy with the main advantage being that it eliminates transmitter-side non-determinism (Sumra, Hasbullah, Bin, & Manan, 2013).

Most time synchronization protocols rely on a time-sensitive message exchange. To mislead these protocols, an adversary may forge and modify time synchronization messages or, jam the communication channel to launch DoS attacks by initially jamming the receipt of time synchronization for messages sent and later replaying buffered copies. Thus, the targeted system is rendered defenseless against all such attacks. To achieve a secure network-wide synchronization, each node in the network examines every path it uses to reach the other nodes in search of misbehaving links (UDP packet), i.e., links under the control of DoS attack attackers. When a misbehaving link is found, its usage is discontinued in order for IP-CHOCK to examine every path to all other nodes in the network. The synchronizer will edit its synch-scale by updating the list of synchronized group members of IP-CHOCK. It will then send a clock adjustment message to all its group members. The message consists of the synchronizers time differences and all receivers' IDs. Each of them should have received the broadcast very close to the same time as one another, at which point vehicle would reset their system clocks to a particular time (see: Table 2).

Table 1. Summary of related work and required modification of DoS attacks detection schemes

Related Work	Strengths	Weaknesses	Required Modification
IP-CHOCK DoS Detection Mechanisms: • ipac functions • IP-CHOCK functions • Change based Signature-based • Anomaly-based CUSUM • (Cumulative Weighted) • EWMA • (Exponentially Weighted Moving Average)	• Minimal delay and low false detection rate statistical properties computationally less expensive and lighter in terms of memory utilization • Uses real traffic traces • Reduces false alarm ratio	• Verification of message from an unknown vehicle involves fragmented transmissions through network causing heavy message overhead • Mitigation of unauthorized location tracking of vehicles • All data goes to location server • Model works only at primary level; verification data and time based data causes slow and costly transmission speed	• Framework for identification and local containment of DoS attacks • Local detection of misbehavior performed individually by each node • Distribute localized protocol for the eviction of an attacker by its neighboring nodes
Filtering DoS Detection Mechanisms: • SPIE (Source Path Isolation Engine) • DCMD (Detection and Correction Malicious Data) • FDS (Flooding Detection System) • MDADF (Making Packet Detection and Flooding) • TTL (Time-To-Time) • IP Trackback • Hash IP Track-back	• Detection of IP Spoofing works well for communication of a predefined source nodes • Filtering of improperly addressed packets is worthwhile • Incremental deployment • Gives priority to frequent packets in case of congestion or attack	• Needs global development • Attacks with real IP addresses cannot be detected • Needs wider implementation for effectiveness • Ineffective when attacks come from real IP addresses • Requires offline database to keep track of IP addresses • Depends on collected data during transient period valid packets can be dropped	• Probabilistic method using Bloom-filter to securely evaluate the integrity of a node with the help of modified BF using the hash function • Proactively filter out a large fraction of spoofed packets • Reactively find origins of unfiltered nodes • Spoof packets within a small scope
Traffic Capacity DoS Detection Mechanisms: • Network Traffic Analysis • Synthetic Traffic • Existing Traffic	• Detection of incoming network traffic • Early detection of IP spoofing, detection without FE consideration • FE tagging an abnormal activity for further analysis • Detection of early counter by SYN+ACK • Stores all IP addresses in Bloom-filter • Threshold values is markedly reduced • Uses public domain database (e.g., KDD99, CAIDA), uses software and hardware platforms (SmartBits 600, D-ITG, Harpoon, Fudp5, Hping, Curl-loader)	• Difficult to filter attack traffic from background traffic • Precludes detection strategies relying • Large public domain not available • Poor software-based traffic generation • Software is obsolete • Software and hardware parameters such as traffic volume and distribution, packet size and protocols	• Less-memory database that stores all incoming IP addresses using modified Bloom-filter based hashing • Checks data from vehicle nodes and further evaluates whether the incoming or generated message is a valid position verification • Position claims of independence or use of special software or hardware to change traffic flow

Table 2. Summary of related work and required modification of DoS attacks prevention (synchronization mechanisms)

Related Work	Strengths	Weaknesses	Required Modification
FTSP (Flooding Time Synchronization Protocol)	• Uses global time (time-stamps) • Collects all data then sends to the reference point • Achieves high synchronization accuracy and multiple transmissions	• Many collisions • Significant communication overhead • Too complex	• Main approach to achieving max. synchronization of all communication nodes • Packets with spoofed source address cannot pass
ETSP (Energy Efficient Synchronization Protocol)	• Saves energy and minimizes number of synchronizations • Synchronizes 'sender to receiver' only when number of nodes is small	• High threshold • High overhead • Does not provide full synchronization for entire network • Very high reference time	• Reference model to improve local clock with less communication time • Offset value less than $0(t{\geq}0)$ • Uses 'less than or equal to' a defined threshold
RATS (Rate Adaptive Time Synchronization)	• Less synchronization time • Uses reference node, stores in database • Uses BF database • Chooses optimal periods during which numbers of time-stamps are sent	• Synchronization interval varies • Synchronization error for reference node • Collision in large database • Very high synchronization overhead	• Can complement other DoS attack defense models • Estimates local time on other node's clock • Able to synchronize mobile nodes in dynamic environment
RBS (Reference broadcast Synchronization)	• Calculates offset with respect to clock of other nodes • Uses least-square linear regression • Synchronizes receiver to receiver • Uses Bloom-filter to reference nodes and offset values • Database: stores values, clock and distance • Records when packet received according to local clock • Calculates timing interval based on range of offset values	• High synchronize errors • Needs more space to store reference nodes and reference vector values • Reference node allocation and reduction in capacity of memory for the expansion of filtering • Cannot store large number of control packets in database.	• Proposed prevention model to reduce DoS attacks and message collision rate when calculating offset value • Broadcasts authentication then generates and sends reference to all mobile nodes. • Uses a modified Bloom-filter store for all reference node values and clock times • Reduces time synchronization errors, uses perfect clock $C_p(t){=}t$

The Possible Combined Scheme for Detection and Prevention of DoS Attacks

The combined method is combination of filtration (detection) and clock synchronization (prevention). The fundamental aim for this method is to detect and prevent DoS attacks with features of filtration mechanism and clock synchronization jointly as single method. In this process, a communication link for all mobile nodes is generated using the clock maintenance service ability. The IP-CHOCK works as a firewall for filtering purposes of the packet on the master node and that master node works as a central control device. The link for synchronization is provided by the clock. The clock maintains network capability for all nodes during communication. The IP-CHOCK scans the packet to discover if it is normal or abnormal.

Foreseeable Solution for a Combined Approach

The primary aims of VANET are to improve traffic safety and driving comfort to road users, through its safety and non-safety applications. It is achieved through the exchange of warning and information messages in V2V and V2I about any incidents and road conditions, as well as about its environment. In supporting these applications however, VANET infrastructure is exposed to external and internal attacks, which these attacks need to be detected (as a proactive measure) and prevented (as a reactive measure). While most attacks from external attackers may be easily resolved, the internal attackers are absolutely having more chances to misuse, and subsequently to attack the system by injecting volume of fake messages into the network, leading to a denial of service (DoS) attack. For example, DoS attack can be made by flooding/spoofing the UDP/TCP packets, which blocks the provided bandwidth of communication. The task of detection and prevention of DoS attacks is a complex process, involving multiple inter-related components, such as filtration and time synchronization. It is anticipated that these components are to work inter-dependently in providing an effective and robust solution to the DoS attacks problem. In this research work, the full length of IP addresses is possible to be used to filter and detect DoS attacks, which increases the number of memory segments, and hence maximizing the false positive rate. As for the prevention, it is possible to rely on a time-sensitive message exchange for synchronization of those memory segments, so that fall positive rate is reduced. The sensitivity of synchronization time needs to be detected for any attempts of tempering by attackers, such that there is a chance for them to send forged time relay messages that mislead the time relay process. It works in the reverse way as well, where the packets are sent in time synchronism, thus providing prevention to chances of DoS attacks during user communication. However, the UDP/TCP packets may have been altered during their perfect synchronization, which needs to be filtered and detected for reduced false positive rate. Hence, it is foreseeable that the detection and prevention mechanisms to work together. If they are not working as a single mechanism, then it is possible that the DoS attacks could not be effectively identified and robustly prevented. Therefore, a combined approach of detection and prevention can be expected to provide a complete and solid solution to the problem of DoS attacks in VANET.

COMBINED APPROACH OF DETECTION AND PREVENTION TO HADLE THE DOS ATTACKS

The combined model is based on a filtration that distinguishes attack packets from the normal packets which is send by the legitimate users and thus filters out the most of attack packets before reaching the victim. In this combined model the source IP addresses is spoofed by attackers; the paths packets take to the destination are totally decided by the network topology and routers in the internet, which are not controllable by the attackers. By recording the path information, the packets from different sources can be precisely differentiated, no matter what the IP addresses appeared in the packets. A router puts its IP address into the marking space of each packet it receivers; if there is already a number in the space, it calculates the exclusive-or (XOR) of its address with the previous values in the marking space and puts the new value back. Each cooperating router on the path of an IP packet would insert a mark on the ID-field of the packet. It used BF based hash function, provides space and speed efficiency with the low false positive rate while it offers a quick decision making function that filters mobile vehicle attack messages. The (IP address, marking) pairs are stored in a filter table, which are used to stored and verify each incoming packets and filter-out the spoofed and flooded packets. RBS is used when there is no difference in failure ratios and it contains different types of scanners to empower as well as capable of detecting nodes. RBS (prevention) compare computed offset values from newly received exchange messages with mean values already stored in the BF through the hash function based database. Values greater than a predefined threshold, are rejected without affecting phase offset or skew computations.

However, the two components of detection and prevention approaches need to be discussed separately for clarity, as well as to highlight their research contribution individually.

Bloom-Filter Based IP-CHOCK (BFICK) for Detection of DoS Attacks in VANET

DoS attacks comprise of the actual volume of traffic flow (e.g. normal or random) and script kiddie, used by attackers for flooding; i.e. they send exorbitant amounts of useless traffic aimed at the victim (Ramakrishnan, Rajesh, & Shaji, 2010). Malicious entities might launch a DoS attack by overwhelming the communication channel so that crucial messages do not reach their destinations. The intention of such an attack is to disable the entire network by continuously or selectively jamming important transmissions (Ramakrishnan, Rajesh, & Shaji, 2010). Since VANET is a real-time communication system, consequences from losing normal transmissions can be fatal. A straightforward attack of this kind might be launched by a malicious node that simply synchronizes with the broadcast schedule of corresponding service providers to broadcast false messages at the exact same time as service announcements are sent

(Park, S. et al., 2008; Spaho, E. et al., 2008; Karagiannis, G. et al,. 2011). Multiple attackers may focus on the same transmission to increase their chances of success, especially since increasing capacities of traffic volume and the dynamic nature of a vehicular network invite service-oriented attacks that compromise the service (C. Liu & Chigan, 2012). For filtering, a BFICK scheme has been applied for identifying, monitoring and fast detection against spoofed and flooding attacks. It's a common practice in network management activities and is commonly used to filter and monitor network equipment such as mobile vehicles, servers, and routers.

Nevertheless, generally speaking, there is insufficient attack traffic from links close to an attack source during the early stages, making it simple to bundle legitimate and attack traffic together. Hence, it is particularly challenging to precisely detect such attacks early on at their source (Raya, M. et al., 2007 & Liu, J. K., et al., 2007). However, the detection and sensitivity may decline as the number of attack sources increases. In a large-scale DoS attack, the attack sources can be orchestrated so that attack traffic generated by each source is scarce and looks similar to legitimate traffic. Consequently, the attack traffic close to the source will cause only an insignificant deviation from the normal traffic pattern.

Request Detector

The request is deployed at the edge router on the innocent request side. One of the main tasks of the request detector is to monitor UDP control packets entering and leaving the domain. The detector scheme was developed from a BF based hash table. The design of the new hash table is based on the BF method. Each state of the UDP connection is recorded in the hash table and the abnormal asymmetric connection is recorded and observed within the request detector. After an accumulation of suspicious alarms, the request detector reaches the threshold and issues a DoS attack warning that is sent to all response nodes. To detect attacking traffic with a spoofed source request IP, the destination response IP is recorded in the monitoring table. When a *SYN* packet - the first time round-is captured from outgoing traffic, the destination IP (response's IP) is split into several segments and hashed into the monitoring table.

If the corresponding count is 0, the corresponding count is turned on. If the count is already turned on, the count is incremented by 1. If the corresponding *ACK/SYN* packet for the second round of the BF is captured in incoming traffic, the source IP (the response's IP) is hashed into the hash table again.

But this time, the corresponding count is decremented by 1. When a count changes from 1 to 0, the corresponding bit is turned off; meaning there is space made for other packets.

The count will remain unchanged if the first two rounds of UDP/TCP connections are completely captured by request and response detectors on the source side. These counts are reset to 0 and the monitoring process is restarted for every period t. If there is no *ACK* or *SYN* packet sent in response to the previous *SYN* the count is not decremented for the connection. The value in the count then grows larger as it increases by 1 for each spoofed *SYN* packet. When DoS attacks occur, an exceptionally heavy volume of packets is sent towards victim IP addresses. If there is at least one count in the table containing a suspicious value, it is recorded in the data-base for further analysis. Hence, when a value of a count exceeds the predefined threshold during period t, this value is regarded as suspicious and the DoS attack alarm is sent the detection scheme only requires simple hash,and addition/subtraction operations at little overhead cost to mobile users.

When a new suspicious alarm (SA) is reported, the request detector analyzes the source IP distribution of SAs in the database. During a DoS attack, the request detector searches for irregularities of SAs in its database of *ACK* or *SYN* packets sent from victim vehicles.When SAs are reported from packets with the same vehicle's request IP within a short period, there is probably a DoS attack targeting the mobile host. However, each SA comes from a different vehicle request IP. To evaluate the distribution of the vehicle request IP of the SAs, a score is calculated as follows:

$$S = \sum\nolimits_{s \in IP_{list}} \left(\left| X_s \right| - 1 \right)^2 \tag{1}$$

where X_s stands for a subset of the IP list that contains reported SAs and S is the score value. All elements in X_s have the same IP values in a certain period. The score will increase when the number of SAs containing the same source vehicle IP increases. On the other hand, if each SA has a different source vehicle IP, the score will be 0. This score value can be an indicator of DoS attacks. To save computation when a new SA arrives, the following expression is used to calculate the score value:

$$S_c = \begin{cases} S_p + 2 \times \left| X_s \right| - 1 & S \ not \ in \ the \ history \ IP \ list \\ S_p & S \ in \ the \ history \ IP \ list \end{cases} \tag{2}$$

where S_c is the score of the current value and S_p is the score of the previous value. This equation describes the arrival of an SA whose source IP is not in the IP history list where upon the score remains unchanged; but if it is in the history list(s) the score is renewed and increased. As the score is the sum of $(|X_s|-1)^2$, the new score equals the previous score plus the current $(|X_s|-1)^2$. When the score exceeds a predefined threshold, the reported SAs with the IP of the victim are sent to the vehicle detector address. To the contrary, whenever a query is received from a vehicle detector, SAs with the server's IP in the client vehicle's detector database are returned.

Response Detector

The response detector is deployed at the protected master node. With the assistance of the vehicle's request detector, a master node, as the response detector, can detect a 0 forthcoming DoS attack at an early stage. The components operate independently but concurrently and issue a confirmed DoS attack alarm. Since this confirmation has no negative effect on the protected master node, the master node can perform a query as soon as any suspicious vehicle request connections are observed. This is a distinct advantage over many other DoS detection methods (Lin, X. et al., 2007 & Ramakrishnan, B. et al., 2010), which must wait to capture sufficient DoS attack evidence before taking further action; a requirement that delays DoS attack detection (Kaur, & Verma, 2012). In the proposed scheme, cooperation between the vehicle request and vehicle response detectors ensures that the vehicle response detector launches DoS alarms at a very early stage.

The response detector scheme comprises two parts. Part one shows that the master node may passively wait for a potential DoS alarm from the vehicle request detector, which, when enough potential DoS attack alarms arrive, sends the master node a confirmed DoS attack alarm. Part two shows that the master node performs even more active detection by sending queries to the vehicle request detector when too many vehicle requests are observed. It is possible that request IPs of spoofed packets are so widely distributed that the number of SA's at the request detector is insufficient to provoke the sending of an SA to the master node. But in this scheme, the master node selects several cooperative request detectors to query the number of SA's. The selection of request detectors depends on the request vehicle's IP address connections as reserved by the master node. A query is first sent to a request detector in the routing domain containing the most pending connections. After receiving replies, the master node knows if the connection was caused by a spoofed DoS packet (in which case an alarm is sent) or whether it was caused by something else requiring no action.

A DoS attack can be detected based on the updated monitoring table. Since the list maintains the distance, energy, number of hops, packet delivery rate, and acceptance rate of every optimal node taken, then a random validation between the current node and the listed path is matched for any distance or energy variation expected threshold. If an error falls within an expected threshold, nodes along that route are assumed as 'legitimate', otherwise the entire route is penalized for a time instant t seconds. Random validation ensures greater longevity of routes and resources. If networks are found to be real emergency vehicles then the request information is sent to the master node, then emergency vehicles are found as new IP addresses and stored in the BF. However, if DoS attacks are found with any emergency vehicles, then the master node generates the same reference link for all malicious emergency vehicles.

Reference Broadcast Synchronization (RBS) Using IP-CHOCK for Prevention of DoS Attacks in VANET

Vehicular networks are typically deployed in unattended environments that are usually not trusted as all communications using wireless channels are subject to eavesdropping. Therefore, vehicular networks are easily breached by malicious adversaries. Every time synchronization protocols rely on a time-sensitive exchange message, adversaries can easily tamper with rely protocols with attacks. They may launch a message manipulation attack in which the attacker may drop, modify, or even forge time relay messages to mislead the time relay process; this is a reason why mobile channels are jammed by attackers, who then launch such DoS attacks. Hence, the DoS attacker may snoop messages and then jam the receiving synchronization messages at his/her discretion. Time synchronization in wireless communication is not only essential, but also grants administrators mechanisms that determine movement, location, and proximity (Chen, Hsu, & Yi, 2012). Time synchronization schemes embrace four major issues: sending time, access time, propagating time, and receiving time. Three existing synchronization protocols, namely:

1. Reference Broadcast Synchronization (RBS);
2. Timing-sync Protocol for Sensor Networks; and
3. Flooding Time Synchronization Protocol are presently available (Defrawy, & Tsudik, 2009).

Most protocols utilize sender-receiver synchronization in which the sender imprints the timestamp and the receiver coordinates, accordingly; unlike RBS, which uses receiver to receiver synchronization. This study's proposition is for an arbiter to relay a signal to all receivers, one that holds no time data. Instead, receivers will contrast respective clock settings to compute relative phase offsets. The timing is, of course, completely based on when the node receives the reference beacon.

The recent growth and popularity of VANET and its use in numerous settings has provoked new scenarios where greater security is highly valued. This is mainly due to VANET's increasingly important roles in various infrastructure-less environments and applications; even more so in exceptionally critical settings such as vehicular and emergency rescue as well as military and law enforcement venues. Positioning data has lately become increasingly available through smaller and less expensive Global Positioning System (GPS) receivers (Kopetz & Ochsenreiter, 1987; Sundararaman, Buy, & Kshemkalyani, 2005). This was partially encouraged by the emerging incorporation of location-sensing in personal handheld and other wireless devices (Kopetz, & Ochsenreiter, 2012). A natural step, therefore, was to adapt such location-based operations to VANET, where devices were equipped with location-sensing capabilities. Nevertheless, although these relied on location data for operations, they proved insufficient (Ma, Wilson, & Trivedi, 2012). Furthermore, accurate proximity data is essential to secure both applications and basic networking functions; e.g., the prevention of DoS attacks or secure localization, both of which require efficient, reliable, and secure verification of distances between nodes. These and other security and privacy challenges in VANET remain largely unresolved due to node mobility and the dynamic infrastructure of a network that is not secure and is open to offensive intrusions. A diversity of attackers uses different approaches and performs illegal maneuvers to disturb the service of VANET. From an informed security perspective, secured communication by means of a new scheme with *RBS using IP-CHOCK* is proposed. This combined method employs clock synchronization with the Reference Broadcast system. The process generates a communication link for all mobile nodes through the clock maintenance service. The IP-CHOCK point works like a firewall for packet filtering purposes in addition to the master node, which is transformed to a central control device. This model is able to locate malicious nodes without the requirements of any secret information exchange and special hardware support. The detection rate also increases when optimal numbers of nodes are forged by the attackers. It also deals in the field of DoS attack and prevention used cryptography technique and puzzle for the prevention of DoS attack.

The fundamental property of RBS is that a broadcast message is used to synchronize a set of receivers with each other. Doing so eliminates both sending and access time from the critical path; as these parameters are typically the greatest source of error and largest contributors to latent non-determinism. In addition, the minimized operating system modification that reads a clock interrupt at reception time is optimized. Therefore the critical path length in RBS only includes the time from the injection of the packet into the channel to the last clock's reading it. RBS is only sensitive to the difference in the propagation time between a pair of receivers.

In this method, a RBS using IP-CHOCK (master filter) sent by the node is called the reference node. And those nodes accepting the joint query from the reference node generate tokens with the help of the IP-CHOCK. This IP-CHOCK is a combined model of the well-known RBS (reference broadcast method) and clock synchronization. In addition, it uses symmetric key cryptography for data privacy. Basically, IP-CHOCK works as a packet filter because the current trend is DoS assault by the flooding of packets. These packets are either UDP or TCP. Such flooding blocks the communication bandwidth and jams the network without generating other interference or jamming attacks. Hence, a strong filter was designed for the *unknown* control request packet at a point in time marking the node's mobility. With this model, the system generates a link that correlates a mobile node with its respective speed as all nodes connect to the master node. Basically, the master node becomes an IP-CHOCK control section and maintains all links from the mobile node.

The vector value is a bit value in the IP-CHOCK filter of the proposed model. This value shows the attack variation in a network. Initially, the vector value is 0 and the change in the reference node reaction value is 0. The frequency of 0 and 1 is counted. The behavior of the mobile node in VANET is measured. The link for synchronization is provided by the clock. The clock maintains network capability for all nodes during communications. If an unknown mobile node sends a request to any node and that node does not reply, the reference node transfers that message to the IP-CHOCK section. The IP-CHOCK scans the packet to discover if it is normal or abnormal. If the latter, the chock takes action to block it and also generates a security alarm sent to all nodes

RESULTS

Based on the developed system's model, simulations using NS-2.34 evaluated the performance of the combined model under normal and random traffic, as well as reference nodes and without reference nodes, AODV performance. The following discussion concerns details of the simulation parameters and results.

Detection Efficiency for the Traffic Density and Request Density Functions

In this simulation, detection efficiency for traffic density was measured in terms of percentage (%) by varying the number of attacks from 0 to 35%. Figure 3 shows increases in traffic loads (i.e., the number of vehicles within communication range). Detection efficiency was minimally varied with less than the maximum allowable end-to-end message transmission latency of 0 to 100 m/s.

Moreover, the message false positive rate decreased as the traffic load increased. The detection rate is as high as 60% when the detection load increased by 100%. However, such traffic flow can only be simulated for a severe traffic jam according to relationships between:

1.   Communication range;
2.   Inter-vehicle distances; and
3.   Attack vehicles.

In this situation, it is acceptable if a large number of messages are lost as most are repeatedly sent by attack vehicles.

Figure 3. Detection of response for traffic density and false positives

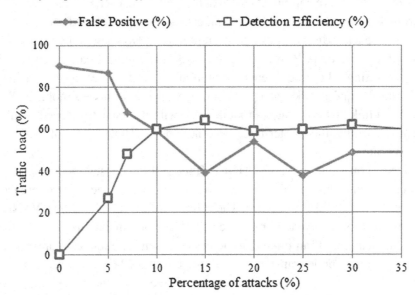

Normal traffic load occurred when the load was less than 50 where a 35% false positive rate was observed. Table 3 summarizes the finding from this detection performance of the combined model.

Table 3. Detection performance of the combined model

Number of New IP Addresses	Detection Efficiency (%)	Detection Time (Seconds)
15	89.79	0.923
18	91.0	0.675
40	92.23	0.546
60	93.32	0.187
200	93.65	0.125

In this simulated the detection rate was measured in terms of percentages (%) by varying the number of attackers from 0% to 5%. Figure 4 shows comparative results from running the proposed scheme's Bloom-filter vs. the modified Bloom-filter.

Simulation results in Figures 5 shows that with an increased traffic load (i.e., the number of vehicles within communication range), the detection efficiency varied only minimally and was less than the maximum allowable message end-to-end transmission latency of 0 to 80m/s. Furthermore, the false positive rate decreased as the traffic load increased. Compared to the false postive rate for the Bloom-filter under different traffic conditions (street and highway) and AODV, the FPR also decreased.

Figure 4. Comparison between proposed and modified Bloom-filter

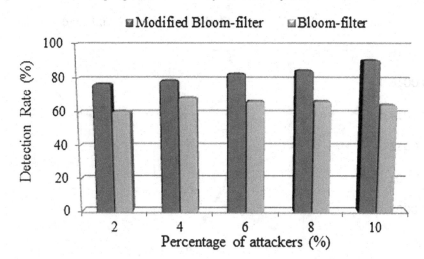

Figure 5. False positive rate vs. load factor

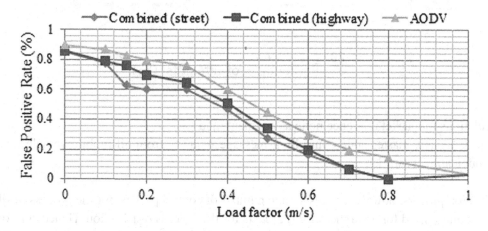

The gap in the detection rates between the proposed and improved Bloom-filter was 89%, and the gap in the detection rate between the proposed and improved Bloom-filter was 64%.

In this simulated, the measurement of the error rate for the three models with varying number of attempts (0-100) is done Figure 6. The error rate AODV model was increases and BF and proposed (combined) was decreases as the number of attempts increases.

FUTURE RESEARCH DIRECTIONS

This section briefly discusses the future directions of the Combined (IP-CHOCK Reference) detection and prevention of the DoS attacks in VANET. The following are a few interesting research directions where work presented in this thesis can be extended in the future. The diversity of network and service oriented attacks in VANET examined by this research worked via:

Figure 6. Error rate vs. percentage of attempts

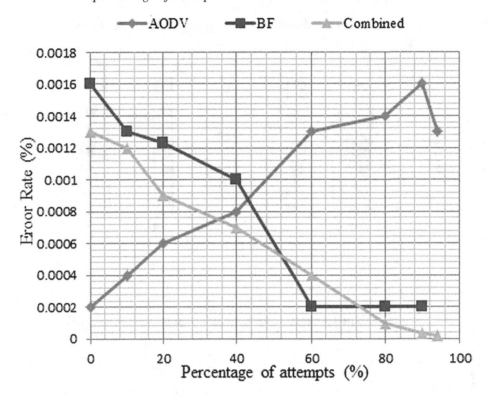

1. Calculations for packet reference node assignment; and
2. The process as a master node controlling message requests from all mobile vehicle nodes in a communicating network.

The filtration process, however, stores a huge number of control packets for the process of filtration and there remains a need for extra memory segments for the process of filtration. Hence, an expansion of this work and optimization of the process of reference node allocation and reduction would involve memory capacity to extend the filtration process.

CONCLUSION

This work has achieved a combined approach of detection and prevention of DoS attacks in a VANET system utilizing two approaches, namely: the Bloom-filter-based IP-CHOCK detection (BFICK), and the Reference Broadcast Synchronization (RBS) using IP-CHOCK for VANET.

As safety is the primary concern for drivers, critical life-saving messages must be transmitted from node to node in a reliable and timely manner. After analyzing various management of VANET, it is a challenging task to count nodes for corresponding locations by changing bits of the bit vector. Due to vehicular mobility in an open channel area, it requests other vehicles to give way it or nearby OBUs for changing traffic lights. The work has targeted on the filtration processes which suffer from bit changing in incoming and outgoing packets. To achieve this, secure communications and network availability must be established during the VANET set-up. IP sniffing will cause to support in the design of VANETs on the UDP suite. Moreover, IP spoofing helps to exploit the characteristics of UDP/IP. The detection DoS attacks during their early stages, the BFICK scheme has been conceived comprising request and response (OTS and OFS) algorithms. An IP-CHOCK method has been applied to detect abrupt changes in vehicle traffic characteristics that correspond with the incidence of flooding attacks. The adopted method uses the Bloom-filter as a detection process, which is suitable for small and large scale DoS attacks. BFICK using IP-CHOCK makes it possible to capture abnormal connections even when the volume of the traffic is large. It also avoids traffic collision within a fixed space efficient data structure and also provided very low rate for false positives rate. The produced results also demonstrate that BFICK detection of DoS attacks is efficient in the large traffic flow. The Reference Broadcast Synchronization using IP-CHOCK prevention model of DoS attacks in VANET has been proposed. The proposed RBS using IP-CHOCK model consists of clock and reference synchronization components, filters the packets on the behalf of the traffic statistics of filtering rules. The receiver used to receive message from another receiver with the help of broadcasting, which is being executed before the broadcast. To achieve the secure end-to-end synchronization, each node (vehicle) in the network examines every path it uses to reach the other nodes in search of misbehaving links:

1. Link to link checking,
2. Neighborhood checks,
3. Network consistency check,
4. Admissibility of network inconsistencies.

When a misbehaving link has found, its usage is discontinued. The IP-CHOCK works as packet filtering process in addition to the master node which is transformed to a central control device.

REFERENCES

Amadeo, M., Campolo, C., & Molinaro, A. (2013). Enhancing content-centric networking for vehicular environments. *Computer Networks*, *57*(16), 3222–3234. doi:10.1016/j.comnet.2013.07.005

Antolino Rivas, D., Barceló-Ordinas, J. M., Guerrero Zapata, M., & Morillo-Pozo, J. D. (2011). Security on VANETs: Privacy, misbehaving nodes, false information and secure data aggregation. *Journal of Network and Computer Applications*, *34*(6), 1942–1955. doi:10.1016/j.jnca.2011.07.006

Aslam, B., Park, S., Zou, C. C., & Turgut, D. (2010). Secure traffic data propagation in vehicular ad hoc networks. *International Journal of Ad Hoc and Ubiquitous Computing*, *6*(1), 24–39. doi:10.1504/IJAHUC.2010.033823

Biswas, S., Mi˘sic, J., & Mi˘sic, V. (2012). *DDoS attack on WAVE-enabled VANET through synchronization.* Paper presented at the Global Communications Conference (GLOBECOM). 10.1109/GLOCOM.2012.6503256

Bloom, B. H. (1970). Space/time trade-offs in hash coding with allowable errors. *Communications of the ACM*, *13*(7), 422–426. doi:10.1145/362686.362692

Bregni, S. (1997). Clock stability characterization and measurement in telecommunications. *Instrumentation and Measurement. IEEE Transactions on, 46*(6), 1284–1294.

Chen, Y., & Hwang, K. (2006). Collaborative detection and filtering of shrew DDoS attacks using spectral analysis. *Journal of Parallel and Distributed Computing, 66*(9), 1137–1151. doi:10.1016/j.jpdc.2006.04.007

Chen, Y.-S., Hsu, C.-S., & Yi, W.-H. (2012). An IP passing protocol for vehicular ad hoc networks with network fragmentation. *Computers & Mathematics with Applications (Oxford, England), 63*(2), 407–426. doi:10.1016/j.camwa.2011.07.062

Chen, Y.-Y., Wang, Y.-J., & Jan, J.-K. (2013). The design of speedy seamless safe messaging mechanism in VANET. *International Journal of Computer Mathematics, 90*(12), 2614–2630. doi:10.1080/00207160.2013.807916

Cheng, J., Yin, J., Wu, C., Zhang, B., & Liu, Y. (2009). *DDoS attack detection method based on linear prediction model. In Emerging Intelligent Computing Technology and Applications* (pp. 1004–1013). Springer. doi:10.1007/978-3-642-04070-2_106

El Defrawy, K., & Tsudik, G. (2008). *PRISM: Privacy-friendly routing in suspicious MANETs (and VANETs)*. Paper presented at the Network Protocols, 2008. ICNP 2008. IEEE International Conference on.

Geravand, S., & Ahmadi, M. (2013). Bloom filter applications in network security: A state-of-the-art survey. *Computer Networks, 57*(18), 4047–4064. doi:10.1016/j.comnet.2013.09.003

Gillani, S., Shahzad, F., Qayyum, A., & Mehmood, R. (2013). *A Survey on Security in Vehicular Ad Hoc Networks. In Communication Technologies for Vehicles* (pp. 59–74). Springer.

Hamieh, A., Ben-Othman, J., & Mokdad, L. (2009). *Detection of radio interference attacks in VANET.* Paper presented at the Global Telecommunications Conference. 10.1109/GLOCOM.2009.5425381

Isaac, J. T., Zeadally, S., & Cámara, J. S. (2010). Security attacks and solutions for vehicular ad hoc networks. *Communications, IET, 4*(7), 894–903. doi:10.1049/iet-com.2009.0191

Jingle, I. D. J., & Rajsingh, E. B. (2014). ColShield: An effective and collaborative protection shield for the detection and prevention of collaborative flooding of DDoS attacks in wireless mesh networks. *Human-centric Computing and Information Sciences, 4*(1), 1–19. doi:10.118613673-014-0008-8

Karagiannis, G., Altintas, O., Ekici, E., Heijenk, G., Jarupan, B., Lin, K., & Weil, T. (2011). Vehicular networking: A survey and tutorial on requirements, architectures, challenges, standards and solutions. *IEEE Communications Surveys and Tutorials, 13*(4), 584–616. doi:10.1109/SURV.2011.061411.00019

Kaur, T., & Verma, A. (2012). Simulation and Analysis of AODV routing protocol in VANETs. *International Journal of Soft Computing andEngineering (IJSCE). ISSN, 2231*, 2307.

Kopetz, H., & Ochsenreiter, W. (1987). Clock synchronization in distributed real-time systems. *Computers. IEEE Transactions on, 100*(8), 933–940.

Li, C.-T., Hwang, M.-S., & Chu, Y.-P. (2008). A secure and efficient communication scheme with authenticated key establishment and privacy preserving for vehicular ad hoc networks. *Computer Communications*, *31*(12), 2803–2814. doi:10.1016/j.comcom.2007.12.005

Lin, X., Sun, X., Ho, P.-H., & Shen, X. (2007). GSIS: A secure and privacy-preserving protocol for vehicular communications. *Vehicular Technology. IEEE Transactions on*, *56*(6), 3442–3456.

Liu, C., & Chigan, C. (2012). RPB-MD: Providing robust message dissemination for vehicular ad hoc networks. *Ad Hoc Networks*, *10*(3), 497–511. doi:10.1016/j.adhoc.2011.09.003

Liu, J. K., Yuen, T. H., Au, M. H., & Susilo, W. (2014). Improvements on an authentication scheme for vehicular sensor networks. *Expert Systems with Applications*, *41*(5), 2559–2564. doi:10.1016/j.eswa.2013.10.003

Lo, N.-W., & Tsai, H.-C. (2007). *Illusion attack on VANET applications-A message plausibility problem*. Paper presented at the Globecom Workshops. 10.1109/GLOCOMW.2007.4437823

Ma, X., Wilson, M., Yin, X., & Trivedi, K. S. (2013). *Performance of VANET safety message broadcast at rural intersections*. Paper presented at the Wireless Communications and Mobile Computing Conference (IWCMC), 2013 9th International. 10.1109/IWCMC.2013.6583798

Mishra, T., Garg, D., & Gore, M. M. (2011). *A publish/subscribe communication infrastructure for VANET applications*. Paper presented at the Advanced Information Networking and Applications (WAINA), 2011 IEEE Workshops of International Conference on.

Mohandas, B. K., & Liscano, R. (2008). *IP address configuration in VANET using centralized DHCP*. Paper presented at the Local Computer Networks, 2008. LCN 2008. 33rd IEEE Conference on. 10.1109/LCN.2008.4664252

Muraleedharan, R., & Osadciw, L. A. (2009). *Cognitive security protocol for sensor based VANET using swarm intelligence*. Paper presented at the Signals, Systems and Computers, 2009 Conference Record of the Forty-Third Asilomar Conference on. 10.1109/ACSSC.2009.5470101

Park, S., & Zou, C. C. (2008). *Reliable traffic information propagation in vehicular ad-hoc networks*. Paper presented at the Sarnoff Symposium. 10.1109/SARNOF.2008.4520100

Rahim, A., Ahmad, I., Khan, Z. S., Sher, M., Shoaib, M., Javed, A., & Mahmood, R. (2009). A Comparative Study of Mobile and Vehicular Adoc Networks. *International Journal of Recent Trends in Engineering*, *2*(4), 195–197.

Ramakrishnan, B., Rajesh, R., & Shaji, R. (2010). Performance analysis of 802.11 and 802.11 p in cluster based simple highway model. *International Journal of Scientific & Engineering Research*, *1*(5), 420–426.

Raya, M., & Hubaux, J.-P. (2007). Securing vehicular ad hoc networks. *Journal of Computer Security*, *15*(1), 39–68. doi:10.3233/JCS-2007-15103

Sarela, M., Rothenberg, C. E., Aura, T., Zahemszky, A., Nikander, P., & Ott, J. (2011). *Forwarding anomalies in Bloom filter-based multicast*. Paper presented at the INFOCOM. 10.1109/INFCOM.2011.5935060

Sichitiu, M. L., & Kihl, M. (2008). Inter-vehicle communication systems: A survey. *IEEE Communications Surveys and Tutorials*, *10*(2), 88–105. doi:10.1109/COMST.2008.4564481

Spaho, E., Ikeda, M., Barolli, L., Xhafa, F., Younas, M., & Takizawa, M. (2013). *Performance Evaluation of OLSR and AODV Protocols in a VANET Crossroad Scenario*. Paper presented at the Advanced Information Networking and Applications (AINA), 2013 IEEE 27th International Conference on. 10.1109/AINA.2013.111

Sumra, I. A., Hasbullah, H. B., Bin, J.-L., & Manan, A. (2013). Comparative study of security hardware modules (EDR, TPD and TPM) in VANET. *International Journal of Information*, *7*(5), 289–304.

Sundararaman, B., Buy, U., & Kshemkalyani, A. D. (2005). Clock synchronization for wireless sensor networks: A survey. *Ad Hoc Networks*, *3*(3), 281–323. doi:10.1016/j.adhoc.2005.01.002

Tang, D., Chen, K., Chen, X., Liu, H., & Li, X. (2014). Adaptive EWMA Method based on abnormal network traffic for LDoS attacks. *Mathematical Problems in Engineering*.

Tarkoma, S., Rothenberg, C. E., & Lagerspetz, E. (2012). Theory and Practice of Bloom Filters for Distributed Systems. *IEEE Communications Surveys and Tutorials*, *14*(1), 131–155. doi:10.1109/SURV.2011.031611.00024

Wang, H., Zhang, D., & Shin, K. G. (2004). Change-point monitoring for the detection of DoS attacks. *Dependable and Secure Computing. IEEE Transactions on*, *1*(4), 193–208.

Wang, J., & Yan, W. (2009). *RBM: a role based mobility model for VANET*. Paper presented at the Communications and Mobile Computing, 2009. CMC'09. WRI International Conference on. 10.1109/CMC.2009.36

Wu, B., Chen, J., Wu, J., & Cardei, M. (2007). A survey of attacks and countermeasures in mobile ad hoc networks *Wireless Network Security*, 103–135.

Xiong, H., Chen, Z., & Li, F. (2012). Efficient and multi-level privacy-preserving communication protocol for VANET. *Computers & Electrical Engineering*, *38*(3), 573–581. doi:10.1016/j.compeleceng.2011.11.009

Zeadally, S., Hunt, R., Chen, Y.-S., Irwin, A., & Hassan, A. (2012). Vehicular ad hoc networks (VANETS): Status, results, and challenges. *Telecommunication Systems*, *50*(4), 217–241. doi:10.100711235-010-9400-5

Zhang, G., Xu, Y., Wang, X., Tian, X., Liu, J., Gan, X. Y., ... Qian, L. (2012). Multicast capacity for VANETs with directional antenna and delay constraint. *Selected Areas in Communications. IEEE Journal on*, *30*(4), 818–833.

Zhang, Y., & Cao, G. (2011). V-PADA: Vehicle-platoon-aware data access in VANETs. *Vehicular Technology. IEEE Transactions on*, *60*(5), 2326–2339.

Zhao, J., Zhang, Y., & Cao, G. (2007). Data pouring and buffering on the road: A new data dissemination paradigm for vehicular ad hoc networks. *Vehicular Technology. IEEE Transactions on*, *56*(6), 3266–3277.

KEY TERMS AND DEFINITIONS

Bloom–Filter: Its structure offers a way to perform member queries that may result in false positives but never false negatives.

Clock Synchronization: It is extremely important for basic communication as it provides an ability to detect movement, location and proximity.

IP-Address: An Internet Protocol address (IP address) is a numerical label assigned to each device (e.g., computer, printer) participating in a computer network that uses the Internet Protocol for communication.

IP-CHOCK: IP-CHOCK is a monitoring, filtering, speedy detection, and defense against flooding and spoofing attacks. It is standard for network management activities and is commonly used to filter and monitor network equipment.

MANET: Mobile ad hoc network (MANET) is a continuously self-configuring, infrastructure-less network of mobile devices connected without wires. *Ad hoc* is Latin and means "for this" (i.e., for this purpose).

Reference Synchronization: It is that a broadcast message is used to synchronize a set of receivers with each other.

RSU: An RSU is a grant valued in terms of company stock, but company stock is not issued at the time of the grant. After the recipient of a unit satisfies the vesting requirement, the company distributes shares or the cash equivalent of the number of shares used to value the unit.

UDP: It is a transport layer protocol defined for use with the IP network layer protocol. It is defined by RFC 768 written by John Postel. It provides a best-effort datagram service to an End System (IP host).

VANET: Vehicular Ad Hoc Networks (VANETs) are created by applying the principles of mobile ad hoc networks (MANETs) - the spontaneous creation of a wireless network for data exchange - to the domain of vehicles.

WAVE: It is protocol stack is designed to provide multi-channel operation (even for vehicles equipped with only a single radio), security, and lightweight application layer protocols.

This research was previously published in the Handbook of Research on Advanced Trends in Microwave and Communication Engineering edited by Ahmed El Oualkadi and Jamal Zbitou; pages 398-420, copyright year 2017 by Information Science Reference (an imprint of IGI Global).

Chapter 31
A Detailed Study on Security Concerns of VANET and Cognitive Radio VANETs

M. Manikandakumar
(iD) https://orcid.org/0000-0003-2648-7139
Thiagarajar College of Engineering, India

Sri Subarnaa D. K.
Thiagarajar College of Engineering, India

Monica Grace R.
Thiagarajar College of Engineering, India

ABSTRACT

Wireless ad hoc networks are dynamic networks in which nodes can move freely in the network. A new type of Vehicular Ad Hoc Network (VANET) that allows smart transport system to provide road security and reduces traffic jams through automobile-to-automobile and automobile-to-roadside communication. In this, vehicles rely on the integrity of received data for deciding when to present alerts to drivers. Because of wireless network the VANET messages are vulnerable to many attacks and the security concerns are also major issues. So, with respect to these methods, this article will discuss the Denial of Service (DoS) attack, masquerading, and their vulnerabilities. Also, it classifies the securities and their prevention mechanisms in overcoming these security issues in VANET and Cognitive Radio VANET perspectives.

INTRODUCTION

Nowadays VANET are the most important and upcoming recent technology which allow many vehicles to communicate with each other with in a network. In common, a VANET is formed from a number of vehicles which are in the same road to form ad-hoc network. In the presence of these networks will create the way for a wide range of applications such as travelling safely, mobility and connectivity for both

DOI: 10.4018/978-1-7998-5348-0.ch031

driver and passengers to exploit the transport systems in a smoothly, efficiently and safer way. There are three most common component in VANET they are onboard unit (OBU), Road side unit (RSU) and Application unit (AU) for communication among vehicles. And it is the challenging research area to provide an Intelligent Transportation System (ITS) services to every user in the network. Every vehicle with in that network will be installing (OBU), which will integrate the respective vehicles where the micro-sensors, embedded systems, wireless communications, and Global Positioning System (GPS) would be there in the vehicle (Al-Sultan et al., 2014; Jiang et al., 2006). In this VANET the Cognitive Radio (CR) is introduced and it is used as extended application in wireless communications. This Cognitive radio verifies the availability of electromagnetic spectrum and permits the waves for the transmission parameter. Here the communication takes places in open air medium. Wireless networks lack the complexities of infrastructure setup and administration, enabling devices to create and join networks "on the fly" – anywhere, anytime. A wireless ad hoc network is a type of computer-to-computer connection. In ad hoc mode, one can set up a wireless connection directly to another computer without having to connect to a Wi-Fi access point or router.

COMPONENTS

On Board Unit (OBU)

This OBU is the central processing power where the vehicular node is installed in vehicle. This unit can contain a variety of devices that are used for communication and information processing like:

- A processor that are processing the application to obtain the communication protocols.
- A wireless transceiver is used to transmit and receive data among itself, other vehicles and with road side units.
- A GPS is used here for viewing the vehicles location.
- A set of sensors is used to measure various parameters which can then be processed in a distributed network. Special sensors can also be used to measure driver's mental status.
- Network interfaces used for VANET are IEEE 802.11p card and other networks like Bluetooth and infrared for communication.

Mode of Operation

Once the data has been entered, the vehicle gets activated for automatic system by comparing the GPS signal and information from positioning sensors with the motor network information, the OBU automatically detects whether the vehicle is on a route segment, and determines which segments are used. Based on the route and vehicle data that has been saved automatically, OBU can calculate the toll charges, saves this information, and transmit it through radio signal (GSM) to the computing center.

Application Unit (AU)

The application layer of the network is intended to provide a safety measures and non-safety applications. AU is a device with input output interfaces like monitor, keypad, headphone jack, USB port etc

(Anandakumar, Umamaheswari, & Arulmurugan, 2018). The AU is connected by either wired connection or wirelessly connected to OBU.

Road Side Unit (RSU)

This RSU is fixed device located on road side that helps in maintaining the network. It is also equipped with network interfaces like IEEE 802.11p. IEEE 802.11p is a standard to add wireless access in vehicular environments (WAVE), a vehicular communication system. This RSU requires a support Intelligent Transportation Systems (ITS) applications. This RSU includes data exchange between high-speed vehicles and the vehicles on the roadside infrastructure, so it is called as V2X communication. The RSU also facilitates the routing mechanism. The RSU receives the information and provide a warning message to the drivers about the accidents occurred in some area.

VANET

VANETs deal with movement of nodes. There are different types of VANET communications exist. Here a vehicle can contact another vehicle, known as Vehicle-to-Vehicle (V2V) communication. These vehicles can also transmit the information with roadside infrastructures, known as Vehicle to Infrastructure (V2I) communication. The road-side infrastructures at the roadside communicate with one another. Communication in VANET is a challenging fact due to its faster mobility. VANET has been classified into two categories and the one is comfort applications and other is safety related applications (Haldorai & Ramu, 2018).

COMFORT APPLICATIONS

The main objective of comfort applications is to improve the passenger comfort and traffic efficiency. These applications can be included in Value Added Services (VASs) which can be used by VANET. Passengers in a vehicle for a long period would be interested to use some applications from vehicular networks. Some of the applications are as follows:

- **Automatic Toll Collection:** By using this type of service, payment is done through automatic process. So, the vehicle does not need to stop to pay the fees.
- **Location Based Applications:** Information about the location of restaurants, shopping malls, ATMs, Gas and filling stations etc., can be uploaded to the vehicles. Vehicles can exchange this information through vehicular network to facilitate travelling.
- **Internet Connectivity:** Vehicle passengers can access the Internet to send or receive emails using internet. Distributing this information using vehicular networks reduces the cost of infrastructure installation along roadside.
- **Entertainment applications:** Movies, songs, games, etc., can be shared among vehicles using VANET Where one or more vehicles can store those data.
- **Safety Applications:** It aims to save human lives on the roads. The feature of these safety applications is to deliver the safety related data to the actual receiver in time. Safety related applications are as follows:

- **Assistance Messages (AM):** These messages include cooperative collision avoidance (CCA), navigating and lane switching messages. Preventing collisions is the main goal of CCA. If there is a possibility of a collision among the vehicles nearby, these applications will trigger automatically to warn the driver to steer the vehicle or reduce the speed, thereby avoiding possible collision(s). Vehicles detecting an accident may start sending messages to other vehicles so that others may take a detour.
- **Warning Messages (WMs):** Some of the basic examples of WMs are obstacle, post-crash, toll point or road condition warnings; stop light ahead in a highway. Vehicles may start transmitting WMs to other vehicles in a certain zone after sensing it, thereby helping other subsequent vehicles reducing their speed to avoid accidents.
- **Information Messages (IMs):** Some of the basic examples of Information Messages are speed limit, work zone information in the highway, toll point ahead.

COGNITIVE RADIO (CR)

Cognitive radio will extend the spectral efficiency, with the available frequencies in a region. This CR monitors the available spectrum and when a spectral is identified it adapts the transceiver to operate in the same frequency channel when frequency is not occupied by users or even when the interference levels do not harm other users. This Spectrum will allow the users to classify as Primary Users (PU) or Licensed users else Secondary Users (SU) or Cognitive Users. Licensed users are authorized users those operate in a specific frequency band, while the secondary users do not have a permission to transmit and receive the frequency bands. Cognitive user should monitor the frequency spectrum to find out if there is any authorized user occupying the spectrum or if there is a spectral opportunity. Cognitive users verify the presence and absence of spectrum holes via spectrum sensing. Spectrum holes are defined as temporarily non-used spectrum bands that can be accessed by cognitive users. If a band is available, the cognitive user can opportunistically use that channel, although the priority will be given to authorized user if they are present, then the CR will not be allowed to benefit from that frequency band. Spectrum Sensing (SS) is fundamental in a cognitive radio network. Higher bandwidth and lower error rates in the transmission can be observed with the monitoring of channel occupancy. Different spectrum sensing techniques can be adopted by cognitive networks. There are some techniques which is used to improve spectral detection and they are Energy Detection Matched Filtering detection. Also, the combination of two or more spectrum sensing techniques sometimes referred as hybrid sensing is a new approach in recent researches. New applications in different scenarios are arising grace to cognitive radio. Some of the major applications of CR are:

- TV white spaces and regulation
- Smart grids
- Wireless sensor networks (WSN)
- Public safety and medical networks
- Power line communications
- Vehicular networks

COGNITIVE RADIO VEHICULAR AD HOC NETWORKS (CRVs)

Recently, almost all automatic vehicles are investing the dangers and traffic in road side and providing an infotainment solutions and new alternatives to drivers and passengers. Internet access or Bluetooth connections inside cars are already suffering interferences in heavy-traffic roads. So that this Cognitive radio has been introduced and inserted to vehicular communication. Cognitive radio for vehicular Ad hoc Networks (CRVs or CRVANETs) led the cars to monitor the available frequency bands and provide an opportunistically to operate only on these specified frequencies. CRVs can improve the throughput; also, these CR-VANETs enable more users to operate in high user density scenarios (Anandakumar & Umamaheswari, 2018).

Spectrum users are classified as primary users (Licensed) users or secondary user (Cognitive) users. Licensed users are authorized user that they can operate in a specific frequency band, while secondary users do not have a permission to transmit and receive in that frequency bands. Cognitive user should monitor the frequency spectrum to find out if there is any licensed user occupying the spectrum or if there is a spectral opportunity.

Spectrum sensing properly detect the presence or absence of PUs or SUs in a specific frequency band; this optimizes the usage of spectrum holes opportunistic. Spectrum sensing schemes are classified as:

- Per-vehicle sensing
- Spectrum database techniques
- Cooperation

In per-vehicle sensing method each car will performs the spectrum sensing mechanism automatically and be independent from others. The spectrum sensing is performed with traditional SS strategies as cyclostationary detection, matched filter, and energy detection. Spectrum database techniques are used to establish a centralized database for collecting the information from all PUs operating in a geographic region. This centralized database can reduce the limitations of observing the per-vehicle sensing, however the control of this database is complex and expensive. Based on the CR concept, the information collected from all vehicles are forwarded to a fusion center and transmitted to all users within the central node range.

Security Attacks in VANET

Security and privacy issues are most effective design for implementation of CR enabled VANETs due to potential threats like traffic flow, malicious attacks, or sending fake message by using the authorized user ID by which it leads to a traffic disruption and some accidents. This VANET provide a wireless access to random vehicles for transforming the information on the road sides, where else this CRNs enable an efficient sharing of available spectrum bandwidth between the random vehicles. Hence, guaranteeing security, privacy, anonymity, and liability in CR assisted vehicular networks. Due to open wireless nature of communication various security threats and attacks occurs in VANET network and disrupts the services provided. The attacks on VANET network in the different layer is presented and focused mainly on network layer attack, especially Denial of Service (DoS) attack.

The requirements for security in VANET are:

Authentication

Authentication is a process in which the credentials provided are compared to those on file in a database of authorized users' information on a local operating system or within an authentication server. Since the large volume of vehicular data has transmitted and need to be processed in big data environment, security of big vehicular data is essential (Manikandakumar & Ramanujam, 2018). If the credentials match, the process is completed, and the user is granted authorization for access. The permissions and folders returned define both the environment the user sees and the way he can interact with it, including hours of access and other rights such as the amount of allocated storage space. The process of granting an administrator rights and the process of checking user account for access specific resources are referred to as authorization. The privileges and preferences granted for the authorized account depend on the user's permissions, which are either stored locally or on the authentication server. The settings defined for all these environment variables are set by an administrator.

Integrity

It involves maintaining the consistency, accuracy, and trust worthiness of data over its entire life cycle. Data must not be changed in transit, and steps must be taken to ensure that data cannot be altered by unauthorized people. These measures include user access controls and file permissions. Version control is used to prevent accidental deletion or erroneous changes by authorized users becoming a problem. As with data confidentiality, cryptography plays a very major role in ensuring data integrity. The most commonly used methods are to protect the data integrity which includes hashing the data you receive and comparing it with the hash of the original message. However, this means that the hash of the original data must be provided to you in a secure fashion.

Confidentiality

The confidentiality ensures that no unauthorized gain of information is possible. Requirements regarding confidentiality are application specific in a VANET. It ensures that sensitive information is accessed only by an authorized person and kept away from those not authorized to possess them. It is implemented using security mechanisms such as access control lists (ACLs), usernames, passwords, and encryption method. It is also common for information to be categorized according to the extent of damage that could be done should it fall into unintended hands. Security measures can then be implemented accordingly.

Non-Repudiation

Non-repudiation is the assurance that someone cannot deny something. Typically, non-repudiation refers to the ability to ensure that a party to a contract or a communication cannot deny the authenticity of their signature on a document or the sending of a message that they originated. The email non-repudiation process which involves email tracking mechanism which is designed to ensure that the sender cannot deny having sent a message and/or that the recipient cannot deny having received it.

Possible Attacks in VANET

For a secured transformation of messages, a dissemination protocol has to provide cognitive security solution for a secure communication in vehicular networks through the usage of distributed sensor technology. This distributed sensor technology helps us to guarantee high reliability and priorities an efficient QoS, robustness against denial of service (DoS) security attacks, and the prevention of data aging. In general, wireless access in vehicular network like other wireless networks is highly vulnerable to both DoS and distributed DoS security attacks, such as radio jamming attack.

Then some of the possible attacks are:

Masquerade Attacks

A masquerade attack is a attack on network side which uses a fake identity, this false network identity will work as an authorized user to access their personal computer to gain information through legitimate access identification. If an authentication process is not fully protected, it will become extremely vulnerable to a masquerade attack. These attacks can be perpetrated using stolen passwords and logons, by locating gaps in programs, or by finding a way around the authentication process. These attacks can be triggered either by employees within the organization or by an outsider if the organization is connected to a public network. The amount of masquerade attackers will depend on the level of authorization that they have managed to attain. It allows one machine to act on behalf of other machines. That is one machine can pretend to be another and can misuse the information obtained via conversation. The problem of masquerading is also eliminated in our proposed algorithm by mutual authentication. As such, masquerade attackers can have a full smorgasbord of cybercrime opportunities if they've gained the highest access authority to a business organization. Personal attacks, although less common, can also be harmful.

DoS Attack

Due to the wireless medium in VANET, there are a number of possible DoS attacks will occur in VANET. Hence, there will be many chances for high attacks. The purpose of the denial of service attack is to create a problem for legitimate users, and as a result the user cannot access the services. Some of the DOS attacks are.

Sybil Attack

The Sybil attack is an attack where reputation system is subverted by forging identities in peer-to-peer networks. A Sybil attack happens when an insecure computer is hijacked to claim multiple identities. A Sybil attack is a type of network attack where the multiple nodes are controlled by single adversary Avoiding Sybil attacks is a difficult problem. In centralized systems they are typically avoided through heuristics that do not provide cryptographic assurance of Sybil resilience. In a Sybil attack, the attacker subverts the reputation system of a peer-to-peer network by creating a large number of pseudonymous identities, using them to gain a disproportionately large influence (Hasbullah, & Soomro, 2010). For example, in a centralized entity every time it will try to avoid this Sybil attacks by requiring an individual IP, but it cannot create to more user with a specific number for every user account in a given time interval.

Node Impersonation

It is an attempt by a node to send a modified version of a message received from the real originator for the wrong purpose and claim the message has come from the originator. In order to overcome these types of problems, a unique identifier is assigned to each vehicle node in VANET, which will be used to verify from where the message is originating (Hasbullah & Soomro, 2010).

Sending False Information

It is type of attack where it produces a wrong or fake information to the user which was purposely sent by a node to other nodes in the network to create a chaos traffic scenario, which it may lead to misinterpretation of the actual situation. With the falsified information, the users would likely to leave the road, thus it makes the road free for the attacker to use it for their own purposes (Hasbullah, & Soomro, 2010).

Impersonate

This attack happens when the adversaries pretend to be authenticated vehicles or RSUs. The adversaries use the legitimate identities they hacked into to insert malicious information in the network, which would not only fool other vehicles but also make the innocent drivers whose identities were taken be removed from the network and denied service.

Hardware Tampering

This attack happens when the sensors, other onboard hardware RSUs are manipulated by adversaries. For example, an adversary can relocate a tampered RSU to launch a malicious attack, such as tampering the traffic lights to always be green when the malicious attack is approaching an intersection.

Black Hole Attack

In this Black hole attack, data packets may get lost while travelling through the Black Hole because it does not have any nodes, so it refuses to transmit data packets to the next destination.

Deception

Some vehicles may pretend to another by its movement. For example, a private car may pretend itself as an emergency vehicle to clear the congestion ahead, thereby making its movement faster.

Malware and Spam

These types of attacks are caused by malicious insider nodes of the network rather than outsider. The attack is performed when the software is getting updated for both OBUs and RSUs. These attacks can be mitigated by centralized administration.

Timing Attack

One of the basic requirements of VANET is to broadcast VANET security messages at the right time and at right place. When a malicious car receives an emergency message, it may delay the forwarding and transmission of message. The neighboring vehicles don't receive the message at the proper time. In order to avoid a dangerous situation a malicious car receives a message "accident ahead" from neighbor but it doesn't transmit the message immediately.

Global Positioning System (GPS) Spoofing

Identifying the location based on the location table is carried out by the GPS satellites with the help of that uniqueness of the vehicle and geographic location in the network is found. A malicious vehicle may alter the information in the location table to some other random location. In that case, a vehicle will decide to think that it is in a different position by reading the false information, due to that there will be accidents to the vehicle. An attacker can also use a GPS simulator to produce signals stronger than the original satellite. Initially the attacks will take place on GPS receivers concentrated on GPS jamming to simply ban receivers from location information and acquiring time. A more powerful attack is given by GPS spoofing. This kind of attack allows the attacker to manipulate the received GPS signal inside the attacked area in an arbitrary way. Thus, receivers report time and location information as controlled by the attacker. An attacker can easily empower the original GPS signal, when it arrives at the earth surface with very low power i.e., about 10-20 dB below the receiver's noise floor. Thereby, GPS receivers of attacked ITS-S will synchronize to the spoofed time signal. Studies on countermeasures to GPS spoofing concentrate on detection of the attack. Thereby, usage of antennas or multi-antenna systems with well-known micro movement has been suggested. Both the systems are currently not used in the automotive domain. Instead, a fixed single antenna is typically used in vehicles. And the usage of the detection systems would significantly increase the costs of on VANET deployment as every ITS-S has to be equipped with them. And the use of classical GPS spoofing detection on the physical layer, by using a multi antenna system, with trustworthiness model on higher layers. This model is based in the fact that a smart grid can be controlled by a central entity VANET.

PREVENTION MEASURES OF DOS ATTACK IN VANET CRYPTOGRAPHIC SOLUTIONS

ECDSA (Elliptic Curve Digital Signature Algorithm)

In authentication process the VANET messages uses the public key cryptography (i.e) it uses both the private and public keys is achieved. This technique generates digital signatures for messages using elliptic curve parameters and sends the message along with digital signature and certificate issued by the central authority. This ECDSA achieves broadcast authentication and non-repudiation in VANET with computational overhead on the OBU and also it has to verify one ECDSA signature the OBU which lead to computational identify for computation-based DoS under highly dense VANET environment.

TESLA (Timed Efficient Stream Loss-Tolerant Authentication)

In TESLA it authenticates messages through symmetric key cryptography. The source authentication, it uses one-way hash chains with key and provide a source and destination time that are synchronized. To generate one-way hash chain, selects a random number An, apply hash to get a previous value An-1, repeatedly apply hash to get new values up to A0. To authenticate a message m in the time t_i, it uses hash a_i to create MAC (m), send it along with the message to the receiver. The receiver buffers the message along with the MAC until the key is communicate with each other. After some duration of time (d), the source will send the key, which the receiver uses to verify the message it buffered. TESLA achieves an coherent authentication with low communication and computation overhead since it uses hashing and single key cryptography.

FastAuth and SelAuth

This prevention mechanism defines another two efficient broadcast authentication techniques as a countermeasure for signature flooding. Fast Authentication (FastAuth), secures single-hop beam messages by predicting the future beam messages using chained Huffman hash trees, which is used to generate one-time signature scheme which is 50 times faster and generation time is 20 times faster than ECDSA. Selective Authentication (SelAuth), this also secures the multi-hop messages. It provides fast isolation of malicious vehicles due to which invalid signatures are constrained to a small area without impacting the whole network and uses forwarder identification mechanism to distinguish between original and misbehaving vehicles.

ID-Based Cryptography

By implementing this ID-based cryptography the computing cost is reduced. ID-based cryptography will make use of online/offline signature (IBOOS) scheme for verification purpose. Online process is performed during V2V communications among the vehicles. Offline method is performed first in the vehicles or in the RSUs. IBOOS is a best method for Verification process than IBS. Using IBS and IBOOS proposed an ID-based scheme. This scheme does not provide a vehicle privacy using real-world IDs rather it uses self-constructed pseudonyms. In this approach, IBOOS is used during V2V authentications and IBS is used for V2I authentication. This approach will provide the privacy of VANET in an efficiently manner.

Symmetric and Hybrid Methods

In symmetric and hybrid methods, vehicles can contact each other when they both share a secret key. Security methods use either symmetric key or public key. Recently a new method is proposed which uses both symmetric key and public key. This method is known as hybrid system. Two types of communications are used in this approach: group communication and pair wise communication. The key pair is used to reduce overhead; symmetric key is used for pair wise communication in hybrid system.

Certificate Revocation Methods

This certificate revocation will invalidate the association of a vehicle by using centralized and decentralized certification process. In centralized system certificate authority (CA) will start revocation. In decentralized approach, revocation decision is taken by the neighboring vehicles. CA transmits messages to the RSU when an invalid certificate is detected. When vehicles get the message from RSU, then the vehicles will cancel that certificate and no longer communicate with it.

Ant-Colony Optimization

In an Ant-Colony Optimization (ACO) algorithm is proposed to provide an efficient, optimized and secure technique for securing routing process by isolating the malicious attacker in the path to the destination. It defends against a Blackhole attack, a form of DoS attack, ACO based routing algorithm creates the path with trust and pheromone value, to detect the malicious node. The main goal is to maintain the maximum lifetime of network, during data transmission in an efficient manner. The node with low trust and pheromone value are identified as malicious and any route through the node is cancelled. This ACO is one of the bio-inspired mechanisms. ACO is a dynamic and reliable protocol. It provides data gathering structure and aware-of-energy in wireless network. It can avoid network congestion and fast consumption of energy of individual node. Then it can prolong the life cycle of the whole network. ACO algorithm reduces the energy consumption. It optimizes the routing paths, and provides an effective multi-path data transmission structure to obtain a reliable communications in the case of fault node.

Applications

The main objectives of VANETs and CR-VANETs are public safety. The primary concern is the improvement of safety for drivers and passengers by optimization technique. Driving Safety Support Systems (DSSS) is a development process to reduce traffic accidents and to increase drivers' awareness. Vehicle-to-Person applications aim to provide security measures to pedestrians, motorcycles and bicycles. To eliminate V2P collisions, the pedestrian will use of Dedicated Short-Range Communications (DSRC) and enable the Smartphone to sends a navigation screen alert and audible warning to the vehicle. On the side, the system detects a vehicle close to the person or motorcycle or bicycle, and alerts are forwarded to the walker. Company like Honda also develops these solutions for the named Vehicle-to-Motorcycle (V2M) safety.

SUMMARY

This Vehicular Adhoc Networks is an emerging technology with many features to offer. Only if the security hazards in these types of networks are taken care of, VANET can be integrated with the upcoming automobile technology that is essential for VANET. Here the authors have discussed about VANET security via digital certificate and attempted to secure the network against the most common form of network attacks like DOS and Masquerade. The main focus is to do the task with minimum overhead on network and using the available resources.

REFERENCES

Al Hasan, A. S., Hossain, M. S., & Atiquzzaman, M. (2016, September). Security threats in vehicular ad hoc networks. In *2016 International Conference on Advances in Computing, Communications and Informatics (ICACCI)* (pp. 404-411). IEEE.

Al-Sultan, S., Al-Doori, M. M., Al-Bayatti, A. H., & Zedan, H. (2014). A comprehensive survey on vehicular ad hoc network. *Journal of Network and Computer Applications, 37*, 380–392. doi:10.1016/j.jnca.2013.02.036

Anandakumar, H., & Umamaheswari, K. (2018). Cooperative Spectrum Handovers in Cognitive Radio Networks. In Cognitive Radio, Mobile Communications and Wireless Networks (pp. 47–63). Springer. doi:10.1007/978-3-319-91002-4_3

Anandakumar, H., Umamaheswari, K., & Arulmurugan, R. (2019). A Study on Mobile IPv6 Handover in Cognitive Radio Networks. In *International Conference on Computer Networks and Communication Technologies* (pp. 399-408). Springer Singapore. doi:10.1007/978-981-10-8681-6_36

Biglieri, E., Goldsmith, A. J., Greenstein, L. J., Mandayam, N. B., & Poor, H. V. (2013). *Principles of cognitive radio*. Cambridge University Press.

Bouabdallah, F., Bouabdallah, N., & Boutaba, R. (2009). On balancing energy consumption in wireless sensor networks. *IEEE Transactions on Vehicular Technology, 58*(6), 2909–2924. doi:10.1109/TVT.2008.2008715

Haldorai, A., & Ramu, A. (2018). An Intelligent-Based Wavelet Classifier for Accurate Prediction of Breast Cancer. In *Intelligent Multidimensional Data and Image Processing* (pp. 306–319). doi:10.4018/978-1-5225-5246-8.ch012

Hasbullah, H., & Soomro, I. A. (2010). Denial of service (dos) attack and its possible solutions in VANET. *International Journal of Electrical, Computer, Energetic, Electronic and Communication Engineering, 4*(5), 813–817.

Haykin, S. (2005). Cognitive radio: Brain-empowered wireless communications. *IEEE Journal on Selected Areas in Communications, 23*(2), 201–220. doi:10.1109/JSAC.2004.839380

Jiang, D., Taliwal, V., Meier, A., Holfelder, W., & Herrtwich, R. (2006). Design of 5.9 GHz DSRC-based vehicular safety communication. *IEEE Wireless Communications, 13*(5), 36–43. doi:10.1109/WC-M.2006.250356

Li, H., & Irick, D. K. (2010, May). Collaborative spectrum sensing in cognitive radio vehicular ad hoc networks: belief propagation on highway. In 2010 IEEE 71st Vehicular technology conference (VTC 2010-spring) (pp. 1-5). IEEE.

Manikandakumar, M., & Ramanujam, E. (2018). Security and Privacy Challenges in Big Data Environment. In Handbook of Research on Network Forensics and Analysis Techniques (pp. 315-325). Hershey, PA: IGI Global.

Naik, M. (2015). Early Detection and Prevention of DDOS attack on VANET [Doctoral dissertation].

Patel, K. N., & Jhaveri, R. H. (2015). Isolating Packet Dropping Misbehavior in VANET using Ant Colony Optimization. *International Journal of Computers and Applications, 120*(24).

Petit, J. (2009, December). Analysis of ecdsa authentication processing in vanets. In *2009 3rd International Conference on New Technologies, Mobility and Security (NTMS)* (pp. 1-5). IEEE.

Qian, Y., & Moayeri, N. (2008, May). Design of secure and application-oriented VANETs. In *IEEE Vehicular Technology Conference VTC Spring 2008* (pp. 2794-2799). IEEE. 10.1109/VETECS.2008.610

Shabbir, M., Khan, M. A., Khan, U. S., & Saqib, N. A. (2016, December). Detection and Prevention of Distributed Denial of Service Attacks in VANETs. In *2016 International Conference on Computational Science and Computational Intelligence (CSCI)* (pp. 970-974). IEEE.

Singh, K. D., Rawat, P., & Bonnin, J. M. (2014). Cognitive radio for vehicular ad hoc networks (CR-VANETs): Approaches and challenges. *EURASIP Journal on Wireless Communications and Networking, 2014*(1), 49. doi:10.1186/1687-1499-2014-49

Thilak, K. D., & Amuthan, A. (2016, February). DoS attack on VANET routing and possible defending solutions-A survey. In *2016 International Conference on Information Communication and Embedded Systems (ICICES)* (pp. 1-7). IEEE.

Varshney, N., Roy, T., & Chaudhary, N. (2014, April). Security protocol for VANET by using digital certification to provide security with low bandwidth. In *2014 International Conference on Communications and Signal Processing (ICCSP)* (pp. 768-772). IEEE.

Vijay, G., Bdira, E. B. A., & Ibnkahla, M. (2011). Cognition in wireless sensor networks: A perspective. *IEEE Sensors Journal, 11*(3), 582–592. doi:10.1109/JSEN.2010.2052033

This research was previously published in Cognitive Social Mining Applications in Data Analytics and Forensics edited by Anandakumar Haldorai and Arulmurugan Ramu; pages 252-264, copyright year 2019 by Information Science Reference (an imprint of IGI Global).

Chapter 32
Design and Development of Secured Framework for Efficient Routing in Vehicular Ad–Hoc Network

Mamata Rath

iD https://orcid.org/0000-0002-2277-1012

Birla School of Management, Birla Global University, Bhubaneswar, India

Bibudhendu Pati

iD https://orcid.org/0000-0002-2544-5343

Department of Computer Science, Rama Devi Women's University, Bhubaneswar, India

Binod Kumar Pattanayak

Department of Computer Science and Engineering, Siksha 'O' Anusandhan (Deemed to be) University, Bhubaneswar, India

ABSTRACT

Due to many challenging issues in vehicular ad-hoc networks (VANETs), such as high mobility and network instability, this has led to insecurity and vulnerability to attacks. Due to dynamic network topology changes and frequent network re-configuration, security is a major target in VANET research domains. VANETs have gained significant attention in the current wireless network scenario, due to their exclusive characteristics which are different from other wireless networks such as rapid link failure and high vehicle mobility. In this are, the authors present a Secured and Safety Protocol for VANET (STVAN), as an intelligent Ad-Hoc On Demand Distance Vector (AODV)-based routing mechanism that prevents the Denial of Service attack (DoS) and improves the quality of service for secured communications in a VANET. In order to build a STVAN, the authors have considered a smart traffic environment in a smart city and introduced the concept of load balancing over VANET vehicles in a best effort manner. Simulation results reveal that the proposed STVAN accomplishes enhanced performance when compared with other similar protocols in terms of reduced delay, better packet delivery ratio, reasonable energy efficiency, increased network throughput and decreased data drop compared to other similar approach.

DOI: 10.4018/978-1-7998-5348-0.ch032

1. INTRODUCTION

Safety and security are two major aspects while designing any efficient routing model for vehicular ad-hoc networks. The way toward navigation in Vehicular Ad hoc Networks (VANET) is a difficult task in city conditions. Finding the briefest end-to-end associated way fulfilling defer limitation and insignificant overhead is gone up against with numerous imperatives and troubles (Kaur et al., 2016). Such troubles are because of the high portability of vehicles, the successive way disappointments, and the different obstacles, which may influence the dependability of the information transmission and directing. Business Unmanned Aerial Vehicles or what are usually alluded to as drones can prove to be useful in managing these imperatives (Chunha et al., 2016). A Detail contemplate has been done on how they are working in impromptu mode can collaborate with VANET on the ground to aid the directing procedure and enhance the dependability of the information conveyance by spanning the correspondence hole at whatever point it is conceivable (Singh et al., 2014).

In this way, an augmentation of the convention has been modified by supporting two distinctive methods for steering information: (I) conveying information (Singh et al., 2017) parcels only on the ground utilizing UVAR-G; and (ii) transmitting information bundles in the sky utilizing a responsive directing in light of UVAR-S. Recreation comes about exhibit that the half and half correspondence amongst vehicles and UAVs is in a perfect world suited for VANETs contrasted with customary vehicle-to-vehicle (V2V) interchanges. Vehicular Adhoc Networks (VANETS) empower the vehicles to communicate with each other vehicle and in addition with road side units (Lai et al., 2018). However, building up a dynamic routing policy (Rath et al., 2016) for these networks conceivably because of the substantial portability and normal changes in these networks is a tough work. In VANETS transmission joins are at the danger of separation (Abdelgadir et al., 2017).

Along these lines the advancement of the proficient directing component is required in VANETS. It is seen in writing study that the many VANET protocols solves conventional challenges in the network. Yet at the same time issues identified with blockage control should be tended to. Ant Colony Optimization based protocols for better information collection (Pournaghi et al., 2018) and route determination has been suggested by some researchers that utilized a strategy which has indicated very huge change over accessible ones. Figure1. shows a representative traffic scenario in VANET with RSU and Server. An UVAR – a UAV-Assisted VANETs directing convention was proposed, which enhances information steering and availability of the vehicles on the ground using UAVs. Be that as it may, UVAR does not completely misuse UAVs in the sky for information sending since it utilizes UAVs just when the network is ineffectively thick.

VANETS may really make to end up valuable for throughout the way with security and additionally a few business purposes activities. For example; vehicular network might be utilized to educate drivers with the goal that the likelihood of guests jams; offering higher solace and also adequacy. Remote association frameworks have permitted the majority of the advantages inside our lives and moreover enhanced our everyday productivity additionally (Halim et al., 2018). Specially appointed networks work without a characterized preset looked after foundation. VANETS working with 802.11-organized WLAN development currently got critical intrigue Due to this reason the vehicles worked with Wi-Fi mechanism (Rath et al., 2015). Another locale in which there is a ton prospect of remote advancements to make a gigantic impact might be the district of between vehicular interchanges (IVC) (Oubbati et. al, 2017). Intervehicle association (IVC) is increasing huge enthusiasm from the investigation territory and the engine vehicle industry; in which it will valuable in giving shrewd transportation framework (ITS) alongside drivers and explorers relate administrations (Ngo et al., 2014). The idea of IVC is regularly called vehicle-to-vehicle correspondences (V2V) and notwithstanding framework it alluded vehicle-to-foundation inside their transmission extend and vehicular adhoc networks (VANET) (Rahim et al., 2018).

Basic Objective of our proposed Research Work are as follows:

1. Design and development of Secured Network Layer Protocol in VANET;
2. Communication Improvement among vehicles in Congested Traffic using Improved Routing Algorithm for Security Purpose;
3. Investigational simulation and result with better network performance.

The rest of the paper is organized as follows: Literature Review has been presented in Section II, section 3 depicts the encouragement & motivation behind this research; Then our main contribution of the proposed approach and design of the proposed system has been illustrated over section 4. Next, section 5 projects simulation and last section 6 concludes the paper with future scope.

2. LITERATURE REVIEW

The following exploring literatures were studied in detail to review and attain knowledge about the existing research scenario in basic security status of VANET with respect to protocols and data communication. Table 1 shows the description of our literature study regarding basic routing protocols and issues used in them.

Table 1. Description of contributions on routing protocols in VANET with variant issues

Routing Protocols Study and Design in VANET				
Sl. No	Literature	Year	Related Topic	Related Domain
1	Singh et al.	2014	Study and Analysis of VANET Routing Protocols	VANET Protocols
2	Cunha et al.	2016	Applications and Issues of VANET Routing Protocols	VANET Protocols and applications
3	Ngo et al.	2014	Link quality prediction metric for shadowing and fading effects in VANET	Routing Metric in VANET
4	Wang et al.	2018	Reliable routing in IP-Based VANET with network gaps analysis	Reliable Routing in VANET
5	Saleh et al.	2017	Reliable Routing Protocols in VANET	Reliable Routing in VANET
6	Hossain et al.	2017	Novel MAC Protocol Design in VANET	Protocol Design in VANET
7	Filho et al.	2016	Technical Survey on DTN and VDTN Routing Protocols in VANET	Routing Protocol in VANET
8	Brik et al.	2016	Distributed Data Gathering Protocol Design for VANET	Routing Protocol in VANET

VANETs have been developed as an exciting network system and application domain. Progressively vehicles are being furnished with implanted sensors, handling and wireless correspondence abilities. Article (FChunha et al., 2016) refers that this special network has opened various possible outcomes for intense and potential extraordinary applications on security, effectiveness, comfort, open joint effort and interest. The location-based routing protocol has been given (C. Ngo et al., 2014) attention as one of the effective routing approaches in vehicular adhoc network on the subject of low overhead and high adaptability. Its basic influence lies in playing out a pathless routing with the end objective that a node having a group communication message to its neighbour node that gives the most limited physical separation to goal and this procedure proceeds until the point when the parcel achieves goal. Route Establishment Algorithm (Wang et al., 2018) describes that in a route with a network gap, a vehicle usually drops messages if it cannot find the next hop. In this case, communications may be disrupted. Therefore, it is very important to avoid network gaps when routing paths are established. A reliable routing scheme (Rath et al., 2017) indicates and aims to establish routing paths without network gaps to improve the packet delivery rate. Reliable Protocol for VANET named as R2P has been outlined (Ahmed et al., 2017), which separates the network into covering zones. For each zone, an extraordinary node is elevated to be the Master Node (MN), which keeps up an exceptional routing sheets for bury/intra-zone communication. R2P relies upon two kinds of sheets, in particular; Internal Routing Board (IRB) and External Routing Board (ERB). A novel Distributed Data Gathering Protocol (DDGP) has been projected (Brik et al., 2016) for dealing the delay tolerant factor in VANET routing and in addition constant information in both urban and interstate situations has been planned. The fundamental commitment of DDGP is another medium access procedure that empowers vehicles to get to the direct distributedly in light of their area data.

Chaki et al. in (2010) presents an analysis and detailed study on various IDS structures specially the way they Have been transformed from normal IDS systems of the primitive wireless ad-hoc networks to the ambient intelligent scenario of the computing systems. To investigate the DDOS (Distributed Denial of Service) attack, using non-address spoofing flood in Ad-hoc networks. Collaboration mechanism between station vehicles is highly required in VANETs, for appropriate execution of comfortable routing and deployment of effectiveness applications. A non-inconsequential logical test in VANETs is the plan of a versatile communicate convention, which can give effective and end-to-end solid cautioning messages scattering. As a rule, communicate conventions for VANETs utilize reference point messages, spread among the vehicles, with a specific end goal to get neighborhood data. At the point when the vehicles are beside each other attempting to communicate in the meantime, this may prompt regular dispute, and communicate challenges. An elaborated literature review has been presented in this section to discuss the challenges and security concerns in this spectacular area of VANET routing. Table 2 shows the description of our literature study regarding basic secured routing protocols and contributed literatures to prevent security issues used in VANET.

It gives enhanced administration by executing activity markers to refresh the movement related data at each example of occasions occurring in the network. In this approach ease sensors with limit of vehicle identifying framework applications are installed amidst the street at an interim of each 500 meters and 1000 meters. IoT gadgets are utilized to procure the activity related on-line data (Singh et al., 2016) quickly and additionally sent for preparing at the Big information investigation focuses. Knowledge based logical apparatuses (Ding et al., 2016) are utilized to examine the movement thickness and arrangement procedures are demonstrated. Congested activity is overseen by a versatile application (Rath et al., 2018) in view of the investigated movement thickness and substitute arrangement of this. An on-street air quality checking and controlling strategy has been proposed (Fazziki et al., 2017) with advancement of operator based model that incorporates urban street network framework and surveys ongoing and inexact air contamination list in various portions of the street and produces prescribed systems for street clients.

Table 2. Description of safety and secured protocols in VANET

Sl. No	Literature	Year	Related Topic	Related Domain
			**Safety and Security Protocols in VANET**	
1	Morteza et al.	2018	Privacy Preserving Authentication scheme for VANET	Security & Privacy in VANET
2	Sattar et al.	2018	Energy efficiency Analysis and reliability of safety messages broadcast in VANET	Reliability Safety VANET
3	Hasrouny et al.	2017	VANET Security Challenges & Solutions	Security VANET
4	Baiad et al.	2016	Cross layer detection scheme to detect black hole attack in VANET	Network Security Safety VANET
5	Sharma et al.	2018	VANET Based Intrusion detection System using Cluster Head	Security Cluster Computing VANET
6	Oliveira et al.	2017	Reliable Protocol in VANET with Safety Applications	Safety Security VANET

The security of Vehicular Ad hoc Networks is very basic necessity. Initially survey and investigation are being done by prominent specialists and after that the fundamental confirmation conspires in VANET are contrasted and their advantages and disadvantages. Another confirmation conspire which gives secure interchanges in VANET has been introduced (Pournaghi et al., 2018). The method used is a mix of Road Side Unit Based (RSUB) and Tamper Proof Device Based (TPDB) plans. An original thought in NECPPA (Pournaghi et al., 2018) (Novel and Efficient Conditional Privacy-Preserving Authentication Scheme) is to let the keys and the principle parameters of the framework be put away in the Tamper Proof Device (TPD) of Road Side Units (RSUs). Since, there is dependably a safe and quick communicational connection amongst TA and RSU, embeddings TPD in RSUs is substantially more productive than embeddings them in OBUs.

Solid and on-time conveyance of safety messages is basic in VANETs that requires effective communicate models. Model of the unwavering quality of flooding utilized as the basic information dispersal protocol for time-basic safety messages has been delineated (Sattar et al., 2018) with a multi-bounce VANET and end-to-end dependability gave by the network layer. The investigative outcomes release imperative bits of knowledge about the flooding system.

VANET is an eminent modernization technology with promising future and also incredible difficulties particularly in its security. VANET security systems are introduced in three noteworthy practical parts (Hasrouny et al., 2017). The initial segment shows a broad outline of VANET security qualities and difficulties and in addition necessities. These prerequisites ought to be mulled over to empower the execution of secure VANET framework with productive correspondence between parties. We give the subtle elements of the ongoing security models and the notable security measures protocols.

Such procedures incorporate lessening number of vehicles use in most dirtied street portions, decreasing the contamination levels with expanding vehicle stream (Dai et al., 2016) on the streets. Informational indexes utilized for this reason for existing are gathered from traffic control towers are sent at each movement point and they are remotely associated with each other through VANET (Miao et al., 2013).

In an area of quality checking framework, street network data accessible and installed minimal effort e-participatory contamination sensors. Mobile cloud computing underpins specialized advancement in shrewd urban communities. Essential qualities of outlining an enhanced activity control framework incorporates interfacing movement signals and activity control focuses with GIS empowered advanced guide of the town utilizing wise computational energy of information examination (Lahlah et al., 2018) as a key module. In this unique situation, the fundamental test lies in utilization of constant investigation on-line activity data and accurately applying it to some essential movement stream. Activity control towers are ordinarily sent at each movement point in savvy city and they are remotely associated with each other through VANET (Venkataramana et al., 2017). Setting up a clever transportation framework (Rath et al., 2018) with a network security component in an Internet of Vehicles (IoV) condition, with accentuation on incorporating it with activity signal control to help crisis vehicles all the more immediately touching base towards its destination.

A software defined network (SDN) empowered availability mindful topographical steering convention of VANETs for urban condition has been proposed (H. Wu et al., 2017) that courses the movement amid clog in a controlled manner. A constant disseminated framework (Mallah et al., 2017) has been proposed to arrange the urban street network blockage level utilizing VANET. The article proposes models in light of idea of spatial and fleeting measures on manufactured information extricated from a particular contextual analysis. An optimized AIC technique has been used to improve traffic performance (Dai et al., 2016). To avoid collision, a scheduled rule has been formulated that determines priority of vehicles in the traffic point considering the travel time of vehicles. Performance evaluation of the projected algorithm has been simulated and the superior results were projected demonstrating the usefulness of the approach. We have considered this novel approach of AIC to compare the results of our proposed approach for route diversion.

3. MOTIVATION

Many conventional routing protocols have been designed by eminent researchers in this field, but they are not fully feasible to handle substantial network payload in VANET with an optimized network life time.There are still many challenges that are very difficult to be addressed and to be computed to accurately compute the efficiency. The following challenges in VANET routing and technical concerns have motivated us to design an energetic, safe, improved and reliable protocol in VANET. We found from our extensive experimental review and investigation of existing challenging VANET based issues that there are many conventional routing protocols designed but the still the following challenges are always there:

1. **Power supply to Network Devices:** Vehicular Adhoc Networks (VANETS) empower the vehicles to communicate with each other vehicle and in addition with road side units. However, building up a dynamic routing policy for these networks conceivably because of the substantial portability and normal changes in these networks is a tough work. As the road side units depend on battery life (Rath et al., 2016), so power supply to such network devices as well as to the mobile vehicles is a challenge in VANET;
2. **IVC-Inter Vehicular Communication:** Another challenge in which there is a lot prospect of wireless innovations to create an enormous effect is be the region of inter-vehicular communications

(IVC). Vehicles should be correctly communicated and signalled during transit in order to skip any attack or accident (Rath et al., 2019);

3. **V2V and V2R Communication:** With a sharp increment of vehicles out and about, new technology is imagined to give offices to the travelers including wellbeing application, help to the drivers, crisis cautioning and so forth. Ad-hoc network is a sort of wireless correspondence network which built up by utilizing a group of portable vehicles with wireless communication facility. The network which is totally versatile and which require practically no framework is a special feature of VANET. So, such framework must be dynamic in order to spontaneously react to external stimuli;

4. **Data Scheduling Policy in VANET:** Wireless technology gives compelling and effective correspondence between the cell phones. Vehicular Ad-hoc Network (VANET) is the most affecting field to scientists because of vehicle thickness, movement clog, mishaps, and so on. So as to conquer these issues, a few research works are going on particularly in the field of the correspondence among moving vehicles and assets. The need of proficient resource reservation and resource scheduling (Rath et al., 2014) is very required for effective use of a communicate medium and information transmission. Information scheduling turns into a critical issue when vehicles get to information through Road Side Unit (RSU);

5. **Secured Group Access Management in VANET:** Currently, the integrated communication between vehicles in vehicular ad-hoc network (VANET) and cellular network can suit rich applications since coordinated VANET-Cellular network empowers portable administrators to furnish vehicle clients with consistent information access to the administrators' administrations. In built-in VANET-Cellular networks, the clustering algorithm partners vehicles into cluster groups and can give elite information transmission benefit and have been broadly examined. Therefore, the big challenge is How to effectively and safely set up and manage communication in a group.

From our wide-ranging experimental assessment and exploration of existing challenging VANET based issues, it is watched that the designed conventional protocols are not feasible to handle substantial network payload. Most of them use normal shortest path routing algorithm for data transmission, whereas it is very much challenging to transmit critical information in a VANET mostly in a real-time basis. As the data shared between vehicles and other road side units are meant for controlling the routing in emergency situation or in real time road congestion system, or in emergency medical event related to critical patients in ambulance. Therefore, it is highly challenging to design a very dynamic and robust protocol in VANET environment. Again, as the power consumption by vehicles and RSU are also a major concern, therefore conventional protocols are not suitable to be used as they chose a route for routing without considering total network load and station(vehicle)s' energy capability, while choosing the reasonable way among station(vehicle)s. Also, the station(vehicle)s, who participate in sending the activity over same course, gets depleted losing their valuable vitality. Notwithstanding that, we felt, there should be satisfactory Quality of Service (QoS) while vehicles and cell phones are moving freely. That there are diverse prerequisites of QoS for information and ongoing administrations.

To avoid frequent data drop due to longest route, link failure or frequent topology change, very special real time protocols should be developed to prevent such network challenges. All the above-mentioned issues motivated and inspired us to develop a dynamic and robust real-time protocol for very challenging network called VANET. The idea is that the real time and critical information over a wireless connection can be retransmitted with some reasonable postponement, if they are lost. Hardly any conceded information packets won't imperil much to the system clients, however same thing isn't appropriate for voice and video packets. The continuous multimedia administrations are to a great degree defer delicate, and are futile, on the off chance that they neglect to meet the conveyance due date by missing arrangement of edges or packets. All the previously mentioned bottlenecks motivated us to consider inside and out, and to design an unequivocal routing scheme for constant VANET arrange. This motivated us for designing STVAN routing system, which would adjust the uneven load i.e. message appropriation over a troubled VANET. This approach is considering neighbouring vehicle's energy and time delay factor as routing measurements while broadcasting message to next station in a network.

4. PROPOSED SECURED PROTOCOL

In the current research work, we have designed an energy efficient and reliable VANET based protocol that selects a shortest path among vehicles to transmit control message from vehicle to vehicle, so that emergency message can be passed to neighbour vehicles quickly and network throughput can be increased. In VANET systems, vehicles have to be informed a large number of important information for example starting from climate conditions, traffic data, multimedia information, alert signs and some other sort of information. Today, VANETs have vital advantages contrast with cellular and devoted systems. Such advantages have roused makers to contribute on them to make them grew independently. The most critical piece of VANET is the sensors that ought to be actualized in various parts of the vehicle to report the circum-position of the vehicle and the outer condition to the driver. It can tune in to the orders of the driver or get data of different vehicles. The intrinsic properties of specially appointed systems make them valuable for the wellbeing of vehicles and traffic. These properties incorporate being short-go, framing a system promptly, changing the topology and exchanging signals from the inception to the objective. An Intelligent and safe traffic management routing protocol has been proposed in VANET here as depicted in Figure 1. The proposed framework deals with traffic controlling system with security module to prevent malicious attack as the ruling section.

Figure 1. A VANET scene at a traffic square from the proposed approach STVAN

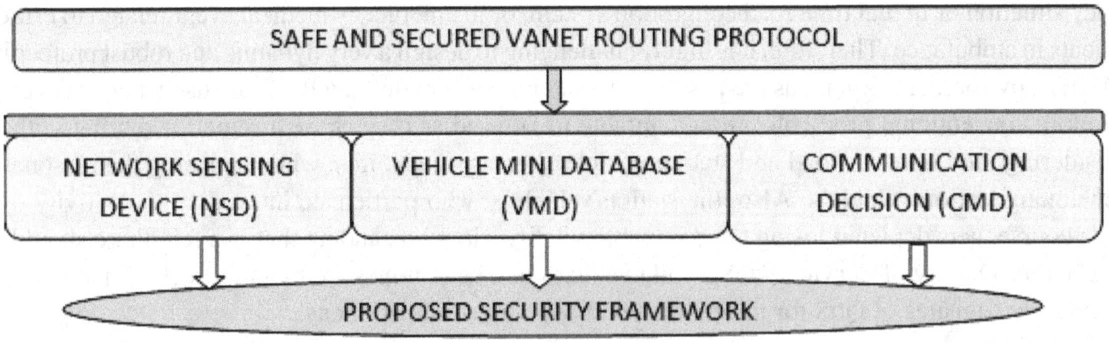

The description of the proposed Safe and Secured VANET protocol (STVAN) is given in this section. The proposed protocol has been designed with energy efficiency management in the network layer of TCP/IP Protocol stack in VANET. In the proposed network all the intelligent vehicles are considered to be the mobile stations and they have a central controller routing engine, that controls the routing task during communication. Each of these engines has three components at their core design. NSD refers to network sensing device that senses the incoming communication message from other smart vehicles or a road side unit (RSU). It stores the details of the source in the mini-database (VMD). Next with the help of the security framework (our proposed work), authentication of the source is checked in order to prevent from any external suspicious attack. Details of the proposed scheme has been explained in the next section. Then depending on the security function, Communication Decision (CMD) part either sends reply to the source or denies communication. When a source vehicle (controlling vehicle) or RSU initiates a message transmission to a destination vehicle during mobility in a dynamic and congested traffic scenario in VANET, our proposed protocol STVAN uses an intelligent analytical engine to select the intermediate hub vehicle or a next hop station to forward the message till destination. To select a suitable station out of many of its own neighbouring vehicles, is a challenging execution. The proposed algorithm to select next hop vehicle in a given VANET scenario is explained here.

4.1. Functionality of the Proposed System

The Smart Data Analytic Module for controlling Message Transmission & traffic congestion works as follows:

Step 1: Total number of vehicle information transiting, crossing and waiting for a specific traffic at a particular time range is sent by the traffic signal sensor device of STVAN to the central server.

Step 2: The above real time data from sensors serves as input to the data analytic engine at the STVAN server i.e. supervisory computer control system which is connected to the GIS mapping of the roads.

Step 3: When the congestion level crosses a particular threshold value, the data analytic engine sends a broadcast message to all the agent computers situated at traffic controllers to divert the next two and four wheeler passengers to an alternate route.

Step 4: When the congestion level decreases the threshold value, again another broadcast message goes to the traffic computer controllers to again divert the next passengers back to the same route. Figure 2. displays a VANET Scenario of traffic with RSU and Smart Vehicles.

4.2. Security Mechanism Used in the Proposed System

A malicious effort to disturb normal traffic of a targeted server, service or network is caused by denial-of-service (DoS) attack. It is done by overpowering the destination station or its surrounding infrastructure with a flood of Internet traffic. DoS attacks accomplish efficiency by utilizing multiple compromised vehicular systems as sources of attack traffic. Exploited vehicles can include mobile vehicles in the traffic, road side units or other sensing devices and may be other networked resources such as IoT devices. From a high level, a DoS attack is like a traffic jam blockage up with highway, preventing customary traffic from arriving at its desired destination.

In the proposed STVAN Framework, a group communication targeted security protocol has been designed in the proposed approach for real time group vehicles intending to send sensitive real-time communication. Figure 3 presents an attack set-up and its prevention mechanism. When a vehicle V1 sends a route request packet to V2 with an intention to send an information to some destination towards V2, an Intruder vehicle silently collects the source_vehicle_id, destination_id and next-hop information

Figure 2. A VANET scenario of traffic with RSU and smart vehicles

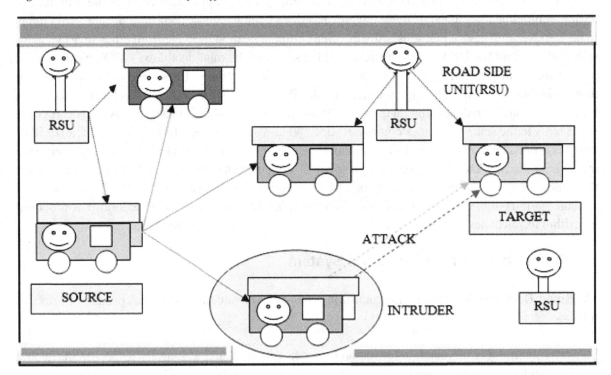

Figure 3. The proposed security framework

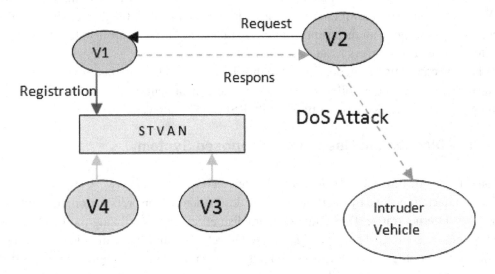

from the sending station using malicious code that it periodically transmits to its neighbour vehicles. Figure 4 shows the flow chart of the proposed system.

As per the flow chart, every smart vehicle in the proposed system that wants to send any communication to another vehicle has to undergo a registration process with STVAN protocol. For every communication its authenticity as a user is checks, in this way the entire network platform is kept secured

Figure 4. Flow chart of the proposed system

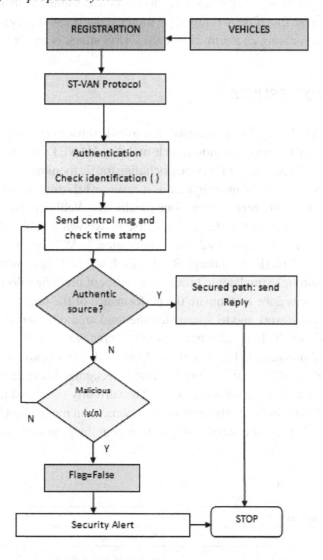

where every external communication by any intruder can be easily detected. If the authentication check fails within the stipulated time, then authentication Flag bit is assigned to False with a security message "don't send reply", else for every valid vehicle, the communication is carried out with the positive signal "send reply". As a part of attack activity (Figure 3) and taking advantages of VANET vulnerability, the Intruder observes that V1 frequently sends request to V2. Hence in idle times it attacks V1 to isolate it from other vehicles and consumes the network resources illegally. It does so by sending false request message to vehicle V2 presuming itself as vehicle V1. But actually, it is sent from Intruder vehicle. In normal scenario, V2 would have sent the reply, confirming a path from V1 to V2, but as vehicle V2 has registered with STVAN Protocol, now the security system authenticates every vehicle every time any incoming request arrives. During the authentication process, it executes an RSA algorithm to generate a public and private key pair specifically for source and destination. Hence, whenever there is any false request, the STVAN protocol validates the source_id, IP- address of the source vehicle and the equivalent encoded code generated for those two parties. But this is not accessible to any third-party intruder. So STVAN can easily recognise that if there is any false source request and it prevents the vehicle V2 from sending reply frame by generating an alarm. Hence the DDoS attack is prevented.

5. SIMULATION AND RESULTS

Vehicular Ad hoc Network (VANET) are considered as mobile sensor networks and featured with challenging topology change and increasing station vehicle mobility. VANET vehicles can sense versatile data in its neighboring area to offer a number of services including traffic monitoring, velocity controlling, lost vehicle identifying and environmental investigation as it covers everlastingly a wide geographical region. Vehicles are configured with different communiqué parameters. Vehicles moves within the particular network margin. Station vehicles in VANET can converse in two ways: vehicle-to-vehicle (V2V) communication and Vehicle-to-infrastructure (V2I) communication. In V2I communication model, vehicles communicate to Road-Side-Unit (RSU) through Road-Side-Routers. This section elaborates the simulation scenarios deployed through simulator to proof our concept of providing decent QoS for multimedia packets. Further analysis was done to compare the performance of the proposed routing protocol with best effort technique. Our network model speculated the total area of simulation as 1000m x 1000m. Numbers of mobile station(vehicle)s that roam around this area were 60. We used Random Waypoint mobility model for users' movement. The underlying MAC and wirelessphy protocol was 802_11. The simulation was observed for 900 sec.ata communication is recognized between station(vehicle)s using UDP agent and CBR traffic (R. Oliveira et al., 2017). The currently simulated program in tcl designs a VANET with sensor station(vehicle) configuration, communication model, mobility model, and energy model component. Table 3 shows the simulation parameters in the proposed system.

Table 3. Simulation parameters

Parameter	Value
Channel Type	Wireless Channel
Propagation	Radio-propagation model
Network Interface	Wireless Phy
MAC Type	MAC/802_11
Interface Queue Type	Drop Tail
Antenna Model	Antenna/OmniAntenna
Max Packet Size in ifq	100
X Dimension	1000
Y Dimension	1000
Simulation Tool	NetSim

Figure 5. Performance evaluation and comparison- Throughput

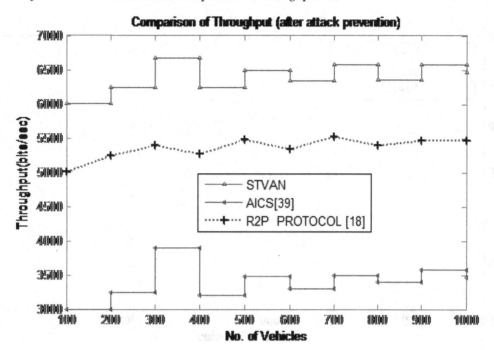

The proposed traffic model has been simulated using NetSim Simulator. Netsim has been extensively used, to crate the road topology, the map editor is used and to create the vehicle movements, the vehicle movement editor is used. This editor also helps the users to specify vehicle (ambulance) route information such as total number of ambulances to be included in the simulation scenario in a particular route, the vehicle departure time, origin and destination of vehicle, transit period of the vehicle, speed etc which are configured during simulation. The simulation result shows improved performance in terms of quick message communication between smart health care centres and increasing the throughput of the proposed system.

The station(vehicle)s in a VANET can sense moving information around them which helps in monitoring the traffic, controlling the speed of the vehicles and many other traffic congestion parameters. In a VANET, the vehicles which act as mobile vehicles move within the VANET network range. Mobile vehicles are configured with various communication parameters. Two types of communication are possible using the VANET station(vehicle)s, vehicle to vehicle communication and vehicle to infrastructure(V2I). In this simulation work, we have used the V2I approach in which vehicles interact and response with the road side sensor units through network routing devices at the road side.

Throughput – Due to varying number of malicious station(vehicle)s in the network during the attack, throughput in the transmission is greatly affected, hence it has been considered as an important routing metric. Throughput can be computed as number of effectively received packets in unit time and its unit is bps (bits per second), Kbps or Mbps. We have calculated throughput using awk script (Chaki et al., 2010) that processed the output trace file during simulation. Figure 5 represents the throughput analysis of the proposed protocol STVAN with other protocols.

Figure 6. No. of Vehicles vs. Security processing time

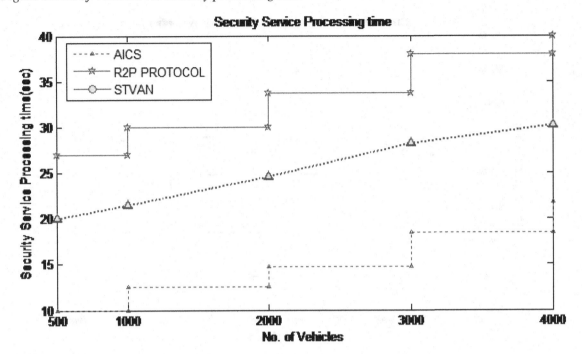

During running time of the simulation, energy of a station(vehicle) represents its energy level. Initial energy of the station(vehicle) is an input parameter. For every packet transmitted the station(vehicle) consumes some power which reduces its energy level. So, at any point of time, the energy consumption level can be found out by scheming the variation between the present energy and the initial energy. Gradually due to more consumption, when the energy level of a station(vehicle) reaches to zero, it cannot do any network operation such as packet sending, receiving, forwarding or processing. The energy consumption amount in a station(vehicle) has been computed and printed in the trace file. The total energy level of a network can be calculated by adding the energy level of all the station (vehicle)s. Figure 6 shows security service processing time by our proposed protocol.

End to end delay - This can be distinctly noted as the time taken by a data message to reach from source station to destination station. This delay includes the time used up by route discovery method and the delay at queue of the station router. Data packets that are fruitfully delivered to the destination are considered:

Total end to end delay = $\sum$ (arrive time – send time) / $\sum$ Number of connections

Performance of a protocol is better if it exhibits a lower value for end to end delay.

Figure 7. displays performance evaluation and comparison of average end to end delay in our proposed system. Here delay refers to the time consumed to execute the security algorithm in the proposed system and delay due to it. When it is compared with other protocols, it can be observed that the delay is between 10 to 50 milliseconds (ms) which is a comparatively better result than others.

Figure 7. Performance evaluation and comparison- Avg. end to end delay

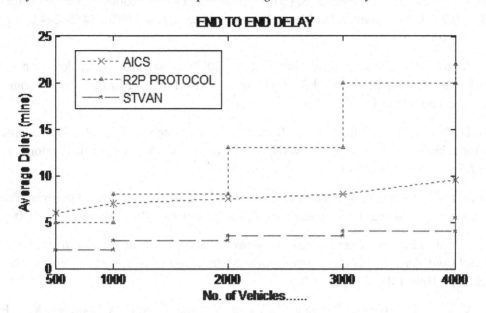

The above simulation results show that our proposed secured protocol performs better in comparison to other similar protocols in terms of Packet Delivery ratio, throughput, energy efficiency and it uses a fewer number of control packets to disseminate security messages to other vehicles hence reducing the total end to end delay of data transmission up to a greater extent.

6. CONCLUSION AND FUTURE WORK

This article presents a secured and intelligent protocol for VANETs. In reviewing the simulation results it can be observed that our proposed STVAN protocol outperforms other similar approaches up to little better extent which ensures the validity and suitability of the technically sound improved protocol. Its enhanced performance is ensured when compared with other similar protocols in terms of reduced delay, better packet delivery ratio, reasonable energy efficiency and increased network throughput. There are a lot of future research scope for this emerging wireless network security project. As this is related to dynamic vehicular network it can be extended in various direction such as using security approach and novel power consumption schemes using machine learning algorithms, the network can be optimized in VANET using optimized techniques, VANET based vehicle information can be more analytically reviewed using big data analytics tools and can be further processed to increase the network performance using data mining techniques.

REFERENCES

Abdelgadir, M., Saeed, R. A., & Babiker, A. (2017). Mobility Routing Model for Vehicular Ad-hoc Networks (VANETs). *Vehicular Communications*, *9*, 154–161.

Al Mallah, R., Quintero, A., & Farooq, B. (2017). Distributed Classification of Urban Congestion Using VANET. *IEEE Transactions on Intelligent Transportation Systems*, *18*(9), 2435–2442. doi:10.1109/TITS.2016.2641903

Baiad, R., Alhussein, O., Otrok, H., & Muhaidat, S. (2016). Novel cross layer detection schemes to detect blackhole attack against QoS-OLSR protocol in VANET. Vehicular Communications, 5, 9–17. doi:10.1016/j.vehcom.2016.09.001

Boussoufa-Lahlah, S., Semchedine, F., & Bouallouche-Medjkoune, L. (2018). Geographic routing protocols for vehicular ad hoc networks (VANETs): A survey. Vehicular Communications, 11, 20–31. doi:10.1016/j.vehcom.2018.01.006

Brik, B., Lagraa, N., Lakas, A., & Cheddad, A. (2016). DDGP: Distributed Data Gathering Protocol for vehicular networks. Vehicular Communications, 4, 15–29. doi:10.1016/j.vehcom.2016.01.001

Chaki, R. (2010). *Intrusion detection: Ad-hoc networks to ambient intelligence framework. In 2010 International Conference on Computer Information Systems and Industrial Management Applications.* CISIM., doi:10.1109/CISIM.2010.5643700.

Cunha, F., Villas, L., Boukerche, A., Maia, G., Viana, A., Mini, R. A. F., & Loureiro, A. A. F. (2016). Data communication in VANETs: Protocols, applications and challenges. *Ad Hoc Networks*, *44*, 90–103. doi:10.1016/j.adhoc.2016.02.017

Dai, P., Liu, K., Zhuge, Q., Sha, E. H. M., Lee, V. C. S., & Son, S. H. (2016, July). A convex optimization based autonomous intersection control strategy in vehicular cyber-physical systems. In 2016 Intl IEEE Conferences on Ubiquitous Intelligence & Computing, Advanced and Trusted Computing, Scalable Computing and Communications, Cloud and Big Data Computing, Internet of People, and Smart World Congress (UIC/ATC/ScalCom/CBDCom/IoP/SmartWorld) (pp. 203-210). IEEE. doi:10.1109/UIC-ATC-ScalCom-CBDCom-IoP-SmartWorld.2016.0050

Ding, Z., Yang, B., Chi, Y., & Guo, L. (2016). Enabling Smart Transportation Systems: A Parallel Spatio-Temporal Database Approach. *IEEE Transactions on Computers*, *65*(5), 1377–1391. doi:10.1109/TC.2015.2479596

El Fazziki, A., Benslimane, D., Sadiq, A., Ouarzazi, J., & Sadgal, M. (2017). An Agent Based Traffic Regulation System for the Roadside Air Quality Control. *IEEE Access : Practical Innovations, Open Solutions*, *5*, 13192–13201. doi:10.1109/ACCESS.2017.2725984

Filho, J. G., Patel, A., Bruno, L. A. B., & Celestino, J. (2016). A systematic technical survey of DTN and VDTN routing protocols. *Computer Standards & Interfaces*, *48*, 139–159. doi:10.1016/j.csi.2016.06.004

Frank, M., Hwu, T., Jain, S., Knight, R. T., Martinovic, I., Mittal, P., ... Song, D. (2017, October). Using EEG-Based BCI Devices to Subliminally Probe for Private Information. In *Proceedings of the 2017 on Workshop on Privacy in the Electronic Society* (pp. 133-136). ACM.

Geeks for geeks. (n.d.). RSA algorithm cryptography. Retrieved from http://www.geeksforgeeks.org/rsa-algorithm-cryptography

Hasrouny, H., Samhat, A. E., Bassil, C., & Laouiti, A. (2017). VANet security challenges and solutions: A survey. Vehicular Communications, 7, 7–20. doi:10.1016/j.vehcom.2017.01.002

Kaur, K., & Kad, S. (2016). Enhanced clustering based AODV-R protocol using Ant Colony Optimization in VANETS. In IEEE 1st International Conference on Power Electronics, Intelligent Control and Energy Systems (ICPEICES), Delhi, India (pp. 1-5). doi:10.1109/ICPEICES.2016.7853381

Lai, C., Zheng, D., Zhao, Q., & Jiang, X. (2018). SEGM: A secure group management framework in integrated VANET-cellular networks. *Vehicular Communications*, *11*, 33–45.

Miao, L., Djouani, K., Van Wyk, B. J., & Hamam, Y. (2013). Performance evaluation of IEEE 802.11p MAC protocol in VANETs safety applications. In 2013 IEEE Wireless Communications and Networking Conference (WCNC), Shanghai, China (pp. 1663-1668).

Ngo, C. T., & Oh, H. (2014). A Link Quality Prediction Metric for Location based Routing Protocols under Shadowing and Fading Effects in Vehicular Ad Hoc Networks. *Procedia Computer Science*, *34*, 565–570. doi:10.1016/j.procs.2014.07.071

Oliveira, R., Montez, C., Boukerche, A., & Wangham, M. S. (2017). Reliable data dissemination protocol for VANET traffic safety applications. *Ad Hoc Networks*, *63*, 30–44. doi:10.1016/j.adhoc.2017.05.002

Oubbati, O. S., Lakas, A., Zhou, F., Güneş, M., Lagraa, N., & Yagoubi, M. B. (2017). Intelligent UAV-assisted routing protocol for urban VANETs. *Computer Communications*, *107*, 93–111. doi:10.1016/j.comcom.2017.04.001

Pournaghi, S. M., Zahednejad, B., Bayat, M., & Farjami, Y. (2018). NECPPA: A novel and efficient conditional privacy-preserving authentication scheme for VANET. *Computer Networks*, *134*, 78–92. doi:10.1016/j.comnet.2018.01.015

Qiu, H. J. F., Ho, I. W. H., Tse, C. K., & Xie, Y. (2015). A Methodology for Studying 802.11p VANET Broadcasting Performance With Practical Vehicle Distribution. *IEEE Transactions on Vehicular Technology*, *64*(10), 4756–4769. doi:10.1109/TVT.2014.2367037

Rahim, A., Kong, X., Xia, F., Ning, Z., Ullah, N., Wang, J., & Das, S. K. (2018). Vehicular Social Networks: A survey. *Pervasive and Mobile Computing*, *43*, 96–113. doi:10.1016/j.pmcj.2017.12.004

Rath, M. (2017). Resource provision and QoS support with added security for client side applications in cloud computing. *International Journal of Information Technology*, *9*(3), 1–8.

Rath, M. (2017). Resource provision and QoS support with added security for client side applications in cloud computing. *International Journal of Information Technology*, *9*(3), 1–8.

Rath, M., & Panda, M. R. (2017). MAQ system development in mobile ad-hoc networks using mobile agents. In IEEE 2nd International Conference on Contemporary Computing and Informatics (IC3I), Noida, Japan (pp. 794-798).

Rath, M., & Panda, M. R. (2017). MAQ system development in mobile ad-hoc networks using mobile agents. In IEEE 2nd International Conference on Contemporary Computing and Informatics (IC3I), Noida, Japan (pp. 794-798).

Rath, M., Pati, B., Panigrahi, C. R., & Sarkar, J. L. (2019). QTM: A QoS Task Monitoring System for Mobile Ad hoc Networks. In P. Sa, S. Bakshi, I. Hatzilygeroudis, & M. Sahoo (Eds.), *Recent Findings in Intelligent Computing Techniques*. Springer., doi:10.1007/978-981-10-8639-7_57.

Rath, M., Pati, B., & Pattanayak, B. K. (2017). *Cross layer based QoS platform for multimedia transmission in MANET. In 11th International Conference on Intelligent Systems and Control*. ISCO., doi:10.1109/ISCO.2017.7856026.

Rath, M., Pati, B., Pattanayak, B. K., Panigrahi, C. R., & Sarkar, J. L. (2017). Load balanced routing scheme for MANETs with power and delay optimisation. *International Journal of Communication Networks and Distributed Systems*, *19*(4), 394–405.

Rath, M., Pati, B., Pattanayak, B. K., Panigrahi, C. R., & Sarkar, J. L. (2017). Load balanced routing scheme for MANETs with power and delay optimisation. *International Journal of Communication Networks and Distributed Systems*, *19*(4), 394–405.

Rath, M., & Pattanayak, B. (2017). MAQ: A Mobile Agent Based QoS Platform for MANETs. *International Journal of Business Data Communications and Networking*, *13*(1), 1–8. doi:10.4018/IJBDCN.2017010101

Rath, M., & Pattanayak, B. (2017). MAQ: A Mobile Agent Based QoS Platform for MANETs. *International Journal of Business Data Communications and Networking*, *13*(1), 1–8. doi:10.4018/IJBDCN.2017010101

Rath, M., & Pattanayak, B. (2018). Technological improvement in modern health care applications using Internet of Things (IoT) and proposal of novel health care approach. International Journal of Human Rights in Healthcare. doi:10.1108/IJHRH-01-2018-0007

Rath, M., & Pattanayak, B. (2018). Technological improvement in modern health care applications using Internet of Things (IoT) and proposal of novel health care approach. International Journal of Human Rights in Healthcare. doi:10.1108/IJHRH-01-2018-0007

Rath, M., & Pattanayak, B. K. (2017, December). SCICS: A Soft Computing Based Intelligent Communication System in VANET. In *International Conference on Intelligent Information Technologies* (pp. 255-261). Springer, Singapore.

Rath, M., & Pattanayak, B. K. (2018). SCICS: A Soft Computing Based Intelligent Communication System in VANET. Smart Secure Systems – IoT and Analytics Perspective. *Communications in Computer and Information Science*, *808*, 255–261. doi:10.1007/978-981-10-7635-0_19

Rath, M., & Pattanayak, B. K. (2018). Monitoring of QoS in MANET Based Real Time Applications. In S. Satapathy & A. Joshi (Eds.), *Information and Communication Technology for Intelligent Systems ICTIS 2017* (Vol. 2, pp. 579–586). Springer., doi:10.1007/978-3-319-63645-0_64.

Rath, M., & Pattanayak, B. K. (2018). Monitoring of QoS in MANET Based Real Time Applications. In S. Satapathy & A. Joshi (Eds.), *Information and Communication Technology for Intelligent Systems* (Vol. 2, pp. 579–586). Springer., doi:10.1007/978-3-319-63645-0_64.

Rath, M., Pattanayak, B. K., & Pati, B. (2017). Energetic Routing Protocol Design for Real-time Transmission in Mobile Ad hoc Network. In *Computing and Network Sustainability*. Springer.

Rath, M., Pattanayak, B. K., & Pati, B. (2017). Energetic routing protocol design for real-time transmission in mobile ad hoc network. In *Computing and Network Sustainability* (pp. 187–199). Springer.

Hossain, M. K., Datta, S., Hossain, S. I., & Edmonds, J. (2017). ResVMAC: A Novel Medium Access Control Protocol for Vehicular Ad hoc Networks. *Procedia Computer Science*, *109*, 432–439. doi:10.1016/j.procs.2017.05.413

Rtah, M. (2018). Big Data and IoT-allied challenges associated with healthcare applications in smart and automated systems. *International Journal of Strategic Information Technology and Applications*, *9*(2). Advance online publication. doi:10.4018/IJSITA.201804010

Rtah, M. (2018). Big Data and IoT-Allied Challenges Associated With Healthcare Applications in Smart and Automated Systems. *International Journal of Strategic Information Technology and Applications*, *9*(2). Advance online publication. doi:10.4018/IJSITA.201804010

Saleh, A. I., Gamel, S. A., & Abo-Al-Ez, K. M. (2017). A Reliable Routing Protocol for Vehicular Ad hoc Networks. *Computers & Electrical Engineering*, *64*, 473–495. doi:10.1016/j.compeleceng.2016.11.011

Sattar, S., Qureshi, H. K., Saleem, M., Mumtaz, S., & Rodriguez, J. (2018). Reliability and energy-efficiency analysis of safety message broadcast in VANETs. *Computer Communications*, *119*, 118–126. doi:10.1016/j.comcom.2018.01.006

Singh, D., Vishnu, C., & Mohan, C. K. (2016). Visual Big Data Analytics for Traffic Monitoring in Smart City. In IEEE International Conference on Machine Learning and Applications (ICMLA), Anaheim, CA (pp. 886-891). doi:10.1109/ICMLA.2016.0159

Singh, S., & Agrawal, S. (2014). *VANET routing protocols: Issues and challenges. In 2014 Recent Advances in Engineering and Computational Sciences*. RAECS.

Singh, S., Negi, S., Verma, S. K., & Panwar, N. (2018). Comparative Study of Existing Data Scheduling Approaches and Role of Cloud in VANET Environment. *Procedia Computer Science*, *125*, 925–934. doi:10.1016/j.procs.2017.12.118

Venkatramana, D. K. N., Srikantaiah, S. B., & Moodabidri, J. (2017). SCGRP: SDN-enabled connectivity-aware geographical routing protocol of VANETs for urban environment. IET Networks, 6(5), 102-111. doi:10.1049/iet-net.2016.0117

Wang, X., Wang, D., & Sun, Q. (2018). Reliable routing in IP-based VANET with network gaps. *Computer Standards & Interfaces*, *55*, 80–94. doi:10.1016/j.csi.2017.05.002

Wu, H. T., & Horng, G. J. (2017). Establishing an intelligent transportation system with a network security mechanism in an Internet of vehicle environment. *IEEE Access : Practical Innovations, Open Solutions*, *5*, 19239–19247. doi:10.1109/ACCESS.2017.2752420

This research was previously published in the International Journal of Business Data Communications and Networking (IJBDCN), 15(2); edited by Zoubir Mammeri; pages 55-72, copyright year 2019 by IGI Publishing (an imprint of IGI Global).

Chapter 33
UWDBCSN Analysis During Node Replication Attack in WSN

Harpreet Kaur
Thapar University, India

Sharad Saxena
Thapar University, India

ABSTRACT

Wireless sensor network is an emerging area in which multiple sensor nodes are present to perform many real-time applications like military application, industrialized automation, health monitoring, weather forecast, etc. Sensor nodes can be organized into a group which is led by a cluster head; this concept is known as clustering. Clustering of wireless sensor network is used when sensor nodes want to communicate simultaneously in a single network. The author organizes the sensor nodes by applying UWDBCSN (underwater density-based clustering sensor network) clustering approach in which routing of the packets is controlled by cluster head. The author also considers the security of sensor nodes which are harmful to different types of mischievous attacks like wormhole attack, denial of service attack, replication or cloning attack, blackhole attack, etc. Node replication is one of the types in which an attacker tries to capture the node and generate the replica or clone of that node in the same network. So, this chapter describes how to deal with these types of attacks. The author used the intrusion detection process to deal with this type of attack. All the detection procedure is combined with sleep/wake scheduling algorithm to increase the performance of sensor nodes in the network.

INTRODUCTION

Wireless sensor networks include the large number of multiple sensor nodes which are used for monitoring purposes such as elementary monitoring, forecast monitoring, early earthquake detection, military application etc. The sensor nodes are grouped together to perform the multiple tasks simultaneously which is monitored by a head selected by clusters of nodes in the network. The selection of cluster head is done by the sensor nodes and this overall concept of sending the data through cluster head is known

DOI: 10.4018/978-1-7998-5348-0.ch033

as Clustering (Boyinbode, Le, Mbogho, Takizawa, & Poliah, 2010). Clustering is important when the multiple sensor nodes are targeted to perform the single important task. It is energy efficient and less time is used for the packet transmission because the nodes communicate through cluster head. The different clustering algorithm has been proposed like LEACH, LEACH-C, UWDBCSN, LNCA etc. are consider of having same clustering approach but routing mechanisms are different. Figure 1 below shows the clustering of various sensor nodes. The sensor nodes are organized into clusters which tend to perform similar type of tasks like in data mining.

Figure 1.Clustering in WSN

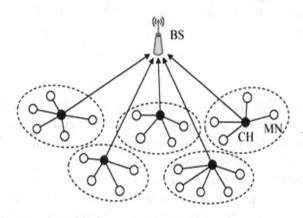

Attacks on Wireless Sensor Networks

The author discussed about the various types of malicious attacks (Savner & Gupta, 2014) which are responsible for destroying the security of wireless sensor networks such as node replication attack, wormhole attack, jellyfish attack, Sybil attack etc. Security is major important concern because many applications directly or indirectly depend upon sensor network. They are used in everywhere in today's era. The author considered one of the dangerous types of attacks in which malicious user try to inject the attacking or malicious nodes in order to generate many insider threats. This attack is known as node replication attack. The different types of attacks on wireless sensor network are explained in Figure 2.

- **Jamming Attack (Li, Koutsopoulos, & Poovendran, 2010):** Jamming attack blocks the channel due to which the genuine nodes are unable to access the wireless communication. It is also known as denial of service attack which disrupts the normal functioning of the network and leads to many insider threats.
- **Wormhole Attack (Alajmi, 2014):** In wormhole attack, the malicious user creates the fake tunnel in the routing path of the sender and the destination nodes so that the sending node will use the fake tunnel for the immediate packet transmission and redirected them to their malicious network in order to halt the communication.
- **Sybil Attack:** In Sybil attack, the malicious attacking nodes possess the different fake identities in the same network and generate the confusion among different genuine nodes in order to increase the network delay.

Figure 2. Different types of attacks in WSN

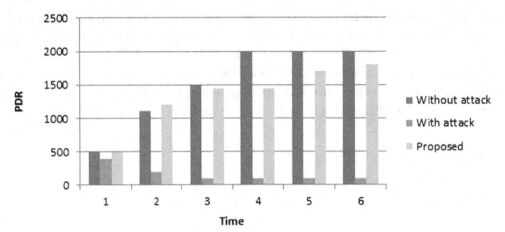

- **Jellyfish Attack (Kaur, Sarangal, & Nayyar, 2014):** In jellyfish attack, the malicious user injects the jellyfish node in the routing path and takes participation in all the communication between sender and receiver node. The jellyfish node appears as a genuine node which will steal the packet information and use in an inefficient way.
- **Routing Attack (Abdelaziz, Nafaa, & Salim, 2013):** In routing attack, the malicious adversary tries to route the packets in order to perform various attacks and mislead the normal functioning of the network. This type of attack is proved to be dangerous because they disrupt the network's activity by introducing the fake routes between the paths of the network.
- **Node Replication Attack (Mishra & Turuk, 2015):** Replication is considered to be great threat to the security of wsn. In this attack, an attacker tries to capture the sensor nodes by extracting the credentials of genuine sensor nodes, after capturing the attacker create the clone or replica of the genuine node in the same network in order to pretend that the injected clone is same as that of genuine node (Game & Raut, 2014). Replicas are very difficult to identify because they appear as legitimitate node in the network. There may be case that attacker targets the multiple sensor nodes by capturing the whole cluster or cluster head and generate the clone or replica of whole cluster (Ho, 2009). Figure 3 below shows the node replication attack in sensor network.

BACKGROUND

Background study includes the concept of clustering applied to the sensor nodes using clustering algorithms like LNCA, UWDBCSN, LEACH, LEACH-C, NI-LEACH etc. Then secure communication is ensuring in these routing protocols. The previous study showed that the hierarchical clustering is used during node replication attack in sensor network using different-different clustering routing protocols that the author discussed below:

(Znaidi, Minier, & Ubeda, 2013) introduced the hierarchical node replication attack detection in sensor network and the algorithm used is LNCA (Local Negotiated Clustering Approach) (Xia & Vlajic, 2007). LNCA is a hierarchical distributed clustering routing protocol in which election mechanism is done using node degree which means the node with high number of immediate neighbor is considered as

Figure 3. Node replication attack

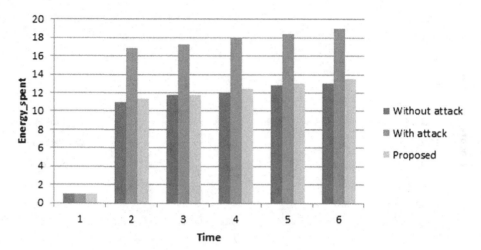

cluster head and other becomes its member. This election is done dynamically in which the node degree is calculated by each node in the network. Then the author analyses the behavior of node replication attack and detection is done using Bloom filter mechanism (Tarkoma, Rothenberg, & Lagerspetz, 2011). Each cluster head calculates the hash function and check the authenticity of each member in its circle. When the cluster head found the two different locations of same node Id, then alert is generated which indicate that there is a presence of cloning or replicated node in the network.

(Cheng, Guo, Yang, & Wang, 2015) proposed the energy efficient clustering protocol NI-LEACH which is an improvement over LEACH. The selection of cluster head is based on the energy value stored by each node and give only number of cluster head which are optimal in number. In addition, an intrusion detection process is introduced by the author who is based on the implementation of monitoring nodes. The detection rate is high in this case because multiple monitor nodes exchange the special encoder function and detect the replicated node in an efficient way.

(Tripathi & Gaur, 2013) proposed the centralized clustering detection of node replication attack in wireless sensor network. In this, the author used LEACH-C protocol which is an enhanced version of LEACH. Author used the witness node technique which has the ability to identify the replication of whole cluster if any. The witness nodes identify the replicated node ids which are generated by an attacker and alert the other sensor nodes. This approach is proved to be highly efficient in determining the replication attack.

(Saxena, Mishra, & Singh, 2013) proposed the energy efficient UWDBCSN (under-water density based clustering sensor network) which is used to perform clustering in acoustic sensor networks. The algorithm performs the selection operation of cluster head based on node density. The network model manages energy model where each node is associated with certain amount of energy and the nodes are divided into low level energy nodes and high-level energy nodes. The node which is having highest energy is selected as cluster head and its member nodes are having lowest energy and in the same way the low energy sensor nodes cover the maximum of high energy sensor nodes (Tomar, Kevre, & Shrivastava, 2015). So, in this way overall energy is maintained and hence this is appropriate method as compared to LEACH clustering. Following Figure 4 shows the UWDBCSN clustering of sensor nodes.

Figure 4. UWDBCSN clustering

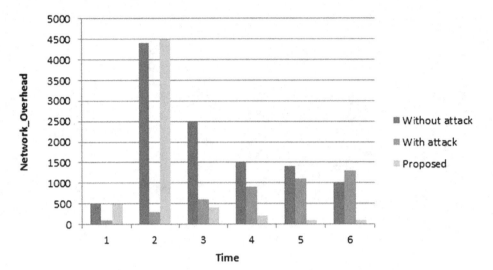

The author performs the UWDBCSN clustering on the randomly deployed nodes in the considered wireless sensor network. Later, the same is analyzed in the presence of node replication attack and network performance is compared.

The objective of this book chapter is to check the network performance under replication attack. The randomly deployed nodes are organized using UWDBCSN algorithm. Then node replication attack is performed in which the author made an assumption that two attacking nodes are injected which increase the packet dropping in the network and fail the communication between sender and the destination nodes. For the detection of node replication attack, the author presented the defending technique Dydog detection which is an intrusion detection process as discussed later in the next section.

MAIN FOCUS OF THE CHAPTER

The main focus of this chapter is to organize the randomly deployed nodes using energy efficient algorithm and furthermore node replication attack is detected which is found to be dangerous among sensor nodes. The author has compared the network performance on the basis of performance parameters.

Issues, Controversies, Problems

- Wireless sensor networks are found to be vulnerable to many attacks such as replication, spoofing, routing, wormhole, Sybil attack etc.
- There should be secure routing of packets which would ensure the authenticity, integrity and confidentiality of packets.
- Every node participated in the transmission procedure so there is a need to organize the node so that overall energy used is less and an efficient energy consuming process is followed by each and every sensor node.

- The replication attack after capturing the node may generate many insider threats which halt the secure communication between the sensor nodes.

- The network performance is degraded when the attacking nodes are introduced because packet drop is more. So, network performance must be a biggest concert.

- The main challenge is to maintain the energy level acquired by each sensor node in which lifetime of the network depends. If the energy is lowest then the network is no more and cannot able to perform further transmission process.

- Different node replication attack detection protocols are introduced by various researchers. But there is still need of improvement because the security of sensor network is biggest area of concern as they are used in various applications.

These are the problems and issues that should be taken into consideration. Keeping all the issues in the mind, the author proposed the solution which is proved to be efficient.

SOLUTIONS AND RECOMMENDATIONS

The author first introduces the clustering approach UWDBCSN in order to locate the multiple sensor nodes into groups which is known as cluster head, then node replication attack is performed to check the network performance, later Dydog intrusion detection process (Janakiraman, Rajasoundaran, & Narayanasamy, 2012) is applied to detect or prevent the node replication attack.

- **Network Model:** The author considered to work upon fixed number of sensor nodes which constructed a wireless sensor network. Author proposed a three-tier structure which includes sensor nodes with low energy or high energy and a base station. All the nodes are equally distributed initially with unique identification number and cluster head election mechanism is done using UWDBCSN algorithm. The structure works as follows: the sensor nodes when want to communicate send their data to the selected cluster head and cluster head then forwards the request to the sink station or base station. The author made an assumption that a malicious user is somewhere present in the network and targets the communication between the sensor nodes. The malicious user extracts all the cryptographic materials of sensor nodes and generates the replica inside the same network. In this way malicious user able to inject the replicated or attacking nodes. Our main focus is on the detection of the replicated or attacking nodes and stops the packet drop so that the sensor nodes are able to communicate securely. The author has used Dydog detection in which monitoring nodes are participating to detect the attacking or replicated nodes and tries to remove or prevent this attack. Figure 5 below represents the graphic view of hierarchical architecture in network simulator that the author considered in his implementation.
- **UWDBCSN Analysis and Detection Procedure:**
  - **UWDBCSN Analysis:** Initially, the author considers there is malicious activity between the communicating entities and the packet transmission is normal between source and the destination nodes. The randomly deployed sensor nodes are organized into clusters using UWDBCSN clustering algorithm which could be explained as follows:
    - Sensor nodes with high energy or low energy are considered.

Figure 5. Network model

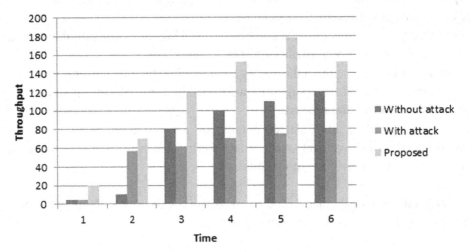

- The selection is based on their energy value, so energy model is main consideration while electing the cluster head.
- The one which is having high value of energy is selected as cluster head and other sensor node start the request message in order to become the member of cluster head.
- Cluster head checks the energy level and authenticity. Cluster head with high energy always likely to cover the more number of low energy sensors. So that the overall energy consume is less.
- After cluster formation, the sensor nodes start the normal packet transmission through their cluster head which forward the request to the sink station or base station.

The figure below shows the graphic view of formation of 4 cluster heads using UWDBCSN algorithm. The pink color nodes are cluster head and all the green color nodes are its member. The blue color node is the sink station which can be the destination node. The Figure 6 only shows the formation of one cluster with one cluster head.

- **Node Replication Attack Detection Procedure:** The author proposed the intrusion detection process based on the clustered hierarchical structure. The algorithm is based on the implementation of monitoring nodes which are responsible for the detection of replicated node in the network. Different detection keys are maintained by these monitoring nodes. The algorithm is divided into five steps which could be explained as follows:

Figure 6. Cluster head Election

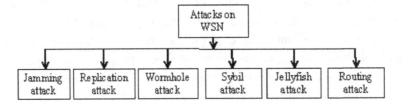

○ **Distribution Step:** The distribution step includes the unique identification key for each node in the wireless sensor network. This also include the cryptographic materials such as public and private key, digital hash signatures and hash function which is computed and verified at each step of authentication.

○ **Election of Cluster Head using UWDBCSN:** When unique identification number has been given to every node, then there is selection of cluster head using UWDBCSN as discussed in previous section. The selection is done on random basis because when the node transmits the data, energy is decreased by 1 factor. At that point the node which is having value of energy as highest is elected as cluster head. The cluster head is the one which is responsible for the overall communication between the sensor and the destination nodes.

○ **Injection of Attacking Nodes:** When the nodes are organized and there is normal transmission of data packets among the sensor nodes. This step assumes that there are two attacking nodes which are injected by the malicious users and packet drop has begun because the malicious nodes continuously tried to send the data packets and generate the flood of requests which lead to many insider threats to the important information. The following Figure 7 shows the packet drop due to the presence of attacking nodes shown in red color.

Figure 7. Injection of two attacking nodes

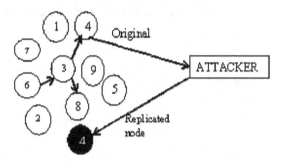

○ **Detection using Dydog Method:** Dydog method (Janakiraman, Rajasoundaran, & Narayanasamy, 2012) is a dynamic intrusion detection method which includes the multiple monitoring nodes that will also act as monitoring nodes or data forwarding nodes. Secure session key management algorithm is used for the selection of monitoring nodes which check the authenticity or verify each and every sensor nodes. This method has been proved to reduce high error rate in the wireless sensor network. The attacker is unable to create or inject the malicious or attacking nodes in the sensor network due to the presence of secure monitoring nodes. In this way the author tries to increase the security of wireless sensor network.

• **Select the Monitoring Nodes:** The nodes which are immediate neighbor of sender nodes are selected as intrusion detection nodes. They may be large in number depending upon the node degree which is the number of nodes present in their immediate area. The selection procedure follows the secure management approach. When the data forwarding nodes are not monitored by their immediate neighbor, then the two-hop neighbor node will act as intrusion detection node. In this way selection is done dynamically, as shown in Table 1.

Table 1.

```
nf :forwarding node
n1 :one-hop neighbor node
n2 :two-hop neighbor node
Ids: Id of the sender node
Idr: Id of the receiver node in nf
datas : data bit of sender node
datar : data bit of receiver node in nf
n: node taken for selection process
```

n_f $\xrightarrow{Id_s || data_s}$ n_1 $\xrightarrow{Id (n_1) \text{ XOR } Id_s || data_s}$ n_2

n_1 $\xrightarrow{Id (n_2)}$ n_f

n_2 $\xrightarrow{Id_s || data_s \text{ XOR } Id (n_1) \text{ XOR } Id (n_2) \text{ via } n_1}$ n_f

```
here, keys are k1 : Ids|| datas XOR Id (n1)
              k2 : Ids|| datas XOR Id (n1) XOR Id (n2)
In k1 → nf or k2 → nf check
    If (Idr == Ids && datar == datas)
    {
        n → IDN (intrusion detection node)
    }
    Else
    {
        n → malicious node
    }
end
```

Table 2.

```
DMIDN: decision making intrusion detection node
IDNs: intrusion detection node
i: initial data packet
ack: acknowledgement
Condition applied:
DMIDN ∈ IDN (s)
```

n_f $\xrightarrow{key+ data\,bit+ TTL}$ IDN (s);

IDN(s) $\xrightarrow[\text{Data bit+TTL}]{\text{Req}}$ n_f;

IDN(s) $\rightarrow$ DMIDN; iff TTL==TTL$_s$;

Then n_f $\xrightarrow{data_i+ ack_i}$ DMIDN ;

- **Secure Routing or Management Algorithm:** Each sensor node in the network will maintain the shared secret key which is used to differentiate the genuine nodes from the attacking nodes. At every step, authentication action is performed by monitoring nodes. When the packet drop starts the neighbor, node will act as watchdog which take care of all the data communication between the sensor nodes and the sink node.

- **Deciding Module of Intrusion Detection Nodes:** Since there are multiple intrusion detection nodes but there is only one deciding node which will decide what should be the secure path followed by the data forwarding nodes in which attacking nodes are not present. The forwarding node shares its private keys with all the monitoring or intrusion detection nodes. All the intrusion detection nodes send their data bits with their TTL (time to live) value. Then forwarding node declares the deciding intrusion detection node which is having low TTL value. Then the intrusion detection node will decide which secure route should be followed in order to prevent the attack. During this process, other nodes will go into idle state to save their energy.

  ◦ **Revocation Message:** After the monitoring nodes perform the detection, if they find any attacking nodes or replicated nodes, then the intrusion detection nodes will generate the alert in order to inform the other sensor nodes to stop their communication for a second until they decide which secure path should be followed for secure communication. The attacker probability to inject the replicated nodes is very less because the Dydog method (Varshney, Sharma, & Sharma, 2014) can be able to detect the multiple attacking nodes in the sensor network. Network replies are verified by each cluster head which will check the authenticity by looking at their data bits or keys associated with them.

  ◦ **Sleep/Wake Scheduling Algorithm (Manirajan & SathishKumar, 2015):** The Dydog detection is combined with sleep/wake scheduling algorithm in order to increase the performance of the network. With sleep/wake approach, all those nodes who do not take part in the transmission can be able to change their state from wake state to sleep state. So, the overall energy of the network can be saved. Figure 8 shows the sleep/wake algorithm applied in addition to Dydog method in which grey nodes are in sleep state and green nodes are in wake state or participate in the transmission process.

Figure 8. Sleep/wake Scheduling algorithm

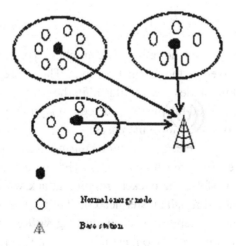

Simulation Results

The author has compared the performance of the hierarchical network considering 500 sensor nodes on the five parameters such as throughput, packet delivery ratio, energy used, network overhead and end to end delay. the results show the efficient detection of the replication attack with Dydog intrusion detection process and the network's lifetime is increased using sleep/wake scheduling algorithm. The simulation results have been shown in the graph.

- **End to End Delay:** A packet will take the total time to reach to the desired destination is called end to end delay. The figure 9 shows the delay with respect to time where the delay in the presence of attacking nodes increased as compared to the normal environment but when the author used Dydog detection integrated with sleep/wake scheduling, then the delay decreased by certain amount.

Figure 9. End to End delay versus time

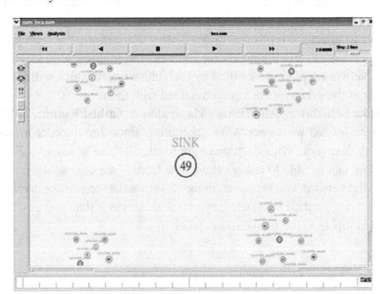

- **Packet Delivery Ratio:** It defines the ratio of the number of packets sent by the source node and the number of packets received by the destination node. The figure 10 shows the delivery of packets reduce when the attacking nodes are introduced in the network as compared to the normal environment. When the author used the intrusion detection Dydog method, then delivery of packets will be more. So delivery of packet ratio increases.
- **Energy Consumption:** It is the energy consumed during the packets transmission by each node and calculates the total energy of the whole network. The energy consumed by the attacking nodes is increased because they perform the packet dropping attack when a genuine node tries to send the packet to the base station through cluster head by duplicating their ids. When the author used Dydog method in addition to sleep/wake scheduling algorithm, the overall energy consumption will be less, and the network lifetime also increased show in Figure 11.

Figure 10. PDR versus time

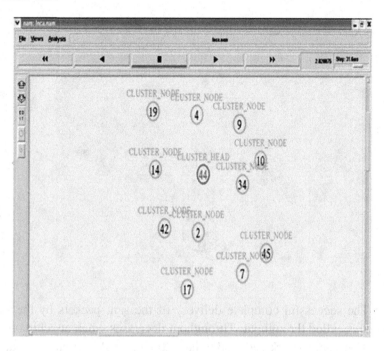

Figure 11. Energy consumption versus time

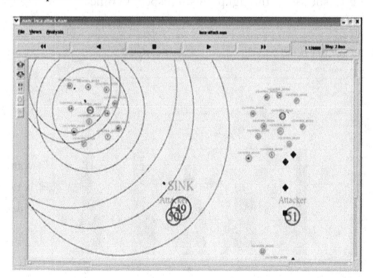

- **Network Overhead:** The amount of resources used by every sensor node in the network such as bandwidth, energy, memory, time etc. the overhead tends to increase in case of attacking nodes because the attacking nodes drop the large amount of packets during transmission and try to send the multiple requests to the destination node or cluster head. Figure 12 shows, when Dydog method is used the overhead is decreased by some amount because the monitoring nodes are only in the active state and other nodes go to the sleep state which decreased the certain amount of overhead in the network.

Figure 12. Network overhead versus time

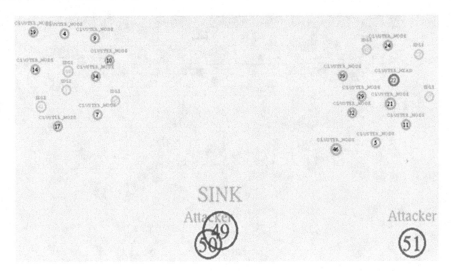

- **Throughput:** The successful complete delivery of the sent packets by the sender node to the destination node is called throughput. Throughput decreases when attacking nodes perform their attacking activity in the network and tend to harm the network security. The author increases the throughput rate by introducing the concept of Dydog detection followed by sleep/wake scheduling algorithm. Figure 13 shows the throughput with respect to time.

Figure 13. Throughput versus time

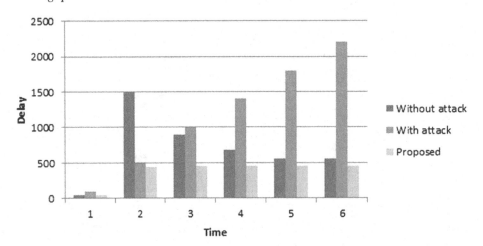

FUTURE RESEARCH DIRECTIONS

The author has proved that the introduced algorithm is efficient for the detection of attacking or replicated nodes in the network. The author suggested that the future work may include the detection of all other different types of attack like Sybil node attack, jellyfish attack, wormhole attack etc. The prevention of the attacking nodes will also be considered by using the same Dydog approach. The security of cluster head will also be considered including optimum number of sensor nodes in the network.

CONCLUSION

The security of sensor nodes should be a major or important consideration in the wireless sensor network because sensors are used everywhere in today's world. Author main focused on the concept of security in the network which can be harmed by various malicious attacks such as jellyfish attack, routing attack, wormhole attack, Sybil attack etc. There is a need to secure the senor node's activity in the network. The author has applied the UWDBCSN clustering algorithm to arrange the sensor nodes under cluster head and then analyses the network behavior under node replication attack. The intrusion detection process is used for detection which is done using monitoring nodes and proved to be efficient and the overall detection procedure is integrated with sleep/wake scheduling algorithm in order to enhance the performance of the network.

REFERENCES

Abdelaziz, A. K., Nafaa, M., & Salim, G. (2013). Survey of Routing Attacks and Countermeasures in Mobile Ad Hoc Networks. Computer Modelling Simulation (UKSim).

Alajmi,N. (2014). Wireless Sensor Networks Attacks and Solutions. *International Journal of Computer Science and Information Security*.

Boyinbode, O., Le, H., Mbogho, A., Takizawa, M., & Poliah, R. (2010). A Survey on Clustering Algorithms for Wireless Sensor Networks. Network-Based Information Systems (NBiS).

Butun, I., Morgera, S. D., & Sankar, R. (2015). A Surevy of Intrusion Detection Systems in Wireless Sensor Networks. *IEEE Communications Surveys and Tutorials*, 266–282.

Cheng, G., Guo, S., Yang, Y., & Wang, Y. (2015). *Replication attack detection with monitor nodes in clustered wireless sensor networks. In IEEE 34th International Performance*. IPCCC.

Game,S.,& Raut,C. (2014). Protocols for Detection of Node Replication Attack on Wireless sensor Network. *IOSR Journal of Computer Engineering*, 1-11.

Gupta,V., & Sangroha,D. (n.d.). Protection against packet drop attack. *Advances in Engineering and Technology Research (ICAETR)*.

Ho, J. (2009). Distributed Detection Replica Cluster Attacks in Sensor Networks using Sequential Analysis. *Distributed Detection Replica Cluster Performance, Computing and Commuincations Conference (IPCCC)*.

Janakiraman, S., Rajasoundaran, S., & Narayanasamy, P. (2012). *The Model- Dynamic and Flexible Intrusion Detection Protocol for high error rate Wireless Sensor Networks based on data flow. In Computing, Communication and Applications (ICCCA)*. Tamilnadu, India: Dindigul.

Jin, H., & Chen, H. (2008). Lightweight session key management scheme in Sensor Networks. *Future Generation Communication and Networking (FGCN 2007)*.

Kaur, M., Sarangal, M., & Nayyar, A. (2014). Simulation of Jelly Fish Periodic Attack in Mobile Ad hoc Networks. *International Journal of Computer Trends and Technology, 15*(1), 20–22. doi:10.14445/22312803/ IJCTT-V15P104

Li, M., Koutsopoulos, I., & Poovendran, R. (2010). Optimal Jamming attack strategies and Network Defense Policies in Wireless Senosr Networks. *IEEE Transactions on Mobile Computing*, 1119–1133.

Li, Y., Zhang, A., & Liang, Y. (2013). *Improvement of leach Protocol for Wireless Sensor Networks. In Instrumentation, Measurement, Computer, Communication and Control*. Shenyang, China: IMCCC.

Manirajan, R., & Sathishkumar, R.K. (2015). Sleep/Wake Scheduling for Target Coverage Problem in Wireless Sensor Networks. *International Journal of Advanced Research in Computer and Communication Engineering*.

Mishra, A. K., & Turuk, A. K. (2015). A Comparative Analysis of Node Replica Detection Scheme in Wireless Sensor Networks. *Journal of Network and Computer Applications*, 21–32.

Nazir, B., & Hasbullah, H. (2011). Dynamic sleep scheduling for minimizing delay in Wireless Sensor Network. *Electronics, Communications and Photonics Conference (SIECPC)*.

Pelechrinis, K., Lliofotou, M., & Krishnamurthy, S. V. (2011). *Denial of Service Attacks in Wireless Networks: The Case of Jammers*. IEEE Communications Surverys & Tutorials.

Salva-Garau, F., & Stojanovic, M. (2003). Multi-Cluster Protocol for Ad-hoc Mobile Underwater Acoustic Network. *IEEE OCEANS'03 Conference*.

Savner, J., & Gupta, V. (2014). *Clustering Of Mobile Ad-hoc Networks: An approach for black hole prevention. In Issues and Challenges in Intelligent Computing Techniques*. Ghaziabad, India: ICICT.

Saxena, S., Mishra, S., & Singh, M. (2013). Clustering Based on Node Density in Hetergeneous Under-Water Sensor Networks. *Information Technology and Computer Science*, 49-55.

Tamane, S., Kumar Solanki, V., & Dey, N. (2017). Privacy and Security Policies in Big Data. *Advances in Information Security, Privacy, and Ethics*, 305.

Tarkoma,S., Rothenberg, C.E.,& Lagerspetz,E. (2011). Theory and Practice of Bloom Filters for Distributed Systems. *IEEE Communication Surveys & Tutorials*, 131-155.

Tomar,G.S., Kevre,P., & Shrivastava,L. (2015). Energy model based performance analysis of cluster based wireless sensor network. *International Journal of Reliable Information and Assurance*.

Tripathi, M., Gaur, M. S., Laxmi, V., & Battula, R. B. (2013). Energy efficient LEACH-C protocol for wireless sensor network. *Third International Conference on Computational Intelligence and Information Technology (CIIT)*. 10.1049/cp.2013.2620

Varshney, T., Sharma, T., & Sharma, P. (2014). *Implementation of Watchdog Protocol with AODV in Mobile Ad Hoc Network. In Communication Systems and Network Technologies*. Bhopal, India: CSNT.

Xia, D., & Vlajic, N. (2007). *Near-Optimal Node Clustering in Wireless sensor Networks for Environment Monitoring*. Niagara Falls, Canada: Advanced Information Networking and Applications. doi:10.1109/AINA.2007.97

Znaidi, W., Minier, M., & Ubeda, S. (2013). Hierarchical Node Replication Attacks Detection in Wireless Sensor Networks. *International Journal of Distributed Sensor Networks*, 12.

KEY TERMS AND DEFINITIONS

Clustering Network: A group of sensor nodes in which multiple nodes are grouped together under cluster head which is elected by them.

Dydog Method: It is the intrusion detection process which detects the multiple attacking nodes in the network with the help of intrusion detection nodes or monitoring nodes.

End to End Delay: The time a packet will take to reach to the desired destination is called end to end delay.

Energy Consumption: It is the amount of energy consumed during the packets transmission by each node and calculates the overall energy of the whole network.

Intrusion Detection: Intrusion detection is a process of detecting any unnecessary activity in the network.

Network Overhead: The amount of resources used by every sensor node in the network such as bandwidth, energy, memory, time, etc.

Node Replication Attack: The dangerous type of attack in which an attacker can harm the functionality of the network by injecting the clone or replica in the network.

Ns2 Simulator: The network simulator which is discrete event and tcl scripts are written in OTcl and C++ language.

Packet Delivery Ratio: It defines the ratio of the number of packets sent by the source node and the number of packets received by the destination node.

Sensor: Sensor is the monitoring device which is equipped with every node in the network in order to measure the physical conditions like temperature, pressure, etc.

Sleep/Wake Scheduling: The algorithm which enhances the performance of the network by increasing the life span of the network.

Throughput: The successful complete delivery of the sent packets by the sender node to the destination node is called throughput.

This research was previously published in the Handbook of Research on Information Security in Biomedical Signal Processing edited by Chittaranjan Pradhan, Himansu Das, Bighnaraj Naik and Nilanjan Dey; pages 210-227, copyright year 2018 by Information Science Reference (an imprint of IGI Global).

APPENDIX

Table 3 represents the simulation parameters taken during implementation in network simulator.

Table 3. Simulation Parameters

Parameters	Value
Channel type	Wireless
Radio propagation model	Two ray ground
Antenna type	Omni
Link layer type	LL
Interface queue type	Droptail
Max packets in interface queue	200
MAC type	IEEE 802.11
No. of mobile nodes	50
Routing protocol	AODV
Simulation time	1000s
Speed	20

Index

Purchase Print, E-Book, or Print + E-Book

IGI Global's reference books are available in three unique pricing formats:
Print Only, E-Book Only, or Print + E-Book.
Shipping fees may apply.

www.igi-global.com

Recommended Reference Books

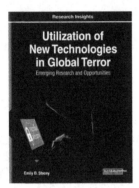

ISBN: 978-1-5225-8876-4
© 2019; 141 pp.
List Price: $135

ISBN: 978-1-5225-8100-0
© 2019; 321 pp.
List Price: $235

ISBN: 978-1-5225-7847-5
© 2019; 306 pp.
List Price: $195

ISBN: 978-1-5225-6313-6
© 2019; 349 pp.
List Price: $215

ISBN: 978-1-5225-7628-0
© 2019; 281 pp.
List Price: $220

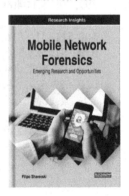

ISBN: 978-1-5225-5855-2
© 2019; 337 pp.
List Price: $185

Do you want to stay current on the latest research trends, product announcements, news and special offers?
Join IGI Global's mailing list today and start enjoying exclusive perks sent only to IGI Global members.
Add your name to the list at **www.igi-global.com/newsletters.**

Publisher of Peer-Reviewed, Timely, and Innovative Academic Research

www.igi-global.com Sign up at www.igi-global.com/newsletters facebook.com/igiglobal twitter.com/igiglobal linkedin.com/igiglobal

IGI Global Proudly Partners With eContent Pro International

Receive a 25% Discount on all Editorial Services

Editorial Services

IGI Global expects all final manuscripts submitted for publication to be in their final form. This means they must be reviewed, revised, and professionally copy edited prior to their final submission. Not only does this support with accelerating the publication process, but it also ensures that the highest quality scholarly work can be disseminated.

English Language Copy Editing

Let eContent Pro International's expert copy editors perform edits on your manuscript to resolve spelling, punctuaion, grammar, syntax, flow, formatting issues and more.

Scientific and Scholarly Editing

Allow colleagues in your research area to examine the content of your manuscript and provide you with valuable feedback and suggestions before submission.

Figure, Table, Chart & Equation Conversions

Do you have poor quality figures? Do you need visual elements in your manuscript created or converted? A design expert can help!

Translation

Need your documjent translated into English? eContent Pro International's expert translators are fluent in English and more than 40 different languages.

Email: customerservice@econtentpro.com   **www.igi-global.com/editorial-service-partners**

www.igi-global.com

Publisher of Peer-Reviewed, Timely, and
Innovative Academic Research Since 1988

IGI Global's Transformative Open Access (OA) Model:
How to Turn Your University Library's Database Acquisitions Into a Source of OA Funding

In response to the OA movement and well in advance of Plan S, IGI Global, early last year, unveiled their OA Fee Waiver (Offset Model) Initiative.

Under this initiative, librarians who invest in IGI Global's InfoSci-Books (5,300+ reference books) and/or InfoSci-Journals (185+ scholarly journals) databases will be able to subsidize their patron's OA article processing charges (APC) when their work is submitted and accepted (after the peer review process) into an IGI Global journal.*

How Does it Work?

1. When a library subscribes or perpetually purchases IGI Global's InfoSci-Databases including InfoSci-Books (5,300+ e-books), InfoSci-Journals (185+ e-journals), and/or their discipline/subject-focused subsets, IGI Global will match the library's investment with a fund of equal value to go toward subsidizing the OA article processing charges (APCs) for their patrons.

   Researchers: Be sure to recommend the InfoSci-Books and InfoSci-Journals to take advantage of this initiative.

2. When a student, faculty, or staff member submits a paper and it is accepted (following the peer review) into one of IGI Global's 185+ scholarly journals, the author will have the option to have their paper published under a traditional publishing model or as OA.

3. When the author chooses to have their paper published under OA, IGI Global will notify them of the OA Fee Waiver (Offset Model) Initiative. If the author decides they would like to take advantage of this initiative, IGI Global will deduct the US$ 1,500 APC from the created fund.

4. This fund will be offered on an annual basis and will renew as the subscription is renewed for each year thereafter. IGI Global will manage the fund and award the APC waivers unless the librarian has a preference as to how the funds should be managed.

Hear From the Experts on This Initiative:

"I'm very happy to have been able to make one of my recent research contributions, 'Visualizing the Social Media Conversations of a National Information Technology Professional Association' featured in the *International Journal of Human Capital and Information Technology Professionals*, freely available along with having access to the valuable resources found within IGI Global's InfoSci-Journals database."

– Prof. Stuart Palmer,
Deakin University, Australia

For More Information, Visit:
www.igi-global.com/publish/contributor-resources/open-access or contact IGI Global's Database Team at eresources@igi-global.com.